Beginning JavaScript

Paul Wilton

Wrox Press Ltd.

Beginning JavaScript

Published by Wrox Press Ltd,
Arden House, 1102 Warwick Road, Acocks Green,
Birmingham, B27 6BH, UK
Printed in the United States
ISBN 1-861004-06-0

Trademark Acknowledgements

Credits

Author
Paul Wilton

Contributing Author
Chris Ullman

Technical Reviewers
Stuart Conway
Brian Donnelly
Denise Geliot
Jeff Hart
Susan Henshaw
Martin Honnen
Nigel McFarlane
Dmitry V. Simonov
Jon Stephens
Andrew Van-Heusen
Cliff Wooton

Category Manager
Dave Galloway

Development Editor
Peter Morgan

Project Manager
Chandima Nethisinghe

Technical Architect
Victoria Hudgson

Technical Editors
Amanda Kay
Simon Mackie
Howard Davies
Phillip Jackson

Production Manager
Simon Hardware

Production Coordinator
Tom Bartlett

Figures
Shabnam Hussain

Proofreader
Christopher Smith

Index
Andrew Criddle

Cover
Shelley Frazier

About the Author

Paul Wilton

After an initial start as a Visual Basic applications programmer at the Ministry of Defense in the UK, Paul found himself pulled into the Net. Having joined an Internet development company, he spent the last 3 years helping create Internet solutions and is currently working on an e-commerce web site for a major British bank.

Paul's main skills are in developing web front ends using DHTML, JavaScript, VBScript, and Visual Basic and back-end solutions with ASP, Visual Basic, and SQL Server. Currently, he's expanding his skill set to include ADSI programming of Windows 2000 Active Directory.

Lots of love to my fiancée Catherine who ensures my sanity chip remains plugged in. Also many thanks to all in the Wrox team, whose dedication and hard work helped create this book and whose editors turned my jumble of words in a language closely resembling English into something truly professional.

Table of Contents

Table of Contents

Table of Contents

Table of Contents

Table of Contents

Online discussion at http://p2p.wrox.com

Introduction

JavaScript is a scripting language that enables you to enhance static web applications, by providing dynamic, personalized, and interactive content. This improves the experience of visitors to your site and makes it more likely that they will visit again. You must have seen the flashy drop down menus, moving text, and changing content that is now widespread on web sites – techniques enabled through JavaScript. Supported by all the major browsers, JavaScript is the language of choice on the Web. JavaScript can even be used outside web applications, to automate administrative tasks, for example.

This book aims to teach you all you need to know to start experimenting with JavaScript – what it is, how it works, and what you can do with it. Starting from the basic syntax, you'll move on to learn how to create powerful web applications. Don't worry if you've never programmed before – this book will teach you all you need to know, step by step. You'll find that JavaScript can be a great introduction into the world of programming; with the knowledge and understanding that you'll gain from this book, you'll be able to move on to learn newer and more advanced technologies in the world of computing.

Who is This Book For?

In order to get the most out of this book, you'll need to have an understanding of HTML and how to create a static web page. You don't need to have any programming experience; this book will teach you all you need to know to incorporate JavaScript into your pages, so that you can create more dynamic and exciting web applications.

This book will also suit you if you have some programming experience already, and would like to turn your hand towards web programming. You will know a fair amount about computing concepts, but maybe not as much about web technologies.

Alternatively, you may have a design background, and know relatively little about the Web and computing concepts. For you, JavaScript will be a cheap and relatively easy introduction to the world of programming, and web application development.

Whoever you are, we hope that this book lives up to your expectations.

What's Covered in This Book?

We'll begin by looking at exactly what JavaScript is, and taking our first steps with the underlying language and syntax. You'll learn all the fundamental programming concepts, including data and data types, and structuring your code to make decisions in your programs or to loop over the same piece of code many times.

Once you're comfortable with the basics, we'll move on to one of the key ideas of JavaScript – the object. You'll learn how to take advantage of the objects that are native to the JavaScript language, such as Dates and Strings, and find out how these objects allow you to manage complex data and simplify your programs. Next, you'll see how we can use JavaScript to manipulate objects made available to us in the browser, such as forms, windows, and other controls. Using this knowledge, we can start to create truly professional-looking applications that allow us to interact with the user.

Long pieces of code are very hard to get right every time – even for the experienced programmer – and JavaScript code is no exception. We look at common syntax and logical errors, how we can spot them, and how to use the Microsoft Script Debugger to aid us with this task. Also, we need to examine how we handle the errors that slip through the net, and ensure that these do not detract from the experience of the end user of our application.

From here, we'll move on to more advanced topics, such as using cookies, and jazzing up our web pages with Dynamic HTML. Finally, we'll move away from manipulation of data and code on the client-side, and discuss ASP, the environment that enables dynamic generation of web content using server-side scripting and back-end databases.

The appendices at the end of the book provide you with a comprehensive reference for the JavaScript language, and for the object models of the major browsers as well as ASP. They also include solutions to the exercises set throughout the book.

All the new concepts that are introduced in this book will be illustrated with practical examples, which allow you to experiment with JavaScript and build on the theory that you have just learned. Throughout the book, we'll also be building up a more complex sample application – an online trivia quiz – which will allow you to see how JavaScript is used in action in a real-world situation.

What You Need to Use This Book

Because JavaScript is a text-based technology, all you really need to create documents containing JavaScript is Notepad (or your equivalent text editor).

Also, in order to try out the code in this book, you will need a web browser that supports JavaScript 1.2 or above, namely version 4 or above of Netscape Navigator or Internet Explorer. (See the table in Chapter 1 for which versions of JavaScript are supported in which versions of Netscape Navigator and Internet Explorer.) Details of where these browsers can be downloaded from are given in Appendix I. Some of the code in later chapters, where we examine Dynamic HTML and scripting of the DOM, is specific to particular browsers, but the majority of the code presented is cross-browser. Where there are exceptions, they will be clearly noted.

In Chapter 15, we introduce scripting on the server-side with JavaScript and ASP. To run the code examples in this and the subsequent chapter you will need a web server. We have used PWS, for which there is an installation guide included in Chapter 15, but any other server is also OK.

Finally, in Chapter 16, we use JavaScript to access a database. For demonstration purposes, the database we use is Microsoft Access 2000, so to run the code examples you will need this software on your machine. The database itself is available for download along with the rest of the code for this book.

Conventions

To help you understand what's going on, and in order to maintain consistency, we've used a number of conventions throughout the book:

When we introduce new terms, we **highlight** them.

> *Advice, hints, and background information comes in an indented, italicized font like this.*

Try It Out

After learning something new, we'll have a *Try It Out* section, which will demonstrate the concepts learned, and get you working with the technology.

How It Works

After a *Try It Out* section, there will sometimes be a further explanation within a *How It Works* section, to help you relate what you've done to what you've just learned.

Words that appear on the screen in menus, like the File or Window menu, are in a similar font to what you see on screen.

Keys that you press on the keyboard, like *Ctrl* and *Enter*, are in italics.

We use two font styles for code. If it's a word that we're talking about in the text, for example, when discussing `functionNames()`, `<ELEMENTS>`, and `ATTRIBUTES`, it will be in a fixed pitch font. URLs and file names are also displayed in this font.

If it's a block of code that you can type in and run, or part of such a block, then it's also in a gray box:

```
<HTML>
   <HEAD>
      <TITLE>Simple Example</TITLE>
   </HEAD>
   <BODY>
      <SCRIPT LANGUAGE=JavaScript>
         document.write(Very simple JavaScript);
      </SCRIPT>
   </BODY>
</HTML>
```

Sometimes you'll see code in a mixture of styles, like this:

```
<HTML>
   <HEAD>
      <TITLE>Simple Example</TITLE>
   </HEAD>
   <BODY>
```

```
        <SCRIPT LANGUAGE=JavaScript>
          document.write(Very simple JavaScript);
        </SCRIPT>
    </BODY>
</HTML>
```

In this case, we want you to consider the code with the gray background in particular, for example to modify it. The code with a white background is code we've already looked at, and that we don't wish to examine further.

Downloading the Source Code

As we move through the chapters, there will be copious amounts of code available for you, so that you can see exactly how the JavaScript principles being explained work. We'll also be stopping frequently to try it out, so that you not only see how things work, but can make them work yourself.

The source code for all of the examples is available for download from the Wrox site (see below). However, you might decide that you prefer to type all the code in by hand. Many readers prefer this, because it's a good way to get familiar with the coding techniques that are being used.

Whether you want to type the code in or not, we have made all the source code for this book available at our web site, at the following address:

```
http://www.wrox.com
```

If you're one of those readers who likes to type in the code, you can use our files to check the results you should be getting – this should be your first stop if you think you might have typed in an error. If you're one of those readers who don't like typing, then downloading the source code from our web site is a must!

Either way, it'll help you with updates and debugging.

Tell Us What You Think

We've worked hard to make this book as relevant and useful as possible, so we'd like to get a feel for what it is you want and need to know, and what you think about how we've presented things.

If you have anything to say, let us know at:

```
feedback@wrox.com
```

Errata & Updates

We've made every effort to make sure there are no errors in the text or the code. However, to err is human, and as such we recognize the need to keep you informed of any mistakes as they're spotted and amended.

More details on obtaining support, finding out about errata, and providing us with feedback, can be found in Appendix J.

Online discussion at http://p2p.wrox.com

Introduction to JavaScript and the Web

In this introductory chapter, we'll take a look at what JavaScript is, what it can do for you, and what you need to be able to use it. With these foundations in place, we will see throughout the rest of the book how JavaScript can help you to create powerful web applications for your web site.

The easiest way to learn something is by actually doing it, so throughout the book we'll be creating a number of useful example programs using JavaScript. We start this process in this chapter, by the end of which you will have created your first piece of JavaScript code.

Additionally over the course of the book, we'll develop a complete JavaScript web application: an online trivia quiz. By seeing it develop, step-by-step, you'll get a good understanding of how to create your own web applications. At the end of this chapter, we'll look at the finished trivia quiz, and discuss the ideas behind its design.

Introduction to JavaScript

In this section, we're going to take a brief look at what JavaScript is, where it came from, how it works, and what sort of useful things we can do with it.

What is JavaScript?

Having bought this book you are probably already well aware that JavaScript is some sort of **computer language**, but what is a computer language? Put simply a computer language is a series of instructions that instruct the computer to do something. That something can be a wide variety of things, including displaying text, moving an image, or asking the user for information. Normally the instructions, or what is termed **code**, are **processed** from the top line downwards. Processed simply means that the computer looks at the code we've written, works out what action we want taken, and then takes that action. The actual act of processing the code is called **running** or **executing** it.

Using natural English, let's see what instructions, or code, we might write to make a cup of coffee.

1. Put coffee in cup

2. Fill kettle with water

3. Put kettle on to boil

4. Has the kettle boiled? If so, then pour water into cup, otherwise continue to wait

5. Drink coffee

We'd start running this code from the first line (instruction 1), and then continue to the next (instruction 2), then the next, and so on until we came to the end. This is pretty much how most computer languages work, JavaScript included. However, there are occasions when we might change the flow of execution, or even miss out code altogether, but we'll see more of this in Chapter 3.

JavaScript is an interpreted language, rather than a compiled language. What do we mean by the terms interpreted and compiled?

Well, to let you into a secret, your computer doesn't really understand JavaScript at all. It needs something to interpret the JavaScript code and convert it into something that it understands; hence it is an **interpreted language**. Computers only understand machine code, which is essentially a string of binary numbers (that is a string of zeros and ones). As the browser goes through the JavaScript, it passes it to a special program called an **interpreter**, which converts the JavaScript to the machine code your computer understands. The important point to note is that the conversion of the JavaScript happens at the time the code is run; it has to be repeated every time the code is run. JavaScript is not the only interpreted language: there are others, including VBScript.

The alternative **compiled language**, is one where the program code is converted to machine code before it's actually run, and this conversion only has to be done once. The programmer uses a compiler to convert the code that they wrote to machine code, and it is this machine code that is run by the program's user. Compiled languages include Visual Basic and C++.

Perhaps this is a good point to dispel a widespread myth: JavaScript is not the same as the Java language. In fact, although they share the same name, that's virtually all they do share. Particularly good news is that JavaScript is much, much easier to learn and use than Java. In fact, languages like JavaScript are the easiest of all languages to learn, but are still surprisingly powerful.

JavaScript and the Web

For most of this book we'll be looking at JavaScript code that runs inside a web page loaded into a browser. All we need to create these web pages is a text editor, for example Windows Notepad, and a web browser, such as Netscape Navigator or Internet Explorer, with which we can view our pages. These browsers come equipped with JavaScript interpreters.

In fact, the JavaScript language first became available in the web browser Netscape Navigator 2, part of the Netscape Communicator suite of web applications. Initially, it was called LiveScript. However, since Java was the hot technology of the time, Netscape decided that JavaScript sounded more exciting. Once JavaScript really took off, Microsoft decided to add their own brand of JavaScript to Internet Explorer, which they named JScript. Since then, both Netscape and Microsoft have released improved versions and included them in their latest browsers. Although these different brands and versions of JavaScript have much in common, there are enough differences to cause problems if we're not careful. In this book we'll make sure that our JavaScript code will work with the versions that come with both Netscape and Microsoft version 4 and later browsers. We'll look into the problems with different browsers and versions of JavaScript later in this chapter, and see how we deal with them.

The majority of the web pages containing JavaScript that we will create in the this book can be stored on your hard drive and loaded directly into your browser from the hard drive itself, just as you'd load any normal file like a text file. However, this is not how web pages are loaded when we browse web sites on the Internet. The Internet is really just one great big network connecting computers together. Web sites are a special service provided by particular computers on the Internet; the computers providing this service are said to **host web services** and are known as **web servers**.

Basically the job of a web server is to hold lots of web pages on its hard drive. Then, when a browser, usually on a different computer, requests a web page that is contained on that web server, the web server loads it from its own hard drive and then passes the page back to the requesting computer via a special communications protocol called **HyperText Transfer Protocol (HTTP)**. The computer running the web browser that makes the request is known as the **client**. Think of the client/server relationship as a bit like a customer/shop keeper relationship. The customer goes into a shop and says, "Give me one of those." The shopkeeper serves the customer by reaching for the item requested and passing it back to the customer. In a web situation, the client machine running the web browser is like the customer and the web server getting the page requested is like the shopkeeper.

When we type an address into the web browser, how does it know which web server to get the page from? Well, just as shops have addresses, say 45 Central Avenue, SomeTownsville, so do web servers. Web servers don't have street names; instead they have Internet Protocol (IP) **addresses**, which uniquely identify them on the Internet. These consist of four sets of numbers, separated by dots, for example `127.0.0.1`.

If you've ever surfed the net, you're probably wondering what on earth I'm talking about. Surely web servers have nice `www.somewebsite.com` names, not IP addresses? In fact, the `www.somewebsite.com` name is the "friendly" name for the actual IP address; it's a whole lot easier for us humans to remember. On the Internet, the friendly name is converted to the actual IP address by computers called **domain name servers**, something your Internet Service Provider will have set up for you.

Towards the end of the book, we'll go through the process of how to set up our own web server in a step-by-step guide. We'll then see that web servers are not just dumb machines that pass pages back to clients, but in fact can do a bit of processing using JavaScript themselves. We'll be looking at this later in the book as well.

Why Choose JavaScript?

JavaScript is not the only scripting language; there are others such as VBScript and Perl. So why choose JavaScript over the others?

The main reason for choosing JavaScript is its widespread use and availability. Both of the most commonly used browsers, Internet Explorer and Netscape Navigator, support JavaScript, as do some of the less commonly used browsers. So, basically we can assume that most people browsing our web site will have a version of JavaScript installed, though it is possible to use a browser's options to disable it.

Of the other scripting languages we mentioned, VBScript, which can be used for the same purposes as JavaScript, is only supported by Internet Explorer, and Perl is not used at all in web browsers.

JavaScript is also very versatile and not just limited to use within a web page. For example, it can be used to automate computer administration tasks. However, the question of which scripting language is the most powerful and useful has no real answer. Pretty much everything that can be accomplished in JavaScript can be done in VBScript and vice versa.

What can JavaScript do for me?

The most common use of JavaScript is interacting with your users, getting information from them and validating their actions. For example, say we wanted to put a drop-down menu on the page so that users can choose where they want to go to on our website. The drop-down menu might be plain old HTML, but it needs JavaScript behind it to actually do something with the user's input. Other examples of using JavaScript for interactions are given by forms, which are used for getting information from the user. Again these may be plain HTML, but we might want to check the validity of the information that the user is entering. For example, if we had a form taking a user's credit card details in preparation for the online purchase of goods, we'd want to make sure they have actually filled in their credit card details before we sent them the goods. We might also want to check that the data being entered is of the correct type, such as a number for their age rather than text.

JavaScript can also be used for various "tricks". One example is switching an image in a page for a different one when the user rolls their mouse over it, something often seen in web page menus. Also if you've ever seen scrolling messages in the browser's status bar (usually at the bottom of the browser window) and wondered how they manage that, then now's your chance to find out as this is another JavaScript trick. We'll demonstrate this later in the book. We'll also see how to create expanding menus that display a list of choices when a user rolls their mouse over them, another commonly seen JavaScript driven trick.

Tricks are OK up to a point, but even more useful can be small applications that provide a real service. Examples of the sort of things I mean are a mortgage seller's web site that has a JavaScript-driven mortgage calculator, or a web site about financial planning that includes a calculator that works out your tax bill for you. With a little inventiveness you'll find it's amazing what can be achieved.

Tools Needed to Create JavaScript Web Applications

All that you need to get started with creating JavaScript code for web applications is a simple text editor, such as Windows Notepad, or one of the many slightly more advanced text editors that provide line numbering, search and replace, and so on. An alternative is a proper HTML editor; you'll need one that allows you to edit the HTML source code, as that's where we need to add our JavaScript. There are also a number of very good tools specifically aimed at developing web-based applications, such as Microsoft's Visual InterDev. However, in this book we'll be concentrating on JavaScript, rather than any specific development tool. When it comes to learning the basics, it's often best to write the code by hand rather than relying on a tool to do it for you. This helps you to understand the fundamentals of the language before you attempt the more advanced logic that is beyond a tool's capability. Once you've got a good understanding of the basics, you can use tools as timesavers so that you can spend more time on the more advanced and more interesting coding.

You'll also need a browser to view your web pages in. It's best to develop your JavaScript code on the sort of browsers you expect visitors to your web site to be using. We'll see later in the chapter that there are different versions of JavaScript, each supported by different versions of the web browsers. Each of these JavaScript versions, while having a common core, also contains various extensions to the language. All the examples that we give in this book have been tested on Netscape Navigator versions 4.0, 4.7, and 6, and Internet Explorer versions 4.0 and 5.0. Wherever a piece of code does not work on any of these browsers, a note of this has been made in the text.

Even if your browser supports JavaScript, it is possible to disable this functionality in the browser. So, before we start on our first JavaScript examples in the next section, you should check whether JavaScript is enabled in your browser.

To do this in Netscape Navigator, choose Preferences from the Edit menu on the browser. In the window that appears, choose the Advanced tab. Check that the checkbox beside Enable JavaScript is checked. If not, then check it.

In Internet Explorer it is harder to turn off scripting. Choose Internet Options from the Tools menu on the browser, click the Security tab, and check whether the Internet or Local intranet options have custom security settings. If either of them do, click the Custom Level button, and scroll down to the Scripting section. Check that Active Scripting is set to Enable.

A final point to note is how to open our code examples in your browser. For most of the book (up to Chapter 15) you simply need to open the file from where it is stored on your hard drive. There are a number of ways to do this. One way you can do this in Internet Explorer is by choosing Open from the File menu, and clicking the Browse button to browse to where you stored the code. Similarly, in Netscape Navigator, you should choose Open Page from the File menu, and click the Choose File button, or in Netscape Navigator 6 choose Open File from the File menu.

The <SCRIPT> Tag and Your First Simple JavaScript Program

We've now talked around the subject of JavaScript for long enough; let's look at how we put it into our web page. We'll write our first piece of JavaScript code.

Inserting JavaScript in a web page is much like inserting any other HTML content; we use tags to mark out the start and end of our script code. The tag we use to do this is the <SCRIPT> tag. This tells the browser that the following chunk of text, bounded by the closing </SCRIPT> tag, is not HTML to be displayed, but rather script code to be processed. We call the chunk of code surrounded by the <SCRIPT> and </SCRIPT> tags a **script block**.

Basically when the browser spots <SCRIPT> tags, instead of trying to display the contained text to the user, it uses the browser's built in JavaScript interpreter to run the code's instructions. Of course, the code might give instructions about changes to the way the page is displayed or what is shown in the page, but the text of the code itself is never shown to the user.

We can put the <SCRIPT> tags inside the header (between the <HEAD> and </HEAD> tags), or inside the body (between the <BODY> and </BODY> tags) of the HTML page. However, we can't put them outside these areas, for example before the <HTML> tag or after the </HTML> tag, since anything outside these areas is not considered by the browser to be part of the web page and is ignored.

The <SCRIPT> tag has a number of attributes, but the most important one for us is the LANGUAGE attribute. As we saw above, JavaScript is not the only scripting language available, and different scripting languages need to be processed in different ways. We need to tell the browser which scripting language to expect, so that it knows how to process it. There are no prizes for guessing that the LANGUAGE attribute, when using JavaScript, takes the value JavaScript. So, our opening script tag will look like this:

```
<SCRIPT LANGUAGE="JavaScript">
```

Including the LANGUAGE attribute is good practice, but within a web page it can be left off. Browsers such as Internet Explorer (IE) and Netscape Navigator (NN) default to a script language of JavaScript. By this I mean that if the browser encounters a <SCRIPT> tag with no LANGUAGE attribute set, it assumes that the script block is written in JavaScript. However, it is good practice to always include the LANGUAGE attribute.

There are situations where JavaScript is not the default language, such as when script is run server-side (see Chapter 15), and in these situations we need to specify the language and sometimes the version of JavaScript that our web page requires. However, when *not* specifying the LANGUAGE attribute will cause problems, I'll be sure to warn you.

OK, let's take a look at our first page containing JavaScript code.

Try It Out – Painting the Document Red

We'll try out a simple example of using JavaScript to change the background color of the browser. In your text editor (I'm using Windows NotePad) type in the following:

```
<HTML>
<BODY BGCOLOR="WHITE">

<P>Paragraph 1</P>

<SCRIPT LANGUAGE="JavaScript">
    document.bgColor = "RED";
</SCRIPT>

</BODY>
</HTML>
```

Save the page as ch1_exampl.htm to a convenient place on your hard drive. Now load it into your web browser. You should see a red web page with the text Paragraph 1 in the top left hand corner. But wait – didn't we set the <BODY> tag's BGCOLOR attribute to white? OK, let's look at what's going on here.

How It Works

The page is contained within <HTML> and </HTML> tags. This then contains a <BODY> element. When we define the opening <BODY> tag, we use HTML to set the page's background color to white:

```
<BODY BGCOLOR="WHITE">
```

Then, we let the browser know that our next lines of code are JavaScript code by using the <SCRIPT> start tag:

```
<SCRIPT LANGUAGE="JavaScript">
```

Everything from here until the close tag, </SCRIPT>, is JavaScript and is treated as such by the browser. Within this script block, we use JavaScript to set the document's background color to red:

```
document.bgColor = "RED";
```

What we might call the page is known as the document when scripting in a web page. The document has lots of properties, including its background color, bgColor. We can reference properties of the document by writing document, then putting a dot, then the property name. Don't worry about use of the document at the moment, as we'll be looking at it in depth later in the book.

Note that this line of code is an example of a JavaScript **statement**. Every line of code between the <SCRIPT> and </SCRIPT> tags is called a statement.

You'll also see that there's a semicolon (;) at the end of the line. We use a semicolon in JavaScript to indicate the end of a line of code. In practice, JavaScript is very relaxed about the need for semicolons and will usually be able to work out, when you start a new line, whether you mean to start a new line of code. However, for good coding practice, you should use a semicolon at the end of statements of code, and a single JavaScript statement should fit onto one line and shouldn't be continued onto two or more lines. Moreover, you'll find there are times when you *must* include a semicolon, which we'll come to later in the book.

Finally, to tell the browser to stop interpreting our text as JavaScript and start interpreting it as HTML, we use the script close tag:

```
</SCRIPT>
```

We've now looked at how the code works, but we've not looked at the order in which it works. When the browser loads in the web page it goes through it, rendering it line by line. This process is called **parsing**. The web browser starts at the top of the page and works its way down to the bottom of the page. The browser comes to the `<BODY>` tag first and sets the document's background to white. Then it continues parsing the page. When it comes to the JavaScript code, it is instructed to change the document's background to red.

Try It Out – The Way Things Flow

Let's extend the previous example to demonstrate the parsing of a web page in action. Type the following into your text editor:

```
<HTML>
<BODY BGCOLOR="WHITE">

<P>Paragraph 1</P>

<SCRIPT LANGUAGE="JavaScript">
    // Script block 1
    alert("First Script Block");
</SCRIPT>

<P>Paragraph 2</P>

<SCRIPT LANGUAGE="JavaScript">
    // Script block 2
    document.bgColor = "RED";
    alert("Second Script Block");
</SCRIPT>

<P>Paragraph 3</P>

</BODY>
</HTML>
```

Save the file to your hard drive as `ch1_examp2.htm`, and then load it into your browser. When you load the page you should see the first paragraph, **Paragraph 1**, appear followed by a message box displayed by the first script block. The browser halts its parsing until you click the **OK** button. As you can see, the page background is white, as set in the `<BODY>` tag, and only the first paragraph is currently displayed.

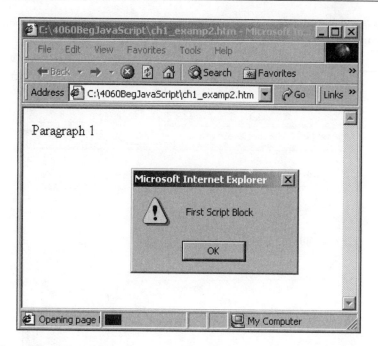

Click the **OK** button and the parsing continues. The browser displays the second paragraph and the second script block is reached, which changes the background color to red. Another message box is also displayed by the second script block.

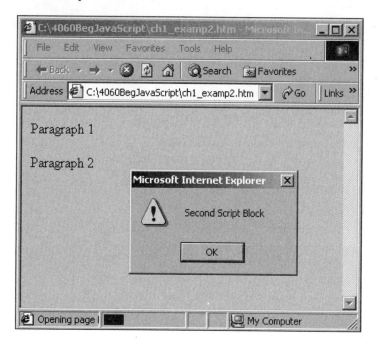

Click **OK** and again the parsing continues, with the third paragraph, Paragraph 3, being displayed. The web page is complete.

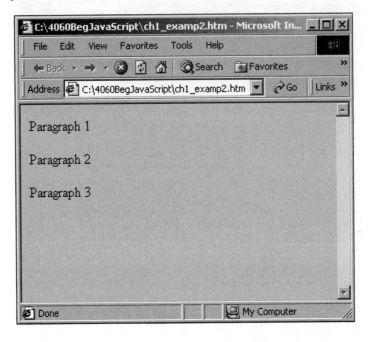

How It Works

The first part of the page is the same as in our earlier example. The background color for the page is set to white in the definition of the `<BODY>` tag, and then a paragraph is written to the page:

```
<HTML>
<BODY BGCOLOR="WHITE">

<P>Paragraph 1</P>
```

The first new section is contained in the first script block:

```
<SCRIPT LANGUAGE="JavaScript">
   // Script block 1
   alert("First Script Block");
</SCRIPT>
```

This script block contains two lines, both of which are new to us. The first line:

```
   // Script block 1
```

is just a **comment**, solely for our benefit. The browser recognizes anything on a line after a double forward slash (//) to be a comment, and does not do anything with it. It is useful for us as programmers, since we can add explanations to our code that make it easier for us to work out what we were doing when we come back to our code at a later date.

The `alert()` function in the second line of code is also new to us. Before we can explain what it does, we need to explain what a **function** is.

We will define functions properly in Chapter 3, but for now we just need to think of them as pieces of JavaScript code that we can use to do certain tasks. If you have a background in math, you may already have some idea of what a function is: it takes some information, processes it, and gives you a result. Functions makes life easier for us as programmers since we don't have to think about *how* the function does the task, but can just concentrate on when we want the task done.

In particular, the `alert()` function enables us to alert or inform the user about something, by displaying a message box. The message to be given in the message box is specified inside the parentheses of the `alert()` function and is known as the function's **parameter**.

The message box that's displayed by the `alert()` function is **modal**. This is an important concept, which we'll come across again. It simply means that the message box won't go away until the user closes it by clicking the **OK** button. In fact, parsing of the page stops at the line where the `alert()` function is used, and doesn't restart until the user closes the message box. This is quite useful for this example, as it allows us to demonstrate the results of what has been parsed so far: the page color has been set to white and the first paragraph has been displayed.

Once you click **OK**, the browser carries on parsing down the page through the following lines:

```
<P>Paragraph 2</P>

<SCRIPT LANGUAGE="JavaScript">
    // Script block 2
    document.bgColor = "RED";
    alert("Second Script Block");
</SCRIPT>
```

The second paragraph is displayed, and the second block of JavaScript is run. The first line of the script block code is another comment, so the browser ignores this. The second line of the script code we saw in our previous example – it changes the background color of the page to red. The third line of code is our `alert()` function, which displays the second message box. Parsing is brought to a halt until we close the message box by clicking **OK**.

When we close the message box, the browser moves on to the next lines of code in the page, displaying the third paragraph and finally ending our web page.

```
<P>Paragraph 3</P>

</BODY>
</HTML>
```

Another important point raised by this example is the difference between setting properties of the page, such as background color, via HTML and doing the same thing using JavaScript. The method of setting properties using HTML is **static**: a value can be set only once and never changed again using HTML. Setting properties using JavaScript enables us to dynamically change their values. By **dynamic**, I simply mean something that can be changed and whose value or appearance is not set in stone.

Our example is just that, an example. In practice if we wanted the page's background to be red, we would set the <BODY> tag's BGCOLOR attribute to "RED", and not use JavaScript at all. Where we *would* want to use JavaScript is where we want to add some sort of intelligence or logic to the page. For example, if the user's screen resolution is particularly low, then we might want to change what's displayed on the page; with JavaScript we can do this. Another reason for using JavaScript to change properties might be for special effects, for example making a page fade in from white to its final color.

A Brief Look at Browsers and Compatibility Problems

We've seen in the example above that using JavaScript we can change a web page's document's background color using the bgColor property of the document. The example worked whether you used a Netscape or Microsoft browser, and the reason for this is that both browsers support a document with a bgColor property. We can say that the example is **cross browser compatible**. However, unfortunately it's not always the case that the property or language feature available in one browser will be available in another browser. This is even sometimes the case between versions of the same browser.

The version numbers for Internet Explorer and Netscape Navigator browsers are usually written as a decimal number, for example Netscape Navigator has a version 4.06. In this book we will use the following terminology to refer to these versions. By version 4.x we mean all versions starting with the number 4. By version 4.0+ we mean all versions with a number greater than 4.

One of the main headaches involved in creating web-based JavaScript is the differences between different web browsers, the level of HTML they support, and the functionality their JavaScript interpreters can handle. You'll find that in one browser, you can move an image using just a couple of lines of code, and in another, it'll take a whole page of code, or even prove impossible. One version of JavaScript will contain a method to change text to upper case, and another won't. Each new release of Microsoft or Netscape browsers sees new and exciting features added to their HTML and JavaScript support. The good news is that with a little ingenuity we can write JavaScript that will work with both Microsoft and Netscape browsers.

Which browsers you want to support is really down to the browsers you think the majority of your web site's visitors, that is your **user base**, will be using. This book has been aimed at both Internet Explorer 4 and above (IE 4.0+) and Netscape Navigator 4 and above (NN 4.0+).

If we want our website to be professional, we need to somehow deal with older browsers. We could make sure our code is backwardly compatible, that is it only uses features that were available in older browsers. However, we may decide that it's simply not worth limiting ourselves to the features of older browsers. In this case we need to make sure our pages degrade gracefully. What is meant by degrade gracefully is that, although our pages won't work in older browsers, they will fail in a way that means the user is either never aware of the failure or is alerted to the fact that certain features on the website are not compatible with their browser. The alternative to degrading gracefully is for our code to raise lots of error messages, cause strange results to be displayed on the page, and generally make us look like idiots who don't know what we're doing!

So how do we make our web pages degrade gracefully? You can do this by using JavaScript to check which browser the web page is running in after it has been partially or completely loaded. We can use this information to determine what scripts to run, or even to re-direct the user to another page written to make best use of their particular browser. In later chapters, we'll see how to check for the browser version and take appropriate action, so that your pages work acceptably on as many browsers as possible.

Below is a table listing the different versions of JavaScript (and JScript) that Microsoft and Netscape browsers support. However, it is a necessary over simplification to some extent, because there is no exact feature-by-feature compatibility. We can only indicate the extent to which different versions have similarities. Also, as we'll see in Chapter 12, it's not just the JavaScript support that is a problem, but also the extent to which the HTML can be altered by code.

On a more positive note, the core of the JavaScript language does not vary too much between JavaScript versions; the differences are mostly useful extra features, which are nice-to-haves but often not essential. We'll concentrate on the core parts of the JavaScript language in the next few chapters.

Language Version	Netscape Navigator Version	Internet Explorer Version
JavaScript 1.0 (equivalent to JScript 1.0)	2.x	3.x
JavaScript 1.1	3.x	–
JavaScript 1.2 (equivalent to JScript 3.0)	4.0 - 4.05	4.x
JavaScript 1.3	4.06+	–
JavaScript 1.4 (equivalent to JScript 5.0)	–	5.x
JavaScript 1.5	6.0	–

Introducing the Trivia Quiz

Over the course of the book, we'll be developing a full web-based application, namely a trivia quiz. The trivia quiz works with both Netscape Navigator 4.0+ and Internet Explorer 4.0+ web browsers, making full use of their JavaScript capabilities. Initially, the quiz runs purely using JavaScript code in the web browser, but later it will also use JavaScript running on a web server to access a Microsoft Access database containing the questions.

Let's take a look at what the quiz will finally look like. The main starting screen is shown below. Here the user can choose the number of questions that they want to answer and whether to set themselves a time limit. Using a JavaScript-based timer, we keep track of when the time that they have allotted themselves is up.

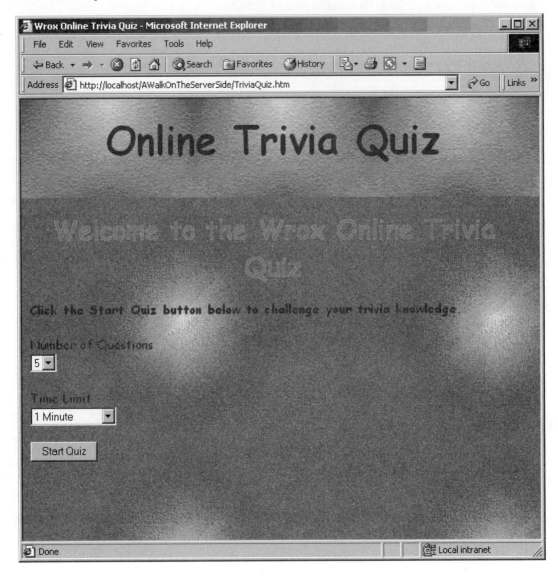

Having clicked the Start Quiz button, the user is faced with a random choice of question pulled from the database that we'll create to hold the trivia questions. There are two types of question. The first, as shown below, is the multiple-choice based question. There is no limit to the number of answer options that we can specify for these types of questions: the JavaScript handles it without the need for each question to be programmed differently.

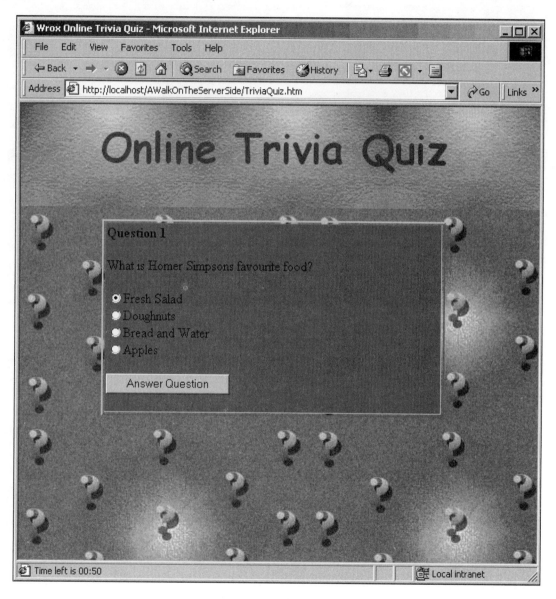

The second question style is a text-based one. The user types the answer into a box provided and then JavaScript does its best to intelligently interpret what they have written. For example, for the question shown overleaf I have entered Richard Nixon, the correct answer. However, the JavaScript has been programmed to also accept R. Nixon, Nixon, Richard M. Nixon and so on, as a correct answer. We'll find out how in Chapter 8 on text manipulation.

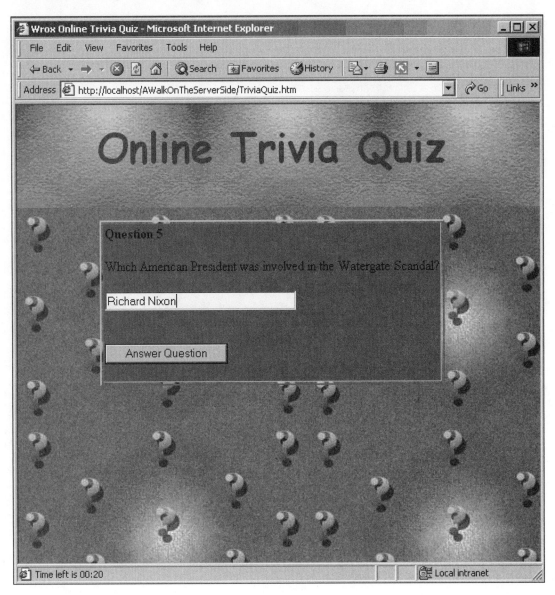

Finally, once the questions have all been answered, the final page of the quiz displays the user's results. This page also contains two buttons: one to restart the quiz and another to reset the quiz statistics for the current user.

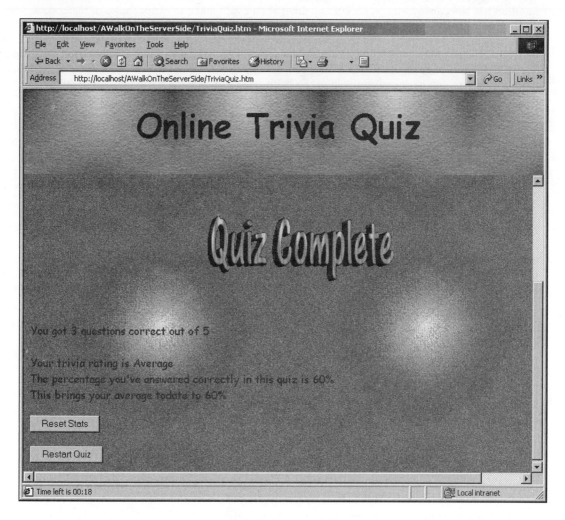

Ideas Behind the Coding of the Trivia Quiz

We've taken a brief look at the final version of the trivia quiz in action and will be looking at the actual code in later chapters, but it's worthwhile considering what the guiding principles behind its design and programming are.

One of the most important ideas that we use is of code reuse. We save time and effort by making use of the same code again and again. Quite often in a web application, you'll find that you need to do the same thing over and over again. For example, we'll need to make use of the code that checks if a question has been answered correctly many times. You could make as many copies of the code as you needed, and add this code to your page wherever you need it. However, this makes maintaining the code difficult, because if you need to correct an error or to add a new feature, then you will need to make the change to the code in lots of different places. Once the code for a web application grows from a few lines in one page to many lines over a number of pages, it's quite difficult actually keeping track of the places where you have copied the code. So, with reuse in mind, the trivia quiz keeps all the important code that will need to be used a number of times in one place.

The same ideas go for any data you use. For example, in the trivia quiz we keep track of the number of questions that have been answered in one place, and update this information in as few places as possible.

Sometimes you have no choice but to put important code in more than one place, for example, when you need information that can only be obtained in a particular circumstance. However, if you can keep it in one place, then you'll find doing so makes coding more efficient.

In the trivia quiz, I've also tried to split the code into specific **functions**. We will be looking at JavaScript functions in detail in Chapter 3. In our trivia quiz, the function that provides us with a randomly selected question for our web page to display is in one place, regardless of whether this is a multiple-choice question or a purely text based question. By doing this, we're not only just writing code once, but we're also making life easier for ourselves by keeping code that provides the same service or function in one place. As you'll see later in the book, the code for creating these different question types is very different, but at least putting it in the same logical place makes it easy to find.

When creating your own web-based applications, you might find it useful to break the larger concept, here a trivia quiz, into smaller ideas. Breaking it down makes writing the code a lot easier. Rather than sitting down with a blank screen and thinking, "Right, now I must write a trivia quiz," you can think, "Right, now I must write some code to create a question." I find this technique makes coding a lot less scary and easier to get started on. This method of splitting the requirements of a piece of code down into smaller and more manageable parts is often referred to as 'divide and conquer'.

Let's use the trivia quiz as an example. Our trivia quiz application needs to do the following things:

- ❑   Ask a question
- ❑   Retrieve and check the answer provided by the user to see if it's correct
- ❑   Keep track of how many questions have been asked
- ❑   Keep track of how many questions the user has got right
- ❑   Keep track of the time remaining if it's a timed quiz, and stop the quiz when the time is up
- ❑   Show a final summary of the number of correct answers given out of the number answered

These are the core ingredients for the trivia quiz. There may be other things that you want to do like keeping track of the number of user visits, but these are really external to the functionality of the trivia quiz.

Once you've broken the whole concept into various logical areas, it's sometimes worth using the 'divide and conquer' technique again to break down the sub-areas into smaller chunks, particularly if the sub-area is quite complex or involved. As an example, let's take the 'Ask a question' item from the above list.

Asking a question will involve:

❑ Retrieving the question data from where it is stored, for example from a database

❑ Processing the data and converting it to a form that can be presented to the user. Here we need to create HTML to be displayed in a web page. How we process the data depends on the question style: multi-choice or text

❑ Displaying the question for the user to answer

As we build up the trivia quiz over the course of the book, we'll look at its design and some of the tricks and tactics that are used in more depth. We'll also break down each function as we come to it, to make it clear what needs to be done.

What Functionality do we Add and Where?

How do we build up the functionality needed in the trivia quiz? The following list should give you an idea of what we add and in which chapter.

In Chapter 2, we start the quiz off by defining the multiple-choice questions that will be asked. We do this using something called an array, which is also introduced in that chapter.

In Chapter 3, where we talk about functions in more detail, we add a function to the code that will check to see if the user has entered the correct answer or not.

After a couple of chapters of theory, in Chapter 6 we get the quiz into its first 'usable' state. We display the questions to the user, and allow the user to answer these questions.

In Chapter 7, we enhance the quiz by turning it into what is called a 'multi-frame application'. We add a button that the user can press to start the quiz, and specify that the quiz must finish after all the questions have been asked, rather than the questions being repeated indefinitely.

In Chapter 8 we add the text-based questions to the quiz. These must be treated slightly differently from multiple-choice questions, both in how they are displayed to the user and in how their answer is checked. As we saw above, the quiz will accept a number of different correct answers for these questions.

In Chapter 9, we allow the user to choose the number of questions that they wish to answer, and also whether they want to have a time limit for the quiz. If they choose to impose a time limit upon themselves, we count down the time in the status bar of the window, and inform them when their time is up.

In Chapter 11, we will store information about the user's previous results, using cookies, which are introduced in that chapter. This enables us to give the user a running average score at the end of the quiz.

In Chapter 15, the quiz goes server-side! We move a lot of the processing of the quiz so that it occurs on the server before the page is sent to the user. We use the server to store information about the number of questions and time limit that the user has chosen, so that these values can be displayed to the user as the default values the next time they start the quiz.

Finally, in Chapter 16, we change the way that the quiz gets the questions, from an array to a server-side database. This way, we can add new questions to the quiz more easily.

Summary

In this brief introduction to JavaScript you should have got a feel for what JavaScript is and what it can do. In particular this chapter covered the following:

❑   We looked into the process the browser follows when interpreting our web page. It goes though the page line by line (parsing), and acts upon our HTML tags and JavaScript code as it comes to it.

❑   When developing for the web using JavaScript, there are two places where we can choose our code to be executed: server-side or client-side. Client-side is essentially the side on which the browser is running – the user's machine. Server-side refers to any processing or storage done on the web server itself.

❑   Unlike many programming languages, JavaScript requires just a text editor to start creating code. Something like Windows NotePad is fine for getting started, though more extensive tools will prove valuable once you get more experienced.

❑   JavaScript code is embedded into the web page itself along with the HTML. Its existence is marked out by the use of <SCRIPT> tags. As with HTML, script executes from the top of the page and works down to the bottom, interpreting and executing the code line by line as it's reached.

❑   We introduced the online trivia quiz, which is the case study that we'll be building over the course of the book. We took a look at some of the design ideas behind the trivia quiz's coding, and explained how the functionality of the quiz is built up over the course of the book.

Data Types and Variables

One of the main uses of computers is to process and display information. By processing we mean that the information is modified, interpreted, or filtered in some way by the computer. For example, on an online banking web site, a customer may request details of all monies paid out from their account in the last month. Here the computer would retrieve the information, filter out any information not relating to payments made in the last month, and then display it in a web page. In some situations, information is processed without display, and at other times, information is obtained directly without being processed. For example, in a banking environment, regular payments may be processed and transferred electronically without any human interaction or display.

In computing we refer to information as **data**. This data comes in all sorts of forms, such as numbers, text, dates, and times to mention just a few. In this chapter, we'll be looking specifically at how JavaScript handles data such as numbers and text. An understanding of how data is handled is fundamental to any programming language.

We start the chapter by looking at the various types of data JavaScript can process. Then we look at how we can store this data in the computer's memory so that we can use it again and again in the code. Finally, we'll see how to use JavaScript to manipulate and process the data.

Types of Data in JavaScript

Data can come in many different forms, or what we term **types**. Some of the data types that JavaScript handles you'll recognize from the world outside programming, for example, numbers and text. Other data types are a little bit more abstract and are used to make programming easier, one example being the object data type, which we won't see in detail until Chapter 4.

Some programming languages are strongly typed languages. In these languages, whenever we use a piece of data we need to explicitly state what sort of data we are dealing with, and use of that data must follow strict rules applicable to its type. For example, we can't add a number and a word together.

JavaScript, on the other hand, is a weakly typed language and is a lot more forgiving about how we use different types of data. When we deal with data, we often don't need to specify what type of data it is; JavaScript will work it out for itself. Furthermore, when we are using different types of data at the same time, JavaScript will workout behind the scenes what it is we're trying to do.

Given how easygoing JavaScript is about data, why do we need to talk about data types at all? Why not just cut to the chase and start using data without worrying about its type?

First of all, while JavaScript is very good at working out what data it's dealing with, there are occasions when it'll get things wrong or at least not do what we want it to do. In these situations, we need to make it explicit to JavaScript what sort of data type we intended and how it should be used. To do that, we first need to know a little bit about data types.

A second reason why there's a need to know about data types is that it enables us to use data effectively in our code. The things that can be done with data and the results you'll get will depend on the type of data being used, even though we don't specify explicitly what type it is. So, while trying to multiply two numbers together makes sense, doing the same thing with text doesn't. Also, the result of adding two numbers together is very different from adding text together. With numbers we get the total of their sum, but with text we get one big piece of text consisting of the other pieces of text joined together.

Let's take a brief look at some of the more commonly used data types: numerical, text, and Boolean. We will see how to use them later in the chapter.

Numerical Data

Numerical data comes in two forms:

❑ Whole numbers, such as 145, which are also known as **integers**. These numbers can be positive or negative and can span a very wide range: -2^{53} to 2^{53}.

❑ Fractional numbers, such as 1.234, which are also known as **floating-point** numbers. Like integers, they can be positive or negative and they also have a massive range.

In simple terms, unless you're writing specialized scientific applications, you're not going to face problems with the size of numbers available in JavaScript. Also, although we can treat integer and floating-point numbers differently when it comes to storing them, JavaScript actually treats them both as floating-point numbers. It kindly hides the detail from us so we don't need to worry about it.

Text Data

Another term for one or more characters of text is a **string**. We tell JavaScript that text is to be treated as text and not as code simply by enclosing it inside quote marks ("). For example, "Hello World" and "A" are examples of strings that JavaScript will recognize. You can also use the single quote marks ('), so 'Hello World' and 'A' are also examples of strings that JavaScript will recognize. However, you must end the string with the same quote mark that you started it with. Therefore, "A' is not a valid JavaScript string, and neither is 'Hello World".

What if you want a string with a single quote mark in the middle, say a string like Peter O'Toole? If you enclose it in double quotes you'll be fine, so "Peter O'Toole" is recognized by JavaScript. However, 'Peter O'Toole' will produce an error. This is because JavaScript thinks that your text string is Peter O (that is, it treats the middle single quote as marking the end of the string) and falls over wondering what the Toole' is.

Another way around this is to tell JavaScript that the middle ' is part of the text and is not indicating the end of the string. You do this by using the \ character, which has special meaning in JavaScript and is referred to as an **escape character**. The \ tells the browser that the next character is not the end of the string, but part of the text. So, `'Peter O\'Toole'` will work as planned.

What if you want to use a double quote inside a string enclosed in double quotes? Well, everything we have just said above about the single quote still applies. So `'Hello "Paul"'` works, but `"Hello "Paul""` won't. However, `"Hello \"Paul\""` will work.

There are a lot of other special characters in JavaScript, which can't be typed in, but can be represented using the escape character in conjunction with other characters to create **escape sequences**. The principle behind this is similar to that used in HTML. For example, more than one space in a row is ignored in HTML, so we represent a space by . Similarly, in JavaScript there are instances where we can't use a character directly, but must use an escape sequence. The table below details some of the more useful escape sequences:

Escape Sequences	Character Represented
\b	Backspace
\f	Form feed
\n	New line
\r	Carriage return
\t	Tab
\'	Single quote
\"	Double quote
\\	Backslash
\xNN	NN is a hexadecimal number which identifies a character in the Latin-1 character set

The least obvious of these is the last, which represents individual characters by their character number in the Latin-1 character set rather than by their normal appearance. Appendix D contains the full Latin-1 character set. Let's pick an example: say we wanted to include the copyright symbol   in our string. What would our string need to look like? The answer is `"\xA9 Paul Wilton"`. If you look in the appendix table, you'll see that the character number of the copyright symbol is the hexadecimal number A9, so this is the number we need.

There is a similar way of referring to characters using their Unicode escape sequence. However, this is only valid in JavaScript version 1.3 and later (that is IE 4.0+ and NN 4.06+). These are written \uNNNN where NNNN refers to the Unicode number for that particular character. For example, to refer to the copyright symbol using this method, you would use `\u00A9`.

Boolean Data

The use of yes or no, positive or negative, and true or false is commonplace in the 'real' world. The idea of true and false is also fundamental to digital computers themselves; they don't understand maybes, only true and false. In fact, the concept of 'yes or no' is so useful it has its own data type in JavaScript: the **Boolean** data type. The Boolean type has two possible values: `true` for yes and `false` for no.

The purpose of Boolean data in JavaScript is just the same as in the world outside programming; it allows us to answer questions and make decisions based on the answer. For example, if I ask you, "Is this book about JavaScript?" you would hopefully answer, "Yes it is," or you might also say, "That's true". Similarly we might say, "If it's false that the subject of the book is JavaScript, then put it down." Here we have a Boolean logic statement (named after its inventor George Boole), which asks a question and then does something based on whether the answer was true or false. In JavaScript, we can use the same sort of Boolean logic to give our programs decision-making abilities. We'll be taking a more detailed look at Boolean logic in the next chapter.

Variables – Storing Data in Memory

Data can be stored either permanently or temporarily.

Important data, such as the details of a person's bank account, we will want to keep in a permanent store. For example, when Ms Bloggs takes 10 dollars or pounds or euros out of her account, we want to deduct the money from her account and keep a permanent record of the new balance. Information like this might be stored in something called a **database**. We'll be looking at databases in detail in Chapter 16.

However, there are other cases where we don't want to permanently store data, but simply want to keep a temporary note of it. Let's look at an example. Say Ms Bloggs has a loan from BigBadBank Inc. and wants to find out how much is still outstanding on this loan. She goes to the online banking page for loans, and clicks a link to find out how much she owes. This is data that will be stored permanently somewhere. However, suppose we also provide a facility for increasing loan repayments to pay off the loan early. If Ms Bloggs enters an increased repayment amount into the text box on the web page, we might want to show how much sooner the loan will be paid. This will involve a few possibly complex calculations, so to make it easier we want to write code that calculates the result in several stages, storing the result at each stage as we go along, before providing a final result. Once we've done the calculation and displayed the results, there's no need to permanently store the results for each stage, so rather than use a database, we need to use something called a **variable**. Why named variable? Well, perhaps because a variable can be used to store temporary data that can be varied.

Another bonus of variables is that unlike permanent storage, which might be saved to disk or magnetic tape, variables are held in the computers memory. This means that it is much, much faster to store and retrieve the data.

So what makes variables good places for temporarily storing your data? Well, variables have a limited lifetime. What I mean by this is that once your visitors close the page or move to a new one, your variables are lost, unless you take some steps to save them somewhere.

Each variable is given a name so that you can refer to it elsewhere in your code. These names must follow certain rules.

As with much of JavaScript code, you'll find that variable names are case sensitive. For example, `myVariable` is not the same as `myvariable`. You'll find that this is a very easy way for errors to slip into your code, even when you become an expert at JavaScript.

There are also certain names and characters that you can't use for your variable names. Names you can't use are called **reserved** words. Reserved words are words that JavaScript uses itself, for example the word `var` or the word `with`, and so reserves for its own use. You'll find a complete list of reserved words in Appendix B. Certain characters are also forbidden in variable names. For example, the ampersand (`&`) and the percent sign (`%`). Again, you'll find a full list in Appendix B. You are allowed to use numbers in your variable names, but the names mustn't begin with numbers. So `101myVariable` is not OK, but `myVariable101` is. Let's look at some more examples.

Invalid names include:

❑   `with`

❑   `99variables`

❑   `my%Variable`

❑   `theGood&theBad`

Valid names include:

❑   `myVariable99`

❑   `myPercent_Variable`

❑   `the_Good_and_the_Bad`

You may wish to use a naming convention for your variables, for example one that describes what sort of data you plan to hold in the variable. There are lots of different ways of notating your variables – none are right or wrong, but it is best to stick with one of them. One common method is **Hungarian notation**, where the beginning of each variable name is a three letter identifier indicating the data type. For example, we may start integer variable names with `int`, floating-point variable names with `flt`, string variable names with `str`, and so on. However, as long as the names you use make sense and are used consistently it really doesn't matter what you use.

Declaring Variables and Giving Them Values

Before you can use a variable, you should declare its existence to the computer using the `var` keyword. This warns the computer that it needs to reserve some memory for your data to be stored in later. To declare a new variable called `myFirstVariable` you would write:

```
var myFirstVariable;
```

Note that the semicolon at the end of the line is not part of the variable name, but instead is used to indicate to JavaScript the end of a line of code. This line is an example of a JavaScript statement.

Once declared, a variable can be used to store any type of data. As we said earlier, many other programming languages, called strongly typed languages, require you to declare not only the variable, but also the type of data, such as numbers or text, that it will be used to store. However, JavaScript is a **weakly typed** language; you don't need to limit yourself to what type of data a variable can hold.

You put data into your variables, a process called **assigning values** to your variables, by using the equals sign (=). For example, if you want your variable named myFirstVariable to hold the number 101, you would write:

```
myFirstVariable = 101;
```

The = sign has a special name when used to assign values to a variable; it's called the **assignment operator**.

Try It Out – Declaring Variables

Let's look at an example in which we declare a variable, store some data in it, and finally access its contents. We'll also see that variables can hold any type of data, and that the type of data being held can be changed. For instance, we can start by storing text, then change to storing numbers, without JavaScript having any problems. Type the following code into your text editor and save it as ch2_examp1.htm:

```
<HTML>
<HEAD>
</HEAD>
<BODY>

<SCRIPT LANGUAGE=JavaScript>

var myFirstVariable;

myFirstVariable = "Hello";
alert(myFirstVariable);

myFirstVariable = 54321;
alert(myFirstVariable);

</SCRIPT>

</BODY>
</HTML>
```

As soon as you load this into your web browser, it should show an alert box with Hello in it. This is the content of the variable myFirstVariable at that point in the code:

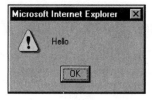

Click OK and another alert box appears with 54321 in. This is the new value we assigned to the variable myFirstVariable.

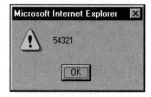

How It Works

Within the script block, we first declare our variable:

```
var myFirstVariable;
```

Currently, its value is undefined as we've only declared its existence to the computer, not actually stored any data inside it. However, in the next line we assign myFirstVariable a string value, namely the value "Hello":

```
myFirstVariable = "Hello";
```

Here we have assigned the variable a **literal** value, that is, a piece of actual data rather than data obtained by a calculation or from another variable. Almost anywhere that you can use a literal string or number, you can replace it with a variable containing number or string data. We see an example of this in the next line of code where we use our variable myFirstVariable in the alert() function that we saw in the last chapter:

```
alert(myFirstVariable);
```

This causes the first alert box to appear. Next we store a new value in our variable, this time a number:

```
myFirstVariable = 54321;
```

The previous value of myFirstVariable is lost forever. The memory space used to store the value is freed up automatically by JavaScript in a process called **garbage collection**. Whenever JavaScript detects that the contents of a variable are no longer usable, such as when we allocate a new value, it performs the garbage collection process and makes the memory available. Without this automatic garbage collection process, more and more of the computer's memory would be consumed, until eventually the computer ran out and the system ground to a halt. However, garbage collection is not always as efficient as it should be and may not occur until another page is loaded.

Just to prove that the new value has been stored, we use the alert() function again to display the variable's new contents:

```
alert(myFirstVariable);
```

Assigning Variables with the Value of Other Variables

We've seen that we can assign a variable with a number or string, but can we assign a variable with the data stored inside another variable? The answer is yes, very easily, and in exactly the same way as giving a variable a literal value. For example, if we have declared two variables myVariable and myOtherVariable, and have given the variable myOtherVariable the value 22, like this:

```
var myVariable;
var myOtherVariable;
myOtherVariable = 22;
```

then we can use the following line to assign myVariable with the same value as myOtherVariable (that is, 22):

```
myVariable = myOtherVariable;
```

Try It Out – Assigning Variables the Values of Other Variables

Let's look at another example, this time assigning variables the values of other variables. Type the code into your text editor and save it as ch2_examp2.htm:

```
<HTML>
<BODY>

<SCRIPT LANGUAGE=JavaScript>

var string1 = "Hello";
var string2 = "Goodbye";

alert(string1);
alert(string2);

string2 = string1;

alert(string1);
alert(string2);

string1 = "Now for something different";

alert(string1);
alert(string2);

</SCRIPT>

</BODY>
</HTML>
```

Load the page into your browser and you'll see a series of six alert boxes appear. Click OK for each one to see the next. The first two show the values of string1 and string2 respectively, Hello and Goodbye.

Then we assign string2 the value that's in string1. The next two alert boxes show string1 and string2's contents; this time both are Hello.

Finally, we change the value of string1. Note that the value of string2 remains unaffected. The final two alert boxes show the new value of string1 (Now for something different) and the unchanged value of string2 (Hello).

How It Works

The first thing we do in the script block is to declare our two variables, string1 and string2. However, notice that we have assigned them with values at the same time as we have declared them. This is a short cut, called **initializing**, that saves us typing too much code.

```
var string1 ="Hello";
var string2 = "Goodbye";
```

Note that we can use this short cut with all data types, not just strings. In the next two lines, we show the current value of each variable to the user using the `alert()` function:

```
alert(string1);
alert(string2);
```

Then, we assign `string2` with the value that's contained in `string1`. To prove that the assignment really has worked, we again show the user the contents of each variable using the `alert()` function:

```
string2 = string1;

alert(string1);
alert(string2);
```

Next, we set `string1` to a new value:

```
string1 = "Now for something different";
```

This leaves `string2` with its current value, demonstrating that `string2` has its own copy of the data assigned to it from `string1` in the previous step. We'll see in later chapters that this is not always the case. However, as a general rule we find that basic data types such as text and numbers are always copied when assigned, while more complex data types, like the objects that we'll come across in Chapter 4, are actually shared and not copied. For example, if we have a variable with the string "Hello" and assign five other variables with the value of this variable, then we now have the original data and five independent copies of the data. However, if it was an object rather than a string and we did the same thing we'd find we still have only one copy of the data, but now six variables share it. Changing it using any of the six variable names would change it for all of them.

Finally, the `alert()` function is used to show the current values of each variable:

```
alert(string1);
alert(string2);
```

Setting Up Your Browser for Errors

Although our code has been fairly simple so far, it is still possible for us to make errors when typing it in. As we start to look at more complex and detailed code, this will become more and more of a problem. So, before we move on to look at how we can use the data stored in variables, it seems like a good point to discuss how to ensure that any errors that arise in our code are shown to us by the browser, so that we can go away and correct them.

When you are surfing other people's websites, you probably won't be interested in seeing when there are errors in their code. In this situation, it's tempting to find a way of switching off the display of error dialog boxes in the browser. However, as JavaScript programmers, we want to know all the gory details about errors in our web pages; that way we can fix them before someone else spots them. It's important, therefore, to make sure the browsers we use to test our web sites are configured correctly to show errors and their details. In this section, this is exactly what we're going to do.

Displaying Errors in Netscape Navigator

There are different ways of displaying errors in Netscape Navigator depending on the version that you have installed.

If you have NN 4.0 – 4.05, then error messages are displayed in dialog boxes that pop up on your screen. This should be set up by default.

If you have NN 4.06+, then you can use the JavaScript console. The console allows you to 'interact' with the error – we leave further discussion of this functionality until Chapter 10.

To set up the JavaScript console to appear whenever an error occurs, you need to set the preferences for displaying errors by modifying the preference file, `prefs.js`:

1. Make sure Navigator is not running. If it is, then it may overwrite your changes when you edit the preferences file.

2. Open `prefs.js` using a text editor such as NotePad. The preference file is in the user's own directory under the `Netscape/Users` directory. For example, for NN 4.7 on Windows NT, you may find `prefs.js` in:

   ```
   <Netscape path>\Users\<user name>
   ```

   Just in case things go wrong, it might be an idea to save a backup version of the file elsewhere, before changing it.

3. Add the following line to the bottom of the `prefs.js` file:

   ```
   user_pref("javascript.console.open_on_error", true);
   ```

4. Save and close the file `prefs.js`.

Another way of opening up the JavaScript console is by typing `javascript:` into the location box of the Netscape browser.

However, at the time of writing, these two methods do not work on Netscape 6. On this browser you need to choose Tools from the Tasts menu, and select the JavaScript Console option.

Displaying Errors in Internet Explorer

Normally, IE will by default display JavaScript errors using dialog boxes.

However, it is possible to turn off the displaying of such errors, in which case we need to follow a few simple steps to re-enable error displaying.

First open up Internet Explorer and select the **Internet Options** menu from the **Tools** menu:

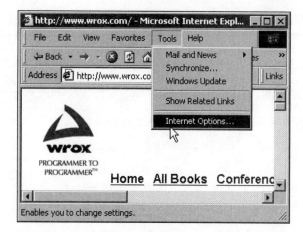

In the dialog box that appears, select the **Advanced** tab. Under **Browsing**, make sure the checkbox next to **Disable script debugging** is not ticked. If it is then clear it. Once you've done this you can click the **OK** button to close the dialog box.

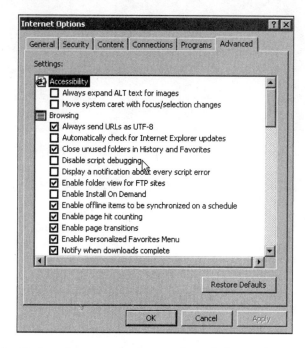

OK, now we've got the display of error messages sorted out, let's see what does happen when we have an error in our code.

What Happens when we get an Error

As we mentioned in the previous section, the use of a reserved word in a variable name will result in a JavaScript error in the browser. However, the error message displayed may not be instantly helpful. It may not indicate that you've used a reserved word in declaring your variables. Let's look at the sort of error messages you might see in this situation. Note that these error messages can also be produced by other mistakes not related to variable naming, which can get confusing at times. We'll look at these other mistakes later in the book and, indeed, the whole of Chapter 10 is devoted to spotting and fixing errors.

Let's assume that we try to define a variable called with like this:

```
var with;
```

The word with is reserved in JavaScript. What errors will we see?

If you load the page in a Netscape browser that is using dialog boxes to show errors, you'll see something like:

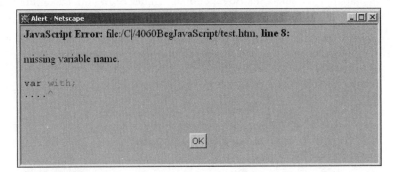

The same mistake in NN using the JavaScript console to show the error, will produce something like:

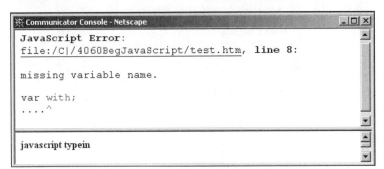

In Internet Explorer, the number of different dialog boxes that can be produced by the same error is more confusing. The messages depend on which version of Internet Explorer you have, and whether you have installed additional components such as the Microsoft Script Debugger, which we'll see in use in Chapter 10.

For example, using a reserved word for a variable name produces an error message telling you that an identifier was expected. On my machine, which has Microsoft's Visual Studio installed, the error message dialog box I get is shown below:

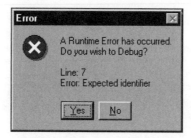

You'll also get the dialog shown above if you have installed the script debugger component available from Microsoft. This message box will appear whether you're using IE 4 or IE 5.

However, if you're using IE 5 and don't have Visual Studio or the script debugger installed, the error dialog you'll see will probably be similar to that below:

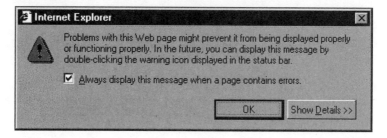

We really want to see what went wrong so we can fix our script. To do this, click the Show Details button and you'll be told where the error is and what it is:

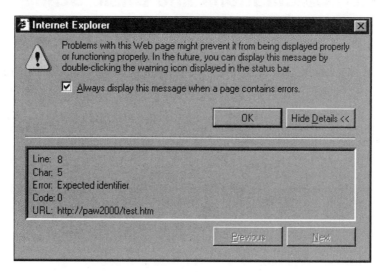

If you have IE 5 and didn't see either of the error messages above, then don't panic. In the browser's status bar (usually at the bottom of the browser window), you'll notice a little yellow triangle with an exclamation mark inside it. Double-click the yellow triangle and the error message dialog box will appear.

Finally, if you have IE 4 installed and no script debugger, then you'll see a plain dialog box pop up like that shown below:

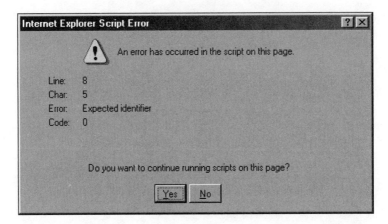

For the rest of the book, I'll show error dialog messages for Internet Explorer 5 with the script debugger installed. Bear in mind, though, that it doesn't matter what your dialog box looks like, so long as you're getting an indication that an error has occurred and what has caused it.

Using Data – Calculations and Basic String Manipulation

Now that we've seen how to cope with errors, we can get back to the main subject of this chapter: data and how to use it. We've seen how to declare variables, and how they can store information, but so far we've not done anything really useful with this – so just why would we want to use variables at all?

What variables allow us to do is temporarily hold information that we can use for processing in mathematical calculations, in building up text messages, or processing words that the user has entered, for example. Variables are a little bit like the memory store button on the average pocket calculator. Say you were adding up your finances. You might first add up all the money you needed to spend, and then store it in temporary memory. Once you had added up all your money coming in, you could deduct the amount stored in the memory to figure out how much is left over. Variables can be used in a similar way; we can first gain the necessary user input and store it in variables, then we can do our calculations using the values obtained.

In this section, we'll see how we can put the values stored in variables to good use in both number crunching and text-based operations.

Numerical Calculations

JavaScript has a range of basic mathematical capabilities, such as addition, subtraction, multiplication, and division. Each of the basic math functions is represented by a symbol, +, -, *, and / respectively. We call these symbols **operators** since they operate on the values we give them. In other words, they perform some calculation or operation and return us a result. You can use the results of these calculations almost anywhere you'd use a number or a variable.

Let's imagine we were calculating the total value of items on a shopping list. We could write this calculation as:

Total cost of shopping $= 10 + 5 + 5$

or, if we actually calculate the sum, it's:

Total cost of shopping $= 20$

Now let's see how we would do this in JavaScript. In actual fact, it is very similar except that we need to use a variable to store the final total:

```
var TotalCostOfShopping;
TotalCostOfShopping = 10 + 5 + 5;
alert(TotalCostOfShopping);
```

First, we declared a variable, `TotalCostOfShopping`, to hold the total cost.

In the second line we have the code `10 + 5 + 5`. This piece of code is known as an **expression**. When we assign the variable `TotalCostOfShopping` with the value of this expression, JavaScript automatically calculates the value of the expression (20) and stores it in the variable. You'll notice that we've used the = sign to tell JavaScript to store the results of the calculation in the `TotalCostOfShopping` variable. We call this **assigning** the value of the calculation to the variable, which is why the single equals sign (=) is called the **assignment operator**.

Finally, we display the value of the variable in an alert box.

The other operators for subtraction and multiplication, - and *, work in exactly the same way. Division is a little different and is represented by the forward slash character /.

Try It Out – Calculations

Let's take a look at an example using the division operator to see how it works. Type in the following code and save it as `ch2_examp3.htm`:

```
<HTML>
<BODY>

<SCRIPT LANGUAGE=JavaScript>
var firstNumber = 15;
var secondNumber = 10;
var answer;
answer = 15 / 10;
```

```
alert(answer);

alert(15 / 10);

answer = firstNumber / secondNumber;
alert(answer);

</SCRIPT>

</BODY>
</HTML>
```

Load this into your web browser. You should see a succession of three alert boxes, each containing the value 1.5. These values are the results of three calculations.

How It Works

The first thing we do in the script block is to declare our three variables and assign the first two of these variables with values that we'll be using later:

```
var firstNumber = 15;
var secondNumber = 10;
var answer;
```

Next, we set the answer variable to the results of the calculation of the expression 15/10. We show the value of this variable in an alert box:

```
answer = 15 / 10;
alert(answer);
```

If you're thinking, "why not just set the answer variable to 1.5", then I agree with you. This example demonstrates one way of doing the calculation, but in reality you'd almost never do it this way.

To demonstrate that we can use expressions in places we'd use numbers or variables, we show the results of the calculation of 15/10 directly by including it in the alert() function:

```
alert(15 / 10);
```

Finally we do the same calculation, but this time using our two variables firstNumber, which was set to 15, and secondNumber, which was set to 10. We have the expression firstNumber / secondNumber, the result of which we store in our answer variable. Then, to prove it has all worked, we show the value contained in answer by using our friend the alert() function:

```
answer = firstNumber / secondNumber;
alert(answer);
```

Most calculations will be done in the third way shown above, that is using variables, or numbers and variables, and storing the result in another variable. The reason for this is that if the calculation used literal values – actual values, such as 15 / 10 – then we might as well program in the result of the calculation, rather than force JavaScript to calculate it for us. For example, rather than writing 15 / 10, we might as well just write 1.5. After all, the more calculations we force JavaScript to do, the more work it has and the slower it will be, though admittedly just one calculation won't tax it too much.

Another reason for using the result rather than the calculation is that it makes code more readable. Which would you prefer to read in code, 1.5 * 45 – 56 / 67 + 2.567, or 69.231? Still better, a variable named, for example, `PricePerKG`, makes code even easier to understand for someone not familiar with it.

Increment and Decrement Operators

There are a number of operations using the above math operators that are so commonly used that they have been given their own operators. The two we'll be looking at here are the **increment** and **decrement** operators, which are represented by ++ and --. Basically, all they do is increase or decrease a variable's value by one. We could use the normal + and – operators to do this, for example:

```
myVariable = myVariable + 1;
myVariable = myVariable – 1;
```

(Note that we can assign a variable a new value that is the result of an expression involving its previous value.) However using the increment and decrement operators shortens this to:

```
myVariable++;
myVariable--;
```

The result is the same – the value of `myVariable` is increased or decreased by one – but the code is shorter. Once you are familiar with the syntax, this becomes very clear and easy to read.

Right now, you may well be thinking that these operators sound as useful as a poke in the eye. However, in the next chapter when we look at how we can run the same code a number of times, we'll see that these operators are very useful and widely used. In fact, the ++ operator is so widely used they named a computer language after it, C++. The 'joke' here is that C++ is one up from C (well, that's programmer humor for you!)

The increment and decrement operators are usually used on their own, but it is possible to use the ++ and -- operators in an expression along with other operators. For example:

```
myVar = myNumber++ - 20;
```

subtract 20 from `myNumber`, assign the result to `myVar`, and then increments `myNumber` by one. However, it's usually best to avoid this syntax, as it makes code more difficult to read and can lead to obscure bugs.

Before we go on, this seems to be a good point to introduce another operator, +=. This operator can be used as a short cut way of increasing the value held by a variable by a set amount. For example:

```
myVar += 6;
```

does exactly the same thing as:

```
myVar = myVar + 6;
```

Operator Precedence

We saw that symbols which perform some function, like +, which adds two numbers together and -, which subtracts one number from another, are called operators. Unlike people, not all operators are created equal; some have a higher **precedence** – that is, they get dealt with sooner. A quick look at a simple example will help demonstrate my point:

```
<HTML>
<BODY>

<SCRIPT LANGUAGE=JavaScript>

var myVariable;

myVariable = 1 + 1 * 2;

alert(myVariable);

</SCRIPT>

</BODY>
</HTML>
```

If you were to type this in, what result would you expect the `alert` box to show as the value of `myVariable`? You might expect that, since 1 + 1 = 2, and 2 * 2 = 4, the answer is 4. Actually, you'll find that the `alert` box shows 3 as the value stored in `myVariable` as a result of the calculation. So what gives? Doesn't JavaScript add up right?

Well, you probably already know the reason why from your understanding of mathematics. The way JavaScript does our calculation is to first calculate 1 * 2 = 2, and then use this result in the addition, so that JavaScript finishes off by doing 1 + 2 = 3.

Why? Because * has a higher precedence than +. The = symbol, also an operator (called the assignment operator), has the lowest precedence – it always gets left until last.

The + and – operators have an equal precedence, so which one gets done first? Well, JavaScript works from left to right, so if operators with equal precedence exist in a calculation, they get calculated in the order in which they appear when going from left to right. The same applies to * and /, which are also of equal precedence.

Try It Out – Fahrenheit to Centigrade

Let's take a look at a more complex example – a Fahrenheit to centigrade converter. (Centigrade is another name for the Celsius temperature scale.) Type in this code and save it as `ch2_examp4.htm`:

```
<HTML>
<BODY>

<SCRIPT LANGUAGE=JavaScript>
```

```
// Equation is °C = 5/9 (°F - 32).
var degFahren = prompt("Enter the degrees in Fahrenheit",50);
var degCent;

degCent = 5/9 * (degFahren - 32);

alert(degCent);

</SCRIPT>

</BODY>
</HTML>
```

If you load the page into your browser, you should see a prompt box that asks you to enter the degrees in Fahrenheit to be converted. The value 50 is already filled in by default:

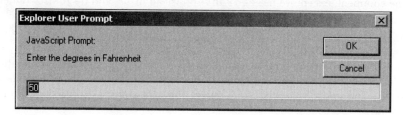

If you leave it at 50 and hit the **OK** button, an `alert` box with the number 10 in it appears. This represents 50 degrees Fahrenheit converted to centigrade.

Reload the page and try changing the value in the prompt box to different values to see what results you get. For example, change the value to 32 and reload the page. This time you should see 0 appear.

How It Works

The first line of the script block is a comment since it starts with two forward slashes (//). It contains the equation for converting Fahrenheit temperatures to centigrade, and is in the example code solely for reference:

```
// Equation is °C = 5/9 (°F - 32).
```

Our task is to represent this equation in JavaScript code. We start by declaring our variables, degFahren and degCent.

```
var degFahren = prompt("Enter the degrees in Fahrenheit",50);
var degCent;
```

Instead of initializing the degFahren variable to a literal value, we get a value from the user using the prompt() function. The prompt() function works in a similar way to an alert() function, except that as well as displaying a message, it also contains a text box in which the user can enter a value. It is this value that will be stored inside the degFahren variable.

We pass two pieces of information to the prompt() function:

- ❑   The text to be displayed – usually a question that prompts the user for input
- ❑   The default value that is contained in the input box when the prompt dialog first appears

These two pieces of information must be specified in the given order, and separated by a comma. If you don't want a default value to be contained in the input box when the prompt box opens, you should use an empty string (" ") for the second piece of information.

As you can see in the code above, our text is, "Enter the degrees in Fahrenheit" and the default value in the input box is 50.

Next in our script block comes the equation represented in JavaScript. We store the result of the equation in the degCent variable. You can see that the JavaScript looks very much like the equation we have in the comment, except we use degFahren instead of °F, and degCent rather than °C.

```
degCent = 5/9 * (degFahren - 32);
```

The calculation of the expression on the right-hand side of the equals sign raises a number of important points. First, just as in math, the JavaScript equation is read from left to right, at least for the basic math functions like +, - and so on. Secondly, as we saw earlier, just as there is precedence in math, so there is too in JavaScript.

Starting from the left, first JavaScript works out 5/9 = .5555 (approximately). Then it comes to the multiplication, but wait... the last bit of our equation, degFahren - 32, is in parentheses. This raises the order of precedence and causes JavaScript to calculate the result of degFahren - 32 before doing the multiplication. For example, when degFahren is set to 50, (degFahren - 32) = (50 - 32) = 18. Now JavaScript does the multiplication, .5555 * 18, which is 10.

What if we didn't use the parentheses? Then our code would be:

```
degCent = 5/9 * degFahren - 32;
```

The calculation of 5/9 remains the same, but then JavaScript would have calculated the multiplication, 5/9 * degFahren. This is because the multiplication takes precedence over the subtraction. When degFahren is 50 this equates to 5/9 * 50 = 27.7778. Finally JavaScript would have subtracted the 32, leaving the result as -4.2221; not the answer we want!

Finally, in our script block, we display the answer using the alert() function:

```
alert(degCent);
```

That concludes our brief look at basic calculations with JavaScript. However, in Chapter 4 we'll be looking at something called the **Math object**, which enables us to do more complex calculations like finding cosines, square roots and much more.

Basic String Operations

In an earlier section, we looked at the text or string data type, as well as numerical data. Just as numerical data has associated operators, strings have operators too. In this section we'll introduce some basic string manipulation techniques available using such operators. We'll be covering strings in more depth in Chapter 4 and looking at advanced string handling in Chapter 8.

One thing you'll find yourself doing again and again in JavaScript is joining two strings together to make one string – a process that's termed **concatenation**. For example, we may want to concatenate the two strings "Hello " and "Paul" to make the string "Hello Paul". So how do we concatenate? Easy! We use the + operator. Recall that when applied to numbers, the + operator adds them up, but when used in the context of two strings, it joins them together.

```
var concatString = "Hello " + "Paul";
```

The string now stored in the variable concatString is "Hello Paul". Notice that the last character of the string "Hello " is a space – if we left this out then our concatenated string would be "HelloPaul".

Try it Out – Concatenating Strings

Let's look at an example using the + operator for string concatenation. Type the following code in and save it as ch2_examp5.htm.

```
<HTML>
<BODY>

<SCRIPT LANGUAGE=JavaScript>

var greetingString = "Hello";
var myName = prompt("Please enter your name", "");
var concatString;

document.write(greetingString + " " + myName + "<BR>");

concatString = greetingString + " " + myName;

document.write(concatString);

</SCRIPT>

</BODY>
</HTML>
```

If you load it into your web browser you should see firstly a prompt box asking for your name.

Enter your name and click the OK button. You should see a greeting and your name displayed twice on the web page.

How It Works

We start the script block by declaring three variables. We set the first variable, `greetingString`, to a string value. The second variable, `myName`, is assigned to whatever is entered by the user in the prompt box. The third variable, `concatString`, we do not initialize here. It will be used to store the result of the concatenation we'll do later in the code:

```
var greetingString = "Hello";
var myName = prompt("Please enter your name", "");
var concatString;
```

In the last chapter, we saw how the web page was represented by the word `document` and that it had a number of different properties such as the `bgColor`. We can also use `document` to write text and HTML directly into the page itself. We do this by using the word `document`, followed by a dot, and then `write()`. We then use `document.write()` much as we do the `alert()` function, in that we put the text that we want displayed in the web page inside the parentheses following the word write. Don't worry too much about this here though, as it will all be explained in detail in Chapter 4. However, we now make use of `document.write()` in our code to write the result of an expression to the page:

```
document.write(greetingString + " " + myName + "<BR>");
```

The expression written to the page is the concatenation of the value of the `greetingString` variable, a space (`" "`), the value of the `myName` variable, and the HTML `<BR>` tag. For example, if I enter Paul into the prompt box, the value of this expression will be:

```
Hello Paul<BR>
```

In the next line of code we have a similar expression. This time it is just the concatenation of the value in the variable `greetingString`, a space, and the value in the variable `myName`. We store the result of this expression in the variable `concatString`. Finally, we write the contents of the variable `concatString` to the page using `document.write()`:

```
concatString = greetingString + " " + myName;
document.write(concatString);
```

Mixing Numbers and Strings

What if we want to mix text and numbers in an expression? A prime example of this would be in the temperature converter we saw earlier. In the example, we just display the number without telling the user what it actually means. What we really want to do is display the number with descriptive text wrapped around it, such as "The value converted to degrees centigrade is 10".

Mixing numbers and text is actually very easy. We can simply join them together using the + operator. JavaScript is intelligent enough to know that when a both a string and a number are involved, we're not trying to do numerical calculations, but rather we want to treat the number as a string and join it to the text. For example, to join the text My age is and the number 101 together, we could simply do the following:

```
alert("My age is " + 101);
```

This would produce an `alert` box with My age is 101 inside it.

Try It Out – Making the Temperature Converter User Friendly

We can try out this technique of concatenating strings and numbers in our temperature converter example. We'll output some explanatory text, along with the result of the conversion calculation. The changes that we need to make are very small, so load ch2_examp4.htm into your text editor and change the line shown below. Then save it as ch2_examp6.htm.

```
<HTML>
<BODY>

<SCRIPT LANGUAGE=JavaScript>

// Equation is °C = 5/9 (°F - 32).

var degFahren = prompt("Enter the degrees in Fahrenheit",50);
var degCent;

degCent = 5/9 * (degFahren - 32);

alert(degFahren + "\xB0 Fahrenheit is " + degCent + "\xB0 centigrade");

</SCRIPT>

</BODY>
</HTML>
```

Load the page into your web browser. Click **OK** in the prompt box to submit the value 50, and this time you should see:

How It Works

This example is identical to ch2_examp4.htm above, except for one line:

```
alert(degFahren + "\xB0 Fahrenheit is " + degCent + "\xB0 centigrade");
```

so we will just look at this line here. You can see that the alert() function contains an expression. Let's look at that expression more closely.

Firstly we have the variable degFahren, which contains numerical data. We concatenate that to a string "\xB0 Fahrenheit is ". JavaScript realizes that because you are adding a number and a string, you want to join them together into one string rather than trying to take their sum, and so automatically converts the number contained in degFahren to a string. We next concatenate this string to the variable degCent, containing numerical data. Again JavaScript converts the value of this variable to a string. Finally we concatenate to the string "\xB0 centigrade".

Note also, that we have used an escape sequence to insert the degree character in the strings. You'll remember from earlier in the chapter that \xNN can be used to insert special characters not available to type in directly. Remember NN are hexadecimal numbers representing a character from the Latin-1 character table (see Appendix D for more details). So, when JavaScript spots \xB0 in a string, instead of showing those characters, it does a lookup to see what character is represented by B0 and shows that instead.

Something to be aware of when using special characters is they are not necessarily cross-platform compatible. While we can use \xNN for a certain character on a Windows computer, we may find it's a different character on an Apple Mac or a Unix machine. We'll see in Chapter 4 how we can detect what operating system a user has and use this information to make sure our code works with different operating systems.

We'll be looking at more string manipulation techniques in Chapter 4 – we'll see how to search strings, and insert characters in the middle of them.

Data Type Conversion

As we saw above, if you add a string and a number together, JavaScript makes the sensible choice and converts the number to a string, then concatenates the two. Usually JavaScript has enough sense to make data type conversions like this whenever it needs to, but there are some situations where we need to convert the type of a piece of data ourselves. For example, in some situations, we may be given a piece of string data that we want to think of as a number. This is especially true in the case of using forms to collect data from the user. Any values input by the user are treated as strings, even though they may contain numerical data, such as the user's age.

Why is changing the type of the data so important? Consider the following situation where we collect two numbers from the user using a form, and want to calculate their sum. The two numbers are available to us as strings, for example "22" and "15". When we try to calculate the sum of these values using "22" + "15" we get the result "2215", since JavaScript thinks we are trying to concatenate two strings rather than trying to find the sum of two numbers.

In this section we'll look at two conversion functions that convert strings to numbers: parseInt() and parseFloat().

Let's take parseInt() first. This function will take a string and convert it to an integer. The name is a little confusing at first – why parseInt() rather than convertToInt()? The main reason for the name comes from the way that the function works. It actually goes through (that is, parses) each character of the string you ask it to convert, and sees if it's a valid number. If it is valid, then parseInt() uses it to build up the number; if it is not valid, then the command simply stops converting and returns the number it has converted so far.

For example, if your code was parseInt("123"), then JavaScript will convert the string "123" to the number 123. For the code parseInt("123abc"), JavaScript will also return the number 123. When the JavaScript interpreter gets to the letter a, it assumes the number has ended and gives 123 as the integer version of the string "123abc".

The parseFloat() function works in the same way as parseInt(), except that it returns floating point numbers – fractional numbers – and that a decimal point in the string that it is converting is considered to be part of the allowable number.

Try It Out – Converting Strings to Numbers

Let's look at an example using parseInt() and parseFloat(). Type in the following code and save it as ch2_examp7.htm:

```
<HTML>
<BODY>

<SCRIPT LANGUAGE=JavaScript>

var myString = "56.02 degrees centigrade";
var myInt;
var myFloat;

document.write("\"" + myString + "\" is " + parseInt(myString) +
    " as an integer" + "<BR>");

myInt = parseInt(myString);
document.write("\"" + myString + "\" when converted to an integer equals " +
    myInt + "<BR>");

myFloat = parseFloat(myString);
document.write("\"" + myString +
    "\" when converted to a floating point number equals " + myFloat);

</SCRIPT>

</BODY>
</HTML>
```

Load it into your browser and you'll see three lines written in the web page as shown below:

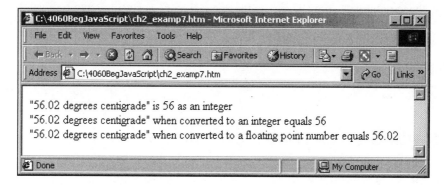

How It Works

Our first task in the script block is to declare some variables. The variable myString is declared and initialized to the string we want to convert. We could just as easily have used the string directly in this example rather than storing it in a variable, but in practice you'll find that you use variables more often than literal values. We also declare the variables myInt and myFloat, which will hold the converted numbers:

```
var myString = "56.02 degrees centigrade";
var myInt;
var myFloat;
```

Next, we write to the page the converted integer value of `myString` displayed inside a user-friendly sentence we build up using string concatenation. Notice that we use the escape sequence \ " to display quotes (") around the string that we are converting.

```
document.write("\"" + myString + "\" is " + parseInt(myString) +
    " as an integer" + "<BR>");
```

As you can see, you can use `parseInt()` and `parseFloat()` in the same places you would use a number itself or a variable containing a number. In fact, in this line the JavaScript interpreter is doing two conversions. First it converts `myString` to an integer, because that's what we asked for by using `parseInt()`. Then it automatically converts that integer number back to a string, so it can be concatenated with the other strings to make up our sentence. Also note that only the 56 part of the `myString` variable's value is considered a valid number when dealing with integers. Anything after the 6 is considered invalid and ignored.

Next we do the same conversion of `myString` using `parseInt()`, but this time store the result in the `myInt` variable. On the following line we use the result in some text we display to the user.

```
myInt = parseInt(myString);
document.write("\"" + myString + "\" when converted to an integer equals " +
    myInt + "<BR>");
```

Again, though `myInt` holds a number, the JavaScript interpreter knows that +, when a string and a number are involved, means we want the `myInt` value converted to a string and concatenated to the rest of the string so it can be displayed.

Finally, we use `parseFloat()` to convert the string in `myString` to a floating-point number, which we store in the variable `myFloat`. This time the decimal point is considered to be a valid part of the number, so it's anything after the 2 that is ignored. Again we use `document.write()` to write the result to the web page inside a user-friendly string:

```
myFloat = parseFloat(myString);
document.write("\"" + myString +
    "\" when converted to a floating point number equals " + myFloat);
```

Dealing with Strings That Won't Convert

There are some strings that are simply not convertible to numbers, such as strings that don't contain any numerical data. What happens if we try to convert these strings? As a little experiment, try changing the example above so that `myString` holds something that is not convertible. For example, change the line:

```
var myString = "56.02 degrees centigrade";
```

to:

```
var myString = "I'm a name not a number";
```

Now reload the page in your browser and you should see the following:

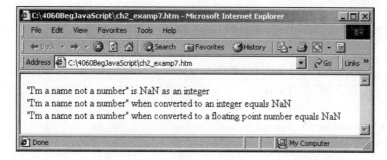

You can see that in the place of the number's we got before we get **NaN**. What sort of number is that? Well, it's **N**ot **a** **N**umber at all!

If you use parseInt() or parseFloat() with any string that is empty or does not start with a least one valid digit, then you get NaN, meaning Not a Number.

NaN is actually a special value in JavaScript. It has its own function isNaN() which checks whether something is NaN or not. For example:

```
myVar1 = isNaN("Hello");
```

will store the value true in the variable myVar1, since "Hello" is not a number, whereas:

```
myVar2 = isNaN(34);
```

will store the value false in the variable myVar2, since 34 is a number.

In the next chapter we'll see how you can use the isNaN() function to check the validity of strings as numbers, something that proves invaluable when dealing with user input, as we'll see in Chapter 6.

Arrays

We're now going to introduce a new concept – something called an **array**. An array is similar to a normal variable, in that you can use it to hold any type of data. However, it has one important difference, which we illustrate below.

As we have already seen, a normal variable can only hold one piece of data at a time. For example, I can set myVariable to be equal to 25 like so:

```
myVariable = 25;
```

and I can then go and set it to something else, say 35:

```
myVariable = 35;
```

However, when I set the variable to 35, the first value of 25 is lost. The variable `myVariable` now holds just the number 35.

We can illustrate the variable using the following table:

Variable name	myVariable
Value	35

The difference between such a normal variable and an array is that an array can hold *more than one* item of data at the same time. For example, we could use an array with name `myArray` to store both the numbers 25 and 35. Each place where a piece of data can be stored in an array is called an **element**.

How do we distinguish between these two pieces of data in an array? We give each piece of data an **index** value. To refer to that piece of data we enclose its index value in square brackets after the name of the array. For example, an array called `myArray` containing the data 25 and 35 could be illustrated using the following table.

Element name	myArray[0]	myArray[1]
Value	25	35

Notice that the index values start at 0 and not 1. Why is this? Surely 1 makes more sense – after all, we humans tend to say the first item of data, followed by the second item, and so on. Unfortunately, computers start from 0, and think of the first item as the zero item, the second as the first item, and so on. Confusing I know, but you'll soon get used to the fact.

Arrays can be very useful since you can store as many (within the limits of the computer) or as few items of data in an array as you want. Also, you don't have to say up front how many pieces of data you want to store in an array, though you can if you wish.

So how do we create an array? This is done in a slightly different way from declaring a normal variable. To create a new array, you need to declare a variable name and tell JavaScript that you want it to be a new array using the `new` keyword and the `Array()` function. For example, the array `myArray` could be defined like this:

```
var myArray = new Array();
```

Note that, as with everything in JavaScript, the code is case sensitive, so if you type `array()` rather than `Array()` the code won't work. This way of defining an array will be explained further in Chapter 4.

As with normal variables, you can also declare your variable first, and then tell JavaScript you want it to be an array. For example:

```
var myArray;
myArray = new Array();
```

Above we said that we could say up front how many elements the array will hold if we wanted to, although this is not necessary. This is done by putting the number of elements you want to specify between the parentheses after `Array`. For example, to create an array that will hold 5 elements, we write:

```
var myArray = new Array(5);
```

We have seen how to declare a new array, but how do we store our pieces of data inside it? You can do this when you define your array by including your data inside the parentheses with each piece of data separated by a comma. For example:

```
var myArray = new Array("Paul",345,"John",112,"Bob",99);
```

Here, the first item of data, `"Paul"`, will be put in the array with an index of 0. The next piece of data, `345`, will be put in the array with an index of 1, and so on. This mean that the element with name `myArray[0]` contains the value "Paul", and the element with name `myArray[1]` contains the value 345, and so on.

Note that you can't use this method to declare an array containing just one piece of numerical data, such as 345, since JavaScript assumes that you are declaring an array that will hold 345 elements.

This leads us on to another way of declaring data in our array. We could write the above line as:

```
var myArray = new Array();
myArray[0] = "Paul";
myArray[1] = 345;
myArray[2] = "John";
myArray[3] = 112;
myArray[4] = "Bob";
myArray[5] = 99;
```

We use each element name as we would a variable, assigning them with values. We explain this method of declaring the values of array elements in the *Try It Out* section below. Obviously, in this example the first way of defining the data items is much easier. However, there will be situations where you want to change the data stored in a particular element in an array after it has been declared. In that case you will have to use the latter method of defining the values of the array elements.

You'll also spot from the above example that we can store different data types in the same array. JavaScript is very flexible in what you can put in an array and where you can put it.

Before we go on to an example, note here that if, for example, you had defined your array called `myArray` as holding 3 elements like this:

```
var myArray = new Array(3);
```

and then defined a value in the element with index 130:

```
myArray[130] = "Paul";
```

JavaScript would not complain, but would happily assume that you had changed your mind and wanted an array that had (at least) 131 elements in it.

Try It Out – An Array

In the example below, we'll create an array to hold some names. We'll use the second method described above to store these pieces of data in the array. We'll then display this data to the user. Type the code in and save it as ch2_examp8.htm.

```
<HTML>
<BODY>

<SCRIPT LANGUAGE=JavaScript>

var myArray = new Array();
myArray[0] = "Bob";
myArray[1] = "Pete";
myArray[2] = "Paul";

document.write("myArray[0] = " + myArray[0] + "<BR>");
document.write("myArray[2] = " + myArray[2] + "<BR>");
document.write("myArray[1] = " + myArray[1] + "<BR>");

myArray[1] = "Mike";
document.write("myArray[1] changed to " + myArray[1]);

</SCRIPT>

</BODY>
</HTML>
```

If you load this into your web browser, you should see a web page that looks something like this:

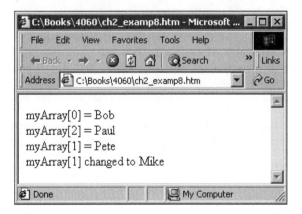

How It Works

Our first task in our script block is to declare a variable and tell the JavaScript interpreter we want it to be a new array:

```
var myArray = new Array();
```

Now that we have our array defined, we can store some data in it. Each time we store an item of data with a new index, JavaScript automatically creates a new storage space for it. Remember that the first element will be at myArray[0].

Let's take each addition to our array in turn and see what's happening. Before we add anything, our array is empty. Then we add an array element with the line:

```
myArray[0] = "Bob";
```

Our array now looks like this:

Index	0
Data Stored	Bob

Then we add another element to the array, this time with an index of 1:

```
myArray[1] = "Pete";
```

Index	0	1
Data Stored	Bob	Pete

Finally we add another element to the array with an index of 2:

```
myArray[2] = "Paul";
```

Our array now looks like this:

Index	0	1	2
Data Stored	Bob	Pete	Paul

Next, we use a series of document.write() functions to insert the values that each element of the array contains into the web page. I've accessed the array out of order just to demonstrate that you can:

```
document.write("myArray[0] = " + myArray[0] + "<BR>");
document.write("myArray[2] = " + myArray[2] + "<BR>");
document.write("myArray[1] = " + myArray[1] + "<BR>");
```

You can treat each particular position in an array as if it's a standard variable. So you can use it to do calculations, transfer its value to another variable or array, and so on. However, if you try to access the data inside an array position before you have defined it, then you'll get an error message.

Finally, we change the value of the second array position to "Mike". I could have changed it to a number since, just as with normal variables, you can store any data type at any time in each individual data position in an array.

```
myArray[1] = "Mike";
```

Now our array's contents look like this:

Index	0	1	2
Data Stored	Bob	Mike	Paul

Just to show that the change we made has worked, we use `document.write()` to display the second element's value:

```
document.write("myArray[1] changed to " + myArray[1]);
```

A Multi-dimensional Array

Imagine we have the situation where we want to store a company's personnel information in an array. We might have data such as names, ages, addresses, and so on. One way to do this would be to store the information sequentially. What I mean is that we store the first name in the first element of the array, then the corresponding age in the next element, the address in the third, and then the next name in the fourth element, and so on. Our array could look something like this:

Index	0	1	2	3	4	5	6	7	8
Data Stored	Name1	Age1	Address1	Name2	Age2	Address2	Name3	Age3	Address3

This would work, but there is a neater solution using a **multi-dimensional array**. Up to now we have been using single dimension arrays. In these arrays each element is specified using just one index, that is, one dimension. So, taking the example above, we can see `Name1` is at index `0`, `Age1` is at index `1`, and so on.

A multi-dimensional array is one with two or more indexes for each element. For example, this is how our personnel array could look as a two dimensional array:

Index	0	1	2
0	Name1	Name2	Name3
1	Age1	Age2	Age3
2	Address1	Address2	Address3

We'll see how to create such multi-dimensional arrays in the next *Try It Out* section.

Try It Out – A Two Dimensional Array

The following example illustrates how we can create such a multi-dimensional array in JavaScript code, and how we can access the elements of this array. Type in the code and save it as ch2_examp9.htm.

```
<HTML>
<BODY>

<SCRIPT LANGUAGE=JavaScript>

var personnel = new Array();

personnel[0] = new Array();
personnel[0][0] = "Name0";
personnel[0][1] = "Age0";
personnel[0][2] = "Address0";

personnel[1] = new Array();
personnel[1][0] = "Name1";
personnel[1][1] = "Age1";
personnel[1][2] = "Address1";

personnel[2] = new Array();
personnel[2][0] = "Name2";
personnel[2][1] = "Age2";
personnel[2][2] = "Address2";

document.write("Name : " + personnel[1][0] + "<BR>");
document.write("Age : " + personnel[1][1] + "<BR>");
document.write("Address : " + personnel[1][2]);

</SCRIPT>

</BODY>
</HTML>
```

If you load it into your web browser you'll see three lines written into the page, which represent the name, age and address of the person whose details are stored in the personnel[1] element of the array.

How It Works

The first thing we do in our script block is to declare a variable, `personnel`, and tell JavaScript that we want it to be a new array:

```
var personnel = new Array();
```

Then we do something new; we tell JavaScript we want index 0 of the personnel array, that is the element `personnel[0]`, to be another new array:

```
personnel[0] = new Array();
```

So what's going on? Well, the truth is that JavaScript doesn't actually support multi-dimensional arrays, only single ones. However, JavaScript allows us to fake multi-dimensional arrays by creating an array inside another array. So, what the above line is doing is creating a new array inside the element with index 0 of our `personnel` array.

In the next three lines we put values into the newly created `personnel[0]` array. JavaScript makes it easy for us to do this; we just state the name of the array, `personnel[0]`, followed by another index in square brackets. The first index (0) belongs to the `personnel` array; the second index belongs to the `personnel[0]` array.

```
personnel[0][0] = "Name0";
personnel[0][1] = "Age0";
personnel[0][2] = "Address0";
```

After these lines of code, our array looks like this:

Index	0
0	Name0
1	Age0
2	Address0

The numbers at the top, at the moment just 0, refer to the `personnel` array. The numbers going down the side, 0, 1, and 2, are actually indices for the new array `personnel[0]` array inside the `personnel` array.

For the second person's details, we repeat the process again, but this time we are using the `personnel` array element with index 1:

```
personnel[1] = new Array();
personnel[1][0] = "Name1";
personnel[1][1] = "Age1";
personnel[1][2] = "Address1";
```

Now our array looks like this:

Index	0	1
0	Name0	Name1
1	Age0	Age1
2	Address0	Address1

We create a third person's details in the next few lines. We are now using the element with index 2 inside the `personnel` array to create a new array.

```
personnel[2] = new Array();
personnel[2][0] = "Name2";
personnel[2][1] = "Age2";
personnel[2][2] = "Address2";
```

Our array now looks like this:

Index	0	1	2
0	Name0	Name1	Name2
1	Age0	Age1	Age2
2	Address 0	Address1	Address2

We have now finished creating our multi-dimensional array. We end the script block by accessing the data for the second person (Name1, Age1, Address1) and displaying it in the page by using `document.write()`. As you can see, accessing the data is very much the same as storing it. We can use the multi-dimensional array anywhere we would use a normal variable or single dimension array:

```
document.write("Name : " + personnel[1][0] + "<BR>");
document.write("Age : " + personnel[1][1] + "<BR>");
document.write("Address : " + personnel[1][2]);
```

Try changing the `document.write()` commands so that they display the first person's details. The code would look like this:

```
document.write("Name : " + personnel[0][0] + "<BR>");
document.write("Age : " + personnel[0][1] + "<BR>");
document.write("Address : " + personnel[0][2]);
```

It's possible to create multi-dimensional arrays of three, four, or even a hundred dimensions, but things can start to get very confusing, and you'll find you'll rarely, if ever, need more than two dimensions. To give you an idea, here's how to declare and access a five dimensional array:

```
var myArray = new Array();
myArray[0] = new Array();
myArray[0][0] = new Array();
myArray[0][0][0] = new Array();
myArray[0][0][0][0] = new Array();

myArray[0][0][0][0][0] = "This is getting out of hand"

document.write(myArray[0][0][0][0][0]);
```

Well, I don't know about you, but my head is starting to hurt!

That's it for arrays for now, but we'll return to them in Chapter 4 where we find out something shocking about them. We'll also learn about some of their more advanced features.

The Trivia Quiz – Storing the Questions Using Arrays

OK, it's time to make our first steps in building the online trivia quiz. We're going to lay the foundations by defining the data that makes up the questions and answers used in the quiz.

In this chapter, we're just going to define multiple-choice based questions, which have a single letter answer. We'll be using arrays to store the questions and answers; a two-dimensional array for the questions and a single dimensional one for the matching answers.

The format of each multiple-choice question will be the question followed by each of the possible choices for answers. The correct answer to the question is specified using the letter corresponding to that answer. For example:

The Beatles were:

❏   A sixties rock group from Liverpool

❏   Four musically gifted insects

❏   I don't know – can I have the questions on Baseball please

has an answer specified by the letter A.

So how do we store this information in our arrays? Let's look at the array holding the questions first. We will define the array something like this:

Index	0	1	2
0	Text for Question0	Text for Question1	Text for Question2
1	Possible Answer A for Question 0	Possible Answer A for Question 1	Possible Answer A for Question
2	Possible Answer B for Question 0	Possible Answer B for Question 1	Possible Answer B for Question 2
3	Possible Answer C for Question 0	Possible Answer C for Question 1	Possible Answer C for Question 2

Of course we can extend this array if we create further questions or have more than three possible answers for a question.

The answers array will then be defined something like this:

Index	0	1	2
Value	Correct answer to Question 0	Correct answer to Question 1	Correct answer to Question 2

Again, we can extend this array as we add more questions.

Now that we have an idea of how we are going to store the question data, let's have a look at the code. We start by creating the HTML at the top of the page.

```
<HTML>
<HEAD>
<TITLE>Wrox Online Trivia Quiz</TITLE>
</HEAD>
<BODY>
```

Then, in the body of the page, we start a JavaScript block, in which we declare two variables, questions and answers, and define them as new arrays. The purpose of these variables should be pretty self-explanatory! However, as in the rest of the code, we add comments so that it is easy to work out what we are doing.

```
<SCRIPT LANGUAGE=JavaScript>

// questions and answers arrays will holds questions and answers
var questions = new Array();
var answers = new Array();
```

Next we move straight on to define our first question. Since the questions will be in a two-dimensional array, our first task is to set questions[0] to a new array. We assign the first element in this array, questions[0][0], to the text of the question, and the following elements to the possible answers.

```
// define question 1
questions[0] = new Array();

// the question
questions[0][0] = "The Beatles were";

// first choice
questions[0][1] = "A sixties rock group from Liverpool";

// second choice
questions[0][2] = "Four musically gifted insects";

// third choice
questions[0][3] = "I don't know - can I have the questions on Baseball please";
```

Having defined the first question, let's set the first answer. For multiple-choice questions we just need to set the element with the corresponding index in the `answers` array to the character representing the correct choice. In the question above the correct answer is "A sixties rock group from Liverpool". As this is the first choice, its letter is A.

```
// assign answer for question 1
answers[0] = "A";
```

Let's define two more questions for the quiz. They both take the same format as the first question, though they differ in having four options for the user to choose from. In the next chapter, you'll see that our code can handle this and indeed we can have as many options as we like.

```
// define question 2
questions[1] = new Array();
questions[1][0] = "Homer Simpson's favorite food is";
questions[1][1] = "Fresh salad";
questions[1][2] = "Doughnuts";
questions[1][3] = "Bread and water";
questions[1][4] = "Apples";

// assign answer for question 2
answers[1] = "B";

// define question 3
questions[2] = new Array();
questions[2][0] = "Lisa Simpson plays which musical instrument";
questions[2][1] = "Clarinet";
questions[2][2] = "Oboe";
questions[2][3] = "Saxophone";
questions[2][4] = "Tubular Bells";

// assign answer for question 3
answers[2] = "C";
```

We end the script block by creating an alert box that tells us that the array has been initialized.

```
alert("Array Initialized");

</SCRIPT>
</BODY>
</HTML>
```

Save the page as `trivia_quiz.htm`. That completes the definition of our quiz's questions and answers. In the next chapter we can move on to write code that checks the answers of the questions against the answers supplied by the user.

Summary

In this chapter we have built up knowledge of the fundamentals of JavaScript's data types and variables, and how to use them in operations. In particular we saw that:

❑   JavaScript supports a number of types of data such as numbers, text, and Booleans.

❑   Text is represented by strings of characters and surrounded by quotes. You must match the quotes surrounding strings. Escape characters allow you to include characters in your string that cannot be typed.

❑   Variables are JavaScript's way of storing data, such as numbers and text, in memory so that they can be used again and again in your code.

❑   Variable names must not include certain illegal characters, like % and &, or be a reserved word, like with.

❑   Before we can give a value to a variable, we must declare its existence to the JavaScript interpreter.

❑   JavaScript has the four basic math operators, represented by the symbols +, -, *, and /. To assign values of a calculation to a variable we use the = sign, termed the assignment operator.

❑   Operators have a different precedence, so multiplication and division will be calculated before addition and subtraction.

❑   Strings can be joined together, or concatenated, to produce one big string, using the + operator. When numbers and strings are concatenated with the + operator, JavaScript automatically converts the number into a string.

❑   Although JavaScript's automatic data conversion suits us most of the time, there are occasions when we need to force the conversion of data. We saw how parseInt() and parseFloat() can be used to convert strings to numbers. Attempting to convert strings that won't convert will result in NaN (Not a Number) being returned.

❑   Arrays are a special type of variable that can hold more than one piece of data. The data is inserted and accessed using a unique index number.

Exercise Questions

Suggested solutions to these questions can be found in Appendix A.

Question 1

Write a JavaScript program to convert degrees centigrade into degrees Fahrenheit and write the result to the page in a descriptive sentence. The JavaScript equation for Fahrenheit to centigrade is:

```
degFahren = 9 / 5 * degCent + 32
```

Question 2

The following code uses the prompt() function to get two numbers from the user. It then adds those two numbers together and writes the result to the page.

```
<HTML>
<BODY>
<SCRIPT LANGUAGE=JavaScript>

var firstNumber = prompt("Enter the first number","");
var secondNumber = prompt("Enter the second number","");
var theTotal = firstNumber + secondNumber;
document.write(firstNumber + " added to " + secondNumber + " equals " +
    theTotal);

</SCRIPT>
</BODY>
</HTML>
```

However, if you try the code out you'll spot that it doesn't work, why not?

Change the code so that it does work.

Online discussion at http://p2p.wrox.com

Decisions, Loops, and Functions

So far in this book, we've seen how we can use JavaScript to get user input, perform calculations and tasks with that input, and write the results to a web page. However, a pocket calculator can do all this, so what is it that makes computers different? That is to say, what gives computers the appearance of having intelligence? The answer is the ability to make decisions based on information gathered.

How will decision making help us when creating web sites? In the last chapter we wrote some code that converted temperature in degrees Fahrenheit to centigrade. We obtained the degrees Fahrenheit from the user using the `prompt()` function. This worked fine if the user entered a valid number, such as 50. If, however, the user entered something invalid for the Fahrenheit temperature, such as the string `"aaa"`, then we find that our code no longer works as expected. Now, if we had some decision-making capabilities in our program, we could check to see if what the user has entered is valid. If it is, we could do the calculation, and if it isn't we can tell the user why and ask them to enter a valid number.

Validation of user input is probably one of the most common uses of decision making in JavaScript, but it's far from being the only use. Our trivia quiz also needs some decision-making capabilities so that we can check if the answer given by the user is right or wrong. If it's right, then we need to take certain steps, such as telling the user they are right and increasing their score. If the answer is wrong, then a different set code needs to be executed to tell them that they're wrong.

In this chapter we'll look at how decision-making is implemented in JavaScript and how we can use it to make our code smarter.

Decision Making – The if and switch Statements

All programming languages allow you to make decisions. By this I mean that they allow the program to follow a certain course of action depending on whether or not a particular **condition** is met. This is what gives programming languages their intelligence.

For example, in a situation where we use JavaScript code that is only compatible with version 4 or later browsers, the condition could be that the user is using a version 4 or later browser. If we discovered that this condition is not met, then we could direct them to a set of pages that are compatible with earlier browsers.

Conditions are comparisons between variables and data, such as:

- ❑ "Is *A* bigger than *B*?"

- ❑ "Is this *X* equal to *Y*?"

- ❑ "Is *M* not equal to *N*?"

In our above example, if the variable `browserVersion` held the version of the browser that the user was using, the condition would be:

- ❑ "Is `browserVersion` greater than or equal to 4?"

You'll notice that all of these questions have a yes or no answer – that is, they are Boolean-based and can only evaluate to `true` or `false`. How do we use this to create decision-making abilities in our code? We get the browser to test whether the condition is `true`. If (and only if) it is `true`, we execute a particular section of code.

Let's look at another example. Recall from Chapter 1 the natural English instructions we used to demonstrate how code flows. One of these instructions for making a cup of coffee was:

- ❑ Has the kettle boiled? If so, then pour water into the cup. Otherwise continue to wait.

This is an example of making a decision. The condition in this instruction is "Has the water boiled?" It has a `true` or `false` answer. If the answer is `true`, we pour the water into the cup. If it isn't `true`, we continue to wait.

In JavaScript, we can change the flow of the code depending on whether a condition is `true` or `false`, using an `if` statement or a `switch` statement. We will look at these shortly, but first we need to introduce some new operators that are essential for the definition of conditions – **comparison operators**.

Comparison Operators

In the last chapter, we saw how mathematical functions, such as addition and division, were represented by symbols, such as + and /, called operators. We also saw that if we wanted to give a variable a value, we can assign to it a value or the result of a calculation using the equals sign (=), termed the assignment operator.

Decision-making also has its own operators, which allow you to test conditions. Comparison operators, just like the mathematical operators we saw in the last chapter, have a left-hand side (LHS) and a right-hand side (RHS) and the comparison is made between the two. For example, the less than operator, with symbol <, is a comparison operator. We could write 23 < 45, which translates as "Is 23 less than 45?" Here, the answer would be `true`.

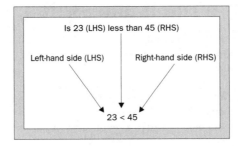

There are other comparison operators, the more useful of which are summarized in the table below:

Operator Symbol	Purpose
==	Tests if LHS is equal to RHS
<	Tests if LHS is less than RHS
>	Tests if LHS is greater than RHS
<=	Tests if LHS is less than or equal to RHS
>=	Tests if LHS is greater than or equal to RHS
!=	Tests if LHS is not equal to RHS

We'll see these comparison operators in use in the next section when we look at the `if` statement.

Precedence

Recall from Chapter 2 that operators have an order of precedence. This applies also to the comparison operators. The == and != comparison operators have the lowest order of precedence, and the rest of the comparison operators, <, >, <=, and >=, have an equal precedence.

All the comparison operators above have a precedence that is below operators such as +, -, * and /. This means that if you make a comparison such as 3 * 5 > 2 * 5, the multiplication calculations are worked out first, before their results are compared. However, in these circumstances it's both safer and clearer if you wrap the calculations on either side inside parentheses, for example, (3 * 5) > (2 * 5). As a general rule, it's a good idea to use parentheses to ensure that the precedence is clear, or you may find yourself surprised by the outcome.

Assignment versus Comparison

One final important point to mention is the ease of which the assignment operator (=) and the comparison operator (==) can be mixed up. Remember that the = operator assigns a value to a variable and that the == operator compares the value of two variables. Even once you have this idea clear, it's amazingly easy to put one equals where you meant to put two – it's a mistake I make all too often, even now.

The if Statement

The `if` statement is one you'll find yourself using in almost every program that is more than a couple of lines long. It works very much like our understanding of the word 'if' in the English language. For example, we might say in English, "If the room temperature is more than 80 degrees Fahrenheit, then I'll turn the air conditioning on." In JavaScript, this would translate into something like this:

```
if (roomTemperature > 80)
{
    roomTemperature = roomTemperature - 10;
}
```

How does this work?

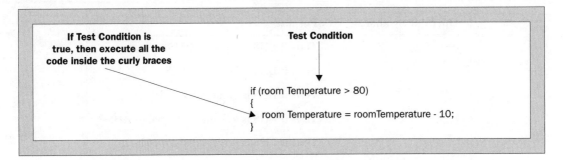

Notice that the test condition is placed in parentheses, and follows the `if` keyword. Also, note that there is no semi-colon at the end of this line. The code to be executed if the condition is true is placed in curly braces on the line after the condition, and each of these lines of code does end with a semi-colon.

The curly braces, { }, have a special purpose in JavaScript – they mark out a **block** of code. Marking out lines of code as belonging to a single block means that JavaScript will treat them all as one piece of code. If the condition of an `if` statement is `true`, JavaScript executes the next line or block of code following the `if` statement. In the above example, we have only one statement in the block of code, so we could equally as well have written:

```
if (roomTemperature > 80)
    roomTemperature = roomTemperature - 10;
```

However, if you have a number of lines of code that you want to execute, then you need the braces to mark them out as a single block of code. For example, a modified version of the above example with three lines of code would have to include the braces:

```
if (roomTemperature > 80)
{
    roomTemperature = roomTemperature - 10;
    alert("Its getting hot in here");
    alert("Air conditioning switched on");
}
```

A particularly easy mistake to make is to forget the braces when marking out a block of code to be executed. Instead of the code in the block being executed when the condition is true, you'll find *only the first line* after the `if` statement is executed. However, the other lines will always be executed regardless of the outcome of the test condition. To avoid mistakes like these, it's a good idea to always use braces, even where there is only one statement. If you get into this habit, you'll be less likely to miss them out when they are actually needed.

Try It Out – The if Statement

Let's return to our temperature converter example from Chapter 2, and add some decision-making functionality. Enter the code shown below, and save it as `ch3_exampl.htm`:

```
<HTML>
<BODY>

<SCRIPT LANGUAGE=JavaScript>

var degFahren = prompt("Enter the degrees Fahrenheit",32);
var degCent;

degCent = 5/9 * (degFahren - 32);

document.write(degFahren + "\xB0 Fahrenheit is " + degCent +
   "\xB0 centigrade<BR>");

if (degCent < 0)
{
   document.write("That's below the freezing point of water");
}

if (degCent == 100)
   document.write("That's the boiling point of water");

</SCRIPT>

</BODY>
</HTML>
```

Load the page into your browser, and enter 32 into the prompt box for the Fahrenheit value to be converted. With a value of 32 neither of the `if` statement's conditions will be true, so the only line written in the page will be:

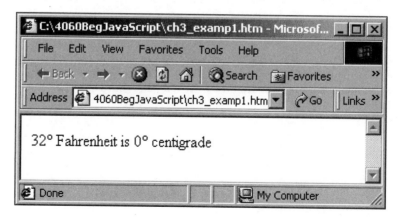

Now reload the page and enter 31 for the Fahrenheit value. This time we'll see two lines in the page:

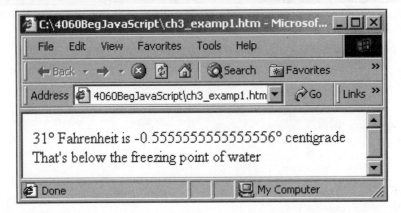

Finally, reload the page again, but this time enter 212 in the prompt box. The following two lines will appear in the page:

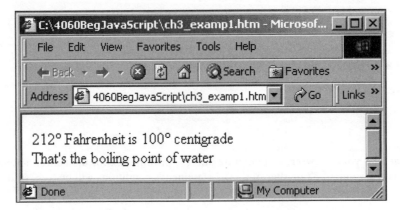

How It Works

The first part of the script block in this page is taken from the example ch2_examp4.htm in Chapter 2. We declare two variables, degFahren and degCent. The variable degFahren is given an initial value obtained from the user with the prompt() function. The variable degCent is then set to the result of the calculation 5/9 * (degFahren - 32), which is our Fahrenheit to centigrade conversion calculation.

```
var degFahren = prompt("Enter the degrees Fahrenheit",32);
var degCent;

degCent = 5/9 * (degFahren - 32);
```

Then we write the result of our calculation to the page:

```
document.write(degFahren + "\xB0 Fahrenheit is " + degCent +
    "\xB0 centigrade<BR>");
```

Now we come to the new code; the first of our two `if` statements:

```
if (degCent < 0)
{
    document.write("That's below the freezing point of water");
}
```

This `if` statement has the condition that asks, "Is the value of the variable `degCent` less than zero?" If the answer is yes – `true` – the code inside the curly braces executes. In this case, we write a sentence to the page using `document.write()`. If the answer is no – `false` – then the processing moves on to the next line after the closing brace. Also worth noting is the fact that the code inside the `if` statement's opening brace is indented. This is not necessary, but it is a good practice to get into as it makes your code much easier to read.

When trying out the example, we started by entering 32 so that `degFahren` will be initialized to 32. In this case, the calculation, `degCent = 5/9 * (degFahren - 32)` will set `degCent` to 0. So, the answer to the question "Is `degCent` less than zero?" is `false`, since `degCent` is equal to zero, not less than zero. The code inside the curly brackets will be skipped and never executed. In this case, the next line to be executed will be the second if statement's condition, which we'll talk about shortly.

When we entered 31 in the prompt box, `degFahren` is set to 31, so the variable `degCent` will be -0.55555555556. So how does our `if` statement look now? It evaluates to "Is –0.55555556 less than zero?" The answer this time is `true`, and the code inside the braces, here just a `document.write()` statement, will execute.

Finally, when we entered 212, how does this alter our `if` statement? The variable `degCent` is set to 100 by the calculation, so the `if` statement now asks the question, "Is 100 less than zero?" The answer is `false`, and the code inside the braces will be skipped over.

In the second `if` statement we evaluate the condition "Is the value of variable `degCent` equal to 100?"

```
if (degCent == 100)
    document.write("That's the boiling point of water");
```

There are no braces here so, if the condition is `true`, the only code to execute is the first line below the `if` statement. When we want to execute multiple lines in the case of the condition being `true`, then braces are required.

We saw above that when `degFahren` is 32, `degCent` will be 0. So our `if` statement will be "Is 0 equal to 100?" The answer is clearly `false` and the code won't execute. Again, when we set `degFahren` to 31, `degCent` will be calculated to be -0.55555555556, so "Is –0.5555556 equal to 100?" is also `false` and the code won't execute.

Finally, when `degFahren` is set to 212, `degCent` will be 100. This time the `if` statement is "Is 100 equal to 100?" and the answer is `true`, so the `document.write()` statement executes.

As we have seen already, one of the most common errors in JavaScript, even for experts, is using one equals sign for evaluating, rather than the necessary two. Take a look at the following code extract:

```
if (degCent = 100)
    document.write("That's the boiling point of water");
```

This condition will always evaluate to `true` and the code below the `if` statement will always execute. Worse still, your variable `degCent` will be set to 100. Why? Because a single equals sign assigns values to a variable; only a double equals sign compares values.

Logical Operators

You should have a general idea of how to use conditions in `if` statements now, but how do we use a condition such as "Is degFahren greater than zero, but less than 100?". There are two conditions to test here. We need to test whether degFahren is greater than zero *and* whether degFahren is less than 100.

JavaScript allows us to use such multiple conditions. To do this we need to learn about three more operators, the logical operators AND, OR, and NOT. The symbols for these are listed in the table below:

Operator	Symbol
AND	&&
OR	||
NOT	!

Notice that the AND and OR operators are *two* symbols repeated: `&&` and `||`. If you type just one symbol, `&` or `|`, then strange obscure things will happen – you should always use two.

Once we have discussed the three logical operators, we'll be taking a look at how to use them in `if` statements, with plenty of practical examples. So if it seems a bit confusing on first read, don't panic. All will become clear. Let's look at how each of these works, starting with the AND operator.

AND

Recall from above that we talked about the left-hand side (LHS) of the operator and the right-hand side (RHS). The same is true with the AND operator. However, now the LHS and RHS of the condition are Boolean values (usually the result of a condition).

The AND operator works very much like our understanding of the word in English. For example, we might say, "If I feel cold and I have a coat, then I'll put my coat on". Here, the left-hand side of the 'and' word is, "Do I feel cold?" and this can be evaluated as `true` or `false`. The right-hand side is, "Do I have a coat?", which again is evaluated to either `true` or `false`. If the left-hand side is true (I am cold) *and* the right hand side is true (I do have a coat), then I put my coat on.

This is very similar to how the AND operator works in JavaScript. The AND operator actually produces a result, rather like adding two numbers together produces a result. However, the AND operator takes two Boolean values (on its LHS and RHS) and results in another Boolean value. If the LHS and RHS conditions evaluate to `true` then the result will be `true`. In any other circumstance, the result will be `false`.

Below is a **truth table** of possible evaluations of left-hand sides and right-hand sides, and the result when AND is used.

Left-Hand Side	Right-Hand Side	Result
true	true	true
false	true	false
True	false	false
false	false	false

Now although the table above is strictly speaking true, its worth noting that JavaScript doesn't like doing unnecessary work. Well, who does! If the left-hand side is false, then even if the right-hand side does evaluate to true it won't make any difference to the final result – it'll still be false. So to avoid wasting time, if the left-hand side is false, JavaScript doesn't even bother checking the right-hand side, but just returns a result of false.

OR

Just like AND, OR also works in a similar way to our English language understanding. For example, we might say that if it is raining or if it is snowing, then we'll take an umbrella. If either of the conditions 'it is raining', or 'it is snowing' is true, then we will take an umbrella.

Again, just like AND, the OR operator acts on two Boolean values (one from its left-hand side, and one from its right-hand side) and returns another Boolean value. If the left-hand side evaluates to true, or the right-hand side evaluates to true, then the result returned is true. Otherwise the result is false. The table below shows the possible results:

Left-Hand Side	Right-Hand Side	Result
true	true	true
false	true	true
true	false	true
false	false	false

As with the AND operator, JavaScript likes to avoid doing things which make no difference to the final result. If the left-hand side is true, then whether the right-hand side is true or false makes no difference to the final result – it'll still be true. So, to avoid work, if the left-hand side is true the right-hand side is not evaluated, and JavaScript simply returns true. The end result is the same – the only difference is in how JavaScript does the working out. However, it does mean you should not rely on the right hand side of the OR operator to be executed.

NOT

In English we might say "If I'm not hot, then I'll eat soup." The condition being evaluated is whether I'm hot. The result is true or false, but in this example we act (eat soup) if the result is false.

However, JavaScript is used to executing code only if a condition is true. So if we want a false condition to cause code to execute, we need to switch that false value to true (and any true value to false). That way we can trick JavaScript into executing code after a false condition.

We do this using the NOT operator. This operator reverses the logic of a result; it takes one Boolean value and changes it to the other Boolean value. So it changes true to false and false to true. This is sometimes called **negation**.

To use the NOT operator we put the condition we want reversed in parentheses and put the ! symbol in front of the parentheses. For example:

```
if (!(degCent < 100))
{
    // Some code
}
```

Any code within the braces will be executed only if the condition degCent < 100 is false.

The table below details the possible results when using NOT.

Right-Hand Side	Result
true	false
false	true

Multiple Conditions Inside an if Statement

The previous section started by asking how we could use the condition "Is degFahren greater than zero, but less than 100?" One way of doing this would be to use two if statements, one **nested** inside another. Nested simply means that there is an outer if statement, and nested inside this is an inner if statement. If the condition for the outer if statement is true, then (and only then) the nested inner if statement's condition will be tested.

Using nested if statements, our code would be:

```
if (degCent < 100)
{
    if (degCent > 0)
    {
        document.write("degCent is between 0 and 100");
    }
}
```

This would work, but it is a little verbose, and can be quite confusing. JavaScript offers a better alternative – using multiple conditions inside the condition part of the if statement. The multiple conditions are strung together with the logical operators we just looked at. So, the above code could be rewritten as:

```
if (degCent > 0 && degCent < 100)
{
    document.write("degCent is between 0 and 100");
}
```

The if statement's condition first evaluates whether degCent is greater than 0. If that is true, then the code above goes on to evaluate whether degCent is less than 100. Only if both of these conditions are true, will the document.write() code line execute.

Try It Out – Multiple Conditions

In this example, we'll demonstrate multi-condition `if` statements using the AND, OR, and NOT operators. Type in the following code, and save it as `ch3_examp2.htm`:

```
<HTML>
<BODY>

<SCRIPT LANGUAGE=JavaScript>

var myAge = prompt("Enter your age",30);

if (myAge >= 0 && myAge <= 10)
{
    document.write("myAge is between 0 and 10<BR>");
}

if ( !(myAge >= 0 && myAge <= 10) )
{
    document.write("myAge is NOT between 0 and 10<BR>");
}

if ( myAge >= 80 || myAge <= 10 )
{
    document.write("myAge is 80 or above OR 10 or below<BR>");
}

if ( (myAge >= 30 && myAge <= 39) || (myAge >= 80 && myAge <= 89) )
{
    document.write("myAge is between 30 and 39 or myAge is between 80 and 89");
}

</SCRIPT>

</BODY>
</HTML>
```

When you load it into your browser, you should see a prompt box appear. Enter the value 30, then hit return and the following lines are written to the web page:

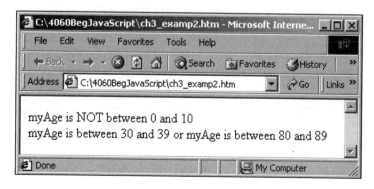

How It Works

We start the script block by defining the variable myAge and initializing it to the value entered by the user in the prompt box:

```
var myAge = prompt("Enter your age",30);
```

After this we have four if statements, each using multiple conditions. We'll look at each in detail in turn.

The easiest way to work out what multiple conditions are doing is to split them up into smaller pieces, and then evaluate the combined result. In our example we have entered the value 30, which has been stored in variable myAge. We'll substitute this value into the conditions to see how they work.

Here's the first if statement:

```
if (myAge >= 0 && myAge <= 10)
{
    document.write("myAge is between 0 and 10<BR>");
}
```

The first if statement is asking the question "Is myAge between 0 and 10?" We'll take the LHS of the condition first, substituting in our particular value for myAge. This asks "Is 30 greater than or equal to 0?" – answer true. The question posed by the RHS condition is, "Is 30 less than or equal to 10" – answer false. These two halves of the condition are joined using && which indicates the AND operator. Using the AND results table above, we can see that if LHS is true and RHS is false, we have an overall result of false. So the end result of the condition for the if statement is false, and the code inside the braces won't execute.

Let's move on to the second if statement:

```
if ( !(myAge >= 0 && myAge <= 10) )
{
    document.write("myAge is NOT between 0 and 10<BR>");
}
```

The second if statement is posing the question "Is myAge not between 0 and 10?" Its condition is similar to that of the first if statement, but with one small difference: we have enclosed our condition inside parentheses and put the NOT operator (!) in front.

The part of the condition inside the parentheses will be evaluated and, as before, produces the same result – false. However, the NOT operator reverses the result and makes it true. As the if statement's condition is true, the code inside the braces *will* execute this time causing a document.write() to write a response to the page.

What about the third if statement?

```
if ( myAge >= 80 || myAge <= 10 )
{
    document.write("myAge is either 80 and above OR 10 and below<BR>");
}
```

The third `if` statement asks, "Is myAge greater than or equal to 80, or less than or equal to 10?" Taking the LHS condition first – "Is 30 greater than or equal to 80?" – the answer is `false`. The answer to the RHS condition, "Is 30 less than or equal to 10?", is again `false`. These two halves of the condition are combined using || which indicates the OR operator. Looking at the OR result table above we see that `false` OR `false` produces a result of `false`. So again the `if` statement's condition evaluates to `false` and the code within the curly braces does not execute.

The final `if` statement is a little more complex:

```
if ( (myAge >= 30 && myAge <= 39) || (myAge >= 80 && myAge <= 89) )
{
    document.write("myAge is either between 30 and 39 or myAge is between 80 and
89<BR>");
}
```

It asks the question "Is myAge between 30 and 39 or between 80 and 89?" Let's break the condition down into its component parts. We have a left-hand side and a right-hand side condition, combined using an OR operator. However, the LHS and RHS themselves have a LHS and RHS which are combined using AND operators. Notice how we use parentheses to tell JavaScript which parts of the condition we want to be evaluated first, just as we would with numbers in a mathematical calculation.

Let's look at the LHS of the condition first, namely (myAge >= 30 && myAge <= 39). By putting the condition into parentheses we ensure it's treated as a single condition; no matter how many conditions are inside the parentheses, it only produces a single result, either `true` or `false`. Breaking down the conditions in the parentheses, we have "Is 30 greater than or equal to 30?" with a result of `true`, and "Is 30 less than or equal to 39?" again with result `true`. From our AND table, we know `true` AND `true` produces a result of `true`.

Now let's look at the RHS of the condition, namely (myAge >= 80 && myAge <= 89). Again breaking the condition down, we see that the LHS asks, "Is 30 greater than or equal to 80?" which gives a `false` result, and the RHS asks, "Is 30 less than or equal to 89?" which gives a `true` result. We know that `false` AND `true` gives a `false` result.

Now we can think of our `if` statement's condition as looking like (true || false). Looking at our OR results table, we can see that `true` OR `false` gives a result of `true`, so the code within the braces following the `if` statement will execute and a line will be written to the page.

However, now remember that JavaScript does not evaluate conditions where they won't affect the final result, and the above condition is one of those situations. The LHS of the condition evaluated to `true`. After that, it does not matter if the RHS of the condition is `true` or `false` as only one of the conditions in an OR operation needs to be `true` for a `true` result. Thus JavaScript does not actually evaluate the RHS of the above condition. We did so simply for demonstration purposes.

As we have seen, the easiest way to approach understanding or creating multiple conditions is to break them down into the smallest logical chunk. You'll find that with experience, you will do this almost without thinking, unless you have a particularly tricky condition to evaluate.

Although using multiple conditions is often better than using multiple `if` statements, there are times when it makes your code harder to read and therefore harder to understand and debug. It's possible to have 10, 20, or over 100 conditions inside your `if` statement, but can you imagine trying to read an `if` statement with even 10 conditions? If you feel like your multiple conditions are getting too complex, then break them down into smaller logical chunks.

For example, imagine we wanted to execute some code if myAge is in the ranges 30 - 39, 80 - 89, or 100 - 115. We could write the statement like so:

```
if ( (myAge >= 30 && myAge <= 39) || (myAge >= 80 && myAge <= 89) ||
     (myAge >= 100 && myAge <= 115) )
{
    document.write("myAge is either between 30 and 39 or myAge is between 80
                   and 89 or myAge is between 100 and 115");
}
```

There's nothing wrong with this, but it is starting to get a little long and difficult to read. Instead we could create another if statement for the 100 - 115 range part.

else and else if

Imagine a situation where you want some code to execute if a certain condition is true, and some other code to execute if it is false. We can achieve this by having the two if statements, as shown in the example below:

```
if (myAge >= 0 && myAge <= 10)
{
    document.write("myAge is between 0 and 10");
}

if ( !(myAge >= 0 && myAge <= 10) )
{
    document.write("myAge is NOT between 0 and 10");
}
```

The first if statement tests whether myAge is between 0 and 10, and the second for the situation where myAge is not between 0 and 10. However, JavaScript provides an easier way of achieving this, by using an else statement. Again, the use of the word else is similar to its use in the English language. We may say, "If it is raining, I will take an umbrella, else I will take a sun hat". In JavaScript we can say if the condition is true, then execute one block of code, else execute an alternative block. Rewriting the code above using this technique, we would have:

```
if (myAge >= 0 && myAge <= 10)
{
    document.write("myAge is between 0 and 10");
}
else
{
    document.write("myAge is NOT between 0 and 10");
}
```

Writing the code like this makes it simpler and therefore easier to read, and also saves JavaScript testing a condition that we already know the answer to.

We could also include another `if` statement with the `else` statement. For example:

```
if (myAge >= 0 && myAge <= 10)
{
    document.write("myAge is between 0 and 10");
}
else if ( (myAge >= 30 && myAge <= 39) || (myAge >= 80 && myAge <= 89) );
{
    document.write("myAge is either between 30 and 39 or myAge is between 80 and
89");
}
else
{
    document.write("myAge is NOT between 0 and 10, nor is it between 30 and 39, nor
is it between 80 and 89");
}
```

The first `if` statement checks whether `myAge` is between 0 and 10 and executes some code if that's true. If it's `false`, then an `else if` statement checks if `myAge` is between 30 and 39 or 80 and 89, and executes some other code if it's `true`. Failing that, we have a final `else` statement, which catches the situation where the value of `myAge` did not trigger `true` in any of the earlier `if` conditions.

When using `if` and `else if`, we need to be extra careful with our curly braces to ensure that the `if` and `else if` statements start and stop where we expect, and we don't end up with an `else` that doesn't belong to the right `if`. This is quite tricky to describe with words – it's easier to see what I mean with an example:

```
if (myAge >= 0 && myAge <= 10)
{
document.write("myAge is between 0 and 10");
if (myAge == 5)
{
document.write("Your 5 years old")
}
else
{
document.write("myAge is NOT between 0 and 10");
}
```

Notice I've not indented the code. While it does not matter to JavaScript, it does make it more difficult for humans to read and hides the missing curly brace that should be before the final `else` statement.

Correctly formatted and with the missing bracket inserted the code looks like this:

```
if (myAge >= 0 && myAge <= 10)
{
    document.write("myAge is between 0 and 10");
    if (myAge == 5)
    {
        document.write("Your 5 years old")
    }
}
```

```
   else
   {
      document.write("myAge is NOT between 0 and 10");
   }
```

As you can see, as well as working now, it is also a lot easier to see which code is part of which `if` block.

Comparing Strings

Up to this point we have been looking exclusively at using comparison operators with numbers. However, they work just as well with strings. All that's been said and done with numbers applies to strings, but with one important difference. We are now comparing data alphabetically rather than numerically, so there are a few traps to watch out for.

In the following code, we compare the variable `myName`, which contains the string `"Paul"`, with the string literal `"Paul"`:

```
var myName ="Paul";
if (myName == "Paul")
{
    alert("myName is Paul");
}
```

How does JavaScript deal with this? Well, it goes though each letter in turn on the LHS and checks it with the letter in the same position on the RHS to check if it's actually the same. If at any point it finds a difference then it stops and the result is `false`. If having checked each letter in turn all the way to the end, it confirms that they are all the same, then it returns `true`. The condition in the above `if` statement will return `true`, and so we'll see an `alert` box.

However, string comparison in JavaScript is case sensitive. So, `"P"` is not the same as `"p"`. Taking the example above, but changing the variable `myName` to `"paul"`, we find that the condition is `false` and the code inside the `if` statement does not execute:

```
var myName ="paul";
if (myName == "Paul")
{
    alert("myName is Paul");
}
```

The `>=`, `>`, `<=`, and `<` operators work with strings as well as with numbers, but again it is an alphabetical comparison. So `"A"` `<` `"B"` is true, because A comes before B in the alphabet. However, JavaScript's case sensitivity comes into play again. `"A"` `<` `"B"` is `true`, but `"a"` `<` `"B"` is `false`. Why? Because upper case letters are treated as always coming *before* lower case letters. Why is this? Each letter has a code number in the ASCII character set, and the code numbers for upper case letters are lower than the code numbers for lower case letters. This is something to watch out for when writing your own code.

The simplest way to avoid confusion with different cases is to convert both strings to either upper case or lower case before you compare them. This can easily be achieved using the `toUpperCase()` or `toLowerCase()` functions we'll be coming to in the next chapter.

The switch Statement

We saw above how the `if` and `else if` statements could be used for checking various conditions; if the first condition is not valid then another is checked, and another, and so on. However when you want to check the value of a particular variable for a large number of possible values, there is a more efficient alternative, namely the `switch` statement. Note that the `switch` statement is strictly a version 4 and later browser language feature, so if you want to support NN 3 and earlier or IE 3 browsers, then don't use it.

The structure of the `switch` statement is given below:

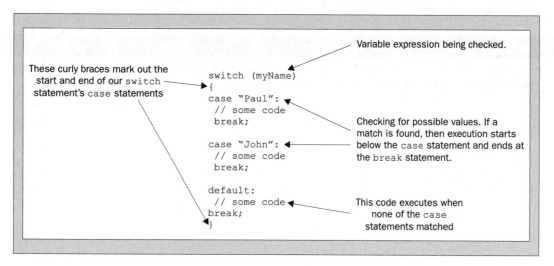

The best way to think of the `switch` statement is, "switch to the code where the case matches". There are four important elements to the `switch` statement:

- ❏ The test expression
- ❏ The `case` statements
- ❏ The `break` statements
- ❏ The `default` statement

The test expression is given in the parentheses following the `switch` keyword. In the above example, we are testing using the variable `myName`. Inside the parentheses, however, we could have any valid expression.

Next we come to the `case` statements. It's the `case` statements that do the condition checking. To indicate which `case` statements belong to our `switch` statement we must put them inside the curly braces following the test expression. Each `case` statement specifies a value, for example `"Paul"`. The `case` statement then acts like `if (myName == "Paul")`. If the variable `myName` did contain the value `"Paul"`, then execution would commence from the code starting below the `case: "Paul"` statement, and would continue to the end of the `switch` statement unless a `break` statement is encountered. There are only two `case` statements in this example, but you can have as many as you like.

In most cases, you just want the block of code directly underneath the relevant `case` statement to execute, and not *all* the code below the relevant `case` statement, including any other `case` statements. To achieve this, we put a `break` statement at the end of the code that we want executed. This tells JavaScript to stop executing at that point and leave the `switch` statement.

Finally we have the `default` case, which (as the name suggests) is the code that will execute when none of the other `case` statements matched. The `default` statement is optional; if you have no default code that you want to execute then you can leave it out, but remember that in this case, no code will execute if no `case` statements match. It is a good idea to include a `default` case, unless you are absolutely sure that you have all your options covered.

Try It Out – Using the switch Statement

Let's take a look at the `switch` statement in action. The example below illustrates a simple guessing game. Type in the code and save it as ch3_examp3.htm:

```
<HTML>
<BODY>

<SCRIPT LANGUAGE=JavaScript>

var secretNumber = prompt("Pick a number between 1 and 5:", "");
secretNumber = parseInt(secretNumber);

switch (secretNumber)
{
case 1:
    document.write("Too low!");
    break;

case 2:
    document.write("Too low!");
    break;

case 3:
    document.write("You guessed the secret number!");
    break;

case 4:
    document.write("Too high!");
    break;

case 5:
    document.write("Too high!");
    break;

default:
    document.write("You did not enter a number between 1 and 5.");
    break;
}
document.write("<BR>Execution continues here");

</SCRIPT>

</BODY>
</HTML>
```

Load this into your browser and enter, for example, the value 1 in the prompt box. You should then see something like this:

If, on the other hand, you enter the value 3, then you should see a friendly message letting you know that you guessed the secret number correctly:

How It Works

First we declare the variable `secretNumber` and set it to the value entered by the user via the `prompt()` box. Note that we use `parseInt()` function to convert the string that is returned from `prompt()` to an integer value:

```
var secretNumber = prompt("Pick a number between 1 and 5:", "");
secretNumber = parseInt(secretNumber);
```

Next we create the start of the `switch` statement:

```
switch (secretNumber)
{
```

The expression in parentheses is simply the variable `secretNumber`, and it's this number that the `case` statements will be compared against.

We specify the block of code encompassing our `case` statements using curly braces. Each `case` statement checks one of the numbers between 1 and 5, as this is what we have specified to the user that they should enter. The first simply outputs a message that the number they have entered is too low:

```
case 1:
    document.write("Too low!");
    break;
```

The second `case` statement, for the value 2, has the same message, so the code is not repeated here. The third `case` statement lets the user know that they have guessed correctly:

```
case 3:
    document.write("You guessed the secret number!");
    break;
```

Finally, the fourth and fifth `case` statements output a message that the number the user has entered is too high:

```
case 4:
    document.write("Too high!");
    break;
```

We do need to add a `default` case in this example, since the user might very well (despite the instructions) enter a number that is not between 1 and 5, or even perhaps a letter. In this case we add a message to let them know that there is a problem:

```
default:
    document.write("You did not enter a number between 1 and 5.");
    break;
```

A `default` statement is also very useful for picking up bugs – if you have coded some of the `case` statements incorrectly, then you will pick that up very quickly if you see the `default` code being run when it shouldn't.

We finally have added the closing brace indicating the end of the `switch` statement. After this we output a line to indicate where the execution continues:

```
}
document.write("<BR>Execution continues here");
```

Note that each `case` statement ends with a `break` statement. This is important to ensure that execution of the code moves to the line after the end of the `switch` statement. If we forgot to include this, then we could end up executing the code for each `case` following the `case` that matched.

Executing the Same Code for Different cases

You may have spotted a problem with the `switch` statement in our example above – we want to execute the same code if the user enters a 1 or a 2, and the same code for a 4 or a 5. However, in order to achieve this, we have had to repeat the code in each case. What we would like is an easier way of getting JavaScript to execute the same code for different cases. Well, that's easy! Simply change the above code, so that it looks like this:

```
switch (secretNumber)
{
case 1:
case 2:
    document.write("Too low!");
    break;

case 3:
    document.write("You guessed the secret number!");
    break;

case 4:
case 5:
    document.write("Too high!");
    break;

default:
    document.write("You did not enter a number between 1 and 5.");
    break;
}
```

If you load this into your browser and experiment with entering some different numbers, then you should see that it behaves in exactly the same way as it did before.

Here, we are making use of the fact that if there is no break statement underneath the code for a certain case statement, execution will continue through each following case statement, until a break statement or the end of the switch is reached. Think of it as a sort of free fall through the switch statement until we hit the break.

If the case statement for the value 1 is matched, then execution simply continues until the break statement under case 2, so effectively we can execute the same code for both cases. The same technique is used for the case statements with values 4 and 5.

Looping – The for and while Statements

Looping means repeating a block of code while a condition is true. This is achieved in JavaScript using two statements, the while statement and the for statement – we'll be looking at these shortly. But why would we want to repeat blocks of code anyway?

Well, take the situation where you have a series of results, say average temperatures for each month in a year, and you want to plot these on a graph. The code needed for plotting each point will most likely be the same. So, rather than write out the code twelve times, once for each point, it's much easier to execute the same code twelve times, but using the next item of data in the series. This is where the for statement would come in handy, since we know how many times we want the code to execute.

In another situation, you might want to repeat the same piece of code all the while a certain condition is true, for example while the user keeps clicking on a Start Again button. In this situation, the while statement would be very useful.

The for Loop

The `for` statement allows you to repeat a block of code a certain number of times. The syntax is illustrated in the diagram below:

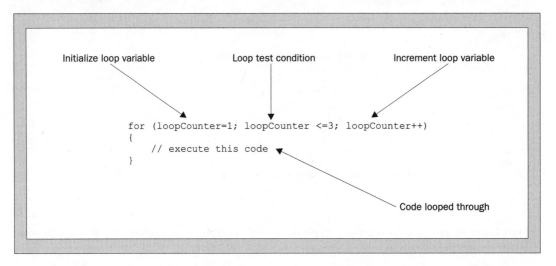

Let's look at the make up of a `for` statement. We can see from the above diagram that, just like the `if` and `switch` statements, the `for` statement also has its logic inside parentheses. However, this time it's split into three parts, each part separated by a semicolon. For example, in the above example we have the logic:

```
(loopCounter = 1; loopCounter <= 3; loopCounter++)
```

The first part of the `for` statement's logic is the **initialization** part of the `for` statement. To keep track of how many times we have looped through the code, we need a variable to keep count. It's in the initialization part that we initialize this variable. In the above example we have set the `loopCounter` variable to the value of `1`. This part is only executed once during the execution of the loops, unlike the other parts.

Following the semicolon, we have the **test condition** part of the `for` statement. The code inside the `for` statement will keep executing for as long as this test condition evaluates to `true`. After the code is looped through each time, this condition is tested. In the diagram above, we execute for as long as `loopCounter` is less than or equal to three. You'll often see the number of times a loop is performed called the number of **iterations**.

Finally, we have the **increment** part of the `for` loop, where variables in our loop's test condition have their values incremented. Here we can see that `loopCounter` is incremented by one using the `++` operator we saw in Chapter 2. Again this part of the `for` statement is repeated with every loop of the code. Although we call it the increment part, it can actually be used to decrease or **decrement** the value, for example if we wanted to count down from the top element in an array to the first.

After the `for` statement, we have the block of code that will be executed repeatedly, as long as the test condition is `true`. This block of code is contained within curly braces. If the condition is never `true`, even at the first test of the loop condition, then the code inside the `for` loop will be skipped over and never be executed.

Putting all the above together, how does the `for` loop work?

1. Execute initialization part of the `for` statement.

2. Check the test condition. If `true`, continue, if not exit the `for` statement.

3. Execute code in the block after the `for` statement.

4. Execute the increment part of `for` statement.

5. Repeat steps 2 to 4 until the test condition is `false`.

Try It Out – Converting a Series of Fahrenheit Values

Let's change our temperature converter so that it converts a series of values, stored in an array, from Fahrenheit to centigrade. We will be using the `for` statement to go through each element of the array. Type in the code and save it as `ch3_examp4.htm`.

```
<HTML>
<BODY>

<SCRIPT LANGUAGE=JavaScript>

var degFahren = new Array(212, 32, -459.15);
var degCent = new Array();
var loopCounter;

for (loopCounter = 0; loopCounter <= 2; loopCounter++)
{
    degCent[loopCounter] = 5/9 * (degFahren[loopCounter] - 32);
}

for (loopCounter = 2; loopCounter >= 0; loopCounter--)
{
    document.write("Value " + loopCounter + " was " + degFahren[loopCounter] +
                " degrees Fahrenheit");
    document.write(" which is " + degCent[loopCounter] +
                " degrees centigrade<BR>");
}

</SCRIPT>

</BODY>
</HTML>
```

On loading this into your browser, you'll see a series of three lines in the page containing the results of converting our array of Fahrenheit values into centigrade.

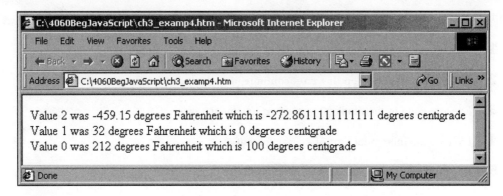

How It Works

Our first task is to declare the variables we are going to use. First, we declare and initialize degFahren to contain an array of three values, 212, 32 and -459.67. Next, degCent is declared as an empty array. Finally, loopCounter is declared and will be used to keep track of which array index we are accessing during our looping:

```
var degFahren = new Array(212, 32, -459.67);
var degCent = new Array();
var loopCounter;
```

Following this comes our first for loop:

```
for (loopCounter = 0; loopCounter <= 2; loopCounter++)
{
   degCent[loopCounter] = 5/9 * (degFahren[loopCounter] - 32);
}
```

In the first line, we start by initializing the loopCounter to zero. Then the for loop's test condition, loopCounter <= 2, is checked. If this condition is true, then the loop executes for the first time. Once the code inside the curly brackets has executed, the incrementing part of the for loop, loopCounter++, will be executed and then the test condition will be re-evaluated. If it's still true then another execution of the loop code is performed. This continues until the for loop's test condition evaluates to false, at which point looping will end, and the first statement after the closing curly bracket will be executed.

The code inside the curly braces is the equation we saw in earlier examples, only this time we are placing its result into the degCent array, with the index being the value of loopCounter.

In the second for loop we write the results contained in our degCent array to the screen:

```
for (loopCounter = 2; loopCounter >= 0; loopCounter--)
{
   document.write("Value " + loopCounter + " was " + degFahren[loopCounter] +
                  " degrees Fahrenheit");
   document.write(" which is " + degCent[loopCounter] +
                  " degrees centigrade<BR>");
}
```

This time we're counting *down* from 2 to 0. The variable `loopCounter` is initialized to 2 and the loop condition remains `true` until `loopCounter` is less than zero. This time `loopCounter` is actually decremented each time rather than incremented, using `loopCounter--`. Again, `loopCounter` is serving a dual purpose: it keeps count of how many loops we have done and also provides the index position in the array.

Note that in these examples, we've used whole numbers in our loops. However, there is no reason why you can't use fractional numbers, although it's much less common to do so.

The for...in Loop

The `for...in` loop was introduced in JavaScript version 1.3 (Internet Explorer 5.0+ and Netscape 4.06+). This loop works primarily with arrays. It allows us to loop through each element in the array, without having to know how many elements the array actually contains. In plain English, what this loop says is, "For each element in the array, execute some code." Rather than us having to work out the index number of each element, the `for...in` loop does it for us, and automatically moves to the next index with each iteration (loop through).

Its syntax for use with arrays is:

```
for (index in arrayName)
{
    //some code
}
```

In the above code extract, `index` is a variable we declare prior to the loop, which will automatically be populated with the next index value in the array. `arrayName` is the name of the variable holding the array we want to loop through.

Let's look at an example to make things clearer. We'll define an array and initialize it with three values:

```
var myArray = new Array("Paul","Paula","Pauline");
```

To access each element using a conventional `for` loop, we'd write:

```
var loopCounter;
for (loopCounter = 0; loopCounter < 3; loopCounter++)
{
    document.write(myArray[loopCounter]);
}
```

To do exactly the same thing with the `for...in` loop, we write:

```
var elementIndex;
for (elementIndex in myArray)
{
    document.write(myArray[elementIndex]);
}
```

As you can see, the code in the second example is a little clearer, as well as being shorter. Both methods work equally well, and will iterate three times. However, if you increase the size of the array, for example by adding the element myArray[3] = "Philip", the first method will still only loop through the first three elements in the array, whereas the second method will loop through all four elements.

The while Loop

Whereas the for loop is used for looping a certain number of times, the while loop allows you to test a condition and keep on looping while it's true. The for loop is useful where you know how many times you need to loop, for example where you are looping through an array that you know has a certain number of elements. The while loop is more useful where you don't know how many times you'll need to loop. For example, if you are looping through an array of temperature values and want to continue looping while the temperature value contained in the array element is less that 100, then you will need to use the while statement.

Let's take a look at the structure of the while statement.

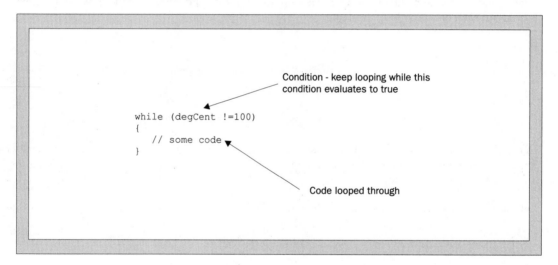

We can see that the while loop has fewer parts to it than the for loop. The while loop consists of a condition which, if it evaluates to true, causes the block of code inside the curly braces to execute once, and then the condition is re-evaluated. If it's still true, then the code is executed again and the condition is re-evaluated again, and so on until the condition evaluates to false.

One thing to watch out for is that if the condition is false to start with, then the while loop never executes. For example:

```
degCent = 100;

while (degCent != 100)
{
        // some code
}
```

Here, the loop will run if degCent does not equal 100, but as degCent is 100 the condition is false and the code never executes.

In practice we would normally expect the loop to execute once; whether it executes again will depend on what the code inside the loop has done to variables involved in the loop condition. For example:

```
degCent = new Array();
degFahren = new Array(34, 123, 212);
var loopCounter = 0;
while (loopCounter < 3)
{
    degCent[loopCounter] = 5/9 * (degFahren[loopCounter] - 32);
    loopCounter++;
}
```

The loop will execute so long as loopCounter is less than three. It's the code inside the loop (loopCounter++;) that increments loopCounter and will eventually cause loopCounter < 3 to be false so that the loop stops. Execution will then continue on the first line after the closing brace of the while statement.

Something to watch out for is the **infinite loop** – a loop that will never end. Suppose we forgot to include the loopCounter++; line in the above code. Leaving this line out would mean that loopCounter will remain at zero, so the condition (loopCounter < 3) will always be true and the loop will continue until the user gets bored, cross, and shuts down their browser. However, it is an easy mistake to make and one JavaScript won't warn you about.

It's not just missing out lines that can cause infinite loops, but also mistakes inside the loop's code. For example:

```
var testVariable = 0;
while (testVariable <= 10)
{
    alert("Test Variable is " + testVariable);
    testVariable++;
    if (testVariable = 10)
    {
        alert("The last loop");
    }
}
```

Spot the deliberate mistake that leads to an infinite loop – yes, it's the if statement that will cause this code to go on forever. Instead of using == as the comparison operator in the condition of the if statement, we have put =, so testVariable is *set* to 10 again in each loop, despite the line, testVariable++. This means that at the start of each loop the test condition always evaluates to true, since 10 is less than or equal to 10. Put the extra = in to make, if (testVariable == 10), and everything is fine.

The do...while loop

With the `while` loop, we saw that the code inside the loop only executes if the condition is `true`; if it's `false` the code never executes, and execution instead moves to the first line after the `while` loop. However, there may be circumstances when you want the code in the `while` loop to execute at least once, regardless of whether or not the condition in the `while` statement evaluates to `true`. It might even be that code inside the `while` loop needs to be executed before we can test the `while` statement's condition. It's situations like this that the do...while loop is ideal for.

Let's look at an example where we want to get the user's age via a prompt box. We want to show the prompt box, but also make sure that what they have entered is a number:

```
var userAge;
do
{
    userAge = prompt("Please enter your age","")
}
while (isNaN(userAge) == true)
```

The code line within the loop:

```
userAge = prompt("Please enter your age","")
```

will be executed regardless of the `while` statement's condition. This is because the condition is not checked *until* one loop has been executed. If the condition is `true`, then the code is looped through again. If it's `false`, then looping stops.

Note that within the `while` statement's condition, we are using the `isNaN()` function that we saw in Chapter 2. This checks whether the `userAge` variable's value is NaN (not a number). If it is not a number, the condition returns a value of `true`, otherwise it returns `false`. As we can see from the example, it allows us to test the user input to ensure the right data has been entered. The user might lie about their age, but at least we know they have entered a number!

The do...while loop is fairly rare; there's not much you can't do with the `while` loop that can only be done with a do...while loop, so it's best avoided unless really necessary.

The break and continue Statements

We met the `break` statement earlier when we looked at the `switch` statement. Its function inside a `switch` statement is to stop code execution and move execution to the next line of code after the closing curly brace of the `switch` statement. However, the `break` statement can also be used as part of the `for` and `while` loops when you want to exit the loop prematurely. For example, suppose you're looping through an array, like we did with the temperature conversion example, and you hit an invalid value? In this situation, you might want to stop the code in its tracks, notify the user that the data is invalid, and leave the loop. This is one situation where the `break` statement comes in handy.

Let's see how we could change the example where we converted a series of Fahrenheit values (`ch3_examp4.htm`), so that if we hit a value that's not a number we stop the loop and let the user know about the invalid data.

```
<SCRIPT LANGUAGE=JavaScript>
var degFahren = new Array(212, "string data", -459.67);
var degCent = new Array();
var loopCounter;

for (loopCounter = 0; loopCounter <= 2; loopCounter++)
{
    if (isNaN(degFahren[loopCounter]))
        {
            alert("Data '" + degFahren[loopCounter] + "' at array index " +
                loopCounter + " is invalid");
            break;
        }

    degCent[loopCounter] = 5/9 * (degFahren[loopCounter] - 32);
}
```

We have changed the initialization of the degFahren array so that it now contains some invalid data. Then, inside the for loop, an if statement is added to check whether the data in the degFahren array is not a number. This is done using the isNaN() function; it returns true if the value passed to it in the parentheses, here degFahren[loopCounter], is not a number. If the value is not a number, then we tell the user whereabouts in the array we have the invalid data. Then we break out of the for loop altogether, using the break statement, and code execution continues on the first line after the end of the for statement.

That's the break statement, but what about continue? The continue statement is similar to break in that it stops the execution of a loop at the point it is found, but instead of leaving the loop, it starts execution at the next iteration, starting with the for or while statement's condition being re-evaluated, just as if the last line of the loop's code had been reached.

In the break example above it was all or nothing – if even one piece of data was invalid we broke out of the loop. It might be better if we tried to convert all the values in degFahren, but if we hit an invalid item of data in the array we notify the user and continue with the next item, rather than giving up as our break statement example above does.

```
    if (isNaN(degFahren[loopCounter]))
        {
            alert("Data '" + degFahren[loopCounter] + "' at array index " +
                loopCounter + " is invalid");
            continue;
        }
```

Just change the break statement to a continue. We will still get a message telling us about the invalid data, but the third value will also be converted.

Functions

A function is something that performs a particular task. Take a pocket calculator as an example. It provides lots of basic calculations, such as addition and subtraction. However, many also have function keys that do something more complex. For example, some calculators have a button for calculating the square root of a number, and others even provide statistical functions, such as calculating an average. Most of these functions could be done using just the basic mathematical operations of add, subtract, multiply and divide. However, the number of calculations needed could be quite extensive, so the calculation is greatly simplified for the user if they can just use one button to do all the stages of the calculation. All they need do is provide the data – numbers in this case – and the function key does all the rest.

Functions in JavaScript work a little like the function buttons on a pocket calculator; they encapsulate a block of code that performs a certain task. Over the course of the book so far, we have come across a number of handy built-in functions that perform a certain task, such as the `parseInt()` and `parseFloat()` functions, which convert strings to numbers, and the `isNaN()` function, which tells us whether a particular variable can be converted to a number. Some of these functions return data, such as `parseInt()`, which returns an integer number; others simply perform an action, but return no data. You'll also notice that some functions can be passed data, while others cannot. For example, the `isNaN()` function needs to be passed some data, which it checks to see if it is NaN. The data that a function requires to be passed is known as its **parameter(s)**.

As we work our way through the book, we'll be coming across many more useful built-in functions, but wouldn't it be great to be able to write our own functions? Having worked out, written and debugged a block of code to perform a certain task, it would be nice to be able to call it again and again when we need it. JavaScript gives us the ability to do just that, and this is what we'll be concentrating on in this section.

Creating Your Own Functions

Creating and using your own functions is very simple. The diagram below shows a sample of a function:

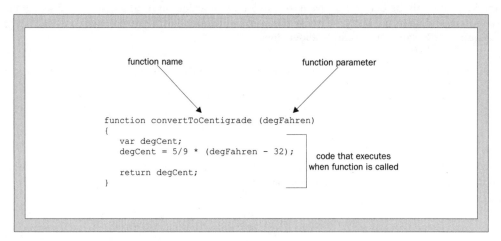

You've probably already realized what this function does and how the code works. Yes, it's the infamous Fahrenheit to centigrade conversion code again.

Each function you define in JavaScript must be given a unique name for that particular page. The name comes immediately after the `function` keyword. To make life easier for yourself try using meaningful names so that when you see it being used later in your code you'll know exactly what it does. For example, a function that takes as its parameters someone's birthday and today's date, and returns their age could be called `getAge()`. However, the names you can use are limited in a similar way to variable names. For example, you can't use words reserved by JavaScript, so you couldn't call your function `with()` or `while()`.

The parameters for the function are given in parentheses after the function's name. A parameter is just an item of data that the function needs to be given to do its job. Not passing the required parameters will result in an error. A function can have zero or more parameters, though even if it has no parameters you must still put the open and close parentheses after its name. For example, the top of your function definition must look like:

```
function myNoParamFunction()
```

We then write the code, which the function will execute when called on to do so. All the function code must be put in a block by using a pair of curly braces.

Functions also give us the ability to return a value from a function to the code that called it. We use the `return` statement to return a value. In the example function given above, we return the value of the variable `degCent`, which we have just calculated. You don't have to return a value if you don't want to, but you should always include a `return` statement at the end of your function, although JavaScript is a very forgiving language and won't have a problem if you don't use a `return` statement at all.

When JavaScript comes across a `return` statement in a function, it treats it a bit like `break` statement in a `for` loop – it exits the function, returning any value specified after the `return` keyword.

You'll probably find it useful to build up a 'library' of functions that you use frequently in JavaScript code, which you can cut and paste into your page whenever you need them.

Having created our functions, how do we use them? Unlike the code we've seen so far which executes when JavaScript reaches that line, functions only execute if you ask them to, which is termed **calling** or **invoking** the function. We call a function by writing its name at the point we want it to be called and making sure that we pass any parameters it needs, separated by commas. For example:

```
myTemp = convertToCentigrade(212);
```

This line would call the `convertToCentigrade()` function we saw above, passing `212` as the parameter and storing the `return` value from the function (that is, `100`) in the `myTemp` variable.

Let's have a go at creating our own functions now, taking a closer look at how parameters are passed. Parameter passing can be a bit confusing, so we'll first create a simple function that takes just one parameter (the user's name) and writes it to the page in a friendly welcome string. First, we need to think of a name for our function. A short, but descriptive, name is `writeUserWelcome()`. Now we need to define what parameters the function expects to be passed. There's only one parameter – the user name. Defining parameters is a little like defining variables, we need to stick to the same rules for naming, so that means no spaces, special characters, or reserved words. Let's call our parameter `userName`. We need to add it inside parentheses to the end of the function name (note we don't put a semi-colon at the end of the line):

```
function writeUserWelcome(userName)
```

OK, now we have defined our function name and its parameters, all that's left is to create the function body – that is, the code that will be executed when the function is called. We mark out this part of the function by wrapping it in curly braces:

```
function writeUserWelcome(userName)
{
    document.write("Welcome to my website" + userName + "<BR>");
    document.write("Hope you enjoy it!");
}
```

The code is simple enough, we write out a message to the web page using document.write(). You can see that userName is used just as we'd use any normal variable; in fact, it's best to think of parameters just as normal variables. The value that the parameter has will be that specified by the JavaScript code where the function was called.

Let's see how we would call this function:

```
writeUserWelcome("Paul");
```

Simple really – just write the name of the function we want to call, and then in parentheses add the data to be passed to each of the parameters, here just one. When the code in the function is executed, the variable userName, used in the body of the function code, will contain the text "Paul".

Suppose we wanted to pass two parameters to our function – what would we need to change? Well first we'd have to alter the function definition. Imagine that the second parameter will hold the user's age – we could call it userAge since that makes it pretty clear what the parameter's data represents. Here is the new code:

```
function writeUserWelcome(userName, userAge)
{
    document.write("Welcome to my website" + userName + "<BR>");
    document.write("Hope you enjoy it");
    document.write("Your age is " + userAge);
}
```

We've added a line to the body of the function that uses the parameter we have added. To call the function we'd write:

```
writeUserWelcome("Paul",31);
```

The second parameter is a number so there is no need for quotes around it. Here the userName parameter will be Paul and the second parameter userAge will be 31.

Try It Out – Fahrenheit to Centigrade Function

Let's rewrite our temperature converter page using functions. You can cut and paste most of this code from ch3_examp4.htm – the parts that have changed have been highlighted. Once you've finished, save it as ch3_examp5.htm:

```
<HTML>
<BODY>

<SCRIPT LANGUAGE=JavaScript>

function convertToCentigrade(degFahren)
{
   var degCent;
   degCent = 5/9 * (degFahren - 32);

   return degCent;
}

var degFahren = new Array(212, 32, -459.67);
var degCent = new Array();
var loopCounter;

for (loopCounter = 0; loopCounter <= 2; loopCounter++)
{
   degCent[loopCounter] = convertToCentigrade(degFahren[loopCounter]);
}

for (loopCounter = 2; loopCounter >= 0; loopCounter--)
{
   document.write("Value " + loopCounter + " was " + degFahren[loopCounter] +
                  " degrees Fahrenheit");
   document.write(" which is " + degCent[loopCounter] +
                  " degrees centigrade<BR>");
}

</SCRIPT>

</BODY>
</HTML>
```

When you load this page into your browser, you should see exactly the same results that you had with ch3_examp4.htm.

How It Works

At the top of our script block we declare our convertToCentigrade() function. We saw this function above:

```
function convertToCentigrade(degFahren)
{
   var degCent;
   degCent = 5/9 * (degFahren - 32);

   return degCent;
}
```

If you're using a number of separate `script` blocks in a page, then it's very important that the function is defined before any script calls it. If you have a number of functions you may want to put them all in their own script block at the top of the page – between the `<HEAD>` and `</HEAD>` tags is good. That way you know where to find all your functions and you can be sure that they have been declared before they have been used.

You should be pretty familiar with how the code in the function works. We declare a variable `degCent`, do our calculation and store its result in `degCent`, then return `degCent` back to the calling code. The function's parameter is `degFahren`, which provides the information the calculation needs.

Following the function declaration is the code that executes when the page loads. First we define the variables we need, and then we have the two loops that calculate and then output the results. This is mostly the same as before, apart from the first `for` loop:

```
for (loopCounter = 0; loopCounter <= 2; loopCounter++)
{
    degCent [loopCounter] = convertToCentigrade (degFahren [loopCounter]);
}
```

The code inside the first `for` loop puts the value returned by our function `convertToCentigrade ()` into the `degCent` array.

There is a subtle point to the code in this example. Notice that we declare the variable `degCent` within our function `convertToCentigrade ()`, and we also declare it as an array after the function definition.

Surely, this isn't allowed?

Well, this leads neatly on to the next topic of this chapter – variable scope.

Variable Scope and Lifetime

What do we mean by **scope**? Well, put simply, it's the scope or extent of a variable's availability – where it can be seen and used. Any variables declared in a web page outside of a function will be available to all script on the page, whether that script is inside a function or otherwise – we term this a **global** or **page level scope**. However, variables declared inside a function are *only* visible inside that function – no code outside the function can access them. So, we could declare a variable `degCent` in every function we have on a page *and* once on the page outside any function. However, we can't declare the variable *more* than once inside any one function or *more* than once on the page outside the functions. Note that reusing a variable name throughout a page in this way, while not *illegal*, is not standard good practice – it can make the code very confusing to read.

Function parameters are similar to variables: they can't be seen outside the function, and we can't declare a variable in a function with the same name as one of its parameters.

So what happens when the code inside a function ends and execution returns to the point the code was called? Do the variables defined within the function retain their value when we call the function the next time?

The answer is no; variables not only have the scope property – where they are visible – they also have a **lifetime**. When the function finishes executing, the variables in that function die and their values are lost, unless we return one of them to the calling code. Every so often JavaScript performs garbage collection (which we talked about in the last chapter), whereby it scans through the code and sees if any variables are no longer in use; if so, the data they hold is freed from memory to make way for other variables.

Given that global variables can be used anywhere, why not make all of them global? Global variables are great when you need to keep track of data on a global basis. However, because they are available for modification anywhere in your code, it does mean that if they are changed incorrectly, due to a bug, then that bug could be anywhere within the code, making debugging difficult. It's best, therefore, to keep global variable use to a minimum, though sometimes they are a necessary evil, for example, when you need to share data among different functions.

The Trivia Quiz – Building One of the Basic Functions

In the last chapter we declared the arrays that hold the questions and answers for our trivia quiz. We also populated these arrays with the first three questions. At that point we didn't have enough knowledge to actually make use of the data, but with what we've learnt in this chapter, we can create a function that uses the information in the arrays to check whether an answer is correct.

Load in `trivia_quiz.htm` and alter it to that shown below:

```
<HTML>
<HEAD>
<TITLE>Wrox Online Trivia Quiz</TITLE>

<SCRIPT LANGUAGE=JavaScript>

function answerCorrect(questionNumber, answer)
{
   // declare a variable to hold return value
   var correct = false;

   // if answer provided is same as correct answer then correct variable is true
   if (answer == answers[questionNumber])
      correct = true;

   // return whether the answer was correct (true or false)
   return correct;
}

</SCRIPT>
</HEAD>

<BODY>
<SCRIPT LANGUAGE=JavaScript>

// Questions variable will holds questions
var questions = new Array();
var answers = new Array();
```

```
// define question 1
questions[0] = new Array();

// the question
questions[0][0] = "The Beatles were";

// first choice
questions[0][1] = "A sixties rock group from Liverpool";

// second choice
questions[0][2] = "Four musically gifted insects";

// third choice
questions[0][3] = "I don't know - can I have the questions on Baseball please";

// assign answer for question 1
answers[0] = "A";

// define question 2
questions[1] = new Array();
questions[1][0] = "Homer Simpson's favorite food is";
questions[1][1] = "Fresh salad";
questions[1][2] = "Doughnuts";
questions[1][3] = "Bread and water";
questions[1][4] = "Apples";

// assign answer for question 2
answers[1] = "B";

// define question 3
questions[2] = new Array();
questions[2][0] = "Lisa Simpson plays which musical instrument";
questions[2][1] = "Clarinet";
questions[2][2] = "Oboe";
questions[2][3] = "Saxophone";
questions[2][4] = "Tubular Bells";

// assign answer for question 3
answers[2] = "C";

</SCRIPT>

</BODY>
</HTML>
```

The only changes here are that we've removed the `alert()` function, which told the user that the array was initialized, and added a function, `answerCorrect()`, which checks whether a trivia question has been answered correctly. This function has been added inside a script block in the head of the page. The `answerCorrect()` function takes two parameters: the question index from the arrays in parameter `questionNumber` and the answer the user has given in parameter `answer`. It then checks whether the user's answer is in fact correct – if it is, then the function returns `true`, otherwise it returns `false`.

Currently the code checks the answer given by the user by checking to see whether the element of the answers array with an index of questionNumber is equal to the answer parameter. Given how simple this function is, could we not have just included the code wherever it's needed? Why go to the bother of creating a function? The answer to this query is that we have plans for that function. Currently, its role is simply to check whether the multiple-choice response, a single letter given by the user, is the same as the letter stored in the answers array. However, later we'll be expanding the trivia quiz to handle text-based questions such as, "Which President was involved in the Watergate scandal?" and we want the answer to be considered correct whether the user enters Richard Nixon, Nixon, or R Nixon and so on. This involves more than a simple comparison, so at some point we'll be expanding the answerCorrect() function to incorporate this extra intelligence. By including it in just one function, we need to change our code in only one place and can do so without breaking other parts of our program. Code using our function expects only a true or false result – how this function comes by this result is irrelevant.

To test our new answerCorrect() function, let's write some code that goes through each of the questions in the questions array and uses the answerCorrect() function to work out which answer is correct. Insert the lines shown below into the body of the page, inside the script block after the questions and answers array have been defined. Once you've finished testing, you can delete this code, as it does not form part of the final trivia quiz.

```javascript
// define question 3
questions[2] = new Array();
questions[2][0] = "Lisa Simpson plays which musical instrument";
questions[2][1] = "Clarinet";
questions[2][2] = "Oboe";
questions[2][3] = "Saxophone";
questions[2][4] = "Tubular Bells";

// assign answer for question 3
answers[2] = "C";
```

```javascript
var possibleAnswers = new Array("A","B","C","D","E");
var questionNumber;
var arrayIndex;

for (questionNumber = 0; questionNumber < answers.length; questionNumber++)
{
   for (arrayIndex = 0; arrayIndex < 5; arrayIndex++)
   {

      if (answerCorrect(questionNumber,possibleAnswers[arrayIndex]))
      {
         alert("The Answer to Question " + questionNumber + " is " +
            possibleAnswers[arrayIndex]);
         break;
      }
   }
}
```
```
</SCRIPT>
</BODY>
</HTML>
```

First we define the three variables that we'll be using:

❑ possibleAnswers is an array of five characters, each representing one of the choices a user could make to answer a question

❑ questionNumber will be used to loop through the answers to the questions in the answers array

❑ arrayIndex will be used as the array index for our possibleAnswers array

Next we have two for loops, one contained within the other. The outer for loop loops through each question's answer in the answers array. How do we know how many questions there are? Easy – we use the length property that arrays have built in. We'll be looking further at this in the next chapter. However, for now all that you need to know is that answers.length gives us the number of elements in the answers array, that is 3 in this case. Recall that the indices for an array start at 0. So the array indices that we need to loop through are 0, 1, and 2. Therefore the test condition in the outer for loop needs only to be questionNumber < answers.length, rather than questionNumber <= answers.length.

For each question looped through in the outer for loop, the inner for loop goes through each possible answer in the possibleAnswers array and tests it against the correct answer of the current question using our answerCorrect() function. If we find an answer that is correct, then we cause an alert box to tell us the result and break out of the loop. Note that the break only breaks out of the inner for loop, not both loops.

If you load trivia_quiz.htm into your browser, you should see the following three alert boxes:

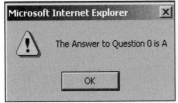
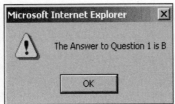
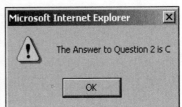

Note that the questions and answers arrays holding the question and answer data have global scope within the page, something that I warned you about in the previous section. However, here it is necessary since the arrays need to be accessed by both the function and the JavaScript code within the page.

Summary

In this chapter, we have concluded our look at the core of the JavaScript language and its syntax. Everything from now on builds on these foundations, and with the less interesting syntax under our belts, we can move on to more interesting things in the remainder of the book.

The chapter looked at:

- ❑ Decision making with the `if` and `switch` statements – the ability to make decisions is essentially what gives the code its 'intelligence'. Based on whether a condition is `true` or `false` we can decide on a course of action to follow.

- ❑ Comparison operators – the comparison operators compare the value on the left of the operator (left-hand side, LHS) with the value on the right of the operator (right-hand side, RHS) and return a Boolean value. The main comparison operators are:

    - ❑ `==`   Is the LHS equal to the RHS?
    - ❑ `!=`   Is the LHS not equal to the RHS
    - ❑ `<=`   Is the LHS less than or equal to the RHS?
    - ❑ `>=`   Is the LHS greater than or equal to the RHS?
    - ❑ `<`   Is the LHS less than the RHS?
    - ❑ `>`   Is the LHS greater then the RHS?

- ❑ The `if` statement – using the `if` statement, we can choose to execute a block of code (defined by being in curly braces) when a condition is `true`. The `if` statement has a test condition, specified in parentheses. If this evaluates to `true`, the code after the `if` statement will execute.

- ❑ The `else` statement – if we want code to execute when the `if` statement is `false`, then we can use the `else` statement which appears after the `if` statement.

- ❑ Logical operators – to combine conditions we can use the three logical operators AND, OR and NOT represented by `&&`, `||` and `!`

    - ❑ The AND operator only returns true if both sides of the expression are true
    - ❑ The OR operator returns true when either one or both sides of an expression are true
    - ❑ The NOT operator reverses the logic of an expression

- ❑ The switch statement – this compares the result of an expression with a series of possible cases, similar in effect to a multiple if statement.

- ❑ Looping with `for`, `for...in`, `while`, and `do...while` – it's often necessary to repeat a block of code a number of times, something JavaScript enables by looping.

    - ❑ The `for` loop – useful for looping through code a certain number of times. It consists of three parts, the initialization, test condition, and increment parts. Looping continues while the test condition is `true`. Each loop executes the block of code and then executes the increment part of the `for` loop before re-evaluating the test condition to see if the results of incrementing have changed it.

    - ❑ The for   in loop – this is useful when we want to loop through an array without knowing the number of elements there are in the array. JavaScript works this out for us so that no elements are missed.

❑ The `while` loop – useful for looping through some code so long as a test condition remains `true`. It consists of a test condition and the block of code that's executed only if the condition is `true`. If the condition is never `true` then the code never executes.

❑ The `do...while` loop – similar to a `while` loop, except that it executes the code once and then keeps executing the code as long as the test condition remains `true`.

❑ `break` and `continue` statements – sometimes we have a good reason why we want to break out of a loop prematurely, in which case we need to use the `break` statement. On hitting a `break` statement, code execution stops for the block of code marked out by the curly braces and starts immediately after the closing brace. The `continue` statement is similar to `break`, except that while code execution stops at that point in the loop, the loop is not broken out of, but instead continues as if the end of that re-iteration had been reached.

❑ Functions are reuseable bits of code – JavaScript has a lot of built-in functions, which provide us as programmers a service, such as converting a string to a number. However, JavaScript also allows us to define and use our own functions using the `function` keyword. Functions can have zero or more parameters passed to them and can return a value if we so wish.

❑ Variable scope and lifetime – variables declared outside of a function are available globally, that is, anywhere in the page. Any variables defined inside a function are private to that function and can't be accessed outside of it. Variables have a lifetime, the length of which depends on where the variable was declared. If it's a global variable then its lifetime is that of the page – while the page is loaded in the browser, the variable remains alive. For variables defined in a function, the lifetime is limited to the execution of that function. Once the function has finished being executed, the variables die and their values are lost. If the function is called again later in the code, then the variables will be empty.

Exercise Questions

Suggested solutions to these questions can be found in Appendix A.

Question 1

A junior programmer comes to you with some code that appears not to work. Can you spot where they have gone wrong? Give them a hand and correct the mistakes.

```
var userAge = prompt("Please enter your age");

if (userAge = 0);
{
    alert("So you're a baby!");
}
else if ( userAge < 0 | userAge > 200)
    alert("I think you may be lying about your age");
else
{
    alert("That's a good age");
}
```

Question 2

Write code that displays, using document.write(), the results of the 12 times table. Its output should be the results of the calculations:

```
12 * 1 = 12
12 * 2 = 24
12 * 3 = 36
...
12 * 11 = 132
12 * 12 = 144
```

Question 3

Change the code of Question 2 so that it's a function that takes as parameters the times table required and what values it should start and end at. So we might want the 4 times table displayed starting with 4 * 4 and ending at 4 * 9.

Question 4

Modify the code of Question 3 to request the times table to be displayed from the user, the code should continue to request and display times tables until the user enters -1. Additionally do a check to make sure that the user is entering a valid number; if it's not valid ask them to re-enter it.

Online discussion at http://p2p.wrox.com

JavaScript – An Object-Based Language

In this chapter, we'll be looking at a concept that is central to JavaScript, namely **objects**. But what are objects, and why are they useful?

Firstly, I have to make a confession. All the way through this book you have been using objects. For example, an `Array` is an object. I just kept it quiet for simplicity, but now you're ready to learn the 'horrible' truth. JavaScript is an object-based language and therefore much of what we do involves manipulating objects. We'll see that by making full use of these objects, the range of things we can do with JavaScript is expanded immensely.

We'll start this chapter by introducing the idea of what objects are and why they are important. We'll move on to see what kind of objects we use in JavaScript, how to create them and use them, and how they simplify many programming tasks for us. Finally, we'll look in more detail at some of the most useful objects that JavaScript provides for us, and see how to use these in practical situations.

Not only does JavaScript itself consist of a number of these things called objects (which we term native JavaScript objects), but also the browser itself is modeled as a collection of objects available for our use. We'll learn about these objects in particular in the next chapter.

Object-Based Programming

Object-based programming is a slightly scarier way of saying programming using objects. But what are these objects that we will be programming with? Where are they, and how and why would we want to program with them? In this section, we'll be look at the answers to these questions, both in general programming terms, and more specifically within JavaScript.

A Brief Introduction to Objects

To start our introduction to objects, let's think about what is meant by an object in the 'real world' outside computing. The world is composed of things, or objects, such as tables, chairs, and cars (to name just a few!). Let's take a car as an example, so we can explore what an object really is.

How would we define our car? We might say it's a blue car with 4-wheel drive. We may specify the speed that it's traveling at. When we do this, we are specifying **properties** of the object. For example, the car has a color property, which in this instance has the value blue.

How do we use our car? We turn the ignition key, press the gas pedal, beep the horn, change the gear (that is, choose between 1, 2, 3, 4, and reverse on a manual car, or drive and reverse on an automatic), etc. When we do this, we are using **methods** of the object.

We can think of methods as being a bit like functions. Sometimes, we may need to use some information with the method, or pass it a parameter, to get it to work. For example, when we use the changing gear method, we need to say what gear we want to change to. Other methods may pass information back to the owner. For example, the dipstick method will tell the owner how much oil is left in the car.

Sometimes using one or other of the methods may change one or more of the object's properties. For example, using the accelerator method will probably change the car's speed property. Other properties can't be changed, for example the body shape property of the car (unless you hit a brick wall with the speed property at 100 miles per hour!).

We could say that the car is defined by its collection of methods and properties. In object-based programming, the idea is to model real-world situations by objects, which are defined by their methods and properties.

Objects in JavaScript

You should now have a basic idea of what an object is – a 'thing' with methods and properties. But how do we use this in JavaScript?

In the previous chapters, we have (for the most part) been dealing with **primitive** data. This is *actual* data such as strings and numbers. This type of data is not too complex, and is fairly easy for us to deal with. However, not all information is as simple as primitive data. Let's look at an example to clarify things a little.

Suppose you had written a web application that displayed timetable information for buses or trains. Once the user has selected a journey, you might want to let them know how long that journey would take. To do that, you would need to subtract the arrival time from the departure time.

However, that's not quite as simple as it may appear at first glance. For example, consider a departure time of 14.53 and an arrival time of 15.10. If we tell JavaScript to evaluate the expression 15.10-14.53, we get the result 0.57, that is fifty seven minutes. However, we know that the real difference in time is seventeen minutes. Using the normal mathematical operators on times doesn't work!

What would we need to do to calculate the difference between these two times? We would firstly need to separate out the hours from the minutes in each time. Then, to get the minutes difference between the two times, we would need to check whether the minutes of the arrival time were greater than the minutes of the departure. If so, we can simply take the departure time minutes from the arrival time minutes. If not, we need to add 60 to the arrival time minutes, and take away one from the arrival time hours to compensate, before taking the departure time minutes from the arrival time minutes. We then need to take the departure time hours from the arrival time hours, before putting the minutes and hours that we have arrived at back together.

This would work okay, so long as the two times were in the same day. It wouldn't work, for example, with the times 23.45 and 04.32.

This way of working out the time difference obviously has its problems, but it also seems very complex. Is there an easier way to deal with more complex data such as times and dates?

This is where objects come in. We can define our departure and arrival times as Date objects. Because they are Date objects, they come along with a variety of properties and methods that we can use when we need to manipulate or calculate with the times. For example, it has the getTime() method that we can use to get the number of milliseconds between the time in the Date object and 1st January 1970, 00:00:00. Once we have these millisecond values for the arrival and departure times, we can simply take one away from the other and store the result in another Date object. To retrieve the hours and minutes of this time, we simply use the getHours() and getMinutes() methods of the Date object. We'll see more examples of this later in the chapter.

The Date object is not the only object that JavaScript has to offer. Another object was introduced in Chapter 2, but to keep things simple, I didn't tell you it was an object at the time. That object was the Array object. Recall that an array is a way of holding a number of pieces of data at the same time.

Array objects have a property called length that tells us how many pieces of data, or rather how many elements, the array holds. We actually used this property in the Trivia Quiz in Chapter 3 to work out how many times we needed to loop through the array.

Array objects also have a number of methods. One example is the sort() method, which can be used to sort the elements within the array into alphabetical order.

You should now have an idea why objects are useful in JavaScript. We have seen the Date and Array objects, but there are many other objects that JavaScript makes available so that we can achieve more with our code. These include the Math and String objects, which we will talk more about later in the chapter.

Using JavaScript Objects

Now that we have seen the 'Why?' of JavaScript objects, we need to look at the 'What?' and 'How?'

Each of the JavaScript objects has a collection of related properties and methods that can be used to manipulate a certain kind of data. For example, the Array object consists of methods to manipulate arrays, and properties to find out information from them. In most cases, to make use of these methods and properties we need to define our data as one of these objects. In other words, we need to create an object.

In this section, we'll look at how we go about creating an object and, having done that, how we use its properties and methods.

Creating an Object

We have already seen an example of an object being created. This was for `Array` objects. To create an `Array` object, we used the JavaScript statement:

```
var myArray = new Array();
```

So how is this statement made up?

The first half of the statement is familiar to us. We use the `var` keyword to define a variable called `myArray`. This variable is initialized, using the assignment operator (=), to the right-hand side of the statement.

The right-hand side of the statement consists of two parts. First we have the keyword new. This tells JavaScript that we want to create a new object. Next we have `Array()`. This is the **constructor** for an `Array` object. It tells JavaScript what type of object we want to create. Most objects have constructors like this. For example, the `Date` object has the `Date()` constructor. The only exception we see in this book is the `Math` object, and this will be explained in a later part of the chapter.

We also saw in Chapter 2 that we can pass parameters to the constructor `Array()` to add data to our object. For example, to create an `Array` object that has three elements containing the data `"Paul"`, `"Paula"` and `"Pauline"`, we use:

```
var myArray = new Array("Paul", "Paula", "Pauline");
```

Let's see some more examples, this time using the `Date` object. The simplest way of creating a `Date` object is:

```
var myDate = new Date();
```

This will create a `Date` object containing the date and time that it was created. However,

```
var myDate = new Date("1 Jan 2000");
```

will create a `Date` object containing the date 1st January 2000.

How object data is stored in variables differs from how primitive data, such as text and numbers, is stored. With primitive data, the variable holds the data's actual value. For example:

```
var myNumber = 23;
```

means that the variable `myNumber` will hold the data 23. However, variables assigned to objects don't hold the actual data, but rather a **reference** to the memory address where the data can be found. This doesn't mean we can get hold of the memory address, as this is something only JavaScript has details of and keeps to itself in the background. All you need to remember is that when we say that a variable references an object, this is what we mean.

To summarize this section, we create a JavaScript object using the following basic syntax:

```
var myVariable = new ObjectName(optional parameters);
```

Using an Object's Properties

Accessing the values contained in an object's properties is very simple. We write the name of the variable containing (or referencing) our object, followed by a dot, and then the name of the object's property.

For example, if we had defined an `Array` object contained in the variable `myArray`, we could access its `length` property using:

```
myArray.length
```

This would give us the number of elements contained in the array.

But what can we do with this property now that we have it? We can use this property as we would any other piece of data. We can store it in a variable:

```
var myVariable = myArray.length;
```

or show it to the user:

```
alert(myArray.length);
```

In some cases, we can even change the value of the property, such as:

```
myArray.length = 12;
```

However, unlike variables, some properties are read-only – we can get information from them, but we can't *change* information inside them.

Calling an Object's Methods

Methods are very much like functions in that they can be used to perform useful tasks, such as getting the hours from a particular date or generating a random number for us. Again like functions, some methods return a value, such as the `Date` object's `getHours()` method, while others perform a task, but return no data, such as the `Array` object's `sort()` method.

Using the methods of an object is very similar to using properties in that you put the object's variable name first, then a dot, and then the name of the method. For example, to sort the elements of an `Array` in the variable `myArray`, you may use the following code:

```
myArray.sort();
```

Just like functions, some methods can be passed parameters, which are placed between the parentheses following the method's name. However, whether a method takes parameters or not, we must still put parentheses after the method's name, just as we did with functions. As a general rule anywhere you can use a function, you can use a method of an object.

Primitives and Objects

You should now have a good idea about the difference between primitive data, such as numbers and strings, and object data, such as `Dates` and `Arrays`. However, didn't I mention earlier that there is also a `String` object? Where does this fit in?

In fact there are `String`, `Number`, and `Boolean` objects corresponding to the three string, number. and Boolean primitive data types. For example, to create a `String` object containing the text "I'm a String object", we may use:

```
var myString = new String("I'm a String object");
```

The `String` object has the `length` property just as the `Array` object does. This returns the number of characters in the `String` object. For example:

```
var lengthOfString = myString.length;
```

would store the data 19 in the variable `lengthOfString` (remember that spaces are referred to as characters too).

But what if we had declared a primitive string called `mySecondString` holding the text `"I'm a primitive string"` like this:

```
var mySecondString = "I'm a primitive string";
```

and wanted to know how many characters could be found in this primitive string?

This is where JavaScript helps us out. Recall from previous chapters that JavaScript can handle the conversion of one data type to another automatically. For example, if we tried to add a string primitive to a number primitive:

```
theResult = "23" + 23;
```

JavaScript assumes that we want to treat the number as a string and concatenate the two together, the number being converted to text automatically. The variable, `theResult` would contain `"2323"` – the concatenation of 23 and 23, and not the sum of 23 + 23, which is 46.

The same applies to objects. If we declare a primitive string and then treat it as an object, such as by trying to access one of its methods or properties, JavaScript would work out that what we're trying to do is not correct for a primitive string, but would be valid if it was a `String` object. In this case, JavaScript converts the plain text string into a temporary `String` object, just for that operation.

So, for our primitive string `mySecondString`, we can use the `length` property of the `String` object to find out the number of characters it contains:

```
var lengthOfSecondString = mySecondString.length;
```

would store the data 22 in the variable `lengthOfSecondString`.

The same ideas as we have expressed here are also true for number and Boolean primitives and their corresponding `Number` and `Boolean` objects. However, these objects are not used very often, so we will not be discussing them further in this book.

The JavaScript Native Objects

So far we have just been looking at what objects are, how to create them and how to use them. Now, let's take a look at some of the more useful objects that are native to JavaScript, that is those that JavaScript makes available for us to use.

We won't be looking at all of the native JavaScript objects, just some of the more commonly used ones, namely the `String` object, the `Math` object, the `Array` object, and the `Date` object. However, Appendix B gives a full listing of the JavaScript native objects. Later in the book, we'll also be dedicating a whole chapter to each of the more complex objects, such as the `String` object (Chapter 8) and the `Date` object (Chapter 9).

String Objects

Like most objects, `String` objects need to be created before they can be used. To create a `String` object we can write:

```
var string1 = new String("Hello");
var string2 = new String(123);
var string3 = new String(123.456);
```

However, as we have seen, we can also declare a string primitive and use it as if it was a `String` object, letting JavaScript do the conversion to an object for us behind the scenes. For example:

```
var string1 = "Hello";
```

Using this technique is fine so long as it's clear to JavaScript what object we expect to be created in the background. If the primitive data type is a string then this won't be a problem, JavaScript will work it out.

The `String` object has a vast number of methods and properties of which you can find full details in Appendix B. In this section, we'll only be looking at some of the less complex and more commonly used methods. However, in Chapter 8, we'll be looking at some of the trickier, but very powerful, methods associated with strings and the regular expression object (`RegExp`). Regular expressions provide a very powerful means of searching strings for patterns of characters. For example, if we wanted to find "Paul" where it exists as a whole word in the string "Pauline, Paul, Paula" we need to use regular expressions. However, they can be a little tricky to use and so we won't discuss them further in this chapter – we want to save some fun for later!

When using most of the `String` object's methods, it helps to remember that a string is just a series of individual characters and that each character has a position or index, a little like arrays. Just like arrays, the first position, or index, is labeled 0 and not 1. So, for example, the string "Hello World" has the following character positions.

Character Index	0	1	2	3	4	5	6	7	8	9	10
Character	H	e	l	l	o		W	o	r	l	d

The length Property

The length property simply returns the number of characters in the string. For example:

```
var myName = new String("Paul");
document.write(myName.length);
```

will write the length of the string "Paul" (that is, 4) to the page.

The charAt() and charCodeAt() Methods – Selecting a Single Character from a String

If you want to find out information about a single character within a string, then you need the charAt() and charCodeAt() methods. These methods can be very useful for checking the validity of user input, something we'll see more of in Chapter 6 when we look at HTML forms.

The charAt() method takes one parameter: the index position of the character you want in the string. It then returns that character. As discussed above, charAt() treats the positions of the string characters as starting at 0, so the first character is at index 0, the second at index 1 and so on.

For example, to find the last character in a string, we could use the code:

```
var myString = prompt("Enter some text","Hello World!");
var theLastChar = myString.charAt(myString.length - 1);
document.write("The last character is " + theLastChar);
```

In the first line we prompt the user for a string, with the default of "Hello World!", and store this string in the variable myString.

In the next line, we use the charAt() method to retrieve the last character in the string. We use the index position of (myString.length - 1). Why? Let's take the string "Hello World!" as an example. The length of this string is 12, but the last character position is 11 since the indexing starts at 0. Therefore, we need to subtract 1 from the length of the string to get the last character position.

In the final line, we write the last character in the string to the page.

The charCodeAt() method is similar in use to the charAt() method, but instead of returning the character itself, it returns a number which represents the decimal character code in the Latin-1 character set for that character. (See Appendix D.) Recall that computers only understand numbers – to the computer all our strings are just number data. When we request text rather than numbers, the computer does a conversion, based on its internal understanding of each number and provides the respective character.

For example, to find the character code of the first character in a string, we could write:

```
var myString = prompt("Enter some text","Hello World!");
var theFirstCharCode = myString.charCodeAt(0);
document.write("The first character code is " + theFirstCharCode);
```

which will get the character code for the character at index position zero in the string given by the user, and write it out to the page.

Character codes go in order, so for example the letter A has the code 65, B has 66 and so on. Lower case letters start at 97 (a is 97, b is 98, and so on). Digits go from 48 (for the number 0) to 57 (for the number 9). You can use this information for various purposes, as we'll see in the next example.

Try It Out – Checking a Character's Case

Shown below is an example that detects the type of the character at the start of a given string, that is, whether the character is upper case, lower case, numeric, or other.

```
<HTML>
<BODY>

<SCRIPT LANGUAGE=JavaScript>

function checkCharType(charToCheck)
{
    var returnValue = "O";
    var charCode = charToCheck.charCodeAt(0);

    if (charCode >= "A".charCodeAt(0) && charCode <= "Z".charCodeAt(0))
    {
        returnValue = "U";
    }
    else if (charCode >= "a".charCodeAt(0) && charCode <= "z".charCodeAt(0))
    {
        returnValue = "L";
    }
    else if (charCode >= "0".charCodeAt(0) && charCode <= "9".charCodeAt(0))
    {
        returnValue = "N";
    }
    return returnValue;
}

var myString = prompt("Enter some text","Hello World!");
switch (checkCharType(myString))
{
    case "U":
        document.write("First character was upper case");
        break;
    case "L":
        document.write("First character was lower case");
        break;
    case "N":
        document.write("First character was a number");
        break;
    default:
        document.write("First character was not a character or a number");
}

</SCRIPT>
</BODY>
</HTML>
```

Type in the code and save it as ch4_exampl.htm.

When you load the page into your browser, you will be prompted for a string. A message will then be written to the page informing you of the type of the first character that you entered – whether it is uppercase, lowercase, a number, or something else, such as a punctuation mark.

How It Works

In the head of the page, we define a function `checkCharType()`, which is used in the body of the page. We start this function by declaring the variable `returnValue` and initializing it to the character `"O"`:

```
function checkCharType(charToCheck)
{
    var returnValue = "O";
```

We use this variable as the value to be returned at the end of the function, indicating the type of character. It will take the values U for upper case, L for lower case, N for number, and O for other.

The next line in the function uses the `charCodeAt()` method to get the character code of the first character in the `string` stored in `charToCheck`, which is the function's only parameter. The character code is stored in the variable `charCode`:

```
var charCode = charToCheck.charCodeAt(0);
```

In the following lines we have a series of `if` statements, which check what range of values the character code falls within. We know that if it falls between the character codes for A and Z, it's uppercase, and so we assign the variable `returnValue` the value U. If the character code falls between the character codes for a and z, then it's lowercase, and so we assign the variable `returnValue` the value L. If the character code falls between the character codes for 0 and 9, then it's a number, and we assign the variable `returnValue` the value N. If the value falls into none of these ranges, then the variable retains its initialization value of O for other, and we need do nothing:

```
if (charCode >= "A".charCodeAt(0) && charCode <= "Z".charCodeAt(0))
{
    returnValue = "U";
}
else if (charCode >= "a".charCodeAt(0) && charCode <= "z".charCodeAt(0))
{
    returnValue = "L";
}
else if (charCode >= "0".charCodeAt(0) && charCode <= "9".charCodeAt(0))
{
    returnValue = "N";
}
```

This probably seems a bit weird at first, so let's see what JavaScript is doing with our code. When we write:

```
"A".charCodeAt(0)
```

it appears that we are trying to use a method of the `String` object on a string literal, which is the same as primitive string in that it's just characters and not an object. However, JavaScript realizes what we are doing and does the necessary conversion of literal character `"A"` into a temporary `String` object containing `"A"`. Then, and only then, JavaScript performs the `charCodeAt()` method on the `String` object it has created in the background. When it has finished, the `String` object is disposed of. Basically, this a shorthand way of writing:

```
var myChar = new String("A");
myChar.charCodeAt(0);
```

In either case the first (and in this string the only) character's code is returned to us. For example, on the Windows operating system, `"A".charCodeAt(0)` will return the number 65.

Finally we come to the end of the function, and return the `returnValue` variable to where the function was called:

```
    return returnValue;
}
```

You might wonder why we bother using the variable `returnValue` at all, instead of just returning its value. For example, we could write the code as follows:

```
if (charCode >= "A".charCodeAt(0) && charCode <= "Z".charCodeAt(0))
{
    return "U";
}
else if (charCode >= "a".charCodeAt(0) && charCode <= "z".charCodeAt(0))
{
    return "L";
}
else if (charCode >= "0".charCodeAt(0) && charCode <= "9".charCodeAt(0))
{
    return "N";
}
return "O";
```

This would work fine, so why not do it this way? The disadvantage of this way is that it's difficult to follow the flow of execution of the function, which is not that bad in a small function like this, but can get tricky in bigger functions. With the original code we always know exactly where the function execution stops: it stops at the end with the only `return` statement. The version of the function shown above finishes when any of the `return` statements is reached, so there are four possible places where the function might end.

In the body of our page, we have some test code to check that the function works. We first use the variable `myString`, initialized to `"Hello World!"` or whatever the user enters into the prompt box, as our test string:

```
var myString = prompt("Enter some text","Hello World!");
```

Next, the `switch` statement uses the `checkCharType()` function that we defined above in its comparison expression. Depending on what is returned by the function, one of the `case` statements will execute and let the user know what the character type was:

```
switch (checkCharType(myString))
{
    case "U":
        document.write("First character was upper case");
        break;
    case "L":
```

```
        document.write("First character was lower case");
        break;
    case "N":
        document.write("First character was a number");
        break;
    default:
        document.write("First character was not a character or a number");
}
```

That completes the example, but before we move on it's worth noting that this example is just that, an example of using `charCodeAt()`. In practice, it would be much easier to just write:

```
if (char >= "A" && char <= "Z")
```

rather than:

```
if (charCode >= "A".charCodeAt(0) && charCode <= "Z".charCodeAt(0))
```

which we have used here.

The fromCharCode() Method – Converting Character Codes to a String

The method `fromCharCode()` can be thought of as the opposite to `charCodeAt()`, in that you pass it a series of comma-separated numbers representing character codes, and it converts them to a single string.

However, the `fromCharCode()` method is unusual in that it's a **static** method – we don't need to have created a `String` object to use it with. Instead, we can use the `String` statement.

For example, the following lines put the string "ABC" into the variable `myString`:

```
var myString;
myString = String.fromCharCode(65,66,67);
```

The `fromCharCode()` method can be very useful when used with variables. For example, to build up a string consisting of all the upper case letters of the alphabet, we could use the following code:

```
var myString = "";
var charCode;

for (charCode = 65; charCode <= 90; charCode++)
{
    myString = myString + String.fromCharCode(charCode);
}

document.write(myString);
```

We use the `for` loop to select each character from A to Z in turn and concatenate this to `myString`. Note that, while this is fine as an example, it is more efficient and less memory hungry to simply write:

```
var myString = "ABCDEFGHIJKLMNOPQRSTUVWXYZ"
```

The indexOf() and lastIndexOf() Methods – Finding a String Inside Another String

The methods `indexOf()` and `lastIndexOf()` are used for searching for the occurrence of one string inside another. A string contained inside another is usually termed a **substring**. They are useful when we have a string of information, but only want a small part of it. For example, in our trivia quiz when someone enters a text answer, we want to check if certain keywords are present within the string.

Both `indexOf()` and `lastIndexOf()` take two parameters:

❑ The string you want to find

❑ The character position you want to start searching from (optional)

As with the `charAt()` method, character positions start at zero. If you don't include the second parameter, then searching starts from the beginning of the string.

The return value of `indexOf()` and `lastIndexOf()` is the character position in the string at which the substring was found. Again, it's zero based, so if the substring is found at the start of the string, then 0 is returned. If there is no match then the value `-1` is returned.

For example, to search for the substring `"Paul"` in the string `"Hello paul. How are you Paul"`, we may use the code:

```
<SCRIPT LANGUAGE=JavaScript>

var myString = "Hello paul. How are you Paul";
var foundAtPosition;

foundAtPosition = myString.indexOf("Paul");
alert(foundAtPosition);

</SCRIPT>
```

This code should result in a message box containing the number 25, which is the character position of `"Paul"`. You might be wondering why it's 25, which clearly refers to the second `"Paul"` in the string, rather than 6 for the first `"paul"`. Well, this is due to case sensitivity again. It's laboring the point a bit, but JavaScript takes case sensitivity very seriously, both in its syntax and when making comparisons. If you type `IndexOf()` instead of `indexOf()`, JavaScript will complain. Similarly, `"paul"` is not the same as `"Paul"`. Mistakes with case are so easy to make, even for experts, that it's best to be very aware of case when programming.

We've seen `indexOf()` in action, but how does `lastIndexOf()` differ? Well, whereas `indexOf()` starts searching from the beginning of the string, or the position you specified in the second parameter, and works towards the end, `lastIndexOf()` starts at the end of the string, or the position you specified, and works towards the beginning of the string.

In the example overleaf we first search using `indexOf()`, which finds the first `"Paul"` (changed to the correct case from the last example). The `alert` box displays this result, which is character position 6. Then we search using `lastIndexOf()`. This starts searching at the end of the string, and so the first Paul it comes to is the last one in the string at character position 25. Therefore, the second alert box displays the result 25.

125

```
<SCRIPT LANGUAGE=JavaScript>

var myString = "Hello Paul. How are you Paul";
var foundAtPosition;

foundAtPosition = myString.indexOf("Paul");
alert(foundAtPosition);

foundAtPosition = myString.lastIndexOf("Paul");
alert(foundAtPosition);

</SCRIPT>
```

Try It Out – Counting Occurrences of Substrings

In this example, let's look at how we can use the start character position parameter of indexOf(). Here, we will count how many times the word Wrox appears in the string.

```
<HTML>
<BODY>
<SCRIPT LANGUAGE=JavaScript>
var myString = "Welcome to Wrox books. "
myString = myString + "The Wrox website is www.wrox.com. "
myString = myString + "Visit the Wrox website today. Thanks for buying Wrox"

var foundAtPosition = 0;
var wroxCount = 0;

while ( foundAtPosition != -1)
{
    foundAtPosition = myString.indexOf("Wrox",foundAtPosition);
    if (foundAtPosition != -1)
    {
        wroxCount++;
        foundAtPosition++;
    }
}

document.write("There are " + wroxCount + " occurrences of the word Wrox");

</SCRIPT>
</BODY>
</HTML>
```

Save this example as ch4_examp2.htm.

When you load the page into your browser, you should see the sentence:

There are 4 occurrences of the word Wrox

written to the page.

How It Works

At the top of the script block, we have built up a string inside the variable `myString`, which we then want to search for the occurrence of the word `Wrox`. We also define two variables: `wroxCount` will contain the number of times `Wrox` is found in the string, and `foundAtPosition` will contain the position in the string of the current occurrence of the substring `Wrox`.

We have then used a `while` loop, which continues looping all the while we are finding the word `Wrox` in the string, that is while the variable `foundAtPosition` is not equal to `-1`. Inside the `while` loop, we have the line:

```
foundAtPosition = myString.indexOf("Wrox",foundAtPosition);
```

Here we search for the next occurrence of the substring `Wrox` in the string `myString`. How do we make sure that we get the next occurrence? We use the variable `foundAtPosition` to give us the starting position of our search, since this contains the index after the index position of the last occurrence of the substring `Wrox`. We assign the variable `foundAtPosition` to the result of our search, the index position of the next occurrence of the substring `Wrox`.

Each time `Wrox` is found (that is `foundAtPosition` is not `-1`) we increase the variable `wroxCount`, which counts how many times we have found the substring, and we increase `foundAtPosition` so that we recommence the search at the next position in the string:

```
if (foundAtPosition != -1)
{
    wroxCount++;
    foundAtPosition++;
}
```

Finally, we `document.write()` the value of the variable `wroxCount` to the page.

In the previous chapter we talked about the danger of infinite loops and you can see that there is a danger of one here. If the `foundAtPosition++` was removed, we'd keep searching from the same starting point and never move to find the next occurrence of the word `Wrox`.

The `indexOf()` and `lastIndexOf()` methods are more useful when coupled with the `substr()` and `substring()` methods, which we'll be looking at in the next section. Using a combination of these methods allows us to cut substrings out of a string.

The substr() and substring() Methods – Copying Part of a String

If we wanted to cut out part of a string and assign that cut out part to another variable or use it in an expression, then we would use the `substr()` and `substring()` methods. Both methods provide the same end result, that is a part of a string, but they differ in the parameters they require.

The method `substring()` takes two parameters: the character start position and the character end position of the part of the string we want. The second parameter is optional; if you don't include it then all characters from the start position to the end of the string are included.

For example, if our string is `"JavaScript"` and we want the just the text `"Java"`, we could call the method like so:

```
var myString = "JavaScript";
var mySubString = myString.substring(0,4);
alert(mySubString);
```

As with all the methods of the `String` object so far, the character positions start at zero. However you might be wondering why we specified the end character as 4. This method is a little confusing because the end character is the end marker; it's not included in the substring that is cut out. It helps to think of the parameters as specifying the *length* of the string being returned: the parameters 0 and 4 will return (4 - 0) characters starting at and including the character at position 0. Depicted graphically it looks like this:

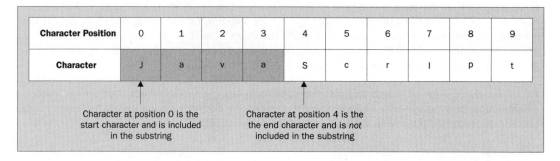

Character Position	0	1	2	3	4	5	6	7	8	9
Character	J	a	v	a	S	c	r	I	p	t

Character at position 0 is the start character and is included in the substring

Character at position 4 is the the end character and is *not* included in the substring

Like `substring()`, the method `substr()` again takes two parameters, the first being the start position of the first character you want included in your substring. However, this time the second parameter specifies the length of the string of characters that you want to cut out of the longer string. For example, we could rewrite the code above as:

```
var myString = "JavaScript";
var mySubString = myString.substr(0,4);
alert(mySubString);
```

As with the `substring()` method, the second parameter is optional. If you don't include it then all the characters from the start position onward will be included.

The main reason for using one method rather than the other is that the `substring()` method is supported by IE 3+ and by NN 2+ browsers. However, the `substr()` method only works with version 4 (and later) browsers.

Let's look at the use of the `substr()` and `lastIndexOf()` methods together. In the next chapter, we'll see how we can retrieve the file path and name of the currently loaded web page. However, there is no way of just retrieving the file name alone. So if, for example, your file is `"D:\mywebsite\temp\myfile.htm"`, you may need to extract the `myfile.htm` part. This is where `substr()` and `lastIndexOf()` come in useful:

```
var fileName = window.location.href;
fileName = fileName.substr(fileName.lastIndexOf("/") + 1);
document.write("The file name of this page is " + fileName);
```

The first line sets the variable `fileName` to the current file path and name, such as `D:\mywebsite\temp\myfile.htm`. Don't worry about understanding this line, as we'll be looking at it in the next chapter.

The second line is where the interesting action is. You can see that I've used the return value of the `lastIndexOf()` method as a parameter for another method, something that's perfectly correct and very useful. Our goal in using `fileName.lastIndexOf("\")` is to find the position of the final backslash, \, which will be the last character before the name of the file. We add one to this value, because we don't want to include that character, and then pass this new value to the `substr()` method. There's no second parameter here (the length), because we don't know it. As a result, `substr()` will return all the characters right to the end of the string, which is what we want.

This example retrieves the name of the page on the local machine, as we're not accessing the page from a web server. However don't let this mislead you into thinking that accessing files on a local hard drive from a web page is something you'll be able to do with JavaScript alone. To protect users from malicious hackers, JavaScript is very limited in what access it has to the user's system, such as access to files. We'll talk more about this later in the book.

The toLowerCase() and toUpperCase() Methods – Changing the Case of a String

If we want to change the case of a string, for example to remove case sensitivity when comparing strings, then we need the `toLowerCase()` and `toUpperCase()` methods. It's not hard to guess what these two methods do. Both of them return a string that is the value of the string in the `String` object, but with its case converted to either upper or lower depending on the method invoked. Any non-alphabetical characters remain unchanged by these functions.

In the following example, we can see that by changing the case of both strings we can compare them without case sensitivity being an issue:

```
var myString = "I Don't Care About Case"

if (myString.toLowerCase() == "i don't care about case")
{
    alert("Who cares about case?");
}
```

Even though `toLowerCase()` and `toUpperCase()` don't take any parameters, you must remember to put the two empty parentheses at the end, that is, `()`.

The Math Object

The `Math` object provides a number of useful mathematical functions and number manipulation methods. We'll be taking a look at some of them here, but you'll find the rest described in Appendix B.

The `Math` object is a little unusual in that JavaScript automatically creates it for you. There's no need to declare a variable as a `Math` object, or define a new `Math` object before being able to use it, making it a little bit easier to use.

The properties of the Math object include some useful math constants, such as the PI property (giving the value 3.14159 etc.). We access these properties, as usual, by placing a dot after the object name (Math) and then writing the property name. For example, to calculate the area of a circle, we may use the following code:

```
var radius = prompt("Give the radius of the circle", "");
var area = (Math.PI)*radius*radius;
document.write("The area is " + area);
```

The methods of the Math object include some operations that are impossible, or complex to perform, using the standard mathematical operators (+, -, *, /). For example, the cos() method returns the cosine of the value passed as a parameter. We'll look at a few of these methods now.

The abs() Method

The abs() method returns the absolute value of the number passed as its parameter. Essentially, this means that it returns the positive value of the number. So -1 is returned as 1, -4 as 4 and so on. However, 1 would be returned as 1 because it's already positive.

For example, the following code would write the number 101 to the page:

```
var myNumber = -101;
document.write(Math.abs(myNumber));
```

The ceil() Method

The ceil() method always rounds a number up to the next largest whole number or integer. So 10.01 becomes 11, and -9.99 becomes -9 (because -9 is greater than -10). The ceil() method has just one parameter, namely the number you want rounded up.

Using ceil() is different from using the parseInt() function we saw in Chapter 2, because parseInt() simply chops off any numbers after the decimal point to leave a whole number, whereas ceil() rounds the number up.

For example, the following code write two lines in the page, the first containing the number 102 and the second containing the number 101:

```
var myNumber = 101.01;
document.write(Math.ceil(myNumber) + "<BR>");
document.write(parseInt(myNumber));
```

The floor() Method

Like the ceil() method, the floor() method removes any numbers after the decimal point, and returns a whole number or integer. The difference is that floor() always rounds the number down. So if we pass 10.01 we would be returned 10, and if we pass -9.99, we will see -10 returned.

The round() Method

The round() method is very similar to ceil() and floor(), except that instead of always rounding up, or always rounding down, it rounds up only if the decimal part is .5 or greater, and rounds down otherwise.

For example:

```
var myNumber = 44.5;
document.write(Math.round(myNumber) + "<BR>");

myNumber = 44.49;
document.write(Math.round(myNumber));
```

would write the numbers 45 and 44 to the page.

Summary of Rounding Methods

As we have seen, the ceil(), floor(), and round() methods all remove the numbers after a decimal point and return just a whole number. However, which whole number they return depends on the method used: floor() returns the smallest, ceil() the highest, and round() the nearest equivalent integer. This can be a little confusing, so shown below is a table of values and what whole number would be returned if these values were passed to the parseInt() function, and ceil(), floor(), and round() methods.

Parameter	parseInt() returns	ceil() returns	floor() returns	round() returns
10.25	10	11	10	10
10.75	10	11	10	11
10.5	10	11	10	11
-10.25	-10	-10	-11	-10
-10.75	-10	-10	-11	-11
-10.5	-10	-10	-11	-10

Remember that parseInt() is a native JavaScript function, and not a method of the Math object, like the other methods presented in this table.

Try It Out – JavaScript's Rounding Functions Results Calculator

If you're still not sure about rounding numbers, then the following example should help. Here, we'll look at a calculator that gets a number from the user, then writes out what the result would be when we pass that number to parseInt(), ceil(), floor(), and round().

```
<HTML>
<BODY>
<SCRIPT Language=JavaScript>

var myNumber = prompt("Enter the number to be rounded","");

document.write("<H3>The number you entered was " + myNumber + "</H3><BR>");
document.write("<P>The rounding results for this number are</P>");
document.write("<TABLE WIDTH=150 BORDER=1>");
```

```
document.write("<TR><TH>Method</TH><TH>Result</TH></TR>");
document.write("<TR><TD>parseInt()</TD><TD>"+ parseInt(myNumber) +"</TD></TR>");
document.write("<TR><TD>ceil()</TD><TD>" + Math.ceil(myNumber) + "</TD></TR>");
document.write("<TR><TD>floor()</TD><TD>"+ Math.floor(myNumber) + "</TD></TR>");
document.write("<TR><TD>round()</TD><TD>" + Math.round(myNumber) +"</TD></TR>");
document.write("</TABLE>")

</SCRIPT>
</BODY>
</HTML>
```

Save this as ch4_examp3.htm and load into a web browser. In the prompt box, enter a number, for example -12.354, and OK. The results of this number being passed to parseInt(), ceil(), floor(), and round() will be displayed in the page formatted inside a table as shown below.

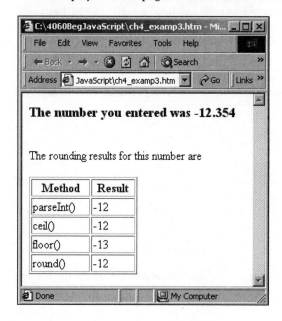

How It Works

Our first task is to get the number to be rounded from the user:

```
var myNumber = prompt("Enter the number to be rounded","");
```

Then, we write out the number and some descriptive text:

```
document.write("<H3>The number you entered was " + myNumber + "</H3><BR>");
document.write("<P>The rounding results for this number are</P>");
```

Notice how this time some HTML tags for formatting have been included, the main header being in <H3> tags and the description of what the table means being inside a paragraph <P> tag.

Next we create our table of results:

```
document.write("<TABLE WIDTH=150 BORDER=1>");
document.write("<TR><TH>Method</TH><TH>Result</TH></TR>");
document.write("<TR><TD>parseInt()</TD><TD>"+ parseInt(myNumber) +"</TD></TR>");
document.write("<TR><TD>ceil()</TD><TD>" + Math.ceil(myNumber) + "</TD></TR>");
document.write("<TR><TD>floor()</TD><TD>"+ Math.floor(myNumber) + "</TD></TR>");
document.write("<TR><TD>round()</TD><TD>" + Math.round(myNumber) +"</TD></TR>");
document.write("</TABLE>")
```

We create the table header first before actually displaying the results of each rounding function on a separate row. You can see how easy it is to create HTML inside the web page dynamically using just JavaScript. The principles are the same as with HTML in a page: we must make sure our tag's syntax is valid or otherwise things will appear strange or not appear at all.

Each row follows the same principle just using a different rounding function. Let's look at the first row which displays the results of parseInt():

```
document.write("<TR><TD>parseInt()</TD><TD>"+ parseInt(myNumber) +"</TD></TR>");
```

Inside the string to be written out to the page, we start by creating the table row with the <TR> tag. Then we create a table cell with a <TD> tag and insert the name of the method from which the results are being displayed on this row. Then we close the cell with </TD> and open a new one with <TD>. Inside this next cell we are placing the actual results of the parseInt() function. Although a number is returned by parseInt(), because we are concatenating it to a string JavaScript automatically converts the number returned by parseInt() into a string before concatenating. All this happens in the background without us needing to do a thing. Finally, we close the cell and the row with </TD></TR>.

The random() Method

The random() method returns a random floating point number in the range between 0 and 1, where 0 is included and 1 is not. This can be very useful for displaying random banner images, or if you're writing a JavaScript game.

Let's look at how you would mimic the roll of a single die. In the page below 10 random numbers are written to the page. Hit the browser's refresh button to get another set of random numbers.

```
<HTML>
<BODY>
<SCRIPT LANGUAGE=JavaScript>
var throwCount;
var diceThrow;
for (throwCount = 0; throwCount < 10; throwCount++)
{
    diceThrow = (Math.floor(Math.random() * 6) + 1);
    document.write(diceThrow + "<BR>");
}

</SCRIPT>
</BODY>
</HTML>
```

We want `diceThrow` to be between 1 and 6. The `random()` function returns a floating point number between 0 and just under 1. By multiplying this number by 6 we get a number between 0 and just under 6. Then by adding 1 we get a number between 1 and just under 7. By using `floor()` to always round it down to the next lowest whole number, we can ensure that a we'll end up with a number between 1 and 6.

If we wanted a random number between 1 and 100, we would just change the code so that `Math.random()` is multiplied by 100 rather than 6.

The pow() Method

The `pow()` method raises a number to a specified power. It takes two parameters, the first being the number you want raised to a power, and the second being the power itself. For example, to raise 2 to the power of 8, that is to calculate 2 * 2 * 2 * 2 * 2 * 2 * 2, we would write `Math.pow(2,8)` – the result being 256. Unlike some of the other mathematical methods, like `sin()`, `cos()`, and `acos()` which are not commonly used in web programming unless it's a scientific application you're writing, the `pow()` method can often prove very useful.

Try It Out – Using pow()

In the example below, we write a function using `pow()`, which fixes the number of decimal places in a number – a function that's missing from JavaScript. This helps demonstrate that even where a function is missing from JavaScript, you can usually use existing functions to create what you want.

```
<HTML>
<HEAD>
<SCRIPT LANGUAGE=JavaScript>

function fix(fixNumber, decimalPlaces)
{
    var div = Math.pow(10,decimalPlaces);
    fixNumber = Math.round(fixNumber * div) / div;
    return fixNumber;
}
</SCRIPT>
</HEAD>
<BODY>
<SCRIPT LANGUAGE=JavaScript>

var number1 = prompt("Enter the number with decimal places you want to fix","");
var number2 = prompt("How many decimal places do you want?","");

document.write(number1 + " fixed to " + number2 + " decimal places is: ");
document.write(fix(number1,number2));

</SCRIPT>
</BODY>
</HTML>
```

Save the page as `ch4_examp4.htm`.

When you load the page into your browser, you will be presented with two prompt boxes. In the first enter the number that you want to fix the number of decimal places of, for example 2.2345. In the second, enter the number of decimal places you want fixed, for example 2. Then the result of fixing the number you have given to the number of decimal places you have given will be written to the page. For the example numbers I have given, this will be 2.23.

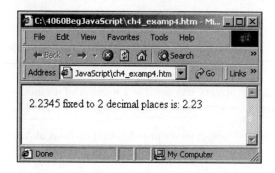

How It Works

In the head of the page we define the function `fix()`. This function will fix its `fixNumber` parameter to a maximum of its `decimalPlaces` parameter's number of digits after the decimal place. For example, fixing 34.76459 to a maximum of 3 decimal places will return 34.765.

The first line of code in the function sets the variable `div` to the number 10 raised to the power of the number of decimal places we want:

```
function fix(fixNumber, decimalPlaces)
{
    var div = Math.pow(10,decimalPlaces);
```

Then, in the next line, we calculate the new number:

```
    fixNumber = Math.round(fixNumber * div) / div;
```

What the code `Math.round(fixNumber * div)` does is to move the decimal point in the number that we are converting to after the point in the number that we want to keep. So for 2.2345, if we want to keep two decimal places, we convert it to 223.45. The `Math.round()` method rounds this number to the nearest integer (in this case 223) and so removes any undesired decimal part.

We then convert this number back into the fraction it should be, but of course only the fractional part we want is left. We do this by dividing by the same number (`div`) that we multiplied by. In our example, we divide 223 by 100, which leaves 2.23. This is 2.2345 fixed to two decimal places. This value is returned to the calling code in the line:

```
    return fixNumber;
}
```

In the body of the page we use two prompt boxes to get numbers from the user. We then display the results of using these numbers in our `fix()` function to the user using `document.write()`.

Array Objects

We saw how to create and use arrays in the Chapter 2, and earlier in this chapter I admitted to you that they are actually objects.

As well as storing data, `Array` objects also provide a number of useful properties and methods we can use to manipulate the data in the array and find out information such as the size of the array.

Again, this is not an exhaustive look at every property and method of `Array` objects, but rather just some of the more useful ones. You'll find details of the rest in Appendix B.

The length Property – Finding Out How Many Elements are in an Array

The `length` property gives us the number of elements within an array. Recall that we have already seen this in use in the Trivia Quiz in Chapter 3. Sometimes we know exactly how long the array is, but there are situations where we may have been adding new elements to an array with no easy way of keeping track of how many have been added.

The `length` property can be used to find the index of the last element in the array. This is illustrated in the example below:

```
var names = new Array();

names[0] = "Paul";
names[1] = "Catherine";
names[11] = "Steve";

document.write("The last name is " + names[names.length - 1]);
```

Note that we have inserted data in the elements with index positions 0, 1, and 11. The array index starts at 0, so the last element is at index `length - 1`, that is 11, rather than the value of the `length` property, which is 12.

Another situation in which the `length` property proves useful is where a JavaScript method returns an array it has built itself. For example, in Chapter 8 on advanced string handling, we'll see that the `String` object has the `split()` method, which splits text into pieces and passes back the result as an `Array` object. As it's JavaScript that created the array, there is no way for us to know, without the `length` property, what the index is of the last element in the array.

The concat() Method – Joining Arrays Together

If we want to take two separate arrays and join them together into one big array, then we can use the `Array` object's `concat()` method. The `concat()` method returns a new array, which is the combination of the two arrays: the elements of the first array, then the elements of the second array. To do this, we use the method on our first array and pass the name of the second array as its parameter.

For example, say we have two arrays, `names` and `ages`, and separately they look like this:

names array:

Element Index	0	1	2
Value	Paul	Catherine	Steve

ages array:

Element Index	0	1	2
Value	31	29	34

If we combine them using names.concat(ages), we will get an array like this:

Element Index	0	1	2	3	4	5
Value	Paul	Catherine	Steve	31	29	34

In the code below this is exactly what we are doing:

```
var names = new Array("Paul","Catherine","Steve");
var ages = new Array(31,29,34);

var concatArray;

concatArray = names.concat(ages);
```

It's also possible to combine two arrays into one, but assign the new array to the name of the existing first array, using names = names.concat(ages).

If we were to use ages.concat(names), what would be the difference? Well, as you can see below, the difference is that now the ages array elements are first, then concatenated on the end are the elements from the names array:

Element Index	0	1	2	3	4	5
Value	31	29	34	Paul	Catherine	Steve

When using the concat() method it is important to note that it is only available in version 4 or later browsers.

The slice() Method – Copying Part of an Array

When we just want to copy a portion of an array, we can use the slice() method. Using the slice() method, we can slice out a portion of the array and assign that to a new variable name. The slice() method has two parameters:

- ❏ The index of the first element you want to be copied
- ❏ The index of the element marking the end of the portion you are slicing out (optional)

Just like string copying with `substr()` and `substring()`, the start point is included in the copy, but the end point is not. Again, if you don't include the second parameter, then all elements from the start index onwards are copied.

Suppose we have the array `names` shown below:

Index	0	1	2	3	4
Value	Paul	Sarah	Louise	Adam	Bob

If we want to create a new array with elements 1, Sarah, and 2, Louise, we would specify a start index of 1 and an end index of 3. The code for this would look something like:

```
var names = new Array("Paul","Sarah","Louise","Adam","Bob");
var slicedArray = names.slice(1,3);
```

Note that when JavaScript copies the array, it copies the new elements to an array where they have indexes 0 and 1, and not their old indexes of 1 and 2. After slicing, the `slicedArray` looks like this:

Index	0	1
Value	Sarah	Louise

The first array, `names`, is unaffected by the slicing.

As with the `concat()` method, the `slice()` method is only available in version 4 and later browsers.

The join() Method – Converting an Array into a Single String

The `join()` method concatenates all the elements in an array and returns them as a string. It also allows you to specify any characters you want to insert *between* each element as they are joined together. The method has only one parameter, and that's the string we want between each element.

Things will be clearer if we look at an example. Let's imagine I have my weekly shopping stored in an array, which looks something like this:

Index	0	1	2	3	4
Value	Eggs	Milk	Potatoes	Cereal	Banana

Now I want to write out my list of shopping to the page using `document.write()`. I want each item to be on a different line, so this means using the `<BR>` tag between each element. First, I need to declare my array:

```
var myShopping = new Array("Eggs","Milk","Potatoes","Cereal","Banana");
```

Now, let's convert the array that into one string with the `join()` method:

```
var myShoppingList = myShopping.join("<BR>");
```

Now the variable `myShoppingList` will hold the following text:

```
"Eggs<BR>Milk<BR>Potatoes<BR>Cereal<BR>Banana"
```

which we can write out to the page with `document.write()`:

```
document.write(myShoppingList);
```

Now the shopping list will appear in the page with each item on a new line:

The sort() Method – Putting Your Array in Order

If you have an array that contains similar data, such as a list of names or a list of ages, then you may want to put them in alphabetical or numerical order. This is something that the `sort()` method makes very easy. In the code below, we define our array and then put it in ascending alphabetical order using `names.sort()`. Finally, we output it so that we can see that it's in order:

```
var names = new Array("Paul","Sarah","Louise","Adam","Bob");
var elementIndex;

names.sort();
document.write("Now the names again in order" + "<BR>");

for (elementIndex = 0; elementIndex < names.length; elementIndex++)
{
    document.write(names[elementIndex] + "<BR>");
}
```

Don't forget that the sorting is case sensitive, so Paul will come before paul. In fact the array elements are sorted by the Unicode character numbers for their characters. So the array with elements Adam, adam, Zoë, zoë, will be sorted to the order Adam, Zoë, adam, zoë.

Note that in our `for` statement we've used the `Array` object's `length` property in the condition statement, rather than inserting the length of the array (5) ourselves, like this:

```
for (elementIndex = 0; elementIndex < 5; elementIndex++)
```

Why do this? After all we know in advance that there are 5 elements in the array. Well, what would happen if we altered the number of elements in our array by adding two more names?

```
var names = new Array("Paul","Sarah","Louise","Adam","Bob","Karen","Steve");
```

If we had inserted 5 rather than `names.length`, our loop code wouldn't work as we want it to. It wouldn't display the last two elements, unless we altered the condition part of the `for` loop so it was 7. By using the `length` property, we've made life easier for ourselves, as now there is no need to change code elsewhere if we add array elements.

OK, we've put things in ascending order, but what if we wanted descending order? That is where the `reverse()` method comes in.

The reverse() Method – Putting Your Array into Reverse Order

The final method for the `String` object we'll look at is the `reverse()` method, which – no prizes for guessing – reverses the order of the array so that the elements at the back are moved to the front. Let's take our shopping list again as an example:

Index	0	1	2	3	4
Value	Eggs	Milk	Potatoes	Cereal	Banana

If we used the `reverse()` method:

```
var myShopping = new Array("Eggs","Milk","Potatoes","Cereal","Banana");
myShopping.reverse();
```

we end up with the array elements in this order:

Index	0	1	2	3	4
Value	Banana	Cereal	Potatoes	Milk	Eggs

To prove this we could write it to the page with the `join()` method we saw earlier:

```
var myShoppingList = myShopping.join("<BR>")
document.write(myShoppingList);
```

Try It Out – Sorting an Array

When used in conjunction with the sort() method, the reverse() method can be used to sort an array so that its elements appear in reverse alphabetical or numerical order. This is shown in the following example:

```
<HTML>
<BODY>
<SCRIPT LANGUAGE=JavaScript>

var myShopping = new Array("Eggs","Milk","Potatoes","Cereal","Banana");

var ord = prompt("Enter 1 for alphabetical order, and -1 for reverse order", 1);

if (ord == 1)
{
    myShopping.sort();
    document.write(myShopping.join("<BR>"));
}
else if (ord == -1)
{
    myShopping.sort();
    myShopping.reverse();
    document.write(myShopping.join("<BR>"));
}
else
{
document.write("That is not a valid input");
}
</SCRIPT>
</BODY>
</HTML>
```

Save the example as ch4_examp5.htm. When you load this into your browser, you will be asked to enter some input depending on whether you want the array to be ordered in forward or backward order. If you enter 1, the array will be displayed in forward order. If you enter –1, the array will be displayed in reverse order. If you enter neither of these values, you will be told that your input was invalid.

How It Works

At the top of the script block we define the array containing our shopping list that we have been using throughout this section. Next we define the variable ord to be the value entered by the user in a prompt box:

```
var ord = prompt("Enter 1 for alphabetical order, and -1 for reverse order", 1);
```

This value is used in the conditions of the if statements that follows. The first if checks whether the value of ord is 1, that is whether the user wanted the array in alphabetical order. If so the following code is executed:

```
myShopping.sort();
document.write(myShopping.join("<BR>"));
```

141

The array is sorted, and then displayed to the user on separate lines using the `join()` method. Next in the `else if` statement, we check whether the value of `ord` is `-1`, that is whether the user wants the array in reverse alphabetical order. If so, the following code is executed:

```
myShopping.sort();
myShopping.reverse();
document.write(myShopping.join("<BR>"));
```

Here, we sort the array before reversing its order. Again the array is displayed to the user using the `join()` method.

Finally, if `ord` has neither the value `1` nor the value `-1`, we tell the user that their input was invalid:

```
document.write("That is not a valid input");
```

Date Objects

The `Date` object handles everything to do with date and time in JavaScript. Using it, we can find out the date and time now, store our own dates and times, do calculations with these dates, and convert the dates into strings.

The `Date` object has a lot of methods and can be a little tricky to use, which is why there's a whole chapter later on in the book dedicated to the date, time, and timers in JavaScript (Chapter 9). We'll also see in Chapter 11 how we can use dates to work out if there's been anything new added to the web site since the user last visited it. However, in this section, we'll focus on how to create a `Date` object and some of its more commonly used methods.

Creating a Date Object

There are four ways of declaring and initializing a `Date` object. In the first method, we just declare a new `Date` object, without initializing its value. In this case, the date and time value will be set to the current date and time on the PC that the script is run on:

```
var theDate1 = new Date();
```

Secondly, we can define a `Date` object by passing the number of milliseconds since on January 1 1970 at 00:00:00. In the example shown below, the date is 31 January 2000 00:20:00 GMT (that is, twenty minutes passed midnight):

```
var theDate2 = new Date(949278000000);
```

It's unlikely that you'll be using this way of defining a `Date` object very often, but this is how JavaScript actually stores the dates. The other formats for giving a date are simply for our convenience.

Next, we can pass a string representing a date, or a date and time. In the example below, we have "31 January 2000":

```
var theDate3 = new Date("31 January 2000");
```

However, we could have written 31 Jan 2000, Jan 31 2000, 01-31-2000, or any of a number of valid variations you'd commonly expect when writing down a date normally – if in doubt try it out. If you are writing your web pages for an international audience outside of the USA, then you need to be aware of the different way of specifying dates. In the UK and many other places, the standard is day, month, year, whereas in the US the standard is month, day, year. This can cause problems if you only specify numbers – JavaScript may think you're referring to a day when you meant a month. The easiest way to avoid such headaches is to, where possible, always use the name of the month. That way there can be no confusion.

In the fourth and final way, we initialize the `Date` object by passing the following parameters separated by commas: year, month, day, hours, minutes, seconds, and milliseconds. For example:

```
var theDate4 = new Date(2000,0,31,15,35,20,20);
```

This date is actually 31 January 2000 at 15:35:20 and 20 milliseconds. You can just specify the date part if you wish and ignore the time.

Something to be aware of is that in this instance January is month 0, not month 1, as you'd expect, and December is month eleven. It's a very easy mistake to make.

Getting Date Values

It's all very nice having stored a date, but how do we get the information out again? Well, we just use the get methods. These are summarized in the table below:

Method	Returns
getDate()	The day of the month.
getDay()	The day of the week as an integer, with Monday as 0, Tuesday as 1, and so on.
getMonth()	The month as an integer, with January as 0, February as 1 and so on.
getFullYear()	The year as a four digit number.

For example, if we want to get the month in `ourDateObj`, then we can simply write:

```
theMonth = myDateObject.getMonth();
```

All of the methods work in a very similar way, and all values returned are based on local time, that is local to the machine the code is running on. It's also possible to use Universal Time, previously known as GMT, but we'll save looking at this until Chapter 9.

Note that the `getFullYear()` method is only available in IE 4+ and NN 4.06+.

Try it Out – Using the Date Object to Retrieve the Current Date

In the example below, we use the get date type methods we have been looking at to write the current day, month, and year to a web page.

```
<HTML>
<BODY>

<SCRIPT LANGUAGE=JavaScript>

var months = new Array("January","February","March","April","May","June","July",
                       "August","September","October","Novemeber","Decemeber");
var dateNow = new Date();
var yearNow = dateNow.getFullYear();
var monthNow = months[dateNow.getMonth()];
var dayNow = dateNow.getDate();
var daySuffix;

switch (dayNow)
{
case 1:
case 21:
case 31:
   daySuffix = "st";
   break;
case 2:
case 22:
   daySuffix = "nd";
   break;
case 3:
case 23:
   daySuffix = "rd";
   break;
default:
   daySuffix = "th";
   break;
}

document.write("It is the " + dayNow + daySuffix + " day ");
document.write("in the month of " + monthNow);
document.write(" in the year " + yearNow);

</SCRIPT>
</BODY>
</HTML>
```

Save the code as `ch4_examp6.htm`. If you load up the page you should see a well-formed sentence telling you what the current date is.

How It Works

The first thing we do in the code is to declare an array and populate it with the months of a year. Why do this? Well, there is no method of the `Date` object that'll give us the month by name rather than as a number. However, this poses no problem, we just declare an array of months and use the month number as the array index to select the correct month name:

```
var months = new Array("January","February","March","April","May","June","July",
                       "August","September","October","Novemeber","Decemeber");
```

Next we create a new `Date` object and, by not initializing with our own value, we allow it to initialize itself to the current date and time:

```
var dateNow = new Date();
```

Following this we set the `yearNow` variable to the current year, as returned by the `getFullYear()` method:

```
var yearNow = dateNow.getFullYear();
```

Note that `getFullYear()` only became available with version four browsers, such as IE 4 and NN 4.06 and above. Prior to this, there was only the `getYear()` method, which on some browsers only returned a two digit year.

We then populate our `monthNow` variable with the value contained in the array element with an index of that returned by `getMonth()`. Remember that `getMonth()` returns the month as an integer value, starting with 0 for January – this is a bonus, since arrays also start at zero so no adjustment is needed to find the correct array element:

```
var monthNow = months[dateNow.getMonth()];
```

Finally, the current day of the month is put into variable `dayNow`:

```
var dayNow = dateNow.getDate();
```

Next we used a `switch` statement that we learned about in the last chapter. This is a useful technique for adding the correct suffix to the date that we already have. After all, our application will look more professional if we can say, "it is the 1st day", rather than, "it is the 1 day." This is a little tricky, however, as the suffix we want to add depends on the number that precedes it. So, for the 1st, 21st and 31st days of the month we have:

```
switch (dayNow)
{
case 1:
case 21:
case 31:
   daySuffix = "st";
   break;
```

For the 2nd and 22nd days we have

```
case 2:
case 22:
   daySuffix = "nd";
   break;
```

and for the 3rd and 23rd days we have:

```
case 3:
case 23:
    daySuffix = "rd";
    break;
```

Finally, we need the `default` case for everything else. As you will have guessed by now, this is simply `"th"`:

```
default:
    daySuffix = "th";
    break;
}
```

In the final lines we simply write the information to the HTML page, using `document.write()`.

Setting Date Values

In order to change part of the date in a `Date` object, we have a group of set functions, which pretty much replicate the get functions described above, except that we are setting not getting the values. These are summarized in the table below:

Method	Description
setDate()	The date of the month is passed in as the parameter to set the date
setMonth()	The month of the year is passed in as an integer parameter, where 0 is January, 1 is February, and so on
setFullYear()	Sets the year to the 4 digit integer number passed in as a parameter

Note that for security reasons, there is no way from web based JavaScript to change the current date and time on a user's computer.

So, to change the year to 2001, the code would be:

```
myDateObject.setFullYear(2001);
```

Again, the `setFullYear()` method is only available in IE 4+ and NN 4.06+ browsers.

Setting the date and month to the 27th of February looks like:

```
myDateObject.setDate(27);
myDateObject.setMonth(1);
```

One minor point to note here is that there is no direct equivalent to the `getDay()` method. Once the year, date and month have been defined, the day is automatically set for you.

Calculations and Dates

Take a look at the following code:

```
var myDate = new Date("1 Jan 2000");
myDate.setDate(32);
document.write(myDate);
```

Surely there is some error – since when has January had 32 days? The answer to this query is that of course it doesn't, and JavaScript knows that. Instead JavaScript sets the date to 32 days from the 1st of January – that is, it sets it to the 1st of February.

The same also applies to the `setMonth()` method. If you set it to a value greater than 11, then the date automatically rolls over to the next year. So if we use `setDate(12)`, that will set the date to January of next year, and similarly `setDate(13)` is February of next year.

How can we use this feature of `setDate()` and `setMonth()` to our advantage? Well, let's say we wanted to find out what date it is 28 days from now. Given that different months have different numbers of days and that we could roll over to a different year, it's not as simple a task as it might first seem. Or at least that would be the case if it were not for `setDate()`. The code to achieve this task is below:

```
var nowDate = new Date();
var currentDay = nowDate.getDate();
nowDate.setDate(currentDay + 28);
```

First we get the current system date by setting `nowDate` variable to a new `Date object` with no initialization value. In the next line we put the current day of the month into a variable called `currentDay`. Why? Well, when we use `setDate()` and pass it a value outside of the maximum number of days for that month, it starts from the first of the month and counts that many days forward. So, if today's date is the 15th of January and we use `setDate(28)`, then it's not 28 days from the 15th of January, but 28 days from the 1st of January. What we want is 28 days from the current date so we need to add the current date onto the number of days ahead we want. So, we want `setDate(15 + 28)`. In the third line we set the date to the current date, plus 28 days. We stored the current day of the month in `currentDay`, so now we just add 28 to that to move 28 days ahead.

If we wanted the date 28 days prior to the current date then we would just pass the current date minus 28. Note that this will most often be a negative number. We need only change one line and that's the third one, which we change to:

```
nowDate.setDate(currentDay - 28);
```

We can use exactly the same principles for `setMonth()` as we have used for `setDate()`.

Getting Time Values

Retrieving the individual time data works much like the get methods for date values. The methods we use here are summarized below:

❑ `getHours()`

❑ `getMinutes()`

❑ `getSeconds()`

❑ `getMilliseconds()`

These methods return respectively the hours, minutes, seconds, and milliseconds of the specified Date object, where the time is based on the 24 hour clock: 0 for midnight and 23 for eleven p.m.

Note that the getMilliseconds() method is only available in IE 4+ and NN 4.06+ browsers.

Try It Out – Writing the Current Time into a Web Page

Let's look at an example that writes out the current time to the page:

```
<HTML>
<BODY>
<SCRIPT LANGUAGE=JavaScript>

var greeting;

var nowDate = new Date();
var nowHour = nowDate.getHours();
var nowMinute = nowDate.getMinutes();
var nowSecond = nowDate.getSeconds();

if (nowMinute < 10)
{
    nowMinute = "0" + nowMinute;
}

if (nowSecond < 10)
{
    nowSecond = "0" + nowSecond;
}

if (nowHour < 12)
{
    greeting = "Good Morning";
}
else if (nowHour < 17)
{
    greeting = "Good Afternoon";
}
else
{
    greeting = "Good Evening";
}

document.write("<H4>" + greeting + " and welcome to my website</H4>")
document.write("According to your clock the time is ");
document.write(nowHour + ":" + nowMinute + ":" + nowSecond);

</SCRIPT>
</BODY>
</HTML>
```

Save this page as ch4_examp7.htm.

When you load it into a web browser it writes a greeting based on the time of day and also the current time into the page:

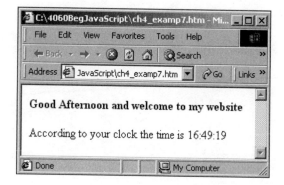

How It Works

The first two lines of code declare two variables – greeting and nowDate:

```
var greeting;
var nowDate = new Date();
```

The greeting variable will be used shortly to store the welcome message on the web site, whether this is good morning, afternoon, or evening. The nowDate variable is initialized to a new Date object. Note that the constructor for the Date object is empty, so JavaScript will store the current date and time in it.

Next, we get the information on current time from nowDate and store it in various variables. You can see that getting time data is very similar to getting date data, just using different methods:

```
var nowHour = nowDate.getHours();
var nowMinute = nowDate.getMinutes();
var nowSecond = nowDate.getSeconds();
```

You may wonder why the following lines are included in the example:

```
if (nowMinute < 10)
{
   nowMinute = "0" + nowMinute;
}

if (nowSecond < 10)
{
   nowSecond = "0" + nowSecond;
}
```

These lines are there just for formatting reasons. If the time is nine minutes past 10, then you expect to see something like 10:09. You don't expect 10:9, which is what we would get if we used the getMinutes() method without adding the extra zero. The same goes for seconds. If you're just using the data in calculations, then you don't need to worry about formatting issues – we do here because we're inserting the time the code executed into the web page.

149

Next, in a series of `if` statements, we decide what greeting to create for displaying to the user based on the time of day:

```
if (nowHour < 12)
{
    greeting = "Good Morning";
}
else if (nowHour < 17)
{
    greeting = "Good Afternoon";
}
else
{
    greeting = "Good Evening";
}
```

Finally we write out the greeting and the current time to the page:

```
document.write("<H4>" + greeting + " and welcome to my website</H4>");
document.write("According to your clock the time is ");
document.write(nowHour + ":" + nowMinute + ":" + nowSecond);
```

We'll see in Chapter 9 on dates, times, and timers how we can write a continuously updating time to the web page, making it look like a clock.

Setting Time Values

When we want to set the time in our `Date` objects, we have a similar series of methods to those used for getting the time, but now it's:

❑   `setHours()`

❑   `setMinutes()`

❑   `setSeconds()`

❑   `setMilliseconds()`

Again, the `setMilliseconds()` method is only available in IE4+ and NN 4.06+ browsers.

These work in a similar way to setting the date, in that if we set any of the time parameters to an illegal value then JavaScript assumes you mean the next or previous time boundary. If it's 9:57 and you set minutes to 64, then the time will be set to 10:04, that is, 64 minutes from 9:00.

This is demonstrated in the code below:

```
var nowDate = new Date();
nowDate.setHours(9);
nowDate.setMinutes(57);
alert(nowDate);

nowDate.setMinutes(64);
alert(nowDate);
```

First we declare the nowDate variable and assign it to a new Date object, which will contain the current date and time. In the following two lines we set the hours to 9 and the minutes to 57. We show the date and time using an alert box, which should show a time of 9.57. The minutes are then set to 64 and again an alert box is used to show the date and time to the user. Now the minutes have rolled over the hour so the time shown should be 10.04.

If the hours were set to 23 instead of 9, setting the minutes to 64 would not just move the time to another hour, but also cause the day to change to the next date.

Summary

In this chapter we've taken a look at the concept of objects and seen how vital they are to an understanding of JavaScript, which represents virtually everything with objects. We also looked at some of the various native objects that the JavaScript language provides to add to its functionality.

We saw that:

❑ JavaScript is object-based – it represents things, such as strings, dates, and arrays, using the concept of objects.

❑ Objects have properties and methods. For example, an Array object has the length property and the sort() method.

❑ To create a new object we simply write new ObjectType(). We can choose to initialize an object when we create it.

❑ To set an object's property's value or get that value we simply write ObjectName.ObjectProperty.

❑ Calling the methods of an object is similar to calling functions. There may be parameters to be passed and return values may be passed back. Accessing the methods of an object is identical to accessing a property, except we must remember to add parentheses at the end, even when there are no parameters. We write ObjectName.ObjectMethod()

❑ The String object provides a handy wrapper object for text and gives us ways of finding out how long the text is, searching for text inside the string, and selecting parts of the text.

❑ The Math object is created automatically and provides a number of mathematical properties and methods. For example to obtain a random number between 0 and 1 we use the method, Math.random().

❑ The Array object provides ways of manipulating arrays. Some of the things we can do are to find the length of an array, sort its elements, and join two arrays together.

❑ The Date object provides a way of storing, calculating with, and later accessing dates and times.

In the next chapter, we'll be turning our attention to the web browser itself, and particularly the various objects that it makes available for our JavaScript programming. We'll see that the use of the browser objects is key to creating powerful web pages.

Exercise Questions

Suggested solutions to these examples can be found in Appendix A.

Question 1

Using the `Date` object, calculate the date 12 months from now and write this into a web page.

Question 2

Obtain a list of names from the user storing each name entered in an array. Keep getting another name until the user enters nothing. Sort the names into ascending order then write them out to the page, each name being on its own line.

Question 3

We saw earlier in the chapter when looking at the `pow()` method how we could use it inventively to fix a number to a certain number of decimal places. However, there is a flaw in the function we created. A proper `fix()` function should return 2.1 fixed to three decimal places as:

```
2.100
```

However our `fix()` function instead returns it as:

```
2.1
```

Change the `fix()` function so that the additional zeros are added where necessary.

Online discussion at http://p2p.wrox.com

Programming the Browser

Over the last three chapters, we've examined the core JavaScript language. We've seen how to work with variables and data, perform operations on that data, make decisions in our code, loop repeatedly over the same section of code, and even how to write our own functions. In the last chapter we moved on to learn how JavaScript is an object-based language, and saw how to work with the native JavaScript objects. However, we are not just interested in the language itself – we want to find out how to write script for the web browser. Using this, we can start to create more impressive web pages.

Not only is JavaScript object-based, the browser is also made up of objects. When JavaScript is running in the browser, we can access the browser's objects in exactly the same way as we used JavaScript's native objects in the last chapter. But what kinds of objects does the browser provide for us to use?

There are a remarkable number of objects that the browser makes available to us. For example, there is a window object corresponding to the window of the browser. We have already been using two methods of this object, namely the alert() and prompt() methods. For simplicity we previously called these functions, but they are in fact methods of the browser's window object.

Another object made available by the browser is the page itself, represented by the document object. Again, we have already used methods and properties of this object. Recall from Chapter 1 that we used the document object's bgColor property to change the background color of the browser. We have also been using the write() method of the document object to write information to the page.

There are a variety of other objects, representing a lot of the HTML that we write in the page. For example, there is an IMG object for each <IMG> tag that we use to insert an image into our document.

The collection of objects that the browser makes available to us for use with JavaScript is generally called the **Browser Object Model (BOM)**.

> *You will often see this termed the Document Object Model (DOM). However, throughout this book, we'll use the term DOM to refer to the W3C's standard Document Object Model, which is discussed in Chapter 13.*

There is a downside to all this added functionality that JavaScript is given. The collections of objects that are made available to us are highly dependent on the brand and version of the browser that we are using. Some objects are made available in some browsers and not in others, while other objects have different properties and methods in different browsers. The details of the BOM of IE 4, IE 5, and NN 4 can be found in Appendices E, F, and G respectively. We will see more about the differences between the BOM of IE and NN browsers in Chapter 12.

However, in this chapter we will concentrate on the core functionality of the BOM, that is the objects that are common to all browsers. There is still a lot that we can achieve in JavaScript by just sticking to such objects. More information can be found on them in Appendix C.

Introduction to the Browser Objects

In this section we will give an introduction to the objects of the BOM that are common to all browsers.

In Chapter 4, we saw that JavaScript has a number of native objects that we have access to and can make use of. Most of the objects are those that we need to create ourselves, such as the `String` and `Date` objects. Others, such as the `Math` object, exist without us needing to create them and are ready for use immediately the page starts loading.

When JavaScript is running in a web page it has access to a large number of other objects made available by the web browser. Rather like the `Math` object, these are created for us rather than us needing to create them explicitly. As we mentioned above, the objects, their methods, properties, and events are all mapped out in something called the Browser Object Model or BOM.

The BOM is very large, and potentially overwhelming at first. However you'll find that initially you won't be using more than 10% of the available objects, methods, and properties in the BOM. We'll start in this chapter looking at the more commonly used parts of the BOM, shown in the diagram below. These parts of the BOM are, to a certain extent, common across all browsers. Later chapters will build on this so that by the end of the book you'll be able to really make the BOM work for you.

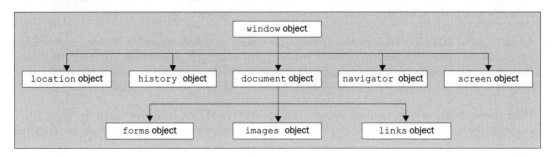

The BOM has a hierarchy. At the very top of this hierarchy is the `window` object. You can think of this as representing the frame of the browser and everything associated with it such as the scrollbars, navigator bar icons, and so on.

Contained inside our window frame is the page. The page is represented in the BOM by the `document` object. You can see this represented graphically below:

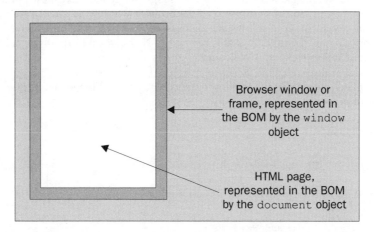

Browser window or frame, represented in the BOM by the `window` object

HTML page, represented in the BOM by the `document` object

We'll now go on to discuss each of these objects in more detail.

The window Object – Our Window onto the Page

The `window` object represents the browser's frame or window in which your web page is contained. To some extent, it also represents the browser itself and includes a number of properties that are there simply because they don't fit anywhere else. For example, via the properties of the `window` object, we can find out what browser is running, the pages the user has visited, the size of the browser window, the size of the user's screen (if we're using IE) and much more. We can also use the `window` object to access and change the text in the browser's status bar, change the page that is loaded, and even open new windows.

The window object is a **global object**, which means we don't need to use its name to access its properties and methods. For example, the `alert()` function we have been using since the beginning of the book is, in fact, the `alert()` method of the `window` object. Although we have been using this simply as:

```
alert("Hello!");
```

we could write:

```
window.alert("Hello!");
```

However, since the `window` object is a global object, it is perfectly correct to use the first version.

Some of the properties of the `window` object are themselves objects. Those common to both IE and NN include the `document`, `navigator`, `history`, `screen`, and `location` objects. The `document` object represents our page, the `history` object contains the history of pages visited by the user, the `navigator` object holds information about the browser, the `screen` object contains information about the display capabilities of the client, and the `location` object contains details on the current page's location. We'll look at these important objects individually later in the chapter.

Using the window Object

Let's start with a nice simple example in which we change the default text shown in the browser's status bar. The status bar (usually in the bottom left of the browser window) is usually used by the browser to show the status of any document loading into the browser. For example, on IE once a document has loaded you'll normally see Done in the status bar and in Navigator it normally says Document : Done. Let's change that so it says Hello and Welcome.

To change the default message in the window's status bar, we need to use the window object's defaultStatus property.

To do this we can write:

```
window.defaultStatus = "Hello and Welcome";
```

or, because the window is a global object, we can just write:

```
defaultStatus = "Hello and Welcome";
```

Either way works and both are valid, though personally I normally prefer to write window in front as it makes clear exactly where the defaultStatus property came from. Otherwise we might think that defaultStatus is a variable name. This is particularly true when using less common properties and methods, such as defaultStatus. For properties like document or methods like alert(), you'll find that you become so familiar with them that you don't need to put window in front to remind you of their context.

Let's put our code in a page:

```
<HTML>
<HEAD>
<SCRIPT LANGUAGE=JavaScript>

window.defaultStatus = "Hello and Welcome";

</SCRIPT>
</HEAD>
</HTML>
```

Save the page as ch5_examp1.htm and load it into your browser. You should see the specified message in the status bar.

At this point, it's worth highlighting the point that within a web page you shouldn't use names for your functions or variables that conflict with names of BOM objects or their properties and methods. If you do, you may not get an error, but instead unexpected results. For example, in the code below we declare a variable named defaultStatus. We then try to set the defaultStatus property of the window object to "Welcome to my website". However, this won't change the default message in the status bar; instead the value in the defaultStatus variable will be changed.

```
var defaultStatus;
defaultStatus = "Welcome to my website";
```

In this situation we need to either use a different variable name, or add `window` in front of the `defaultStatus` property we want to change:

```
var defaultStatus;
window.defaultStatus = "Welcome to my website";
```

This will have the effect that we want, that is the message in the status bar will change. However, this way of writing things can obviously make code very confusing, so it is usually best not to use BOM object, property, or method names as variable names.

As with all the BOM objects, there are lots of properties and methods we could look at for the `window` object. However, in this chapter we'll concentrate on the, `history`, `location`, `navigator`, `screen`, and `document` properties. All five of these properties contain objects, the `history`, `location`, `navigator`, `screen`, and `document` objects, each with its own properties and methods. In the next few pages, we'll look at each of these objects in turn and find out how they can help us make full use of the BOM.

The history Object

The `history` object keeps track of each page that the user visits. This list of pages is commonly called the history stack for the browser. It enables the user to click the browser **Back** and **Forward** buttons to re-visit pages. We have access to this object via the `window` object's `history` property.

Like the native JavaScript `Array` object, the `history` object has a `length` property. This can be used to find out how many pages are in the history stack.

As you might expect, the `history` object has the `back()` and `forward()` methods. When they are called, the location of the page currently loaded in the browser is changed to the previous or next page that the user has visited. (Note that on Netscape 6 the `back()` and `forward()` methods of the `history` object do not always work as expected.)

The `history` object also has the `go()` method. This takes one parameter that specifies how far forward or backward in the history stack you want to go. For example, if you wanted to return the user to the page previous to the previous page then you'd write:

```
history.go(-2);
```

To go forward three pages you'd write:

```
history.go(3);.
```

Note that `go(-1)` and `back()` are equivalent, as are `go(1)` and `forward()`.

The location Object

The location object contains lots of potentially useful information about the current page's location. Not only does it contain the URL (Uniform Resource Locator) for the page, but also the server hosting the page, the port number of the server connection, and the protocol used. This information is made available through the location object's href, hostname, port, and protocol properties. However, many of these values are only really relevant when we are loading the page from a server and not, as we are doing in our examples at present, loading the page directly from a local hard drive.

As well as retrieving the current page's location, we can also use the methods of the location object to change the location and refresh the current page.

Changing Locations

There are two ways of navigating to another page. We can either set the location object's href property to point to another page, or we can use the location object's replace() method. The effect of the two is the same; the page changes location. However, they differ in that the replace() method removes the current page from the history stack and replaces it with the new page we are moving to, whereas using the href property simply adds the new page to the top of the history stack. This means that if the replace() method has been used and the user hits the **Back** button in their browser, they can't go back to the original page loaded. If the href property has been used, the user can use the **Back** button as normal.

For example, to replace the current page with a new page called myPage.htm, we'd use the replace() method and write:

```
window.location.replace("myPage.htm");
```

This will load myPage.htm and replace any occurrence of the current page in the history stack with myPage.htm.

To load the same page, but to add it to the history of pages navigated to, we use the href property:

```
window.location.href = "myPage.htm"
```

In both cases I've added window at the front of the expression, but as the window object is global throughout the page we could have written:

```
location.replace("myPage.htm")
```

or:

```
location.href = "myPage.htm"
```

The navigator Object

The navigator object is another object that is a property of the window object and is available in both IE and NN browsers, despite the name. Its name is more of a historical thing, rather than being very descriptive. Perhaps a better name would be the 'browser object', as the navigator object contains lots of information about the browser and the operating system it's running in.

Probably the most common use of the navigator object is for handling browser differences. Using its properties, we can find out which browser, version, and operating system the user has. We can then act on that information and make sure they are directed to pages that will work with their browser. The last section in this chapter is dedicated to this important subject, so we will not discuss it further here.

The screen Object

The screen object property of the window object contains lot of information about the display capabilities of the client machine. Its properties include the height and width properties, which indicate the vertical and horizontal range of the screen in pixels.

Another property of the screen object, which we will be using in an example below, is the colorDepth property. This tells us the number of bits used for colors on the client's screen.

This object is newer than the other objects we have mentioned – it is only available in version 4 and later browsers.

The document Object – The Page Itself

Along with the window object, the document object is probably one of the most important and commonly used objects in the BOM. Via this object you can gain access to the properties and methods of some of the objects defined by HTML tags inside your page.

Unfortunately, it's here that the BOMs of IE 4 and IE 5, and NN 4 differ greatly. The former's BOM implementation allows you easy access to nearly every element on a page, whereas the latter's only allows limited access to some elements. If we go back to earlier browsers, such as IE 3 and NN 3, we find the BOM and our ability to program with it even more limited. We will go into the details of the differences between the BOMs of IE 4.0+ and NN 4.x in Chapter 12.

While IE 5 supports all the proprietary BOM of IE 4 (that is, it is backwards compatible), NN 6 does not support all the proprietary BOM of NN 4. Instead, NN6 supports the W3C DOM, also somewhat supported by IE 5. We will leave this more advanced topic until Chapter 13.

In this chapter we will concentrate on those properties and methods of the document object that are common to all browsers.

The document object has a number of properties associated with it, which are also arrays. The main ones are the forms, images, and links arrays. IE 4 and IE 5 support a number of other array properties, such as the all array property, which is an array of all the tags represented by objects in the page. Netscape also has a few additional arrays that are not supported by IE, for example the tags array. However, we'll be concentrating on using objects that have cross-browser support, so that we are not limiting our web pages to just one browser.

We'll be looking at the images and links arrays shortly. A third array, the forms array, will be one of the topics of the next chapter when we look at forms in web browsers. First though we'll look at a nice simple example of how to use the document object's methods and properties.

Using the document Object

We've already come across some of the document object's properties and methods, for example the write() method and the bgcolor property. Appendix C has a full list of the available properties and methods and we'll be using more of them later in the book.

Try It Out – Settings Colors According to the User's Screen Color Depth

In the next example we set the background color of the page to a color dependent on how many colors the user's screen supports. This is termed screen color depth. If the user has a display that supports just two colors, black and white, there's no point in us setting the background color to bright red. We accommodate this by using JavaScript to set a color the user can actually see.

```
<HTML>
<BODY>
<SCRIPT LANGUAGE=JavaScript>

switch (window.screen.colorDepth)
{
   case 1:

   case 4:
      document.bgColor = "white";
      break;

   case 8:

   case 15:

   case 16:
      document.bgColor = "blue";
      break;

   case 24:

   case 32:
      document.bgColor = "skyblue";
      break;

   default:
      document.bgColor = "white";
}
   document.write("Your screen supports " + window.screen.colorDepth +
                  "bit color");
</SCRIPT>

</BODY>
</HTML>
```

Save the page as ch5_examp2.htm.

When you load it into your browser, the background color of the page will be determined by your current screen color depth. Also, a message in the page will tell you what the color depth currently is.

You can test that the code is working properly by changing the colors supported by your screen. On Windows, you can do this by right clicking on the desktop, and choosing the **Properties** option. Under the **Settings** tab, there is a section called colors in which you can change the number of colors supported. By refreshing the browser, you can then see what difference this makes to the color of the page.

On Netscape 6, we found that you need to shut down and restart the browser to observe any effect.

How It Works

As we saw above, the window object has the screen object property. One of the properties of this object is the colorDepth property, which returns a value of 1, 4, 8, 15, 16, 24 or 32. This represents the number of bits assigned to each pixel on your screen – a pixel is just one of the dots that your screen is formed of. To work out how many colors we have, we just calculate the value of 2 to the power of the colorDepth property. For example, a colorDepth of 1 means that there are 2 colors available, a colorDepth of 8 means that there are 256 colors available, and so on. Currently, most people have a screen color depth of at least 8, but usually of 16 or 24, with 32 becoming more common.

The first task of our script block is to set the color of the background of the page based on the number of colors the user can actually see. We do this in a big switch statement. The condition that is checked for in the switch statement is the value of window.screen.colorDepth:

```
switch (window.screen.colorDepth)
```

We don't need to set a different color for each colorDepth possible, as many of them are not that different for general web use. Instead, we set the same background color for different, but similar, colorDepth values. For a colorDepth of 1 or 4, we set the background to white. We do this by declaring the case 1: statement, but not giving it any code. If the colorDepth matches this case statement, it will fall through to the case 4: statement below, where we do set the background color to white. We then call a break statement, so that the case matching will not fall any further through the switch statement:

```
{
    case 1:

    case 4:
        document.bgColor = "white";
        break;
```

We do the same with colorDepth values of 8, 15 and 16, setting the background color to blue:

```
    case 8:

    case 15:
```

163

```
        case 16:
            document.bgColor = "blue";
            break;
```

Finally, we do the same for `colorDepth` values of 24 and 32, setting the background color to skyblue:

```
        case 24:

        case 32:
            document.bgColor = "skyblue";
            break;
```

We end the `switch` statement with a `default` case, just in case the other `case` statements did not match. In this `default` case, we again set the background color to white:

```
        default:
            document.bgColor = "white";
    }
```

In our next bit of script, we use the `document` object's `write()` method, something we've been using in our examples for a while now. We use it to write to the document, that is the page, the number of bits the color depth is currently set at:

```
        document.write("Your screen supports " + window.screen.colorDepth +
                        "bit color")
```

We've already been using the `document` object in our examples throughout the book so far. We used its `bgColor` property in Chapter 1 to change the background color of the page, and we've also made good use of its `write()` method in our examples to write HTML and text out to the page.

Now let's look at some of the slightly more complex properties of the `document` object. These properties have in common the fact that they all contain arrays. The first one we look at is an array containing an object for each image in the page.

The images Array

As we know, we can insert an image into an HTML page using the following tag:

```
    <IMG NAME=myImage SRC="usa.gif">
```

The browser makes this image available for us to script in JavaScript by creating an `IMG` object for it with the name `myImage`. In fact, each image on your page has an `IMG` object created for it.

Each of the `IMG` objects in a page is stored in the `images[]` array. This array is a property of the `document` object. The first image on the page is found in the element `document.images[0]`, the second in `document.images[1]`, and so on.

If we want to, we can assign a variable to reference an IMG object in the images[] array. It can make code easier to read. For example, if we write:

```
var myImage2 = document.images[1];
```

then the myImage variable will contain a reference to the IMG object inside the images[] array at index position 1. Now we can write myImage2 instead of document.images[1] in our code, with exactly the same effect.

We can also access IMG objects in the images array by name. For example, the IMG object created by the <IMG> tag above, which has the name myImage can be accessed in the document object's images array property like this:

```
document.images["myImage"];
```

As the document.images property is an array, it has the properties of the native JavaScript Array object, such as the length property. For example, if we want to know how many images there are on the page, then the code document.images.length will tell us.

Try It Out – Image Selection

The IMG object itself has a number of useful properties we can utilize. The most important of these is its src property. By changing this we can change the image that's loaded, even after the page has finished loading. We demonstrate this in the next example:

```
<HTML>
<BODY>

<IMG NAME=img1 SRC="" BORDER=0 WIDTH=200 HEIGHT=150>

<SCRIPT LANGUAGE=JavaScript>
    var myImages = new Array("usa.gif","canada.gif","jamaica.gif","mexico.gif");
    var imgIndex = prompt("Enter a number from 0 to 3","");
    document.images["img1"].src = myImages[imgIndex];
</SCRIPT>

</BODY>
</HTML>
```

Save this as ch5_examp3.htm. You will also need four image files, called usa.gif, canada.gif, jamaica.gif, and mexico.gif. You can create these yourself, or obtain the ones provided with the code download for the book.

When this page is loaded into the browser, a prompt box asks you to enter a number from 0 to 3. A different image will be displayed depending on the number you enter.

How It Works

At the top of the page we have our HTML `<IMG>` tag. Notice that the SRC attribute is left empty and it is given the NAME value img1:

```
<IMG NAME=img1 SRC="" BORDER=0 WIDTH=200 HEIGHT=150>
```

Next we come to the script block where the image to be displayed is decided:

We first define an array containing a list of image sources. My images are in the same directory as the HTML file, so I haven't specified a path. If yours are not, make sure you enter the full path, for example `C:\myImages\mexico.gif`.

```
var myImages = new Array("usa.gif","canada.gif","jamaica.gif","mexico.gif");
```

Then we ask the user for a number from 0 to 3, which will be used as the array index to access the image source in the `myImages` array:

```
var imgIndex = prompt("Enter a number from 0 to 3","");
```

Finally we set the `src` property of the IMG object to the source text inside the `myImages` array element with the index number provided by the user:

```
document.images["img1"].src = myImages[imgIndex];
```

Don't forget that when we write `document.images["img1"]` we are accessing the IMG object stored in the `images` array. We've used the image's name, as defined in the NAME attribute of the `<IMG>` tag, but we could have used `document.images[0]`. It's an index position of 0, because it's the first (and only) image on this page.

The links Array

For each hyperlink tag `<A>` defined with an HREF attribute, the browser creates an A object. The most important property of the A object is the `href` property, corresponding to the HREF attribute of the tag. Using this, we can find out where the link points to and can change this, even after the page has loaded.

The collection of all A objects in a page is contained within the `links[]` array, in a similar way to the IMG objects in the `images[]` array that we saw above.

Connecting Code to Web Page Events

In Chapter 4 when we introduced objects, we said that they were defined by their methods and properties. However, this is not the whole story. Objects also have events associated with them. We did not mention it before since native JavaScript objects do not have these events, but the objects of the BOM do.

So what are these events?

Events occur when something in particular happens. For example, the user clicking on the page, or clicking on a hyperlink, or moving their mouse pointer over some text all cause events to occur. Another example, which is used quite frequently, is the load event for the page.

Why are we interested in events?

Take as an example the situation where we want to make a menu pop up when the user clicks anywhere in our web page. Assuming that we can write a function that will make the popup menu appear, how do we know *when* to make it appear, that is *when* to call the function? We somehow need to intercept the event of the user clicking in the document, and make sure our function is called when that event occurs.

To do this, we need to use something called an **event handler**. We associate this with the code that we want to execute when the event occurs. This provides us with a way of intercepting events and making our code execute when they have occurred. You will find that adding an event handler to our code is often known as 'connecting our code to the event'. It's a bit like setting an alarm clock – you set the clock to make a ringing noise when a certain event happens. With alarm clocks, the event is when a certain time is reached.

Event handlers are made up of the word on and the event that they will handle. For example, the click event has the `onclick` event handler and the load event has the `onload` event handler.

There are quite a number of ways of connecting your code to an event using event handlers; we're going to look at two of the more useful ways.

Event Handlers as Attributes

The first, and most common, method is to add the event handler's name and the code we want executing to the HTML tag's attributes.

Let's create a simple HTML page with a single hyperlink, given by the element <A>. Associated to this element is the A object. One of the events the A object has is the click event. The click event fires, not surprisingly, when the user clicks on the hyperlink.

```
<HTML>
<BODY>

<A HREF="somepage.htm" NAME="linkSomePage">
   Click Me
</A>

</BODY>
</HTML>
```

As it stands this page does nothing a normal hyperlink doesn't do. You click it and it navigates this window to another page. There's been no event handler added to the link – yet!

As we said above, one very common and easy way of connecting the event to our code is to add it directly to the tag of the object whose event we are capturing. In this case it's the click event of the A object, as defined by the <A> tag. On clicking the link, we want to capture the event and connect it to our code. We need to add the event handler, in this case `onclick`, as an attribute to our <A> tag. We set the value of the attribute to the code we want executing when the event occurs.

Let's re-write our <A> tag to do this:

```
<A HREF="somepage.htm" NAME="linkSomePage" onclick="alert('You Clicked?')">
    Click Me
</A>
```

You can see that we have added `onclick="alert('You Clicked?')"` to the definition of the <A> tag. Now, when the link is clicked we see an alert box. After this, the hyperlink does its 'usual stuff' and takes us to the page defined in the HREF attribute.

This is fine if you just have one line of code to connect to the event handler, but what if you want a number of lines to execute when the link is clicked?

Well all you need to do is define the function you want to execute and call it in the `onclick` code. Let's do that now:

```
<HTML>
<BODY>

<SCRIPT LANGUAGE="JavaScript">
function linkSomePage_onclick()
{
    alert('You Clicked?');
    return true;
}
</SCRIPT>

<A HREF="somepage.htm" NAME="linkSomePage"
    onclick="return linkSomePage_onclick()">
        Click Me
</A>

</BODY>
</HTML>
```

Within the script block we have created a function, just a standard function, and given it a descriptive name to help us when reading the code. I'm using *ObjectName_event()* as my function names. That way you can instantly see what object on the page this relates to and which event is being connected to. So, in the example above, the function is called `linkSomePage_onclick()` since we are referring to the `onclick` event handler for the A object with name `linkSomePage`.

Our `onclick` attribute is now connected to some code that calls the function `linkSomePage_onclick()`. Therefore, when the user clicks the hyperlink, this function will be executed.

You'll also see that the function returns a value, `true` in this case. Also, where we define our `onclick` attribute, we return the return value of the function by using the `return` statement before the function name. Why do we do this?

The value returned by `onclick="return linkSomePage_onclick()"` is used by JavaScript to decide whether the normal action of the link, that is going to a new page, should occur. If we return `true`, then the action continues and we go to `somepage.htm`. If we return `false`, then the normal chain of events, that is going to `somepage.htm`, does not happen. We say that the action associated with the event is canceled. Try changing the function to this:

```
function linkSomePage_onclick()
{
    alert('This link is going nowhere');
    return false;
}
```

Now you'll find, you just get a message, but no attempt is made to go to somepage.htm.

Not all objects and their events make use of the return value, so sometimes it's redundant. Also it's not always the case that returning false cancels the action. For reasons of browser history rather than logic, it's sometimes true that cancels the action. Generally speaking, it's best to return true and deal with the exceptions to this as you find them.

Some events are not directly linked with the user's actions as such. For example, the window object has the load event, which fires when a page is loaded, and unload event, which fires when the page is unloaded, that is either the user closes the browser or moves to another page.

Event handlers for the window object actually go inside the <BODY> tag. For example, to add an event handler for the load and unload events, we'd write:

```
<BODY LANGUAGE=JavaScript onload="myOnLoadfunction()"
    onunload="myOnUnloadFunction()">
```

Notice that we have specified the LANGUAGE attribute of the <BODY> tag as JavaScript. This is because the <BODY> tag is not contained within a JavaScript script block defined with the <SCRIPT> tag. As usual, since JavaScript is the default scripting language, this can be left off.

Event Handlers as Properties

I promised you two ways of connecting to events, so now let's look at the second.

In this way of connecting to events, we first need to define the function that will be executed when the event occurs. Then we need to set that object's event handler property to the function we defined.

This is illustrated in the following example:

```
<HTML>
<BODY>

<SCRIPT LANGUAGE="JavaScript">

function linkSomePage_onclick()
{
    alert('This link is going nowhere');
    return false;
}

</SCRIPT>

<A HREF="somepage.htm" NAME="linkSomePage">
    Click Me
</A>
```

```
<SCRIPT LANGUAGE=JavaScript>
   window.document.links[0].onclick = linkSomePage_onclick;
</SCRIPT>

</BODY>
</HTML>
```

Save this as ch5_examp4.htm.

We define the function linkSomePage_onclick(), much as we did before. As before we can return a value indicating whether we want the normal action of that object to happen.

Next we have the <A> tag, whose object's event we are connecting to. You'll notice there is no mention of the event handler or the function within the attributes of the tag.

The connection is made between the object's event and our function on the final lines of script:

```
<SCRIPT LANGUAGE=JavaScript>
   document.links[0].onclick = linkSomePage_onclick;
</SCRIPT>
```

As we saw before, document.links[0] returns the A object corresponding to the first link in our web page, which is our linkSomePage hyperlink. We set this object's onclick property to reference our function name – this makes the connection between the object's event handler and our function. Note that no parentheses are added after the function name. Now whenever we click the link, our function gets executed.

The first method of connecting code to events is easier, so why would we ever want to use the second?

Perhaps the most common situation in which you would want to do this is where you want to capture an event for which there is no HTML tag to write your event handler as an attribute. It is also useful in situations where you want the code attached to an event handler to be changed dynamically.

Try It Out – Displaying a Random Image when the Page Loads

Let's look at another example in which we connect to a hyperlink's click event to randomly change the image loaded in a page.

```
<HTML>
<HEAD>

<SCRIPT LANGUAGE=JavaScript>

var myImages = new Array("usa.gif","canada.gif","jamaica.gif","mexico.gif");

function changeImg(imgNumber)
{
   var imgClicked = document.images[imgNumber];
   var newImgNumber = Math.round(Math.random() * 3);
```

```
        while (imgClicked.src.indexOf(myImages[newImgNumber]) != -1)
        {
            newImgNumber = Math.round(Math.random() * 3);
        }

        imgClicked.src = myImages[newImgNumber];
        return false;
    }

    </SCRIPT>
    </HEAD>

    <BODY>

    <A HREF="" NAME="linkImg1" onclick="return changeImg(0)">
        <IMG NAME=img1 SRC="usa.gif" BORDER=0 >
    </A>

    <A HREF="" NAME="linkImg2" onclick="return changeImg(1)">
        <IMG NAME=img1 SRC="mexico.gif" BORDER=0 >
    </A>

    </BODY>
    </HTML>
```

Save the page as ch5_examp5.htm. Again, you will need four image files for the example, which you can create or retrieve from the code download available with this book.

Load the page into your browser. You should see a page like that below:

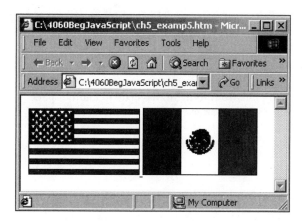

If you click on an image, you'll see it change to a different image, that image being selected randomly.

How It Works

The first line in the script block at the top of the page defines a variable with page level scope. This is an array that contains our list of image sources:

```
var myImages = new Array("usa.gif","canada.gif","jamaica.gif","mexico.gif");
```

Next we have the `changeImg()` function, which will be connected to the `onclick` event handler of an <A> tag surrounding each of our images. This time we are using the same function for both link's `onclick` event handlers and indeed can connect one function to as many event handlers as we like. We pass this function one parameter – the index in the `images` array of the `IMG` object related to that click event, so that we know which image we need to act on.

In the first line of the function we use the passed parameter to declare a new variable that points to the IMG object in the `images[]` array corresponding to the image that was clicked:

```
function changeImg(imgNumber)
{
    var imgClicked = document.images[imgNumber];
```

Following this we set `newImgNumber` variable to a random integer between 0 and 3. The `Math.random()` method provides a random number between 0 and 1 and we multiply that by 3 to get a number between 0 and 3. This number is converted to an integer (either 0, 1, 2, or 3) using `Math.round()`. This integer will provide the index for the image `src` we'll be selecting from the `myImages` array.

```
    var newImgNumber = Math.round(Math.random() * 3);
```

The next lines are a `while` loop, the purpose of which is to ensure we don't select the same image as the current image. If the string contained in `myImages[newImgNumber]` is found inside the `src` property of the current image, then we know it's the same and that we need to get another random number. We keep looping until we get a new image, at which point `myImages[newImgNumber]` will not be found in the existing `src` and `-1` will be returned by the `indexOf()` method, breaking out of the loop:

```
    while (imgClicked.src.indexOf(myImages[newImgNumber]) != -1)
    {
        newImgNumber = Math.round(Math.random() * 3);
    }
```

Finally we set the `src` property of the `IMG` object to the new value contained in our `myImages` array. We return `false` to stop the link from trying to navigate to another page – the link is only there to provide a way of capturing an `onclick` event handler:

```
    imgClicked.src = myImages[newImgNumber];
    return false;
}
```

In IE you'll find that the `IMG` object itself has an `onclick` event, but unfortunately in Netscape browsers this is not so. To make our code Netscape-compatible, we need to use workarounds – the goal is the same, just a little more convoluted. As the A object does support the `onclick` event handler, we wrap the image inside <A> tags and use the A object's `onclick` event handler instead:

```
<A HREF="" NAME="linkImg1" onclick="return changeImg(0)">
    <IMG NAME=img1 SRC="usa.gif" BORDER=0 >
</A>
```

If we were using only IE, we could just use <IMG> tags and add onclick event handlers like this:

```
<IMG NAME=img1 SRC="usa.gif" BORDER=0 ID="img1" onclick="return changeImg(0)">
```

Browser Version Checking Examples

There are many browsers, versions of the same browser, and operating systems out there on the Internet, each with its own version of the BOM and its own particular quirks. It's therefore important that you make sure your pages will work correctly on all browsers, or at least **degrade gracefully**, such as by displaying a message suggesting that the user upgrade their browser.

While you can go a long way with cross-browser compatible code, there may come a time when you want to add extra features that only one browser supports. The answer is to write script that checks the browser name, version and, if necessary, operating system and executes script that is compatible with these variants.

Our main tool in checking browser details is the navigator object property of the window object. In particular, we use the appName and userAgent properties of the navigator object.

The appName property returns the model of the browser, such as Microsoft Internet Explorer or Netscape Navigator.

The userAgent property returns a string containing various bits of information, such as the browser version, operating system, and browser model. However, the value returned by this property varies from browser to browser, so we have to be careful when using it. For example, we can't assume that it starts with the browser version. It does under NN, but under IE the browser version is embedded in the middle of the string.

It's important that the browser checking code does not itself use features only available in the latest browsers. For example, IE 3 did not support arrays. If we used them in our checking code, it would throw up errors and fail.

Try It Out – Checking for and Dealing with Different Browsers

In this example, we create a page that uses the above-mentioned properties to discover the client's browser, version, and operating system. It then can forward the user to a page that matches their specifications.

```
<HTML>
<HEAD>

<SCRIPT LANGUAGE=JavaScript>
<!--

function getBrowserName()
{
    var lsBrowser = navigator.appName;
    if (lsBrowser.indexOf("Microsoft") >= 0)
    {
        lsBrowser = "MSIE";
```

```
      }
      else if (lsBrowser.indexOf("Netscape") >= 0)
      {
         lsBrowser = "NETSCAPE";
      }
      else
      {
         lsBrowser = "UNKNOWN";
      }
      return lsBrowser;
}

function getOS()
{
      var userPlat = "unknown";
      var navInfo = navigator.userAgent;

      if ((navInfo.indexOf("windows NT") != -1)
         || (navInfo.indexOf("windows 95") != -1 )
         || (navInfo.indexOf("windows 98") != -1 )
         || (navInfo.indexOf("WinNT") != -1 )
         || (navInfo.indexOf("Win95") != -1 )
         || (navInfo.indexOf("Win98") != -1 ))
      {
         userPlat = "Win32";
      }
      else if(navInfo.indexOf("Win16") != -1)
      {
         userPlat = "Win16";
      }
      else if(navInfo.indexOf("Macintosh") != -1)
      {
         userPlat = "PPC";
      }
      else if(navInfo.indexOf("68K") != -1)
      {
         userPlat = "68K";
      }
      return userPlat;
}

function getBrowserVersion()
{
      var findIndex;
      var browserVersion = 0;
      var browser = getBrowserName();

      if (browser == "MSIE")
      {
      browserVersion = navigator.userAgent;
      findIndex = browserVersion.indexOf(browser) + 5;
      browserVersion = parseInt(browserVersion.substring(findIndex,findIndex + 1));
      }
```

```
        else
        {
            browserVersion = parseInt(navigator.appVersion.substring(0,1));
        }
        return browserVersion;
}

//-->
</SCRIPT>
</HEAD>

<BODY>
<SCRIPT LANGUAGE=JavaScript>
<!--

var userOS = getOS();
var browserName = getBrowserName();
var browserVersion = getBrowserVersion();

if (browserVersion < 4 || browserName == "UNKNOWN" || userOS == "Win16")
{
    document.write("<H2>Sorry this browser version is not supported</H2>")
}
else if (browserName == "NETSCAPE")
{
    location.replace("NetscapePage.htm");
}
else
{
    location.replace("MSIEPage.htm");
}

//-->
</SCRIPT>
<NOSCRIPT>
    <H2>This website requires a browser supporting scripting</H2>
</NOSCRIPT>

</BODY>
</HTML>
```

Save the script as ch5_examp6.htm. You'll also need to create two more simple pages, one called MSIEPage.htm for IE 4 and IE 5 browsers, and one called NetscapePage.htm for Netscape 4 and above. These are just dummy pages, which we re-direct to. (Example dummy pages are provided with the code download.) In practice they would be your browser-specific pages, implementing code that simply can't be changed to be cross browser compatible.

If the code differences are small, then it is possible to incorporate them in one page and put them inside if statements, making sure the code is run only by a suitable browser.

If the browser detected is not version 4 or above, or it's a Win16 operating system, such as Windows 3.1, or it's not a Microsoft or Netscape browser, then we display a message informing the user that the pages are not compatible with their browser. While this is not ideal, it's certainly better than just letting the pages fail with a battery of error messages.

175

How It Works

The script block in the head of the page defines three important functions. The `getBrowserName()` function finds out the name of the browser, the `getOS()` function returns the operating system, and the `getBrowserVersion()` function finds out the browser version.

Let's look at the first of these, `getBrowserName()`. First we get the name of the browser, as returned by `navigator.appName`, and store it in the variable `lsBrowser`. This will also be used as the variable to store the return value for the function.

```
function getBrowserName()
{
    var lsBrowser = navigator.appName;
```

The string returned by this property tends to be quite long, and does vary slightly sometimes. However, by checking for the existence of certain keywords, such as Microsoft or Netscape we can determine the browser name. We start with the lines:

```
if (lsBrowser.indexOf("Microsoft") >= 0)
{
    lsBrowser = "MSIE";
}
```

which search the `lsBrowser` string for `Microsoft`. If the `indexOf` value of this substring is zero or greater, then we know we have found it and so we set the return value to `MSIE`.

The following `else if` statement does the same, but for Netscape:

```
else if (lsBrowser.indexOf("Netscape") >= 0)
{
    lsBrowser = "NETSCAPE";
}
```

If neither of these two are found then we return `UNKNOWN` as the browser name. If you want to support a wider range of browser, then you could add on extra `if` statements to handle other browsers.

```
else
{
    lsBrowser = "UNKNOWN";
}
```

The value of `lsBrowser` is then returned to the calling code:

```
    return lsBrowser;
}
```

Next we'll turn to the `getOS()` function. This starts by defining two variables: `userPlat` is initialized to the string `unknown`, and `navInfo` is initialized to the value of the `userAgent` property of the `navigator` object.

```
function getOS()
{
    var userPlat = "unknown";
    var navInfo = navigator.userAgent;
```

The sort of information the `userAgent` property returns is:

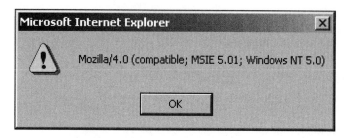

for Internet Explorer 5 and:

for Netscape Navigator 4.7. Even though these were both running on the same operating system, namely Windows 2000, you can see that the results returned by two different browsers for `userAgent` are very different.

The next part of the function consists of a giant `if` statement where we test the `userAgent` property for the name of various operating systems.

The first part of the `if` statement is checking for all the possible Windows permutations, such as windows NT, WinNT, windows 98, Win98 and so on, by searching `navInfo` with the `indexOf()` method. If any of the 32 bit operating systems of Microsoft are found then we set our return value to Win32.

```
    if ((navInfo.indexOf("windows NT") != -1)
        || (navInfo.indexOf("windows 95") != -1 )
        || (navInfo.indexOf("windows 98") != -1 )
        || (navInfo.indexOf("WinNT") != -1 )
        || (navInfo.indexOf("Win95") != -1 )
        || (navInfo.indexOf("Win98") != -1 ))
    {
        userPlat = "Win32";
    }
```

Our next `else if` statement checks to see if Win16 is anywhere in the `userAgent` string, if so the user has a Win16 operating system such as windows 3.1:

```
else if(navInfo.indexOf("Win16") != -1)
{
    userPlat = "Win16";
}
```

The final two `if` statements are checking for variations of Apple Mac operating systems. We could go further and check for Unix and Linux.

```
else if(navInfo.indexOf("Macintosh") != -1)
{
    userPlat = "PPC";
}
else if(navInfo.indexOf("68K") != -1)
{
    userPlat = "68K";
}
```

Finally if no match is found then the return value will be "unknown":

```
    return userPlat;
}
```

How important is it to check for an operating system? Unfortunately IE on Win32 is not the same as IE on the Mac or on Win16. The same goes for NN though perhaps to a lesser extent. For example, the Mac version of IE does not support ActiveX controls. However most of the time you don't need to use the OS checking code – it tends to be the more complex or exotic things that won't work on different operating systems.

We now turn to the final function `getBrowserVersion()`.

How we deduce the browser version depends on the type of browser. For Netscape this is simply the first character of the `Navigator` object's `appVersion` property. However for IE this does not distinguish between version 4 and version 5 so we need a different approach.

For these reasons, our first task in the function is to find out which browser we are dealing with. We declare and initialize the `browser` variable to the name of the browser, using the `getBrowserName()` function we just wrote:

```
function getBrowserVersion()
{
    var findIndex;
    var browserVersion = 0;
    var browser = getBrowserName();
```

If the browser is MSIE (Internet Explorer) then we need to use the `userAgent` property again. Under IE the `userAgent` property always contains MSIE followed by the browser version. So what we need to do is search for MSIE, then get the number following that.

We set findIndex to the character position of MSIE, plus 5, which selects the number after MSIE. browserVersion is set to the integer value of that number which we obtain using the substring() method. This selects the character starting at findIndex, our number, and whose end is one before findIndex + 1. This ensures that we just select one character.

```
if (browser == "MSIE")
{
browserVersion = navigator.userAgent;
findIndex = browserVersion.indexOf(browser) + 5;
browserVersion = parseInt(browserVersion.substring(findIndex, findIndex + 1));
}
```

Finding out the browser version number for Netscape and other browsers is easier; we just convert the first character in appVersion to an integer. The first character is obtained using substring() method, starting at character 0 and ending one before character 1:

```
else
{
    browserVersion = parseInt(navigator.appVersion.substring(0,1));
}
```

At the end of the function we return browserVersion to the calling code:

```
    return browserVersion;
}
```

We've seen the supporting functions but how do we make use of them? Well in the code below, which executes as the page is loaded, we obtain the three bits of information: operating system, browser, and version and we use this to filter out unsupported browsers.

```
<SCRIPT LANGUAGE=JavaScript>
<!--

var userOS = getOS();
var browserName = getBrowserName();
var browserVersion = getBrowserVersion();

if (browserVersion < 4 || browserName == "UNKNOWN" || userOS == "Win16")
{
    document.write("<H2>Sorry this browser version is not supported</H2>")
}
else if (browserName == "NETSCAPE")
{
    location.replace("NetscapePage.htm");
}
else
{
    location.replace("MSIEPage.htm");
}

//-->
</SCRIPT>
```

The first if statement says that if the browser version is less than 4 or it's an unknown browser or the user is running a 16 bit version of windows, then we write a message into the page telling them that their browser is not supported. We could, if we wanted, give more exact details.

Knowing that we are dealing with a version 4 browser or better we then check if the browser is Netscape. If it is, we re-direct the user to a Netscape-specific page using the replace() method of the location object. Then in the else statement we re-direct to the Internet Explorer compatible page.

You may notice I've used <!-- at the beginning and //--> at the end of the script block. This simply wraps the script in HTML comment tags. Doing this prevents older browsers, that is version two and earlier, which don't support JavaScript, from displaying the text in the web page.

```
<NOSCRIPT>
    <H2>This website requires a browser supporting scripting</H2>
</NOSCRIPT>
```

Finally, I've added some <NOSCRIPT> tags for very early browsers and for users who have chosen to disable JavaScript. These will display a message informing the user that they need a JavaScript-enabled browser.

Summary

We've covered a lot in this chapter, but now we have all the grounding we need to move on to more useful things, such as forms and user input, and later on to more advanced areas of text and date manipulation.

- ❏ We turned our attention to the browser, the environment in which JavaScript exists. Just as JavaScript has native objects, so do web browsers. The objects within the web browser, and the hierarchy they are organized in, are described by something called the Browser Object Model. This is essentially a map of a browser's objects. Using it we can navigate our way round each of the objects made available by the browser together with their properties, methods, and events.

- ❏ The first of the main objects we looked at was the window object. This sits at the very top of the BOM's hierarchy. The window object contains a number of important sub-objects, including the location object, the navigator object, the history object, the screen object, and the document object.

- ❏ The location object contains information about the current page's location such as its filename, the server hosting the page, and the protocol used. Each of these is a property of the location object. Some properties are read-only, but others, such as the href property, not only allow us to find out the location of the page, but also can be changed so that we can navigate the page to a new location.

- ❏ The history object is a record of all the pages the user has visited since opening their browser. Sometimes pages are not noted, for example when the location object's replace() method is used for navigation. We can move the browser forward and backward in the history stack and discover what pages the user has visited.

- ❏ The navigator object represents the browser itself and contains useful details of what type of browser, version, and operating system the user has. These details enable us to write pages dealing with various types of browser, even where they may be incompatible.

❑ The `screen` object contains information about the display capabilities of the user's computer.

❑ The `document` object is one of the most important objects. It's an object representation of our page and it contains all of the elements, also represented by objects, within that page. The differences between Netscape and Microsoft browsers are particularly prominent here. If we want cross, browser compatible pages then we find we are quite limited as to which elements we can access.

❑ The `document` object contains three properties that are actually arrays. These are the `links[]`, `images[]`, and `forms[]` arrays. Each contains all the objects created by the `<A>`, `<IMG>`, and `<FORM>` tags on the page, and it's our way of accessing those tags.

❑ The `images[]` array contains an `IMG` object for each `<IMG>` element on the page. We found that even after the page has loaded, we can change the properties of images. For example, we can make the image change when clicked. The same principles for using the `images[]` array apply to the `links[]` array.

❑ We next saw that BOM objects have events as well as methods and properties. These events are handled in JavaScript by using event handlers, which we connect to code that we want to execute when the event occurs. The events available for use depend on the object we were dealing with.

❑ Connecting functions that we have written to event handlers is simply a matter of adding an attribute to the element corresponding to the particular object we are interested in. The attribute has the name of the event handler we want to capture and the value of the function we want to connect to it.

❑ In some instances, such as for the `document` object, a second way of connecting event handlers to code is necessary. Setting the object's property, with the name of the event handler, to our function produces the same effect as if we did it using the event handler as an attribute.

❑ In some instances returning values from event functions allowed us to cancel the action associated with the event. For example, to stop a clicked link from navigating to a page, we returned `false` from the event handler's code.

❑ Finally, we looked at how we can check what type of browser the user has so that we can make sure they only see pages or parts of a page that their browser is compatible with. The `navigator` object provides us with the details we need, in particular the `appName` and `userAgent` properties.

That's it for this chapter. In the next chapter we can move on to more exciting scripting of forms, where you can add various controls to your page to help you gather information from the user.

Exercise Questions

Suggested solutions to these questions can be found in Appendix A.

Question 1

Create a page with a number of links. Then write code that fires on the window onload event, displaying the href's of each of the links on the page.

Question 2

Create two pages, one called IEOnly.htm and the other called NNOnly.htm. Each page should have a heading telling you what page is loaded, for example:

```
<H2>Welcome to the Internet Explorer only page</H2>
```

Using the functions for checking browser type, connect to the window object's onload event handler and detect what browser the user has. Then if it's the wrong page for that browser, redirect to the other page.

Question 3

Insert an image in the page with the <IMG> tag. When the mouse pointer rolls over the image it should switch to a different image. When it rolls out, that is leaves the image, it should swap back again. You'll need to wrap the images inside <A> tags as IMG objects don't have the onmouseover and onmouseout events.

Online discussion at http://p2p.wrox.com

HTML Forms: Interacting with the User

Web pages would be very boring if we could not interact with the user, or obtain information from them, such as text, numbers, or dates. Luckily, with JavaScript we can. We can use this information within the web page, or it can be posted to the web server where we can manipulate it and store it in a database if we so wish. In this chapter we'll concentrate on using the information within the web browser, termed client-side processing. In Chapters 14 and 15, we'll see how to send this information to a web server and store it in a database, termed server-side processing.

When using your computer you'll be quite accustomed to various user interface elements. For example, the Windows operating system has a number of standard elements such as buttons you can click, lists, drop down list boxes, and radio buttons you can select from, and checkboxes you can tick. The same applies with any Graphical User Interface (GUI) operating system, whether it's on the Apple Mac, Unix, or Linux. These elements are the way we now interface with applications. The good news is that we can include many of these types of element in our web page and, even better, it's very easy to do so. Once we have such an element, say a button, inside our page we can then tie code to its events. For example, when the button is clicked, we can fire off a JavaScript function we've created.

It's important to note at this point that the elements I'm talking about in this chapter are the common elements made available by HTML, and not ActiveX elements, Java Applets or plug-ins. We'll look at some of these in Chapter 14.

All of the HTML elements used for interaction must be placed inside an HTML form. Let's start by taking a look at HTML forms and how we interact with them in JavaScript.

HTML Forms

Forms provide us with a way of grouping HTML interaction elements with a common purpose together. For example, a form may contain elements that enable the input of a user's data for registering on a web site. Another form may contain elements that enable the user to ask for a car insurance quote. It's possible to have a number of separate forms in a single page. Pages containing multiple forms need not worry us until we are submitting information to a web server – then we need to be aware that only the information from one of the forms on a page can be submitted to the server at once.

To create a form, we use the `<FORM>` and `</FORM>` tags to declare where it starts and where it ends. The `<FORM>` tag has a number of attributes, such as the `ACTION` attribute, which determines where the form is submitted to, the `METHOD` attribute, which determines how the information is submitted, and the `TARGET` attribute, which determines the frame to which the response to the form is loaded.

Generally speaking, for client-side scripting where we have no intention of submitting information to a server, these attributes are not necessary. When in a later chapter we look at programming server pages, then these properties will come into play. For now the only attribute we need to set in the `<FORM>` tag is the `NAME` attribute, so that we can reference the form.

So, to create a blank form, the tags required would look something like:

```
<FORM NAME="myForm">
</FORM>
```

You won't be surprised to hear that these tags create a `Form` object, which we can use to access the form. We access this object in two ways.

Firstly, we can access the object directly using its name, here `document.myForm`.

Alternatively we can access the object through the `document` object's `forms[]` array property. Remember in the last chapter we talked about the `document` object's `images[]` array, and how we could manipulate it like any other array. Exactly the same applies to the `forms[]` array, except that instead of each element in the array holding an `IMG` object, it now hold a `Form` object. For example, if our `Form` was the first `Form` in the page, we would reference it using `document.forms[0]`.

Many of the attributes of the `<FORM>` tag can be accessed as properties of the `Form` object. In particular, the name property of the `Form` object mirrors the `NAME` attribute of the `<FORM>` tag.

Try It Out – The forms Array

Let's have a look at an example that uses the `forms` array. Here we have a page with three forms on it. Using the `forms[]` array we access each `Form` object in turn and show the value of its name property in a message box.

```
<HTML>
<HEAD>
<SCRIPT LANGUAGE=JavaScript>

function window_onload()
{
```

```
        var numberForms = document.forms.length;
        var formIndex;
        for (formIndex = 0; formIndex < numberForms; formIndex++)
        {
            alert(document.forms[formIndex].name);
        }
}

</SCRIPT>
</HEAD>
<BODY LANGUAGE=JavaScript onload="window_onload()">

<FORM NAME="form1">
<P>This is inside form1</P>
</FORM>

<FORM NAME="form2">
<P>This is inside form2</P>
</FORM>

<FORM NAME="form3">
<P>This is inside form3</P>
</FORM>

</BODY>
</HTML>
```

Save this as `ch6_examp1.htm`. When you load it into your browser, you should see three alert boxes, each of which shows a name of a form.

How It Works

Within the body of the page we define three forms. Each form is given a name, and contains a paragraph of text.

Within the definition of the `<BODY>` tag, the `window_onload()` function is connected to the `window` object's `onload` event handler.

```
<BODY LANGUAGE=JavaScript onload="return window_onload()">
```

This means that when the page is loaded, our `window_onload()` function will be called.

The `window_onload()` function is defined in a script block in the head of the page. Within this function we loop through the `forms[]` array. Just like any other JavaScript array, the `forms[]` array has a `length` property, which we can use to determine how many times we need to loop. Actually, as we know how many forms there are, we could just write the number in. However, here I'm demonstrating the `length` property, since it is then easier to add to the array without having to change the function. Generalizing your code like this is a good practice to get into.

187

The function starts by getting the number of Form objects within the forms array and stores it in variable numberForms.

```
function window_onload()
{
    var numberForms = document.forms.length;
```

Next we define a variable, formIndex, to be used in our for loop. After this comes the for loop itself.

```
var formIndex;
for (formIndex = 0; formIndex < numberForms; formIndex++)
{
    alert(document.forms[formIndex].name);
}
```

Remember that since the indices for arrays start at zero, our loop needs to go from an index of 0 to an index of numberForms - 1. We do this by initializing the formIndex variable to zero, and setting the condition of the for loop to formIndex < numberForms.

Within the for loop's code, we pass the index of the form we want (that is, formIndex) to document.forms[], which gives us the Form object at that array index in the forms array. To access the Form object's name property, we put a dot at the end and the name of the property, name.

Other Form Object Properties and Methods

The HTML elements commonly found in forms, which we will look at in more detail shortly, also have corresponding objects. One way of accessing these is through the elements[] property of the Form object. This is an array just like the forms[] array property of the document object that we have just seen. The elements[] array contains all the objects corresponding to the HTML interaction elements within the form, with the exception of the little used <INPUT TYPE=image> element. As we'll see later, this property is very useful for looping through each of the elements in a form. For example, we could loop through each element checking that it contains valid data prior to submitting the form.

Being an array, the elements[] property of the Form object has the length property, which tells us how many elements are in the form. The Form object also has the length property, which also gives us the number of elements in the form. Which of these you use is up to you since both do the same job, although writing document.myForm.length is shorter, and so quicker to type and less lengthy to look at in code, than document.myForm.elements.length.

When we submit data from a form to a server, we normally use the submit button, which we will come to shortly. However, the Form object also has the submit() method which does nearly the same thing. It differs in Netscape Navigator since it does not call the onsubmit event handler for the submit event of the Form object.

Recall that in the last chapter we saw how return values passed back from an event handler's code can affect whether the normal course of events continues or is cancelled. We saw, for example, that returning `false` from a hyperlink's `onclick` event handler causes the link's navigation to be cancelled. Well, the same principle applies to the `Form` object's `onsubmit` event handler, which fires when the user submits the form. If we return `true` to this event handler, then the form submission goes ahead; if we return `false` then the submission is cancelled. This makes the `onsubmit` event handler's code a great place to do form validation; checking that what the user has entered into the form is valid. For example, if we ask for their age and they enter "mind your own business" we can spot that this is text rather than a valid number, and stop them from continuing. We'll see this in action when we look at server-side scripting in Chapter 15.

As well as there being a reset button, which we will discuss later in the chapter, the `Form` object has the `reset()` method, which clears the form, or restores default values if these exist.

Creating blank forms is not exactly exciting or useful, so now let's turn our attention to the HTML elements that provide interaction functionality inside our forms.

HTML Elements in Forms

There are about ten elements commonly found within `<FORM>` elements. The most useful are shown below, ordered into general types. We give each its name and, in parentheses, the HTML needed to create it, though note this is not the full HTML but only a portion.

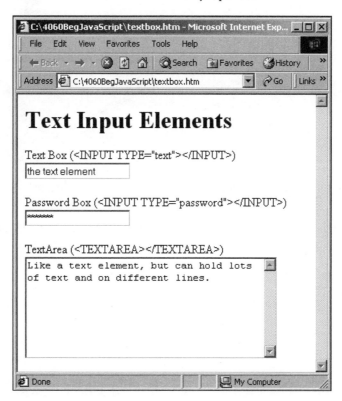

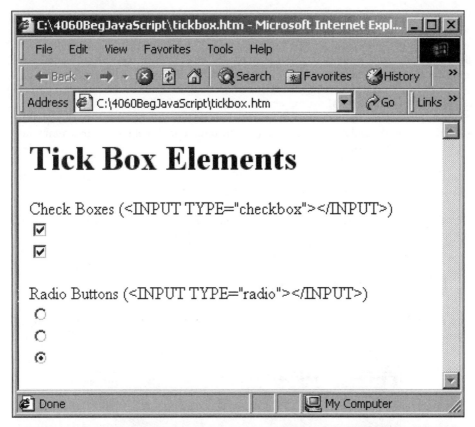

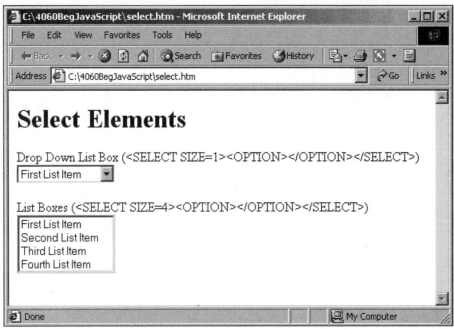

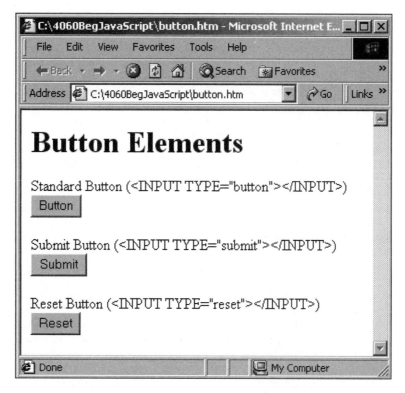

As you can see, most of the form elements are created using the <INPUT> tag. One of the <INPUT> tag's attributes is the TYPE attribute. It's this attribute that decides which of the HTML elements this will be. Examples of values for this attribute include button, to create a button, and text to create a text box.

Each form element inside the web page is made available to us as, yes, you guessed it, an object. As with all the other objects we have seen, each element's object has its own set of distinctive properties, methods and events. We'll be taking a look at each form element in turn and how to use its particular properties, methods, and events. But, before we do that, let's look at properties and methods that the objects of the form elements have in common.

Common Properties and Methods

One property that all the objects of the form elements have in common is the name property. We can use the value of this property to reference that particular element in our script. Also, if we are sending the information in the form to a server, then the element's name property is sent along with any value of the form element, so that the server knows what the value relates to.

Most form element objects also have the value property in common, which returns the value of the element. For example, for a text box the value property returns the text that the user has entered in the text box. Also, by setting the value of the value property, it allows us to put text inside the text box. However, the use of the value property is specific to each element, so we'll look at what it means as we look at each individual element below.

All form element objects also have the form property, which returns the Form object in which the element is contained. This can be useful in cases where you have a generic routine that checks the validity of data in a form. For example, when the user clicks a submit button, we can pass the Form object referenced by the form property to our data checker which can use it to loop through each element on the form in turn, checking that data in the element is valid. This is handy if you have more than one form defined on the page or where you have a generic data checker that you cut and paste to different pages – this way you don't need to know the form's name in advance.

Sometimes it's useful to know what type of element you're dealing with, particularly where you're looping through the elements in a form using the elements[] array property of the Form object. This information can be retrieved using the type property, which each element's object has. This property returns the type of the element, for example button or text.

All form element objects also have the focus() and blur() methods. **Focus** is a concept you might not have come across yet. If an element is the center of the focus then any key presses made by the user will be passed directly to that element. For example, if a text box has focus, then hitting keys will enter values into the text box. Also, if a button has the focus, then hitting the *enter* key will cause the button's onclick event handler code to fire, just as if a user had clicked the button with their mouse.

The user can set which element currently has the focus by clicking on it or using the *tab* key to select it. However we, as the programmer, can also decide which element has the focus by using the form element's object's focus() method. For example, if we have a text box for the user's age to be put into and the user enters an invalid value, such as a letter rather than a number, then we can tell them that their input is invalid and send them back to that text box to correct their mistake.

Blur, which perhaps could be better named 'lost focus', is the opposite of focus. If we want to remove a form element from being the focus of the user's attention, then we can use the blur() method. The blur() method, when used with a form element, usually results in the focus shifting to the containing window.

As well as the focus() and blur() methods, all the form element's objects have the onfocus and onblur event handlers. These are fired, as you'd expect, when an element gets the focus or loses the focus, due to user action or the focus() and blur() methods. The onblur event handler can be a good place to check the validity of data in the element that has just lost the focus. If invalid you can set the focus back to the element and let the user know why the data they entered is wrong.

One thing to be careful of is using the focus() or blur() methods in the onfocus or onblur event handler code. There is a danger of an infinite loop occurring. For example, consider two elements, each of whose onfocus events passes the focus to the other element. Then, if one element gets the focus, its onfocus event will pass the focus to the second element, whose onfocus event will pass the focus back to the first element, and so on until the only way out is to close the browser down. This is not likely to please your users!

Also be very wary of using the focus() and blur() methods to put focus back in a problem field if that field or others depend on some of the user's input. For example, say we have two text boxes, one in which we want the user to enter their city and the other in which we want them to enter their state. Also say that the input into the state text box is checked to make sure that the specified city is in that state. If the state does not contain the city, we put the focus back on the state text box so that the user can change the name of the state. However, if the user actually input the wrong city name and the right state name, they may not be able to go back to the city text box to rectify the problem.

Button Form Elements

I'm starting our look at form elements with the standard button element, as it's probably the most commonly used and is fairly simple. The HTML tag to create a button is the <INPUT> tag. For example, to create a button called myButton, which has the words Click Me on its face, the <INPUT> tag would need to be:

```
<INPUT TYPE="button" NAME="myButton" VALUE="Click Me">
```

The TYPE attribute is set to button and the VALUE attribute is set to the text we want to appear on the face of the button. We can leave the VALUE attribute off, but we'll end up with a blank button, which will leave our users guessing as to its purpose.

This element creates an associated Button object; in this example it is called myButton. This object has all the common properties and methods described above, including the value property. This allows you to change the text on the button face using JavaScript, though this is probably not something you'll need to do very often. What the button is really all about is the onclick event.

We connect to the button's onclick event handler just as we did for the onclick events of other HTML tags such as the <A> tag. All we need do is to define a function that we want to execute when the button is clicked (say, button_onclick()) and then add the onclick event handler as an attribute of the <INPUT> tag:

```
<INPUT TYPE="button" onclick="button_onclick()">
```

Try It Out – Counting Button Clicks

In the example below we use the methods described above to record how often a button has been clicked on the button face.

```
<HTML>
<HEAD>

<SCRIPT LANGUAGE=JavaScript>

var numberOfClicks = 0;

function myButton_onclick()
{
    numberOfClicks++;
    window.document.form1.myButton.value = 'Button clicked ' + numberOfClicks +
    ' times';
}

</SCRIPT>
</HEAD>
<BODY>
<FORM NAME=form1>
    <INPUT TYPE='button' NAME='myButton' VALUE='Button clicked 0 times'
    onclick="myButton_onclick()">
</FORM>
</BODY>
</HTML>
```

Save this page as ch6_examp2.htm. If you load this page into your browser, you will see a button with Button clicked 0 times on it. On repeatedly pressing this button, you will see the number of button clicks recorded on the top of the button.

How It Works

We start the script block in the head of the page by defining a global variable, accessible anywhere inside our page, called numberOfClicks. We record the number of times the button has been clicked in this variable, and use this information to update the button's text.

The other piece of code in the script block is the definition of the function myButton_onclick(). This function is connected to the onclick event handler in the <INPUT> tag in the body of the page. This tag is for a button element called myButton, and is contained within a form called form1.

```
<FORM NAME=form1>
    <INPUT TYPE='button' NAME='myButton' VALUE='Button clicked 0 times'
    onclick="myButton_onclick()">
</FORM>
```

Let's look at the myButton_onclick() function a little more closely. First, the function increments the value of the variable numberOfClicks by one.

```
function myButton_onclick()
{
    numberOfClicks++;
```

Next, we update the text on the button face using the Button object's value property.

```
    window.document.form1.myButton.value = 'Button clicked ' + numberOfClicks +
    ' times';
}
```

The function is specific to this form and button, rather than a generic function we'll be using in other situations. Therefore I've referred to the form and button directly using window.document.form1.myButton. Remember that the window object has a property containing the document object, which itself holds all the elements in a page, including the <FORM> element, and that the button is embedded inside our form.

Try It Out – onmouseup and onmousedown

Two less commonly used events supported by the Button object in version 4 or higher browsers are the onmousedown and onmouseup events. You can see these two events in action in the next example.

```
<HTML>
<HEAD>

<SCRIPT LANGUAGE=JavaScript>

function myButton_onmouseup()
{
```

```
        document.form1.myButton.value = "Mouse Goes Up"
    }

    function myButton_onmousedown()
    {
        document.form1.myButton.value = "Mouse Goes Down"
    }

</SCRIPT>
</HEAD>
<BODY>
<FORM NAME=form1>
    <INPUT TYPE='button' NAME='myButton' VALUE=' Mouse Goes Up '
    onmouseup="myButton_onmouseup()"
    onmousedown="myButton_onmousedown()">
</FORM>
</BODY>
</HTML>
```

Save this page as ch6_examp3.htm and load it into your browser. If you click the button with your left mouse button and keep it held down, you'll see the text on the button change to "Mouse Goes Down". As soon as you release the button, the text changes to "Mouse Goes Up".

How It Works

In the body of the page we define a button called myButton within a form called form1. Within the attributes of the <INPUT> tag, we attach the function myButton_onmouseup() to the onmouseup event handler, and the function myButton_onmousedown() to the onmousedown event handler.

```
<FORM NAME=form1>
    <INPUT TYPE='button' NAME='myButton' VALUE=' Mouse Goes Up '
    onmouseup="myButton_onmouseup()"
    onmousedown="myButton_onmousedown()">
</FORM>
```

The myButton_onmouseup() and myButton_onmousedown() functions are defined in a script block in the head of the page. Each function consists of just a single line of code, in which we use the value property of the Button object to change the text that is displayed on the button's face.

An important point to note is that events like onmouseup and onmousedown only trigger when the mouse pointer is actually over the element in question. For example if you click and keep held down the mouse button over our button, then move the mouse away from the button before releasing the mouse button, you'll find that the onmouseup event does not fire and the text on the button's face does not change. In this instance it would be the document object's onmouseup event handler code that would fire, if we'd connected any code to it.

Don't forget that, like all form element objects, the Button object also has the onfocus and onblur events, though they are rarely used in the context of buttons.

The Submit and Reset Buttons

Two additional types of button are the submit and reset buttons. Defining the submit and reset buttons is done in the same way as defining a standard button, except that the TYPE attribute of the <INPUT> tag is set to submit or reset rather than button. For example, the submit and reset buttons in the earlier screenshot were created using:

```
<INPUT TYPE="submit" VALUE="Submit" NAME="submit1">
<INPUT TYPE="reset" VALUE="Reset" NAME="reset1">
```

These buttons have special purposes, which are not related to script.

When the submit button is clicked, the form data from the form that the button is inside gets automatically sent to the server, without the need for any script.

When the reset button is clicked, all the elements in a form are cleared and returned to their default values; the values they had when the page was first loaded.

The submit and reset buttons have corresponding objects called Submit and Reset, which have exactly the same properties, methods, and events as a standard Button object.

Text Elements

The standard text element allows users to enter a single line of text. This information can then be used in JavaScript code, or be submitted to a server for server-side processing.

A text box is created using the <INPUT> tag, much as our button was, but by setting the TYPE attribute to text. Again, you can choose not to include the VALUE attribute, but if you do include it, then this value will appear inside the text box when the page is loaded.

In the example below, the <INPUT> tag has two additional attributes of SIZE and MAXLENGTH. The SIZE attribute determines how many characters wide the text box is, and MAXLENGTH determines the maximum number of characters the user can enter into the box. Both attributes are optional and use defaults determined by the browser.

For example, to create a text box 10 characters wide, with a maximum character length of 15, and initially containing the words 'Hello World', our <INPUT> tag would be as follows:

```
<INPUT TYPE="text" NAME="myTextBox" SIZE=10 MAXLENGTH=15 VALUE="Hello World">
```

The Text object that this element creates has a value property, which we can use in our scripting to set or read the text contained inside the text box. In addition to the common properties and methods we discussed earlier, the Text object also has the select() method, which selects or highlights all the text inside the text box. This may be used if the user has entered an invalid value, and we can set the focus to the text box and select the text inside it. This then puts the user's cursor in the right place to correct the data and makes it very clear to the user where the invalid data is.

The `value` property of `Text` objects always returns a string data type, even though it may be that number characters are being entered. If we use the value as a number then JavaScript normally does a conversion from a string data type to a number data type for us, but this is not always the case. For example, JavaScript won't do the conversion if the operation you're doing is valid for a string. If we have a form with two text boxes and we added the values returned from these, JavaScript will concatenate rather than add the two values, so 1 + 1 will be 11 and not 2. To fix this, we need to convert all the values involved to numerical data type, for example by using `parseInt()` or `parseFloat()`. However, if we subtracted the two values, an operation only valid for numbers, then JavaScript says "ah ha this can only be done with numbers so I'll convert the values to a number data type". So, 1 – 1 will be returned as 0 without using `parseInt()` or `parseFloat()`. This is a tricky bug to spot, so it's best to get into the habit of converting explicitly to save problems later.

As well as the common event handlers such as `onfocus` and `onblur`, the `Text` object also has the `onchange`, `onselect`, `onkeydown`, `onkeypress`, and `onkeyup` event handlers.

The `onselect` event fires when the user selects some text in the text box.

More useful is the `onchange` event which fires when the element loses focus if (and only if) the value inside the text box is different from the value it had when it got the focus. This enables us to do things like validity checks that occur only if something has changed.

As mentioned before, the `onfocus` and `onblur` events can be used for validating user input. However, they also have another purpose and that's to make a text box read-only. In IE 4.0+ and NN 6 we can use the `READONLY` attribute of the `<INPUT>` tag or the `readOnly` property of the `Text` object to prevent the contents being changed. However, this won't work on NN 4.x. We can get around this using the `blur()` method. All we need do is add an `onfocus` event handler to the `<INPUT>` tag defining the textbox, and connect it to some code that blurs the focus from the text box with the `blur()` method:

```
<INPUT TYPE="text" NAME=txtReadonly VALUE="Look but don't change"
    onfocus="window.document.form1.txtReadonly.blur()"
    READONLY=true>
```

The `onkeypress`, `onkeydown`, and `onkeyup` events fire, as their names suggest, when the user presses a key, when they press a key down, and when a key pressed down is let back up.

Try It Out – A Simple Form with Validation

Let's put all the above information on text boxes and buttons together into an example. In this example we have a simple form consisting of two text boxes and a button. The top text box is for the user's name, the second for their age. We do various validity checks. We check the validity of the age text box when it loses focus. However, the name and age text boxes are only checked to see if they are empty when the button is clicked.

```
<HTML>
<HEAD>

<SCRIPT LANGUAGE=JavaScript>

function butCheckForm_onclick()
{
```

```
      var myForm = document.form1;
      if (myForm.txtAge.value == "" || myForm.txtName.value == "")
      {
         alert("Please complete all the form");
         if (myForm.txtName.value == "")
         {
            myForm.txtName.focus();
         }
         else
         {
            myForm.txtAge.focus();
         }
      }
      else
      {
         alert("Thanks for completing the form " + myForm.txtName.value);
      }
}

function txtAge_onblur()
{
   var txtAge = document.form1.txtAge;
   if (isNaN(txtAge.value) == true)
   {
      alert("Please enter a valid age");
      txtAge.focus();
      txtAge.select();
   }
}

function txtName_onchange()
{
   window.status = "Hi " + document.form1.txtName.value;
}

</SCRIPT>
</HEAD>
<BODY>
<FORM NAME=form1>
   Please enter the following details:
   <P>
   Name:
   <BR>
   <INPUT TYPE="text" NAME=txtName onchange="txtName_onchange()">
   <BR>
   Age:
   <BR>
   <INPUT TYPE="text" NAME=txtAge onblur="txtAge_onblur()" SIZE=3 MAXLENGTH=3>
   <BR>
   <INPUT TYPE="button" VALUE="Check Details" NAME=butCheckForm
      onclick="butCheckForm_onclick()">
</FORM>
</BODY>
</HTML>
```

After you've entered the text, save the file as ch6_examp4.htm and load it into your web browser.

Type your name into the name text box. When you leave the text box you'll see Hi *yourname* appear in the status bar at the bottom of the window.

Enter an invalid value into the age text box, such as 'aaaa', and when you try to leave the box it'll tell you of the error and send you back to correct it.

Finally click the Check Details button and both text boxes will be checked to see that you have completed them. If either is empty, you'll get a message telling you to complete the whole form and it'll send you back to the box that's empty.

If everything is filled in correctly, you'll get a message thanking you.

Note that, at the time of writing, this example does not work properly on NN 6.

How It Works

Within the body of the page, we create the HTML tags that define our form. Inside our form, which is called form1, we create the three form elements with names txtName, txtAge, and butCheckForm.

```
<FORM NAME=form1>
   Please enter the following details:
   <P>
   Name:
   <BR>
   <INPUT TYPE="text" NAME=txtName onchange="txtName_onchange()">
   <BR>
   Age:
   <BR>
   <INPUT TYPE="text" NAME=txtAge onblur="txtAge_onblur()" SIZE=3 MAXLENGTH=3>
   <BR>
   <INPUT TYPE="button" VALUE="Check Details" NAME=butCheckForm
      onclick="butCheckForm_onclick()">
</FORM>
```

You'll see that for the second text box, that is the txtAge text box, we have included the SIZE and MAXLENGTH attributes inside the <INPUT> tag. Setting the SIZE attribute to 3 gives the user an idea of how much text we are expecting, and setting the MAXLENGTH attribute to 3 helps ensure that we don't get too large numbers entered for our age value!

The first text box's onchange event handler is connected to the function txtName_onchange(), the second text box's onblur event handler is connected to the function txtAge_onblur(), and the button's onclick event handler is connected to the function butCheckForm_onclick(). These functions are defined in a script block in the head of the page. We will look at each of them in turn, starting with butCheckForm_onclick().

The first thing we do is define a variable, myForm, and set it to reference the Form object created by our <FORM> tag later in the page.

```
function butCheckForm_onclick()
{
    var myForm = document.form1;
```

Doing this reduces the size of our code each time we want to use the form1 object. Instead of document.form1 we can just type myForm. It makes our code a bit more readable and therefore easier to debug, and it saves typing. When we set a variable to be equal to an existing object, we don't (in this case) actually create a new form1 object. Instead we just point our variable to the existing form1 object. So when we type myForm.name JavaScript checks our variable, finds it's actually storing the location in memory of the object form1 and uses that object instead. All this goes on behind the scenes so we don't need to worry about it and can just use myForm as if it was document.form1.

Having got our reference to the Form object, we then use it in an if statement to check whether the value in the text box named txtAge or the text box named txtName actually contains any text.

```
if (myForm.txtAge.value == "" || myForm.txtName.value == "")
{
    alert("Please complete all the form");
    if (myForm.txtName.value == "")
    {
        myForm.txtName.focus();
    }
    else
    {
        myForm.txtAge.focus();
    }
}
```

If we do find an incomplete form, we alert the user. Then in an inner if statement we check which text box was not filled in. We set the focus to the offending text box, so that the user can start filling it in straight away without having to move the focus to it themselves. It also lets the user know which text box our program considers needs filling in. To avoid annoying your users, make sure that text in the page tells them which fields are required.

If the original outer if statement found that the form was complete, then it would let the user know with a thank you message.

```
    else
    {
        alert("Thanks for completing the form " + myForm.txtName.value);
    }
}
```

In this sort of situation, it's probably more likely that at this point, having validated the form, we'd submit it to the server for processing. We can do this using the Form object's submit() method as we'll see in the chapters on server-side programming.

The next of our three functions is txtAge_onblur(), which is connected to the onblur event of our txtAge text box. The purpose of this function is to check that the string value the user entered into the age box actually consists of number characters.

```
function txtAge_onblur()
{
    var txtAge = document.form1.txtAge;
```

Again at the start of the function we declare a variable and set it to reference an object; this time it's the Text object created for the txtAge text box that we define further down the page. Now instead of having to type document.form1.txtAge every time we just type txtAge and it acts as the same thing. It certainly helps save those typing fingers, especially since it's a big function with multiple use of the txtAge object.

The following if statement checks to see if what has been entered in the txtAge text box can be converted to a number. We use the isNaN() function to do this for us. If the value in txtAge test box is not a number then it's time to tell the user and set the focus back to the offending element with the focus() method of the corresponding Text object. Additionally, this time we also highlight the text by using the Text object's select() method. It makes it even clearer to the user, and they can rectify the problem without needing to delete text first.

```
    if (isNaN(txtAge.value) == true)
    {
        alert("Please enter a valid age");
        txtAge.focus();
        txtAge.select();
    }
}
```

We could go further and check that the number inside the text box is actually a valid age, for example – 191 is not a valid age, nor is 255 likely to be. We just need to add another if statement to check for these possibilities, but I'll leave that as an extra exercise!

This function is connected to the onblur event handler of the txtAge text box, but why didn't we use the onchange event handler, with the advantage that we only recheck the value when it's actually been changed? The onchange would not fire in the situation where the box was empty before focus was passed to it, and after focus was passed away from it. However, leaving the checking of the form completion until just before the form is submitted is probably better as some users prefer to fill in information out of order and come back to some form elements later.

The final function is for the `txtName` text box's onchange event. Its use here is a little flippant, and more as an example of the `onchange` event.

```
function txtName_onchange()
{
    window.status = "Hi " + document.form1.txtName.value;
}
```

When the `onchange` event fires, when focus is passed away form the name text box and its contents have changed, we take the value of the `txtName` box and put it into the window's status bar at the bottom of the window. It simply says Hi *yourname*. We access the status bar using the `window` object's `status` property. Although we could just put:

```
status = "Hi " + document.form1.txtName.value;
```

I've actually put `window` in front of this just to make it clear what we are actually accessing. It would be very easy when reading the code to mistake `status` for a variable, so in this situation, although strictly unnecessary, putting `window` in front does make the code easier to read, understand, and therefore debug.

The Password Text Box

The only real purpose of the password box is to allow users to type in a password on a page and to have its characters hidden, so that no one can look over their shoulder at it. However, when sent to the server the text in the password is sent as plain text – there is no encryption or attempt at hiding the text – so it's not a secure way of passing information.

Defining a password box is identical to a text box, except that the `TYPE` attribute is `password`:

```
<INPUT NAME=password1 TYPE=password>
```

This form element creates an associated `Password` object, which is almost identical to the `Text` object in its properties, methods, and events.

The Hidden Text Box

The hidden text box can hold text and numbers just like a normal text box, the difference being that it's not visible to the user. A hidden element? It may sound as useful as an invisible painting, but in fact it proves to be very useful.

To define a hidden text box we have the following HTML:

```
<INPUT TYPE="hidden" NAME=myHiddenElement>
```

The hidden text box creates a `Hidden` object. This is available in the `elements` array property of the `Form` object and can be manipulated in JavaScript like any other object. Although it's only through its HTML definition or through JavaScript that we can actually set its value, like a normal text box its value is submitted to the server when the user submits the form.

So why are they useful? Let's imagine we had a lot of information that we need to obtain from the user, but to avoid having a page stuffed full of elements and looking like the control panel of the space shuttle, we decide to obtain the information over more than one page. The problem is how do we keep a note of what was entered in previous pages? Easy – we use hidden text boxes and put the values in there. Then, in the final page, all the information is submitted to the server – it's just that some of it is hidden. Anyway, we'll see more about this in the server-side scripting chapter.

Textarea Element

The text area element allows multi-line input of text. Other than this, it acts very much like the text box element.

However, unlike the text box, the textarea element has its own tag, the <TEXTAREA> tag. It also has two additional attributes: COLS and ROWS. The COLS attribute defines how many characters wide the textarea will be and the ROWS attribute defines how many character rows there will be. Setting the text inside the element is not done by using the VALUE attribute, but by putting it between the start and close tags. So if we want a textarea element 40 characters wide by 20 rows deep with initial text of "Hello World" on the first line and "Line 2" on the second line, then we would define this as:

```
<TEXTAREA NAME=myTextArea COLS=40 ROWS=20>
    Hello World
    Line 2
</TEXTAREA>
```

Another additional attribute of the <TEXTAREA> tag is the WRAP attribute, which determines what happens when the user types to the end of a line. The default value for this is off so that if the user does not hit return at the end of a line then it just keeps going, with a horizontal scroll bar appearing. To switch wrapping on we have two possible values we can use: nothing (that is just including the WRAP attribute on its own) and hard. As far as client-side processing goes both do the same thing: they switch wrapping on. However when we come to server-side processing they do make a difference to what information is sent to the server when the form is posted.

If we set the WRAP attribute on by including it in the tag definition, or setting it to soft, then wrapping will occur client side, but the carriage returns won't be posted to the server, just the text. If the WRAP attribute is set to hard then any carriage returns caused by wrapping will be converted to hard returns, that is, as if the user had hit the return key, and these will be sent to the server. Also we need to be aware that what a carriage return character actually is, is determined by the operating system that the browser is running on. For example, on Windows a carriage return is \r\n, whereas on a Macintosh the carriage return is \r and on Unix a carriage return is \n.

The Textarea object created by the <TEXTAREA> tag has the same properties, methods and events as the Text object we saw previously. Note that there is a value property even though the <TEXTAREA> tag does not have a VALUE attribute. The value property simply returns the text between the <TEXTAREA> and </TEXTAREA> tags. The events supported by the Textarea object include the onkeydown, onkeypress, onkeyup and onchange event handlers.

To help demonstrate how the onkeydown, onkeypress, onkeyup, and onchange events work, in particular the order in which they fire, let's create an example that tells us what events are firing:

```
<HTML>
<HEAD>

<SCRIPT LANGUAGE=JavaScript>
function DisplayEvent(eventName)
{
    var myMessage = window.document.form1.textarea2.value;
    myMessage = myMessage + eventName;
    window.document.form1.textarea2.value = myMessage;
}
</SCRIPT>
</HEAD>

<BODY>
<FORM NAME=form1>
    <TEXTAREA ROWS=15 COLS=40 NAME=textarea1
        onchange="DisplayEvent('onchange\n');"
        onkeydown="DisplayEvent('onkeydown\n');"
        onkeypress="DisplayEvent('onkeypress\n');"
        onkeyup="DisplayEvent('onkeyup\n\n');">
    </TEXTAREA>
    <TEXTAREA ROWS=15 COLS=40 NAME=textarea2>
    </TEXTAREA>
    <BR><BR>
    <INPUT TYPE="button" VALUE="Clear Event TextArea"
        NAME=button1 onclick="window.document.form1.textarea2.value=''">
</FORM>

</BODY>
</HTML>
```

Save this page as ch6_examp5.htm.

Load the page into your browser and see what happens when you type any letter into the first textarea box. You should see the events being fired listed in the second textarea box (onkeydown, onkeypress, onkeyup). If you click outside of the first textarea box you'll see the onchange event fire.

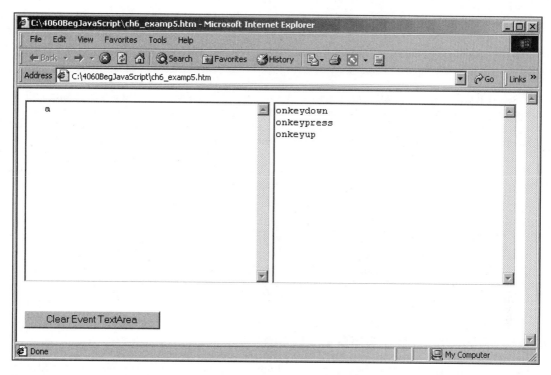

Experiment with the example to see what events fire, and when. Sometimes you will not get quite the results you expect. For example, if you press and hold a key down then in IE and NN 6 onkeydown and onkeypress will fire continuously until you let go, when just one onkeyup event will fire. In NN 4.x, onkeydown will fire once, then onkeypress will fire continuously until you let go, when just one onkeyup will fire.

How It Works

Within a form called form1 in the body of the page, we define two textareas and a button. The first textarea is the one whose events we are going to monitor. We attach code which calls the DisplayEvent() function to each of the onchange, onkeydown, onkeypress, and onkeyup event handlers. The value passed to the function reflects the name of the event firing.

```
<TEXTAREA ROWS=15 COLS=40 NAME=textarea1
    onchange="DisplayEvent('onchange\n');"
    onkeydown="DisplayEvent('onkeydown\n');"
    onkeypress="DisplayEvent('onkeypress\n');"
    onkeyup="DisplayEvent('onkeyup\n\n');">
</TEXTAREA>
```

Next we have an empty textarea, the same size as the first textarea.

```
<TEXTAREA ROWS=15 COLS=40 NAME=textarea2>
</TEXTAREA>
```

Finally we have our button element:

```
<INPUT TYPE="button" VALUE="Clear Event TextArea"
    NAME=button1 onclick="window.document.form1.textarea2.value=''">
```

Notice that the onclick event handler for the button is not calling a function, but just executing a line of JavaScript. Although we do normally call functions it's not compulsory; if we have just one line of code to execute, it's easier just to insert that rather than create a function and call it. In this case, the onclick event handler is connected to some code that sets the contents of the second textarea to empty (' ').

Now let's look at the DisplayEvent() function. This is defined in a script block in the head of the page. It adds the name of the event that it has been passed as a parameter to the text already contained in the second textarea:

```
function DisplayEvent(eventName)
{
    var myMessage = window.document.form1.textarea2.value;
    myMessage = myMessage + eventName;
    window.document.form1.textarea2.value = myMessage;
}
```

Checkboxes and Radio Buttons

I've put the discussion of checkboxes and radio buttons together, because their objects have identical properties, methods, and events. A checkbox allows the user to tick and untick it. It is similar to the paper surveys you may get where you are asked to "check the boxes that apply to you". Radio buttons are basically a group of checkboxes, with the property that only one can be checked at once. Of course, they also look different and their group nature means that they are treated differently.

Creating checkboxes and radio buttons requires our old friend the <INPUT> tag. Its TYPE attribute is set to "checkbox" or "radio" to determine which box or button is created. To set a checkbox or a radio button to be checked when the page is loaded, we simply insert the keyword CHECKED into the <INPUT> tag. So to create a checkbox, which is already checked, our <INPUT> tag will be:

```
<INPUT TYPE="checkbox" NAME=chkDVD CHECKED VALUE="DVD">
```

To create a checked radio button the <INPUT> tag would be:

```
<INPUT TYPE="radio" NAME=radCPUSpeed CHECKED VALUE="1 GHz">
```

I mentioned above that radio buttons are group elements. In fact, there is little point in putting just one on a page as the user won't be able to choose between any alternative boxes.

To create a group of radio buttons we simply give each radio button the same NAME. This creates an array of radio buttons going by that name which we can access, as we would with any array, using its index.

For example, to create a group of three radio buttons, our HTML would be:

```
<INPUT TYPE="radio" NAME=radCPUSpeed CHECKED VALUE="800 MHz">
<INPUT TYPE="radio" NAME=radCPUSpeed VALUE="1 GHz">
<INPUT TYPE="radio" NAME=radCPUSpeed VALUE="1.5 GHz">
```

We can have as many groups of radio buttons in a form as we want, by just giving each group their own unique name. Note that we have only used one CHECKED attribute, since only one of the radio buttons in the group can be checked. If we had used the CHECKED attribute in more than one of the radio buttons, only the last of these would have actually been checked.

Using the VALUE attribute of the checkbox and radio button elements is different from previous elements we've looked at. Firstly it tells you nothing about the user's interaction with an element, as it's predefined in our HTML or by our JavaScript. Whether a checkbox or radio button is checked or not, it still returns the same value. Secondly, when a form is posted to a server, only the values of the checked checkboxes and radio buttons are sent. So, if you have a form with 10 checkboxes on and the user submits the form with none of these checked, then nothing would be sent to the server except a blank form. We'll learn more about this when we look at server-side scripting.

Each checkbox has an associated Checkbox object and each radio button in a group has a separate Radio object. As mentioned above, with radio buttons of the same name, we can access each Radio object in a group by treating the group of radio buttons as an array, with the name of the array being the name of the radio buttons in the group. As with any array, we have the length property, which will tell us how many radio buttons there are in that group.

For determining whether a user has actually checked or unchecked a checkbox, we need to use the checked property of the Checkbox object. This property returns true if the checkbox is currently checked, and false if not.

Radio buttons are slightly different. Because radio buttons with the same name are grouped together, we need to test each Radio object in the group in turn to see if it has been checked. Only one of the radio buttons in a group can be checked, so if you check another one in the group, the previously checked one will become unchecked and the new one will be checked in its place.

Both Checkbox and Radio have the event handlers, onclick, onfocus, and onblur, and these operate as we saw for the other elements.

Try It Out – Checkboxes and Radio Buttons

Let's look at an example that makes use of all the properties, methods, and events we have just talked about. The example is a simple form, which allows a user to build a computer system. Perhaps it could be used in an e-commerce situation for buying computers online with the exact specification determined by the customer.

```
<HTML>
<HEAD>

<SCRIPT LANGUAGE=JavaScript>

var radCpuSpeedIndex = 0;
```

```
function radCPUSpeed_onclick(radIndex)
{
   var returnValue = true;

   if (radIndex == 1)
   {
      returnValue = false;
      alert("Sorry that processor speed is currently unavailable");
      document.form1.radCPUSpeed[radCpuSpeedIndex].checked = true;
   }
   else
   {
      radCpuSpeedIndex = radIndex;
   }
   return returnValue;
}

function butCheck_onclick()
{
   var controlIndex;
   var element;
   var numberOfControls = document.form1.length;
   var compSpec = "Your chosen processor speed is ";
   compSpec = compSpec + document.form1.radCPUSpeed[radCpuSpeedIndex].value;
   compSpec = compSpec + "\nWith the following addtional components\n";
   for (controlIndex = 0; controlIndex < numberOfControls; controlIndex++)
   {
      element = document.form1[controlIndex];
      if (element.type == "checkbox")
      {
         if (element.checked == true)
         {
            compSpec = compSpec + element.value + "\n";
         }
      }
   }
   alert(compSpec);
}

</SCRIPT>
</HEAD>
<BODY>

<FORM NAME=form1>
<P>
Tick all of the components you want included on your computer
<BR><BR>
<TABLE>
<TR>
   <TD>DVD-ROM</TD>
   <TD><INPUT TYPE="checkbox" NAME=chkDVD VALUE="DVD-ROM"></TD>
</TR>
<TR>

   <TD>CD-ROM</TD>
   <TD><INPUT TYPE="checkbox" NAME=chkCD VALUE="CD-ROM"></TD>
</TR>
<TR>
   <TD>Zip Drive</TD>
```

```
        <TD><INPUT TYPE="checkbox" NAME=chkZip VALUE="ZIP Drive"></TD>
    </TR>
    </TABLE>
    <P>
    Select the processor speed you require
    <TABLE>
    <TR>
        <TD><INPUT TYPE="radio" NAME=radCPUSpeed CHECKED
            onclick="return radCPUSpeed_onclick(0)" VALUE="800 MHz"></TD>
        <TD>800 MHz</TD>
        <TD><INPUT TYPE="radio" NAME=radCPUSpeed
            onclick="return radCPUSpeed_onclick(1)" VALUE="1 GHz"></TD>
        <TD>1 GHz</TD>
        <TD><INPUT TYPE="radio" NAME=radCPUSpeed
            onclick="return radCPUSpeed_onclick(2)" VALUE="1.5 GHz"></TD>
        <TD>1.5 GHz</TD>
    </TR>
    </TABLE>
    </P>
    <INPUT TYPE="button" VALUE="Check Form" NAME=butCheck
        onclick="return butCheck_onclick()">

    </FORM>

    </BODY>
    </HTML>
```

Save the page as `ch6_examp6.htm` and load it into your web browser. You should see a form like the one below:

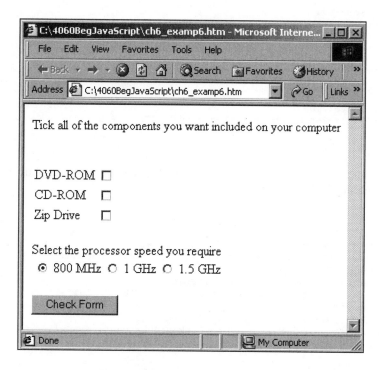

Tick some of the checkboxes, change the processor speed and hit the **Check Form** button. A message box will appear giving details of which components and what processor speed you selected. For example, if you select a DVD-ROM and a Zip Drive, and 1.5GHz processor speed, you will see the following:

Note that the 1 GHz processor is out of stock, so if you choose that, a message box will appear telling you that it's out of stock, and the 1 GHz processor speed radio button won't be selected. The previous setting will be restored once the user dismisses the message box.

How It Works

Let's first look at the body of the page, where we define the checkboxes, radio buttons and standard button inside a form called `form1`. We start with the checkboxes. They are put into a table simply for formatting purposes. No functions are called or events are hooked into.

```
<TABLE>
<TR>
    <TD>DVD-ROM</TD>
    <TD><INPUT TYPE="checkbox" NAME=chkDVD VALUE="DVD-ROM"></TD>
</TR>
<TR>
    <TD>CD-ROM</TD>
    <TD><INPUT TYPE="checkbox" NAME=chkCD VALUE="CD-ROM"></TD>
</TR>
<TR>
    <TD>Zip Drive</TD>
    <TD><INPUT TYPE="checkbox" NAME=chkZip VALUE="ZIP Drive"></TD>
</TR>
</TABLE>
```

Next come the radio buttons for selecting the required CPU speed, which are a little more complex. Again they are put into a table for formatting purposes.

```
<TABLE>
<TR>
    <TD><INPUT TYPE="radio" NAME=radCPUSpeed CHECKED
        onclick="return radCPUSpeed_onclick(0)" VALUE="800 MHz"></TD>
    <TD>800 MHz</TD>
    <TD><INPUT TYPE="radio" NAME=radCPUSpeed
        onclick="return radCPUSpeed_onclick(1)" VALUE="1 GHz"></TD>
    <TD>1 GHz</TD>
    <TD><INPUT TYPE="radio" NAME=radCPUSpeed
        onclick="return radCPUSpeed_onclick(2)" VALUE="1.5 GHz"></TD>
    <TD>1.5 GHz</TD>
</TR>
</TABLE>
```

The radio button group name is `radCPUSpeed`. I've set the first one to be checked by default by including the word `CHECKED` inside the `<INPUT>` tag's definition. It's a good idea to ensure that you have one radio button checked by default. Without this, if the user did not select a button, the form would be submitted with no value for that radio group.

We're making use of the `onclick` event of each `Radio` object. For each button we're connecting to the same function, `radCPUSpeed_onclick()`, but for each radio button we are passing a value, the index of that particular button in the `radCPUSpeed` radio button group array. This makes it easy to work out which radio button was selected. We'll look at this function a little later, but first let's look at the standard button that completes our form.

```
<INPUT TYPE="button" VALUE="Check Form" NAME=butCheck
    onclick="return butCheck_onclick()">
```

This button is for the user to click when they have completed filling in the form, and has its `onclick` event handler connected to the `butCheck_onclick()` function.

So, we have two functions, `radCPUSpeed_onclick()` and `butCheck_onclick()`. These are both defined in the script block in the head of the page. Let's look at this script block now. It starts by declaring a variable `radCpuSpeedIndex`. This will be used to store the currently selected index of the `radCPUSpeed` radio button group.

```
var radCpuSpeedIndex = 0;
```

Next we have the `radCPUSpeed_onclick()` function which is called by the `onclick` event handler in each radio button. Our function has one parameter, namely the index position in the `radCPUSpeed[]` array of the radio object selected.

```
function radCPUSpeed_onclick(radIndex)
{
    var returnValue = true;
```

The first thing we do in the function is declare the `returnValue` variable and set it to `true`. We'll be returning this as our return value from the function. In this case the return value is important as it decides whether the radio button remains checked as a result of the user clicking it. If we return `false` then that cancels the user's action and the radio button remains unchecked. In fact no radio button becomes checked, which is why we keep track of the index of the checked radio button so we can check the previously checked button. To allow the user's action to go ahead we return `true`.

As an example of this in action, on the next line we have an `if` statement. If the radio button's index value passed is 1, that is the user checked the box for a 1 GHz processor, then we tell them that it's out of stock and cancel the clicking action by setting `returnValue` to `false`.

```
    if (radIndex == 1)
    {
        returnValue = false;
        alert("Sorry that processor speed is currently unavailable");
        document.form1.radCPUSpeed[radCpuSpeedIndex].checked = true;
    }
```

I mentioned above that canceling the clicking action results in no radio buttons being checked, so to rectify this we set the previously checked box to be checked again in the line:

```
document.form1.radCPUSpeed[radCpuSpeedIndex].checked = true;
```

What we are doing here is using the `Array` object for the `radCpuSpeed` radio group. Each array element actually contains an object, namely each of our three `Radio` objects. We use the `radCpuSpeedIndex` variable as the index of the `Radio` object that was last checked, since this is what it holds.

Finally in the `else` statement we set `radCpuSpeedIndex` to the new checked radio button's index value.

```
    else
    {
        radCpuSpeedIndex = radIndex;
    }
```

In the last line of the function the value of `returnValue` is returned to where the function was called and will either cancel or allow the clicking action.

```
    return returnValue;
}
```

Our second function, `butCheck_onclick()`, is the one connected to the button's `onclick` event. In a real e-commerce situation this button would be the place where we'd check our form and then submit it to the server for processing. Here we use the form to show a message box confirming which boxes you have checked, as if you didn't already know!

At the top we declare the four local variables, which will be used in the function. Variable `numberOfControls` is set to the form's `length` property, which is the number of elements on the form. Variable `compSpec` is be used to build up the string that we'll display in a message box.

```
function butCheck_onclick()
{
    var controlIndex;
    var element;
    var numberOfControls = document.form1.length;
    var compSpec = "Your chosen processor speed is ";
    compSpec = compSpec + document.form1.radCPUSpeed[radCpuSpeedIndex].value;
    compSpec = compSpec + "\nWith the following addtional components\n";
```

In the line:

```
compSpec = compSpec +
document.form1.radCPUSpeed[radCpuSpeedIndex].value;
```

we add the value of the radio button the user has selected to our message string. The global variable `radCpuSpeedIndex`, which was set by the radio button group's `onclick` event, contains the array index of the selected radio button.

An alternative way of finding out which radio button was clicked would be to loop through the radio button group's array and test each radio button in turn to see if it was checked. The code would look something like:

```
var radIndex;
for (radIndex = 0; radIndex < document.form1.radCPUSpeed.length; radIndex++)
{
    if (document.form1.radCPUSpeed[radIndex].checked == true)
    {
        radCpuSpeedIndex = radIndex;
        break;
    }
}
```

Anyway back to the actual code. You'll notice I've thrown in a few new line (\n) characters into the message string for formatting reasons.

Next we have our big `for` statement.

```
for (controlIndex = 0; controlIndex < numberOfControls; controlIndex++)
{
    element = document.form1[controlIndex];
    if (element.type == "checkbox")
    {
        if (element.checked == true)
        {
            compSpec = compSpec + element.value + "\n";
        }
    }
}
alert(compSpec);
```

It's here that we loop through each element on the form using `document.form1[controlIndex]`, which returns a reference to the element object stored at the `controlIndex` index position.

You'll see that I've set the `element` variable to reference the object stored in the `form1[]` array at the index position stored in variable `controlIndex`. Again this is for convenient shorthand purposes, as now to use that particular object's properties or methods, we just type `element` and dot and then the method or property name, making our code easier to read and debug, and saving on typing.

We only want to see which check boxes have been checked, so we use the `type` property, which every HTML element object has, to see what element type we are dealing with. If the `type` is `checkbox` then we go ahead and see if it's a checked checkbox. If this is so, we append its value to the message string in `compSpec`. If it is not a checkbox, it can be safely ignored.

The final thing to do is use the `alert()` method to display the contents of our message string.

The Select Elements

Although they look quite different, the drop-down list and the list boxes are actually both elements created with the <SELECT> tag, and strictly speaking they are both select elements. The select element has one or more options in a list that you can select from; each of these options is defined using the <OPTION> tag. Your list of <OPTION> tags goes in between the <SELECT> and </SELECT> tags.

The SIZE attribute of the <SELECT> tag is used to specify how many of the options are visible to the user.

For example, to create a list box that is 5 rows deep and populate it with 7 options, our <SELECT> tag would look like this:

```
<SELECT NAME=theDay SIZE=5>
<OPTION VALUE=0 SELECTED>Monday
<OPTION VALUE=1>Tuesday
<OPTION VALUE=2>Wednesday
<OPTION VALUE=3>Thursday
<OPTION VALUE=4>Friday
<OPTION VALUE=5>Saturday
<OPTION VALUE=6>Sunday
</SELECT>
```

Notice that the Monday <OPTION> tag also contains the word SELECTED; this will make this option the default selected one when the page is loaded. The values of the options have been defined as numbers, but text would be equally valid.

If we wanted this to be a drop-down list, then we just need to change the SIZE attribute in the <SELECT> tag to 1 and hey presto it's a drop-down list.

If we want to let the user choose more than one item from a list at once, we simply need add the MULTIPLE attribute to the <SELECT> definition.

The <SELECT> tag creates a Select object. This object has an options[] array property, and this array is made up of Option objects, one for each <OPTION> element inside the <SELECT> element associated with the Select object. For example, in the above example if the <SELECT> element was contained in a form called theForm, with

```
document.theForm.theDay.options[0]
```

we would access the option created for Monday.

How can we tell which option has been selected by the user? Easy; we use the Select object's selectedIndex property. We can use the index value returned by this property to access the selected option using the options[] array.

The Option object also has index, text, and value properties. The index property returns the index position of that option in the options[] array. The text property is what's displayed in the list and the value property is the value defined for the option, which would be posted to the server if the form were submitted.

If you want to find out how many options there are in a select element, you can use the `length` property of either the `Select` object itself or of its `options[]` array property.

Let's see how we could loop through the `options[]` array for the above select box:

```
var theDayElement = window.document.form1.theDay;
document.write("There are " + theDayElement.length + "options");
var optionCounter;
for (optionCounter = 0; optionCounter < theDayElement.length; optionCounter++)
{
    document.write("Option text is " + theDayElement.options[optionCounter].text)
    document.write(" and its value is ");
    document.write(theDayElement.options[optionCounter].value);
    document.write("")
}
```

First we set the variable `theDayElement` to reference the `Select` object. Then we write the number of options to the page, in this case 7.

Next we use a `for` loop to loop through the `options[]` array, displaying the text of each option, such as Monday, Tuesday etc., and its value, such as 0, 1 etc. If you create a page based on this code, it must be placed after the `<SELECT>` tag has been defined.

It's also possible to add options to a select element after the page has finished loading. We'll look at how this is done next.

Adding New Options

To add a new option to a select element, we simply create a new `Option` object using the new operator, and then insert it into the `options[]` array of the `Select` object at an empty index position.

When creating a new `Option` object there are two parameters to pass, the first is the text you want to appear in the list, the second the value to be assigned to the option.

```
var myNewOption = new Option("TheText","TheValue");
```

We then simply assign this `Option` object to an empty array element, for example:

```
document.theForm.theSelectObject.options[0] = myNewOption;
```

If you want to remove an option you simply set that part of the `options[]` array to `null`. For example, to remove the element we just inserted above, we need:

```
document.theForm.theSelectObject.options[0] = null;
```

When you remove an `Option` object from the `options[]` array, the array is reordered so that the array index values of all the options above the removed one have their index value decremented by one.

When you insert a new option at a certain index position, beware that it will overwrite any `Option` object that is already there.

Try It Out – Adding and Removing List Options

Let's use the 'list of days' example we saw above to demonstrate adding and removing list options.

```
<HTML>
<HEAD>

<SCRIPT LANGUAGE=JavaScript>

function butRemoveWed_onclick()
{
   if (document.form1.theDay.options[2].text == "Wednesday")
   {
      document.form1.theDay.options[2] = null;
   }
   else
   {
      alert('There is no Wednesday here!');
   }
}

function butAddWed_onclick()
{
   if (document.form1.theDay.options[2].text != "Wednesday")
   {
      var indexCounter;
      var days = document.form1.theDay;
      var lastoption = new Option();
      days.options[6] = lastoption;

      for (indexCounter = 6;indexCounter > 2; indexCounter--)
      {
      days.options[indexCounter].text = days.options[indexCounter - 1].text;
      days.options[indexCounter].value = days.options[indexCounter - 1].value;
      }

      var option = new Option("Wednesday",2);
      days.options[2] = option;
   }
   else
   {
      alert('Do you want to have TWO Wednesdays?????');
   }
}

</SCRIPT>
</HEAD>
<BODY>

<FORM NAME=form1>
<SELECT NAME=theDay SIZE=5>
   <OPTION VALUE=0 SELECTED>Monday
   <OPTION VALUE=1>Tuesday
   <OPTION VALUE=2>Wednesday
```

```
       <OPTION VALUE=3>Thursday
       <OPTION VALUE=4>Friday
       <OPTION VALUE=5>Saturday
       <OPTION VALUE=6>Sunday
  </SELECT>
  <BR>
  <INPUT TYPE="button" VALUE="Remove Wednesday" NAME=butRemoveWed
     onclick="butRemoveWed_onclick()">
  <INPUT TYPE="button" VALUE="Add Wednesday" NAME=butAddWed
     onclick="butAddWed_onclick()">
  <BR>
  </FORM>
  </BODY>
  </HTML>
```

Save this as ch6_examp7.htm.

If you type the page in and load it into your browser, you should see the form below. Click the **Remove Wednesday** button and you'll see it disappear from the list. Add it back by clicking the **Add Wednesday** button. If you try and add a second Wednesday or remove a non-existent Wednesday, then you'll get a polite warning telling you that you can't do that.

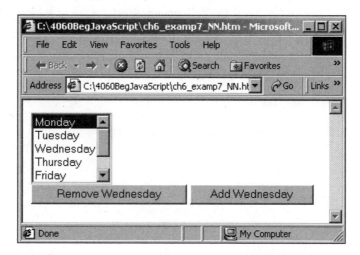

How It Works

Within the body of the page, we define a form with the name form1. This contains the select element containing day of the week options that we have seen above. The form also contains two buttons:

```
<INPUT TYPE="button" VALUE="Remove Wednesday" NAME=butRemoveWed
   onclick="butRemoveWed_onclick()">
<INPUT TYPE="button" VALUE="Add Wednesday" NAME=butAddWed
   onclick="butAddWed_onclick()">
```

Each of these buttons has its onclick event handler connected to some code that calls one of two functions: butRemoveWed_onclick() and butAddWed_onclick(). These functions are defined in a script block in the head of the page. We'll take a look at each of them in turn.

At the top of the page we have our first function, butRemoveWed_onclick(), which removes the Wednesday option.

```
function butRemoveWed_onclick()
{
    if (document.form1.theDay.options[2].text == "Wednesday")
    {
        document.form1.theDay.options[2] = null;
    }
    else
    {
        alert('There is no Wednesday here!');
    }
}
```

The first thing we do in the function is a sanity check: we must only try to remove the Wednesday option if it's there in the first place! We do this by seeing if the third option in the array, with index 2 because arrays start at index 0, has the text "Wednesday". If it does we can remove the Wednesday option by setting that particular option to null. If the third option in the array is not Wednesday, then we alert the user to the fact that there is no Wednesday to remove. Although I've used the text property in the if statement's condition, we could just have easily used the value property; it makes no difference.

Next we come to the butAddWed_onclick() function, which, as the name suggests, adds the Wednesday option.

This is slightly more complex than the code required to remove an option. First we use an if statement to check that there is not already a Wednesday option.

```
function butAddWed_onclick()
{
    if (document.form1.theDay.options[2].text != "Wednesday")
    {
        var indexCounter;
        var days = document.form1.theDay;
        var lastoption = new Option();
        days.options[6] = lastoption;

        for (indexCounter = 6;indexCounter > 2; indexCounter--)
        {
        days.options[indexCounter].text = days.options[indexCounter - 1].text;
        days.options[indexCounter].value = days.options[indexCounter - 1].value;
        }
```

If there is no Wednesday option, we then need to make space for the new Wednesday option to be inserted.

Before we do this we define two variables indexCounter and days, which refers to theDay select element and is a shorthand reference for our convenience. Next we create a new option with the variable name lastoption and assign this new option to the element at index position 6 in our options array. This previously had no contents. We next assign the text and value properties of all the Option objects from Thursday to Sunday to the Option that is at a one higher index in the options array, leaving a space in the options array at position 2 to put Wednesday in. This is the task for the for loop within the if statement.

Next, we create a new `Option` object by passing the text, `"Wednesday"` and the value 2 to the `Option` constructor. The `Option` object is then inserted into the `options[]` array at position 2, and hey presto it appears in our select box.

```
        var option = new Option("Wednesday",2);
        days.options[2] = option;
    }
```

We end the function by alerting the user to the fact that there is already a Wednesday option in the list, if the condition in the `if` statement is false.

```
    else
    {
        alert('Do you want to have TWO Wednesdays?????');
    }
}
```

Adding New Options with Internet Explorer

In IE there are many more additional properties, methods, and events associated with objects. In particular, the `options[]` array we are interested in has the additional `add()` and `remove()` methods, which add and remove options. These make life a little simpler.

Before we add an option, we need to create it. This is done in exactly the same way as before, using the new operator.

The `add()` method allows us to insert an `Option` object that we have created, and takes two parameters. We pass the option that we want to add as the first parameter. The optional second parameter allows us to specify which index position we want to add the option in. This won't overwrite any `Option` object already at that position, but simply moves the `Option` objects up the array to make space. This is basically the same as what we had to code into the `butAddWed_onclick()` function using our `for` loop.

Using the `add()` method, we can rewrite the `butAddWed_onclick()` function in our `ch6_examp7.htm` example to look like this:

```
    function butAddWed_onclick()
    {
        if (document.form1.theDay.options[2].text != "Wednesday")
        {
            var option = new Option("Wednesday",2);
            document.form1.theDay.options.add(option,2);
        }
        else
        {
            alert('Do you want to have TWO Wednesdays?????');
        }
    }
```

The `remove()` method takes just one parameter, namely the index of the option we want removed. When an option is removed, the options at higher index positions are moved down the array to fill the gap.

Using the `remove()` method, we can rewrite the `butRemoveWed_onclick()` function in our `ch6_examp7.htm` example to look like this:

```
function butRemoveWed_onclick()
{
    if (document.form1.theDay.options[2].text == "Wednesday")
    {
        document.form1.theDay.options.remove(2);
    }
    else
    {
        alert('There is no Wednesday here!');
    }
}
```

Modify the previous example and save it as `ch6_examp8_IE.htm`, before loading it into IE. You'll see that it works just as the previous version did.

Select Element Events

Select elements have three event handlers, `onblur`, `onfocus`, and `onchange`. We've seen all these events before. We saw the `onchange` event with the text box element, where it fired when focus was moved away from the text box *and* the value in the text box had changed. Here it fires when the user changes which option in the list is selected.

Try It Out – Using the Select Element for Date Difference Calculations

Let's take a look at an example that uses the `onchange` event and makes good use of the select element in its drop-down list form. Its purpose is to calculate the difference, in days, between two dates as set by the user via drop-down list boxes.

```
<HTML>
<HEAD>
<SCRIPT LANGUAGE=JavaScript>

function writeOptions(startNumber, endNumber)
{
  var optionCounter;
  for (optionCounter = startNumber; optionCounter <= endNumber; optionCounter++)
  {
      document.write('<OPTION value=' + optionCounter + '>' + optionCounter);
  }
}

function writeMonthOptions()
{
    var theMonth;
    var monthCounter;
    var theDate = new Date();

    for (monthCounter = 0; monthCounter < 12; monthCounter++)
    {
        theDate.setMonth(monthCounter);
        theMonth = theDate.toString();
```

```
            theMonth = theMonth.substr(4,3);
            document.write('<OPTION value=' + theMonth + '>' + theMonth);
        }
}

function recalcDateDiff()
{
    var myForm = document.form1;

        var firstDay = myForm.firstDay.options[myForm.firstDay.selectedIndex].value;
        var secondDay =
            myForm.secondDay.options[myForm.secondDay.selectedIndex].value;

        var firstMonth =
            myForm.firstMonth.options[myForm.firstMonth.selectedIndex].value;
        var secondMonth =
            myForm.secondMonth.options[myForm.secondMonth.selectedIndex].value;

        var firstYear =
            myForm.firstYear.options[myForm.firstYear.selectedIndex].value;
        var secondYear =
            myForm.secondYear.options[myForm.secondYear.selectedIndex].value;

        var firstDate = new Date(firstDay + " " + firstMonth + " " + firstYear);
        var secondDate = new Date(secondDay + " " + secondMonth + " " + secondYear);

        var daysDiff = (secondDate.valueOf() - firstDate.valueOf());
        daysDiff = Math.floor(Math.abs((((daysDiff  / 1000) / 60) / 60) / 24));
        myForm.txtDays.value = daysDiff;

        return true;
}

function window_onload()
{
    var theForm = document.form1;
    var nowDate = new Date();

    theForm.firstDay.options[nowDate.getDate() - 1].selected = true;
    theForm.secondDay.options[nowDate.getDate() - 1].selected = true;

    theForm.firstMonth.options[nowDate.getMonth()].selected = true;
    theForm.secondMonth.options[nowDate.getMonth()].selected = true;

    theForm.firstYear.options[nowDate.getFullYear()- 1970].selected = true;
    theForm.secondYear.options[nowDate.getFullYear() - 1970].selected = true;
}

</SCRIPT>
</HEAD>
<BODY LANGUAGE=JavaScript onload="return window_onload()">
```

221

```
<FORM NAME=form1>
<P>
First Date<BR>

<SELECT NAME=firstDay SIZE=1 onchange="return recalcDateDiff()">
<SCRIPT LANGUAGE=JavaScript>
    writeOptions(1,31);
</SCRIPT>
</SELECT>

<SELECT NAME=firstMonth SIZE=1 onchange="return recalcDateDiff()">
<SCRIPT LANGUAGE=JavaScript>
    writeMonthOptions();
</SCRIPT>
</SELECT>

<SELECT NAME=firstYear SIZE=1 onchange="return recalcDateDiff()">
<SCRIPT LANGUAGE=JavaScript>
    writeOptions(1970,2010);
</SCRIPT>
</SELECT>
</P>

<P>
Second Date<BR>

<SELECT NAME=secondDay SIZE=1 onchange="return recalcDateDiff()">
<SCRIPT LANGUAGE=JavaScript>
    writeOptions(1,31);
</SCRIPT>
</SELECT>

<SELECT NAME=secondMonth SIZE=1 onchange="return recalcDateDiff()">
<SCRIPT LANGUAGE=JavaScript>
    writeMonthOptions();
</SCRIPT>
</SELECT>

<SELECT NAME=secondYear SIZE=1 onchange="return recalcDateDiff()">
<SCRIPT LANGUAGE=JavaScript>
    writeOptions(1970,2010);
</SCRIPT>
</SELECT>
</P>

Total difference in days
<INPUT TYPE="text" NAME=txtDays VALUE=0>
<BR>
</FORM>

</BODY>
</HTML>
```

Call the example `ch6_examp9.htm` and load it into your web browser. You should see the form below, but with both date boxes set to the current date.

If you change any of the select boxes, then the difference between the days will be recalculated and shown in the text box.

How It Works

In the body of the page, the form in the web page is built up using six drop-down list boxes, and one text box. Let's look at an example of one of these select elements; take the first `<SELECT>` tag, the one that allows the user to choose the day part of the first date.

```
<SELECT NAME=firstDay SIZE=1 onchange="return recalcDateDiff()">
<SCRIPT LANGUAGE=JavaScript>
    writeOptions(1,31);
</SCRIPT>
</SELECT>
```

The `SIZE` attribute has been set to 1 so that we have a drop-down list box rather than a list box. The `onchange` event handler has been connected to the `recalcDateDiff()` function that we'll be looking at shortly.

However, there are no `<OPTION>` tags defined within the `<SELECT>` element. With all the options that the drop-down list boxes need to be populated with, I'd have to be one cruel person to make you type it all in! Instead we populate the options using the functions, which make use of the `document.write()` method.

The date and year options are populated using the `writeOptions()` function declared in the head of the page. The function is passed two values, the start number and the end number of the options that we want the select element to be populated with. Let's look at the `writeOptions()` function.

```
function writeOptions(startNumber, endNumber)
{
  var optionCounter;
  for (optionCounter = startNumber; optionCounter <= endNumber; optionCounter++)
  {
      document.write('<OPTION value=' + optionCounter + '>' + optionCounter);
  }
}
```

The function is actually quite simple, consisting of a `for` loop that loops from the first number (`startNumber`) through to the last (`endNumber`) using the variable `optionCounter`, and writes out the HTML necessary for each <OPTION> tag. The text for the option and the VALUE attribute of the <OPTION> tag are specified to be the value of the variable `optionCounter`. It's certainly a lot quicker than typing out the 31 <OPTION> tags necessary for the dates in a month.

You might wonder why the `document.write()` method is being used at all; why not use the methods of adding new options we saw before?

Firstly this way works with both IE and NN, so there is no need to write two separate bits of code. Secondly, adding new options to <SELECT> elements when the page is being loaded sometimes proves difficult in NN as a page refresh may be required before the changes take effect.

For the year select box the same function can be re-used. We just pass 1970 and 2010 as parameters to the `writeOptions()` function to populate the year select box.

```
<SELECT NAME=firstYear SIZE=1 onchange="return recalcDateDiff()">
<SCRIPT LANGUAGE=JavaScript>
   writeOptions(1970,2010);
</SCRIPT>
</SELECT>
```

To populate the month select box with the names of each month, a different function will be needed. However, the principle behind populating the <SELECT> element remains the same, using `document.write()`. The function in this case is `writeMonthOptions()` as you can see from the month select element below.

```
<SELECT NAME=firstMonth SIZE=1 onchange="return recalcDateDiff()">
<SCRIPT LANGUAGE=JavaScript>
   writeMonthOptions();
</SCRIPT>
</SELECT>
```

The new function, `writeMonthOptions()`, is defined in the head of the page. Let's take a look at it now. We start the function by defining three variables, and initializing the variable, `theDate`, to today's date.

```
function writeMonthOptions()
{
  var theMonth;
  var monthCounter;
  var theDate = new Date();
```

We use the Date object we have stored to get the months as text (Jan, Feb,... ,Dec). We get these months by setting the month in the theDate variable from 0 up to 11 using the setMonth() method in a for loop. Although the Date object does not provide a method for returning the date as anything other than a number, it does have the toString() method, which returns the value, as a string, of the date stored in the variable. It returns it in the format day of week, month, day of the month, time and finally year, for example Sat Feb 19 19:04:34 2000. We just need the month part. As we always know where it will be in the string and that its length is always 3, we can easily use the String object's substr() method to extract the month.

```
for (monthCounter = 0; monthCounter < 12; monthCounter++)
{
    theDate.setMonth(monthCounter);
    theMonth = theDate.toString();
    theMonth = theMonth.substr(4,3);
    document.write('<OPTION value=' + theMonth + '>' + theMonth);
}
}
```

Having got our month as a string of three characters, we can then create the <OPTION> tag and populate its text and value with the month.

For user convenience it would be nice on page load to set both of the dates in the select elements to today's date. This is what we do in the window_onload() function, which is connected to the window's onload event using the <BODY> tag:

```
<BODY LANGUAGE=JavaScript onload="return window_onload()">
```

The window_onload() function is defined in the head of the page. We start the function by setting the theForm variable to reference our Form object, as it shortens the reference needed in our code. Next we create a variable to hold a Date object to store today's date.

```
function window_onload()
{
    var theForm = document.form1;
    var nowDate = new Date();
```

Setting each of the <SELECT> box's initial values is easy; the value returned by the Date object nowDate can be modified to provide the required index of the options[] array. For the day, the correct index is simply the day of the month minus 1 – remember that arrays start at zero, so day 1 is actually at index 0. The selected property is set to true to make that day the currently selected option in the list.

```
theForm.firstDay.options[nowDate.getDate() - 1].selected = true;
theForm.secondDay.options[nowDate.getDate() - 1].selected = true;
```

The month is even easier as the getMonth() function returns a value from 0 to 11 for the month, which exactly matches the necessary index value for our options[] array.

```
theForm.firstMonth.options[nowDate.getMonth()].selected = true;
theForm.secondMonth.options[nowDate.getMonth()].selected = true;
```

For the year, because we are starting with 1970 as our first year, we need to take 1970 from the current year to get the correct index value.

```
    theForm.firstYear.options[nowDate.getFullYear() - 1970].selected = true;
    theForm.secondYear.options[nowDate.getFullYear() - 1970].selected = true;
}
```

The final part of our code that needs looking at is the function connected to the onchange event of each select element, namely the `recalcDateDiff()` function. Our first task in this function is to build up the two dates the user has selected using the drop down lists.

```
function recalcDateDiff()
{
  var myForm = document.form1;

  var firstDay = myForm.firstDay.options[myForm.firstDay.selectedIndex].value;
  var secondDay =
    myForm.secondDay.options[myForm.secondDay.selectedIndex].value;

  var firstMonth =
    myForm.firstMonth.options[myForm.firstMonth.selectedIndex].value;
  var secondMonth =
    myForm.secondMonth.options[myForm.secondMonth.selectedIndex].value;

  var firstYear =
    myForm.firstYear.options[myForm.firstYear.selectedIndex].value;
  var secondYear =
    myForm.secondYear.options[myForm.secondYear.selectedIndex].value;
```

We go through each select element and retrieve the value of the selected Option object. The selectedIndex property of the Select object provides the index we need to reference the selected Option object in the options[] array. For example in:

```
var firstDay = myForm.firstDay.options[myForm.firstDay.selectedIndex].value;
```

the index is provided by `myForm.firstDay.selectedIndex`. We then use that value inside the square brackets as the index value for the options[] array of the firstDay select element. This provides the reference to the selected Option object, whose value property we store in the variable firstDay.

We use this technique for all the remaining select elements.

We can then create new Date objects based on the values obtained from the select elements and store them in variables firstDate and secondDate.

```
    var firstDate = new Date(firstDay + " " + firstMonth + " " + firstYear);
    var secondDate = new Date(secondDay + " " + secondMonth + " " + secondYear);
```

Finally we need to calculate the difference in days between the two dates.

```
    var daysDiff = (secondDate.valueOf() - firstDate.valueOf());
    daysDiff = Math.floor(Math.abs((((daysDiff / 1000) / 60) / 60) / 24));
```

The `Date` object has a method, `valueOf()`, which returns the number of milliseconds from 1st Jan 1970 to the date stored in the `Date` object. We subtract the value of the `valueOf` property of `firstDate` from the value of the `valueOf` property of `secondDate` and store this in the variable `daysDiff`. At this point, it holds the difference between the two dates in milliseconds, so we convert this to days in the following line. By dividing by 1000 we make the value seconds, dividing by 60 makes this minutes, by 60 again makes it hours, and finally we divide by 24 to convert to our final figure of days difference. The `Math` object's `abs()` method makes negative numbers positive. The user may have set the first date to a later date than the second and as we just want to find the number of days difference, not find out which is the earlier day, we make any negative results positive. The `Math.floor()` method removes the fractional part of any result and returns just the integer part rounded down to the nearest whole number.

Finally we write the number of days difference to the `txtDays` text box in the page.

```
myForm.txtDays.value = daysDiff;

return true;
}
```

That completes our look at the more useful form elements available in web pages. The next section returns to the trivia quiz, where we can put our new found knowledge to good use and actually create a working quiz page.

The Trivia Quiz

It's time to return to the Trivia Quiz as we left it in Chapter 3. So far we have defined the questions and answers in arrays, and defined a function to check whether the user's answer is correct. Now we know how to create HTML forms and elements, we can start using them in the quiz to provide the user input. By the end of this section the question form will look like the picture below.

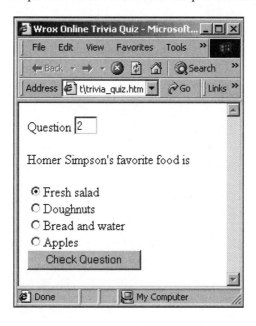

At present our questions are multi-choice; we represent the multi-choice options by a radio button group.

We create the form elements dynamically using our old friend `document.write()` and the information contained in the `questions` array. Once the user has selected the radio button representing the answer, they then click the **Check Question** button, which calls our `checkAnswer()` function, works out if the user got the question right, and lets them know. We then move on to the next question.

Let's start by creating the form elements.

Creating the Form

The first thing we need to do is add a form to our page in which the radio buttons will be written. Load in `trivia_quiz.htm` and change the bottom of the page, below where the questions and answers arrays are defined as follows:

```
// assign answer for question 3
answers[2] = "C";

</SCRIPT>

<FORM NAME="QuestionForm">

Question
<INPUT TYPE="text" NAME=txtQNumber SIZE=1>

<SCRIPT LANGUAGE=JavaScript>
   document.write(getQuestion());
</SCRIPT>

<INPUT TYPE="button" VALUE="Check Question" NAME=buttonCheckQ
   onclick="return buttonCheckQ_onclick()">
</FORM>

</BODY>
</HTML>
```

We're inserting the new form, named `QuestionForm`, inside the body of the page.

The elements on the form are a text box, defined by the line:

```
<INPUT TYPE="text" NAME=txtQNumber SIZE=1>
```

which will hold the current question number, and a button named `buttonCheck`:

```
<INPUT TYPE="button" VALUE="Check Question" NAME=buttonCheckQ
   onclick="return buttonCheckQ_onclick()">
```

which when clicked will check the answer supplied by the user and let them know if they got it correct or not. The button has its `onclick` event connected to a function, `buttonCheckQ_onclick()`, which we'll create in a moment.

Where are the radio buttons you can see in the picture above? Well, we'll be using the `document.write()` method again to dynamically insert the questions as the page is loaded. That way we can pick a random question each time from our question array. It's the code:

```
<SCRIPT LANGUAGE=JavaScript>
   document.write(getQuestion());
</SCRIPT>
```

that inserts the question using the second function we need to add, `getQuestion()`.

Creating the Answer Radio Buttons

We saw in the code above, that the radio buttons required will be inserted by the `getQuestion()` function, and the `buttonCheckQ_onclick()` function is connected to the button's `onclick` event handler. We'll now add these functions to the top of the page in the same script block as the `answerCorrect()` function that we defined in Chapter 3.

Add the following lines to the top of the `trivia_quiz.htm` page.

```
<HTML>
<HEAD>
<TITLE>Wrox Online Trivia Quiz</TITLE>

<SCRIPT LANGUAGE=JavaScript>

var questionNumber;

function answerCorrect(questionNumber, answer)
{
   // declare a variable to hold return value
   var correct = false;

   // if answer provided is same as answer then correct answer is true
   if (answer == answers[questionNumber])
      correct = true;

   // return whether the answer was correct (true or false)
   return correct;
}

function getQuestion()
{
   questionNumber = Math.floor(Math.random() * (questions.length));
   var questionHTML = "<P>" + questions[questionNumber][0] + "</P>";
   var questionLength = questions[questionNumber].length;
   var questionChoice;

   for (questionChoice = 1;questionChoice < questionLength;questionChoice++)
   {
      questionHTML = questionHTML + "<INPUT TYPE=radio NAME=radQuestionChoice"
      if (questionChoice == 1)
      {
```

```
            questionHTML = questionHTML + " CHECKED";
        }
        questionHTML = questionHTML + ">";
        questionHTML = questionHTML + questions[questionNumber][questionChoice];
        questionHTML = questionHTML + "<BR>";
    }

    document.QuestionForm.txtQNumber.value = questionNumber + 1;
    return questionHTML;
}

function buttonCheckQ_onclick()
{
    var answer = 0;

    while (document.QuestionForm.radQuestionChoice[answer].checked != true)
    {
        answer++;
    }

    answer = String.fromCharCode(65 + answer);

    if (answerCorrect(questionNumber,answer) == true)
    {
        alert("You got it right");
    }
    else
    {
        alert("You got it wrong");
    }

    window.location.reload();
}
```

```
</SCRIPT>
</HEAD>
<BODY>
```

We will discuss the getQuestion() function first, which is used to build up the HTML needed to display the question to the user. We first want to select a random question from our questions array, so we need to generate a random number, which will provide the index for the question. We store this number in the global variable questionNumber that we declared at the top of the script block.

```
function getQuestion()
{
    questionNumber = Math.floor(Math.random() * (questions.length));
```

We generate a random number between 0 and 1 using the Math.random() method, and then multiply that by the number of questions in the questions array. This number is converted to an integer using the Math object's floor() method, which returns the lowest integer part of a floating point number. This is exactly what we want here: a randomly selected number from 0 to questions.length - 1. Don't forget that arrays start at an index of 0.

Our next task is to create the radio buttons, which allow the user to answer the question. We do this by building up the HTML that needs to be written to the page inside the variable questionHTML. We can then display the question using just one document.write(), which writes the whole question out in one go.

We start this process by declaring the questionHTML variable and setting it to the HTML needed to write the actual question to the page. This information is stored in the first index position of the second dimension of our questions array, that is questions[questionNumber][0], where questionNumber is the random index we generated before.

```
var questionHTML = "<P>" + questions[questionNumber][0] + "</P>";
var questionLength = questions[questionNumber].length;
var questionChoice;
```

To create the possible answers for the user to select from, we need to know how many radio buttons are required, information that's stored in the length property of the second dimension of our questions array. Remember that the second dimension is really just an Array object stored in a particular position of our questions array and Array objects have a length property. We use the variable questionLength to store the length of the array, and also declare another variable, questionChoice, which we will use to loop through our array.

Now we can start looping through the question options and build up the radio button group. We do this in the next for loop. If it's the first radio button that we are creating the HTML for, then we add the CHECKED word to the <INPUT> tag. We do this to ensure that one of the radio buttons is checked, just in case the user tries to press the Check Answer button without actually providing one first.

```
for (questionChoice = 1;questionChoice < questionLength;questionChoice++)
{
    questionHTML = questionHTML + "<INPUT TYPE=radio NAME=radQuestionChoice"
    if (questionChoice == 1)
    {
        questionHTML = questionHTML + " CHECKED";
    {
    questionHTML = questionHTML + ">";
    questionHTML = questionHTML + questions[questionNumber][questionChoice];
    questionHTML = questionHTML + "<BR>";
}
```

For example, on one loop of the for loop, the HTML built up in questionHTML may be:

```
<INPUT TYPE=radio NAME=radQuestionChoice CHECKED> A sixties rock group from
Liverpool<BR>
```

With the looping finished and questionHTML containing the complete HTML needed to display one question, all that remains to do is to display the question number for the current question in the text box in the form, and then return the questionHTML string to the calling code. We use questionNumber + 1 as the question number purely for user friendliness. Even though it might be a question at index 0, most people think of starting at question 1 not question 0.

```
        document.QuestionForm.txtQNumber.value = questionNumber + 1;
        return questionHTML;
    }
```

That completes the getQuestion() function. The final new code that needs looking at is the buttonCheckQ_onclick() function that fires when the button is clicked. We saw this added to our code above.

We start the function by declaring the variable answer and initializing it to 0. We'll be using this as the index when looping through the radio button group, and also to hold the actual answer.

```
function buttonCheckQ_onclick()
{
    var answer = 0;
```

The then use a while statement to loop through each of the radio buttons, incrementing the answer variable until it hits upon a radio button which is checked. At which point the loop ends and we now know which radio button the user chose as their answer, namely that at the index stored in the answer variable.

```
    while (document.QuestionForm.radQuestionChoice[answer].checked != true)
    {
        answer++;
    }
```

As our answers array holds the answers as A, B, C, D and so on, we need to convert the radio button index contained in answer into a character. We do this in the next line:

```
    answer = String.fromCharCode(65 + answer);
```

This makes use of the fact that character code for A is 65, so if the user choose the first radio button, that is the one with an index of 0, we just need to add 65 and the index number contained in answer to get the answer's character code. This is converted to a character using the String object's fromCharCode() method. Remember that some methods of the String object can be used without having to actually create a String object ourselves (called static methods); we can use the native String object which is always present.

The answerCorrect() function we created in Chapter 3 is then used as part of an if statement. We pass the question number and the answer character to the function, and it returns true if the answer was correct. If it does return true, then we show a message box telling the user that they got the question right, otherwise the else statement lets them know that they got it wrong

```
    if (answerCorrect(questionNumber,answer) == true)
    {
        alert("You got it right");
    }
    else
    {
        alert("You got it wrong");
    }
```

Finally, we reload the page to select another random question.

```
      window.location.reload();
 }
```

In the next chapter we'll be making the Trivia Quiz a more sophisticated multi-frame based application, also adding necessary features like making sure the user doesn't get the same question twice!!!

Summary

In this chapter we looked at how to add a user interface onto our JavaScript so that we can interact with our user and acquire information from them. Let's look at some of the things discussed in this chapter.

❑ The HTML form is where we place elements making up the interface in a page.

❑ Each HTML form groups together a set of HTML elements. When a form is submitted to a server for processing, all the data in that form is sent to the server. We can have multiple forms on a page, but only the information in one form can be sent to the server.

❑ A form is created using the opening tag <FORM> and ended with a close tag </FORM>. All the elements we want included in that form are placed in between the open and close <FORM> tags. The <FORM> tag has various attributes – for client-side scripting the NAME attribute is the important one. We can access forms with either their NAME attribute or ID attribute.

❑ Each <FORM> element creates a Form object, which is contained within the document object. To access a form named myForm we write document.myForm. The document object also has a forms[] property which is an array containing every form inside the document. The first form in the page is document.forms[0], the second is document.forms[1], and so on. Using the length property of an Array object, document.forms.length tells us how many forms there are on the page.

❑ Having discussed forms, we then went on to look at the different types of HTML elements available that can be placed inside forms, how to create them, and how they are used in JavaScript.

❑ The objects associated with the form elements have a number of properties, methods, and events that are common to them all. They all have the name property, which we can use to reference them in our JavaScript. They also all have the form property that provides a reference to the Form object that element is contained inside. The type property returns a text string telling us what type of element this is; types include text, button, and radio.

❑ We also saw that the methods focus() and blur(), and the events onfocus and onblur, are available to every form element object. Such an element is said to receive the focus when it becomes the active element in the form, either because the user has selected that element or because we used the focus() method. However an element got the focus, its onfocus event will fire. When another element is set as the currently active element the previous element is said to lose its focus, or to blur. Again loss of focus can be the result of the user selecting another element or the use of the blur() method; either way when it happens the onblur event fires. We saw that onfocus and onblur can, if used carefully, be a good place to check things like the validity of data entered by a user into an element.

❏ All elements return a value, which is the string data assigned to that element. The meaning of the value depends on the element; for a text box it is the value inside the text box and for a button it's the text displayed on its face.

❏ Having discussed the common features of elements we then looked at each of the more commonly used elements in turn, starting with the button element.

❏ The button element's purpose in life is to be clicked by the user, where that clicking fires some script we have written. We can capture the clicking by connecting to the button's onclick event. A button is created using the <INPUT> tag with the TYPE attribute set to button. The VALUE attribute determines what text appears on the button's face. Two variations on a button are the submit and reset buttons. As well as acting as buttons, they also provide a special service not linked to code. The submit button will automatically submit the form to the server. The reset button clears the form back to its default state when loaded in the page.

❏ The text element allows the user to enter a single line of plain text. A text box is created using the <INPUT> tag, with the TYPE attribute set to text. We can set how many characters the user can enter and how wide the text box is with the MAXLENGTH and SIZE attributes of the <INPUT> tag. The text box has the associated object called Text, which has the additional events onselect and onchange. The onselect event fires when the user selects text in the box, and the more useful onchange event fires when the element loses focus and its contents have changed since the element gained the focus. The onchange event is a good place to do validation of what the user has just entered. If they entered illegal values, such as letters when we wanted numbers, then we can let the user know and send them back to correct their mistake. A variation on the text box is the password box, which is almost identical to the textbox except the values typed into it are hidden and shown as an asterisk. Additionally the text box also has the onkeydown, onkeypress, and onkeyup events

❏ The next element we looked at was the textarea, which is similar to the text box except it allows multiple lines of text to be entered. This element is created with the open tag <TEXTAREA> and closed with the </TEXTAREA> tag, the width and height in characters of the text box being determined by the COLS and ROWS attributes. Whether the textarea wraps text that reaches the end of a line and whether that wrapping is sent when the contents are posted to the server is determined by the WRAP attribute. If left off, or set to off, then no wrapping occurs; if set to soft it causes wrapping client-side, but it's not sent to the server when the form is sent; if set to hard it causes wrapping client-side and for that to be sent to the server. The associated Textarea object has virtually the same properties, methods and events as a Text object.

❏ We then looked at the checkbox and radio button elements together. Essentially they are the same type of element except that the radio button is a grouped element. By this I mean that only one in a group can be checked at once. Checking another one causes the previously checked button to be unchecked. Both elements are created with the <INPUT> tag, the TYPE attribute being checkbox or radio. If CHECKED is put inside the <INPUT> tag, then that element will be checked when the page is loaded. Creating radio buttons with the same name creates a radio button group. The name of a radio button actually refers to an array, each element within which is a radio button defined on the form to be within that group. These elements have associated objects called Checkbox and Radio. Using the checked property of these objects, we can find out whether a checkbox or radio button is currently checked. Both objects also have the onclick event in addition to the common events, onfocus and onblur.

❑ Next in our look at elements were the drop-down list and list boxes, both in fact actually the select element. The <SELECT> tag creates these elements, the SIZE attribute determining how many list items are visible at once. If a SIZE of 1 is given, then a drop-down box rather than list box is created. Each item in a select element is defined by the <OPTION> tag, or added to later using the Select object's options[] array property, which is an array containing each Option object for that element. However, adding options after the page is loaded is different for Netscape and Microsoft browsers. The Select object's selectedIndex property tells us which option is selected; we can then use that value to access that option in the options[] array and use the Option object's value property. The Option object also has the text and index properties, text being the displayed text in the list and the index being its position in the Select object's options[] array property. We can loop through the options[] array, finding out its length from the Select object's length property. The Select object has the onchange event which fires when the user selects another item from the list.

❑ Finally we added a basic user interface to the Trivia Quiz. Now questions are created dynamically with the document.write() method and the user can select their answer from a group of radio buttons.

In the next chapter we'll be looking at how, once you have created a frameset in a page, you can access code and variables between frames. We'll also look at how to open new windows using JavaScript and methods of manipulating them once they are open. We'll see the trivia quiz become a frame based application.

Exercises

Suggested solutions to these questions can be found in Appendix A.

Question 1

Using the code from the temperature converter example we saw in Chapter 2, create a user interface for it and connect it to the existing code so that the user can enter a value in degrees Fahrenheit and convert it to centigrade.

Question2

Create a user interface that allows the user to pick the computer system of their dreams, similar in principle to the e-commerce sites selling computers over the Internet. For example, they could be given a choice of processor type, speed, memory, hard drive size, and the option to add additional components like DVD-ROM drives, sound cards, and so on. As the user changes the selection the price of the system should update automatically and notify the user of the cost of the system as they have specified it either by using an alert box or updating the contents of a text box.

Online discussion at http://p2p.wrox.com

Windows and Frames

Until now, the pages we have been looking at have just been single pages. However, many web applications make use of frames to split up the browser's window, much as panes of glass split up a real window. It's quite possible that you'll want to build web sites which make use of such frames and the good news is that JavaScript allows you not only to manipulate the various frame's objects and their methods and properties, but also to use functions and variables defined in one frame in another frame. We'll start this chapter by looking at how we can script across such frames.

Apart from having a frames based website there are a number of other good reasons for wanting to access variables and functions in another frame. Two important reasons are making your code **modular** and having the ability to maintain information between pages.

What do we mean by **modular**? In other programming languages, like Visual Basic, you can create a module, that is an area to hold general functions and variables, and reuse it from different places in your program. Well, when using frames we can put all of our general functions and variables into one area, such as the top frame, which we can think of as our code module. Then we can call the functions repeatedly from different pages and different frames.

If we put the general functions and variables in a page that defines the frames that it contains (that is, a frameset defining page), then if we need to make changes to the pages inside the frames, any variables defined in the frameset page will retain their value. This provides a very useful way of holding information even when the user is navigating our web site. A further advantage is that any functions defined in the frameset defining page can be called by subsequent pages and only have to be loaded into the browser once, making our page's loading faster.

The second subject of this chapter is how you can open up and manipulate new browser windows. There are plenty of good uses for new windows, for example you may wish to open up an 'external' web site in a new window from your web site, but leave your web site still open for the user. Perhaps even more useful is using small windows as dialog boxes, which you can use to obtain information from the user. Just as you can script between frames, you can do similar things between certain windows. We'll find out how later in the chapter, but let's start by looking at scripting between frames.

Frames and the window Object

Frames are a way of splitting up the browser window into various panes, into which we can then load different HTML documents. The frames are defined in a frameset defining page by the <FRAMESET> and <FRAME> tags. The <FRAMSET> tag is used to contain the <FRAME> tags, and specifies how the frames should look on the page. The <FRAME> tags are then used to specify each frame and to include the required documents in the page.

We saw in Chapter 5 that the window object represents the browser's frame onto your page or document. If you have a page with no frames then there will be just one window object. However, if you have more than one frame, then for each frame there will be one window object. Except for the very top-level window of a frameset, each window object is contained inside another.

The easiest way to demonstrate this is through an example in which we create three frames, a top frame with two frames inside it.

Try It Out – Multiple Frames

For this multi-frame example, we'll need to create three HTML files. The first is the frameset defining page:

```
<HTML>
<FRAMESET ROWS="50%,*" ID=TopWindow>
    <FRAME NAME="UpperWindow" SRC="UpperWindow.htm">
    <FRAME NAME="LowerWindow" SRC="LowerWindow.htm">
</FRAMESET>
</HTML>
```

Save this as TopWindow.htm. Note that the SRC attributes for the two <FRAME> tags in this page are UpperWindow.htm and LowerWindow.htm. We will create these next:

```
<HTML>
<HEAD>
<SCRIPT LANGUAGE=JavaScript>

function window_onload()
{
    alert("The name of the upper frame's window object is " + window.name);
    alert("The location of UpperWindow's parent is " +
        window.parent.location.href);
}

</SCRIPT>
</HEAD>
<BODY LANGUAGE=JavaScript onload="return window_onload()">

<P>Upper Frame</P>

</BODY>
</HTML>
```

This page is the source page for the top frame with the name `UpperWindow` and needs to be saved as `UpperWindow.htm`. The final page is very similar to this:

```
<HTML>
<HEAD>
<SCRIPT LANGUAGE=JavaScript>

function window_onload()
{
    alert("The name of the lower frame's window object is " + window.name);
    alert("The location of LowerWindow's parent is " +
        window.parent.location.href);
}

</SCRIPT>
</HEAD>
<BODY LANGUAGE=JavaScript onload="return window_onload()">

<P>Lower Frame</P>

</BODY>
</HTML>
```

This is the source page for the lower frame; save it as `LowerWindow.htm`.

These three pages fit together so that `UpperWindow.htm` and `LowerWindow.htm` are contained within the `TopWindow.htm` page.

When loaded into the browser, we have three window objects. One is the **parent** window object, and contains the file `TopWindow.htm`, and two are **child** window objects, containing the files `UpperWindow.htm` and `LowerWindow.htm`. The two child window objects are contained within the parent window, as shown in the diagram below:

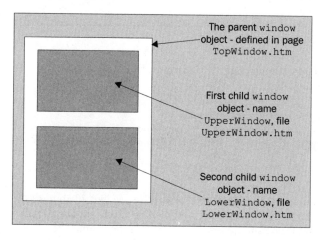

If any of the frames had frames contained inside them, then these would have window objects that were children of the window object of that frame.

When you load `TopWindow.htm` into your browser, you'll see a series of four message boxes. These are making use of the `window` object's properties to gain information and demonstrate the `window` object's place in the hierarchy.

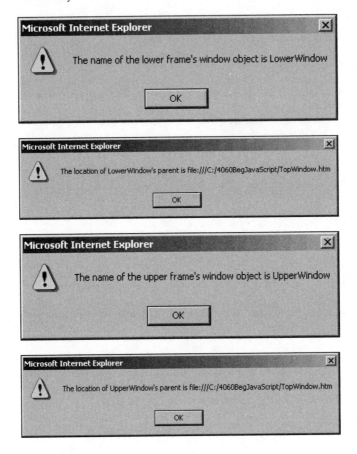

How It Works

Lets look at the frameset defining page, `TopWindow.htm`, first:

```
<HTML>
<FRAMESET ROWS="50%,*" ID=TopWindow>
    <FRAME NAME="UpperWindow" SRC="UpperWindow.htm">
    <FRAME NAME="LowerWindow" SRC="LowerWindow.htm">
</FRAMESET>
</HTML>
```

The frameset is defined using the `<FRAMESET>` tag. We use two attributes `ROWS` and `ID`. The `ROWS` attribute takes the value `"50%,*"` meaning that the first frame should take up half of the length of the window, and the second frame should take up the rest of the room. The `ID` attribute is used to give a name that we can use to reference the page.

The two child windows are created using <FRAME> tags. In each of the <FRAME> tags, we specify a NAME by which the window objects will be known and the SRC attribute of the page that will be loaded into the newly created windows and will form the basis of the document object that each window object contains.

Let's take a look at the UpperWindow.htm file next. In the <BODY> tag of the page, we attach a function window_onload() to the window object's onload event handler. This event handler is called when the browser has finished loading the window, the document inside the window, and all the objects within the document. It's a very useful place to put initialization code or code that needs to change things once the page has loaded, but before control passes back to the user.

```
<BODY LANGUAGE=JavaScript onload="return window_onload()">
```

This function is defined in a script block in the head of the page:

```
function window_onload()
{
    alert("The name of the upper frame's window object is " + window.name);
    alert("The location of UpperWindow's parent is " +
        window.parent.location.href);
}
```

The window_onload() function makes use of two properties of the window object for the frame that the page is loaded in: its name and parent properties. The name property is self-explanatory – it's the name we defined in the frameset page. In this case, the name is UpperWindow.

The second property, the parent property, is very useful. It gives you access to the window object of the frame's parent. This means you can access all of the parent window object's properties and methods. Through these, you can access the document within the parent window as well as any other frames defined by the parent. Here, we display a message box giving details of the parent frame's filename by using the href property of the location object (which itself is a property of the window object).

The code for LowerWindow.htm is identical to the UpperWindow.htm, but with different results because it's a different window object that we are accessing. The name of the window object this time is LowerWindow. However, it shares the same parent window as UpperWindow and so when we access the parent property of the window object, we get a reference to the same window object as we did in UpperWindow. The message box proves this as the filename, or href property, it gives is identical to UpperWindow's parent's filename.

If you load the example in Internet Explorer, and then load it into Netscape browser, you may notice a very important difference and one which highlights the often subtle ways that browsers are incompatible. In IE, the message boxes for the LowerWindow object may appear first meaning that the onload event handler of that window has fired before the onload event handler of the UpperWindow. However, in Netscape it's the other way round; the UpperWindow object's onload event handler fires first and then the LowerWindow object's event handler. This may not be important here, but there will be times when the order that events fire in is important and affects the working of your code. It's an incompatibility that's worth noting and watching out for in your own programs.

Coding Between Frames

We've seen above that each frame exists as a different window and gets its own `window` object. In addition, we saw that we can access the `window` object of a frameset defining page from any of the frame pages it specifies, by using the `window` object's `parent` property. Having got a reference to the parent window's `window` object, we can access its properties and methods in the same way we access the `window` object of the current page. In addition, we have access to all the JavaScript variables and functions defined in that page.

Try It Out – Using the Frameset Page as a Module

Let's look at a more complex example, where we use the top frame to keep track of pages as the user navigates the web site. We're creating five pages in this example, but don't panic, as four of the pages are almost identical. The first page that needs creating is the frameset defining page:

```
<HTML>
<HEAD>

<TITLE>The Unchanging frameset page</TITLE>
<SCRIPT Language=JavaScript>

var pagesVisited = new Array();

function returnPagesVisited()
{
    var returnValue = "So far you have visited the following pages\n";
    var pageVisitedIndex;
    var numberOfPagesVisited = pagesVisited.length;
    for (pageVisitedIndex = 0; pageVisitedIndex < numberOfPagesVisited;
        pageVisitedIndex++)
    {
        returnValue = returnValue + pagesVisited[pageVisitedIndex] + "\n";
    }

    return returnValue;
}

function addPage(fileName)
{
    var fileNameStart = fileName.lastIndexOf("/") + 1;
    fileName = fileName.substr(fileNameStart);
    pagesVisited[pagesVisited.length] = fileName;

    return true;
}

</SCRIPT>

</HEAD>
<FRAMESET COLS="50%,*">
    <FRAME NAME=fraLeft SRC="page_a.htm">
    <FRAME NAME=fraRight SRC="page_b.htm">
</FRAMESET>
</HTML>
```

Save this page as `frameset_page.htm`.

Notice that the two frames have the SRC attributes initialized as page_a.htm and page_b.htm. However, we also need to create page_c.htm and page_d.htm since we will be allowing the user to choose the page loaded into each frame from these four pages. We'll create the page_a.htm page first:

```
<HTML>
<HEAD>

<SCRIPT LANGUAGE=JavaScript>

function butShowVisited_onclick()
{
    document.form1.txtaPagesVisited.value = window.parent.returnPagesVisited();
}

</SCRIPT>
</HEAD>
<BODY onload="window.parent.addPage(window.location.href);">

<CENTER>
    <FONT SIZE=6 COLOR=MidnightBlue FACE=verdana>
       This is Page A
    </FONT>
</CENTER>
<P>
<A HREF="page_a.htm">Page A</A>
<A HREF="page_b.htm">Page B</A>
<A HREF="page_c.htm">Page C</A>
<A HREF="page_d.htm">Page D</A>
</P>

<FORM NAME=form1>
<TEXTAREA ROWS=10 COLS=35 NAME=txtaPagesVisited WRAP=hard>
</TEXTAREA>
<BR>
<INPUT TYPE="button" VALUE="List Pages Visited" NAME=butShowVisited
    onclick="butShowVisited_onclick()">
</FORM>
</BODY>
</HTML>
```

Save this page as page_a.htm.

The other three pages are identical to page_a.htm, except for one line, so you can just cut and paste the text from page_a.htm. Change the HTML that displays the name of the page loaded to:

```
<CENTER>
    <FONT SIZE=6 COLOR=MidnightBlue FACE=verdana>
       This is Page B
    </FONT>
</CENTER>
```

Then save this as page_b.htm.

Do the same again, to create the third page (page C):

```
<CENTER>
    <FONT SIZE=6 COLOR=MidnightBlue FACE=verdana>
        This is Page C
    </FONT>
</CENTER>
```

Save this as page_c.htm.

The final page is again a copy of page_a.htm except for the lines:

```
<CENTER>
    <FONT SIZE=6 COLOR=MidnightBlue FACE=verdana>
        This is Page D
    </FONT>
</CENTER>
```

Save this as page_d.htm.

Load frameset_page.htm into your browser. Then click the **List Pages Visited** button on Page A in the left hand frame, and you should see a screen similar to the one below.

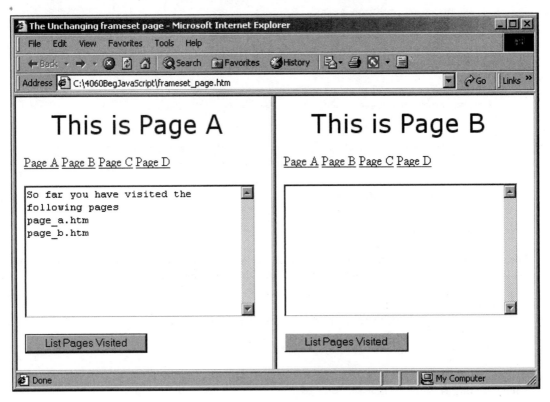

Click the links in either frame to navigate the page to a new location. For example, click the **Page C** link in the right frame, then the **Page D** link in the left frame, then click the left frame's **List Pages Visited** button and you'll see page_c.htm and page_d.htm have been added to the list.

Normally when a new page is loaded any variables and their values in the previous page are lost, but with framesets it does not matter which page is loaded into each frame – the top frame remains loaded and its variables keep their values. What we are seeing in this example is that, regardless of which page is loaded in each frame, some global variable in the top frame is keeping track of the pages that have been viewed and the top frame's variables and functions can be accessed by any page loaded into either the left or right frames.

How It Works

Let's first look at the JavaScript in frameset_page.htm, which is the frameset defining page. The head of the page contains a script block. The first thing we do in this script block is to declare the variable pagesVisited and set it to reference a new Array object. In the array, we'll be storing the filename of each page visited as the user navigates the site.

```
var pagesVisited = new Array();
```

We then have two functions. The first of the two functions, returnPagesVisited(), does what its name suggests – it returns a string containing a message and a list of each of the pages visited. It does this by looping through the pagesVisited array, building up the message string inside the variable returnValue, which is then returned to the calling function:

```
function returnPagesVisited()
{
    var returnValue = "So far you have visited the following pages\n";
    var pageVisitedIndex;
    var numberOfPagesVisited = pagesVisited.length;
    for (pageVisitedIndex = 0; pageVisitedIndex < numberOfPagesVisited;
        pageVisitedIndex++)
    {
        returnValue = returnValue + pagesVisited[pageVisitedIndex] + "\n";
    }

    return returnValue;
}
```

The second function, addPage(), adds the name of a page to the pagesVisited array:

```
function addPage(fileName)
{
    var fileNameStart = fileName.lastIndexOf("/") + 1;
    fileName = fileName.substr(fileNameStart);
    pagesVisited[pagesVisited.length] = fileName;

    return true;
}
```

The `fileName` parameter passed to this function is the full filename and path of the visited page, so we need to strip out the path to leave us with just the filename. The format of the string will be something like `file:///D:/myDirectory/page_b.htm` and we need just the bit after the last `/` character. So in the first line of code we find the position of that character and add one to it as we want to start at the next character.

Then using the `substr()` method of the `String` object in the following line, we extract everything from character position `fileNameStart` right up to the end of the string. Remember that the `substr()` method takes two parameters, namely the starting character we want, and the length of the string we want to extract, but if the second parameter is missing then all characters from the start position to the end are extracted.

We then add the filename into the array, the `length` property of the array providing the next free index position.

We'll now turn to look collectively at the frame pages, namely `page_a.htm`, `page_b.htm`, `page_c.htm`, and `page_d.htm`. In each of these pages, we create a form called `form1`:

```
<FORM NAME=form1>
<TEXTAREA ROWS=10 COLS=35 NAME=txtaPagesVisited WRAP=hard>
</TEXTAREA>
<BR>
<INPUT TYPE="button" VALUE="List Pages Visited" NAME=butShowVisited
   onclick="butShowVisited_onclick()">
</FORM>
```

This contains the `textarea` control that will display the list of pages visited, and a button the user can click to populate the `textarea`.

When one of these pages is loaded, its name is put into the `pagesVisited` array defined in `frameset_page.htm` by connecting the `window` object's `onload` event handler to the `addPage()` function that we also created in `frameset_page.htm`. We connect the code to the event handler in the `<BODY>` tag of the page:

```
<BODY onload="window.parent.addPage(window.location.href);">
```

Recall that all the functions we declare in a page are contained, like everything else in a page, inside the `window` object for that page, but because the `window` object is a global object, we don't need to prefix the name of our variables or functions with `window`.

However, this time the function is not in the current page, but in the `frameset_page.htm` page. The `window` containing this page is the parent `window` to the `window` containing the current page. We need, therefore, to refer to the parent frame's `window` object using the `window` object's `parent` property. The code `window.parent` gives us a reference to the `window` object of `frameset_page.htm`. With this reference, we can now access the variables and functions contained in `frameset_page.htm`. Having stated which `window` object we are referencing, we just add the name of the function we are calling, in this instance the `addPage()` function. We pass this function the `location.href` string, which contains the full path and filename of the page, as the value for its one parameter.

As we saw above, the button on the page has its `onclick` event handler connected to a function called `butShowVisited_onclick()`. This is defined in the head of the page:

```
function butShowVisited_onclick()
{
    document.form1.txtaPagesVisited.value = window.parent.returnPagesVisited();
}
```

In this function we call the parent `window` object's `returnPagesVisited()` function, which, as we saw earlier, returns a string containing a list of pages visited. The `value` property of the `Textarea` object is set to this text.

That completes our look at the code in the frame pages and, as you can see, there's not much of it because we have placed all the general functions in the frameset page. Not only does this code reuse make for less typing, but it also means that all your functions are in one place. If there is a bug in a function, then fixing the bug fixes it not just for one page but also for all pages that use it. Of course, it only makes sense to put general functions in one place; functions that are specific to a page and are never used again outside it are best kept in that page.

Code Access between Frames

We've just seen how a child window can access its parent window's variables and functions, but how can frames inside a frameset access each other?

We saw a simple example earlier in this chapter of how to do this, so this time let's look at a much more complex example. Once created our page will look like this:

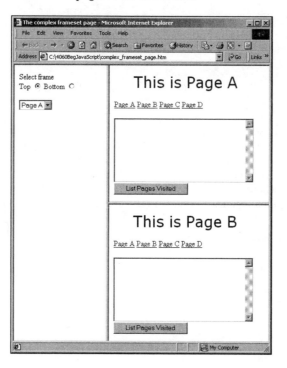

A diagram of the frame layout is shown below. The text labels indicate the names that each frame has been given in the <FRAMESET> and <FRAME> tags, with the exception of the top frame, which is simply the window at the top of the frameset hierarchy.

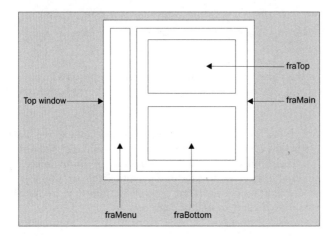

The easiest way to think of the hierarchy of such a frames-based web page is similar to how you would think of family relationships which can be shown in a family tree diagram. If we represent our frameset like that, it looks something like the diagram below:

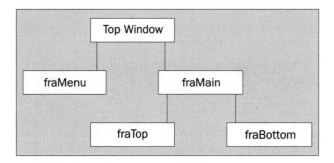

From the diagram we can see that fraBottom, the right-hand frame's bottom frame, has a parent frame called fraMain, which itself has a parent, the top window. Therefore, if we wanted to access a function in the top window from the fraBottom window, we would need to access fraBottom's parent's parent's window object. We know that the window object has the parent property, which is a reference to the parent window of that window object. So, let's use that and create the code to access a function, for example called myFunction(), in the top window:

```
window.parent.parent.myFunction();
```

Let's break this down. First:

```
window.parent
```

gets us a reference to the parent `window` object of the window the code is running in. The code is in `fraBottom`, so `window.parent` will be `fraMain`. However, we want the top window, which is `fraMain`'s parent, so we add to the above code to make:

```
window.parent.parent
```

Now we have a reference to the top window. Finally, we call `myFunction()` by adding that to the end of the expression:

```
window.parent.parent.myFunction();
```

What if we wanted to access the `window` object of `fraMenu` from code in `fraBottom`? Well, we have most of the code we need already. We saw that `window.parent.parent` gives us the top window, so now we just want that window's child `window` object called `fraMenu`. There are three ways of doing this, all with identical results.

We could use its index in the `frames[]` array property of the `window` object:

```
window.parent.parent.frames[0]
```

Alternatively, we could use its name in the `frames[]` array:

```
window.parent.parent.frames["fraMenu"]
```

Finally, we can reference it directly by using its name as we can with any `window` object:

```
window.parent.parent.fraMenu
```

The third method is the easiest unless you have a situation where you don't know the name of a frame and need to access it by its index value in the `frames[]` array, or perhaps where you are looping through each child frame in turn.

As `window.parent.parent.fraMenu` gets us a reference to the `window` object associated with `fraMenu`, to access a function `myFunction()` or variable `myVariable` we would just type:

```
window.parent.parent.fraMenu.myFunction
```

or:

```
window.parent.parent.fraMenu.myVariable.
```

What about the situation where we want to access not a function or variable in a page within a frame, but a control on a form or even the links on that page? Well, let's imagine we want to access a control named `myControl`, on a form called `myForm` in the `fraMenu` page from the `fraBottom` page.

We found that `window.parent.parent.fraMenu` gives us the reference to `fraMenu`'s `window` object from `fraBottom`, but how do we reference a form there?

249

Basically, it's the same as the situation where we access a form from the inside of the same page as the script, except that we need to reference not the `window` object of that page but the `window` object of `fraMenu`, the page we're interested in.

Normally, we write `document.myForm.myControl.value`, with `window` being assumed since it is the global object. Strictly speaking, it's `window.document.myForm.myControl.value`.

Now we're accessing another window we just reference the window we want and then use the same code, so we need:

```
window.parent.parent.fraMenu.document.myForm.myControl.value
```

if we want to access the `value` property of `myControl` from `fraBottom`. As you can see references to other frames can get pretty long and in this situation it's a very good idea to store the reference in a variable. For example, if we are accessing `myForm` a number of times we could write:

```
var myFormRef = window.parent.parent.fraMenu.document.myForm;
```

so that now we can write:

```
myFormRef.myControl.value;
```

rather than:

```
window.parent.parent.fraMenu.document.myForm.myControl.value;
```

The top Property

Using the `parent` property can get a little tedious when you want to access the very top window from a frame quite low down in the hierarchy of frames and `window` objects. An alternative is the `window` object's `top` property. This returns a reference to the `window` object of the very top window in a frame hierarchy. In our example, this is top window.

For example, in the example we just saw:

```
window.parent.parent.fraMenu.document.myForm.myControl.value;
```

could be written as:

```
window.top.fraMenu.document.myForm.myControl.value;
```

although, because the `window` is a global object, we could shorten that to just:

```
top.fraMenu.document.myForm.myControl.value;
```

So when should you use `top` rather than `parent` or vice versa?

There are advantages and disadvantages to both properties. The `parent` property allows you to specify `window` objects relative to the current `window`. The `window` above this `window` is `window.parent`, its parent is `window.parent.parent`, and so on. The `top` property is much more generic; `top` is always the very top `window` regardless of the frameset layout being used. There will always be a `top`, but there's not necessarily going to always be a `parent.parent`. If you put all your global functions and variables that you want accessible from any page in the frameset in the very top window, then `window.top` will always be valid regardless of changes to framesets beneath it, whereas using the `parent` property is dependant on the frameset structure above it. However, if someone else loads your web site inside a frameset page of their own, then suddenly the `top` window is not yours but theirs, and `window.top` is no longer valid. You can't win, or can you?

One trick is to check to see that the `top` window contains your page, if not then reload the `top` page again and specify that your `top` page is the one to be loaded. For example, check to see that the file name of the `top` page actually matches the name you expect. The `window.top.location.href` will give us the name and path – if they don't match what we want, then use `window.top.location.replace("myPagename.htm")` to load the correct `top` page.

Try It Out – Scripting Frames

Let's put all we've learnt about frames, and scripting between them, into an example based on the frameset we've been looking at. We're going to be reusing a lot of the pages and code from the previous example in this chapter.

The first page we're creating is the top window page:

```
<HTML>
<HEAD>
<TITLE>The complex frameset page</TITLE>
<SCRIPT LANGUAGE=JavaScript>

var pagesVisited = new Array();

function returnPagesVisited()
{
   var returnValue = "So far you have visited the following pages\n";
   var pageVisitedIndex;
   var numberOfPagesVisited = pagesVisited.length;
   for (pageVisitedIndex = 0; pageVisitedIndex < numberOfPagesVisited;
      pageVisitedIndex++)
   {
      returnValue = returnValue + pagesVisited[pageVisitedIndex] + "\n";
   }

   return returnValue;
}

function addPage(fileName)
{
   var fileNameStart = fileName.lastIndexOf("/") + 1;
   fileName = fileName.substr(fileNameStart);
   pagesVisited[pagesVisited.length] = fileName;
 return true;
}

</SCRIPT>

</HEAD>
```

251

```
<FRAMESET COLS="200,*">
   <FRAME NAME=fraMenu SRC="menu_page.htm">
   <FRAME NAME=fraMain SRC="main_page.htm">
</FRAMESET>
</HTML>
```

As you can see, we've reused a lot of the code from `frameset_page.htm`, so you can cut and paste the script block from there. The only different code lines are highlighted. Save this page as `complex_frameset_page.htm`.

Next, create the page that will be loaded into `fraMenu`, namely `menu_page.htm`:

```
<HTML>
<HEAD>

<SCRIPT LANGUAGE=JavaScript>

function choosePage_onchange()
{
   var choosePage = document.form1.choosePage;
   var windowobject;

   if (document.form1.radFrame[0].checked == true)
   {
       windowobject = window.parent.fraMain.fraTop;
   }
   else
   {
       windowobject = window.parent.fraMain.fraBottom;
   }

   windowobject.location.href =
       choosePage.options[choosePage.selectedIndex].value;

   return true;
}
</SCRIPT>

</HEAD>
<BODY>

<FORM NAME=form1>
Select frame<BR>
Top <INPUT NAME="radFrame" CHECKED TYPE=radio>
Bottom <INPUT NAME="radFrame" TYPE=radio>
<BR><BR>
<SELECT NAME=choosePage LANGUAGE=JavaScript onchange="choosePage_onchange()">
   <OPTION VALUE=page_a.htm>Page A
   <OPTION VALUE=page_b.htm>Page B
   <OPTION VALUE=page_c.htm>Page C
   <OPTION VALUE=page_d.htm>Page D
</SELECT>
</FORM>

</BODY>
</HTML>
```

Save this as `menu_page.htm`.

The `fraMain` frame contains a page that is simply a frameset for the `fraTop` and `fraBottom` pages:

```
<HTML>
<FRAMESET ROWS="50%,*">
    <FRAME NAME=fraTop SRC="page_a.htm">
    <FRAME NAME=fraBottom SRC="page_b.htm">
</FRAMESET>
</HTML>
```

Save this as `main_page.htm`.

For the next four pages, we reuse the four pages, `page_a.htm`, `page_b.htm`, `page_c.htm`, and `page_d.htm` from the first example. There have been a few changes, as shown below, that you'll need to make. Again, all the pages are identical except for the text shown in the page, so only `page_a.htm` is shown. Amend the rest in a similar way.

```
<HTML>
<HEAD>

<SCRIPT LANGUAGE=JavaScript>

function butShowVisited_onclick()
{
    document.form1.txtaPagesVisited.value = window.top.returnPagesVisited();
}

function setFrameAndPageControls(linkIndex)
{
    var formobject = window.parent.parent.fraMenu.document.form1;
    formobject.choosePage.selectedIndex = linkIndex;
    if (window.parent.fraTop == window.self)
    {
        formobject.radFrame[0].checked = true;
    }
    else
    {
        formobject.radFrame[1].checked = true;
    }

    return true;
}

</SCRIPT>
</HEAD>
<BODY LANGUAGE=JavaScript
    onload="return window.top.addPage(window.location.href);">

<CENTER>
    <FONT size=6 color=MidnightBlue face=verdana>
        This is Page A
    </FONT>
</CENTER>
<P>
```

```
<A HREF="page_a.htm" name="pageALink"
   onclick="return setFrameAndPageControls(0)">Page A</A>
<A HREF="page_b.htm" name="pageBLink"
   onclick="return setFrameAndPageControls(1)">Page B</A>
<A HREF="page_c.htm" name="pageCLink"
   onclick="return setFrameAndPageControls(2)">Page C</A>
<A HREF="page_d.htm" name="pageDLink"
   onclick="return setFrameAndPageControls(3)">Page D</A>
</P>
<FORM NAME=form1>
<TEXTAREA ROWS=8 COLS=35 NAME=txtaPagesVisited>
</TEXTAREA>
<BR>
<INPUT TYPE="button" VALUE="List Pages Visited" NAME=butShowVisited
   onclick="butShowVisited_onclick()">
</FORM>
</BODY>
</HTML>
```

Re-save the pages under their old names.

Load `complex_frameset_page.htm` into your browser and you'll see a screen similar to that shown earlier, which we repeat below:

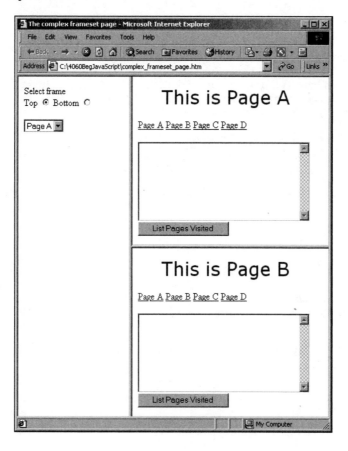

The radio buttons allow the user to determine which frame they want to navigate to a new page. By changing the currently selected page in the drop-down list, the selected page is loaded into the frame selected by the radio buttons.

If you navigate using the links in the pages inside the fraTop and fraBottom frames, then you'll notice that the selected frame radio buttons and the drop-down list in fraMenu on the left will be automatically updated to the page and frame just navigated to.

The List Pages Visited buttons display a list of visited pages, as they did in the previous example.

How It Works

We've already seen how the code in the complex_frameset_page.htm defining the Top window works, as it is very similar to our previous example. However, we'll just look quickly at the <FRAMESET> tags where, as you can see, the names of the windows are defined in the names of the <FRAME> tags:

```
<FRAMESET COLS="200,*">
    <FRAME name=fraMenu src="menu_page.htm">
    <FRAME name=fraMain src="main_page.htm">
</FRAMESET>
```

Notice also that the COLS attribute of the <FRAMESET> tag is set to "200,*". This means that the first frame will occupy a column of width 200 pixels, and the other frame will occupy a column taking up the remaining space.

Let's look in more detail at the fraMenu frame containing menu_page.htm. At the top of the page, we have our main script block. This contains the function choosePage_onchange(), which is connected to the onchange event handler of the select box lower down the page. The select box has options containing the various page URLs.

The function starts by defining two variables. One of these, choosePage, is a shortcut reference to the choosePage Select object lower down the page.

```
function choosePage_onchange()
{
    var choosePage = document.form1.choosePage;
    var windowobject;
```

The if...else statement then sets our variable windowobject to reference the window object of whichever frame the user has chosen in the radFrame radio button group:

```
    if (document.form1.radFrame[0].checked == true)
    {
        windowobject = window.parent.fraMain.fraTop;
    }
    else
    {
        windowobject = window.parent.fraMain.fraBottom;
    }
```

As we saw above, it's just a matter of following through the references, so `window.parent` gets us a reference to the parent `window` object. In this case, `window.top` would have done the same thing. Then `window.parent.fraMain` gets us a reference to the `window` object of the `fraMain` frame. Finally, depending on which frame we want to navigate, we reference the `fraTop` or `fraBottom` `window` objects contained within `fraMain`, using `window.parent.fraMain.fraTop` or `window.parent.fraMain.fraBottom`.

Now that we have a reference to the `window` object of the frame in which we want to navigate, we can go ahead and change its `location.href` property to the value of the selected drop down list item, causing the frame to load that page:

```
windowobject.location.href =
    choosePage.options[choosePage.selectedIndex].value;

return true;
}
```

As we saw before, `main_page.htm` is simply a frameset defining page for `fraTop` and `fraBottom`. Let's now look at the pages we're actually loading into `fraTop` and `fraBottom`. As they are all the same, we'll just look at `page_a.htm`.

Let's start by looking at the top script block. This contains two functions, `butShowVisited_onclick()` and `setFrameAndPageControls()`. We saw the function `butShowVisited_onclick()` in the previous example:

```
function butShowVisited_onclick()
{
    document.form1.txtaPagesVisited.value = window.top.returnPagesVisited();
}
```

However, as the frameset layout has changed, we do need to change the code. Whereas previously the `returnPagesVisited()` function was in the parent window, it's now moved to the top window. As you can see, all we need do is change the reference from `window.parent.returnPagesVisited();` to `window.top.returnPagesVisited();`.

As it happens, in the previous example the `parent` window was also the `top` window, so if we had written our code in this way in the first place, there would have been no need for changes here. It's often quite a good idea to keep all your general functions in the top frameset page. That way all your references can be `window.top`, even if the frameset layout is later changed.

The new function in this page is `setFrameAndPageControls()`, which is connected to the `onclick` event handler of the links defined lower down the page. This function's purpose in life is to make sure that if the user navigates to a different page using the links rather than the controls in the `fraMenu` window, then those controls will be updated to reflect what the user has done.

The first thing we do is set the `formobject` variable to reference the `form1` in the `fraMenu` page:

```
function setFrameAndPageControls(linkIndex)
{
    var formobject = window.parent.parent.fraMenu.document.form1;
```

Let's break this down. So:

```
window.parent
```

gets us a reference to fraMain's window object. Moving up the hierarchy we use:

```
window.parent.parent
```

to get a reference to the window object of the top window. Yes, you're right, we could have used window.top instead and this would have been a better way to do it. I'm doing it the long way here just to demonstrate how the hierarchy works.

Now we move down the hierarchy, but on the other side of our tree diagram, to reference the fraMenu's window object:

```
window.parent.parent.fraMenu
```

Finally, we are only interested in the form and its controls, so we reference that object like this:

```
window.parent.parent.fraMenu.form1
```

Now that we have a reference to the form, we can use it just as we would if this was code in fraMenu itself.

The function's parameter linkIndex tells us which of the four links was clicked and we use this value in the next line of the function's code to set which of the options is selected in the drop-down list box on fraMenu's form:

```
formobject.choosePage.selectedIndex = linkIndex;
```

The if...else statement is where we set the fraMenu's radio button group radFrame to the frame the user just clicked on, but how can we tell which frame this is?

```
if (window.parent.fraTop == window.self)
{
    formobject.radFrame[0].checked = true
}
else
{
    formobject.radFrame[1].checked = true
}
```

We check to see whether the current window object is the same as the window object for fraTop. We do this using the self property of the window object, which returns a reference to the current window object, and window.parent.fraTop, which returns a reference to fraTop's window object. If one is equal to the other, then we know that they are the same thing and that the current window is fraTop. If that's the case, then the radFrame radio group in the fraMenu frame has its first radio button checked. Otherwise, we check the other radio button for fraBottom.

The last thing we do in the function is return true. Remember that this function is connected to an A object, so returning false cancels the link's action, and true allows it to continue, which is what we want.

```
    return true;
}
```

Opening New Windows

So far in this chapter, we have been looking at frames, and scripting between them. In this section, we'll change direction slightly and look at how you can open up additional browser windows.

Why would we want to bother opening up new windows? Well, they can be useful in all sorts of different situations:

❑   You might want a page of links to web sites where clicking a link opens up a new window with that web site in.

❑   Additional windows can be useful for displaying information. For example, if you had a page with products on, the user could click a product image and up would pop a new small window with details of that product. This can be less intrusive for browsing products than navigating the existing window to a new page with product details, and then the user having to click Back to return to the list of products. We'll be creating an example demonstrating this.

❑   Dialog windows can be very useful for obtaining information from a user, although overuse can annoy the user.

Opening up a New Browser Window

The window object has an open() method, which opens up a new window. It takes three parameters, although the third is optional, and it returns a reference to the window object of the new browser window.

The first parameter of the open() method is the URL of the page you want to be opened in the new window. However, if you wish, you can pass an empty string for this parameter and get a blank page, then use the document.write() method to insert HTML into the new window dynamically. We will give an example of this later.

The second parameter is the name we want to allocate to the new window. This is not the name we use for scripting, but instead is used for the TARGET attribute of things like hyperlinks and forms. For example, if we set this parameter to myWindow and set a hyperlink on the original page to:

```
<A HREF="test3.htm" TARGET=myWindow>Test3.htm</A>
```

then clicking that hyperlink will cause the hyperlink to act on the new window opened. By this I mean that test3.htm will be loaded into the new window and not the current window. The same applies to the <FORM> tag's TARGET attribute, which we'll be looking at in the chapters on server-side JavaScript. In this case, if a form is submitted from the original window, the response from the server can be made to appear in the new window.

When a new window is opened, it is opened (by default) with a certain set of properties, such as width and height, and with the normal browser window features. What we mean by browser window features are things like a location entry field or a menu bar with navigation buttons.

The third parameter of the open() method can be used to specify values for the height and width properties. Also, since by default most of the browser window features are switched off, we can switch them back on using the third parameter of the open() method. We'll look at browser features in more detail shortly.

Let's first look at an example of the code we need to open a basic window. We'll name this window myWindow, and give it a width and height of 250 pixels. We want the new window to open with the test2.htm page inside.

```
var newWindow;
newWindow = window.open("test2.htm","myWindow","width=250,height=250");
```

You can see that test2.htm has been passed as the first parameter; that is the URL of the page we want to open. We've named the window myWindow in the second parameter. In the third parameter, we've set the width and height properties to 250.

You'll also notice that we've set the variable newWindow to the return value returned by the open() method, which is a reference to the window object of the new window just opened. We can now use newWindow to manipulate the new window just opened, and gain access to the document contained inside it using the window.document property. We can do everything with this reference that we did when dealing with frames and their window objects. For example, if we wanted to change the background color of the document contained inside the new window we would type:

```
newWindow.document.bgColor = "RED";
```

How would we close the window we just opened? Easy, we just use the window object's close() method like this:

```
newWindow.close();
```

Try It Out – Opening up New Windows

Let's look at the example we mentioned earlier of a products page where clicking a product brings up a window with details of that product. In a shameless plug, we'll be using a couple of Wrox books as examples, though, with just two products on our page, it's not exactly the world's most extensive online catalogue.

```
<HTML>
<HEAD>
<TITLE>Online Books</TITLE>
<SCRIPT LANGUAGE="JavaScript">

var detailsWindow;

function showDetails(bookURL)
{
    detailsWindow = window.open(bookURL,"bookDetails","width=400,height=350");
    detailsWindow.focus();
    return false;
}

</SCRIPT>
</HEAD>
<BODY>
<H2 ALIGN=center>Online Book Buyer</H2>
```

```
<P>
Click any of the images below for more details
</P>
<STRONG>Beginning Active Server Pages 3</STRONG>
<BR>
<A NAME="begASPLink" HREF=""
   onclick="return showDetails('beg_asp3_details.htm')">
      <IMG SRC="beg_asp3.gif" BORDER=0>
</A>
<BR><BR>
<STRONG>Professional JavaScript</STRONG>
<BR>
<A NAME="profJSLink" HREF=""
   onclick="return showDetails('prof_js_details.htm')">
      <IMG SRC="prof_js.gif" BORDER=0>
</A>
</BODY>
</HTML>
```

Save this page as `online_books.htm`. You'll also need to create two images and name them `beg_asp3.gif` and `prof_js.gif`. Alternatively, you can find these files in the code download.

We now need to create the two details pages, both plain HTML:

```
<HTML>
<HEAD>
<TITLE>Beginning Active Server Pages 3.0</TITLE>
</HEAD>
<BODY>
<STRONG>Beginning Active Server Pages 3.0</STRONG>
<BR>
Subjects
<BR>
ASP
<BR>
Internet
<BR>


<HR COLOR=#cc3333>

<P>ASP 3.0 is the most recent version of ASP, and is released with version 5.0
of Microsoft's <B>Internet Information Server</B> (IIS 5.0) web server, with
<B>Windows 2000</B>. It is also ported for use on UNIX.
</P>
<P>ASP is an easy way to control content - giving us the
flexibility to handle complex professional commercial sites. If you want to
program a web page, pure HTML is fine, however this book shows how to add
dynamism to web site generation and will utilize components, objects and
databases to achieve that.
</P>

</BODY>
</HTML>
```

Save this as `beg_asp3_details.htm`.

```
<HTML>
<HEAD>
<TITLE>Professional JavaScript</TITLE>
</HEAD>
<BODY>
<STRONG>Professional JavaScript</STRONG>
<BR>
<STRONG>Subjects</STRONG>

    ECMAScript<BR>
    Internet<BR>
    JavaScript<BR>
    XML and Scripting<BR>

<HR COLOR=#cc3333>
<P>This book covers the broad spectrum of programming JavaScript - from the core
language to browser applications and server-side use to stand-alone and embedded
JavaScript.
</P>
<P>
It includes a guide to the language - when where and how to get the
most out of JavaScript - together with practical case studies demonstrating
JavaScript in action. Coverage is bang up-to-date, with discussion of
compatibility issues and version differences, and the book concludes with a
comprehensive reference section. </P>

</BODY>
</HTML>
```

The final page needs to be saved as `prof_js_details.htm`.

Load `online_books.htm` into your browser and click either of the two images. A new window with the book's details should appear above the existing browser window. Click the other book image and the window will be replaced by one with details of that book.

> *Note that on IE 4, if you open one book's details window without closing a previous details window, the focus is kept with the opening window. In other words, the opening window is above the opened details window.*

How It Works

The files `beg_asp3_details.htm` and `prof_js_details.htm` are both plain HTML files so we won't look at them. However, in `online_books.htm` we find some scripting action, which we *will* look at here.

In the script block at the top of the page, we first define a variable `detailsWindow`:

```
var detailsWindow;
```

We then have the function that actually opens the new windows:

```
function showDetails(bookURL)
{
    detailsWindow = window.open(bookURL,"bookDetails","width=400,height=350");
    detailsWindow.focus();
    return false;
}
```

This function is connected to the `onclick` event handlers of the two hyperlinks surrounding the book images that appear later in the page. The parameter `bookURL` is passed by the code in the `onclick` event handler and will be either `beg_asp3_details.htm` or `prof_js_details.htm`.

We create the new window with the `window.open()` method. We pass the `bookURL` parameter as the URL to be opened. We pass `bookDetails` as the name we want applied to the new window. If the window already exists then another new window won't be opened and the existing one will be navigated to the URL that we pass. This only occurs because we are using the same name (`bookDetails`) when opening the window for each book. If we used a different name then a new window would be opened.

By storing the reference to the `window` object just created in the variable `detailsWindow`, we can access its methods and properties. On the next line, you'll see that we use the `window` object, referenced by `detailsWindow`, to set the focus to the new window – otherwise it will appear behind the existing window.

Finally, we need to return `false` so that the normal action of the hyperlink is canceled.

Although it's the user's action of clicking the images that we're interested in, because under Netscape 4 `IMG` objects don't have an `onclick` event handler, we need to wrap the images in a hyperlink tag and use the `onclick` event associated with the A object. You can see this in the code below where we create the images and hyperlinks and connect the `onclick` event handlers to our function. Although for each of the links' `onclick` event handlers we are using the same function, we pass a different parameter, namely the URL of the details page for that book.

```
<STRONG>Beginning Active Server Pages 3</STRONG>
<BR>
<A NAME="begASPLink" HREF=""
   onclick="return showDetails('beg_asp3_details.htm')">
      <IMG SRC="beg_asp3.gif" BORDER=0>
</A>
<BR><BR>
<STRONG>Professional JavaScript</STRONG>
<BR>
<A NAME="profJSLink" HREF=""
   onclick="return showDetails('prof_js_details.htm')">
      <IMG SRC="prof_js.gif" BORDER=0>
</A>
```

Adding HTML to a New Window

We mentioned above that we can pass an empty string as the first parameter of the window object's open() method, and then write to the page using HTML. Let's see how we would do that.

First, we need to open a blank window by passing an empty value to the first parameter that specifies the filename to load:

```
var newWindow = window.open("","myNewWindow","width=150,height=150");
```

Now we can open the window's document to receive our HTML:

```
newWindow.document.open();
```

This is not essential when a new window is opened as the page is blank, but with a document that already contains HTML, it has the effect of clearing out all existing HTML and blanking the page ready for writing.

Now we can write out any valid HTML using the document.write() method:

```
newWindow.document.write("<H4>Hello</H4>")
newWindow.document.write("<P>Welcome to my new little window</P>")
```

Each time we use the write() method, the text is added to what's already there until we use the document.close() method:

```
newWindow.document.close()
```

If we then use the document.write() method again, the text passed will replace existing HTML rather than adding to it.

Adding Features to your Windows

As we have seen, the window.open() method takes three parameters and it's the third of these parameters that we'll be looking at in this section. Using this third parameter, you can control things like the size of the new window created, its start position on the screen, whether the user can resize it, whether it has a toolbar, and so on.

Features like menu bar, status bar, and tool bar can be switched on or off using yes or 1 for on and no or 0 for off. To switch them on we can also just include their name without specifying a value.

The list of possible options shown below is not complete, and not all of them work with both IE and NN browsers.

Window Feature	Possible Values	Description
copyHistory	yes, no	Copies the history of the window doing the opening to the new window
directories	yes, no	Show directory buttons
height	*integer*	Height of new window in pixels
left	*integer*	Window's left starting position in pixels
location	yes, no	Show location text field
menubar	yes, no	Show menubar
resizable	yes, no	User can re-size the window once opened
scrollbars	yes, no	Show scrollbars if page too large to fit in window
status	yes, no	Show status bar
toolbar	yes, no	Show toolbar
top	*integer*	Window's top starting position in pixels
width	*integer*	Width of new window in pixels

As we said above, this third parameter is optional. If you don't include it then all the window features default to yes, except the window's size and position properties, which default to a set position and size. For example, if you try this code:

```
<HTML>
<HEAD>
<SCRIPT LANGUAGE=JavaScript>

var newWindow;
newWindow = window.open("","myWindow");

</SCRIPT>
</HEAD>
</HTML>
```

then you'll see a window something like this:

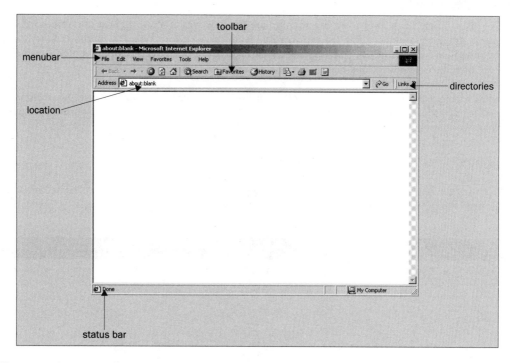

However, if you specify even one of the features, then all the others (except size and position properties) are set to no by default. For example:

```
var newWindow;
newWindow = window.open("","myWindow","width=200,height=120")
```

produces a window with no features as shown below, although we have defined its size this time.

Let's see another example. The following creates a 250 by 250 pixels window, with a location and menu bar, and which is resizable:

```
var newWindow;
newWindow =
window.open("","myWindow","width=250,height=250,location,menubar,resizable")
```

A word of warning, however. Never include spaces inside the features string, otherwise Netscape browsers will consider it invalid and ignore your settings.

Scripting between Windows

We've taken a brief look at how we can manipulate the new window's properties and, methods, and access its `document` object using the return value from the `window.open()` method. Now, we're going to look at how the newly opened window can access the window that opened it and, just as with frames, how it can use functions there.

The key to accessing the `window` object of the window that opened the current window is the `window` object's `opener` property. This returns a reference to the `window` object of the window that opened the current window. So:

```
window.opener.document.bgcolor = "RED"
```

will change the background color of the `opener` window to red. We can use the reference pretty much as we used the `window.parent` and `window.top` properties when using frames.

Try It Out – Inter Window Scripting

Let's look at an example where we open a new window and access a form on the opener window from the new window:

```
<HTML>
<HEAD>
<SCRIPT LANGUAGE=JavaScript>

var newWindow;

function butOpenWin_onclick()
{
    var winTop = (screen.height / 2) - 125;
    var winLeft = (screen.width / 2) - 125;
    var windowFeatures = "width=250,height=250,";
    windowFeatures = windowFeatures + "left=" + winLeft + ",";
    windowFeatures = windowFeatures + "top=" + winTop;

    newWindow = window.open("newWindow.htm","myWindow",windowFeatures);
}

function butGetText_onclick()
{
    if (typeof(newWindow) == "undefined" || newWindow.closed == true)
    {
        alert("No window is open");
    }
    else
    {
        document.form1.text1.value = newWindow.document.form1.text1.value;
    }
}
```

```
function window_onunload()
{
    if (typeof(newWindow) != "undefined")
    {
        if (newWindow.closed == false)
        {
            newWindow.close();
        }
    }

}

</SCRIPT>
</HEAD>
<BODY onunload="window_onunload()">
<FORM NAME=form1>
<INPUT TYPE="button" VALUE="Open newWindow" NAME=butOpenWin
    onclick="butOpenWin_onclick()">
<BR><BR>
NewWindow's Text
<BR>
<INPUT TYPE="text" NAME=text1>
<BR>
<INPUT TYPE="button" VALUE="Get Text" NAME=butGetText
    onclick="return butGetText_onclick()">
</FORM>
</BODY>
</HTML>
```

This is the code for our original window. Save it as `openerwindow.htm`. Now we'll look at the page that will be loaded by the opener window:

```
<HTML>
<HEAD>
<SCRIPT LANGUAGE=JavaScript>

function butGetText_onclick()
{
    document.form1.text1.value = window.opener.document.form1.text1.value;
}

</SCRIPT>
</HEAD>
<BODY>
<FORM NAME=form1>
Opener window's text<BR>
<INPUT TYPE="text" NAME=text1>
<BR>
<INPUT TYPE="button" VALUE="Get Text" NAME=butGetText LANGUAGE=JavaScript
    onclick="butGetText_onclick()">
</FORM>
</BODY>
</HTML>
```

Save this as `newWindow.htm`.

Open `openerwindow.htm` in your browser and you'll see a page with the following simple form:

Click the **Open newWindow** button and you'll see the following window open above the original page:

Type something into the text box of the new window, then returning to the original opener window, click on the **Get Text** button and you'll see what you just typed into `newWindow` appear in the text box on the opener window's form.

Change the text in the opener window's text box and then return to the `newWindow` and click the **Get Text** button, and the text you typed into the opener window's text box will appear in `newWindow`'s text box.

How It Works

Let's look at the opener window first. In the head of the page is a script block in which a variable and three functions are defined. At the top, we have declared a new variable, `newWindow`, which will hold the `window` object reference returned by the `window.open()` method we'll use later. Being outside any function gives this variable a global scope so we can access it from any function on the page.

```
var newWindow;
```

Then we have the first of the three functions in this page, butOpenWin_onclick(), which is connected lower down the page to the **Open newWindow** button's onclick event handler. Its purpose is simply to open the new window.

Rather than have the new window open up anywhere on the page, we use the built-in screen object, which is a property of the window object, to find out the resolution of the user's display and place the window in the middle of the screen. The screen object has a number of read-only properties, as you can see from Appendix B, but we're interested in the width and height properties. Variable winTop is initialized to the position we want the top of the window to be set at. Variable winleft is set to the left position we want the new window at to be in the middle of the screen.

```
function butOpenWin_onclick()
{
    var winTop = (screen.height / 2) - 125;
    var winLeft = (screen.width / 2) - 125;
```

We build up a string for the window features and store it in variable windowFeatures. We set the width and height to 250 and then use the winLeft and winTop variables we just populated to create the initial start positions of the window:

```
    var windowFeatures = "width=250,height=250,";
    windowFeatures = windowFeatures + "left=" + winLeft + ",";
    windowFeatures = windowFeatures + "top=" + winTop;
```

Finally, we open the new window, making sure we put the return value from window.open() into global variable newWindow so we can manipulate it later:

```
    newWindow = window.open("newWindow.htm","myWindow",windowFeatures);
}
```

The next function is used to obtain the text from the text box on the form in newWindow.

In this function we use an if statement to check two things. Firstly we check that newWindow is defined and secondly that the window is actually open. The reasons for checking are that we don't want to try to access a non-existent window, for example if no window has been opened or a window has been closed by the user. The typeof() function returns what type of information is held in a variable, for example number, string, Boolean, object, and undefined. Undefined is returned if the variable has never been given a value, as newWindow won't have been if no new window has been opened.

Having confirmed that a window has been opened at some point, we now need to check whether it's still open, and the window object's closed property does just that. If it returns true the window is closed, and if it returns false then it's still open. (Do not confuse this closed property with the close() method we saw previously.)

In the if statement you'll see that checking if newWindow is defined comes first and this is no accident. If newWindow really were undefined, then newWindow.closed would cause an error, as there is no data inside newWindow. However, we are taking advantage of the fact that if an if statement's condition will be true or false at a certain point regardless of the remainder of the condition, then the remainder of the condition is not checked.

```
function butGetText_onclick()
{
    if (typeof(newWindow) == "undefined" || newWindow.closed == true)
    {
        alert("No window is open");
    }
```

If newWindow exists and is open then the else statement's code will execute. Remember that newWindow will contain a reference to the window object of the window opened. This means we can access the form in newWindow, just as we'd access a form on the page the script's running in, by using the document object inside the newWindow window object.

```
    else
    {
        document.form1.text1.value = newWindow.document.form1.text1.value;
    }
}
```

The last of the three functions is window_onunload(), which is connected to the onunload event of this page and fires when either the browser window is closed or the user navigates to another page. In the window_onunload() function, we check to see if newWindow is valid and open in much the same way as we did above. We must put the check to see if the newWindow variable is defined first. With the && operator, JavaScript only checks the second part of the operation if the first part evaluates to true. If newWindow is defined, and does therefore hold a window object (even though it's possibly a closed window), then we can check the closed property of the window. However, if newWindow is undefined then the check for its closed property won't happen and no errors will occur. If we checked the closed property first and newWindow was undefined, then an error would occur since an undefined variable has no closed property.

```
function window_onunload()
{
    if (typeof(newWindow) != "undefined" && newWindow.closed == false)
    {
        newWindow.close();
    }
}
```

If newWindow is defined and open, we close it. This prevents the newWindow's **Get Text** button being clicked when there is no opener window in existence to get text from (since this function fires when the opener window is closed).

Let's now look at the code for the page that will be loaded in our newWindow, namely newWindow.htm. This page contains one function, butGetText_onclick(). This is connected to the onclick event handler of the **Get Text** button in the page, and is used to retrieve the text from the opener window's text box.

```
function butGetText_onclick()
{
    document.form1.text1.value = window.opener.document.form1.text1.value;
}
```

In this function, we use the window.opener property to get a reference to the window object of the window that opened this one and then use that reference to get the value out of the text box in the form in that window. This value is placed inside the text box in the current page.

Moving and Re-sizing Windows

Before we leave the subject of windows, let's look at the methods available to us for re-sizing and moving existing windows. Note that these methods are only available in version 4 and later browsers.

Once you have opened a window, you can change its position on screen and its size using the `window` object's `resizeTo()` and `moveTo()` methods, both of which take two arguments in pixels.

Let's imagine, having just opened a new window, like this:

```
var newWindow = window.open(myURL,"myWindow","width=125,height=150,resizable");
```

that you want to make it 350 pixels wide by 200 pixels high and move it to a position 100 pixels from the left of the screen and 400 pixels from the top. What code would you need?

```
newWindow.resizeTo(350,200);
newWindow.moveTo(100,400);
```

You can see that we can resize our window to 350 pixels wide by 200 pixels high using `resizeTo()`. Then we move it so it's 100 pixels from the left of the screen and 400 pixels from the top of the screen using `moveTo()`.

There are also `resizeBy()` and `moveBy()` methods of the `window` object. These each take two parameters, in pixels. For example:

```
newWindow.resizeBy(100,200);
```

will increase the size of newWindow by 100 pixels horizontally and 200 pixels vertically. Similarly:

```
newWindow.moveBy(20,50);
```

will move the newWindow by 20 pixels horizontally and 50 pixels vertically.

When using these methods, you must bear in mind that the user can manually resize these windows if they so wish. In addition, the size of the client's screen in pixels will vary between users.

Security

Browsers such as Netscape Navigator and Internet Explorer put certain restrictions on what information scripts can access between frames and windows.

If all the pages in these frames and windows are based on the same server, or on the same computer when you're loading them into the browser locally as we are, then you have a reasonably free rein over what your scripts can access and do. However, there are some restrictions. For example, if you try to use the `window.close()` method in a script page loaded into a browser window that the user opened themselves, as opposed to a window opened by your script, then the a message box will appear giving the user the option of canceling your `close()` method and keeping the window open.

271

When a page in one window or frame hosted on one server tries to access the properties of a window or frame that contains a page from a different server, then the "same origin policy" comes into play and you'll find yourself very restricted as to what your scripts can do. This policy is described below.

Imagine you have a page hosted on a web server whose URL is www.myserver.com. Inside the page is the script below.

```
var myWindow = window.open("www.anotherserver.com/anotherpage.htm","myWindow");
```

Now we have two windows, one that is hosted at www.myserver.com and another hosted on a different server, www.anotherserver.com. While this code does work, the same origin policy prevents any access to the document object of one page from another. For example, the following code in the opener page:

```
var myVariable = myWindow.document.form1.text1.value;
```

will cause a security problem and will be prevented by the browser. Although you do have access to the window object of the page on the other server, you only have access to a limited subset of its properties and methods.

The same origin restriction applies equally to frames as it does to windows. The idea behind it is very sound: it is to prevent hackers putting your pages inside their own and extracting information by using code inside their page. However the restrictions are fairly severe, perhaps too severe, and mean that you should avoid scripting across frames or windows where the pages are hosted on different servers.

There is no easy way around the restrictions in Internet Explorer, but Netscape Navigator browsers do support scripts that have been digitally signed to validate their origin. These scripts suffer less restriction than unsigned scripts, but it does mean that your pages won't be accessible from Internet Explorer. Also, the certificate required for signing is quite expensive.

Trivia Quiz

As we left it in the previous chapter, the trivia quiz was simply a single page that asked a single randomly selected question. Our task for the trivia quiz in this chapter is to convert it from a single page application to a multi-frame based application containing six pages. This is not a small change and will require a lot of work. With the enhancements to the trivia quiz in this chapter, this will transform it to something resembling a proper application. When the application is first is loaded, the user will be presented with the following screen:

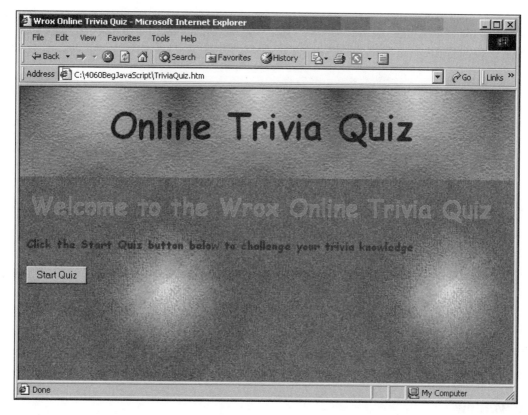

As you can see, this is quite a change from the way the quiz looked in Chapter 6! We'll next look at the strategy for creating this application.

Creating the new trivia quiz

The idea behind using frames is that there will be a page called globalfunctions.htm to hold all the global functions that we use again and again. This will be loaded into a frame called fraDlobalFunctions.

There will also be a page that simply displays the banner, **Online Trivia Quiz**, which you can see in the screenshot above. This page is called menubar.htm and will be loaded into a frame called fraMenuBar.

The third and fourth pages are where all the action takes place as far as the user is concerned. The QuizPage.htm is where the quiz is started – it displays the welcome message and **Start Quiz** button as can be seen above. The AskQuestion.htm page is where the questions are displayed and answered, and finally, when the quiz is finished, where the results are listed. These will be loaded into the frame called fraQuizPage.

There are two other pages called TriviaQuiz.htm and TopFrame.htm whose job is solely to define the framesets for the frames containing the other pages. These frameset pages will be contained in the frames called Top window and fraTopFrame.

The frame structure of the application is shown below, along with the name of each frame. Note that although the `fraGlobalFunctions` frame is shown, it's actually invisible to the user, which has the advantage of making our code and the questions more difficult to read.

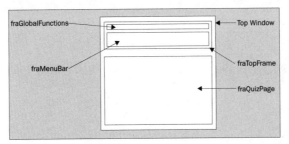

In terms of a tree diagram, the frames look like this:

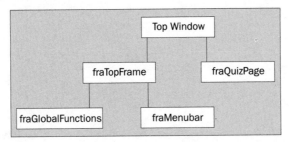

We'll now look at each frame in turn, and give the code for the page or pages that will be loaded into it.

Top window

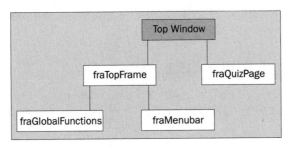

Let's create the frameset page that defines the top and bottom frames that we can see.

```
<HTML>
<HEAD>
    <TITLE>Wrox Online Trivia Quiz</TITLE>
</HEAD>
<FRAMESET ROWS="120,*" BORDER="0">
    <FRAME SRC="TopFrame.htm" NAME="fraTopFrame">
    <FRAME SRC="QuizPage.htm" NAME="fraQuizPage">
</FRAMESET>
</HTML>
```

Save this as `TriviaQuiz.htm`.

This is the page the user loads into their browser. It defines the frames `fraTopFrame` and `fraQuizPage`, and specifies the pages that will be loaded into them.

fraQuizPage

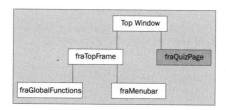

The next frame we're looking at is `fraQuizPage` whose position in the frames hierarchy is shown above. This frame will have two pages loaded into it in turn: `QuizPage.htm` and `AskQuestion.htm`.

QuizPage.htm

In the previous screenshot we saw what the trivia quiz looks like before the quiz has started. We simply have a start page with a bit of text and a button to click that starts the quiz. When the quiz is finished, if the user asks to restart the quiz then this page is loaded again.

Let's create that start page. When you've finished typing the code save the page as `QuizPage.htm`.

```
<HTML>
<HEAD>
<SCRIPT LANGUAGE=JavaScript>

function cmdStartQuiz_onclick()
{
    window.top.fraTopFrame.fraGlobalFunctions.resetQuiz();
    window.location.href = "AskQuestion.htm";
}

</SCRIPT>
</HEAD>

<BODY BACKGROUND="bluewash.jpg">
<H2 ALIGN="center">
    <FONT COLOR=coral FACE="Comic Sans MS" SIZE=6>
        Welcome to the Wrox Online Trivia Quiz
    </FONT>
</H2>
<P>
<FONT COLOR=darkslateblue FACE="Comic Sans MS" >
    <STRONG>
        Click the Start Quiz button below to challenge your trivia knowledge.
    </STRONG>
</FONT>
</P>
<P>
<FORM NAME="frmQuiz">
    <INPUT NAME=cmdStartQuiz TYPE=button VALUE="Start Quiz"
        onclick="return cmdStartQuiz_onclick()">
</FORM>
</P>
</BODY>
</HTML>
```

You can see that the background to the page is set to an image file, namely `bluewash.jpg`. You will need to create this file, or retrieve a copy from the code download.

AskQuestion.htm

Once the start quiz button has been clicked, the next page that is loaded into the `fraQuizPage` frame is `AskQuestion.htm` as shown in the screenshot below (though, as the questions are randomly selected, you may have a different start question).

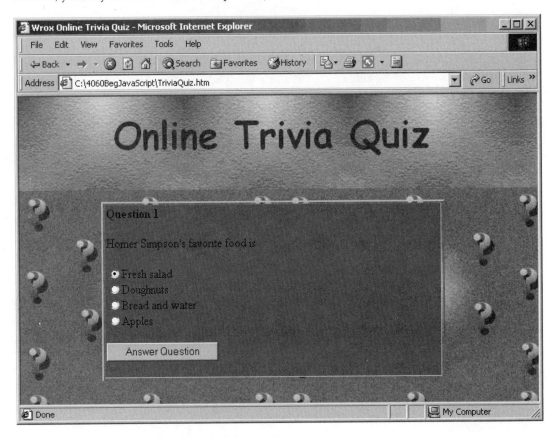

When the **Answer Question** button is clicked, the user's answer is checked and this page is re-loaded. If there are more questions to ask then another, different, randomly selected question is shown. If we've come to the end of the quiz, then a results page like that shown below is displayed. Actually, the results page and question asking pages are the same HTML page, but created dynamically depending on whether the quiz has ended.

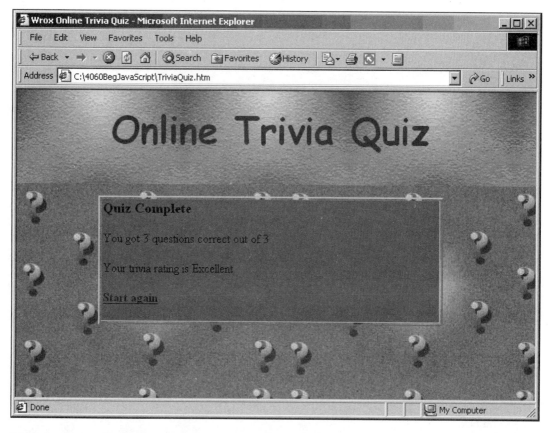

We'll now create that page, which should be saved as `AskQuestion.htm`:

```
<HTML>
<HEAD>
<SCRIPT LANGUAGE=JavaScript>

var globalFunctions;
globalFunctions = window.top.fraTopFrame.fraGlobalFunctions;

function getAnswer()
{
   var answer = 0;

   while (document.QuestionForm.radQuestionChoice[answer].checked != true)
   {
      answer++;
   }

   return String.fromCharCode(65 + answer);
}

function buttonCheckQ_onclick()
```

```
{
    var questionNumber = globalFunctions.currentQNumber;

    if (globalFunctions.answerCorrect(questionNumber,getAnswer()) == true)
    {
        alert("You got it right");
    }
    else
    {
        alert("You got it wrong");
    }

    window.location.reload();
}

</SCRIPT>
</HEAD>
<BODY BACKGROUND="bluewashqs.jpg">
<TABLE ALIGN=center BORDER="2" WIDTH="70%">
<TR>
<TD BGCOLOR=RoyalBlue>
<FORM NAME="QuestionForm">

<SCRIPT LANGUAGE=JavaScript>
    document.write(globalFunctions.getQuestion());
</SCRIPT>

</FORM>
</TD>
</TR>
</TABLE>
</BODY>
</HTML>
```

As you can see, a different background image is needed for this page, namely bluewashqs.jpg. Again, you will need to either create this image or retrieve the one in the code download.

fraTopFrame

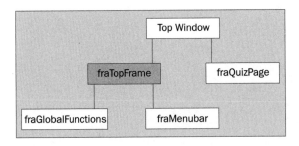

The other frame defined in Topwindow is, in fact, another frameset defining page. It defines one visible frame, the one containing the page heading, and a second frame, which is not visible and contains our global functions, but no HTML. Let's create that frameset defining page next.

```
<HTML>
<FRAMESET ROWS="0,*" BORDER="0">
   <FRAME SRC="GlobalFunctions.htm" NAME="fraGlobalFunctions">
   <FRAME SRC="Menubar.htm" NAME="fraMenubar">
</FRAMESET>
</HTML>
```

Save this page as `TopFrame.htm`.

You can see that it defines the two frames called `fraGlobalFunctions` and `fraMenuBar`, which we will look at next.

fraMenubar

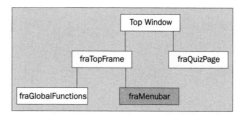

We'll next create the page for the `fraMenubar` frame, whose position in the frames hierarchy is shown above.

```
<HTML>
<BODY BACKGROUND="multicol_heading.jpg">
<H1 ALIGN="center">
<FONT FACE="Comic Sans MS" SIZE=+4 COLOR=DarkRed>
   Online Trivia Quiz
</FONT>
</H1>
</BODY>
</HTML>
```

Save this as `menubar.htm`.

This page just defines the heading that can be seen throughout the trivia quiz. It also uses a background image called `multicol_heading.jpg`, which you will need to create or retrieve from the code download.

fraGlobalFunctions

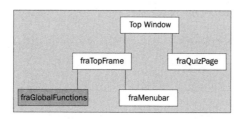

Now let's turn our attention to the final one of our new pages, namely `globalfunctions.htm`, which serves as a module containing all our general JavaScript functions. It is contained in the frame `fraGlobalFunctions`. You may recognize a lot of the code from the `trivia_quiz.htm` page that constituted the trivia quiz we created in Chapter 6.

```
<HTML>
<HEAD>
<SCRIPT LANGUAGE=JavaScript>

 // questions and answers variables will holds questions and answers
var questions = new Array();
var answers = new Array();
var questionsAsked;
var numberOfQuestionsAsked = 0;
var numberOfQuestionsCorrect = 0;
var currentQNumber = -1;

// define question 1
questions[0] = new Array();
questions[0][0] = "The Beatles were";
questions[0][1] = "A sixties rock group from Liverpool";
questions[0][2] = "Four musically gifted insects";
questions[0][3] = "I don't know - can I have the questions on Baseball please";

// assign answer for question 1
answers[0] = "A";

// define question 2
questions[1] = new Array();
questions[1][0] = "Homer Simpson's favorite food is";
questions[1][1] = "Fresh salad";
questions[1][2] = "Doughnuts";
questions[1][3] = "Bread and water";
questions[1][4] = "Apples";

// assign answer for question 2
answers[1] = "B";

// define question 3
questions[2] = new Array();
questions[2][0] = "Lisa Simpson plays which musical instrument";
questions[2][1] = "Clarinet";
questions[2][2] = "Oboe";
questions[2][3] = "Saxophone";
questions[2][4] = "Tubular Bells";

// assign answer for question 3
answers[2] = "C";

function resetQuiz()
{
   var indexCounter;
   currentQNumber = -1;
   questionsAsked = new Array();
```

```
      for (indexCounter = 0; indexCounter < questions.length;indexCounter++)
      {
         questionsAsked[indexCounter] = false;
      }

   numberOfQuestionsAsked = 0;
   numberOfQuestionsCorrect = 0;
}

function answerCorrect(questionNumber, answer)
{
   // declare a variable to hold return value
   var correct = false;

   // if answer provided is same as answer then correct answer is true
   if (answer == answers[questionNumber])
   {
      numberOfQuestionsCorrect++;
      correct = true;
   }

   // return whether the answer was correct (true or false)
   return correct;
}

function getQuestion()
{
   if (questions.length != numberOfQuestionsAsked)
   {
      var questionNumber = Math.floor(Math.random() * questions.length)

      while (questionsAsked[questionNumber] == true)
      {
         questionNumber = Math.floor(Math.random() * questions.length);
      }

      var questionLength = questions[questionNumber].length;
      var questionChoice;

      numberOfQuestionsAsked++;

      var questionHTML = "<H4>Question " + numberOfQuestionsAsked +  "</H4>";
      questionHTML = questionHTML + "<P>" + questions[questionNumber][0];
      questionHTML = questionHTML + "</P>";
      for (questionChoice = 1;questionChoice < questionLength;questionChoice++)
      {
         questionHTML = questionHTML + "<INPUT type=radio "
         questionHTML = questionHTML + "name=radQuestionChoice"
         if (questionChoice == 1)
         {
            questionHTML = questionHTML + " checked";
         }
         questionHTML = questionHTML + ">" +
            questions[questionNumber][questionChoice];
         questionHTML = questionHTML + "<BR>"
```

```
        }

        questionHTML = questionHTML + "<BR><INPUT type='button' "
        questionHTML = questionHTML + " value='Answer Question'";
        questionHTML = questionHTML + "name=buttonNextQ ";
        questionHTML = questionHTML + "onclick='return buttonCheckQ_onclick()'>";

        currentQNumber = questionNumber;
        questionsAsked[questionNumber] = true;
    }
    else
    {
        questionHTML = "<H3>Quiz Complete</H3>";
        questionHTML = questionHTML + "You got " + numberOfQuestionsCorrect;
        questionHTML = questionHTML + " questions correct out of "
        questionHTML = questionHTML + numberOfQuestionsAsked;
        questionHTML = questionHTML + "<BR><BR>Your trivia rating is "

        switch(Math.round(((numberOfQuestionsCorrect / numberOfQuestionsAsked) *
10))))
        {
            case 0:
            case 1:
            case 2:
            case 3:
                questionHTML = questionHTML + "Beyond embarrasing";
                break;
            case 4:
            case 5:
            case 6:
            case 7:
                questionHTML = questionHTML + "Average";
                break;
            default:
                questionHTML = questionHTML + "Excellent"
        }

        questionHTML = questionHTML + "<BR><BR><A "
        questionHTML = questionHTML + "href='quizpage.htm'><STRONG>";
        questionHTML = questionHTML + "Start again</STRONG></A>"
    }

    return questionHTML;
}

</SCRIPT>
</HEAD>
</HTML>
```

Save this page as `GlobalFunctions.htm`. That completes all the pages, so now it's time to load in the new trivia quiz and then find out how it works.

How It Works

Load `TriviaQuiz.htm` into your browser to start the quiz and try it out.

Although there does appear to be a lot of new code, much of it is identical to that in the previous version of the trivia quiz.

We will take a closer look at the pages `QuizPage.htm` and `AskQuestion.htm`, which are loaded into the `fraQuizPage` frame, and `GlobalFunctions.htm`, which is loaded into the `fraGlobalFunction` frame.

Of the other pages, `TriviaQuiz.htm` and `TopFrame.htm` are simply frameset defining pages, and `menubar.htm` simply defines the heading for the page.

QuizPage.htm

This is a simple page. We define a function `cmdStartQuiz_onclick()`, which is connected to the `onclick` event handler of the **Start Quiz** button lower down the page:

```
function cmdStartQuiz_onclick()
{
    window.top.fraTopFrame.fraGlobalFunctions.resetQuiz();
    window.location.href = "AskQuestion.htm";
}
```

In this function, we reset the quiz by calling the `resetQuiz()` function, which is in our `fraGlobalFunctions` frame. We'll be looking at this shortly. To get a reference to the `window` object of `fraGlobalFunctions`, we need to get a reference to the `fraTopFrame` that is under the Top window.

On the second line of the function, we navigate the frame to `AskQuestion.htm`, the page where the questions are asked. Let's look at that next.

AskQuestion.htm

In this page, we'll be accessing the functions in the `fraGlobalFunctions` frame a number of times, so we declare a page-level variable and set it to reference the `window` object of `fraGlobalFunctions`. It saves on typing and makes our code more readable.

```
var globalFunctions;
globalFunctions = window.top.fraTopFrame.fraGlobalFunctions;
```

We then come to `getAnswer()` function, which retrieves from the form lower in the page which one of the options the user chose as their answer. It does this by looping through each option in the form, incrementing the variable `answer` until it finds the option that has been checked by the user. Remember that the answers are stored as A, B, C and so on, so we convert the index number to the correct character using the `fromCharCode()` method of the `String` object. This is identical to the first half of the `buttonCheckQ_onclick()` function that we saw in the previous incarnation of the trivia quiz.

```
function getAnswer()
{
   var answer = 0;

   while (document.QuestionForm.radQuestionChoice[answer].checked != true)
   {
      answer++;
   }

   return String.fromCharCode(65 + answer);
}
```

The second function, butCheckQ_onclick() will be connected to the **Check Answer** button's onclick event. It is similar to the second half of the function with the same name in the previous version of the quiz. However, now it refers to the answerCorrect() function in the fraGlobalFunctions frame rather than the current page, and uses the getAnswer() function rather than the variable answer.

```
function buttonCheckQ_onclick()
{
   var questionNumber = globalFunctions.currentQNumber;

   if (globalFunctions.answerCorrect(questionNumber,getAnswer()) == true)
   {
      alert("You got it right");
   }
   else
   {
      alert("You got it wrong");
   }

   window.location.reload();
}
```

As in Chapter 6, the form that displays the question to the user is populated dynamically, using document.write(). However, this time the function, getQuestion(), is located in the GlobalFunctions.htm page.

GlobalFunctions.htm

Much of this page is taken from the trivia_quiz.htm page that we created in Chapter 6. At the top of the page, we have added four more page-level variables.

```
var questions = new Array();
var answers = new Array();
var questionsAsked;
var numberOfQuestionsAsked = 0;
var numberOfQuestionsCorrect = 0;
var currentQNumber = -1;
```

We then define the `questions` and `answers` arrays exactly as we did previously. The first new function, `resetQuiz()`, is shown below:

```
function resetQuiz()
{
   var indexCounter;
   currentQNumber = -1;
   questionsAsked = new Array();

   for (indexCounter = 0; indexCounter < questions.length;indexCounter++)
   {
      questionsAsked[indexCounter] = false;
   }

   numberOfQuestionsAsked = 0;
   numberOfQuestionsCorrect = 0;
}
```

When the quiz is started or restarted, this function is called to reset all the global quiz variables back to a default state. For example, the `questionsAsked` variable is reinitialized to a new array, the length of which will match the length of the `questions` array, with each element being set to a default value of `false` indicating that the corresponding question has not yet been asked.

We then have the `answerCorrect()` function, which is the same as in the previous chapter. The rest of the page is made up of the `getQuestion()` function, which has undergone major changes since the previous version.

Previously we just asked questions randomly and kept going until the user got bored. Now we're going to keep track of which questions have been asked and how many questions have been asked. The `questionsAsked` array will store which questions have already been asked, so we can avoid repeat questions. The variable `numberOfQuestionsAsked` keeps track of how many have been asked so far, so we can stop when we've used up our question database. The variable `numberOfQuestionsCorrect` will be used to record the number of right answers given. These variables were defined in the head of the page.

Turning to `getQuestion()`, we can see that the very first thing the function does is use an `if` statement to see if we have asked as many questions as there are questions in the database. The `length` property of our `questions` array tells us how many elements there are in our array and `numberOfQuestionsAsked` tells us how many have been asked so far. If we have asked all the questions then we'll see later on that the function writes out an end page with details of how many the user got correct and rates their trivia knowledge.

```
function getQuestion()
{
   if (questions.length != numberOfQuestionsAsked)
   {
      var questionNumber = Math.floor(Math.random() * questions.length)

      while (questionsAsked[questionNumber] == true)
      {
         questionNumber = Math.floor(Math.random() * questions.length);
      }
```

You can see from the code above that the selection of the question is random, as it was in Chapter 6's version of the quiz. However, we have added a `while` loop that makes use of the `questionsAsked` array we declared earlier. Each time a question is asked we set the value of the element in `questionsAsked` array at the same position as its question number to `true`. By checking to see if a particular array position is true we can tell if the question has already been asked, in which case the `while` loop keeps going until it hits a `false` value, that is an unasked question.

Now we know which question we want to ask, we just need to go ahead and ask it, which is the purpose of the next lines of code:

```
var questionLength = questions[questionNumber].length;
var questionChoice;

numberOfQuestionsAsked++;

var questionHTML = "<H4>Question " + numberOfQuestionsAsked +  "</H4>";
questionHTML = questionHTML + "<P>" + questions[questionNumber][0];
questionHTML = questionHTML + "</P>";
for (questionChoice = 1;questionChoice < questionLength;questionChoice++)
{
    questionHTML = questionHTML + "<INPUT type=radio "
    questionHTML = questionHTML + "name=radQuestionChoice"
    if (questionChoice == 1)
    {
        questionHTML = questionHTML + " checked";
    }
    questionHTML = questionHTML + ">" +
        questions[questionNumber][questionChoice];
    questionHTML = questionHTML + "<BR>"
}

questionHTML = questionHTML + "<BR><INPUT type='button' "
questionHTML = questionHTML + " value='Answer Question'";
questionHTML = questionHTML + "name=buttonNextQ ";
questionHTML = questionHTML + "onclick='return buttonCheckQ_onclick()'>";
```

This code is almost identical to its previous form in Chapter 6, except that we now create the button dynamically as well as the answer options. Why? At the beginning of the function we saw that an `if` statement checked whether we had reached the end of the quiz. If not, we created another question as we are doing here. If the quiz has come to an end, then we don't want to create an array of answers to answer the question. Instead we want to create an end of quiz form. The only way to avoid having the answer question button there, is to make it part of the dynamic question creation.

Finally, we see that the `questionsAsked` array is updated, that is the question just asked is added to the array:

```
    currentQNumber = questionNumber;
    questionsAsked[questionNumber] = true;
}
```

The `else` part of the code in the `if` statement at the top of the function is shown above opposite. Its purpose is to create the quiz completed message. We build up the HTML necessary, storing it in variable `questionHTML`. We not only specify how many questions the user got right out of how many were asked, but we also rate their knowledge.

```
    else
    {
        questionHTML = "<H3>Quiz Complete</H3>";
        questionHTML = questionHTML + "You got " + numberOfQuestionsCorrect;
        questionHTML = questionHTML + " questions correct out of "
        questionHTML = questionHTML + numberOfQuestionsAsked;
        questionHTML = questionHTML + "<BR><BR>Your trivia rating is "
```

The rating is done using the `switch` statement, where it's based on questions got right divided by the number of questions asked, which for simplicity we multiply by ten and round to the nearest integer. Then we use the `case` statements to create the correct rating. Remember that code execution starts at the first `case` statement that matches, and continues until either the end of the `switch` statement or when a `break` statement is reached. So if our rating calculation:

```
Math.round(((numberOfQuestionsCorrect / numberOfQuestionsAsked) * 10
```

was to be 1, the code would start executing from the `case 1:` statement and continues until the `break` statement in `case 3`. Essentially this means that a rating of 0 – 3 will be described as "Beyond embarrassing", 4 – 7 as "Average" and anything else, that is the default case, will be "Excellent":

```
        switch(Math.round(((numberOfQuestionsCorrect / numberOfQuestionsAsked) *
10)))
        {
            case 0:
            case 1:
            case 2:
            case 3:
                questionHTML = questionHTML + "Beyond embarrasing";
                break;
            case 4:
            case 5:
            case 6:
            case 7:
                questionHTML = questionHTML + "Average";
                break;
            default:
                questionHTML = questionHTML + "Excellent"
        }
```

Finally, we add a link to allow the user to restart the quiz:

```
        questionHTML = questionHTML + "<BR><BR><A "
        questionHTML = questionHTML + "href='quizpage.htm'><STRONG>"
        questionHTML = questionHTML + "Start again</STRONG></A>"
    }
```

At the end of the function, we return the HTML to be written into the page, either a new question or the end of quiz results:

```
    return questionHTML;
}
```

That completes the discussion of the trivia quiz for this chapter. In the next chapter we'll be using advanced string manipulation to pose questions requiring a text, rather than option-based, answer.

Summary

For various reasons, having a frame-based web site can prove very useful. Therefore, we need to be able to create JavaScript that can interact with frames and with the documents and code within those frames.

- ❑ We saw that an advantage of frames is that, by putting all of our general functions in a single frame, we can create a JavaScript code module which all our web site can use.

- ❑ We saw that the key to coding with frames is getting a reference to the `window` objects of other frames. We saw two ways of accessing frames higher in the hierarchy, using the `window` object's `parent` property and its `top` property.

- ❑ The `parent` property returns the `window` object that contains the current `window` object, which will be the page containing the frameset that created the window. The `top` property returns the `window` object of the window containing all the other frames.

- ❑ Each frame in a frameset can be accessed using two methods. One is by using the name of the frame. The second is by using the `frames[]` array and specifying the index of the frame.

- ❑ If the frame we want to access is defined in another window, we need to get a reference to the `window` object defining that frame, using the `parent` or `top` properties, and then to specify the name or position in the `frames[]` array.

We then looked at how we can open new, additional browser windows using script.

- ❑ Using the `window` object's `open()` method, we can open new windows. The URL of the page we want to open is passed as the first parameter, the name of the new window as the second parameter, and the optional third parameter allows us to define what features the new window will have.

- ❑ The `window.open()` method returns a value, which is a reference to the `window` object of the new window. Using this reference, we can access the document, script, and methods of that window, much as we do with frames. We need to make sure that the reference is stored inside a variable if we want to do this.

- ❑ To close a window we simply use the `window.close()` method. To check if a window is closed we use the `closed` property of the `window` object, which returns `true` if it's closed and `false` if it's still open.

- ❑ For a newly opened `window` object to access the window that opened it, we need to use the `window.opener` property. Like `window.parent` for frames, this gives a reference to the `window` object that opened this one and allows us to access the `window` object and its properties for that window.

- ❑ Once a window is opened we can resize it using `resizeTo(x,y)` and `resizeBy(x,y)`, and move it using `moveTo(x,y)` and `moveBy(x,y)`.

We also looked briefly at security restrictions for windows and frames that are not of the same origin. By not of the same origin, we mean the situation where the document in one frame is hosted on one server and the document in the other is hosted on a different server. In this situation, very severe restrictions apply, which limit the extent of scripting between frames or windows.

In the next chapter, we'll be looking at advanced string manipulation and how we can use this to add different types of questions to our trivia quiz.

Exercise Questions

Suggested solutions to these questions can be found in Appendix A.

Question 1

In the previous chapter's exercise questions we created a form that allowed the user to pick a computer system. They could view the details of their system and its total cost by clicking a button that wrote the details to a `textarea`. Change the example so it's a frames-based web page, and instead of writing to a text area the details should written to another frame.

Question 2

In the first example in this chapter, we had a page with images of books where clicking on a book's image brought up information about that book in a popup window. Amend this so that the popup window also has a button or link that when clicked adds the item to the user's shopping basket. Also on the main page, give the user some way of opening up a shopping basket window with details of all the items the user has purchased so far, and give them a way of deleting items from this basket.

Online discussion at http://p2p.wrox.com

String Manipulation

In Chapter 4 we looked at the `String` object, which is one of the native objects that JavaScript makes available to us. We saw a number of its properties and methods including:

❑   `length` – the length of the string in characters

❑   `charAt()` and `charCodeAt()` – methods for returning the character or character code at a certain position in the string

❑   `indexOf()` and `lastIndexOf()` – methods that allow the searching of a string for the existence of another string, and return the character position of the string if found

❑   `substr()` and `substring()` – methods that return just a portion of a string

❑   `toUpperCase()` and `toLowerCase()` – methods that return a string converted to upper or lower case

In this chapter we'll be looking at four new methods of the `String` object, namely `split()`, `match()`, `replace()`, and `search()`. The last three, in particular, give us some very powerful text manipulation functionality. However, in order to make full use of this functionality, we need to learn about a slightly more complex subject.

The methods `split()`, `match()`, `replace()`, and `search()` can all make use of something called regular expressions, something JavaScript wraps up in an object called the `RegExp` object. Regular expressions allow you to define a pattern of characters, which can be used for text searching or replacement. Say, for example, that you had a string in which you wanted to replace all text enclosed in single quotes with double quotes. This may seem easy – just search the string for `'` and replace with `"` – but what if the string was *Bob O'Hara said 'Hello'*. We would not want to replace the `'` in *O'Hara*. Without regular expressions this could still be done, but it would take more than the two lines of code needed if you use regular expressions.

Although `split()`, `match()`, `replace()`, and `search()` are at their most powerful with regular expressions, they can also be used with just plain text. We'll take a look at how they work in this simpler context first, to familiarize ourselves with the methods.

Additional String Methods

In this section we will take a look at the split(), match(), replace(), and search() methods, and see how they work without regular expressions.

The split() Method

The String object's split() method splits a single string into an array of substrings. Where the string is split is determined by the separation parameter that we pass to the method. This parameter is simply a character or text string.

For example, to split the string "A,B,C" so that we have an array populated with the letters between the commas, the code would be:

```
var myString = "A,B,C";
var myTextArray = myString.split(',');
```

JavaScript creates an array with three elements. In the first element it puts everything from the start of the string myString up to the first comma. In the second element it puts everything from after the first comma to before the second comma. Finally in the third element it puts everything from after the third comma to the end of the string. So, our array myTextArray will look like this:

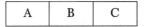

If, however, our string was "A,B,C," JavaScript would split this into four elements, the last element containing everything from the last comma to the end of the string, that is an empty string.

A	B	C	

This is something that can catch you out if you are not aware of it.

Try It Out – Reversing the Order of Text

Let's create a short example using the split() method, in which we reverse the lines written in a <TEXTAREA> element.

```
<HTML>
<HEAD>
<SCRIPT LANGUAGE=JavaScript>
function splitAndReverseText(textAreaControl)
{
    var textToSplit = textAreaControl.value;
    var textArray = textToSplit.split('\r\n');

    var numberOfParts = 0;
    numberOfParts = textArray.length;

    var reversedString = "";
    var indexCount;
```

```
      for (indexCount = numberOfParts - 1; indexCount >= 0; indexCount--)
      {
         reversedString = reversedString + textArray[indexCount];
         if (indexCount > 0)
         {
            reversedString = reversedString + "\r\n";
         }
      }

      textAreaControl.value = reversedString;
}
</SCRIPT>
</HEAD>

<BODY>
<FORM NAME=form1>
<TEXTAREA ROWS=20 COLS=40 NAME=textarea1 WRAP=soft>Line 1
Line 2
Line 3
Line 4</TEXTAREA>
<BR>
<INPUT TYPE="button" VALUE="Reverse Line Order" NAME=buttonSplit
   onclick="splitAndReverseText(document.form1.textarea1)">
</FORM>
</BODY>
</HTML>
```

Save this as ch8_examp1.htm and load it into your browser. You should see the screenshot below:

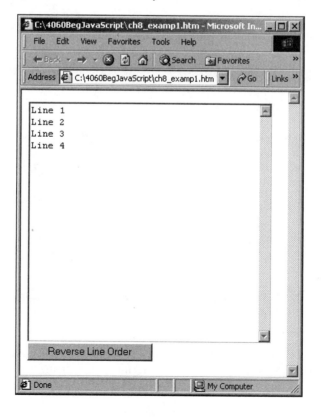

Clicking the Reverse Line Order button reverses the order of the lines:

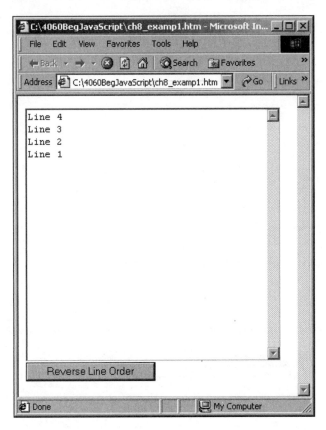

Try changing the lines within the textarea to test it further.

Note that this code is Windows specific – it twice uses the escape characters \r\n. If you are running the code on a Unix machine you will need to replace \r\n with \n, and if you are using a Macintosh machine you will need to replace \r\n with \r. Note also that for Netscape 6 you need to replace the \r\n with \n.

How It Works

The key to how this code works is the function `splitAndReverseText()`. This function is defined in the script block in the head of the page, and is connected to the `onclick` event handler of the button further down the page.

```
<INPUT TYPE="button" VALUE="Reverse Line Order" NAME=buttonSplit
    onclick="splitAndReverseText(document.form1.textarea1)">
```

As you can see, we pass a reference of the textarea that we want reversing as a parameter to the function. By doing it this way, rather than just using a reference to the element itself inside the function, we make the function more generic, so we can use this function with any textarea element.

Now, on with the function. We start by assigning the value of the text inside the textarea element to the `textToSplit` variable. We then split that string into an array of lines of text using the `split()` method of the `String` object and put the resulting array inside the `textArray` variable.

```
function splitAndReverseText(textAreaControl)
{
    var textToSplit = textAreaControl.value;
    var textArray = textToSplit.split('\r\n');
```

So what do we use as the separator to pass as a parameter for the `split()` method? Recall from Chapter 2 that the escape character \n is used for a new line and \r is used for a carriage return. So, on Windows, what we need to use is \r\n. However, just to confuse things, if you have a Unix machine you will need to replace this with \n, and on a Macintosh machine you'll have to use \r. Another point to add to the confusion is that Netscape 6 seems to need \n rather than \r\n even on Windows.

We next define and initialize four more variables.

```
    var numberOfParts = 0;
    numberOfParts = textArray.length;

    var reversedString = "";
    var indexCount;
```

Having got our array of strings, we next want to reverse them. We do this by building up a new string, adding each string from the array, starting with the last and working towards the first. We do this in the `for` loop, where instead of starting at zero and working up as we usually do, we start at a number greater than zero and decrement until we reach zero, at which point we stop looping.

```
    for (indexCount = numberOfParts - 1; indexCount >= 0; indexCount--)
    {
        reversedString = reversedString + textArray[indexCount];
        if (indexCount > 0)
        {
            reversedString = reversedString + "\r\n";
        }
    }
```

When we split the string, all our line formatting is removed. So, in the `if` statement we add a carriage return and linefeed (\r\n) onto the end of each string, except for the last string, that is when the `indexCount` variable is zero. (Remember that if you are using Unix, a Macintosh, or Netscape 6, you will need to use a different escape character, as described above).

Finally we assign the text in the textarea element to the new string we have built up.

```
    textAreaControl.value = reversedString;
}
```

Once we've looked at regular expressions, we'll take another look at the `split()` method.

The replace() Method

The `replace()` method searches a string for occurrences of a substring. Where it finds a match for this substring, it replaces the substring with a third string that we specify.

Let's look at an example. Say we have a string with the word May in:

```
var myString = "The event will be in May, the 21st of May";
```

and we want to replace May with June. We could use the `replace()` method like so:

```
myCleanedUpString = myString.replace("May","June");
```

The value of `myString` will not be changed. Instead, the `replace()` method returns the value of `myString` but with May replaced with June. We assign this returned string to the variable `myCleanedUpString`, which will contain the text:

```
"The event will be in June, the 21st of June"
```

The search() Method

The `search()` method allows you to search a string for a particular piece of text. If the text is found, then the character position at which it was found is returned; otherwise -1 is returned. The method takes only one parameter, namely the text you want to search for.

When used with plain text, the `search()` method provides no real benefit over methods like `indexOf()`, which we've already seen. However, we'll see later that it's when we use regular expressions that the power of this method becomes apparent.

In the example below, we want to find out if the word Java is contained within the string called `myString`:

```
var myString = "Beginning JavaScript, Beginning Java, Professional JavaScript";
alert(myString.search("Java"));
```

The alert box that occurs will show the value 10, which is the character position of the J in the first occurrence of Java, as part of the word JavaScript.

The match() Method

The `match()` method is very similar to the `search()` method, except that instead of returning the position where a match was found, it returns an array. Each element of the array contains the text of each match that is found.

Although you can use plain text with the `match()` method, it would be completely pointless to do so. For example:

```
var myString = "1997, 1998, 1999, 2000, 2000, 2001, 2002";
myMatchArray = myString.match("2000");
alert(myMatchArray.length);
```

This code will result in `myMatchArray` holding two elements, both containing the value 2000. Given that we already know our search string is 2000, you can see it's been a pretty pointless exercise. The only useful information is the array's length, which tells us how many matches were made.

However, the `match()` method makes a lot more sense when we use it with regular expressions. Then we might search for all years in the 21st century, that is those beginning with 2. In this case, our array would contain the values 2000, 2000, 2001 and 2002 – much more useful information!

Regular Expressions

Before we look at the `split()`, `match()`, `search()`, and `replace()` methods of the `String` object again, we need to look at regular expressions and the `RegExp` object. Regular expressions provide a means of defining a pattern of characters, which we can then use to split, search, or replace characters in a string where they fit the defined pattern.

JavaScript's regular expression syntax borrows heavily from the regular expression syntax of Perl, another scripting language. The latest versions of languages such as VBScript have also incorporated regular expressions, as do lots of applications programs such as Microsoft Word in which the Find facility allows regular expressions to be used. You'll find your regular expression knowledge will prove useful even outside JavaScript.

The use of regular expressions in JavaScript is through the `RegExp` object, which is a native JavaScript object, as are `String` and `Array`, etc. There are two ways of creating a new `RegExp` object. The easier is with a regular expression literal, such as:

```
var myRegExp = /\b'|'\b/;
```

The forward slashes (/) mark out the start and end of the regular expression. This is a special syntax that tells JavaScript that the code is a regular expression, much as quote marks define a string's start and end. Don't worry about the actual expression's syntax yet (that is the `\b'|'\b`) – we'll be explaining that in detail shortly.

Alternatively, we could use the `RegExp` object's constructor function `RegExp()` and type:

```
var myRegExp = new RegExp("\\b'|'\\b");
```

Either way of specifying a regular expression is fine, though the former method is shorter, more efficient for JavaScript to use, and therefore generally preferred. For much of the remainder of the chapter, we'll use the first method.

Once we have got to grips with regular expressions, we will come back to the second way of defining them using the `RegExp()` constructor. As you can see from above, the syntax of regular expressions is slightly different when using the second method, and we'll explain this in detail then.

While we'll be concentrating on the use of the `RegExp` object as a parameter for the `String` object's `split()`, `replace()`, `match()`, and `search()` methods, it does have its own methods and properties. For example, the `test()` method allows you to test to see if the string passed to it as a parameter contains a pattern matching that defined in the `RegExp` object. We'll see the `test()` method in use in an example shortly.

Simple Regular Expressions

Defining patterns of characters using regular expression syntax can get fairly complex. In this section we'll be exploring just the basics of regular expression patterns. The best way to do this is through examples.

Let's start by looking at an example where we want to do a simple text replacement using the `replace()` method and a regular expression. Imagine we have the following string:

```
var myString = "Paul, Paula, Pauline, paul, Paul";
```

and we want to replace any occurrence of the name Paul with Ringo.

Well, the pattern of text we need to look for is simply Paul. Representing this as a regular expression, we just have:

```
var myRegExp = /Paul/;
```

As we saw above, the forward slash characters mark the start and end of the regular expression. Now let's use this with the `replace()` method.

```
myString = myString.replace(myRegExp, "Ringo");
```

You can see the `replace()` method takes two parameters, firstly the `RegExp` object that defines the pattern to be searched and replaced, and secondly the replacement text.

If we put this all together in an example, we have:

```
<HTML>
<BODY>
<SCRIPT LANGUAGE=JavaScript>
var myString = "Paul, Paula, Pauline, paul, Paul";
var myRegExp = /Paul/;
myString = myString.replace(myRegExp, "Ringo");
alert(myString);
</SCRIPT>
</BODY>
</HTML>
```

If you load this code into a browser, you will see:

We can see that this has replaced the first occurrence of Paul in our string. But what if we wanted all the occurrences of Paul in the string to be replaced? The two at the far end of the string are still there, so what happened?

Well, by default the RegExp object only looks for the first matching pattern, in this case the first Paul, and then stops. This is common and important behavior for RegExp objects. Regular expressions tend to start at one end of a string and look through the characters until the first complete match is found, then stop.

What we want is a global match, which is for all possible matches to be made and replaced. To help us out, the RegExp object has two attributes we can define. You can see these listed below:

Attribute Character	Description
g	Global match. Look for all matches of the pattern rather than stopping after the first match is found
i	Pattern is case-insensitive. For example, Paul and paul are considered the same pattern of characters

If we change our RegExp object in the above code to:

```
var myRegExp = /Paul/gi;
```

then a global case-insensitive match will be made. Running the code now produces:

This looks like it has all gone horribly wrong. The regular expression has matched the Paul substrings at the start and the end of the string, and the penultimate paul, just as we wanted. However, the Paul substrings inside Pauline and Paula have also been replaced.

The RegExp object has done its job correctly. We asked for all patterns of the characters Paul to be replaced and that's what we got. What we actually meant was for all occurrences of Paul, when it's a single word and not part of another word such as Paula, to be replaced. The key to making regular expressions work is to define exactly the pattern of characters so that only that pattern can match and no other, so let's do that.

So:

1. We want paul or Paul to be replaced.

2. We don't want it replaced when it's actually part of another word, as in Pauline.

How do we specify this second condition? How do we know when the word is joined to other characters, rather than just joined to spaces or punctuation or just the start or end of the string?

To see how we can achieve this with regular expressions, we need to enlist the help of regular expression special characters. We'll look at these in the next section, by the end of which we should be able to solve the above problem.

Regular Expressions : Special Characters

We will be looking at three types of special characters in this section.

Text, Numbers, and Punctuation

The first group of special characters we'll look at are the character class's special characters. By the character class, I mean digits, letters and white space characters. The special characters are displayed in the following table.

Character Class	Characters it matches	Example
\d	Any digit from 0 - 9	\d\d matches 72, but not aa or 7a
\D	Any character not a digit	\D\D\D matches abc, but not 123 or 8ef
\w	Any word character, that is A-Z, a-z, 0-9, and the underscore character _	\w\w\w\w matches Ab_2, but not £$%* or Ab_@
\W	Any non-word character	\W matches @, but not a
\s	Any white space character, including tab, newline, carriage return, formfeed and vertical tab	\s matches *tab*
\S	Any non-white space character	\S matches A, but not *tab*
.	Any single character	. matches a or 4 or @
[...]	Any one of the characters between the brackets	[abc] will match a or b or c, but nothing else.
		[a-z] will match any character in the range a to z.
[^...]	Any one character, but not one of those inside the brackets	[^abc] will match any character except a or b or c.
		[^a-z] will match any character which is not in the range a to z.

Note that uppercase and lowercase characters mean very different things, so you need to be extra careful with case when using regular expressions.

Let's look at an example. To match a telephone number in the format 1-800-888-5474, the regular expression would be

```
\d-\d\d\d-\d\d\d-\d\d\d\d
```

You can see that there's a lot of repetition of characters here, which makes the expression quite unwieldy. To make this simpler, regular expressions have a way of defining repetition. We'll see this in the next section on repetition characters.

Before we go on to this subject, let's look at another example.

Try it out – checking a passphrase for alphanumeric characters

We'll use what we've learnt so far about regular expressions in a full example in which we check that a passphrase contains only letters and numbers, that is alphanumeric characters, and not punctuation or symbols like @ and % and so on.

```
<HTML>
<BODY>
<SCRIPT LANGUAGE=JavaScript>

function regExpIs_valid(text)
{
   var myRegExp = /[^a-z\d ]/i;
   return !(myRegExp.test(text));
}

function butCheckValid_onclick()
{
   if (regExpIs_valid(document.form1.txtPhrase.value) == true)
   {
      alert("Your passphrase contains valid characters");
   }
   else
   {
      alert("Your passphrase contains invalid characters");
   }
}

</SCRIPT>
<FORM NAME=form1>
Enter your passphrase:
<BR>
<INPUT TYPE="text" NAME=txtPhrase>
<BR>
<INPUT TYPE="button" VALUE="Check Character Validity" NAME=butCheckValid
   onclick="butCheckValid_onclick()">
</FORM>
</BODY>
</HTML>
```

Save the page as ch8_examp2.htm then load it into your browser. Type just letters, numbers and spaces into the text box and click the **Check Character Validity** button, and you'll be told that the phrase contains valid characters. Try putting punctuation or special characters like @, ^, $ and so on in the text box, and you'll be informed that it's invalid.

How It Works

Let's start by looking at the regExpIs_Valid() function defined at the top of the script block in the head of the page. That does the validity checking of our passphrase using regular expressions:

```
function regExpIs_valid(text)
{
   var myRegExp = /[^a-z\d ]/i;
   return !(myRegExp.test(text));
}
```

The function takes just one parameter, the text we want to check is valid. We then declare a variable myRegExp and set it to a new regular expression, which implicitly creates a new RegExp object.

The regular expression itself is fairly simple, but first let's think about what pattern we are looking for. What we want to find out is whether our passphrase string contains any characters that are not letters between A and Z, and a and z, numbers between 0 and 9, or a space. Let's see how this translates into a regular expression.

First we've used square brackets with the ^ symbol.

```
[^]
```

This means we want a match any character that is not one of the characters specified inside the square brackets. Next we have added our a-z, which specifies any character in the range a through to z:

```
[^a-z]
```

So far our regular expression matches any character that is not between a and z. Note that, because we added the i to the end of the expression definition, we've made the pattern case insensitive. So our regular expression actually matches any character not between A and Z or a and z.

Next we added \d to indicate any digit character, that is any character between 0 and 9.

```
[^a-z\d]
```

So our expression matches any character that is not between a and z, A and Z, or 0 and 9. Finally, we've decided that a space is valid, so we add that inside the square brackets:

```
[^a-z\d ]
```

Putting this all together, we have a regular expression that will match any character that is not either a letter or a digit or a space.

On the second and final line of the function we use the RegExp object's test() method to return a value:

```
return !(myRegExp.test(text));
```

The test() method of the RegExp object checks the string passed as its parameter to see if the characters specified by the regular expression syntax match anything inside the string. If they do, then true is returned, if not then false is returned. Our regular expression will match the first invalid character found, so if we get a result of true then we have an invalid passphrase. However, it's a bit illogical for an is_valid function to return true when it's invalid, so we reverse the result returned by adding the NOT operator (!).

We've seen above the two line validity checker function using regular expressions. Just to show how much more coding is required to do the same thing without regular expressions, I've created a second function that does the same as regExpIs_valid() but without regular expressions:

```
function is_valid(text)
{
    var isValid = true;
    var validChars = "abcdefghijklmnopqrstuvwxyz1234567890 ";
    var charIndex;
    for (charIndex = 0; charIndex < text.length;charIndex++)
    {
        if ( validChars.indexOf(text.charAt(charIndex).toLowerCase()) < 0)
        {
            isValid = false;
            break;
        }
    }
    return isValid;
}
```

This is probably as small as the non-regular expression version can be, and yet it's still twelve lines long. That's six times the amount of code for the regular expression version.

The principle of this function is similar to the regular expression version. We have a variable, validChars, that contains all the characters we consider to be valid. We then use the charAt() method in a for loop to get each character in the passphrase string and check that it exists in our validChars string. If not, then we know we have an invalid character.

In this example, the non regular expression version of the function is twelve lines, but with a more complex problem we could find it takes twenty or thirty lines to do the same thing a regular expression can do in just a handful of lines of code.

Back to our actual code, the other function defined in the head of the page is butCheckValid_onclick(). As the name suggests, this is called when the butCheckValid button defined in the body of the page is clicked.

This function calls our regExpis_Valid() function in an if statement to check if the passphrase entered by the user in the txtPhrase text box is valid. If it is, then an alert box is used to inform the user.

```
function butCheckValid_onclick()
{
    if (regExpIs_valid(document.form1.txtPhrase.value) == true)
    {
        alert("Your passphrase contains valid characters");
    }
```

If it isn't, then another alert box is used to let the user know that their text was invalid.

```
    else
    {
        alert("Your passphrase contains invalid characters");
    }
}
```

Repetition Characters

Regular expressions include a way of specifying how many of the last item or character, we want to match. This proves very useful, for example, if we want to specify a phone number that repeats a character a specific number of times.

Special Character	Meaning	Example
{n}	Match n of the previous item	x{2} matches xx
{n,}	Match n or more of the previous item	x{2,} matches xx, xxx, xxxx, xxxxx, etc.
{n,m}	Match at least n and at most m of the proceeding item	x{2,4} matches xx, xxx and xxxx
?	Match the previous item zero or one times	x? matches nothing or x.
+	Match the previous item one or more times	x+ matches x, xx, xxx, xxxx, xxxxx, etc.
*	Match the previous item zero or more times	x* matches nothing or x or xx or xxx or xxxx, etc.

We saw earlier that to match a telephone number in the format 1-800-888-5474, the regular expression would be \d-\d\d\d-\d\d\d-\d\d\d\d. Let's see how this would be simplified using the repetition characters.

The pattern we're looking for starts with one digit followed by a dash, so we need:

```
\d-
```

Next are three digits followed by a dash. This time we can use the repetition special characters – \d{3} will match exactly three \d, which is any digit character.

```
\d-\d{3}-
```

Again, next there are three digits followed by a dash, so now our regular expression looks like:

```
\d-\d{3}-\d{3}-
```

Finally the last part of the expression is four digits, which is \d{4}.

```
\d-\d{3}-\d{3}-\d{4}
```

We'd declare this regular expression like this:

```
var myRegExp = /\d-\d{3}-\d{3}-\d{4}/
```

Remember that the first / and last / tell JavaScript that what is in between those characters is a regular expression. JavaScript creates a `RegExp` object based on this regular expression.

As another example, how about if we had the string "Paul Paula Pauline" and we want to replace Paul and Paula with George? To do this, we would need a regular expression that matches both Paul and Paula.

Let's break this down. We know we want the characters 'Paul', so our regular expression starts as

```
Paul
```

Now we also want to match Paula, but if we make our expression `Paula` this will exclude a match on Paul. This is where the special character ? comes in. It allows us to specify that the previous character is optional, that is it must appear zero (not at all) or one times. So, the solution is:

```
Paula?
```

which we'd declare as:

```
var myRegExp = /Paula?/
```

Position Characters

The third group of special characters we'll look at are those that allow you to specify what will be on either side of the character pattern. For example, we might want our pattern to exist at the start or end of a string or line, or we might want it to be between two words.

Position Character	Description
^	The pattern must be at the start of the string, or if it's a multi-line string, then at the beginning of a line. For multi-line text, that is a string that contains carriage returns, we need to set `RegExp.multiline = true`.
$	The pattern must be at the end of the string, or if it's a multi-line string, then at the end of a line. For multi-line text, that is a string that contains carriage returns we need to set `RegExp.multiline = true`.
\b	This matches a word boundary, which is essentially the point between a word character and a non word character.
\B	This matches a position that's not a word boundary.

For example, if we wanted to make sure our pattern was at the start of a line we would type:

```
^myPattern
```

This would match an occurrence of `myPattern` if it was at the beginning of a line.

To match the same pattern, but at the end of a line, we would type:

```
myPattern$
```

The word boundary special characters \b and \B can cause confusion, as they do not match characters but the positions between characters.

Imagine we had the string "Hello world!, let's look at boundaries said 007." defined in the code:

```
var myString = "Hello world!, let's look at boundaries said 007.";
```

To make the word boundaries (that is, the boundaries between the words) of this string stand out, let's convert them to the | character.

```
var myRegExp = /\b/g;
myString = myString.replace(myRegExp, "|");
alert(myString);
```

We've replaced all the word boundaries, \b, with a | and our message box looks like:

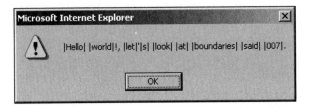

Note that this does not work on Netscape Navigator version 4.0-4.05.

You can see that the position between any word character, that is letters, numbers, or the underscore, and any non word character is a word boundary. You'll also notice that the boundary between the start or end of the string and a word character is considered to be a word boundary. The end of this string is a full stop, so the boundary between that and the end of the string is a non-word boundary and so no | has been inserted.

If we change the regular expression in the example, so that it replaces non-word boundaries:

```
var myRegExp = /\B/g;
```

then we get

Note that this does not work on Netscape Navigator version 4.0-4.05. Also note that on NN version 4.06+ (but not version 6) no | is inserted at the end of the string after the period.

Now the position between a letter, number or underscore and another letter, number or underscore is considered a non-word boundary and is replaced by an | in our example. However, what is slightly confusing is that the boundary between two non-word characters, such as an exclamation mark and a comma, is also considered a non-word boundary. If you think about it, it makes sense, but it's easy to forget about when creating regular expressions.

You'll remember from when we started looking at regular expressions, that I used the example:

```
<HTML>
<BODY>
<SCRIPT LANGUAGE=JavaScript>
var myString = "Paul, Paula, Pauline, paul, Paul";
var myRegExp = /Paul/gi;
myString = myString.replace(myRegExp, "Ringo");
alert(myString);
</SCRIPT>
</BODY>
</HTML>
```

to convert all instances of Paul or paul into Ringo.

However, we found that this code actually converts all instances of Paul to Ringo, even when inside another word.

One option to solve this problem would be to only replace the string Paul where it is followed by a non-word character. The special character for non-word characters is \W, so we need to alter our regular expression to:

```
var myRegExp = /Paul\W/gi;
```

This gives the result:

Note that on Netscape 4.0-4.05, this actually gives the result:

Ringo Paula, Pauline, Ringo Ringo

It's getting better, but still not what we want. Notice that the commas after the second and third Paul substrings have also been replaced since they matched the \W character. Also, we're still not replacing the Paul at the very end of the string. That's because there is no character after the letter l in the last Paul. What is after the l in the last Paul? Nothing, just the boundary between a word character and a non-word character and therein lies our answer. What we want as our regular expression is Paul followed by a word boundary. Let's alter our regular expression to cope with that:

307

```
var myRegExp = /Paul\b/gi;
```

Now we get the result we want:

At last we've got it right and that's this example finished.

Covering All Eventualities

Perhaps the trickiest thing about a regular expression is making sure it covers all eventualities. In the previous example our regular expression works with the string as defined, but does it work with:

```
var myString = "Paul, Paula, Pauline, paul, Paul, JeanPaul";
```

Here the Paul substring in JeanPaul will be changed to Ringo. We really only want to convert the substring Paul where it is on its own, that is with a word boundary on either side. If we change our regular expression code to

```
var myRegExp = /\bPaul\b/gi;
```

then we have our final answer and can be sure only Paul or paul will ever be matched.

Grouping Regular Expressions

Our final topic under regular expressions, before we look at examples using the match(), replace(), and search() methods, is how we can group expressions. In fact it's quite easy. If we want a number of expressions to be treated as a single group, we just enclose them in parentheses, for example /(\d\d)/. Parentheses in regular expressions are special characters that group together character patterns and are not themselves part of the characters to be matched.

The question is, "why would we want to do this?" Well, by grouping characters into patterns, we can use the special repetition characters to apply to the whole group of characters, rather than just one.

Let's take the string defined in myString below as an example:

```
var myString = "JavaScript, VBScript and Perl";
```

How could we match both JavaScript and VBScript using the same regular expression? The only thing they have in common is that they are whole words and they both end in Script. Well, an easy way would be to use parentheses to group the patterns Java and VB. Then we can use the ? special character to apply to each of these groups of characters to make our pattern any word having zero or one instances of the characters Java or VB, and ending in Script.

```
var myRegExp = /\b(VB)?(Java)?Script\b/gi;
```

If we break this expression down, we can see the pattern it requires is:

1. A word boundary: \b

2. Zero or one instances of VB: (VB)?

3. Zero or one instances of Java: (Java)?

4. The characters Script: Script

5. A word boundary: \b

If we put this together we get:

```
var myString = "JavaScript, VBScript and Perl";
var myRegExp = /\b(VB)?(Java)?Script\b/gi;
myString = myString.replace(myRegExp, "xxxx");
alert(myString);
```

And the output of this code is:

If you look back at the special repetition characters table you'll see that they apply to the previous item. This can be a character or, where they have been grouped using parentheses, the previous group of characters.

However, there is a potential problem with the regular expression we just defined. As well as matching VBScript and JavaScript, it also matches VBJavaScript. This is clearly not exactly what we meant.

To get round this we need to make use of both grouping and the special character | which is the alternation character. It has an "or"-like meaning, similar to using || in if statements and will match the characters on either side of itself.

Let's think about the problem again. We want the pattern to match VBScript or JavaScript. Clearly they have the Script part in common, so what we want is a new word starting with Java or starting with VB and either way it must end in Script.

First we know that the word must start with a word boundary:

```
\b
```

Next we know that we want either VB or Java to be at the start of the word. We've just seen that in regular expressions | provides the "or" we need, so in regular expression syntax we want:

```
\b(VB|Java)
```

This would match the pattern VB or Java. Now we can just add the Script part:

```
\b(VB|Java)Script\b
```

So our final code looks like this:

```
var myString = "JavaScript, VBScript and Perl";
var myRegExp = /\b(VB|Java)Script\b/gi;
myString = myString.replace(myRegExp, "xxxx");
alert(myString);
```

Reusing groups of characters

We can reuse the pattern specified by a group of characters later on in our regular expression. To refer to a previous group of characters, we just type \ and the order of the group. For example, the first group can be referred to as \1, the second as \2, and so on.

Let's look at an example. Say we have a list of numbers in a string, with each number separated by a comma. For whatever reason, we are not allowed to have the same numbers repeated after each other, so while:

```
009,007,001,002,004,003
```

would be OK, the following:

```
007,007,001,002,002,003
```

would not be valid, since we have 007 and 002 repeated after themselves.

How can we find instances of repeated digits and replace them with the word ERROR? We need to use the ability to refer to groups in regular expressions.

First let's define our string:

```
var myString  = "007,007,1,02,02,003,002,04";
```

Now we know we need to search for a series of one or more number characters. In regular expressions the \d specifies any digit character and + means one or more of the previous. So far, that gives our regular expression as:

```
\d+
```

We want to match a series of digits followed by a comma, so we just add the comma

```
\d+,
```

This will match any series of digits followed by a comma, but how do we search for any series of digits followed by a comma, then followed again by the same series of digits? As the digits could be any digits we can't add them directly into our expression like so:

```
\d+,007
```

as this will not work with the 002 repeat. What we need to do is put the first series of digits in a group, then we can specify that we want to match that group of digits again. This can be done using \1, which says "match the characters found in the first group defined using parentheses". Put all this together and we have:

```
(\d+),\1
```

This defines a group whose pattern of characters is one or more digit characters. This group must be followed by a comma, and then by the same pattern of characters as were found in the first group. Put this into some JavaScript, and we have:

```
var myString  = "007,007,1,02,02,003,002,04";
var myRegExp = /(\d+),\1/g;
myString = myString.replace(myRegExp,"ERROR");
alert(myString);
```

The alert box will show:

ERROR,1,ERROR,003,002,04

That completes our brief look at regular expression syntax. As regular expressions can get a little complex it's often a good idea to start simple and build them up slowly, as we have above. In fact most regular expressions are just too hard to get right in one step – at least for us mere mortals without a brain the size of a planet.

If it's still looking a bit strange and confusing then don't panic. In the next sections we'll be looking at the String object's split(), match(), search(), and replace() methods with plenty more examples of regular expression syntax.

The String Object – split(), replace(), search(), and match() Methods

The main functions making use of regular expressions are the String object's split(), replace(), search(), and match() methods. We've already seen their syntax, so we'll concentrate on their use with regular expressions and at the same time learn more about regular expression syntax and usage.

The split() method

We've seen that the split() method allows us to split a string into various pieces with the split being made at the character or characters specified as a parameter. The result of this method is an array with each element containing one of the split pieces. For example, the string:

```
var myListString = "apple, banana, peach, orange"
```

could be split into an array where each element contains a different fruit using:

```
var myFruitArray = myListString.split(", ");
```

How about if our string was instead:

```
var myListString = "apple, 0.99, banana, 0.50, peach, 0.25, orange, 0.75";
```

This could, for example, contain both the names and prices of the fruit. How could we split the string, but just retrieve the names of the fruit and not the prices? We could do it without regular expressions, but it would take a number of lines of code. With regular expressions we can use the same code, and just amend the split() method's parameter.

Try it out – splitting the fruit string

Let's create an example that solves the problem described above – it must split our string, but only include the fruit names, not the prices.

```
<HTML>
<BODY>
<SCRIPT LANGUAGE=JavaScript>
var myListString = "apple, 0.99, banana, 0.50, peach, 0.25, orange, 0.75";
var theRegExp = /[^a-z]+/i;
var myFruitArray = myListString.split(theRegExp);
document.write(myFruitArray.join("<BR>"));
</SCRIPT>
</BODY>
</HTML>
```

Save the file as ch8_examp3.htm, and then load it in your browser. You should see the four fruits from our string written out the page with each fruit on a separate line.

How It Works

Within the script block, first we have our string with fruit names and prices:

```
var myListString = "apple, 0.99, banana, 0.50, peach, 0.25, orange, 0.75";
```

How do we split that in such a way that only the fruit names are included. Our first thought might be to use the comma as the `split()` method's parameter, but of course that means we end up with the prices. What we have to ask ourselves is "what is it that's between the items we want", that is what is between the fruit names that we can use to define our split. The answer is that various characters are between the fruit, such as a comma, a space, numbers, a full stop, more numbers and finally another comma. What is it that these things have in common and makes them different from the fruit names that we want? What they have in common is that none of them are the letters from a through z. If we say split the string at the point where there is a group of characters that are not between a and z, then we get the result we want. Now we know what we want we need to create our regular expression.

We know that what we want is not the letters a – z, so we start with:

```
[^a-z]
```

The ^ says "match any character that does not match those specified inside the square brackets". In this case we've specified a range of characters to not to be matched, all those characters between a and z. As specified, this will only match one character, whereas we want to split wherever there is a single group of one or more characters that are not between a and z. To do this we need to add the + special repetition character, which says "match one or more of the preceding character or group specified".

```
[^a-z]+
```

Our final result is:

```
var theRegExp = /[^a-z]+/i
```

The / and / mark the start and end of the regular expression whose `RegExp` object is stored as a reference in variable `theregExp`. We add the i on the end to make the match case insensitive.

Don't panic if creating regular expressions seems a frustrating and less than obvious process. At first, it takes a lot of trial-and-error to get it right, but as you get more experienced you'll find creating them becomes much easier and will enable you to do things that without regular expression would be either very long-winded or virtually impossible.

In the next line of script, we pass the `RegExp` object to the `split()` method, which uses it to decide where to split the string.

```
var myFruitArray = myListString.split(theRegExp);
```

After the split, the variable myFruitArray will contain an Array with each element containing the fruit name as shown below:

Array Element Index	0	1	2	3
Element Value	apple	banana	peach	orange

We then join the string together again using the Array object's join() methods, which we saw in Chapter 4.

```
document.write(myFruitArray.join("<BR>"))
```

The replace() Method

We've already looked at the syntax and usage of the replace() method. However, something unique to the replace() method is its ability to replace text based on the groups matched in the regular expression. We do this using the $ sign and the group's number. Each group in a regular expression is given a number from 1 to 9; any groups greater then 9 are not accessible. To refer to a group we write $ followed by the group's position. For example, if we had:

```
var myRegExp = /(\d) (\W)/g;
```

then $0 refers to the group (\d) and $2 to the group (\W).

You can see this more clearly in the next example. If we had a string defined as below:

```
var myString = "1999, 2000, 2001";
```

and we wanted to change this to "the year 1999, the year 2000, the year 2001", how could we do this with regular expressions?

First we need to work out the pattern as a regular expression, in this case four digits:

```
var myRegExp = /\d{4}/g;
```

But, given that the year is different every time, how can we substitute the year value into the replaced string?

Well, we change our regular expression, so that it's inside a group:

```
var myRegExp = /(\d{4})/g;
```

Now we can use the group, which has group number 1, inside the replacement string like this:

```
myString = myString.replace(myRegExp, "the year $1");
```

The variable myString would then contain the required string "the year 1999, the year 2000, the year 2001".

Let's look at another example in which we want to convert single quotes in text to double quotes. Our test string is:

```
'Hello World' said Mr O'Connerly.
He then said 'My Name is O'Connerly, yes that's right, O'Connerly'.
```

One problem that the test string makes clear is that we only want to replace the single speech mark with a double where it is used in pairs around speech, not when acting as an apostrophe, such as in the word that's, or when part of someone's name, such as in O'Connerly.

Let's start by defining our regular expression. First we know that it must include a single quote:

```
var myRegExp = /'/;
```

However as it is, this would replace every single quote, which is not what we want.

Looking at the text, something else we notice is that quotes are always at the start or end of a word, that is they are at a boundary. On first glance it might be easy to assume that it would be a word boundary. However don't forget that the ' is a non-word character so the boundary will be between it and another non-word character, such as a space. So the boundary will be a non-word boundary, that is \B .

Therefore, the character pattern we are looking for is either a non-word boundary followed by a single quote, or a single quote followed by a non-word boundary. The key is the "or", for which we use | in regular expressions. This leaves our regular expression as:

```
var myRegExp = /\B'|'\B/g;
```

This will match the pattern on the left of the | or the character pattern on the right. We want to replace all the single quotes with double quotes, so the g has been added at the end indicating a global match should take place.

Try It Out – Replacing Single Quotes with Double Quotes

Let's look at an example using the regular expression defined above.

```
<HTML>
<HEAD>
<SCRIPT LANGUAGE=JavaScript>

function replaceQuote(textAreaControl)
{
    var myText = textAreaControl.value;
    var myRegExp = /\B'|'\B/g;

    myText = myText.replace(myRegExp,'"');
    textAreaControl.value = myText;
}

</SCRIPT>
</HEAD>
```

```
<BODY>
<FORM NAME=form1>
<TEXTAREA ROWS=20 COLS=40 NAME=textarea1 WRAP=hard>
'Hello World' said Mr O'Connerly.
He then said 'My Name is O'Connerly, yes that's right, O'Connerly'.
</TEXTAREA>
<BR>
<INPUT TYPE="button" VALUE="Replace Single Quotes" NAME=buttonSplit
    onclick="replaceQuote(document.form1.textarea1)">
</FORM>
</BODY>
</HTML>
```

Save the page as ch8_examp4.htm. Load the page into your browser:

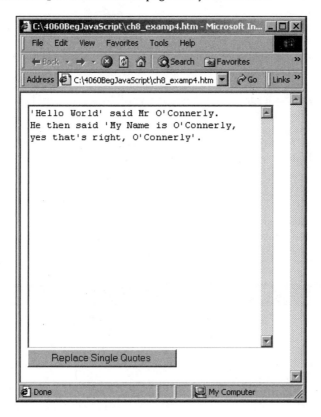

Click the Replace Single Quotes button to see the single quotes in the textarea replaced:

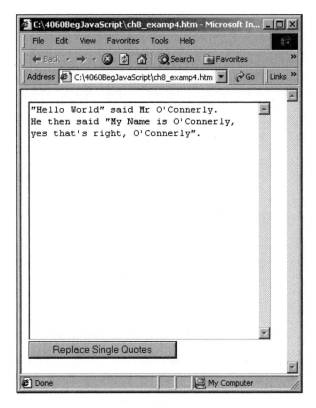

Try entering your own text with single quotes into the textarea and check the results.

How It Works

You can see that using regular expressions we have completed a task in a couple of lines of simple code, that without regular expressions would probably take four or five times that amount.

Lets look first at the `replaceQuote()` function in the head of the page where all the action is:

```
function replaceQuote(textAreaControl)
{
    var myText = textAreaControl.value;
    var myRegExp = /\B'|'\B/g;

    myText = myText.replace(myRegExp,'"');
    textAreaControl.value = myText;
}
```

The function's parameter is the `Textarea` object defined lower down the page – this is the textarea whose text we want the single quotes replaced in. We can see how the `Textarea` object was passed in the button's tag definition:

```
<INPUT TYPE="button" VALUE="Replace Single Quotes" NAME=buttonSplit
    onclick="replaceQuote(document.form1.textarea1)">
```

In the `onclick` event handler we call `replaceQuote()` and pass `document.form1.textarea1` as the parameter – that is the `Textarea` object.

Returning to the function, on the first line we get the value of the `Textarea` and place it in the variable `myText`. Then we define our regular expression as we discussed previously, which matches any non-word boundary followed by a single quote or any single quote followed by a non-word boundary. For example, `'H` will match, as will `H'`, but `O'R` won't as the quote is between two word boundaries. Don't forget that a word boundary is the position between the start or end of a word and a non-word character, such as a space or punctuation mark.

In the function's final two lines we first use the `replace()` method to do the character pattern search and replace, and finally we set the `Textarea` object's value to the changed string.

The search() Method

The `search()` method allows you to search a string for a pattern of characters. If the pattern is found then the character position at which it was found is returned, otherwise –1 is returned. The method takes only one parameter, the `RegExp` object you have created.

While for basic searches the `indexOf()` method is fine, if you want more complex searches, such as a pattern of any digits, or where a word must be in between a certain boundary, then `search()` provides a much more powerful and flexible, but sometimes more complex, approach.

In the example below, we want to find out if the word Java is contained within the string. However, we want to look just for Java as a whole word, not when it's within another word such as JavaScript.

```
var myString = "Beginning JavaScript, Beginning Java 2, Professional JavaScript";
var myRegExp = /\bJava\b/i;
alert(myString.search(myRegExp));
```

First we have defined our string, and then we've created our regular expression. We want to find the character pattern Java when it's on its own, that is between two word boundaries. We've made our search case insensitive by adding the i after the regular expression. Note that with the `search()` method, the g for global is not relevant and its use has no effect.

On the final line we output the position that the search has located the pattern, in this case 32.

The match() Method

The `match()` method is very similar to the `search()` method, except that instead of returning the position where a match was found, it returns an array. Each element of the array contains the text of a match made.

For example, if we had the string:

```
var myString = "The years were 1999, 2000 and 2001";
```

and wanted to extract the years from this string we could do so using the match() method. To match each year, we are looking for four digits in between word boundaries. This requirement translates to the regular expression below:

```
var myRegExp = /\b\d{4}\b/g;
```

We want to match all the years so the g has been added to the end for a global search.

To do the match and store the results, we use the match() method and store the Array object it returns in a variable.

```
var resultsArray = myString.match(myRegExp);
```

To prove it has worked, let's use some code to output each item in the array.

```
var indexCounter;
for (indexCounter = 0; indexCounter < resultsArray.length; indexCounter++)
{
    alert(resultsArray[indexCounter]);
}
```

This would result in three alert boxes containing the numbers 1999, 2000, and 2001.

Try It Out – Splitting HTML

In the next example, we want to take a string of HTML and split it into its component parts. For example, we want the HTML <P>Hello</P> to become an array, the elements having contents:

| <P> | Hello | </P> |

```
<HTML>
<HEAD>
<SCRIPT LANGUAGE=JavaScript>

function button1_onclick()
{
    var myString = "<TABLE align=center><TR><TD>"
    myString = myString + "Hello World</TD></TR></TABLE>"
    myString = myString +"<BR><H2>Heading</H2>";

    var myRegExp = /<[^>\r\n]+>|[^<>\r\n]+/g
    var resultsArray = myString.match(myRegExp);

    document.form1.textarea1.value = "";
    document.form1.textarea1.value = resultsArray.join("\r\n");
}

</SCRIPT>
</HEAD>
```

319

```
<BODY>
<FORM NAME=form1>
   <TEXTAREA ROWS=20 COLS=40 NAME=textarea1></TEXTAREA>
   <INPUT TYPE="button" VALUE="Split HTML" NAME=button1
       onclick="return button1_onclick()">
</FORM>
</BODY>
</HTML>
```

Save this file as ch8_examp5.htm. When you load the page into your browser and click the Split HTML button, a string of HTML is split and each tag is placed on a separate line in the textarea, as shown below:

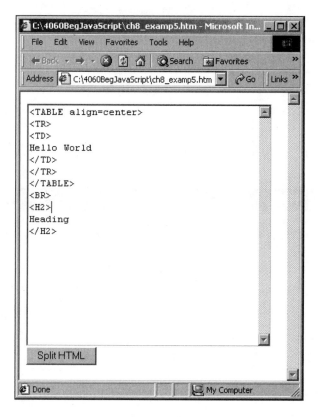

How It Works

The function button1_onclick() defined at the top of the page fires when the Split HTML button is clicked. At the top the lines:

```
function button1_onclick()
{
    var myString = "<TABLE align=center><TR><TD>";
    myString = myString + "Hello World</TD></TR></TABLE>";
    myString = myString +"<BR><H2>Heading</H2>";
```

define our string of HTML that we'll be splitting.

Next we create our `RegExp` object and initialize it to our regular expression.

```
var myRegExp = /<[^>\r\n]+>|[^<>\r\n]+/g
```

Let's break it down to see what pattern we're trying to match. First note that the pattern is broken up by an alternation symbol |. This means that we want the pattern on the left or the right of this symbol. We'll look at these patterns separately. On the left we have:

1. The pattern must start with a <

2. In `[^>\r\n]`+ we specify that we want one or more of any character except the > or a \r (carriage return) or a \n (linefeed)

3. > specifies that the pattern must end with a >

On the right:

4. `[^<>\r\n]`+ specifies that the pattern is one or more of any character so long as that character is not a <, >, \r or \n. This will match plain text.

After the regular expression definition we have a g, which specifies that this is a global match.

So the < `[^>\r\n]`+> regular expression will match any start or close tags such as <P> or </P>. The alternative pattern is `[^<>\r\n]`+ which will match any character pattern that is not an opening or closing tag.

In the following line:

```
var resultsArray = myString.match(myRegExp);
```

we assign the `resultsArray` variable to the `Array` object returned by the `match()` method.

The remainder of the code deals with populating the textarea with the split HTML. We use the `Array` object's `join()` method to join all the array's elements into one string with each element separated by a "\r\n" character, so that each tag or piece of text goes on a separate line:

```
    document.form1.textarea1.value = "";
    document.form1.textarea1.value = resultsArray.join("\r\n");
}
```

Using the RegExp object's Constructor

So far we've been creating `RegExp` objects using the / and / characters to define the start and end of the regular expression, for example:

```
var myRegExp = /[a-z]/;
```

While this is the generally preferred method, it was briefly mentioned that a `RegExp` object can also be created using the `RegExp()` constructor. While we might use the first way most of the time, there are occasions, as we'll see in the trivia quiz shortly, when the second way of creating a `RegExp` object is necessary.

As an example, see that the above regular expression could equally well be defined as:

```
var myRegExp = new RegExp("[a-z]");
```

Here we pass the regular expression as a string parameter to the `RegExp()` constructor function.

A very important difference when using this method is in how we use special regular expression characters, such as \b, which have a backward slash in front of them. The problem is that the backward slash indicates an escape character in JavaScript strings – for example, we may use \b which means a backspace. To differentiate between \b meaning a backspace in a string and the \b special character in a regular expression, we have to put another backward slash in front of the regular expression special character. So \b becomes \\b when we mean the regular expression \b that matches a word boundary, rather than a backspace character.

For example if we have defined our `RegExp` object using:

```
var myRegExp = /\b/;
```

then declaring it using the `RegExp()` constructor, we would need to write:

```
var myRegExp = new RegExp("\\b");
```

and not:

```
var myRegExp = new RegExp("\b");
```

All special regular expression characters, such as \w, \b, \d, and so on must have an extra \ in front when created using `RegExp()`.

When we defined regular expressions with the / and / method, we could add after the final / the special flags g and i to indicate that the pattern matching should be global or case-insensitive. When using the `RegExp()` constructor, how can we do the same thing?

Easy. The optional second parameter of the `RegExp()` constructor takes the flags that specify a global or case-insensitive match. For example:

```
var myRegExp = new RegExp("hello\\b","gi");
```

will do a global case-insensitive pattern match. We can specify just one of the flags if we wish, such as:

```
var myRegExp = new RegExp("hello\\b","i");
```

or

```
var myRegExp = new RegExp("hello\\b","g");
```

The Trivia Quiz

The goal for the trivia quiz in this chapter is to enable it to set questions with answers that have to be typed in by the user, in addition to the multi-choice questions we already have. To do this we'll be making use of our new-found knowledge of regular expressions to search the reply that the user types in for a match with the correct answer.

The problem we face with text answers is that a number of possible answers may be correct and we don't want to annoy the user by insisting that only *one* version is correct. For example, the answer to the question "Which President was involved in the Watergate Scandal?" is Richard Milhous Nixon. However, most people will type Nixon, or maybe Richard Nixon or even R Nixon. Each of these variations is valid, and using regular expressions we can easily check for all of them (or at least many plausible alternatives) in just a few lines of code.

What will we need to change to add this extra functionality? In fact changes are needed in only two pages: the GlobalFunctions.htm page and the AskQuestion.htm page.

In the GlobalFunctions.htm page, we need to define our new questions and answers, change the getQuestion() function, which builds up the HTML to display the question to the user, and change the answerCorrect() function, which checks whether the user's answer is correct.

In the AskQuestion.htm page, we need to change the function getAnswer(), which retrieves the user's answer from the page's form.

We'll start by making the changes to GlobalFunctions.htm that we created in the last chapter, so open this up in your HTML editor.

All the existing multi-choice questions that we define near the top of the page can remain in exactly the same format, so there are no need for any changes there. How can this be if we're using regular expressions?

Previously we checked to see that the answer the user selected, such as A, B, C, and so on, was equal to the character in the answers array. Well, we can do the same thing, but using a very simple regular expression that matches the character supplied by the user with the character in the answers array. If they match then we know the answer is correct.

Now we'll add the first new text based question directly underneath the last multi-choice question and answer.

```
// define question 4
questions[3] = "In the Simpsons, Bleeding Gums Murphy played which instrument?"
// assign answer for question 4
answers[3] = "\\bsax(ophone)?\\b";
```

The question definition is much simpler for text-based questions than for the multi-choice questions: it's just the question text itself.

The answer definition is a regular expression. Note that we use \\b rather than \b, since we'll be creating our regular expressions using new RegExp() rather than using the / and / method. The valid answers to this question are sax and saxophone, so we need to define our regular expression to match either of those. Let's break it down stage by stage:

Expression	Description
\\b	The \\b indicates that the answer must start with a word boundary, in other words the answer must be a whole word and not contained inside another word. We do this just in case the user for some reason puts characters before their answer, such as "my answer is saxophone".
sax	The user's answer must start with the characters sax.
(ophone)?	We've grouped the pattern ophone by putting it in parentheses. Then by putting the ? just after it we are saying that that pattern can appear zero or one times.
	If the user types sax, it appears zero times, if the user types saxophone, it appears once – either way we make a match.
\\b	Finally we want the word to end at a word boundary.

The second question we'll create is:

```
"Which American President was involved in the Watergate Scandal?"
```

The possible correct answers for this are quite numerous and include:

```
Richard Milhous Nixon
Richard Nixon
Richard M. Nixon
Richard M Nixon
R Milhous Nixon
R. Milhous Nixon
R. M. Nixon
R M Nixon
R.M. Nixon
RM Nixon
R Nixon
R. Nixon
Nixon
```

This is a fairly exhaustive list of possible correct answers, we could perhaps just have accepted "Nixon" and "Richard Nixon", but the longer list makes for a more challenging regular expression.

```
// define question 5
questions[4] = "Which American President was involved in the Watergate Scandal?"
// assign answer for question 5
answers[4] = "\\b((Richard |R\\.? ?)(Milhous |M\\.? )?)?Nixon\\b";
```

Add the question and answer code above under the other questions and answers in the `GlobalFunction.htm` file.

Let's analyze this regular expression now.

Expression	Description
`\\b`	The `\\b` indicates that the answer must start with a word boundary, so the answer must be a whole word and not contained inside another word. We do this just in case the user for some reason puts characters before their answer, such as `"my answer is President Nixon"`.
`((Richard |R\\.? ?)`	This part of the expression in fact is grouped together with the next part, `(Milhous |M\\.? )?)`. The first parenthesis creates the outer group. Inside this is an inner group, which can be one of two patterns. Before the | is the pattern `Richard`, after it is the pattern R followed by an optional dot `(.)` followed by an optional space. So either `Richard` or R or R. will match. As the `.` is a special character in regular expressions, we have to tell JavaScript we mean a literal dot and not a special character dot. We do this by placing the \ in front. However, because we are defining this regular expression using the `RegExp()` constructor, we need to place an additional \ in front.
`(Milhous |M\\.? )?)?`	This is the second subgroup within the outer group. It works in a similar way to the first subgroup except it's `Milhous` rather than `Richard` and M rather than R that we are matching. Also, the space after the initial is not optional, since we don't want RMNixon. The second ? outside this inner group indicates that the middle name/initial is optional. The final parenthesis indicates the end of the outer group. The final ? indicates that the outer group pattern is optional, this is to allow the answer `Nixon` alone to be valid.
`Nixon\\b`	Finally the pattern `Nixon` must be matched followed by a word boundary

That completes the two additional text based questions. Now we need to alter the question creation function, `getQuestion()`, again inside the file `GlobalFunctions.htm`:

```
function getQuestion()
{
    if (questions.length != numberOfQuestionsAsked)
    {
        var questionNumber = Math.floor(Math.random() * questions.length);

        while (questionsAsked[questionNumber] == true)
        {
            questionNumber = Math.floor(Math.random() * questions.length);
        }

        var questionLength = questions[questionNumber].length;
        var questionChoice;

        numberOfQuestionsAsked++;

        var questionHTML = "<H4>Question " + numberOfQuestionsAsked +  "</H4>";

        // Check if array or string
        if (typeof questions[questionNumber] == "string")
        {
            questionHTML = questionHTML + "<P>" + questions[questionNumber] + "</P>";
            questionHTML = questionHTML + "<P><INPUT type=text name=txtAnswer ";
            questionHTML = questionHTML + " maxlength=100 size=35></P>"
        }
        else
        {
            questionHTML = questionHTML + "<P>" + questions[questionNumber][0];
            questionHTML = questionHTML + "</P>";
            for (questionChoice = 1;questionChoice < questionLength;questionChoice++)
            {
                questionHTML = questionHTML + "<INPUT type=radio ";
                questionHTML = questionHTML + "name=radQuestionChoice";
                if (questionChoice == 1)
                {
                    questionHTML = questionHTML + " checked";
                }
                questionHTML = questionHTML + ">" +
                    questions[questionNumber][questionChoice];
                questionHTML = questionHTML + "<BR>"
            }
        }

        questionHTML = questionHTML + "<BR><INPUT TYPE='button' ";
        questionHTML = questionHTML + "VALUE='Answer Question'";
        questionHTML = questionHTML + "NAME=buttonNextQ ";
        questionHTML = questionHTML + "onclick='return buttonCheckQ_onclick()'>";

        currentQNumber = questionNumber;
        questionsAsked[questionNumber] = true;
    }
    else
    {
```

```
          questionHTML = "<H3>Quiz Complete</H3>";
          questionHTML = questionHTML + "You got " + numberOfQuestionsCorrect;
          questionHTML = questionHTML + " questions correct out of "
          questionHTML = questionHTML + numberOfQuestionsAsked;
          questionHTML = questionHTML + "<BR><BR>Your trivia rating is "

      switch(Math.round(((numberOfQuestionsCorrect / numberOfQuestionsAsked) *
  10)))
          {
             case 0:
             case 1:
             case 2:
             case 3:
                questionHTML = questionHTML + "Beyond embarrasing";
                break;
             case 4:
             case 5:
             case 6:
             case 7:
                questionHTML = questionHTML + "Average";
                break;
             default:
                questionHTML = questionHTML + "Excellent"
          }

          questionHTML = questionHTML + "<BR><BR><A href='quizpage.htm'><STRONG>"
          questionHTML = questionHTML + "Start again</STRONG></A>"
      }

   return questionHTML;
}
```

You can see that the getQuestion() function is mostly unchanged by our need to ask text based questions. The only real code lines that have changed are:

```
if (typeof questions[questionNumber] == "string")
{
    questionHTML = questionHTML + "<P>" + questions[questionNumber] + "</P>";
    questionHTML = questionHTML + "<P><INPUT type=text name=txtAnswer ";
    questionHTML = questionHTML + " maxlength=100 size=35></P>"
}
else
{
```

The need for this change is that the questions for multiple-choice and text-based questions are displayed differently. Having obtained our question number, we then need to check to see if this is a text question or a multi-choice question. In text based questions we store the string containing the text inside the questions[] array; with the multi-choice questions we store an array inside the questions[] array which contains the question and options. We can check to see whether or not the type of data stored in the questions[] array at the index for that particular question is a string type. If it's a string type, then we know we have a text based question; otherwise we assume it's a multi-choice question.

We use the typeof operator as part of the condition in our if statement in the line:

```
if (typeof questions[questionNumber] == "string")
```

If the condition is true, we then create the HTML for the text-based question; otherwise the HTML for a multi-choice question is created.

The second function inside GlobalFunctions.htm that needs to be changed is the answerCorrect() function, which actually checks the answer given by the user:

```
function answerCorrect(questionNumber, answer)
{
    // declare a variable to hold return value
    var correct = false;

    // if answer provided is same as answer then correct answer is true
    var answerRegExp = new RegExp(answers[questionNumber],"i");
    if (answer.search(answerRegExp) != -1)
    {
        numberOfQuestionsCorrect++;
        correct = true;
    }

    // return whether the answer was correct (true or false)
    return correct;
}
```

Instead of doing a simple comparison of the user's answer to the value in the answers[] array, we're now using regular expressions.

First we create a new RegExp object called answerRegExp and initialize it to the regular expression stored as a string inside our answers[] array. We want to do a case-insensitive match, so we pass the string i as the second parameter.

In our if statement, we search for the regular expression answer pattern in the answer given by the user. This answer will be a string for a text-based question, or a single character for a multi-choice question. If a match is found we'll get the character match position. If no match is found then -1 is returned. Therefore, if the match value is not -1, we know that the user's answer is correct, and the if statement's code executes. This increments the value of the variable numberOfQuestionsCorrect, and sets the correct variable to the value true.

That completes the changes to GlobalFunctions.htm. Remember to save the file before you close it.

Finally we have just one more function we need to alter before our changes are complete. This time the function is in the file AskQuestion.htm. The function is getAnswer(), which is used to retrieve the user's answer from the form on the page. The changes are listed below:

```
function getAnswer()
{
    var answer = 0;
```

```
            if (document.QuestionForm[0].type == "radio")
            {
                while (document.QuestionForm.radQuestionChoice[answer].checked != true)
                    answer++;
                answer =  String.fromCharCode(65 + answer);
            }
            else
            {
                answer = document.QuestionForm.txtAnswer.value;
            }

            return answer;
        }
```

The user's answer can now be given via one of two means: choosing an option in an option group, or through text entered in a text box. We work out which way was used for this question, by using the type property of the first control in the form. If the first control is a radio button, we know this is a multi-choice question, otherwise we assume it's a text based question.

If it is a multi-choice question then we obtain the answer, a character, as we did before we added text questions. If it's a text based question, then it's simply a matter of getting the text value from the text control written into the form dynamically by the getQuestion() function in the GlobalFunctions.htm page.

Save the changes to the page, as we're now ready to give our updated trivia quiz a test run. Load in TriviaQuiz.htm to start the quiz. You should now see the text questions displayed as in the screen shot below.

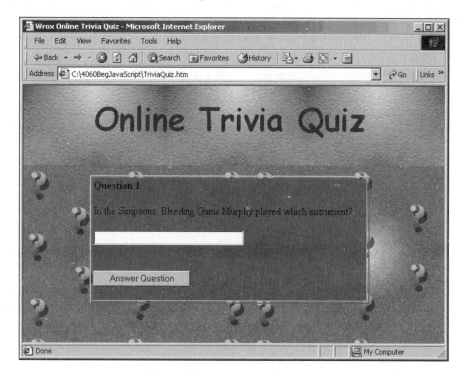

Although we've learnt a bit more about regular expressions while altering the trivia quiz, perhaps the most important lesson has been that using general functions, and where possible placing them inside common code modules, makes later changes quite simple. In less than 20 lines, mostly in one file, we have made a significant addition to the quiz.

Summary

In this chapter we've looked at some more advanced methods of the String object, and how their use can be optimised using regular expressions.

In outline, the chapter covered the following points

❑ The split() method splits a single sting into an array of strings. We pass a string to the method that determines where the split occurs.

❑ The replace() method allows us to replace a pattern of characters with another pattern that we specify as a second parameter.

❑ The search() method returns the character position of the first pattern matching that given as a parameter.

❑ The match() method matches patterns, returning the text of the matches in an array.

❑ We then looked at regular expressions, which allow us to define a pattern of characters that we want to match. Using this pattern we can perform splits, searches, text replacement, and matches on strings.

❑ In JavaScript the regular expressions are in the form of a RegExp object. A RegExp object can be created using either myRegExp = /myRegularExpression/ or with myRegExp = new RegExp("myRegularExpression"). The second form requires that certain special characters that normally have a single \ in front now have a double \\.

❑ The g and i characters at the end of a regular expression ensure a global and case insensitive match is made. For example, myRegExp = /Pattern/gi;

❑ As well as specifying actual characters, regular expressions have certain groups of special characters, which allow any of a certain groups of characters, such as digits, word or non-word characters, to be matched.

❑ Special characters can also be used to specify pattern or character repetition. Additionally we can specify what the pattern boundaries must be, for example at the beginning or end of the string or next to a word or non-word boundary.

❑ Finally we can define groups of characters that can be used later in the regular expression or in the results of using the expression with the replace() method.

❑ We also updated the trivia quiz in this chapter to allow questions to be set that require a text based response from the user, as well as multi-choice questions, which we have already seen.

In the next chapter we'll take a look at using and manipulating dates and times using JavaScript, and time conversion between different world time zones. Also covered is how to create a timer that executes code at regular intervals after the page is loaded. We'll be adapting the trivia quiz so that the user can select a time, within which it must be completed, for example 5 questions in 1 minute.

Exercise Questions

Suggested solutions to these questions can be found in Appendix A.

Question 1

What problem does the code below solve?

```
var myString = "This sentence has has a fault and and we need to fix it."
var myRegExp = /(\b\w+\b) \1/g;
myString = myString.replace(myRegExp,"$1");
```

If we now change our code, so that we create our RegExp object like this:

```
var myRegExp = new RegExp("(\b\w+\b) \1");
```

why would this not work, and how could we rectify the problem?

Question 2

Write a regular expression that finds all of the occurrences of the word "a" in the following sentence, and replaces them with "the":

"a dog walked in off a street and ordered a finest beer"

So the sentence becomes:

"the dog walked in off the street and ordered the finest beer"

Question 3

Imagine you have a web site with a message board. Write a regular expression that would remove barred words. (I'll let you make up your own words!!!)

Online discussion at http://p2p.wrox.com

Date, Time, and Timers

In Chapter 4 we saw that the concepts of date and time are embodied in JavaScript through the `Date` object. We looked at some of the properties and methods of the `Date` object, including the following:

- ❑ The methods `getDate()`, `getDay()`, `getMonth()`, and `getFullYear()` allow us to retrieve date values from inside a `Date` object.

- ❑ The `setDate()`, `setMonth()`, and `setFullYear()` methods allow us to set the date values of an existing `Date` object

- ❑ The `getHours()`, `getMinutes()`, `getSeconds()` and `getMilliseconds()` methods retrieve the time values in a `Date` object

- ❑ The `setHours()`, `setMinutes()`, `setSeconds()` and `setMilliseconds()` methods allow us to set time values of an existing `Date` object

One thing that we didn't cover in that chapter was the idea that the time depends on your location around the world. In this chapter we'll be correcting that omission by looking at date and time in relation to **world time**.

For example, imagine you have a chat room on your web site and want to organize a chat for a certain date and time. Simply stating 15:30 is not good enough if your web site attracts international visitors. The time 15:30 could be Eastern Standard Time, Pacific Standard Time, the time in the United Kingdom, or even the time in Kuala Lumpur. You could of course say 15:30 EST and let your visitors work out what that means, but even that isn't fool proof. There is an EST in Australia as well as in the US. Wouldn't it be great if you could automatically convert the time to the user's time zone? In this chapter we'll see how.

As well as looking at world time, we'll also be looking at how to create a **timer** in a web page. We'll see that using the timer we can trigger code, either at regular intervals or just once, for example five seconds after the page has loaded. We'll see how we can use timers to add a real time clock to a web page, and to create scrolling text in the status bar. Timers can also be useful for creating animations or special effects in our web applications. Finally, we'll be using the timer to enable the users of our trivia quiz to give themselves a time limit for answering the questions.

World Time

The concept of 'now' means the same point in time everywhere in the world. However, when that point in time is represented by numbers, those numbers differ depending on where you are. What is needed is a standard number to represent that moment in time. This is achieved through Coordinated Universal Time (UTC), which is an international basis of civil and scientific time, and was implemented in 1964. It was previously know as GMT (Greenwich Mean Time), and indeed at the time 0:00 UTC it is midnight in Greenwich, London.

The following table shows the local times around the world at 0:00 UTC time.

San Francisco	New York (EST)	Greenwich, London	Berlin, Germany	Tokyo, Japan
4:00 pm	7:00 pm	0:00 midnight	1:00 am	9:00 am

Note that the times given are winter times – no daylight saving hours are taken into account.

The support for UTC in JavaScript comes from a number of methods of the Date object that are similar to those we have already seen. For each of the 'set date' and 'get date' type methods we've seen so far, there is a UTC equivalent. For example, whereas setHours() sets the local hour in a Date object, setUTCHours() does the same thing for UTC time. We'll be looking at these methods in more detail in the next section.

In addition, there are three more methods of the Date object that are to do with world time.

We have the methods toUTCString() and toLocaleString() which return the date and time stored in the Date object as a string based on either UTC or local time.

If we simply want to find out the difference in minutes between the current locale's time and that of UTC time, we can use the getTimezoneOffset() method. If the time zone is behind UTC, such as in the United States, then it will return a positive number. If the time zone is ahead, such as in Australia or Japan, then it will return a negative number.

Try It Out – The World Time Method of the Date Object

In the code below we use the toLocaleString(), toUTCString(), and getTimezoneOffset() methods and write their values out to the page.

```
<HTML>
<HEAD>
<SCRIPT LANGUAGE = JavaScript>
    var localTime = new Date();
</SCRIPT>
</HEAD>
<BODY>
<H4>
    UTC Time is
    <SCRIPT LANGUAGE = JavaScript>
```

```
            document.write(localTime.toUTCString());
        </SCRIPT>
    </H4>
    <H4>
        Local Time is
        <SCRIPT LANGUAGE = JavaScript>
            document.write(localTime.toLocaleString());
        </SCRIPT>
    </H4>
    <H4>
        Time Zone Offset is
        <SCRIPT LANGUAGE = JavaScript>
            document.write(localTime.getTimezoneOffset());
        </SCRIPT>
    </H4>
    </BODY>
    </HTML>
```

Save this as `timetest.htm` and load it into your browser. What you see will, of course, depend on which time zone your computer is set to, but you'll see something like:

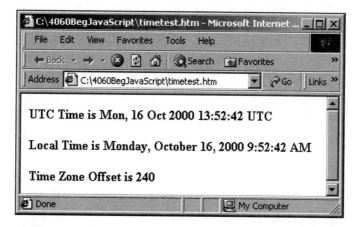

Here I have my computer's time set to the time 9:52 am on 16th October 2000 in America's Eastern Standard Time (for example, New York).

Note that on Netscape 4.0+ browsers, it will actually have GMT at the end of the first line rather than UTC.

How It Works

So how does this work? In the script block at the top of the page we have just one line:

```
    var localTime = new Date();
```

This creates a new `Date` object and initializes it to the current date and time based on the client computer's clock. (Note that in fact the `Date` object simply stores the number of milliseconds between the date and time on your computer's clock and midnight UTC time on the 1 January 1970.)

Within the body of the page we have three more script blocks that use the three world time methods we looked at above. In the line:

```
document.write(localTime.toUTCString());
```

we write to the page the string returned by the `toUTCString()` method. This will convert the date and time stored inside the `localTime Date` object to the equivalent UTC date and time.

Then the line:

```
document.write(localTime.toLocaleString());
```

returns a string with the local date and time value. Since this time is just based on the user's computer's clock, if this clock adjusts for daylight saving time, then the string returned by this method will also adjust for daylight saving time.

Finally, the code:

```
document.write(localTime.getTimezoneOffset());
```

writes out the difference, in minutes, between the local time zone's time and that of UTC time.

You may notice in the screenshot above that the difference between New York time and UTC time is written to be 240 minutes, or 4 hours. Yet, in the table above, we said that New York is 5 hours behind UTC time. So what is happening?

Well, actually in New York on 16th October daylight saving hours are in use. So, while in the summer it is 8:00pm in New York when it is 0:00 UTC time, in the winter it is 7:00 pm in New York when it is 0:00 UTC time. Therefore, in the summer the `getTimeZoneOffset()` method will return 240, while in the winter the `getTimeZoneOffset()` method will return 300.

To illustrate this, compare the previous screenshot to the following one, where I have put the date on my computer's clock forwards by two months.

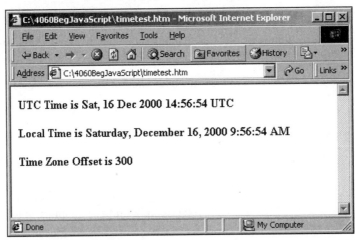

Of course, this example relies on the fact that the user's computer's clock is set correctly.

Setting and Getting a Date Object's UTC Date and Time

When we create a new Date object we can either initialize it with a value or let JavaScript set it to the current date and time. Either way, JavaScript assumes we are setting the *local* time values. If we want to specify UTC time, then we need to use the 'setUTC' type methods, such as setUTCHours().

There are seven methods for setting UTC date and time, which are:

- ❏ setUTCDate()
- ❏ setUTCFullYear()
- ❏ setUTCHours()
- ❏ setUTCMilliseconds()
- ❏ setUTCMinutes()
- ❏ setUTCMonth()
- ❏ setUTCSeconds()

The names pretty much give away exactly what each of the methods does, so let's launch straight into a simple example, which sets the UTC time. These UTC methods were introduced in IE 4.0 and NN 4.06, so you will need one of these or a later version to run the code.

```
<HTML>
<BODY>
<SCRIPT LANGUAGE=JavaScript>

var myDate = new Date();

myDate.setUTCHours(12);
myDate.setUTCMinutes(0);
myDate.setUTCSeconds(0);

document.write("<H3>" + myDate.toUTCString() + "</H3>")
document.write("<H3>" + myDate.toLocaleString() + "</H3>")

</SCRIPT>

</BODY>
</HTML>
```

Save this as settimetest.htm. When you load it in your browser you should see the following in your web page, though the actual date will depend on the current date and where you are in the world:

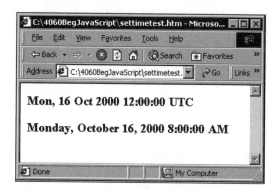

You might want to change your computer's time zone and time of year to see how it varies in different regions and with daylight saving changes. For example, although I'm in the UK, I have changed the settings on my computer for this example to Eastern Standard Time in the USA. In Windows you can make the changes by opening the Control Panel, and then double-clicking the Date/Time icon.

So how does this example work? We declare a variable myDate and set it to a new Date object. As we've not initialized the Date object to any value, it will contain the local current date and time.

Then using the setUTC methods, we set the hours, minutes and seconds so that the time will be 12:00:00 (midday, not midnight) UTC time.

Now, when we write out the value of myDate as a UTC string, we get 12:00:00 and today's date. When we write out the value of the Date object as a local string we get today's date and a time that is the UTC time 12:00:00 converted to the equivalent local time. The local values you'll see will, of course, depend on your time zone. For example, New Yorkers will see 08:00:00 during the summer time and 07:00 during the winter time due to daylight savings. In the UK in the winter, you'll see 12:00:00, however in the summer you'll see 13:00:00.

For getting UTC dates and times we have the same functions as for setting UTC dates and times, except that this time, for example, it's getUTCHours() not setUTCHours().

- ❏ getUTCDate()
- ❏ getUTCDay()
- ❏ getUTCFullYear()
- ❏ getUTCHours()
- ❏ getUTCMilliseconds()
- ❏ getUTCMinutes()
- ❏ getUTCMonth()
- ❏ getUTCSeconds()

Notice that this time there is an additional method, getUTCDay(). This works in the same way as the getDay() method and returns the day of the week as a number, from 0 for Sunday to 6 for Saturday. As the day of the week is decided by the day of the month, the month and the year, there is no setUTCDay() method.

Before we move on to look at timers, let's use our newly gained knowledge of the Date object and world time to create a world time converter. Later in this chapter, when we've learnt how to use timers, we'll update the example to produce a world time clock. Note that this example only works with IE 4.0+ and NN 4.06+. It won't work with IE version 3 or NN version 4.05 and earlier.

Try It Out – World Time Converter (Part I)

The world time converter consists of two pages. The first is a frameset page, and the second the page where the time conversion form exists. Let's start by creating the frameset page.

```
<HTML>
<HEAD>
</HEAD>
<FRAMESET COLS="250,*" BORDER=0>
   <FRAME SRC="worldtimeconverter.htm" NAME=formFrame>
   <FRAME SRC="about:blank" NAME=resultsFrame>
</FRAMESET>
</HTML>
```

This simply divides the page into two frames. However, by setting the border between the frames to 0 we can make it look like just a single page. Save this frameset page as WorldTimeConverterFrameset.htm.

The left frame will contain the form in which the user can select the city that they want the time of, and the right frame will show the results of the conversion. The right frame will be written to using code, so there is no page to create for that.

We'll now create the left frame's page.

```
<HTML>
<HEAD>
<SCRIPT LANGUAGE=javascript>

var timeDiff;
var selectedCity;
var daylightSavingAdjust = 0;

function updateTimeZone()
{
   var lstCity = document.form1.lstCity;
   timeDiff = lstCity.options[lstCity.selectedIndex].value;
   selectedCity = lstCity.options[lstCity.selectedIndex].text;
   updateTime();
}

function getTimeString(dateObject)
{
   var timeString;

   var hours = dateObject.getHours();
   if (hours < 10)
      hours = "0" + hours;

   var minutes = dateObject.getMinutes();
   if (minutes < 10)
      minutes = "0" + minutes;
```

```
      var seconds = dateObject.getSeconds()
      if (seconds < 10)
         seconds = "0" + seconds;

   timeString = hours + ":" + minutes + ":" + seconds;

   return timeString;
}

function updateTime()
{
   var nowTime = new Date();

   var resultsFrame = window.top.resultsFrame.document;

   resultsFrame.open()
   resultsFrame.write("Local Time is " + getTimeString(nowTime) + "<BR>");
   nowTime.setMinutes(nowTime.getMinutes() + nowTime.getTimezoneOffset() +
      parseInt(timeDiff) + daylightSavingAdjust);
   resultsFrame.write(selectedCity + " time is " + getTimeString(nowTime));
   resultsFrame.close();
}

function chkDaylightSaving_onclick()
{
   if (document.form1.chkDaylightSaving.checked)
   {
      daylightSavingAdjust = 60;
   }
   else
   {
      daylightSavingAdjust = 0;
   }

   updateTime();
}

</SCRIPT>
</HEAD>

<BODY LANGUAGE=JavaScript onload="updateTimeZone()">
<FORM NAME=form1>
<SELECT SIZE=5 NAME=lstCity LANGUAGE=JavaScript onchange="updateTimeZone();">
<OPTION VALUE=60 SELECTED>Berlin
<OPTION VALUE=330>Bombay
<OPTION VALUE=0>London
<OPTION VALUE=180>Moscow
<OPTION VALUE=-300>New York (EST)
<OPTION VALUE=60>Paris
<OPTION VALUE=-480>San Francisco (PST)
<OPTION VALUE=600>Sydney
</SELECT>
<P>
```

```
It's summer time in the selected city
and its country adjusts for summertime daylight saving
<INPUT TYPE="checkbox" NAME=chkDaylightSaving LANGUAGE=JavaScript
    onclick="return chkDaylightSaving_onclick()">
</P>
</FORM>

</BODY>
</HTML>
```

Save this page as `WorldTimeConverter.htm`. Then load the `WorldTimeConverterFrameset.htm` page into your browser. (Remember that a NN 4.06+ or an IE 4.0+ browser is needed.)

The form layout looks something like that below. Whenever the user clicks on a city in the list, the user's local time and the equivalent time in the selected city are shown. In the example shown below my local region is set to Eastern Standard Time in the USA (such as New York) and I've clicked on Berlin in the list and checked the box for summer time daylight saving in Berlin.

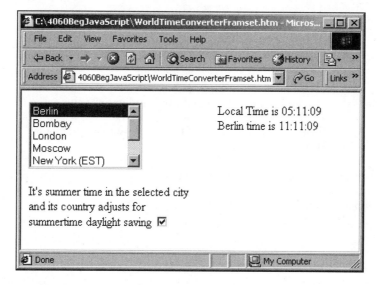

Its worth pointing out that this is an example and not a totally foolproof one due to the problems of daylight saving. Some countries don't have daylight saving, others do and at fixed times of year and yet others do but at varying times of the year. This makes it virtually impossible to accurately predict when a country will have its daylight saving period. We have tried to solve this problem by adding a checkbox for the user to click if the city they choose from the list is using daylight saving hours (which we assume will put the time in the city forwards by one hour).

In addition, don't forget that some users may not even have their regional settings set correctly – there's no easy way round this problem.

How It Works

Before we look at `WorldTimeConverter.htm`, let's just pick up on one point in the frameset defining page `WorldTimeConverterFrameset.htm`:

```
<FRAME SRC="about:blank" NAME=resultsFrame>
```

Notice how we have set the SRC attribute of the right hand frame to `"about:blank"`. This is necessary for some browsers, mainly Netscape – without it, `document.write()` will sometimes fail as there is no page loaded to write to.

Now we'll turn to the page `WorldTimeConverter.htm` where most of the action is to be found. In the body of the page is a form in which we've defined a list box using a `<SELECT>` element.

```
<SELECT SIZE=5 NAME=lstCity LANGUAGE=JavaScript onchange="updateTimeZone();">
<OPTION VALUE=60 SELECTED>Berlin
<OPTION VALUE=330>Bombay
<OPTION VALUE=0>London
<OPTION VALUE=180>Moscow
<OPTION VALUE=-300>New York (EST)
<OPTION VALUE=60>Paris
<OPTION VALUE=-480>San Francisco (PST)
<OPTION VALUE=600>Sydney
</SELECT>
```

Each of the options displays the city's name in the list box and has its value set to the difference in minutes between that city's time zone (in winter) and UTC. So London, which is the same as UTC time has a value of 0. Paris, which is an hour ahead of UTC, has a value of 60, that is 60 minutes. New York, which is 5 hours behind UTC time, has a value of -300.

You'll see that we have captured the onchange event of the `<SELECT>` element and connected it to the function `updateTimeZone()` defined in a script block in the head of the page. This function involves three global variables defined at the top of the script block:

```
var timeDiff;
var selectedCity;
var daylightSavingAdjust = 0;
```

The function `updateTimeZone()` updates two of these, setting variable `timeDiff` to the value of the list's selected option (that is the time difference between the selected city and UTC time) and variable `selectedCity` to the text shown for the selected option (that is the selected city).

```
function updateTimeZone()
{
    var lstCity = document.form1.lstCity;
    timeDiff = lstCity.options[lstCity.selectedIndex].value;
    selectedCity = lstCity.options[lstCity.selectedIndex].text;
```

In the final part of the function `updateTimeZone()`, the function `updateTime()` is called:

```
        updateTime();
    }
```

Before we go on to look at this function, we return to the final part of the form on the page. This is a checkbox, which is clicked by the user if the city they have chosen from the select list is in the summer time of a country that uses daylight saving hours.

```
<INPUT TYPE="checkbox" NAME=chkDaylightSaving LANGUAGE=JavaScript
    onclick="return chkDaylightSaving_onclick()">
```

As you can see, this checkbox's `onclick` event is connected to another function `chkDaylightSaving_onclick()`.

```
function chkDaylightSaving_onclick()
{
    if (document.form1.chkDaylightSaving.checked)
    {
        daylightSavingAdjust = 60;
    }
    else
    {
        daylightSavingAdjust = 0;
    }
```

Inside the `if` statement, the code accesses the checkbox's `checked` property which returns `true` if it is checked and `false` otherwise. If it has been checked, we set the global variable `daylightSavingAdjust` to 60 for summer time daylight saving, else it's set to 0.

```
        updateTime();
    }
```

At the end of this function, as at the end of the function `updateTimeZone()` we saw above, the `updateTime()` function is called. We'll look at that next.

In the function `updateTime()` we write the current local time and the equivalent time in the selected city, to the right-hand frame, named `resultsFrame`, which we defined in the frameset page.

We start at the top of the function by creating a new `Date` object, which is stored in variable `nowTime`. The `Date` object will be initialized to the current local time:

```
function updateTime()
{
    var nowTime = new Date();
```

Next, to make our code more compact and easier to understand, we define a variable `resultsFrame`, which will reference the `document` object contained in the `resultsFrame` window:

```
var resultsFrame = window.top.resultsFrame.document;
```

With our reference to the `resultsFrame` document, we then open the document for writing to. Doing this will clear anything currently in the document and provide a nice blank document to write our HTML into. The first thing we write is the local time based on the new `Date` object we just created. However, we want the time to be nicely formatted as hours:minutes:seconds so we've written another function, `getTimeString()`, which does this for us. We'll look at that shortly.

```
resultsFrame.open()
resultsFrame.write("Local Time is " + getTimeString(nowTime) + "<BR>");
```

Having written the current time to our `resultsFrame`, we now need to calculate what the time would be in the selected city before also writing that to the `resultsFrame`.

We saw in Chapter 4 that if we set the value of a `Date` object's individual parts, such as hours, minutes, and seconds, to a value beyond their normal range, then JavaScript assumes you want to adjust the date, hours or minutes to take account of this. For example, if we set the hours to 36, JavaScript simply sets the hours to 12 and adds one day to the date stored inside the `Date` object. We use this to our benefit in the line:

```
nowTime.setMinutes(nowTime.getMinutes() + nowTime.getTimezoneOffset() +
    parseInt(timeDiff) + daylightSavingAdjust);
```

Let's break this line down to see how it works. Suppose that we're in New York, with the local summer time of 5:11, and we want to know what time it would be in Berlin. How does our line of code calculate this?

First we get the minutes of the current local time; it's 5:11, so `nowTime.getMinutes()` returns 11.

Then we get the difference, in minutes, between the user's local time and UTC time using `nowTime.getTimezoneOffset()`. If we are in New York, which is different from UTC time by 4 hours during the summer, this is 240 minutes.

Then we get the integer value of the time difference between the standard winter time in the selected city and UTC time, which is stored in the variable `timeDiff`. We've used `parseInt()` here as it's one of the few situations where JavaScript gets confused and assumes we want to join two strings together rather than treating the value as a number and adding it together. Remember that we got `timeDiff` from an HTML element's value and HTML element's values are strings, even when they hold characters that are digits. As we want the time in Berlin, which is 60 minutes different from UTC time, this will be 60.

Finally we add the value of `daylightSavingsAdjust`. This variable is set in the function `chkdaylightsaving_onclick()` which we discussed above. Since we are in the summer and Berlin uses daylight saving hours, this value is 60.

So we have:

```
11 + 240 + 60 + 60 = 371
```

Therefore nowTime.setMinutes() is setting the minutes to 371. Clearly, there's no such thing as 371 minutes past the hour, so instead JavaScript assumes we mean 6 hours and 11 minutes after 5:00, that is 11:11 – the time in Berlin that we wanted.

Finally the updateTime() function writes the results to the resultsFrame, then closes off the document writing.

```
    resultsFrame.write(selectedCity + " time is " + getTimeString(nowTime));
    resultsFrame.close();
}
```

In the updateTime() function we looked at above, we saw that it utilizes the function getTimeString() to format the time string. Let's look at that function now. This function is passed a Date object as a parameter and uses that to create a string with the format hours:minutes:seconds.

```
function getTimeString(dateObject)
{
    var timeString;

    var hours = dateObject.getHours();
    if (hours < 10)
        hours = "0" + hours;

    var minutes = dateObject.getMinutes();
    if (minutes < 10)
        minutes = "0" + minutes;

    var seconds = dateObject.getSeconds()
    if (seconds < 10)
        seconds = "0" + seconds;

    timeString = hours + ":" + minutes + ":" + seconds;

    return timeString;
}
```

Why do we need this function? Well, we can't just use:

```
getHours() + ":" + getMinutes() + ":" + getSeconds()
```

because of the case when any of the three results of these functions is less than 10. For example, one minute past twelve would look like 12:1:00 rather than 12:01:00.

The function therefore gets the values for hours, minutes, and seconds and checks each to see if they are below 10. If they are below 10, then a zero is added to the front of the string. When all the values have been retrieved they are concatenated together in the variable `timeString` before being returned to the calling function.

In the next section we're going to look at how, by adding a timer, we can make the displayed time update every second like a clock.

Timers in a Web Page

There are two types of timer we can create in IE 4.0+ and NN 4.0+ browsers. There is a one off timer that triggers just once after a certain period, and a second type of timer that continually triggers at set intervals. We will investigate each of these types of timers in the next two sections. The first type, the "one shot timer" is the only one available in older browsers supporting JavaScript.

Within reasonable limits we can have as many timers as we want and can set them going at any point in our code, such as at the window `onload` event or at the click of a button. Common uses for timers include advertisement banner pictures that change at regular intervals or displaying the changing time in a web page.

One Shot Timer

Setting a one off timer is very easy: we just use the `window` object's `setTimeout()` method.

```
window.setTimeout("your JavaScript code", milliseconds_delay)
```

The method `setTimeout()` takes two parameters. The first is the JavaScript code we want executed, and the second is the delay, in milliseconds (thousandths of a second), until the code is executed.

The method returns a value (an integer), which is the timer's unique ID. If we decide later that we want to stop the timer firing, we use this ID to tell JavaScript which timer we are referring to. However, you must be careful not to halt a timer that has already fired its one shot, as this may crash the browser.

For example, to set a timer that will fire 3 seconds after the page has loaded, we could use the following code:

```
<HTML>
<HEAD>
<SCRIPT LANGUAGE=JavaScript>
var timerID;
function window_onload()
{
    timerID = setTimeout("alert('Times Up!')",3000);
    alert("Timer Set");
}
</SCRIPT>
</HEAD>
<BODY LANGUAGE = JavaScript onload="window_onload()">
</BODY>
</HTML>
```

Save this file as `timertest.htm`, and load it into your browser. In this page a message box will appear 3000 milliseconds (that is 3 seconds) after the `onload` event of the window has fired.

Although `setTimeout()` is a method of the `window` object, you'll remember that because the `window` object is at the top of the hierarchy we don't need to use its name when referring to its properties and methods. Hence, we can use `setTimeout()` instead of `window.setTimeout()`.

It's important to note that setting a timer does not stop script from continuing to execute. The timer runs in the background and fires when its time is up. In the meantime the page runs as normal and any script after we set the timer will run immediately. So, in this example, the alert box telling us that the timer has been set appears immediately after the code setting the timer has been executed.

How about if we decided that we wanted to stop the timer before it fired?

To clear a timer we use the `window` object's `clearTimeout()` method. This takes just one parameter, the unique timer ID that the `setTimeout()` method returns.

Let's alter the example above and provide a button we can click to stop the timer.

```
<HTML>
<HEAD>
<SCRIPT LANGUAGE=JavaScript>
var timerID;
function window_onload()
{
    timerID = setTimeout("alert('Times Up!')",3000);
    alert("Timer Set");
}

function butStopTimer_onclick()
{
    clearTimeout(timerID);
    alert("Timer has been cleared");
}

</SCRIPT>
</HEAD>
<BODY LANGUAGE=JavaScript onload="window_onload()">
<FORM NAME=form1>
<INPUT TYPE="button" VALUE="Stop Timer" NAME=butStopTimer LANGUAGE=JavaScript
    onclick="return butStopTimer_onclick()">
</FORM>
</BODY>
</HTML>
```

Save this as `timertest2.htm`, and load into your browser. Now if we hit the **Stop Timer** button before the three seconds are up, then the timer will be cleared. This is because the button is connected to the `butStopTimer_onclick()` function, which uses the timer's ID `timerID` with the `clearTimeout()` method of the `window` object.

Try It Out – Updating Banner Advertisement

We'll now look at a bigger example using the setTimeout() method. The following example creates a web page with an image banner advertisement, which changes every few seconds.

```
<HTML>
<HEAD>
<SCRIPT LANGUAGE=JavaScript>

var currentImgNumber = 1;
var numberOfImages = 3;

function window_onload()
{
    setTimeout("switchImage()",3000);
}

function switchImage()
{
    currentImgNumber++;
    document.imgAdvert.src = "AdvertImage" + currentImgNumber + ".jpg";

    if (currentImgNumber < numberOfImages)
    {
        setTimeout("switchImage()",3000);    }
    }

</SCRIPT>
</HEAD>
<BODY onload="window_onload()">
<IMG SRC="AdvertImage1.jpg" NAME="imgAdvert">
</BODY>
</HTML>
```

Once you've typed in the code, save the page as Adverts.htm. You'll also need to create three images named AdvertImage1.jpg, AdvertImage2.jpg, and AdvertImage3.jpg (alternatively, the three images are supplied with the downloadable code for the book).

When the page is loaded, we start with a view of AdvertImage1.jpg.

In three seconds this changes to the second image:

Finally, three seconds later, a third and final image loads:

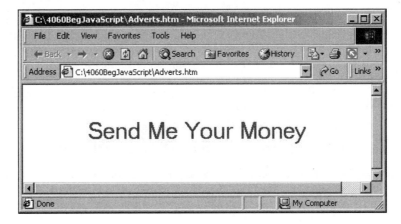

How It Works

When the page loads, the <IMG> tag has its SRC attribute set to the first image.

```
<IMG SRC="AdvertImage1.jpg" name="imgAdvert">
```

Within the <BODY> tag, we connect the window object's onload event handler to the function window_onload() shown below.

```
function window_onload()
{
    setTimeout("switchImage()",3000)
}
```

In this function we use the setTimeout() method to start a timer running that will call the function switchImage() in three seconds. As we've no need to clear the timer, we've not bothered to save the timer ID returned by the setTimeout() method.

The switchImage() function changes the value of the src property of the IMG object corresponding tot he <IMG> tag in our page.

```
function switchImage()
{
    currentImgNumber++;
    document.imgAdvert.src = "AdvertImage" + currentImgNumber + ".jpg";
```

Ouradvertisement images are numbered 1 to 3: AdvertImage1.jpg, AdvertImage2.jpg and AdvertImage3.jpg. We keep track of the number of the advertisement image that is currently loaded in the page in the global variable currentImgNumber, which we defined at the top of the script block and initialized to 1. To get the next image we simply increment that variable by 1, and then update the image loaded by setting the src property of the IMG object, using the variable currentImgNumber to build up its full name.

```
    if (currentImgNumber < numberOfImages)    {
        setTimeout("switchImage()",3000);     }
}
```

We have three advertisement images we want to show. In the if statement we check to see whether currentImgNumber, which is the number of the current image, is less than three. If it is, it means there are more images to show and so we set another timer going, identical to the one we set in the window object's onload event handler. This timer will call this function again in three seconds.

Prior to version 4 browsers, this was the only method of creating a timer that fired continually at regular intervals. However in version 4 and later browsers we'll see next that there's an easier way.

Setting a Timer that Fires at Regular Intervals

The introduction of IE and NN version 4 browsers saw new methods added to the window object for setting timers, namely the setInterval() and clearInterval() methods. These work in a very similar way to setTimeout() and clearTimeout(), except that the timer fires continually at regular intervals rather than just once.

The method setInterval() takes the same parameters as setTimeout(), except that the second parameter now specifies the interval, in milliseconds, between each firing of the timer, rather than just the length of time before the timer fires.

For example, to set a timer that will fire the function myFunction() every 5 seconds, the code would be:

```
var myTimerID = setInterval("myFunction()",5000);
```

As with setTimeout(), the setInterval() method returns a unique timer ID that you'll need if you want to clear the timer with clearInterval(), which works identically to clearTimeout(). So to stop the timer started above, we would use:

```
clearInterval(myTimerID);
```

Try It Out – World Time Convertor (Part 2)

Let's change the world time example that we saw earlier, so that it displays local time and selected city time as a continuously updating clock.

We'll be making changes to the `WorldTimeConverter.htm` file, so open that in your text editor. Add the function shown below, before the functions that are already defined:

```
var daylightSavingAdjust = 0;

function window_onload()
{
    updateTimeZone();
    window.setInterval("updateTime()",1000);
}

function updateTimeZone()
{
```

Next edit the `<BODY>` tag so it looks like this:

```
<BODY LANGUAGE=JavaScript onload="return window_onload()">
```

Resave the file, and then load `WorldTimeConverterFrameset.htm` into your browser. (Remember that a NN 4.06+ or an IE 4.0+ browser is needed.) The page should look the same as the previous version of the time converter, except that the times are continually updated every second.

How It Works

The changes were short and simple. In the function `window_onload()` we have added a timer that will call the `updateTime()` function every 1000 milliseconds, that is every second. It'll keep doing this until we leave the page. Previously our `updateTime()` function was only called when the user clicked either the list box and selected a different city or the summer time checkbox.

The `window_onload()` function is connected to the `window` object's `onload` event in the `<BODY>` tag, so once the page has loaded our clock starts running.

Try It Out – Scrolling Status Bar Text

Let's look at a second example using the `setInterval()` method. This time it's the ubiquitous scrolling status bar text, which you will find on many web sites.

```
<HTML>
<HEAD>
<SCRIPT LANGUAGE = JavaScript>

var message = "Beginning JavaScript from Wrox Press";
var startChar = 0;
var maxLength;
```

```
function window_onload()
{
    var availWidth = 0;
    var spaces = "";
    if (navigator.appName == "Netscape")
    {
        availWidth = window.innerWidth / 10;
    }
    else
    {
        availWidth = document.body.scrollWidth / 10;
    }

    while (availWidth > 0)
    {
        spaces = spaces + " ";
        availWidth--;
    }

    message = spaces + message;

    maxLength = message.length - 1;

    setInterval("scrollMessage()",65);
}

function scrollMessage()
{
    window.status = message.substring(startChar);
    startChar++;
    if (startChar == maxLength)
    {
        startChar = 0;
    }
}

</SCRIPT>
</HEAD>
<BODY LANGUAGE=JavaScript onload="return window_onload()">

<P>Scrolling Status Bar Example</P>

</BODY>
</HTML>
```

Save the page as `scrolling_status.htm` and load into your browser. In the status bar at the bottom of the browser's window you'll see a scrolling message:

Beginning JavaScript from Wrox Press.

How It Works

At the top of the script block we define three global variables:

```
var message = "Beginning JavaScript from Wrox Press";
var startChar = 0;
var maxLength;
```

The message we want scrolled in the status bar is stored in the variable `message`. The variable `startChar` will later be used to determine the portion of the message to be displayed in the scroll bar and will help give the impression of text scrolling from the right and disappearing off to the left. The variable `maxLength` will later store the length of the string to be displayed.

When the message first appears in the status bar, we want it to appear approximately in the middle:

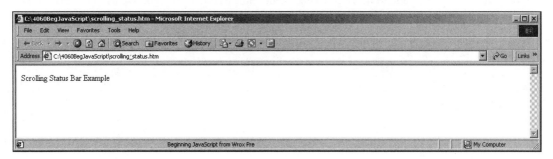

To achieve this, we need to pad the front of the message with enough spaces so that it will be approximately in the middle. Otherwise with no spaces the message will start being displayed at the left of the status bar. The question is how many spaces do we need? This will depend to some extent on the user's screen resolution and on how wide their browser window is. We deal with this in the `window_onload()` function that is connected to the `window` object's `onload` event in the `<BODY>` tag for the page. We find out how many pixels wide the browser window is, and then divide that by ten to give us a very rough guide to the number of spaces required.

Finding out the width of a window requires the use of different properties for Netscape Navigator and Internet Explorer browsers. With Netscape 4.0+, `window.innerWidth` gives us the inner width of the window in pixels.

```
function window_onload()
{
   var availWidth = 0;
   var spaces = "";
   if (navigator.appName == "Netscape")
   {
      availWidth = window.innerWidth / 10;
   }
```

For IE 4.0+ `document.body.scrollWidth` gives roughly the same result.

```
   else
   {
      availWidth = document.body.scrollWidth / 10;
   }
```

Having calculated how many spaces we want, we then use a `while` loop to create a string containing that number of spaces and store it in the variable `spaces`.

```
while (availWidth > 0)
{
    spaces = spaces + " ";
    availWidth--;
}
```

This variable is then concatenated to the front of our message stored in variable `message`.

```
message = spaces + message;
```

Now that we have our padded message string inside the variable `message`, we want to make the text look like it is scrolling to the left:

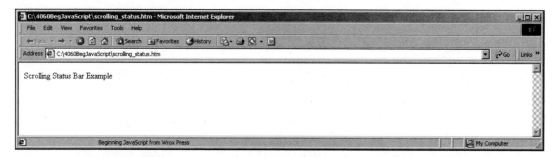

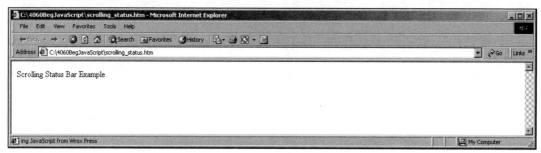

To make this happen, we finish the `window_onload()` function with a timer that calls a function every 65 milliseconds. This function will move the message across the screen to the left by one character.

```
maxLength = message.length - 1;

setInterval("scrollMessage()",65);
}
```

So how can this `scrollMessage()` function make the message move to the left by one character? This is achieved simply by only showing part of the message string. Initially, all of the message string is shown, that is from character position 0 to `maxLength`. When the function is next called, only the portion of the string from character position 1 to `maxLength` is shown. And the next time the function is called, only the portion of the string from character position 2 to `maxLength` is called.

Eventually all the spaces and most of the words will not be displayed in the status bar, and it will look as if our message has rolled off the left hand edge.

Once we are displaying just an empty string in the status bar, we start again by displaying the whole string again. Now we know the principle of how it works, let's look at the code:

```
function scrollMessage()
{
    window.status = message.substring(startChar);
    startChar++;
    if (startChar == maxLength)
    {
        startChar = 0;
    }
}
```

The first thing we do is put our message string into the status bar. However we don't put the whole string in, but instead, using the substring() method, we insert only part of it, the part starting from the character position in variable startChar and ending with the last character. Remember that with substring() if we don't pass a second parameter with the last character index we want displayed, then we get all the string from the start character to the end.

When the page is first loaded startChar is 0, so our substring will be everything from the first character to the end of the string, in other words the whole string. The variable startChar is incremented within the function, so the next time the function is called by the timer, startChar will be 1 so our substring will start from the second character. With each call of the function the start position gets further along the string which means that when displayed in the status bar it appears to the user that the text is moving closer and closer to the left of the window.

Eventually no characters will be displayed in the status bar. This occurs when startChar is the same as the length of the string. Once this point is reached we need to reset the startChar variable back to zero, giving the appearance of the text starting to scroll from the middle of the status bar again. We do this in the if statement at the end of the function.

That completes our look at this example and also our introduction to timers. Next we're going to use this knowledge to alter the trivia quiz so that it is a time-limit-based quiz.

The Triva Quiz

In this chapter we'll be making two changes to the trivia quiz. Firstly we'll allow the user to select how long they have to complete the quiz, and secondly they get to choose how many questions they want to answer.

Converting the quiz to a timer-based one only requires that we change two pages, namely QuizPage.htm and GlobalFunctions.htm.

Our first change in QuizPage.htm will be to the form at the start of the quiz, as we need to allow the user to select their time limit and number of questions. Then we'll change the cmdStartQuiz_onclick() function so that when it calls the resetQuiz() function in the GlobalFunctions.htm page it also passes as parameters the time limit and number of questions that the user has selected.

On to the GlobalFunctions.htm page itself, where we need to alter the resetQuiz() function so that, if necessary, it starts a timer going based on the time limit selected. Then new functions dealing with the time limit need to be created; one puts a message in the scroll bar notifying the user how much time they have left, the other deals with the situation when the time limit is up.

We'll start by making the changes to QuizPage.htm, so open this in your text editor.

The first change we'll make is to the form, which currently just contains a button.

```
<FORM NAME="frmQuiz">
<P>
Number of Questions <BR>
<SELECT name=cboNoQuestions size=1>
    <OPTION value=3>3
    <OPTION value=5>5
</SELECT>
</P>
<P>
Time Limit <BR>
<SELECT name=cboTimeLimit size=1>
    <OPTION value=-1>No Time Limit
    <OPTION value=60>1 Minute
    <OPTION value=180>3 Minutes
    <OPTION value=300>5 Minutes
</SELECT>
</P>
<INPUT NAME=cmdStartQuiz TYPE=button VALUE="Start Quiz"
    onclick="return cmdStartQuiz_onclick()">
</FORM>
```

We've added two new controls; both are drop-down list boxes created using the <SELECT> tag. In the first list box, we enable the user to choose how many questions they want to answer, and in the second the time limit within which they must answer the questions.

Next we need to alter the cmdStartQuiz_onclick() function defined at the top of the page.

```
<SCRIPT LANGUAGE=JavaScript>

function cmdStartQuiz_onclick()
{
    var cboNoQuestions = document.frmQuiz.cboNoQuestions;
    var noQuestions = cboNoQuestions.options[cboNoQuestions.selectedIndex].value;
    var cboTimeLimit = document.frmQuiz.cboTimeLimit;
    var timeLimit = cboTimeLimit.options[cboTimeLimit.selectedIndex].value;
    window.top.fraTopFrame.fraGlobalFunctions.resetQuiz(noQuestions,timeLimit);

    window.location.href = "AskQuestion.htm";
}

</SCRIPT>
```

This function is connected to the `cmdStartQuiz` button's `onclick` event and is how the user kicks the quiz off. Previously we just called the `resetQuiz()` function in the global module then loaded the `AskQuestion.htm` page. Now we need to get the values the user has selected in the select elements for the number of questions and time limit. As we'll see in a minute, the `resetQuiz()` function has been changed and now takes two parameters, namely the number of questions to be answered and a time limit.

At the start of the `cmdStartQuiz_onclick()` function we first set a variable `cboNoQuestions` to reference the `cboNoQuestions` control in the form (where the user chooses how many questions they want to answer). We can then use that reference instead of the more long-winded full reference via the document and form. The benefit here of doing this is to keep the lines shorter and more readable.

On the second line we get the value of the selected option in the select control for the number of questions and store this value in the `noQuestions` variable.

In the following two lines we do exactly the same thing again, except this time it's the time limit control and value we are dealing with.

Finally in the last new line of the function we reset the quiz, this time passing the number of questions to be answered (`noQuestions`) and time limit (`timeLimit`).

That completes all the changes for the page `QuizPage.htm`, so you can resave the page in your text editor and close it.

Let's now turn our attention to the `GlobalFunctions.htm` page and start by looking at the changes we need to make to the `resetQuiz()` function:

```
function resetQuiz(numberOfQuestions, SelectedTimeLimit)
{
    timeLeft = SelectedTimeLimit;
    totalQuestionsToAsk = numberOfQuestions;

    var indexCounter;
    currentQNumber = -1;
    questionsAsked = new Array();

    for (indexCounter = 0; indexCounter < questions.length; indexCounter++)
    {
        questionsAsked[indexCounter] = false;
    }

    numberOfQuestionsAsked = 0;
    numberOfQuestionsCorrect = 0;

    if (timeLeft == -1)
    {
        window.status = "No Time Limit";
    }
    else
    {
        quizTimerId = window.setInterval("updateTimeLeft()",1000);
    }
}
```

The first change is to our function's definition. Previously it took no parameters, now it takes two: the number of questions to be answered and the time limit within which the quiz must be completed.

Our next change is to set two new global variables, timeLeft and totalQuestionsToAsk, to the values passed to the function. We'll see later that these global variables are used elsewhere to determine if enough questions have been asked and to check to see if the time limit has been reached.

The final change to this function is the setting of the timer that will monitor how much time is left. One of the options open to the user is no time limit at all, which is represented by the value -1. If the time limit is -1, we just put a message in the status bar of the browser window using the window object's status property. Note that on Netscape browsers the "No Time Limit" text in the status bar gets overwritten by "Document:Done" when the frames change. If however it's not -1, then we start a timer going, using setInterval(), which will call the function updateTimeLeft() every second.

The updateTimeLeft() function is a new function, so let's create that now. Add it to the script block underneath all the other function definitions.

```
function updateTimeLeft()
{
    timeLeft--;

    if (timeLeft == 0)
    {
        alert("Time's Up");
        numberOfQuestionsAsked = totalQuestionsToAsk;
        window.top.fraQuizPage.location.href = "AskQuestion.htm";
    }
    else
    {
        var minutes = Math.floor(timeLeft / 60);
        var seconds = timeLeft - (60 * minutes);

        if (minutes < 10)
            minutes = "0" + minutes;

        if (seconds < 10)
            seconds = "0" + seconds;

        window.status = "Time left is " + minutes + ":" + seconds;
    }
}
```

This function does three things, it decrements the time left, it stops the quiz if the time left has reached zero, and finally it notifies the user of the time remaining by putting a message in the browser's status bar.

As we saw above, when the quiz is reset using the resetQuiz() function, the global variable timeLeft is set to the amount of time, in seconds, that the user has to complete the quiz. The updateTimeLeft() function is called every second, and in the first line:

```
timeLeft--;
```

we decrement the number of seconds left by 1.

In the following `if` statement we check to see if `timeLeft` is zero. If it is, then it means no seconds are left and we end the quiz. We end the quiz by setting the global variable `numberOfQuestionsAsked` to the same value as the number of questions the user wanted to answer, which is stored in global variable `totalQuestionsToAsk`. Then, when we navigate the page to `AskQuestion.htm`, that page will think that all the questions to be asked have been asked and will end the quiz rather than asking another question.

If there is still time left then the `else` part of the `if` statement executes and updates the status bar with the number of minutes and seconds left.

We need to split `timeLeft`, which is in seconds, into minutes and seconds. First we get the number of minutes using the line:

```
var minutes = Math.floor(timeLeft / 60);
```

This returns just the whole number part of the seconds when divided by 60, which is the minutes we need. We get the seconds in:

```
var seconds = timeLeft - (60 * minutes);
```

which is just `timeLeft`, that is the total seconds, minus the number of seconds represented by the minutes value. So if `timeLeft` is 61, then

```
minutes = 61 / 60 = 1.01667
```

which is 1 as a whole number, and

```
seconds = 61 - (60 * 1) = 1
```

We want to display this as a string in the status bar in the format minutes:seconds, that is 01:01 in this case. However, just concatenating minutes and seconds will leave us with something like 1:1 when the value of either is less than 10. Currently minutes can't go above 5 so we could just add the 0 anyway, but by using an `if` statement we are future proofing it for the situation where we allow the user a time limit over 9 minutes.

To fix this problem we add an extra zero when the values are less than 10.

```
if (minutes < 10)
    minutes = "0" + minutes;

if (seconds < 10)
    seconds = "0" + seconds;
```

Finally we change the value displayed in the window's status bar:

```
window.status = "Time left is " + minutes + ":" + seconds;
```

In the two functions above we have been using some new globally-defined variables we have not yet defined, so let's do that now.

```
var timeLeft =-1;
var totalQuestionsToAsk = 0;
var quizTimerId = 0;
```

Place these at the top of the script block along with the other globally-defined variables.

Finally we've just got two small changes to make to the function getQuestion() and that's the trivia quiz complete for this chapter.

The first change is to the if statement at the top of the function:

```
if (totalQuestionsToAsk != numberOfQuestionsAsked)
{
    var questionNumber = Math.floor(Math.random() * questions.length);
```

Previously we asked another question so long as we had not used up all the questions available. Now we ask another question as long as the totalQuestionsToAsk variable does not equal the number of questions actually asked. The global variable totalQuestionsToAsk had its value determined by the user when they selected the number of questions they wanted to answer from the drop-down list. We passed this value to the resetQuiz() function which did the actual setting of the variable's value.

The second change is to code in the else statement when the quiz is actually ended and we write out the summary of how the user did. Remember we set a timer going that keeps track of how much time is left before the quiz must end. Well, now the quiz has ended we need to stop that timer which we do by using the clearInterval() method, passing the timer ID that we stored in the global variable quizTimerId, which we set when the timer was started. However, we mustn't try to stop the timer if no timer was set, that is if the user did not select a time limit.

```
        currentQNumber = questionNumber;
        questionsAsked[questionNumber] = true;
    }
    else
    {
        if (timeLeft != -1)
        {
            clearInterval(quizTimerId);
        }
        questionHTML = "<H3>Quiz Complete</H3>";
        questionHTML = questionHTML + "You got " + numberOfQuestionsCorrect;
```

Well that's all the changes made, so resave GlobalFunctions.htm. You can start the quiz by loading TriviaQuiz.htm into your browser.

Hopefully you should see a page like that shown below:

If you choose a time limit, then click the Start Quiz button, you'll be presented with the first, randomly selected question, and the timer, which is displayed in the status bar at the bottom of the page, will start counting down.

That completes all the changes to the trivia quiz for this chapter. We'll be returning to the trivia quiz in Chapter 11 to see how we can store information on the user's computer so that we can provide a table of previous results.

Summary

We started the chapter by looking at Universal Time Co-ordination (UTC time), which is an international standard time. We then looked at how to create timers in web pages.

The particular points we covered were:

- ❏ The `Date` object, which allows us to set and get UTC time in a similar way to setting a `Date` object's local time using methods such as `setUTCHours()`, `getUTCHours()` for setting and getting UTC hours with similar methods for months, years, minutes, seconds, and so on.

- ❏ A useful tool in international time conversion is the `getTimezoneOffset()` method which returns the difference, in minutes, between the user's local time and UTC time. One pitfall of this is that we are assuming the user has correctly set their time zone on their computer, If not `getTimezoneOffset()` is rendered useless as will be any local date and time methods if the users clock is incorrectly set.

- ❏ Using the `setTimeout()` method, we found we could start a timer going that would fire just once, after a certain number of milliseconds. `setTimeout()` takes two parameters, the first the code we want executing, the second the delay before that code is executed. It returns a value, the unique timer ID that we can use if we later want to reference the timer; for example to stop it before it fired we used the `clearTimeout()` method.

- ❏ To create a timer that fires at regular intervals we used the `setInterval()` method, which works in the same way to `setTimeout()`, except that it keeps firing unless the user leaves the page or we call the `clearInterval()` method.

- ❏ Finally, using our new knowledge of timers, we changed the trivia quiz so that the user can determine how many questions they want to answer and within what time limit the quiz must be completed.

In the next chapter we'll be looking at the top seven mistakes of all time, ones everyone makes at some point however much of an expert they may claim to be. We'll also be looking at a script debugger for Internet Explorer and how it can be used to step through live code, line by line. Finally we'll be looking at how to avoid errors and how to deal with errors when we get them.

Exercise Questions

Suggested solutions to these questions can be found in Appendix A.

Question 1

Create a web page with an advertisement image at the top. When the page loads, select a random image for that advertisement. Every four seconds change the advertisement to a different image making sure a different advertisement is selected until all the advertisement images have been seen.

Question 2

Create a form that gets the user's date of birth. Then, using that information, tell them what day they were born on.

Online discussion at http://p2p.wrox.com

Common Mistakes, Debugging, and Error Handling

Even once you have become a JavaScript guru, you'll still find that you'll make mistakes, even if they are just annoying typos. In particular, once your code starts to expand into hundreds of lines, then the chance of something going wrong becomes much greater. In proportion the difficulty in finding these mistakes, or bugs, also increases. In this chapter we will look at various techniques that will help us minimize the problems that arise from this situation.

We'll start by taking a look at the top seven JavaScript coding mistakes. Once you know what they are, you'll be able to look out for them when writing code – hopefully, so that you won't make them so often!

Then we'll look at the Microsoft script debugger, which can be used with Internet Explorer. We'll see how we can use it to step through our code and check the contents of variables while the code is running, enabling us to hunt out difficult bugs. We'll also have a briefer look at the debugging tools available through Netscape Navigator.

Finally, we'll look at how we can cope with errors when they do happen, so that we can avoid the user seeing our coding mistakes.

I Can't Believe I Just Did That – Some Common Mistakes

It's time to do a chart run-down of seven common mistakes. Some of these you'll learn to avoid as you become more experienced, but others may haunt you forever!

1: Undefined Variables

JavaScript is actually very easy going when it comes to defining your variables before actually assigning values to them. For example:

```
abc = 23;
```

will implicitly create a new variable abc and assign it to the value 23, although strictly speaking you should define the variable explicitly:

```
var abc = 23;
```

(Actually, whether or not you use the var keyword has a consequence on the scope that the variable has, so in fact it is always best to use the var keyword.)

However, if a variable is actually *used* before it has been defined, then an error will arise. For example, the code:

```
alert(abc);
```

will cause the error shown below if the variable abc has not been previously defined (explicitly or implicitly).

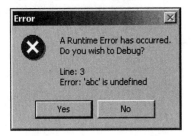

In addition, we must remember that function definitions also have parameters, which if not declared correctly can lead to the same type of error.

Take a look at the code below.

```
function resetQuiz(numberOfQustions, timeLimit)
{
    timeLeft = timeLimit;
    totalQuestionsToAsk = numberOfQuestions;
```

```
        currentQNumber = -1;
        questionsAsked = new Array();
        numberOfQuestionsAsked = 0;
        numberOfQuestionsCorrect = 0;
    }
```

If we call this function, we get an error message something like:

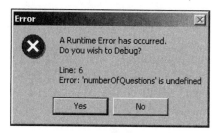

The error here is actually a simple typo in the function definition. The first parameter has the typo: it should read `numberOfQuestions` not `numberOfQustions`. What can be confusing with this type of error is that although the browser tells us the error is on one line, in fact the source of the error is on some other line.

2: Case Sensitivity

This is a major source of errors, particularly as it can be difficult to spot at times.

For example, spot the three case errors in the following code:

```
    var myName = "Paul";
    If (myName == "paul")
        alert(myName.toUppercase());
```

The first error is that we have typed `If` rather than `if`. However, JavaScript won't tell us that the error is an incorrect use of case, but instead IE will tell us 'Object expected' and Netscape will tell us that 'If is not defined'. Although error messages give us some idea of what's gone wrong, they often do so in an oblique way. In this case IE thinks we are trying to use an object called an `If` object and Netscape thinks we are trying to use an undefined variable called `If`.

OK, with that error cleared, we come to the next error, not one of JavaScript syntax, but a logic error. Remember that Paul does not equal paul in JavaScript, so `myName == "paul"` is `false`, even though it's quite likely that we didn't care whether it was `paul` or `Paul`. This type of error will result in no error message at all, just the code not executing as we'd planned.

The third fault is with the `toUpperCase()` method of the `String` object contained in `myName`. We've written `toUppercase`, with the `C` in lower case. IE will tell us that 'Object doesn't support this property or method' and Netscape that 'myName.toUppercase is not a function'. On first glance it would be easy to miss such a small mistake and start checking our JavaScript reference guide for that method. We might wonder why it's there, but our code is not working. Again we always need to be aware of case, something that even experts get wrong from time to time.

3: Incorrect Number of Closing Braces

In the code below we define a function, then call it. However there's a deliberate mistake. See if you can spot where it is.

```
function myFunction()
{
x = 1;
y = 2;

if (x <= y)
{
if (x == y)
{
alert("x equals y");
}
}

myFunction();
```

If we properly format the code it makes it much easier to spot where the error is:

```
function myFunction()
{
    x = 1;
    y = 2;

    if (x <= y)
    {
        if (x == y)
        {
            alert("x equals y");
        }
    }

myFunction();
```

Now we can see that we've forgotten to mark the end of the function with a closing curly brace. Where there are a lot of if, for, or do while statements, it's easy to have too many or too few closing braces. With proper formatting, this problem is much easier to spot.

4: Missing + Signs When Concatenating

In the code below there's a deliberate concatenation mistake:

```
var myName = "Paul";
var myString = "Hello";
var myOtherString = "World";
myString = myName + " said " + myString + " " myOtherString;
alert(myString);
```

There should be a + operator between " " and `myOtherString` in the fourth line of code.

Although easy to spot when in just a few lines of code, this kind of mistake can be harder to spot in large chunks of code. Also the error message that a mistake like this causes can be misleading. Load this code into a browser and we'll be told Error : Expected';' by IE and Missing ; before statement by Netscape. It's surprising how often this error crops up.

5: 'Equals' Rather than 'is Equal to'

Take a look at the code below.

```
var myNumber = 99;

if (myNumber = 101)
{
    alert("myNumber is 101");
}
else
{
    alert("myNumber is " + myNumber);
}
```

You'd expect on first glance that the `alert()` method in the `else` part of the `if` statement would execute telling us that the number in `myNumber` is 99, but it won't. We've made the classic 'one equals sign instead of two equals signs' mistake. Hence, instead of comparing `myNumber` with 101, we have set `myNumber` to equal 101. If, like me, you program in languages such as Visual Basic that only ever use one equals sign for both comparison and assignment, then you'll find that every so often this mistake crops up. It's just so easy to make.

What makes it even trickier is that no error message will be raised; it is just our data and logic that will suffer. Assigning a variable a value in an `if` statement may be perverse, but it's perfectly legal so there will be no complaints from JavaScript. When embedded in a large chunk of code, a mistake like this is easily overlooked. Just remember next time your program's logic seems crazy, that it's worth checking for this error.

One piece of good news is that NN 6 will issue a warning when we make this mistake along the lines of: test for equality (==) mistyped as assignment (=)?.

Note that it's only a warning and not an error, so no error messages will appear. The difference between warnings and errors is that a warning is code that is syntactically correct, but does appear to be flawed logically. Errors are where the syntax of the code is invalid. We'll see later how we can use the Netscape JavaScript console to view errors and warnings.

6: Incorrect Number of Closing Parentheses

Take a look at the code below:

```
if (myVariable + 12) / myOtherVariable < myString.length)
```

Spot the mistake?

The problem is we've missed off a parenthesis at the beginning. We want `myVariable + 12` to be calculated before the division by `myOtherVariable` is calculated, so quite rightly we know we need to put it in parentheses:

```
(myVariable + 12) / myOtherVariable
```

However, the `if` statement's condition must also be in parentheses. Not only is the initial parenthesis missing, but also if you count them you'll find we have one more closing parenthesis than we have opening parentheses – the numbers must match. For each parenthesis opened, there must be a corresponding closing parenthesis. Our code should be:

```
if ((myVariable + 12) / myOtherVariable < myString.length)
```

There will be situations where you'll have lots of opening and closing parentheses and it's very easy to miss one off or have one too many.

7: Using a Method as a Property and Vice Versa

Our final common error is where either we forget to put parentheses after a method with no parameters, or we use a property and do put parentheses after it.

A method must always have parentheses following its name; otherwise JavaScript thinks that it must be a property. For example:

```
var nowDate = new Date;
alert(nowDate.getMonth);
```

In the first line we have use the `Date` constructor, which is simply a method of the `Date` object, with no parentheses. However, even where we don't need to pass any values to the constructor, we must put parentheses after it.

On the second line, we call the `getMonth()` method of the `Date` object, except that we've forgotten the parentheses here also.

The lines should be:

```
var nowDate = new Date();
alert(nowDate.getMonth());
```

Just as we should always have parentheses after a method, we should never have parentheses after a property, otherwise JavaScript thinks we are trying to use a method of that object. For example:

```
var myString = new String("Hello");
alert(myString.length());
```

In the second line we have used parentheses after the `length` property making JavaScript think it is a method. What we should have written is:

```
var myString = new String("Hello");
alert(myString.length);
```

This mistake may seem like an obvious one in two lines of code, but it's easy to slip up when you're pounding out lots and lots of code.

Now that we've seen these top seven mistakes, we'll take a look at one way to make remedying these errors easier. This is through the Microsoft script debugger.

Microsoft Script Debugger

The Microsoft script debugger for use with IE is a very useful tool for helping discover what's gone wrong and why. Using it, you can halt the execution of your script, then step through code line by line, seeing exactly what is happening.

You can also find out what data is being held in variables, and execute statements "on the fly". Without the script debugger the best we can do is use the `alert()` method in our code to show the state of variables at various points.

The script debugger works with IE 3.02+ as long as you have the latest (3.0) version of the language engines. The engines come automatically with IE 5.0+.

Obtaining the Script Debugger

You can currently download the script debugger from the following URL:

```
http://msdn.microsoft.com/scripting/default.htm?/scripting/debugger/
default.htm
```

If this URL changes, then a search on the Microsoft web site, `http://www.microsoft.com`, for 'script debugger' ought to find its new home.

However, if you have installed Personal Web Server (PWS) or Internet Information Services IIS, which we'll be looking at in a later chapter, then the script debugger should already be installed. Other programs, such as Visual InterDev, which is part of Visual Studio, also automatically install the script debugger.

In addition, Windows 2000 comes automatically with the script debugger, although it may not be set up on your system. To install it open the Control Panel and choose Add/Remove Programs. Click on the Add/Remove Windows Components button, and in the window that opens, scroll down the list to the script debugger. If it is not ticked, then tick it and click Next to install it.

To check if the script debugger is already installed, open up Internet Explorer, and select the View menu. If one of the menu options is Script Debugger, as shown in the screenshot overleaf, then the debugger is installed. If you do not find this menu option, then it is still possible that the script debugger is already installed, but that the debugger is disabled. See the end of the next section for how to enable the script debugger, and then check for the menu option again.

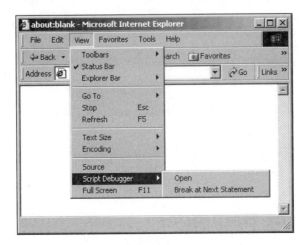

Installing the Script Debugger

Once you've downloaded the script debugger, you need to install it. First, you need to run the file you have just downloaded, for example from the Windows start bar's Run menu option. You should then see the dialog box below asking you whether you want to install the debugger: click the Yes button.

Next the license screen appears. Check through the license, and then click the Yes button if you agree to the conditions and want to install the debugger.

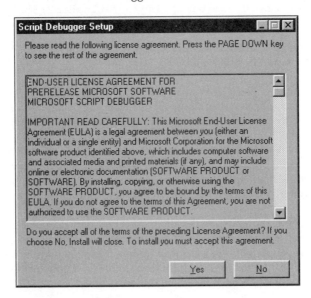

Next you get to choose where you want to install the debugger. Anywhere on your local machine is fine.

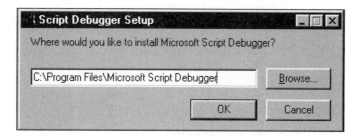

Click on OK, and if you get the following screen, just click Yes.

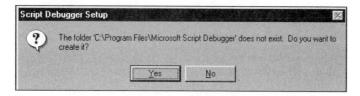

The script debugger will now install. Once it's complete you'll see the following message:

Click OK and you may be asked if you want to restart your computer. If so, click Yes to restart the computer.

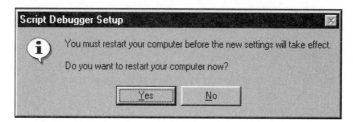

Once the computer has restarted, open up Internet Explorer. If you go to the View menu, you should see the Script Debugger option. If not, then the script debugger may be set as disabled. To enable it, in IE 5 go to the Tools menu, or in IE 4 go to the View menu, and select Internet Options. Select the Advanced tab and you'll see a screen similar to that shown overleaf.

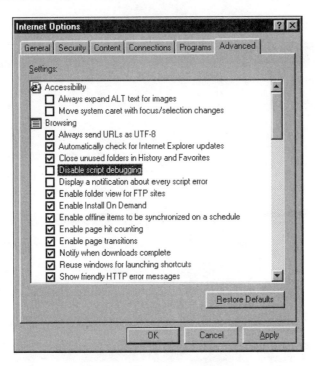

Make sure that the Disable script debugging box is unchecked, as shown in the screenshot above. If not, then uncheck it. Click OK, and then close down the browser. When you reopen the browser you should be able to see the Script Debugger option in the View menu.

Using the Script Debugger

It's important to point out that there are actually two versions of the script debugger: the basic version that we installed above and a more sophisticated version that comes with programs like Personal Web Server and Visual InterDev. The more sophisticated version does everything that the basic version does, but the screen layout and look will vary slightly, as will some of the keys and icons. We'll be looking at just the basic version here, so all screenshots are applicable to that.

Opening a Page in the Debugger

There are quite a number of ways that we can open a page in the script debugger, but here we'll just look at the three most useful. However, before we start let's create a page we can debug. Notice that we have made a deliberate typo in line 14. Be sure to include this typo if you create the page from scratch.

```
<HTML>
<HEAD>
<SCRIPT LANGUAGE=JavaScript>

function writeTimesTable(timesTable)
{
    var counter;
    var writeString;
    for (counter = 1; counter < 12; counter++)
```

```
        {
            writeString = counter + " * " + timesTable + " = ";
            writeString = writeString + (timesTable * counter);
            writeString = writeString + "<BR>";
            documents.write(writeString);
        }
    }

</SCRIPT>
</HEAD>
<BODY>
<P><SCRIPT LANGUAGE=JavaScript>writeTimesTable(2)</SCRIPT></P>
</BODY>
</HTML>
```

Save this page as `debug_timestable.htm`.

Now load this page into Internet Explorer and you'll discover the first way of activating the script debugger – automatically when there is an error in our code.

You should see a message box, similar to that shown overleaf, asking if you wish to debug. Click **Yes**. Note that if you have Visual Studio installed, a second dialog box will give you the option of opening a project. Just click **No** at that point.

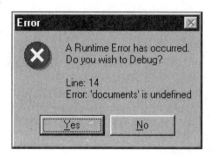

Having said that we want to debug, you should see the screen below. The debugger has opened and has stopped on the line where the error is and highlighted it in yellow, though this may not be obvious from the black and white screen shots in this chapter. The deliberate mistake is that we've written `documents.write` rather than `document.write`. The view is read-only so we can't edit it here, but need to return to our text editor to correct it. Let's do that, and then reload the page.

```
Microsoft Script Debugger                                      _ □ ×
File   Edit   View   Debug   Window   Help

File    Edit    Debug  ▤↓ ▤ ⮧ ⬏ ⬐ ⬑  ✋ ⬤    ▦ ▧ ▤

Read only: file://C:\4060BegJavaScript\debug_timestable.htm [break]    _ □ ×

        var counter;
        var writeString;

        for (counter = 1; counter < 12; counter++)
        {
            writeString = counter + " * " + timesTable + " = ";
            writeString = writeString + (timesTable * counter);
            writeString = writeString + "<BR>"
  ⇨        documents.write(writeString)
        }
    }

    </SCRIPT>
    </HEAD>
    <BODY>
    <P><SCRIPT LANGUAGE=JavaScript>writeTimesTable(2)

Ready                                           Ln 15
```

Having corrected the mistake and reloaded the page, we should see the two times table in our web page:

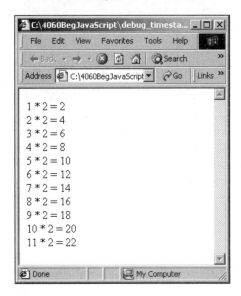

The second way we're going to use to open the debugger is to load the page we want to debug into our browser, then use the Break at Next Statement menu option under Script Debugger on Internet Explorer's View menu.

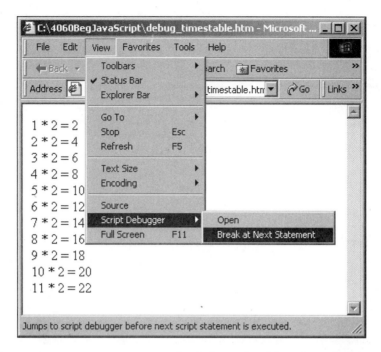

We've already got `debug_timestable.htm` loaded, so select View, Script Debugger, Break at Next Statement as shown above. Not much appears to happen, but reload the page by clicking the refresh icon, or pressing *F5*, and the debugger will open at the next JavaScript statement executed.

Where the 'next JavaScript statement' occurs in your page depends on your code. If you have code in the page other than a function or code connected to an event handler, then the first line the browser executes will be the next JavaScript statement. In our case, this is the code calling the function:

```
<SCRIPT>writeTimesTable(2)</SCRIPT>
```

If there is no code in the page except code inside event handlers or functions, then the next statement executed will be that fired in an event handler such as the `window` object's `onload` event handler or a button's `onclick` event handler.

Note that with some set-ups of the script debugger, the browser brings up a dialog box saying that an exception of type 'Runtime Error' was not handled. This does not mean that there is an error in the code, but simply is the way Break at Next Statement works.

As you can see from the screenshot above, the next statement executed in our example occurs when the browser reaches the script embedded in our web page that calls the writeTimesTable() function, again highlighted in yellow by the debugger.

We're now going to use the **Step Into icon,** illustrated here, that can be found on the top toolbar.

Click this icon and the debugger will execute the current line of code and move to the next line, in this case our function. We'll look more fully at stepping through code and examining the contents of variables shortly.

Finally, let's look at a third way of opening the debugger, which is probably the easiest and most useful.

Imagine we want to stop our code's execution and open the debugger just before the for loop is executed. We can do this by simply adding the keyword debugger to our script, which will stop the execution at that point and open the debugger. Let's do that now.

We need to close down the debugger, return to our text editor and add the following code to debug_timestable.htm:

```
function writeTimesTable(timesTable)
{
   var counter;
   var writeString;
```

```
        debugger
    for (counter = 1; counter < 12; counter++)
    {
        writeString = counter + " * " + timesTable + " = ";
        writeString = writeString + (timesTable * counter);
        writeString = writeString + "<BR>";
        document.write(writeString);
    }
}
```

Now refresh the page in Internet Explorer, and we'll find that the debugger opens, with code execution paused on the line with the `debugger` keyword in it.

```
Microsoft Script Debugger                                              _ □ ×
File   Edit   View   Debug   Window   Help
 File     Edit    Debug  ▤↓ ▨ ░▤ ▚▤ ▙▤ ░▤   ☝ ☜    ▤ ▚▤ ▤
 Read only: file://C:\4060BegJavaScript\debug_timestable.htm [break]    _ □ ×
       function writeTimesTable(timesTable)
       {
           var counter;
           var writeString;

 ⇨         debugger
           for (counter = 1; counter < 12; counter++)
           {
               writeString = counter + " * " + timesTable + " = ";
               writeString = writeString + (timesTable * counter);
               writeString = writeString + "<BR>"
               document.write(writeString)
           }
       }

       </SCRIPT>

Ready                                            Ln 10
```

Again we can click the Step Into icon we used above, and watch the code execute, statement by statement.

Stepping Through Code

There are three important ways of stepping through code, each involving one of the icons from the top toolbar of the script debugger.

We've seen that one way is to step into the code. This simply means that every line of code is executed on a line-by-line basis. If a function is called, then we step into that function and start executing the code inside the function line by line, before stepping out again, at the end and returning to the calling line. To do this we use the **Step Into icon**.

We may find that having stepped into a function we get half way through and decide the function is not the source of the bug and we want to execute the remaining lines of code in the function, then continue step by step from the point at which the function was called. This is called stepping out of the function, and uses the **Step Out icon**.

There may also be times when we have some code with a bug in it that calls a number of functions. If we know that some of the functions are bug free, then we may want to just execute them, and not actually step into them and see them being executed line by line. For this the debugger has the **Step Over icon**, which executes the code within a function but without us having to go through it line by line.

Let's alter our times table code in debug_timestable.htm and demonstrate the three methods of stepping action. Note that the debugger keyword has been removed from inside the writeTimesTable() function and is now in the second script block.

```
<HTML>
<HEAD>
<SCRIPT LANGUAGE=JavaScript>

function writeTimesTable(timesTable)
{
   var counter;
   var writeString;

   for (counter = 1; counter < 12; counter++)
   {
      writeString = counter + " * " + timesTable + " = ";
      writeString = writeString + (timesTable * counter);
      writeString = writeString + "<BR>";
      document.write(writeString);
   }
}

</SCRIPT>
</HEAD>
<BODY>
<P><SCRIPT LANGUAGE=JavaScript>

var timesTable;

debugger

for (timesTable = 1; timesTable <= 12; timesTable++)
{
   document.write("<P>")
   writeTimesTable(timesTable)
   document.write("</P>")
}

</SCRIPT></P>
</BODY>
</HTML>
```

Save this as debug_timestable2.htm. Load this into your browser and the script debugger will be opened by the debugger statement.

Click the Step Into icon and code execution will move to the next statement. In this case, the next statement is the first statement in the for loop where we initialize the variable timesTable to the value of 1.

When we click the Step Into icon again, the `timesTable = 1` statement is executed and we step to the next statement due to be executed, which is the condition part of the `for` loop. Having just seen `timesTable` be set to 1, we know that the condition `timesTable <= 12` is going to be `true`. Click the Step Into icon and the condition executes and indeed we find we're right, the condition is true and the first statement inside the `for` loop, `document.write("<P>")`, is next up for execution.

Click the Step Into icon again and that will take us to the first calling of our `writeTimesTable()` function. We want to see what's happening inside that function, so click Step Into again and we'll step into the function. Your screen should look like that shown below:

```
Microsoft Script Debugger                                                    _ □ ×
File   Edit   View   Debug   Window   Help

 File    Edit   Debug  ▤↓ ▤ ᵗᵢ ⁿ ᵢ ᵗᵢ  🖑 🐾   ᚵ ⬚ ▣

 Read only: file://C:\4060BegJavaScript\debug_timestable2.htm [break]       _ □ ×

        <SCRIPT LANGUAGE=JavaScript>

        function writeTimesTable(timesTable)
        {
            var counter;
            var writeString;


   ⇨     for (counter = 1; counter < 12; counter++)
            {
                writeString = counter + " * " + timesTable + " = ";
                writeString = writeString + (timesTable * counter);
                writeString = writeString + "<BR>";
                document.write(writeString);
            }
        }

Ready                                        Ln 11
```

You might be surprised that the next statement to be executed is not the `var counter;` or `var writeString;` lines, but instead the `for` loop's initialization condition. The first two lines have been executed, but the script debugger does not allow you to step variable declarations line by line.

Click the Step Into icon a few times and you'll soon get the gist of the flow of execution of the function. In fact, as you can see, stepping code line by line can get a little tedious. So let's imagine we're happy with this function and want to run the rest of the function en bloc, then start single stepping from the next line after the function was called. To do this click the Step Out icon, which we discussed above.

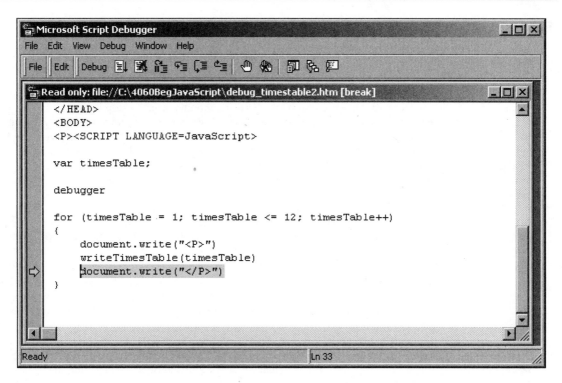

```
🔲 Microsoft Script Debugger                                    _ □ ×
File  Edit  View  Debug  Window  Help

│ File │ Edit │ Debug │ 📄 📄 📄 📄 📄 📄 │ ✋ 🖐 │ 📋 📋 📋

🔲 Read only: file://C:\4060BegJavaScript\debug_timestable2.htm [break]   _ □ ×
      </HEAD>
      <BODY>
      <P><SCRIPT LANGUAGE=JavaScript>

      var timesTable;

      debugger

      for (timesTable = 1; timesTable <= 12; timesTable++)
      {
          document.write("<P>")
          writeTimesTable(timesTable)
  ⇨      document.write("</P>")
      }

◀ │                                                          ▶

Ready                                    │ Ln 33
```

Now the function has been fully executed, and we're back out of it and at the next line, `document.write("</P>")`, as we can see from the screen shot above.

Click the Step Into icon and you'll see that the `document.write()` line will be executed and the next statement in the flow of execution is the increment part of our `for` loop. Click Step Into again and execution will continue to the condition part of the `for` loop. Clicking Step Into twice more brings us back to the calling of the `writeTimesTable()` function. We've already seen this in action, so really we want to step over it and go to the next line. Well, no prizes for guessing that the Step Over icon that we talked about above is what we need to click to do this.

Click the Step Over icon and the function will be executed, but without us having to step through it statement by statement. We should find ourselves back at the `document.write("</P>")` line.

If we've finished debugging, then we can run the rest of the code without stepping through each line by clicking the **Run icon** on the tool bar, which we illustrate here. (However, note that if you are using Visual InterDev, it's a play button icon like that on a video recorder.) Let's do that, then we can return to the browser and see the results of the code we have executed. You should see a page of times tables from 1*1=1 to 11*12=132 in the browser.

Breakpoints

Breakpoints are markers you can set in the debugger which force code execution to stop at that point and start single stepping through the code.

Load up our `debug_timestable2.htm` page into the browser. This will open the debugger and stop execution at the line with our `debugger` statement. Now imagine we want to stop in our `writeTimesTable()` function on the line that writes the results of the times table to the page, namely `document.write(writeString)`. This is the last statement in the `for` loop. However, we're busy people and we don't want to manually step through every line before that. What we can do is set a breakpoint on that line, then hit the Run icon, which will restart the code execution in the normal fashion, that is without single stepping. Then when the breakpoint is reached, code execution will stop and we can start single stepping if we want.

To set the breakpoint we need to scroll up the code window in the debugger until we can see the line we want to put the breakpoint on. Click on that line, then click the **Toggle Breakpoint icon** in the toolbar, illustrated here.

As you can see below, any line with a breakpoint on it is indicated by the reddish brown dot on the left of the code window and by the line itself being set to a reddish brown, though the line may not always be colored. We can set as many or few breakpoints at one time as we wish, so if we want to break on other lines we can add breakpoints there too.

To unset a breakpoint we just click on the relevant line of code, then click the Toggle Breakpoint icon again and that toggles it off. To clear all breakpoints at once we can click the **Clear All Breakpoints icon** illustrated here.

```
Microsoft Script Debugger                                    _ □ ×
File  Edit  View  Debug  Window  Help
File  ┃ Edit ┃ Debug  ≣↓ ⬛ ⌐⬚ ⌐⬚ ⌐⬚ ⌐⬚ ┃ 🖑 🖑 ┃ 🗐 🗐 🗐

  Read only: file://C:\4060BegJavaScript\debug_timestable2.htm [break]   _ □ ×
        <SCRIPT LANGUAGE=JavaScript>

        function writeTimesTable(timesTable)
        {
            var counter;
            var writeString;


            for (counter = 1; counter < 12; counter++)
            {
                writeString = counter + " * " + timesTable + " = ";
                writeString = writeString + (timesTable * counter);
                writeString = writeString + "<BR>";
        ●       document.write(writeString);
            }
        }

  Ready                                    Ln 16
```

OK, now let's start the code running again by hitting the Run icon in the toolbar.

We find that code recommences executing without single stepping until it reaches our breakpoint, at which point it stops. We can either single step using the Step Into icon or hit the Run icon again in which case execution continues, unless a breakpoint is reached again.

Leave the debugger open and with code execution halted on our breakpoint as we'll be using it in a moment.

Command Window

While stepping through code and checking its flow of execution is useful, what would be really useful is the ability to check the values contained inside variables, evaluate conditions and even change things on the fly. We can do all of these things using the debugger's command window.

Hopefully you still have the debugger open with execution halted at the breakpoint we set above. The line stopped on is:

```
document.write(writeString);
```

Let's see how we can find out what the value currently contained in variable writeString is.

First we need to open the command window from within the debugger. We do this by clicking the **Command Window icon**, illustrated here, or by selecting Command Window from the View menu.

In the command window type the name of the variable we want to examine, in this case writeString, then hit return. This will cause the value contained in the variable to be printed below your command in the command window:

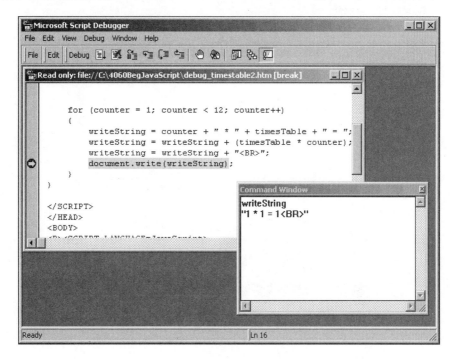

If we want to change a variable, then we can write a line of JavaScript into the command window and hit return.

For example, type:

```
writeString = "Changed on the Fly<BR>"
```

into the command window and hit return. Now remove the breakpoint (see above for how to do this) and hit the Run icon. If we switch to the browser, we see the results of our actions: where the 1*1 times table result should be, our text Changed on the Fly has been inserted instead. Note that this does not change our actual HTML source file, just the page currently loaded in the browser.

The command window can also evaluate conditions. Refresh the browser to reset the debugger and leave execution stopped at our `debugger` statement. Click the Step Into icon twice and execution will stop on the condition in the `for` statement.

Type:

```
timesTable <= 12
```

into the command window and hit return. As this is the first time the loop has been run, `timesTable` is equal to 1 and so the condition `timesTable <= 12` evaluates to `true`. Note that the debugger sometimes represents `true` by the value `-1` and `false` by the value `0`, so you may see the value `-1` instead of `true`.

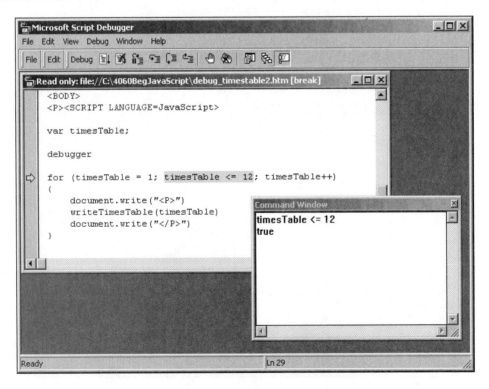

We can also use the command window to access properties of the browser's Browser Object Model (BOM). For example, if we type `window.location.href` into the command window and hit return, it will tell us where the current page is stored.

In fact, the command window can execute any single line of JavaScript including functions.

Call Stack Window

When single stepping through the code, the call stack window keeps a running list of which functions have been called to get to the current point of execution in the code.

Let's create an example web page, which demonstrates the call stack very nicely.

```
<HTML>
<HEAD>

<SCRIPT LANGUAGE=JavaScript>

function firstCall()
{
    secondCall();
}

function secondCall()
{
    thirdCall();
}

function thirdCall()
{
    //
}

function button1_onclick()
{
    debugger
    firstCall();
}

</SCRIPT>
</HEAD>
<BODY>

<INPUT TYPE="button" VALUE="Button" NAME=button1
    onclick="return button1_onclick()">

</BODY>
</HTML>
```

Save this page as `debug_callstack.htm`, and then load it into your IE browser. When loaded, all you'll see is a blank web page with a button. Click the button and the debugger will be opened at the `debugger` statement in the `button1_onclick()` function, which is connected to the button's `onclick` event handler.

To open the call stack window, either click the **Call Stack icon** in the toolbar, illustrated here, or choose Call Stack from the View menu.

Our debugger now looks as below:

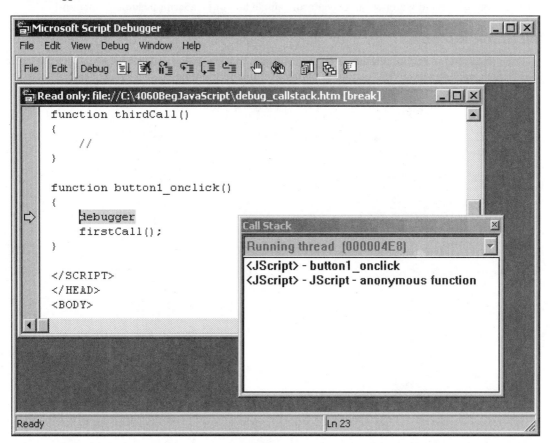

Every time a function is called, the debugger adds the function to the top of the call stack. We can already see that the first function called was actually the code attached to the onclick event handler of our button. Next added to the call stack is the function called by the onclick event, which is the function button1_onclick() shown at the top of the call stack.

If we want to see where each function was first entered from, we just need to double-click the function name in the call stack window. Double-click <JSCRIPT> – Jscript – anonymous function and the calling line, that is the code connected to the onclick attribute of the <INPUT> tag, will be shown. Now double-click the top line <JSCRIPT> – button1_onclick and that will take us back to the current execution point.

Now single step twice, using the Step Into icon. The first step is to the line that calls the firstCall() function, then the second step takes us into that function itself. You'll notice that straight away the function is added to the call stack.

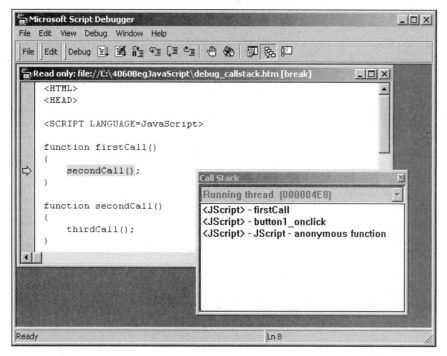

Click the Step Into icon again and we'll step into the second function, `secondCall()`. Again this is added to the call stack. One more click takes us into the third function, `thirdCall()`, again with its name being added to the top of the call stack.

Now click Step Into again and as we leave the function `thirdCall()` we see that its name is removed from the top of the call stack. Another click takes us out of the second function `secondCall()` whose name is also now removed from the stack. Each further click takes us out of a function, with its name removed from the call stack, until eventually all code has been executed and we're back to the browser again.

Our demo page was very simple to follow, but with complex pages, especially multi-frame pages, the call stack can prove very useful for tracking where we are, where we have been, and how we got there.

Running Documents Window

The final window we'll look at is the running documents window. This window lists each instance of Internet Explorer running and what pages, or documents, are currently loaded in that instance of IE.

Let's create some example pages demonstrating the use of the running documents window.

The running documents window proves most useful with frame–based pages, so let's create a page with two frames inside it:

```
<HTML>
<FRAMESET ROWS="50%,*">
   <FRAME NAME="topFrame" SRC="debug_topFrame.htm">
   <FRAME NAME="bottomFrame" SRC="debug_bottomFrame.htm">
</FRAMESET>
</HTML>
```

This first page defines the frameset. Save it as `debug_frameset.htm`.

Next, we see the page for the top window:

```
<HTML>
<HEAD>

<SCRIPT LANGUAGE=JavaScript>

function button1_onclick()
{
    var x;
    x = 1 + 1;
    alert(x)
}

</SCRIPT>
</HEAD>
<BODY>

<H2>Top Frame</H2>
<INPUT TYPE="button" VALUE="Button" NAME=button1 LANGUAGE=JavaScript
    onclick="return button1_onclick()">
</BODY>
</HTML>
```

Save this page as `debug_topFrame.htm`.

Finally the third page:

```
<HTML>
<HEAD>

<SCRIPT LANGUAGE=JavaScript>

function button1_onclick()
{
    var x;
    x = 2 * 2;
    alert(x);
}

</SCRIPT>
</HEAD>
<BODY>

<H2>Bottom Frame</H2>
<INPUT TYPE="button" VALUE="Button" NAME=button1 LANGUAGE=JavaScript
    onclick="return button1_onclick()">
</BODY>
</HTML>
```

Save this page as `debug_bottomFrame.htm`.

Now load `debug_frameset.htm` into the browser. You will see two frames, each containing a button.

We can view all the pages currently loaded in the frames by first opening the debugger by choosing Script debugger, Open from the View menu. Now with the debugger open we need to view the running documents window by either clicking the **Running Documents icon** in the tool bar, illustrated here, or selecting Running Documents from the View menu.

This will initially show each instance of Internet Explorer running on the machine. Click the plus sign (+) to open up which pages are currently loaded, or running, in that instance of Internet Explorer. When pages are in framesets, as ours are, then pages contained within the window frameset page are included, indented underneath the frameset page. You'll need to click the plus sign again to open them up.

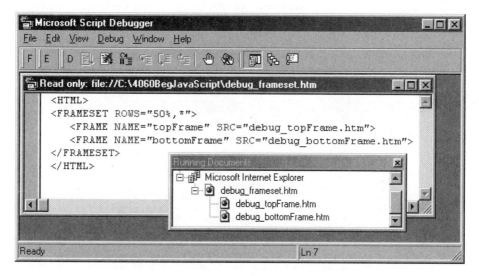

If we wanted to debug the code within the top frame, then the easiest way is to right-click `debug_topFrame.htm` in the Running Documents window and select Break at Next Statement. Then click the button in the top frame and the debugger will open, with execution stopped at the first statement due to be executed (`onclick="return button1_onclick()"`).

That concludes our brief tour of the Microsoft script debugger. This debugger is excellent for debugging pages so that they will work in IE. However, it won't help you spot errors due to cross browser incompatibility. For example, what works in NN might throw an error in IE, and a page that you've debugged successfully in IE could easily throw an error in NN. Aside from this problem, the debugger is a great help for spotting logic errors in your code.

Netscape Debugging

There are a couple of tools provided by Netscape that can help us to debug our pages, namely the JavaScript console and the Netscape script debugger.

The JavaScript Console

The first tool provided by Netscape that we will look at is the JavaScript console, available in NN 4.06+. We saw this earlier in Chapter 2, where we saw that it enables us to see any errors in code loaded into the Netscape browser. We changed the prefs.js file to cause the console to automatically open on an error for NN 4.06+ (not including NN 6).

However, the console also allows you to evaluate JavaScript statements interactively by typing code into a text box in the console. Note that currently NN 6 does have the console, but there is no facility to enter JavaScript code. Later versions may well have this functionality.

To access the JavaScript console on any NN 4.06+ browser (exept NN 6), you can type javascript: into the address bar, as shown below, and hit return:

The console that opens will be something like that shown below for NN 4.06+ browsers:

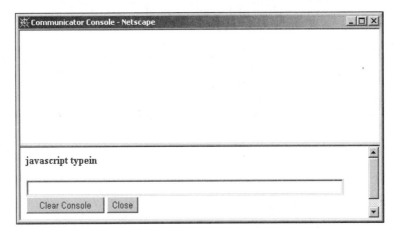

If you're using NN 6, then you'll need to select **Tools, JavaScript Console** from the **Tasks** menu, after which you'll see something like:

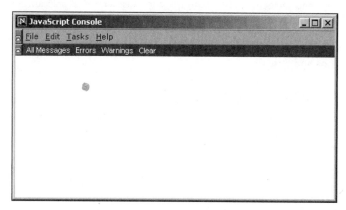

Note that I've opened the console up while the browser contained an empty page, in particular a page with no errors, so the main console screen is blank. Let's create a simple page with an error so that we can see what the console displays.

```
<HTML>
<BODY>

<SCRIPT LANGUAGE=JavaScript>

var myAge = 99;
myAge = myAge -/ 100;
document.write(myAge);

</SCRIPT>

</BODY>
</HTML>
```

Save this as `NN_ConsoleTest.htm` and load it into a Netscape 4.06+ browser.

If you've set your NN browser preferences to display errors in the console automatically (see Chapter 2) then the console will appear as soon as the page is loaded. If not, open the console as described above. The console will appear and display the error message as shown below:

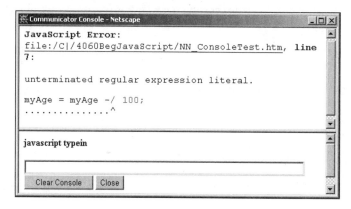

The console not only displays the error message, but also gives us an indication of where it thinks the error occurred. Note that sometimes this can be misleading – although the error actually occurred at that position, we may need to rectify it by changing code elsewhere. For example, a missing curly brace marking out a code block may not produce an error at the position the curly brace should have been.

If you're using Netscape 4.06+, though not currently NN 6, you will notice in the lower frame is a form containing two buttons and a text box.

Evaluating Expressions with the Console

You can use the javascript typein textbox to test comparison operators, and perform math operations. To evaluate an expression simply open the console and type the expression into the javascript typein textbox then press return. The results are displayed in the upper frame.

For example, you could evaluate the following expressions:

```
alert("hello world");
```

which displays an alert dialog box;

```
10-2;
```

which displays 8 in the upper frame;

```
var high=100; var low=45;
```

which creates two variables;

```
high-low;
```

which displays 55 in the upper frame.

However, while the console is very useful for viewing page errors and interactively evaluating JavaScript code it will not allow you to interact with any of the code in the page or with the BOM in any meaningful way. For example, with the test page we used previously we had a variable myAge. Whether you opened the console yourself or it was opened automatically by the error, there is no way of checking the value of myAge or indeed accessing the window or document object of that page or any code inside it. If you type:

```
alert(myAge);
```

into the textbox and hit return, you'd just get the message:

JavaScript Error: [unknown origin]:
myAge is not defined.

This limits the console's use in debugging.

Netscape Debugger

Netscape does, or rather did, have a debugger of its own. This provided some of the debugging power of the IE version, for example you can step into, over and out of your code, can work with breakpoints, and access a call stack window.

However, the debugger has not been updated since 1997. It does not seem to work at all on Windows 2000 or with NN 6 on any platform, and there may be some problems with Windows 98 and ME. Hopefully, Netscape will release an updated version of this in the near future. Bearing in mind its faults, you can still find information about it from:

```
http://developer.netscape.com:80/docs/manuals/jsdebug/contents.htm
```

Also to download it and find more information, follow the links on:

```
http://developer.netscape.com/software/jsdebug.html
```

Error Handling

When writing our programs, we want to be informed of every error. However when we've finally deployed the code to a web server for the whole world to access, the last thing we want the user to be seeing is a lot of error message dialog boxes. Of course, writing bug-free code would be a good start, but:

❑   There are occasions when conditions beyond our control lead to errors. A good example of this is when we are relying on something, such as a Java applet, which isn't on the user's computer and where there is no way of checking for its existence.

❑   'Murphy's Law' states that anything that can go wrong will go wrong!

Preventing Errors

The best way to handle errors is to stop them occurring in the first place. OK, that seems like stating the obvious, but there are a number of things you should do if you want error free pages.

1.   Check your pages thoroughly on as many different platforms and browsers as you can. I realize this is easier said than done given the number of possible variations and that it's easier when it's a professional web site created by a team of people with the hardware, software, and time to check platform and browser compatibility. The alternative is for you to decide which browsers and platforms are supported and state these requirements on your first web page. Then check that it works with the specified combinations. Use the browser and platform checking code we saw earlier in the book to send unsupported users to a nice safe and probably boring web page with reduced functionality or maybe just supply them with a message that their browser/platform is not supported.

2. Validate your data. If there is a way the user can enter dud data that will cause your program to fall over, then they will. As a poster on the wall of somewhere I worked once said, "Users are idiots. Never underestimate the cunning of an idiot". If your code will fall over if a text box is empty, then check that it has got something in it. If you need a whole number, then check that that's what the user has entered. Is the date the user just entered valid? Is the e-mail address `mind your own business` they just entered likely to be valid? No, so check it is in the format `something@something.something`.

OK, so let's say you've carefully checked your pages and there is not a syntax or logic error in sight. You've added data validation that confirms that everything the user enters is in a valid format. There are still things that can go wrong, and problems that you can do nothing about. Let's use a real-world example of a situation that happened to me.

I created an online message board that used something called remote scripting, a Microsoft technology that allows you to transfer data from a server to a web page. This relies on a small Java applet to enable the transfer of data. I checked my code and everything was fine. I launched it live, and again it worked just fine, except in about 5% of cases where the Java applet initialized, but then caused an error. To cut a long story short, remote scripting worked fine, except in a small number of cases where the user was behind a particular type of firewall, a firewall being a method of stopping hackers getting into your local computer network. Now, there is no way of checking that a user is behind a certain type of firewall, so there is nothing that can be done in that sort of exceptional circumstance, or is there?

In fact IE 5 and NN 6 include something called the `try...catch` statement. This allows you to try to run your code – if it fails then the error is caught by the `catch` clause and can be dealt with as you wish. In my message board example, I used a `try...catch` clause to catch the Java applet's failure and re-directed the user to a more basic page that still displayed messages, but without using the applet and therefore was not affected by the firewall.

Let's now look at the `try...catch` statements.

The try...catch Statements

The `try...catch` statements work as a pair; you can't have one without the other.

We use the `try` statement to define a block of code that we want to try to execute.

We use the `catch` statement to define a block of code that will execute if an exception to the normal running of the code occurs in the block of code defined by the `try` statement. The term **exception** is key here: it means a circumstance that is extraordinary and unpredictable to a certain extent, compared to an error, which is something in the code that has been written wrongly. If no exception occurs, then the code inside the `catch` statement is never executed. The `catch` statement also enables us to get the contents of the exception message that would have been shown to the user had we not caught it first.

Let's create a simple example of a `try . . . catch` clause.

```
<HTML>
<BODY>
<SCRIPT LANGUAGE=JavaScript>

try
{
```

```
        alert('This is code inside the try clause');
        alert('No Errors so catch code will not execute');
    }
    catch(exception)
    {
        if (exception.description == null)
        {
            alert("Error is " + exception.message)
        }
        else
        {
            alert("Error is " + exception.description);
        }
    }

    </SCRIPT>
    </BODY>
    </HTML>
```

Save this as `TryCatch.htm`.

First we define the `try` statement – we mark out which block of code is within the `try` statement by enclosing it in curly braces.

Next comes the `catch` statement. We've included `exception` in parentheses straight after the `catch` statement. This `exception` is simply a variable name. It will store an `Exception` object containing information about any exception thrown up during execution of code inside the `try` code block. Although we've used `exception`, we could use any valid variable name. For example, `catch(exceptionObject)` would be fine and certainly more descriptive.

The `Exception` object contains two properties that provide information about the exception that occurred. The bad news is that while both IE 5 and NN 6 support the `Exception` object and both have two properties, the names of these properties differ.

IE's version of the `Exception` object has the `number` and `description` properties. The `number` property is a unique number for that error type. The `description` property is the error message the user would normally see.

With NN 6, the properties of the `Exception` object are `name` and `message`. The `name` property is a unique name for that type of error and the `message` property is much like IE's `description` property in that it gives a more detailed explanation of what went wrong.

Within the curly braces after the `catch` statement is the code block that will execute if and only if an error occurs. In this case the code within the `try` code block is fine, and so the `alert()` inside the `catch` block won't execute.

Let's insert a deliberate error:

```
try
{
    alert('This is code inside the try clause');
    ablert('Exception will be thrown by this code');
}
catch(exception)
{
    if (exception.description == null)
    {
        alert("Error is " + exception.message)
    }
    else
    {
        alert("Error is " + exception.description);
    }
}
```

Now when we load the page the first `alert()` method in the `try` block of code will execute fine and the alert box will be displayed to the user. However, the second `ablert()` statement will cause an error and code execution will start at the first statement in the `catch` block.

As the IE 5 and NN 6 `Exception` objects support different properties, we need different code for each. How do we tell whether the browser is IE or NN?

By checking to see if the `exception.description` property is `null`, we can tell whether the `description` property is supported, and so whether the browser is IE. If it is equal to `null`, then that means the property is not supported and that this is NN 6, so we need to display the `message` property of the `Exception` object instead. If it is not `null`, then it means the `description` property has a value and therefore does exist and can be used.

If you're using Internet Explorer 5.0+, the error description displayed will be 'Object expected'. If you're using Netscape Navigator 6, then the same error is interpreted differently and reported as 'ablert is not defined'.

If we change the code again, so it has a different error, we'll see something important.

```
try
{
    alert('This is code inside the try clause');
    alert('This code won't work');
}
catch(exception)
{
    if (exception.description == null)
    {
        alert("Error is " + exception.message)
    }
    else
    {
        alert("Error is " + exception.description);
    }
}
```

If we were to load this code into an IE 5 or NN 6 browser, instead of the error being handled by our catch clause, we get the normal browser error message telling us Expected ')'.

The reason for this is that this is a syntax error; the functions and methods are valid, but we have an invalid character. The single quote in the word won't has ended the string parameter being passed to the alert() method. At that point JavaScript syntax, or language rules, specifies that a closing parenthesis should appear, which is not the case here. Before executing any code, JavaScript goes through all the code and checks for syntax errors, or code that breaches JavaScript's rules. If a syntax error is found then the browser deals with it as normal; our try clause never gets run and therefore cannot handle syntax errors.

Throwing errors

The throw statement can be used within a try block of code to create your own run-time errors. Why create a statement to generate errors, when a bit of bad coding will do the same?

Throwing errors can be very useful for indicating problems such as invalid user input. Rather than lots of if...else statements, we can check the validity of user input, then use throw to stop code execution in its tracks and cause the error catching code in the catch block of code to take over. In the catch clause, we can determine whether the error is user input based, in which case we can notify the user what went wrong and how to correct it. Alternatively, if it's an unexpected error, we can handle it more gracefully than lots of JavaScript errors.

To use throw, we type throw then include the error message after it. For example:

```
throw "This is my error message";
```

Remember that when we catch the Exception object in the catch statement, we can get hold of the error message that we have thrown. Although I've used a string in my throw statement we can actually throw any type of data, such as numbers and objects.

Try It Out – try...catch and Throwing Errors

In this example we'll be creating a simple factorial calculator. The important part of this example is the try...catch clause and the throw statements. It's a frameset page to enable us to demonstrate that things can go wrong that we can't do anything about. In this case, the page relies on a function defined within a frameset page, so if the page is loaded on its own, a problem will occur.

First let's create the page that will define the frameset and also contains an important function.

```
<HTML>
<HEAD>
<SCRIPT LANGUAGE=JavaScript>

function calcFactorial(factorialNumber)
{
    var factorialResult = 1;
    for (; factorialNumber > 0; factorialNumber--)
    {
        factorialResult = factorialResult * factorialNumber;
    }
return factorialResult;
```

```
}
</SCRIPT>
</HEAD>
<FRAMESET COLS="100%,*">
    <FRAME NAME="fraCalcFactorial" SRC="CalcFactorial.htm">
</FRAMESET>
</HTML>
```

Save this page as `CalcFactorialTopFrame.htm`.

```
<HTML>
<HEAD>
<SCRIPT LANGUAGE=JavaScript>

function butCalculate_onclick()
{
    try
    {
        if (window.top.calcFactorial == null)
            throw "This page is not loaded within the correct frameset";

        if (document.form1.txtNum1.value == "")
            throw "!Please enter a value before you calculate its factorial";

        if (isNaN(document.form1.txtNum1.value))
            throw "!Please enter a valid number";

        if (document.form1.txtNum1.value < 0)
            throw "!Please enter a positive number";

        document.form1.txtResult.value =
            window.parent.calcFactorial(document.form1.txtNum1.value);
    }
    catch(exception)
    {
        if (typeof(exception) == "string")
        {
            if (exception.charAt(0) == "!")
            {
                alert(exception.substr(1));
                document.form1.txtNum1.focus();
                document.form1.txtNum1.select();
            }
            else
            {
                alert(exception);
            }
        }
        else
        {
            if (exception.description == null)
            {
                alert("The following error occurred " + exception.message)
            }
            else
            {
                alert("The following error occurred " + exception.description);
            }
        }
    }
}
```

```
  </SCRIPT>
  </HEAD>
  <BODY>
  <FORM NAME="form1">
     <INPUT TYPE="text" NAME=txtNum1 SIZE=3> factorial is
     <INPUT TYPE="text" NAME=txtResult SIZE=25><BR>
     <INPUT TYPE="button" VALUE="Calculate Factorial"
        NAME=butCalculate onclick="butCalculate_onclick()">
  </FORM>

  </BODY>
  </HTML>
```

Save the page as `CalcFactorial.htm`. Then load the first page, `CalcFactorialTopFrame.htm`, into your browser. Remember that this only works with IE 5.0+ and NN 6.

The page consists of a simple form with two text boxes and a button. Enter the number 4 into the first box, and then click the **Calculate Factorial** button. The factorial of 4, which is 24, will be calculated and put in the second text box:

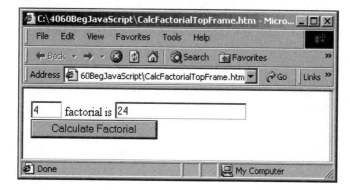

The factorial of a number is the product of all the positive integers less than or equal to that number. For example, the factorial of 4 (written 4!) is $1 * 2 * 3 * 4 = 24$. Factorials are used in various branches of mathematics, including statistics. Here, we just want to create a function that does something complex enough to be worthy of a function, but not so complex as to distract from the main purpose of this example – the `try...catch` and `throw` statements.

If we clear the first text box and click **Calculate Factorial**, then we'll be told that a value needs to be entered. If we enter an invalid non-numeric value into the first text box, then we'll be told to enter a valid value. If we enter a negative value, then we'll be told to enter a positive value.

Also, if you try loading the page `CalcFactorial.htm` into your browser, then enter a value in the text box and click **Calculate Factorial**, you'll be told that the page is not loaded into the correct frameset.

As we'll see, all of these error messages are created using the `try...catch` and `throw` statements.

How It Works

As this example is all about `try...catch` and `throw`, we'll concentrate just on the `CalcFactorial.htm` page, in particular the `butCalculate_onclick()` function, which is connected to the `onclick` event handler of the form's only button.

We'll start by looking at the `try` clause and code inside it. The code consists of four `if` statements, and another line of code that puts the calculated factorial into the second text box. Each of the `if` statements is checking for a condition which, if true, would cause problems for our code.

The first `if` statement checks that the `calcFactorial()` function, in the top frameset window, actually exists. If not, it throws an error, which will be caught by the `catch` block. If the user had loaded the `CalcFactorial.htm` page rather than the frameset page `CalcFactorialTopFrame.htm`, then without this `throw` statement our code would fail.

```
try
{
    if (window.top.calcFactorial == null)
        throw "This page is not loaded within the correct frameset";
```

The next three `if` statements check the validity of the data entered into the text box by the user. First we check that that something has actually been entered in the box, then that what has been entered is a number, and then finally we check that the value is not negative. Again if any of the `if` conditions is true, then we throw an error, which will be caught by the `catch` block. Each of the error messages we define starts with an exclamation mark, the purpose of which is to mark the error as a user input error, rather than an error such as not being in a frameset.

```
    if (document.form1.txtNum1.value == "")
        throw "!Please enter a value before you calculate its factorial";

    if (isNaN(document.form1.txtNum1.value))
        throw "!Please enter a valid number";

    if (document.form1.txtNum1.value < 0)
        throw "!Please enter a positive number";
```

If everything is fine, then the `calcFactorial()` function will be executed and the results text box will be filled with the factorial of the number entered by the user.

```
    document.form1.txtResult.value =
        window.parent.calcFactorial(document.form1.txtNum1.value);
}
```

Finally let's turn our attention to the `catch` part of the `try...catch` statement. First, any message thrown by the `try` code will be caught by the `exception` variable.

```
catch(exception)
{
```

What type of data is contained in exception will depend on how the error was thrown. If it was thrown by the browser and not by our code, then exception will be an object, the Exception object. If it's thrown by our code, then in this instance we've thrown only primitive strings. So the first thing we need to do is decide what type of data exception contains. If it's a string then we know it was thrown by our code and can deal with it accordingly. If it's an object, and given that we know none of our code throws objects, we assume it must be the browser that has generated this exception and that exception is an Exception object.

```
if (typeof(exception) == "string")
{
```

If it was code that generated the exception using a throw (and so exception is a string), then we now need to determine whether the error is a user input error, such as the text box not containing a value to calculate, or whether it was another type of error such as the page not being loaded in our frameset. All the user input exception messages had an exclamation mark at the beginning, so we use an if statement to check the first character. If it is an !, then we notify the user of the error then return focus to our control. If it's not, then we just display an error message.

```
if (exception.charAt(0) == "!")
{
    alert(exception.substr(1));
    document.form1.txtNum1.focus();
    document.form1.txtNum1.select();
}
else
{
    alert(exception);
}
}
```

If exception was not a string, then we know we have an exception object and need to display either the message property if it's NN 6 or the description property if it's IE 5. We use the if e.description == null check to see which property is supported.

```
else
{
    if (exception.description == null)
    {
        alert("The following error occurred " + exception.message)
    }
    else
    {
        alert("The following error occurred " + exception.description);
    }
}
}
```

Nested try...catch Statements

So far we've been using just one try...catch statement, but it's possible to include a try...catch statement inside another try statement. Indeed we could go further and have a try...catch inside the try statement of this inner try...catch, or even another inside that, the limit being what it's actually sensible to do.

So why would we use nested try...catch statements? Well, we can deal with certain errors inside the inner try...catch statement. If, however, it's a more serious error, then the inner catch clause could pass the error to the outer catch clause by throwing it to it.

Let's look at an example.

```
try
{
    try
    {
        ablurt("This code has an error");
    }
    catch(exception)
    {
        var eMessage
        if (exception.description == null)
        {
            eMessage = exception.name;
        }
        else
        {
            eMessage = exception.description;
        }

        if (eMessage == "Object expected" || eMessage == "ReferenceError")
        {
            alert("Inner try...catch can deal with this error");
        }
        else
        {
            throw exception;
        }
    }
}
catch(exception)
{
    alert("Error the inner try...catch could not handle occurred");
}
```

In this code we have two try...catch pairs, one nested inside the other.

The inner try statement contains a line of code that contains an error. The catch statement of the inner try...catch checks the value of the error message caused by this error. If the exception message is either **Object expected** or **ReferenceError** then the inner try...catch deals with it by way of an alert box.

In fact, both the exception messages that are checked for are the same thing, but reported differently by IE and NN. Note that I've used NN's Exception object's name property for comparison rather than the message as name is a much shorter one word description of the exception in comparison to message which is a sentence describing the exception.

However if the error caught by the inner catch statement is any other type of error, it is thrown up in the air again for the catch statement of the outer try...catch to deal with.

Let's change the calcFactorial() function from the previous example CalcFactorial.htm, so that it has an inner and outer try...catch.

```
function butCalculate_onclick()
{
    try
    {
        try
        {
            if (window.top.calcFactorial == null)
                throw ("This page is not loaded within the correct frameset");

            if (document.form1.txtNum1.value == "")
                throw("!Please enter a value before you calcuate its factorial");

            if (isNaN(document.form1.txtNum1.value))
                throw("!Please enter a valid number");

            if (document.form1.txtNum1.value < 0)
                throw("!Please enter a positive number");

            document.form1.txtResult.value =
                window.parent.calcFactorial(document.form1.txtNum1.value);
        }
        catch(exception)
        {
            if (typeof(exception) == "string" && exception.charAt(0) == "!")
            {
                alert(exception.substr(1));
                document.form1.txtNum1.focus();
                document.form1.txtNum1.select();
            }
            else
            {
                throw exception;
            }
        }
    }
    catch(exception)
    {
        switch (exception)
        {
            case "This page is not loaded within the correct frameset":
            alert(exception);
            break;
```

```
            default :
                alert("The following critical error has occurred \n" + exception);
        }
    }
}
```

The inner `try...catch` deals with user input errors. However, if it's not a user input error thrown by us, then the error is thrown for the outer `catch` statement to deal with. The outer `catch` statement has a `switch` statement that checks the value of the error message thrown. If it's the error message thrown by us because the `calcFactorialTopFrame.htm` is not loaded, then it deals with it in the first `case` statement. Any other error is dealt with in the `default` statement. However, there may well be occasions when there are lots of different errors you want to deal with in `case` statements.

And finally

The `try...catch` statement has a `finally` clause which defines a block of script which will execute whether an exception was thrown or not. The `finally` clause can't appear on its own; it must be after a `catch` block. For example:

```
try
{
    ablurt("An exception will occur");
}
catch(exception)
{
    alert("Exception occurred");
}
finally
{
    alert("Whatever happens this line will execute");
}
```

The `finally` part is a good place to put any clean-up code that needs to be executed regardless of any errors occurring previously.

Summary

In this chapter we've looked at the less exciting part of coding, namely bugs. In an ideal world we'd get things right the first time, every time, but in reality any code more than a few lines long is likely to suffer from bugs.

❑   We first looked at some of the more common errors, not just those made when first learning JavaScript, but also by experts with lots of experience.

❑   We then installed the script debugger, which works with Internet Explorer. Without the script debugger any errors throw up messages, but nothing else. With the script debugger we get to see exactly where the error might have been and to examine the current state of variables when the error occurred. Also we can use the script debugger to analyze code as it's being run, seeing its flow step by step, checking variables and conditions.

❑   We had a brief look at the Netscape debugging tools, such as the JavaScript console and the script debugger. The console can be used to run various JavaScript statements.

❑   Some errors are not necessarily bugs in our code, but in fact exceptions to the normal circumstances that cause our code to fail, such as a Java applet failing due to a user being behind a firewall. We saw that the `try...catch` statements are a good way of dealing with this sort of error. Also when used with the `throw` statement, we can use the `catch` clause to deal with errors that are likely to happen, such as user input errors. Finally, we saw that if we want a block of code to execute regardless of any error, then we can use the `finally` clause.

In the next chapter we'll be looking at a way of storing information on the user's computer using something called a cookie. While they may not be powerful enough to hold a user's life history, they are certainly enough for us to keep track of their visits to our web site and what pages they view when they visit and with that information to provide a more customized experience for the user.

Exercise Questions

Suggested solutions to these questions can be found in Appendix A.

Question 1

The example debug_timestable2.htm has a deliberate bug. For each times table it only creates the values from 1 to 11 as you can see from the output for the two times table shown below.

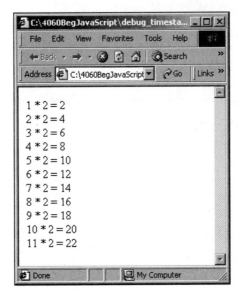

Use the script debugger to work out why this is happening, and then correct the bug.

Question 2

There are a number of common errors in the following code, see if you can spot them:

```
<HTML>
<HEAD>
</HEAD>
<BODY>

<SCRIPT LANGUAGE=JavaScript>

function checkForm(theForm)
{
   var formValid = true;
   var elementCount  = 0;

   while(elementCount =< theForm.length)
   {
      if (theForm.elements[elementcount].type == "text")
      {

         if (theForm.elements[elementCount].value() = "")
            alert("Please complete all form elements")
            theForm.elements[elementCount].focus;
            formValid = false;
            break;

      }
   }

   return formValid;

}

</SCRIPT>

<FORM NAME=form1 onsubmit="return checkForm(document.form1)">
   <INPUT TYPE="text" ID=text1 NAME=text1>
   <BR>
   CheckBox 1<INPUT TYPE="checkbox" ID=checkbox2 NAME=checkbox2>
   <BR>
   CheckBox 1<INPUT TYPE="checkbox" ID=checkbox1 NAME=checkbox1>
   <BR>
   <INPUT TYPE="text" ID=text2 NAME=text2>
   <P>
   <INPUT TYPE="submit" VALUE="Submit" ID=submit1 NAME=submit1>
   </P>
</FORM>

</BODY>
</HTML>
```

Storing Information: Cookies

Our goal as web site programmers should be to make the web site experience as easy and pleasant for the user as possible. Clearly, well-designed pages with easily navigable layout are central to this, but they're not the whole story. We can go one step further by learning about our user and using information gained about them to **personalize** the web site.

For example, when a user returns to our web site, whose name we asked them on their first visit, we could welcome them back to the web site by greeting them by their name. Another good example is given by a web site, such as Amazon's, which incorporates the 1-click purchasing system. By already knowing the user's purchasing details, such as credit card number and delivery address, we can allow the user to go from viewing a book to buying it in just one click, making the likelihood of them purchasing it that much greater. Also, based on information such as the previous purchases and browsing patterns of the user, it's possible to make book suggestions to the user.

Such personalization on web sites requires that information about the user is stored somewhere in between their visits to the web site. We've previously talked about the fact that accessing the user's local file system from a web application is pretty much off limits due to security restrictions included in browsers. However, we, as web site developers, can store small amounts of information in a special place on the user's local disc, using what is called a **cookie**. There may be a logical reason why they are named cookies, but it also provides authors with the opportunity to make a lot of second rate, food related jokes!

Cooking your First Cookie

The key to cookies is the `document` object's `cookie` property. Using this property we can both create and retrieve cookie data from within our JavaScript code.

We can set a cookie by setting `document.cookie` to a **cookie string**. We'll be looking in detail at how this cookie string is made up later in the chapter, but let's first create a simple example of a cookie and see where the information is stored on the user's computer.

A Fresh Baked Cookie

The following code will set a cookie with the information that `UserName` is `Paul`, and with an expiry date of 28 December 2010.

```
<HTML>
<HEAD>
<SCRIPT LANGUAGE=JavaScript>
    document.cookie = "UserName=Paul;expires=Tue, 28 Dec 2010 00:00:00;";
</SCRIPT>
</HEAD>

<BODY>
<P>This page just created a cookie</P>
</BODY>
</HTML>
```

Save the page above as `FreshBakedCookie.htm`. We'll see how the code works as we discuss the parts of a cookie string below, but first let's see what happens when a cookie is created.

How we view cookies without using code varies with the browser you are using. We'll see how this is done, first in IE, and then in NN.

Viewing cookies on IE

In this section we'll see how to look at the cookies that are already stored by IE on our computer. We'll then load in our cookie-creating page created above, to see what effect this has.

First you need to open up IE. I'm using IE 5.5, so if you're using IE 4 you may find the screenshots and menus in slightly different places.

Before we view the cookies, we'll first clear the temporary Internet file folder for the browser, as this will make it easier to view the cookies that our browser has stored. In IE, select Internet Options from the Tools menu, as shown below.

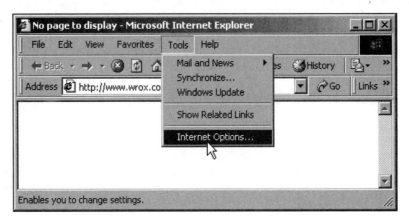

Having selected this option, you'll be presented with the Internet Options dialog box:

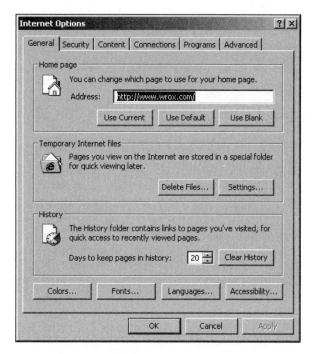

Click the Delete Files button under Temporary Internet files. You'll be asked to confirm your request in another dialog box:

Tick the Delete all offline content checkbox and then click OK. You'll be returned to the Internet Options dialog box.

Let's have a look at the cookies you have currently residing on your machine. From the Internet
Options dialog box, click the Settings button next to the Delete button grouped under Temporary
Internet files. You should see the dialog box below:

Now click the View Files button, and a list of all the temporary pages and cookie files on your computer
will be displayed. If you followed the instructions previously and deleted all temporary Internet files,
then all you should see are the cookie files on your computer, as these are not deleted. The number of
cookie files on your computer will vary, but shown below are those currently on mine:

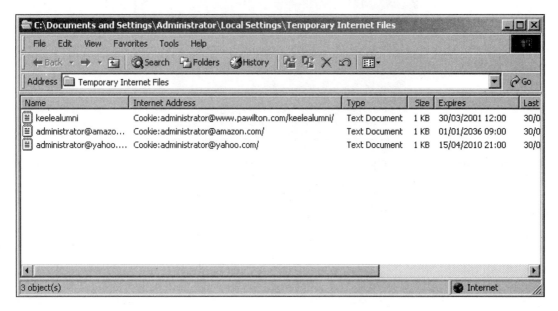

The actual cookies, their names and values, will look slightly different depending on your computer's operating system. In the above screen shot we can see I have three cookie files: one set by the `pawilton.com` website, a second by `amazon.com` and the third by `yahoo.com`.

We can delete each cookie simply by clicking it once, then hitting the *Delete* key, as you would with any file in explorer.

We can examine the contents of the cookies by double clicking them. Note you may get a warning about the potential security risk of opening a text file, though we are fairly safe with cookies as they are simply text files. I've double clicked the cookie file named `keelealumni` set by my web site; we can see its contents below:

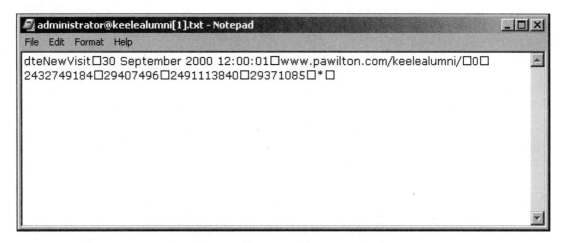

As we can see a cookie is just a plain old text file. Each web site, or **domain name**, has its own text file where all the cookies for that web site are stored. In this case there's just one cookie currently stored for `pawilton.com`, my domain name. Domains like `amazon.com` will almost certainly have many cookies set.

In the screenshot above, we can see that the cookie's details. Here, the name of the cookie is `dteNewVisit`, its value is 30 September 2000 12:00:01, it was set by the domain `pawilton.com`, and it relates only to the directory `/keelealumni`. The contents probably look like a mess of characters, but don't worry – when we see how to program cookies, you'll see that we don't need to worry about setting the details in this format.

Once you have finished, close down the cookie and click OK on the dialog boxes to return to the browser.

Now load the `FreshBakedCookie.htm` page into your IE browser. This will set a cookie – let's see how it has changed things by returning to the Internet Options dialog box (by choosing Internet Options from the Tools menu). Click the Settings button, and then click View Files. On my computer, it now shows the following:

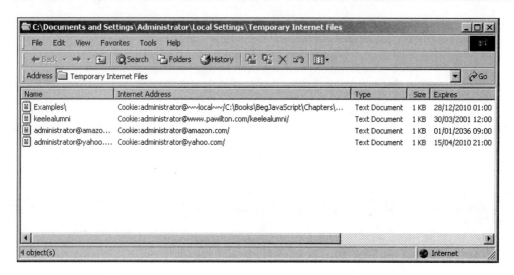

As we are creating a cookie from a web page that is stored on the local hard drive rather than a server, its domain name has been set to `Examples`, the directory my page was stored in. Obviously, this is a little artificial, as in reality people will be loading your web pages from your web site on the Internet and not off your local hard drive. The Internet address is based on the directory the `FreshBakedCookie.htm` file was in. We can also see that it expires on the 28 December 2010 as we specified when we created the cookie. Double click on the cookie to view its contents:

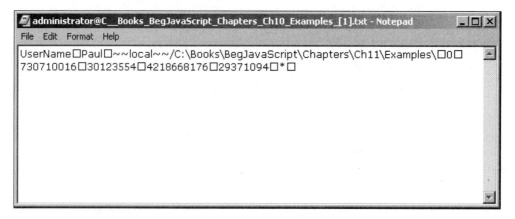

We can see the name we gave to the cookie at the left, `UserName`, then its value, `Paul`, and also the directory it's applicable to. The expiry date is there as well – it's just not in an easily recognizable form.

Viewing cookies on NN

There is no sharing of cookies between browsers, so the cookies stored when you visited web sites using an IE browser won't be available to NN and vice versa.

NN keeps its cookies in a totally different place from IE, and the contents are viewed by a different means. In fact the means of viewing the cookies differs between versions of the browser.

416

Netscape Navigator 4.x

All of the NN 4.x browser cookies are kept in one text file called cookies.txt, which is contained under the directory that you installed Netscape to. However, its exact location will vary, so the easiest way to find this file is to use the operating system to do a search for a file called cookies.txt.

For example, on my computer the file was found in

    C:\Program Files\Netscape\Users\Default

but it'll most likely be different on your computer.

Once you've found the file, open it with a text editor. On my computer it contained the following cookies:

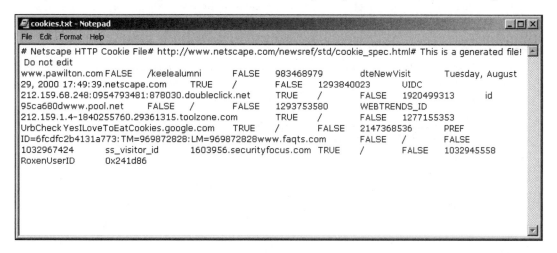

As you can see from the screenshot above, although this was taken from a NN browser on the same machine as IE whose cookies we saw earlier, the cookies have nothing in common. There are no amazon.com or yahoo.com cookies. There is my web site's cookie, from pawilton.com, since I visited it with this browser.

Again you can see the cookie details. This time the first detail is the domain the cookie belongs to, secondly the directory on that domain, then moving along three pieces of data we come to the cookie's name, for example dteNewVisit, and then its value, for example Tuesday, August 29, 2000 17:49:39.

When we know what we are looking for, we can make out individual cookies, their values and so on from this file. However, when viewing the cookies using code, it's much easier.

If we want to delete one or more of the cookies, then we simply need to close the Netscape browser and then delete the cookie's text in the text file, before saving it. Be careful to only delete the cookie text, and not the top line warning you that it is a generated file.

Let's load our FreshBakedCookie.htm page into the NN browser, and see the effects on cookie.txt.

417

If you then re-open the `cookie.txt` file, you should see somewhere within it the following line:

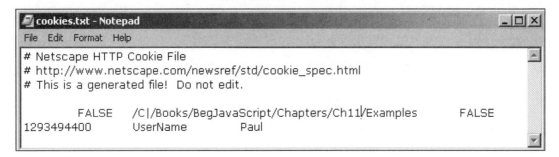

```
# Netscape HTTP Cookie File
# http://www.netscape.com/newsref/std/cookie_spec.html
# This is a generated file!  Do not edit.

        FALSE    /C|/Books/BegJavaScript/Chapters/Ch11/Examples        FALSE
1293494400        UserName        Paul
```

We can see that our code has succeeded and the cookie is in there with the name, UserName, and value, Paul. The expiry date is also contained within the `cookie.txt` file, but not in an obvious form.

Netscape Navigator 6

On Netscape Navigator 6, it is a bit easier to manage the viewing and deletion of cookies. From the **Tasks** menu, choose the **Privacy and Security** option. Click **Cookie Manager**, and then **View Stored Cookies**. This will open the **Cookie Manager**, shown below.

Note that I have no cookies set for NN 6, and so the **Stored Cookies** box is empty.

Click **OK** to get back to the browser, and load `FreshBakedCookie.htm`. Repeat the process above to get to the **Cookie Manager**, and you should find that the UserName cookie has been added to the box. Click on the cookie, and its details are displayed in the spaces below;

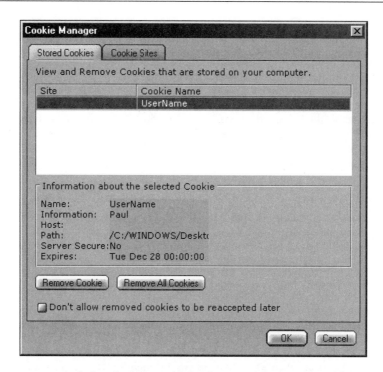

Note that buttons are provided at the bottom of the Cookie Manager to delete the cookie selected or all of the cookies that are stored.

Now we've seen how to view cookies manually, let's look at how we create them and read them using code. We'll start by looking at each of the parts making up a cookie string.

The Cookie String

When creating a cookie there are six parts we can set, namely name, value, expires, path, domain, and security, although the latter four of these are optional. We'll now look at each of these in turn.

name and value

The first part of the cookie string consists of the name and value for the cookie. The name is used so that we can reference the cookie at a later date, and the value is the 'information' part of the cookie.

This name/value part of the cookie string is compulsory – it sort of defeats the point of the cookie if you don't store a name or value, as storing information is what cookies are all about. You should make sure that this part comes first in the cookie string.

The value for the cookie is a primitive string, although of course the string can hold number characters if it is numerical data that you want to store. If we are storing text, then certain characters, such as semi-colons, cannot be used inside the value, unless we use a special encoding which we'll see later. In the case of semicolons, this is because they are used to separate the different parts of the cookie within the cookie string.

In the following line of code we set a cookie with the name `UserName` and the value `Paul`.

```
document.cookie = "UserName=Paul;";
```

This cookie has a very limited **lifespan**. By lifespan, I mean how long the information will continue to exist. If we don't set an expiry date, than a cookie will expire when the user closes their browser. The next time the user opens the browser the cookie will be gone. This is fine if we just want to store information for the life of a user **session**, where a user session is a single visit by the user to our web site. However, if we want to ensure that our cookie is available for longer, then we must set its expiry date, which we'll look at next.

expires

If we want a cookie to exist for longer than just a single user session, we need to set an expiry date using the second part of the cookie string: `expires`. For example:

```
document.cookie = "UserName=Paul;expires=Tue, 28 Dec 2010 00:00:00;";
```

The cookie set by the above line of code will remain available for future use right up until 28 December 2010. Note that the format of the expires date is very important – especially for IE browsers. It should be the same format as is given by the `toGMTString()` method. This method is similar to the `toUTCString()` method that we saw in Chapter 9.

In practice, we'll probably use the `Date` object to get the current date, then set a cookie to expire three or six months ahead of this date. Otherwise, we're going to need to re-write our pages on 28 December 2010. For example, we could write:

```
var expireDate = new Date();
expireDate.setMonth(expireDate.getMonth() + 6);
document.cookie = "UserName=Paul;expires=" + expireDate.toGMTString() + ";";
```

This will create a new cookie called `UserName` with the value of `Paul` and which will expire 6 months from the current date.

path

You'll find that 99% of the time, you will only need to set the `name`, `value` and `expires` parts of a cookie. However, there are times when the other three parts, such as the `path` part that we are looking at here, need to be set. The final two parts, `domain` and `secure` are for more advanced use beyond the scope of a beginners' book, but we'll look at them briefly just for completeness.

You're probably used to the idea of there being directories on your hard drive. Rather than storing everything on your computer in one place on the hard drive, you instead divide it up into these directories. For example, you might keep your word processing files in `My Documents`, your image files in `My Images` and so on. You probably also sub-divide your directories, so under `My Images` you might have sub-directories called `My Family` and `My Holiday`.

Well, web servers use the same principle. Rather than the whole web site being in one web directory, it's common and indeed sensible to divide a web site into various different directories. For example, if you visit the Wrox website at www.wrox.com, then click on one of the book categories, you'll find that the path to the page navigated to is now www.wrox.com/Books/.

This is all very interesting, but why is this relevant to cookies?

The problem is that cookies are specific not only to a particular web domain, such as www.wrox.com, but also to a particular path on that domain. For example, if a page in www.wrox.com/Books/ sets a cookie, then only pages in that directory or its sub-directories will be able to read and change the cookie. If a page in www.wrox.com/academic/ tried to read the cookie, then it would fail. Why are cookies restricted like this?

Take the common example of free web space. There are a lot of companies on the web that allow you to sign up for free web space. Usually everyone who signs up for this web space has a web site at the same domain. For example, Bob's web site might be at www.freespace.com/members/bob/. Belinda might have her web site at www.freespace.com/members/belinda. If cookies could be retrieved and changed regardless of the path, then any cookies set on Bob's web site could be viewed by Belinda and vice versa. This is clearly something neither of them would be happy about. Not only is there a security problem, but if, unknown to each other, they both have a cookie named MyHotCookie, then there would be problems with each of them setting and retrieving the same cookie. When you think how many users a free web space provider often has, you can see that there is potential for chaos.

OK, so now we know that cookies are particular to a certain path, but what if we want to view our cookies from two different paths on our server? Say for example we have an online store at www.mywebsite.com/mystore/ but we sub divide the store into sub-directories such as /Books and /Games. Now let's imagine that our checkout is in the directory www.mywebsite.com/mystore/Checkout. Any cookies set in the /Books and /Games directories won't be visible to each other or pages in the /Checkout directory. To get round this we can either only set cookies in the /mystore directory, since these can be read by that directory and any of its sub-directories, or we can use the path part of the cookie string to specify that the path of the cookie is /mystore even if it's being set in the /Games or /Books or /Checkout sub-directories.

For example, we could do this like so:

```
document.cookie = "UserName=Paul;expires=Tue, 28 Dec 2010 00:00:00" +
";path=/mystore;";
```

Now, even if the cookie is set by a page in the directory /Books, it will still be accessible to files in the /mystore directory and its sub-directories such as /Checkout and /Games.

If we want to specify that the cookie is available to all sub-directories of the domain it is set in, then we can specify a path of the root directory using the / character.

```
document.cookie = "UserName=Paul;expires=Tue, 28 Dec 2010 00:00:00;path=/;";
```

Now, the cookie will be available to all directories on the domain it is set from. If the web site is just one of many at that domain, it's best not to do this as everyone else will also have access to your cookie information.

It's important to note that while Windows computers don't have case sensitive directory names, many other operating systems do. For example, if your web site is on a Unix or Linux based server then the path property will be case sensitive, a mistake it's easy to fall for.

domain

The fourth part of the cookie string is the domain. An example of a domain is wrox.com or pawilton.com. Like the path part of the cookie string, the domain part is optional and it's unlikely that you'll find yourself using it very often.

By default, cookies are only available to pages in the domain they were set in. For example, if we have our first web site running on a server with the domain MyPersonalWebSite.MyDomain.Com and we have a second web site running under MyBusinessWebSite.MyDomain.Com, then a cookie set in one web site will not be available to pages accessed using the other domain name, and vice versa. Most of the time this is exactly what we want, but when this is not the case we can use the domain part of the cookie string to specify that a cookie is available to all sub-domains of the specified domain. For example:

```
document.cookie = "UserName=Paul;expires=Tue, 28 Dec 2010 00:00:00;path=/" +
";domain=MyDomain.Com;";
```

sets a cookie that can be shared across both sub-domains. Note that the domain must be the same: you can't share www.SomeoneElsesDomain.com with www.MyDomain.com.

secure

The final part of the cookie string is the secure part. This is simply a Boolean value; if it's set to true then the cookie will only be sent to a web sever that tries to retrieve it using a secure channel. The default value, which is false, means the cookie will always be sent, regardless of the security. This is only applicable where we have set up a server with SSL (Secure Sockets Layer).

Creating a cookie

To make life easier for ourselves, we'll write a function that allows us to create a new cookie and set certain of its attributes with more ease.

```
function setCookie(cookieName, cookieValue, cookiePath, cookieExpires)
{
    cookieValue = escape(cookieValue);

    if (cookieExpires == "")
    {
        var nowDate = new Date();
        nowDate.setMonth(nowDate.getMonth() + 6);
        cookieExpires = nowDate.toGMTString();
    }

    if (cookiePath != "")
    {
        cookiePath = ";Path=" + cookiePath;
    }

    document.cookie = cookieName + "=" + cookieValue +
        ";expires=" + cookieExpires + cookiePath;
}
```

The secure and domain parts of the cookie string are unlikely to be needed, so we just allow the name, value, expires, and path parts of a cookie to be set by the function. If we don't want to set a path or expiry date, then we just pass empty strings for those parameters. If no path is specified, then the current directory and its sub-directories will be the path. If no expiry date is set, then we just assume a date six months from now.

The first line of the function:

```
cookieValue = escape(cookieValue);
```

introduces the escape() function, which we've not seen before. When we talked about setting the value of a cookie, we mentioned that certain characters cannot be used directly, such as a semicolon. (This also applies to the name of the cookie.) To get around this problem, JavaScript has the built in escape() and unescape() functions. The escape() function converts characters that are not text or numbers into the hexadecimal equivalent of their character in the Latin-1 character set, preceded by a % character. This character set can be found in Appendix D.

For example, a space has the hexadecimal value of 20, and the semi-colon has the value of 3B. So:

```
alert(escape("2001 a space odyssey;"));
```

gives:

We can see that the spaces have been converted to %20, % indicating that it's an "escape" or special character rather than an actual character, and 20 being the ASCII value of the actual character. The semicolon has been converted to %3B, as we'd expect.

As we'll see later, when retrieving cookie values we can use the unescape() function to convert from the encoded version back to plain text.

Back to our function; we next have an if statement:

```
if (cookieExpires == "")
{
    var nowDate = new Date();
    nowDate.setMonth(nowDate.getMonth() + 6);
    cookieExpires = nowDate.toGMTString();
}
```

This deals with the situation where an empty string, "", has been passed for the cookieExpires parameter of the function. As most of the time we want a cookie to last longer than the session it's created in, we set a default value for expires which is six months after the current date.

Next, if a value other than an empty string "" has been passed to the function for the `cookiePath` parameter, then we need to add that value when we create the cookie. We simply put `"path="` in front of whatever value has been passed in the `cookiePath` parameter.

```
if (cookiePath != "")
{
    cookiePath = ";Path=" + cookiePath;
}
```

Finally on the last line we actually create the cookie, putting together the `cookieName`, `cookieValue`, `cookieExpires`, and `cookiePath` parts of the string.

```
document.cookie = cookieName + "=" + cookieValue +
    ";expires=" + cookieExpires + cookiePath;
```

We'll be using the `setCookie()` function again and again whenever we want to create a new cookie as it makes setting a cookie slightly easier than having to remember all the parts we want to set. More importantly, it can be used to set the expiry date to a date six months ahead of now.

For example, to use the function and set a cookie with default values for `expires` and `path` we just type:

```
setCookie("cookieName","cookieValue","","")
```

Try It Out – Using setCookie()

We'll now put this together in a simple example in which we use our `setCookie()` function to set three cookies named `Name`, `Age`, and `FirstVisit`. We then display what is in the `document.cookie` property to see how this has been affected.

```
<HTML>
<HEAD>
<SCRIPT LANGUAGE=JavaScript>

function setCookie(cookieName, cookieValue, cookiePath, cookieExpires)
{
    cookieValue = escape(cookieValue);

    if (cookieExpires == "")
    {
        var nowDate = new Date();
        nowDate.setMonth(nowDate.getMonth() + 6);
        cookieExpires = nowDate.toGMTString();
    }

    if (cookiePath != "")
    {
        cookiePath = ";Path=" + cookiePath;
    }
```

```
        document.cookie = cookieName + "=" + cookieValue +
            ";expires=" + cookieExpires + cookiePath;
    }

    setCookie("Name","Bob","","");
    setCookie("Age","101","","");
    setCookie("FirstVisit","10 May 2000","","");

    alert(document.cookie);

    </SCRIPT>

    </HEAD>
    <BODY>

    </BODY>
    </HTML>
```

Save the example as `CreateCookie.htm`, and then load it into your web browser.

We'll see the following alert box. Note that all three cookies are displayed as name/value pairs separated by semicolons, and also that the expiry date is not displayed. If we had set the path parameter, then this also would not have been displayed.

How It Works

We've already seen how the `setCookie()` function works, so let's look at the three lines that use the function to create three new cookies:

```
    setCookie("Name","Bob","","");
    setCookie("Age","101","","");
    setCookie("FirstVisit","10 May 2000","","");
```

It is all fairly simple. The first parameter is the name that we'll give the cookie. We see shortly how we can retrieve a value of a cookie based on the name we gave it. It's important that the names we use are only alphanumeric characters, with no spaces, punctuation, or special characters. While we can use cookie names with these characters, it's more complex to do so and best avoided. Next we have the value we want to give the cookie. The third parameter is the path, and the fourth the date we want the cookie to expire on.

For example, take the first line where we use the `setCookie()` function above. Here we are setting a cookie which will be named `Name` and have the value `Bob`. We don't want to set the path or expires parts, so we just pass an empty string, that is `""`. Note that we must pass `""` – we can't pass nothing at all.

The remaining two lines above set the cookies named `Age` and `FirstVisit` and set their values to `101` and `10 May 2000`.

If we did want to set the path and the expiry date, how might we change our code?

Well, imagine that we want the path to be `/MyStore` and the expiry date to be 1 year in the future. Then we may use the `setCookie()` function in the following way:

```
var expireDate = new Date();
expireDate.setMonth(expireDate.getMonth() + 12);
setCookie("Name","Bob","/MyStore",expireDate.toGMTString());
```

First we create a new `Date` object and, by passing no parameter to its constructor, we let it initialize itself to today's date. In the next line, we add 12 months on to that date. When setting the cookie using `setCookie()` we pass `"/MyStore"` as the path and `expireDate.toGMTString()` as the expires parameter.

What about the situation where you've created your cookie, say named `Name` with value of `Bob`, and you want to change its value? To do this you can simply set the same cookie again, but with the new value. To change the cookie named `Name` from a value of `Bob` to `Bobby` you'd need the code:

```
setCookie("Name","Bobby","","");
```

What if we want to delete an existing cookie? Well that's easy. Just make it expire by changing its value and setting its expiry date to a date in the past, for example:

```
setCookie("Name","","","Mon, 1 Jan 1990 00:00:00");
```

Getting a Cookie's Value

In the example above, we used `document.cookie` to retrieve a string containing information about the cookies that have been set. However, this string has two limitations.

Firstly, the cookies are retrieved in name/value pairs, with each individual cookie separated by a semi-colon. The expires, path, domain, and secure parts of the cookie are not available to us and cannot be retrieved.

Secondly, the `cookie` property only allows you to retrieve *all* the cookies set for a particular path and, when hosted on a web server, that web server. So, for example, there's no simple way of just getting the value of a `cookie` with the name `Age`. To do this we'll have to use the string manipulation techniques we've learned in previous chapters to cut the information we want out of the returned string.

There are a lot of different ways of getting the value of an individual cookie, but the way we'll use has the advantage of working with all cookie-enabled browsers. We use the following function:

```
function getCookieValue(cookieName)
{
    var cookieValue = document.cookie;
    var cookieStartsAt = cookieValue.indexOf(" " + cookieName + "=");
```

```
    if (cookieStartsAt == -1)
    {
        cookieStartsAt = cookieValue.indexOf(cookieName + "=");
    }

    if (cookieStartsAt == -1)
    {
        cookieValue = null;
    }
    else
    {
        cookieStartsAt = cookieValue.indexOf("=", cookieStartsAt) + 1;
        var cookieEndsAt = cookieValue.indexOf(";", cookieStartsAt);
        if (cookieEndsAt == -1)
        {
            cookieEndsAt = cookieValue.length;
        }
        cookieValue = unescape(cookieValue.substring(cookieStartsAt,
            cookieEndsAt));
    }

    return cookieValue;
}
```

The first task of the function is to get the `document.cookie` string and store it in the variable `cookieValue`.

```
var cookieValue = document.cookie;
```

Next we need to find out where the cookie with the name passed as a parameter to the function is within the `cookieValue` string. We use the `indexOf()` method of the `String` object to find out this information. The method will either return the character position where the individual cookie is found or -1 if no such name, and therefore no such cookie, exists. We search on " " + `cookieName` + "=" so that we don't inadvertently find cookie names or values containing the name that we require. For example, if we have `xFoo`, `Foo`, and `yFoo` as cookie names, a search for `Foo` without a space in front would match the `xFoo` first – not what we want!

```
var cookieStartsAt = cookieValue.indexOf(" " + cookieName + "=");
```

If `cookieStartsAt` is -1, then this means that either the cookie does not exist or it's at the very beginning of the cookie string so there is no space in front of the cookie name. To see which of these is true, we do another search, this time with no space.

```
if (cookieStartsAt == -1)
{
    cookieStartsAt = cookieValue.indexOf(cookieName + "=");
}
```

In the next if statement we check to see if the cookie has been found. If it hasn't, then we set the cookieValue variable to null.

```
if (cookieStartsAt == -1)
{
    cookieValue = null;
}
```

If the cookie has been found, we get the value of the cookie we want from the document.cookie string in an else statement. We do this by finding the start and the end of the value part of that cookie. The start will be immediately after the equals sign following the name. So in the line:

```
else
{
    cookieStartsAt = cookieValue.indexOf("=", cookieStartsAt) + 1;
```

we find the equals sign following the name of the cookie in the string by starting the indexOf() search for an equals sign from the character the cookie name/value pair starts at. We then add one to this value to move past the equals sign.

The end of the cookie value will either be at the next semicolon, or at the end of the string, whichever comes first. We do a search for a semicolon, starting from the cookieStartsAt index in the next line:

```
var cookieEndsAt = cookieValue.indexOf(";", cookieStartsAt);
```

If the cookie we are after is the last one in the string, then there will be no semicolon and the cookieEndsAt variable will be –1 for no match. In this case we know the end of the cookie value must be the end of the string, so we set the variable cookieEndsAt to the length of the string.

```
if (cookieEndsAt == -1)
{
    cookieEndsAt = cookieValue.length;
}
```

We then get the cookie's value using the substring() method to cut the value that we want out of the main string. As we have encoded the string with the escape() function, we need to unescape it to get the real value, hence the use of the unescape() function.

```
    cookieValue = unescape(cookieValue.substring(cookieStartsAt,
      cookieEndsAt));
}
```

Finally we return the value of the cookie to the calling function.

```
    return cookieValue;
```

Try It Out – What's New?

Now we know how to create and retrieve cookies, let's use this knowledge in an example where we check to see if any changes have been made to a web site since the user last visited it.

We'll be creating two pages for this example. The first is the main page for a web site, the second is the page with details of new additions and changes to the web site. A link to the second page will only appear on the first page if the user has visited the page before (that is, a cookie exists) but has not visited since the page was last updated.

Let's create the first page:

```
<HTML>
<HEAD>
<SCRIPT LANGUAGE=JavaScript>

var lastUpdated = new Date("Tue, 28 Dec 2010");

function getCookieValue(cookieName)
{
    var cookieValue = document.cookie;
    var cookieStartsAt = cookieValue.indexOf(" " + cookieName + "=");

    if (cookieStartsAt == -1)
    {
        cookieStartsAt = cookieValue.indexOf(cookieName + "=");
    }

    if (cookieStartsAt == -1)
    {
        cookieValue = null;
    }
    else
    {
        cookieStartsAt = cookieValue.indexOf("=", cookieStartsAt) + 1;
        var cookieEndsAt = cookieValue.indexOf(";", cookieStartsAt);
        if (cookieEndsAt == -1)
        {
            cookieEndsAt = cookieValue.length;
        }
        cookieValue = unescape(cookieValue.substring(cookieStartsAt,
            cookieEndsAt));
    }

    return cookieValue;
}

function setCookie(cookieName, cookieValue, cookiePath, cookieExpires)
{
    cookieValue = escape(cookieValue);
```

```
    if (cookieExpires == "")
    {
        var nowDate = new Date();
        nowDate.setMonth(nowDate.getMonth() + 6);
        cookieExpires = nowDate.toGMTString();
    }

    if (cookiePath != "")
    {
        cookiePath = ";Path=" + cookiePath;
    }

    document.cookie = cookieName + "=" + cookieValue +
        ";expires=" + cookieExpires + cookiePath;
}

</SCRIPT>
</HEAD>

<BODY>
<H2 ALIGN=center>Welcome to my website</H2>
<BR><BR>
<CENTER>
<SCRIPT>

var lastVisit = getCookieValue("LastVisit");
if (lastVisit != null)
{
    lastVisit = new Date(lastVisit);
    if (lastVisit < lastUpdated)
    {
        document.write("<A HREF=\"WhatsNew.htm\">");
        document.write("<IMG SRC=\"WhatsNew.gif\" BORDER=0></A>");
    }
}

var nowDate = new Date();
setCookie("LastVisit", nowDate.toGMTString(),"","")

</SCRIPT>
</CENTER>
</BODY>
</HTML>
```

This page needs to be saved as `MainPage.htm`. Note that it contains our two functions `setCookie()` and `getCookieValue()` that we created earlier. Also note that an image `WhatsNew.gif` is referenced by this page; either create such an image, or retrieve the image from the code download.

Next, we'll just create a simple page to link to for the 'What's New' details.

```
<HTML>
<BODY>
<H2 ALIGN=center>Here's what's new on this website</H2>
</BODY>
</HTML>
```

Save this page as `WhatsNew.htm`.

Load `MainPage.htm` into your browser. The first time we go to the main page, there will be just a heading saying "Welcome to my website". Obviously if this was a real web site, it would have a bit more than that, but it suffices for our example. However, refresh the page and suddenly we'll see:

If we click on the image, we're taken to the `WhatsNew.htm` page detailing all the things added to the web site since we last visited. Obviously nothing has actually changed in our example web site between us loading in the page and then refreshing it. We have got around this for testing purposes by setting the date when the web site last changed, stored in variable `lastUpdated`, to a date in the future (here, 28 Dec 2010).

How It Works

The `WhatsNew.htm` page is just a simple HTML page with no script, so we will confine our attention to `MainPage.htm`. In the head of the page in the first script block we declare the variable `lastUpdated`:

```
var lastUpdated = new Date("Tue, 28 Dec 2010");
```

Whenever we make a change to the web site this variable needs to be changed. It's currently set to `Tue, 28 Dec 2010` just to make sure we see a "What's New" image when we refresh the page. A better alternative for live pages would be the `document.lastModified` property, which returns the date the page was last changed.

The rest of the first script block contains the two functions `getCookieValue()` and `setCookie()` that we looked at earlier. These haven't changed, so we won't discuss them in detail here.

The interesting material is in the second script block that is found within the body of the page. First we get the date of the user's last visit stored in the `LastVisit` cookie using the `getCookieValue()` function:

```
var lastVisit = getCookieValue("LastVisit");
```

If it's `null` then either the user has never been here before, or it's six or more months since they last came here and the cookie has expired. Either way, we'll not put a "What's New" image up as either everything is new if they're a first time visitor, or a lot has probably changed in the last six months – more than what our "what's new" page will detail.

If `lastVisit` is not null, we need to check whether the user last visited the site before the site was last updated, and if so direct them to a page that shows them what is new. We do this within the `if` statement.

```
if (lastVisit != null)
{
    lastVisit = new Date(lastVisit);
    if (lastVisit < lastUpdated)
    {
        document.write("<A HREF=\"WhatsNew.htm\">");
        document.write("<IMG SRC=\"WhatsNew.gif\" BORDER=0></A>");
    }
}
```

We first create a new `Date` object based on the value of `lastVisit` and store that back into the `lastVisit` variable. Then, in the condition of the inner `if` statement, we compare the date of the user's last visit with the date we last updated the web site. If things have changed since the user's last visit, then we write the "What's New" image to the page, so the user can click it and found out what's new. Note that we have used the escape character `\"` for the `"` inside the strings that are written to the page, since otherwise JavaScript will think they indicate the end of the string.

Finally, at the end of the script block, we re-set the `LastVisit` cookie to today's date and time using the `setCookie()` function.

```
var nowDate = new Date();
setCookie("LastVisit", nowDate.toGMTString(),"","")
```

Cookie Limitations

There are a number of limitations that it's important to be aware of when using cookies.

The first is that while all modern browsers support cookies, the user may have disabled them. In NN you can do this from the Preferences option on the Edit menu. The option to disable cookies is under Advanced on NN 4.x, and under the Cookies option under Advanced on NN 6. In IE it's under Internet Options on the Tools menu. Select the Security tab and finally click the Custom Level button. From there, a list of security options appears, some of which relate to the setting of cookies.

Both the functions that we've created for creating and getting cookies will cause no errors when cookies are disabled, but of course the value of any cookie set will be null and we need to make sure our code can cope with this.

We could set a default action for when cookies are disabled. For example, in the example above, if cookies are disabled a 'What's New' image will never appear.

Alternatively, we can let the user know that our web site needs cookies to function, by putting a message in the web page warning users.

Another way is to actively check to see if cookies are enabled and if not then to take some action to cope with this, such as directing them to a page with less functionality that does not need cookies. How do we check to see if cookies are enabled?

In the script below we set a test cookie, and then read back its value. If it's `null`, we know cookies are disabled.

```
setCookie("TestCookie","Yes","","");

if (getCookieValue("TestCookie") == null)
    {
        alert("This website requires cookies to function");
    }
```

A second limitation is on the number of cookies we can set on the user's computer for our web site and how much information can be stored. For each domain and path we can store up to 20 cookies, and each cookie pair, that is the name and value combined, must be not more than 4096 characters in size.

To get around the 20-cookie limit, we can store more than one piece of information per cookie. For example, instead of:

```
setCookie("Name","Karen","","")
setCookie("Age","44","","")
setCookie("LastVisit","10 Jan 2001","","")
```

we could combine this information into one cookie, with each detail separated by a semicolon:

```
setCookie("UserDetails","Karen;44;10 Jan 2001","","")
```

Since the `setCookie()` function escapes the value of the cookie, there is no confusion between the semicolons separating pieces of data in the value of the cookie, and semicolons separating the parts of the cookie. When we get the cookie value back using `getCookieValue()`, we just split it into its constituent parts – just as long as we remember the order we stored it in!

```
var cookieValues = getCookieValue("UserDetails");
cookieValues = cookieValues.split(";")
alert("Name = " + cookieValues[0]);
alert("Age = " + cookieValues[1]);
alert("Last Visit = " + cookieValues[2]);
```

Now we have aquired three pieces of information and still have 19 cookies left in the jar.

Trivia Quiz – Storing Previous Quiz Results

Let's return to the trivia quiz and, using our knowledge of cookies, add the functionality to keep track of previous quiz results. We're going to calculate the user's average score for all the quizzes they have completed. We'll also allow the user to reset the statistics.

We only need to alter one page of the trivia quiz, the GlobalFunctions.htm page. First we need to add the two cookie functions, getCookieValue() and setCookie(), that we introduced earlier in the chapter. These can be added anywhere within the script block – I've added them after all the other functions.

```
function getCookieValue(cookieName)
{
    var cookieValue = document.cookie;
    var cookieStartsAt = cookieValue.indexOf(" " + cookieName + "=");

    if (cookieStartsAt == -1)
    {
        cookieStartsAt = cookieValue.indexOf(cookieName + "=");
    }

    if (cookieStartsAt == -1)
    {
        cookieValue = null;
    }
    else
    {
        cookieStartsAt = cookieValue.indexOf("=", cookieStartsAt) + 1;
        var cookieEndsAt = cookieValue.indexOf(";", cookieStartsAt);
        if (cookieEndsAt == -1)
        {
            cookieEndsAt = cookieValue.length;
        }
        cookieValue = unescape(cookieValue.substring(cookieStartsAt,
            cookieEndsAt));
    }

    return cookieValue;
}

function setCookie(cookieName, cookieValue, cookiePath, cookieExpires)
{
    cookieValue = escape(cookieValue);

    if (cookieExpires == "")
    {
        var nowDate = new Date();
        nowDate.setMonth(nowDate.getMonth() + 6);
        cookieExpires = nowDate.toGMTString();
    }
```

```
    if (cookiePath != "")
    {
       cookiePath = ";Path=" + cookiePath;
    }

    document.cookie = cookieName + "=" + cookieValue +
       ";expires=" + cookieExpires + cookiePath;
}
```

The final change we need is to the getQuestion() function. It's here in this function that either a new question is written to the page or, if all the questions have been asked, that the final results are displayed. Currently we just write out the number of questions that the user got right and rate the result. Now we're going to keep a running average of previous results and display this information as well. The addition is towards the end of the function, after the script that writes a rating to the page.

```
       default:
          questionHTML = questionHTML + "Excellent"
    }
```

```
    var previousNoCorrect = Math.floor(getCookieValue("previousNoCorrect"));
    var previousNoAsked = Math.floor(getCookieValue("previousNoAsked"));
    var currentAvgScore = Math.round(numberOfQuestionsCorrect /
       numberOfQuestionsAsked * 100);

    questionHTML = questionHTML + "<BR>The percentage you've " +
       " answered correctly in this quiz is " + currentAvgScore + "%";

    if (previousNoAsked == 0)
    {
       previousNoCorrect = 0;
    }

    previousNoCorrect = previousNoCorrect + numberOfQuestionsCorrect;
    previousNoAsked = previousNoAsked + numberOfQuestionsAsked;

    currentAvgScore = Math.round(previousNoCorrect / previousNoAsked * 100);

    setCookie("previousNoAsked", previousNoAsked,"","");
    setCookie("previousNoCorrect", previousNoCorrect,"","");

    questionHTML = questionHTML + "<BR>This brings your average todate to " +
       currentAvgScore + "%"
    questionHTML = questionHTML + "<P><INPUT TYPE=button " +
       "VALUE='Reset Stats' " +
       "onclick=\"window.top.fraTopFrame.fraGlobalFunctions.setCookie" +
       "('previousNoAsked', 0,'','1 Jan 1970')\" " +
       "NAME=buttonReset>"
    questionHTML = questionHTML + "<P><INPUT TYPE=button " +
       "VALUE='Restart Quiz' " +
       "onclick=\"window.location.replace('quizpage.htm')\" " +
       "NAME=buttonRestart>"

 }

 return questionHTML;
}
```

So how does this new code work?

First we use cookies to retrieve the number of questions previously answered correctly and the number of questions previously asked in total:

```
var previousNoCorrect = Math.floor(getCookieValue("previousNoCorrect"));
var previousNoAsked = Math.floor(getCookieValue("previousNoAsked"));
```

We then work out the average of the current score, which is simply the number of questions the user got correct in this quiz divided by they number they answered and multiplied by 100:

```
var currentAvgScore = Math.round(numberOfQuestionsCorrect /
    numberOfQuestionsAsked * 100);
```

We then add the average result to questionHTML, the string of HTML we'll be writing to the page:

```
questionHTML = questionHTML + "<BR>The percentage you've " +
    " answered correctly in this quiz is " + currentAvgScore + "%";
```

Next we check to see if the number of questions asked previously was zero. If it is then either the user has reset the stats, or this is the first time they have played the quiz. We reset the number correct to zero, as it would hardly make sense that out of no questions answered they got 10 right!

```
if (previousNoAsked == 0)
{
    previousNoCorrect = 0;
}
```

Then we update the number of previously correctly answered questions and total number of previously answered questions, before using this information to calculate the running average of all the quizzes the user has answered since they first played our quiz or reset the stats:

```
previousNoCorrect = previousNoCorrect + numberOfQuestionsCorrect;
previousNoAsked = previousNoAsked + numberOfQuestionsAsked;

currentAvgScore = Math.round(previousNoCorrect / previousNoAsked * 100);
```

We update our cookies with the new values in the next lines, using the setCookie() function we created earlier:

```
setCookie("previousNoAsked", previousNoAsked,"","");
setCookie("previousNoCorrect", previousNoCorrect,"","");
```

In the final new lines we complete the construction of the results string, adding the running average, then creating two buttons. The first button will reset the number of questions asked by setting the previousNoAsked variable to zero, and the second is a replacement for the link that restarts the quiz.

```
       questionHTML = questionHTML + "<BR>This brings your average todate to " +
          currentAvgScore + "%"
       questionHTML = questionHTML + "<P><INPUT TYPE=button " +
          "VALUE='Reset Stats' " +
          "onclick=\"window.top.fraTopFrame.fraGlobalFunctions.setCookie" +
          "('previousNoAsked', 0,'','1 Jan 1970')\" " +
          "NAME=buttonReset>"
       questionHTML = questionHTML + "<P><INPUT TYPE=button " +
          "VALUE='Restart Quiz' " +
          "onclick=\"window.location.replace('quizpage.htm')\" " +
          "NAME=buttonRestart>"
```

On the button creation lines we need to include single quotes inside double quotes inside more double quotes. This will confuse JavaScript, as it'll think the string has ending before it actually has. It's for this reason that we use the special escape character \ ", which indicates that the double quotes are not delimiting a string, but part of the string itself.

Save the page and load `TriviaQuiz.htm`.

Now when you complete the quiz, you'll see a summary something like that shown below:

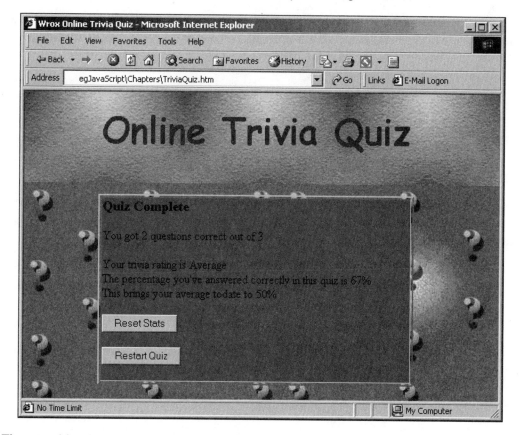

That completes the changes to the trivia quiz for this chapter.

437

Summary

In this chapter we looked at how we can store information on the user's computer and use this to personalize the web site for them. In particular we found that:

❑   The key to cookies is the document object's cookie property.

❑   Creating a cookie simply involves setting the document.cookie property. Cookies have 6 different parts we can set. These are the name, value, when it expires, the path it is available on, the domain it's available on, and finally whether it should only be sent over secure connections.

❑   Although setting a new cookie is fairly easy we found that retrieving its value actually gets all the cookies for that domain and path and we need to split up the cookie name/value pairs to get a specific cookie using String object methods.

❑   There are a number of limitations to cookies. Firstly, the user can set their browser to disable cookies, and secondly we are limited to 20 cookies per domain/path and a maximum of 4096 characters per cookie name/value.

❑   Finally we added the display of a running average for the trivia quiz.

In the next chapter we'll be turning our attention to Dynamic HTML, which allows us to change the contents of a page after it has loaded. We'll be looking at how we can create drop down menus in a web page for both Netscape Navigator 4.x and Internet Explorer 4.0+ browsers.

Exercise Questions

Suggested solutions to these questions can be found in Appendix A.

Question 1

Create a page that keeps track of how many times the page has been visited by the user in the last month.

Question 2

Use cookies to load a different advert every time a user visits a web page.

Dynamic HTML

The term **Dynamic HTML** (DHTML) has rather a loose meaning, but essentially its purpose is to allow the elements and contents of a web page to be dynamically changed after the page has been loaded into the browser. For example, it can be used to change the size of text as the mouse pointer rolls over it. However, in addition, it also aims to enhance user interaction by making many more HTML elements respond to the user doing something.

In plain HTML, we can define what a page will contain and the appearance of its contents. However, once the page is built and downloaded into the user's browser, that's it: no changes can be made to the content within the page or the page's appearance. However, using DHTML we can change the appearance of existing content, add new content,and even remove content. You want some text added inside a table? You got it. You want a heading to change color as the user's mouse pointer rolls over it? You got it.

JavaScript provides us with a means for writing DHTML pages. We've already seen this in action with the example in Chapter 5 where we enabled the user to change an image loaded into the page on the click of a button. The latest browsers go much further than this, and in the case of Internet Explorer 4.0+ we can now change virtually anything in a page. Also, nearly every tag in Internet Explorer is represented by an object with a large selection of events, which make interacting with the user so much easier.

However, the bad news is that the way DHTML is supported by Netscape Navigator 4.x and Internet Explorer 4.0+ browsers is very, very different. This is mainly because we use many of the objects in the Browser Object Model (BOM) to enable us to write Dynamic HTML. Although the parts of the BOM that we have seen so far have been mostly the same, a lot of the rest of the BOMs for the two browsers have large differences. While we'll occasionally find apparent similarities, these are actually sometimes misleading. For example, both IE 4.0+ and NN 4.x have the event object in their BOM and you may think this a wonderful ray of hope for compatibility, until you realize that they are very different objects.

You'll find that you may create an all singing, all dancing DHTML page for IE, only to find that making it work in NN 4.x is either impossible or requires a total re-write. Perhaps even worse, is that DHTML pages written for NN 4 will fail badly in NN 6. You have essentially two choices: either you keep things simple, but limited, so that they are cross-browser compatible, or you go for dazzling pages, but accept that it's most likely that you'll need to write a different version for each browser. There are obviously advantages and disadvantages to each of these strategies.

In this chapter we'll be looking at the DHTML possible with Internet Explorer 4.0+: how we can changes things, add things, and move things around the page. We'll also look at how we can create a dynamic menu system, where the menus appear and disappear as we move the mouse pointer over a series of images.

Next we'll turn our attention to Netscape Navigator 4.x. We'll investigate how DHTML can be achieved on this browser, and have a look at how we can achieve a dynamic menu example with similar functionality to the IE version.

It is possible to write DHTML for the Netscape 6 browser, but this browser does not support the same BOM as Netscape 4.x. Instead it abides by the W3C Document Object Model (DOM). We will be seeing more on this in Chapter 13.

Finally, we'll see how we can make DHTML for IE 4.0+ and NN 4.x cross-browser compatible.

Style Sheets

Before we dive into the DHTML possible with different browsers, we will take a brief look at how we can add styling to HTML documents. For example, how do we specify that a certain paragraph, or a set of paragraphs, or all paragraphs have text that is colored red? There are various ways to do this, including using the STYLE attribute and the <STYLE> tag to include style sheet rules. We will look at how to do this shortly, but first what are style sheets and what problems do they solve?

Style sheets allow us to apply a set of 'styling' rules to various sets of HTML tags. For example, we might want all paragraph tags, <P>, to have the font Verdana, a font size of 12 points, be colored dark blue, and centered in the page. In older browsers, we'd tackle this using various HTML formatting tags, such as <CENTER>, <FONT>, <STRONG>, <U>, and so on, to determine page alignment, font parameters, and whether a font was bold or underlined. However, these formatting tags have various problems.

The first problem with using HTML formatting tags is that we need to wrap every element we want to have a particular style in its own HTML formatting tags. This makes for extra work for us. Also, should we decide we don't like dark blue Verdana any more, and want a bright pink color and Palatino Linotype for our font face instead, we need to change every font tag in the page.

The second problem with HTML formatting tags is that they only provide a limited control over style. For example, we can't specify a 12 point font with the <FONT> tag and its SIZE attribute, as that only allows us to specify that a font should either be bigger or smaller than the normal font size. A value of 1 will be smaller than the normal font size, 3 will be the same, 4 bigger than the normal font size, going all the way up to 7. This is only setting relative sizes – the user might have changed their browser preferences so that their normal font size is very small. When we go and specify that we want a font size smaller than normal, the user ends up with something barely visible.

Related to this lack of fine control over the page is the difficulty of specifying exactly where a HTML element appears on the page. Normally the display of HTML tags is based on where their element appears in the source. So:

```
<P>Hello</P>
<P>Goodbye</P>
```

will display Hello first, then on the next line Goodbye will appear. We can't specify exactly where an element appears, but instead rely on HTML to decide. We can use various tags to format positioning, for example putting things in lists or using tables, but nevertheless we can't specify an exact position.

What style sheets give us is, firstly, the ability to specify in just one place a certain type of style for the whole page, and, secondly, a much, much greater amount of control over how our page looks when loaded by the user.

Adding a Touch of Style

We can add style to an HTML page by creating style sheets within the `<STYLE>` tag or simply specifying `STYLE` attributes for a particular element. There are a number of ways of defining the style, but we'll look at just three of them:

- Defining a style for certain HTML elements, for example a style for all paragraph elements.

- Creating a style class. This style is then applied to all elements for which this class is specified in their attributes.

- Specifying style for just one element.

The <STYLE> Tag

The first two ways mentioned above, that is defining a style for a type of tag or defining a style class, can be achieved by creating a `<STYLE>` tag, which we add inside the `<HEAD>` of a page.

To define the style for a particular element type, say a `<P>` tag, we use the following format:

```
<STYLE>
    ElementName {
        Style Attribute Name : Style Attribute Value;
        Another Style Attribute : Another Value; }
</STYLE>
```

The `ElementName` is the tag we want the style to apply to, but without the `<` and `>`. For example, to define a style for all table cell tags, `<TD>`, the `ElementName` would be `TD` and for the `<P>` tag, the `ElementName` would be `P`.

Inside the curly braces we define the style attributes we want applied to the specified elements. We state the name of the attribute, then rather than an equals sign we put a colon, and then the value we want assigned to that attribute. If we want to define more than one style attribute, we need to separate each with semicolons.

For example, let's say we want all `<P>` tags to be in Verdana font, colored dark blue and 12 points in size. We would need to specify the `font-family`, `font-size` and `color` style attributes:

```
<HTML>
<HEAD>
<STYLE>
    P { font-family: verdana; font-size : 12pt; color : darkblue; }
</STYLE>
```

```
    </HEAD>
    <BODY>
        <P>Some dark blue verdana 12 point text</P>
        <P>Also dark blue verdana 12 point text</P>
    </BODY>
    </HTML>
```

The first attribute we specified is `font-family` with value `verdana`. This is followed by a semicolon to mark the end of that style attribute. Next we define the `font-size` attribute and specify a value of `12pt`. Finally we specify the `color` attribute and value `darkblue`.

Both the paragraphs specified in the page will be in the same font, font size, and color, as specified in the `<STYLE>` tag.

If we wanted to define similar properties for the `<TD>` tag, we'd just add it to the definition inside the `<STYLE>` tag.

```
    <STYLE>
        P { font-family : verdana; font-size : 12pt; color : darkblue; }
        TD { font-family : verdana; font-size : 10pt; color : red; }
    </STYLE>
```

This time I've set the `font-family` attribute to the same as the paragraph, but made the `font-size` `10pt` and the `color` red.

This is fine where we want to define the basic style for a certain type of tag, but what about if we wanted to have some paragraphs in a larger font, say as a heading, while others were still in the 12 point font? For this we could use the second technique we discussed above and define a style class. We can use the style defined in a style class in whichever elements we choose.

Like the styles for certain elements, we define a style class inside the `<STYLE>` tag. The only difference is that instead of the tag name, we create our own class name. A class name is distinguished by putting a dot in front. For example, to define a heading class called `HEADING1` we'd write:

```
    <STYLE>
        P { font-family : verdana; font-size : 12pt; color : darkblue; }
        .HEADING1 { font-size : 24pt; color : orange; }
    </STYLE>
```

The `HEADING1` class's style attributes specify that the `font-size` should be `24pt` and the `color` should be `orange`.

Whenever we want to use the style specified in this class, we need to specify this within the HTML for the element. To do this we use the `CLASS` attribute that most HTML elements support. Let's modify our above example, so that the first of the two paragraphs has the `HEADING1` style applied:

```
    <HTML>
    <HEAD>
    <STYLE>
        P { font-family: verdana; font-size : 12pt; color : darkblue; }
```

```
    .HEADING1 { font-size : 24pt; color : orange; }
  </STYLE>
  </HEAD>

  <BODY>
    <P CLASS="HEADING1">A Heading in dark blue verdana 24 point</P>
    <P>Some dark blue verdana 12 point text</P>
  </BODY>
  </HTML>
```

Now the first paragraph has the HEADING1 class of style applied to it, so it's 24pt in size and colored orange.

However, the style defined for the <P> tags is always applied to all tags of the type <P>. So the first <P> tag has both the P styling and the HEADING1 style class applied to it. Where the P style definition and the style class conflict, that is where the same style attributes are defined by both, then the style class takes precedence. Therefore the first paragraph has the Verdana font applied from the <P> definition, but the size and color style attributes of the class over-ride those defined for all <P> tags.

The STYLE Attribute

The third way we mentioned above of defining styles is the direct route – for each tag we use its STYLE attribute. For example, if we wanted just the second paragraph tag to be in green italics we could change the HTML tag definition to this:

```
<P STYLE="font-style : italic; color: green">
    Some dark blue verdana 12 point text
</P>
```

We define the style attributes inside the STYLE attribute of the tag, just as we did above when it was inside the <STYLE> tag. First we set the font-style attribute to italic, then, separated by a semicolon, we set the color to green. As before, the setting of the color attribute here overrides the setting in the style sheet definition for all <P> tags. However, the paragraph will still take the font-family and font-size attributes set in the <STYLE> tag.

Cascading Style Sheets

Finally, it's worth noting that style sheets, or to give them their full name **Cascading Style Sheets** (CSS), are called cascading because the style attributes defined for one tag may cascade down to tags inside that tag, that is to say some style attributes of a parent tag are inherited by any child tags inside.

For example, in the code below we don't define any style attributes for the two paragraph tags, only for the <DIV> tag. The <DIV> tag is a container tag that does not display anything, and we'll look at it in more detail later. The <P> tag outside the <DIV> has no style applied to it, yet the <P> inside the <DIV> has inherited the style attributes set for the <DIV>.

```
<HTML>
<HEAD>
<STYLE>
    DIV { font-family: verdana; font-size : 12pt; color : darkblue; }
</STYLE>
```

```
    </HEAD>
    <BODY>
        <P>This text has no style</P>
        <DIV>
            <P>This inherits its style from the div tag it's inside</P>
        </DIV>
    </BODY>
</HTML>
```

Positioning Elements

As we said above, HTML content normally flows from the top to the bottom of a page, the position of the output being based on where the tag is defined in the page. So

```
<P>Para 1</P>
<P>Para 2</P>
```

will display the two paragraphs one after the other:

Para 1
Para 2

However, using style sheets we can specify positioning for content in two ways, rather than letting the browser decide where it wants to put things. With **absolute positioning** we can set the position of content in relation to the browser window itself. With **relative positioning** we can set the position of content relative to any content it is inside. For example, in the HTML

```
<DIV><P>My Para</P><DIV>
```

relative positioning of the <P> tag would be relative to the <DIV> tag it's inside. We'll see more about this shortly.

We can specify whether an element is positioned relatively or absolutely using the `position style` attribute, which takes the values relative and absolute.

The keys to positioning an element are the style attributes `left` and `top`. We can use a number of different units for these values, but here I'll stick with those most commonly used – pixels and percentages. I'll start with pixels.

When you set your computer screen's display resolution, you can choose values like 800 * 600 or 1024 * 768 and so on. These values are actually pixels, so 800 * 600 means that your screen will be treated as 800 pixels wide by 600 pixels high. These values are independent of your actual physical monitor size.

As far as absolute positioning is concerned, the top left corner of the screen is 0,0 and the bottom right corner will be whatever the screen resolution determines. So, for 800 * 600 resolutions, the bottom right corner is at the coordinates 800,600, whereas for 1024 * 768 resolutions, it's 1024,768 as you can see in the diagram opposite:

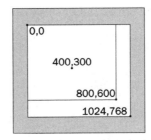

If we specified that a <DIV> tag's left style attribute was set to 400 pixels and top style attribute was set to 300 pixels, then the content's top left corner would be in exactly the middle of a 800 * 600 resolution display. If the display were set to 1024 * 768, then the top left corner would be about two-fifths along the screen by about two-fifths down the screen. This has been marked approximately on the diagram above.

Let's look at an example. Imagine we have an absolutely positioned <DIV> tag at a position left of 200 and top of 100 and with other style attributes specifying it should be 200 pixels wide by 200 pixels deep and have a background color of blue. Our screen would look something like this:

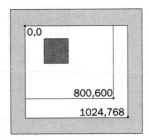

Now how can we position a paragraph contained within the <DIV> relative to the <DIV>? If we think of the <DIV> tag as a sort of screen within a screen, in this case a screen of resolution 200 * 200, then it makes relative positioning easier to understand.

When thinking of the <DIV> as a screen itself, the top left corner of the <DIV> is 0,0 and the bottom right corner is 200,200 in this case (that is, the <DIV> tag's width and height). If we then specified that the <P> tag should be at the relative position left of 100 and top of 100, then that would leave the top, left corner of the <P> in exactly the middle of the <DIV> tag it's contained inside.

What if we relatively position a tag that is not inside another tag? Well in that case it'll be relative to the <BODY> tag, which is the whole page itself – essentially this is the same as absolute positioning, if the whole page fills the screen.

Let's see the HTML for a page with the <DIV> and <P> tags having the positioning we've been discussing:

```
<HTML>
<HEAD>
<STYLE>
    .DivStyle1 {background-color: blue;
        position : absolute;
        width: 200px; height: 200px;}
    .PStyle1 {color: white;
        position : relative;}
</STYLE>
</HEAD>

<BODY>
<DIV STYLE="left: 200px; top: 200px" CLASS="DivStyle1">
    <P CLASS="PStyle1" STYLE="left: 100px;top: 100px">My Paragraph</P>
</DIV>

</BODY>
</HTML>
```

Type this into a text editor and save it as `relativepos.htm`.

In the `<STYLE>` tag, we create two style classes, `DivStyle1` and `PStyle1`. Within these, we specify the style attributes we talked about above. In `DivStyle1` we specify a blue background, that the positioning should be absolute, and finally the width and height in pixels, that is `px`. For the `PStyle1` we just specify the color of the text and that it should be positioned relatively.

Then in the `<DIV>` tag, we apply the style specified in the `DivStyle1` class using the `CLASS` attribute of the tag. Then in the `STYLE` attribute, we specify the `left` and `top` positions of the tag – again we specify pixels as the unit of measurement by adding px at the end of the value. As the `DivStyle1` class specified positioning should be absolute, the values `200` and `200` will be absolute screen values.

In the `<P>` tag, we apply the `PStyle1` class, then specify the position of the tag as `100px` and `100px`. This time it will be relative to the `<DIV>`, with 0,0 being the top, left corner of the `<DIV>` and `200,200` being the bottom right corner.

Note that IE 4 does not support absolute positioning for the <P> tag, but NN 4+ and IE 5+ do.

On an 800 * 600 resolution screen, the example should look like the screenshot below:

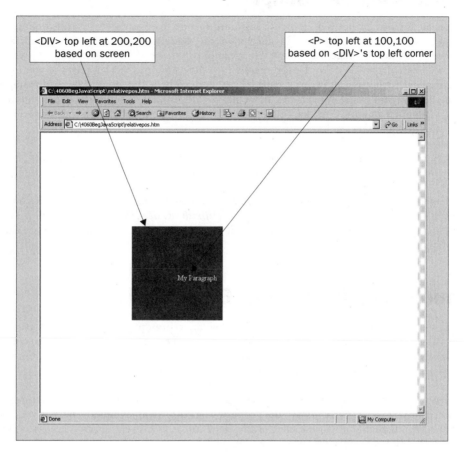

Remember that the left and top style attributes apply to the left and top of the element, so **My Paragraph** has the top left of the letter M at position left 100 and top 100 relative to the <DIV> (that is, in the middle of the <DIV>).

We also mentioned earlier that, as well as specifying position properties as pixels, we can use percentages. To do this we simply put % at the end of the value instead of px. In the case of absolute positioning, it's a percentage of the windows width and height. For relative positioning it's a percentage of the containing tag's width and height.

For example, to position our <DIV> and <P> tags such that the top left of the <DIV> appeared in the middle of the screen and the top left of the <P> appeared in the middle of the <DIV>, regardless of the screen resolution, we'd write:

```
<DIV STYLE="left: 50%; top: 50%" CLASS="DivStyle1">
    <P CLASS="PStyle1" STYLE="left: 50%px;top: 50px">My Paragraph</P>
</DIV>
```

Style Sheets and JavaScript

You might be thinking, "what is the point to this introduction to style sheets in a book about JavaScript?" The point is that by using JavaScript we can manipulate the style of tags to change their appearance even after the page has loaded. For example, as a user's mouse pointer goes over a paragraph we can change its color. Unfortunately how different browsers support the manipulation of style attributes using JavaScript varies greatly. IE 5.0 and 5.5 have the greatest level of manipulation with virtually every tag being changeable. NN 6 has greatly enhanced support when compared with NN 4. IE 4 also supports an ability similar IE 5 for changing style using JavaScript, but with a less extensive range of attributes and tags.

In the remainder of the chapter we'll see how we can use JavaScript and style sheets with IE 4+ and NN 4.x. In the next chapter we'll concentrate on the enhancements in IE 5.5 and NN 6.

Style sheets themselves are a big topic and there are many books exclusively on them if you want to learn more. For example, *Cascading Style Sheets: The Definitive Guide (ISBN 1-56592-622-6)* available from O'Reilly publishers has extensive coverage of the many different attributes available and which tags they apply to.

Dynamic HTML in Internet Explorer 4.0+

Under IE, most tags, even simple tags like the `<P>` tag, are represented by objects. The attributes of these tags are often represented as properties of the objects. The objects also have an amazing number of other properties, as well as methods and events, probably totaling almost a hundred. Some of these properties are themselves objects with even more properties and methods.

In this section we'll be looking at just the fundamentals of DHTML with IE. With the fundamentals under your belt you can explore further the properties, methods and events IE makes available by looking at Appendices E and F at the back of this book for IE BOM references, or referring to the advanced DHTML books available from Wrox Press.

Accessing Page Tags

How do we access the objects of HTML tags, to change their properties, call their methods and hook into their events? We obviously need some way of specifying which individual tag we are referring to. So far in this book we have been giving tags a NAME attribute and using this to access them. For example, a text box within a form could be defined like this:

```
<FORM NAME="myForm">
    <INPUT TYPE="text" NAME="text1">
</FORM>
```

We then referred to the corresponding Form object in JavaScript using the form's name, myForm, and the text box's Text object using the name, text1:

```
document.myForm.text1.value
```

In IE's DHTML, however, we use a different way of uniquely identifying tags, namely with a tag's ID attribute. This works in a very similar way to the NAME attribute. Certain elements, such as forms and controls on forms, still require the NAME attribute, as it's this that's passed to a server if the form is posted. However, for most other elements, we can just use the ID attribute.

For example, if we have a paragraph tag, <P>, which we want to access via script, we write:

```
<P ID="myPara">A Paragraph</P>
```

To access this in our JavaScript code we simple use the ID value. For example, if we wanted to retrieve the text inside the paragraph, we would use the P object's innerText property with the code:

```
myPara.innerText;
```

which will be "A Paragraph" in this example. We will talk about the innerText property in more detail later in this chapter.

Another way of accessing the objects associated with tags is the document object's all array property (or, more precisely, collection property). This property contains all the elements defined in the source code for the page in source code order. We can reference an element by either using its index in the array, or its ID value in square brackets after the all word. For example, to reference the above paragraph we could use:

```
document.all["myPara"];
```

However, for our purposes in this chapter, it is easier to use the former way of referencing tags' objects.

Changing Appearances

The key to changing the look of an HTML tag once the page has been loaded is the style object, which almost every tag's object has as a property. The style object is JavaScript's representation of a tag's style sheet, which we saw earlier, and most properties you can set with style sheets can also be set using the style object. In Appendices E and F you'll find a guide to the properties of the style object.

One example of a property of the style object is color. Quite obviously, this can be used to change the color of an object. For example, to change the color property of the style object property of a paragraph with ID of myPara, we would use:

```
myPara.style.color='red';
```

This technique of using the style object property of the object representing a particular tag to change the tag's appearance works for most tags, with a wide range of appearance changes being available. Everything, from background color to text spacing, text size, and even whether the tag is visible to the user, can be determined using the style object.

Try It Out – Using the style Object

Let's have a go at a simple example using the style object:

```
<HTML>
<HEAD>
<SCRIPT LANGUAGE=JavaScript>

function myPara_onmouseout()
{
    myPara.innerText = "Roll your mouse over my text";
    myPara.style.color = "Black"
}

function myPara_onmouseover()
{
    myPara.innerText = "Wow that feels good!!!";
    myPara.style.color = "Red"
}

</SCRIPT>
</HEAD>

<BODY>
<P ID="myPara"
    onmouseout="return myPara_onmouseout()"
    onmouseover="return myPara_onmouseover()">
        Roll your mouse over my text
</P>
</BODY>
</HTML>
```

Save this as rollover_IE.htm. Load it into your browser, and you should see a paragraph with the text Roll your mouse over my text.

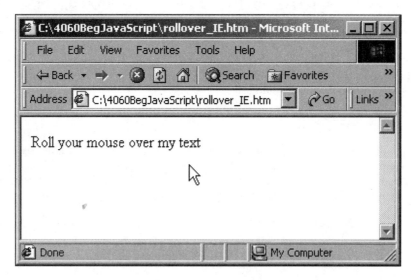

On doing this, the color of the text changes to red, and the text message changes to Wow that feels good!!!

On moving your mouse off of the text, the text returns to the original color and message.

How It Works

In the body of the page, we define a paragraph with ID of myPara. We connect the onmouseout event handler for this paragraph to the function myPara_onmouseout() and the onmouseover event handler to the function myPara_onmouseover(). These functions are defined in a script block in the head of the page.

The myPara_onmouseover() function, which is called when the user's mouse pointer rolls over the paragraph, starts by changing the text of the paragraph. It does this using the innerText property that we saw above:

```
function myPara_onmouseover()
{
    myPara.innerText = "Wow that feels good!!!";
```

Then, the function uses the color property of the style object property of the myPara object to change the color of the paragraph:

```
    myPara.style.color = "Red"
}
```

The myPara_onmouseout() function, which is called when the user's mouse pointer rolls off the paragraph, has very similar functionality. It simply changes the text back to its original value, and changes the color property of the style object back to black.

Positioning and Moving Content

We saw earlier how we can use style sheets to determine the exact position of HTML elements on a page when it's loaded. Well, using JavaScript we can move these absolutely or relatively positioned elements around after the page has loaded, again using the `style` object. In this case we can use the `style` object's `left` and `top` properties to change the `left` and `top` positions of HTML elements.

Try It Out – Moving Text

Let's see an example of how to use JavaScript to move the content around after it has loaded. In this case, we're going to make two paragraphs scroll from left to right, then back again in a continuous loop. We'll use the timer functionality we saw in Chapter 9 to keep the tags moving.

```
<HTML>
<HEAD>
<SCRIPT LANGUAGE=JavaScript>

var paraOneLeft = 100;
var paraTwoLeft = 400;
var switchDirection = false;

function window_onload()
{
    window.setInterval("moveParas()",50);
}

function moveParas()
{
    if (switchDirection == false)
    {
        paraOneLeft++;
        paraTwoLeft--;

        if (paraOneLeft == 400)
        {
            switchDirection = true;
        }
    }
    else
    {
        paraOneLeft--;
        paraTwoLeft++;

        if (paraOneLeft == 100)
        {
            switchDirection = false;
        }
    }

    para1.style.left = paraOneLeft + "px";
    para2.style.left = paraTwoLeft + "px";
}
```

```
    </SCRIPT>
    </HEAD>

    <BODY LANGUAGE=JavaScript onload="window_onload()">

    <P STYLE="position:relative;left:100px;top:30px" ID="para1">Para 1</P>
    <P STYLE="position:relative;left:400px;top:10px" ID="para2">Para 2</P>

    </BODY>
    </HTML>
```

Save the page as `MovingTags_IE.htm` and load it into your Internet Explorer 4.0+ browser. Hopefully, the contents of the two tags (**Para 1** and **Para 2**) will scroll smoothly across the screen in opposite directions and back again continuously.

How It Works

In the body of the page we have two `<P>` elements. Each has been given a unique `ID` value (`para1` and `para2`) and it's this that we'll use to reference the `P` object associated with each tag.

```
    <P STYLE="position:relative;left:100px;top:30px" ID="para1">Para 1</P>
    <P STYLE="position:relative;left:400px;top:10px" ID="para2">Para 2</P>
```

Within the `STYLE` attribute, we have positioned the paragraphs at the co-ordinates `100,30` and `400,10`. Note that this means that `para2` will be above `para1`.

Note that we've positioned the paragraphs relatively rather than absolutely, even though the two `<P>` tags are not inside other tags. Why?

Well this is for browser compatibility. IE 4 does not support the absolute positioning of `<P>` tags but it does support relative positioning of them. IE 5.0+ supports both absolute and relative positioning for `<P>` tags, so we would have no problems. In this example, using relative positioning when not inside another tag gives the same effect as absolute positioning.

An alternative would be to use the `<DIV>` tag, which is a container tag, that is it does not display anything, but allows you to group tags together inside it. This supports absolute and relative positioning in IE 4 and IE 5, so we could have put each paragraph inside a separate absolutely positioned `<DIV>` tag and moved the `<DIV>` tag about instead.

Within the script block in the head of the page, after we've declared three variables that will be used to determine the left positions and the scroll direction of the paragraphs, we then come to the `window_onload()` function.

```
    function window_onload()
    {
        window.setInterval("moveParas()",50);
    }
```

Here we start a timer going using the `setInterval()` method of the `window` object, which will call the `moveParas()` function every 50 milliseconds. The definition of the `moveParas()` function comes next in the script block. This function is used to actually move the paragraph's text.

455

How do we want the paragraph's text moved?

We want the top paragraph, para2, to start with a left position of 400, then move by 1 pixel decrements to the left until the left position is 100. At that point we want to switch directions and start moving the paragraph back to a left position of 400 by increasing the left position by 1 pixel until it's 400, whereupon we switch directions again and the process starts again.

We want the bottom paragraph, para1, to do the exact opposite of the top paragraph: we want it to start at a left position of 100, then scroll to the right by 1 pixel until it hits a left position of 400, then switch direction and scroll back until it has a left position of 100 again.

To achieve this, the first task of the moveParas() function is to determine which way to scroll the paragraphs. It does this by using the switchDirection variable, which will have the value false if para1 is scrolling right, and the value true if para1 is scrolling left. It was initialized to false at the top of the script block.

In the first if statement, the condition checks whether switchDirection has value false. If so, it increments the left position of para1 by 1 and decrements the left position of para2 by 1. It then checks in an inner if statement whether the left position of para1 is 400. If so, then it is time to switch the direction of the scrolling, so it sets the value of the variable switchDirection to true:

```
function moveParas()
{
    if (switchDirection == false)
    {
        paraOneLeft++;
        paraTwoLeft--;

        if (paraOneLeft == 400)
        {
            switchDirection = true;
        }
    }
}
```

Next, in an else statement, we have similar code for the situation where switchDirection is true, that is the scrolling is in the opposite direction:

```
    else
    {
        paraOneLeft--;
        paraTwoLeft++;

        if (paraOneLeft == 100)
        {
            switchDirection = false;
        }
    }
```

Finally we set the left position of the paragraphs in exactly the same way we set the color in our previous example: by using each P object's style object property:

```
        para1.style.left = paraOneLeft + "px";
        para2.style.left = paraTwoLeft + "px";
    }
```

That completes the `moveParas()` function, and the script block.

We'll be looking at moving tags again when we look at the DHTML menus example later in this section.

Changing, Adding, and Deleting Existing Content

We've already seen how in earlier browsers a limited form of DHTML allowed the changing of images loaded in an `<IMG>` tag even after the page had completed loading (see Chapter 5). Now with DHTML in IE 4.0+ we can change all the content after it has loaded.

For IE browsers, there are three properties and two methods available for the objects of most tags that are useful for changing content. These are `innerText`, `innerHTML`, `outerHTML`, `insertAdjacentText()`, and `insertAdjacentHTML()`. Once the page has completed loading, that is once the `onload` event handler of the `window` object has fired, we can use these properties and methods to change the page's contents.

We'll now look at these properties and events in detail, starting with the `innerText` property, which we have already seen in use.

Getting and Setting the innerText Property

The property `innerText` allows us to retrieve, change, or set the plain text contained between a start tag and an end tag, for example `<P>` and `</P>`.

Although many tags support this property, it's not always obvious until you use `innerText` exactly what is returned. For example, although it would work with a `<TABLE>` tag, it would show all the text inside all the contained `<TD>` tags as the retrieved `innerText`.

Try It Out – The innerText property

Let's return to a paragraph example, and use it to examine the `innerText` property.

```
<HTML>
<BODY>

<P ID="para1">Para 1</P>
<BR>
<INPUT TYPE="text" ID=text1 NAME=text1 SIZE=50>
<BR>
<INPUT TYPE="button" VALUE="Get innerText" ID="bttnGetInnerText"
    onclick="text1.value = para1.innerText">
<INPUT TYPE="button" VALUE="Set innerText" ID="bttnSetInnerText"
    onclick="para1.innerText = text1.value">
</BODY>
</HTML>
```

Save the example as `innertext_IE.htm`, then load it into your IE browser. You should see a page with the content shown below:

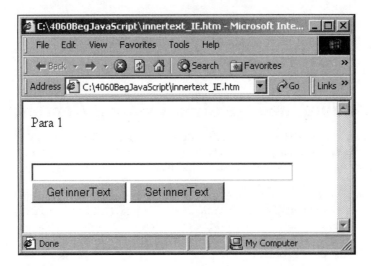

Click on the Get innerText button, and the contents of the paragraph shown above the text box, initially Para 1, are displayed in the text box.

Type something into the text box, and then click the Set innerText button. The text inside the paragraph shown above the text box will change to whatever you added inside the text box.

Try also typing some HTML into the text box (such as `<STRONG>Hello</STRONG>`) and clicking the Set innerText button. Note that the browser does not parse the HTML – it is just dealt with as plain text.

How It Works

At the top of the page, we define our paragraph tag and made sure it has a unique ID value. That way, we can reference it later from JavaScript:

```
<P ID="para1">Para 1</P>
```

We then define two buttons. The first button, Get innerText, has the following code attached to its `onclick` event handler, which fires when the button is clicked:

```
text1.value = para1.innerText
```

This sets the value of the text box to the value of `para1`'s `innerText` property.

When clicked, the second button, Set innerText, changes the text inside the paragraph of the document loaded (not the actual HTML file on our disk drive) setting its value to the value in the `text1` text box. It does this because the following code is attached to its `onclick` event handler:

```
para1.innerText = text1.value
```

Getting and Setting the innerHTML and outerHTML Properties

Whereas the `innerText` property only gives access to any plain text inside a tag, the `innerHTML` property allows us to retrieve and change all the contents of a tag, including any HTML. The `outerHTML` property also allows us to retrieve or change all the contents of a tag, but this time it also includes the HTML defining the tag itself.

For example, if we have the following code:

```
<DIV ID=div1>Some text <H2>A heading</H2></DIV>
```

the value of the `innerHTML` property for `div1` would be;

```
Some text <H2>A heading</H2>
```

The value of the `outerHTML` property for `div1` would be;

```
<DIV ID=div1>Some text <H2>A heading</H2></DIV>
```

When we change the HTML using these properties, IE re-parses it and displays it as if it had been part of the page when it was first loaded.

The `innerHTML` and `outerHTML` properties behave differently depending on the type of tag they are used with.

Certain tags are termed **container** or **grouping** tags – their purpose in life is to group together other tags. Examples of such tags include the `<DIV>` tag and the `<SPAN>` tag. However, the majority of tags are not actually container tags even though other tags can be placed inside them. In particular, the `<P>` tag is not a container tag, even though you could put other HTML inside it, for example `<P>Some <STRONG>Bold</STRONG> text</P>`.

A second and very important distinction that needs to be made is between **block-level** and **inline** elements. The W3C define block and inline elements quite well – you can see the full description at `http://www.w3.org/TR/REC-html40/struct/global.html#h-7.5.3`. However, in brief it says:

Some HTML elements that may appear inside the body of the document are said to be "block-level" while others are "inline" (also known as "text level"). The distinction is founded on several notions:

- ❑ Most block-level elements may contain inline elements and other block-level elements. Most inline elements may contain only data and other inline elements.

- ❑ By default, block-level elements are formatted differently from inline elements. Most block-level elements begin on new lines, whereas inline elements do not.

The sort of elements that are block-level elements include:

```
<ADDRESS>, <BLOCKQUOTE>, <BODY>, <DD>, <DIV>, <DL>, <DT>, <FIELDSET>,
<FORM>, <FRAME>, <FRAMESET>, <H1>, <H2>, <H3>, <H4>, <H5>, <H6>, <IFRAME>,
<NOSCRIPT>, <NOFRAMES>, <OBJECT>, <OL>, <P>, <UL>, <APPLET>, <CENTER>,
<DIR>, <HR>, <MENU>, <PRE>, <LI>, <TABLE>, <TR>, <THEAD>, <TBODY>, <TFOOT>,
<COL>, <COLGROUP>, <TD>, <TH>, <CAPTION>.
```

459

The distinction between container and non-container tags, and block and inline elements is important in DHTML, particularly when dealing with the `innerHTML` and `outerHTML` properties. With most inline elements, we can use these properties to insert formatting HTML tags, for example `<I>` for italics and `<STRONG>` for a bolder typeface, as these are inline elements. However, we can't insert block-level elements. Most block-level elements can have any valid HTML inserted inside them using the `innerHTML` and `outerHTML` properties.

However, note that its only *most* block-level elements – there are exceptions to the rule. For example, although the `<P>` tag is a block-level element, we can't insert other block-level elements inside it, only inline elements.

For example, if we have a `<P>` tag, we could insert the following:

```
<B>Some plain and <I>italicized</I> text with boldness</B>
```

but we can't insert this:

```
Some text, then a <H2>Heading</H2>
```

because of the block-level `<H2>` tag. If you try this you'll find yourself getting strange and unpredictable results.

In reverse, the inline element `<SPAN>` can have other inline elements *and* block-level elements inserted.

In general the two container tags, `<DIV>` and `<SPAN>`, are the safe choice for when you want to insert any valid HTML.

Try It Out – Viewing and Setting Page HTML

Let's look at an example where we demonstrate the `innerHTML` and `outerHTML` properties, and the container, non-container, inline, and block-level tags.

```
<HTML>
<HEAD>
<SCRIPT LANGUAGE=JavaScript>

function setHTML()
{
    var actOnTag = div1;

    if (radTag[0].checked == true)
    {
        actOnTag = para1;
    }

    if (radInnerOuter[0].checked == true)
    {
        actOnTag.innerHTML = textarea1.value
    }
    else
    {
```

```
            actOnTag.outerHTML = textarea1.value;
        }
    }

    function getHTML()
    {
        var actOnTag = div1;

        if (radTag[0].checked == true)
        {
            actOnTag = para1;
        }

        if (radInnerOuter[0].checked == true)
        {
            textarea1.value = actOnTag.innerHTML;
        }
        else
        {
            textarea1.value = actOnTag.outerHTML;
        }
    }

</SCRIPT>
</HEAD>
<BODY>

<DIV ID="div1">
    <P ID="para1">This is a <I>paragraph</I>.</P>
    <H2>A Heading inside the DIV</H2>
</DIV>

<BR><TEXTAREA COLS=60 ROWS=10 ID=textarea1 NAME=textarea1></TEXTAREA>
<BR>
Paragraph <INPUT TYPE="radio" NAME="radTag" CHECKED>
Div <INPUT TYPE="radio" NAME="radTag">
<BR>
InnerHTML <INPUT TYPE="radio" NAME="radInnerOuter" CHECKED>
outerHTML <INPUT TYPE="radio" NAME="radInnerOuter">
<P>
<INPUT TYPE="button" VALUE="Get HTML" NAME="bttnGetInnerText"
    onclick="getHTML()">
<INPUT TYPE="button" VALUE="Set HTML" NAME="bttnSetInnerText"
    onclick="setHTML()">
</P>
</BODY>
</HTML>
```

Save the example page as `innerOuterHTML_IE.htm`.

Load the page into your browser and you should see the page below:

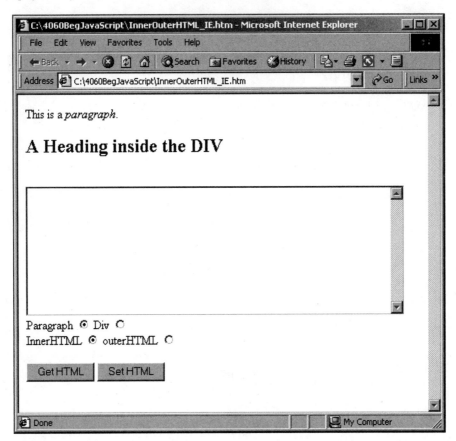

There are two important tags in the page whose `innerHTML` and `outerHTML` properties we are going to try to view or change. The first is `div1`, which contains a paragraph and a heading. The second is the paragraph inside `div1`, which contains some text.

```
<DIV ID="div1">
    <P ID="para1">This is a <I>paragraph</I>.</P>
    <H2>A Heading inside the DIV</H2>
</DIV>
```

The first set of radio buttons on the page allow us to select which of the two elements, `<DIV>` or `<P>`, we want to act on.

The second set of radio buttons allow us to choose whether it's the `innerHTML` or `outerHTML` property we are getting or setting.

Make sure the radio buttons for the **Paragraph** and **innerHTML** are selected, and then click the **Get HTML** button. This will put the value of the `innerHTML` property for the paragraph into the text-area box. We should see:

This is a <I>paragraph</I>.

Now select the outerHTML radio button and click the Get HTML button again. This time, we get:

<P id=para1>This is a <I>paragraph</I>.<P>

Notice that now we have the opening <P> and closing </P> tag as well as the contents of the innerHTML. You'll also notice that the <P> is on the second line of the text area. The reason for this is that <P> is a block-level tag and these normally start on a new line.

If we change the radio buttons so that the Div and innerHTML buttons are selected, and we then click the Get HTML button, we'll see a very different set of tags:

<P ID="para1">This is a <I>paragraph</I>.</P>
<H2>A Heading inside the DIV</H2>

We can see that all the HTML tags inside the container <DIV> tag have been included. If we now click the radio button for the outerHTML and then click the Get HTML button, we see the same as above except that the <DIV> tag itself is included.

<DIV ID="div1"><P ID="para1">This is a <I>paragraph</I>.</P>
<H2>A Heading inside the DIV</H2></DIV>

We can also use the Set HTML button to set the innerHTML and outerHTML properties.

For example, with the Div and innerHTML radio buttons selected, we can enter any valid HTML for the contents of the <DIV> tag into the text area, then set it using the Set HTML button. However, if we do change the HTML, then the existing tags inside the <DIV> will be lost, so unless we define a tag inside the <DIV> with the ID of para1, we'll find that access to para1 will be lost and the Paragraph radio button will no longer have any use.

We'll also face the same problem if we set the HTML for the outerHTML property of the <DIV> without defining another <DIV> with the ID of div1. Setting the outerHTML replaces not just the HTML inside the tag, but also the tag itself.

However, with the Paragraph and innerHTML radio buttons selected, we can only enter plain text or plain text and formatting tags, before we set the HTML.

If we select the outerHTML radio button and delete the paragraph, or even give it another ID, then any future attempts to access para1's inner or outer HTML will fail, since para1 no longer exists. Indeed, doing so will cause an error similar to that shown here:

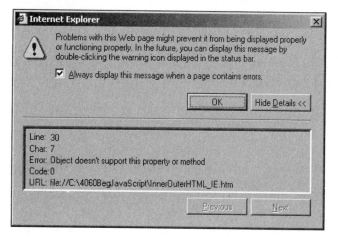

I caused the error above by first setting the outerHTML for the paragraph to:

```
<P ID=para99>This is a <I>paragraph</I>.</P>
```

This has replaced para1 with a paragraph with an ID of para99. Now, when I click either the setHTML or getHTML buttons when the paragraph radio button is selected, I get the error shown above, as para1 no longer exists.

You can use the example to try out various tags and settings to see what information is returned and what tags can be validly set. Just remember that the container tags <DIV> and <SPAN> can contain any valid elements, whether block-level or inline, but that the <P> element can only contain inline elements such as formatting tags.

How It Works

The aim of this example is to experiment with part of the HTML of the document. This piece of HTML occurs at the beginning of the body of the document:

```
<DIV ID="div1">
    <P ID="para1">This is a <I>paragraph</I>.</P>
    <H2>A Heading inside the DIV</H2>
</DIV>
```

Below this we define a text-area control, with the NAME and ID of textarea1:

```
<BR><TEXTAREA COLS=60 ROWS=10 ID=textarea1 NAME=textarea1></TEXTAREA>
```

Next we have two sets of radio buttons. The first two refer to the tag that we want changing. The Paragraph radio button refers to the <P> tag with the ID of para1. The Div radio button refers to the <DIV> tag with an ID of div1, which encloses all the other tags shown above.

```
Paragraph <INPUT TYPE="radio" NAME="radTag" CHECKED>
Div <INPUT TYPE="radio" NAME="radTag">
```

The second set of radio buttons refer to the innerHTML and outerHTML properties:

```
InnerHTML <INPUT TYPE="radio" NAME="radInnerOuter" CHECKED>
outerHTML <INPUT TYPE="radio" NAME="radInnerOuter">
```

Finally we have two buttons to get the HTML or set the HTML. Each button's onclick event handler is connected to a function, either the getHTML() or the setHTML() function, defined in the head of the page.

```
<INPUT TYPE="button" VALUE="Get HTML" NAME="bttnGetInnerText"
    onclick="getHTML()">
<INPUT TYPE="button" VALUE="Set HTML" NAME="bttnSetInnerText"
    onclick="setHTML()">
```

Let's now look at the setHTML() function which we use to set inner or outer HTML properties. The function starts by declaring a variable actOnTag and initializing it to the value div1. Next, if the first of the first set of radio buttons has been checked (the Paragraph radio button), the actOnTag variable's value is changed to para1. Thus this variable actOnTag now contains the ID of the tag that we want to view or change.

```
function setHTML()
{
    var actOnTag = div1;

    if (radTag[0].checked == true)
    {
        actOnTag = para1;
    }
```

The second if statement looks to see if radInnerOuter[0], the innerHTML radio button, is checked. If it is then we set the innerHTML property of the tag referenced by the actOnTag variable to the value of the text-area control. If not, then it must be the outerHTML property that needs to be set.

```
    if (radInnerOuter[0].checked == true)
    {
        actOnTag.innerHTML = textarea1.value
    }
    else
    {
        actOnTag.outerHTML = textarea1.value;
    }
}
```

The getHTML() function works in an identical way, the difference being those lines where instead of setting the HTML using innerHTML or outerHTML properties, we instead get their value and write it out to the <TEXTAREA> tag by using its value property.

Using Methods insertAdjacentText() and insertAdjacentHTML()

The three properties we have looked at so far can be used to retrieve or set content in the page. In comparison, the methods insertAdjacentText() and insertAdjacentHTML() allow us to *add to* the content in the page that already exists.

Just like the innerText and innerHTML properties, the difference between the insertAdjacentText() and insertAdjacentHTML() methods is that for the latter any HTML that is added is parsed and displayed as if it was in the page when it was first loaded, and with the former any addition to the content is simply inserted as plain text.

As with the innerHTML and outerHTML properties, generally speaking we can only insert inline HTML elements inside other inline elements, and inside block-level elements we can insert other block-level elements and inline elements. However, again the exceptions to this are tags such as a <P>, which is a block-level element but can only have inline elements inserted. Both the container tags, <SPAN> and <DIV>, can contain block-level and inline elements, even though <SPAN> is an inline tag.

With either of the two insertion methods, we can insert content at any one of four points in relation to the tag whose object's insert method it is we're using. Both methods take two parameters, the first of which specifies where you want the new HTML to be inserted, and the second of which contains the content to be inserted. The first parameter can take one of four values:

- ❑ `beforeBegin`. This inserts the text or HTML immediately before the start tag

- ❑ `afterBegin`. This inserts the text or HTML after the start tag, but before all other content in the element

- ❑ `beforeEnd`. This inserts the text or HTML immediately before the closing tag, but after all other content in the element

- ❑ `afterEnd`. This inserts the text or HTML immediately after the end of the closing tag

As an example, let's imagine we have the following tags:

```
<DIV ID=div1>
    <P>
        text inside a paragraph
    </P>
</DIV>
```

Using this HTML, we'll use the `insertAdjacentHTML()` method to insert a new `<BR>` tag into the `<DIV>` tag at each of the four possible positions. The code:

```
div1.insertAdjacentHTML("beforeBegin", "<BR>");
```

results in:

```
<BR>
<DIV ID=div1>
    <P>
        text inside a paragraph
    </P>
</DIV>
```

with the `<BR>` tag being placed immediately before the starting `<DIV>` tag.

With the first parameter as `afterBegin`:

```
div1.insertAdjacentHTML("afterBegin", "<BR>")
```

we get:

```
<DIV ID=div1>
<BR>
    <P>
        text inside a paragraph
    </P>
</DIV>
```

If we change the first parameter to `beforeEnd`:

```
div1.insertAdjacentHTML("beforeEnd", "<BR>")
```

we'll find that the HTML will look like this:

```
<DIV ID=div1>
    <P>
        text inside a paragraph
    </P>
<BR>
</DIV>
```

Finally, with the first parameter `afterEnd`:

```
div1.insertAdjacentHTML("afterEnd", "<BR>")
```

the code results in:

```
<DIV ID=div1>
    <P>
        text inside a paragraph
    </P>
</DIV>
<BR>
```

DHTML Events and the IE event Object

As well as providing lots of new methods and properties for every tag in the page, IE provides the tags' objects with many more events and event handlers. These include `ondragstart`, which fires when the user starts selecting content with a mouse drag, `onhelp`, which fires when the user presses *F1* or selects **Help** from the browser menu, and `onscroll`, which fires when the user has adjusted an element's scroll bar. However, we will not look at these events in more detail in this book.

As well as providing many more types of events for each tag, the versions of IE from 4.0 onwards also redefined the chain of events, that is the order in which events fire, so that events bubble up from the inner most tag up to the very outer tag. For example, if we have a table that is contained within a `<DIV>` in a page, and the user moves their mouse pointer over a table cell, then the chain of events will be the `onmouseover` events for the following tags: first the `<TD>` table cell being moved over, next the `<TR>` tag that the `<TD>` is contained within, then the `<TABLE>`, followed by the `<DIV>`, and finally the `document` object. We can handle events at zero or more points along this chain.

DHTML under IE 4.0+ also provides the `event` object. This object is a property of the `window` object, and one such object exists for each open browser window. It provides us with lots of very useful information about the most recent event to fire, such as details regarding the event that was fired, the tag that caused the event to fire, information about where the user's mouse pointer is, what buttons or keys they have pressed and much, much more.

Since the event object only contains information about the most recent event to fire, we must retrieve this information as soon as the event has fired. For this reason, the event object is usually used in the code that is attached to the event handler for an event.

The event object has a lot of properties and methods, but we are going to concentrate only on a few of the more useful ones. We'll take a look at these in the following sections.

Why Did the Event Fire?

The event object allows us to find out information about what the user did to cause the event to fire. For example, we can check to see where the mouse pointer is, which mouse buttons have been clicked and what keys might have been pressed.

The properties screenX and screenY of the event object provide us with the co-ordinates of the user's mouse pointer at the time of the event. As the event object is already created for us, we simply use it by typing its name followed by the property or method we're interested in. So:

```
event.screenX
```

gets us a reference to the horizontal position in pixels of the user's mouse pointer.

Similarly, the code:

```
event.screenY
```

gets us a reference to the vertical position in pixels of the mouse pointer. Remember that screen co-ordinates start at 0,0 in the top left corner of the screen.

The button property of the event object gets us which mouse button, if any, has been pressed by the user. It returns a number between 0 and 7 (inclusive) which indicates the following:

- ❑ 0: No button is pressed.
- ❑ 1: Left button is pressed.
- ❑ 2: Right button is pressed.
- ❑ 3: Left and right buttons are both pressed.
- ❑ 4: Middle button is pressed.
- ❑ 5: Left and middle buttons are both pressed.
- ❑ 6: Right and middle buttons are both pressed.
- ❑ 7: All three buttons (left, right, and middle) are pressed.

Finally we can find out if a key has been pressed and which key it was using the keyCode property of the event object. This returns a number indicating the Unicode character code corresponding to the key pressed. If no key was pressed, then this will be zero.

Finding Out Which Tags are Involved in the Event

The event object has three properties `fromElement`, `srcElement`, and `toElement`, which provide a reference to the objects of the tags involved in the event. For example, in an `onmouseover` event:

❑ The `fromElement` property will refer to the object of whichever tag the user's mouse pointer was on before moving over the tag firing the `onmouseover` event.

❑ The `srcElement` property will be the object of the tag that caused the event to fire. For example, if the mouse pointer just rolled over an image, then the `srcElement` will be that `<IMG>` tag's object.

❑ The `toElement` property is the object of the tag that the user's mouse pointer is about to move to, for example in an `onmouseout` event. How does the browser know where the mouse is going? Well it raises the events for a particular user action after they have actually happened, though we are talking only microseconds delay. It's rather like a live TV broadcast that is actually transmitted with a short delay so that swear words can be bleeped out.

Each of these properties provides the actual object of the tag, which we can use and manipulate as if we had referenced the tag directly. It can be particularly useful in writing generic code that is placed in the event of a higher object like the `document`.

Dynamic Menus in IE

We've taken a brief tour of DHTML in IE, so now it's time to put it into practice with an example that includes everything we've seen so far.

In this example we build a web page with three images on it representing menu choices. When the user's mouse pointer rolls over an image, a menu will appear to the right of the image with various menu options the user can choose from, which take them to a new page.

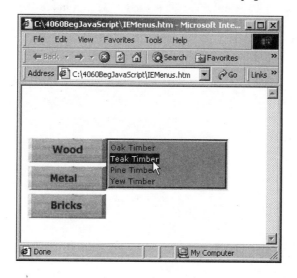

When the user's mouse pointer rolls off the menu, it disappears again.

The IE DHTML Menu System Principles

Let's start by taking a brief high-level overview of how the menu system works. Once we have that explained, we'll look at the HTML and code in much more depth.

The principle is very simple. For each main menu option, that is Wood, Metal, and Bricks, we have an image. For each main menu option we also have a <DIV> tag, which contains a list of menu items. For example, for wood we have Oak Timber, Teak Timber, Pine Timber, and Yew Timber. We capture the onmouseover and onmouseout events of the image – remember that this is IE, so unlike NN the <IMG> tag does have these events and there is no need to wrap it in an <A> tag. When the mouse rolls over the image, we display the <DIV> with its menu items. When the mouse leaves the image, and is not over the <DIV>, we hide the <DIV>.

When the page first loads, the <DIV> is actually located off screen by setting its left style attribute to a large minus number. Concentrating on just the wood menu image and <DIV>, the page screen at start up looks like this:

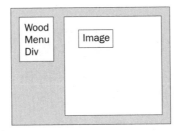

Now the user rolls their mouse pointer over the wood image causing the image's onmouseover event to fire, in which case we move the <DIV> from its off screen position to a position next to the image:

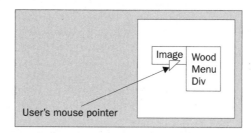

If the user's mouse pointer moves off the image, we want to hide the <DIV> by moving it back to its off screen position. We can do this in the onmouseout event handler. However, if the mouse pointer moves to the right of the image and over the <DIV> containing the menu items, we don't want to move the <DIV> – a menu that disappeared as soon as you tried to put your mouse pointer over it would be fairly pointless.

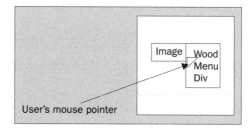

So if the user's mouse pointer is moving from the image to the <DIV> then we won't hide the <DIV>.

If the mouse pointer moves off from the <DIV> to the rest of the page, then by adding code to the <DIV> onmouseout event handler, we can hide the <DIV>, again by setting it to an off screen position.

However, there is a slight problem. When the user's mouse pointer moves from the edge of the <DIV> to the next element inside the <DIV>, then IE considers that the mouse pointer is no longer over the <DIV> but is now over a tag inside the <DIV> and promptly fires the <DIV>'s onmouseout event handler code. The user is trying to select a menu item inside the <DIV>, so again we don't in this circumstance want to hide the <DIV>. We only hide the <DIV> when the mouse pointer moves from the <DIV> to an element that is not contained inside the <DIV> itself.

In summary, we show the <DIV> if:

❑   The mouse pointer moves over the image

and we hide the <DIV> in either of the following two circumstances:

❑   The mouse pointer moves off the image but not onto the <DIV>

❑   The mouse pointer moves off the <DIV>, but not to a tag inside the <DIV>

471

We've covered how the menus appear and disappear, but how do we make each menu item in the <DIV> change font color and background color when the mouse rolls over it? Easy – we simply capture the onmouseover and onmouseout events for each element inside the <DIV>. When the pointer rolls over the element, we change the element's style to the blue background and white text you see in the screenshot. When it moves off the element, we change the style back to its original look. Its very similar to the example we saw earlier in the chapter where we changed the text and appearance of a paragraph when the mouse pointer rolled over or out of it.

Finally, when an element containing the menu item is clicked, we capture the onclick event handler and take the user to the page for that item.

OK, hopefully you now have a good idea of how the basic principles work. It's time to create the first, simple example of the system where we'll explain in much more detail the HTML and code necessary for the basic functionality. Later we'll modify the simple example, so that all the code is created dynamically, based on information in an array.

DHTML Menus Simple Version

In the final version of this example we'll be creating the DHTML using code. However, it's easier to understand the DHTML if we first look at just the DHTML itself. Then we'll look at the style sheets we need, and finally at the basic code required.

We'll first create a simplified version of the menu system, one containing just one menu, the wood menu. We'll look at the DHTML we'll need, then we'll look at the style sheets needed, and finally we'll look at the code required. Then we'll put it all together in a simple example. Once we've done that, we should have a good idea of how the dynamic menu system works and we can create the final version, which not only contains more menus, but also creates the HTML dynamically based on information stored in arrays. That way, adding a menu item or adding a whole new menu just requires changes to the array and possibly an additional image, but no changes to the code.

The DHTML

We'll concentrate on the DHTML required for just the first menu, the wood menu. We have an image on the page saying Wood. When the user's mouse pointer rolls over the image then our menu appears. When it leaves the image or menu, then the menu disappears. Let's look at the image tag itself:

```
<IMG ID="WoodMenuImage"
    SRC="WoodButton.gif"
    STYLE="position:absolute;left:10;top:75"
    onmouseover="showMenu(WoodMenuDiv)"
    onmouseout="hideMenu(WoodMenuDiv,4)">
```

The <IMG> tag is simple enough. It has an ID of "WoodMenuImage" and we've positioned it absolutely. We've set the onmouseover event handler to call a function showMenu() and the onmouseout event handler to call hideMenu(). We'll be creating and looking at how these functions work later, for now we'll stick with looking at what they do. The showMenu() function shows our popup menu, but what is it actually showing? Well, you'll see that it takes just one parameter and this parameter is a reference to the Div object that contains all the menu items. Here we're passing WoodMenuDiv, which is the object representing our Wood Menu <DIV>, which we'll look at in a minute. The function hideMenu() is simply the opposite of showMenu() in that it hides the menu by hiding the <DIV>. Again, we pass a Div object, our WoodMenuDiv.

We've been talking about showing and hiding a `<DIV>`, so let's look at the HTML for this `<DIV>` for the wood menu:

```
<DIV ID="WoodMenuDiv" CLASS="DivMenu"
    onmouseout="return hideMenu(this)">
</DIV>
```

Again this is simple enough. We've given it a unique ID, its style is defined in a style class called `DivMenu`, which we'll look at shortly, and the onmouseout event handler calls the same `hideMenu()` function that the `<IMG>` tag's onmouseout event handler did. This function is passed the same parameters, though on this occasion we pass this as the `Div` object to hide. The this word is JavaScript's way of saying "this object". In the context of an event handler, this always refers to the object of the tag the event handler is part of. In our case this refers to the object representing the `<DIV>` tag. We could have written `WoodMenuDiv` as the parameter and that would have passed exactly the same thing, the wood menu `<DIV>` tag's object. Using this is just convenient shorthand and being non-specific means we can use the same code in different places. For example, this in the `<DIV>` tag for the metal menu will refer to that `Div` object.

The reason we call the `hideMenu()` function in the `<DIV>` tag's onmouseout event handler is that we want to hide the menu if the user's mouse pointer leaves the menu, as well as when it leaves the `<IMG>`.

OK, we have a `<DIV>` for the menu, but there's nothing inside it. Currently it's a blank menu, so let's add each of our menu items for the wood menu, which are: Oak Timber; Teak Timber; Pine Timber; Yew Timber.

The `<DIV>` and the HTML we need inside it are shown below:

```
<DIV ID="WoodMenuDiv" CLASS="DivMenu"
    onmouseout="return hideMenu(this)">
<TABLE BORDER=0 CELLSPACING=1 CELLPADDING=1 ID="WoodTable">
    <TR>
        <TD ID="WoodOak" RollOver RollOut
            onclick="goPage('OakWood.htm')"
            CLASS="TDMenu">
                Oak Timber
        </TD>
    </TR>
</TABLE>
</DIV>
```

So far I've just added the menu item for Oak Timber. We're putting the menu items inside a table for formatting reasons and because it gives us a specific element whose events we can use – the `<TD>` element. The `<TD>` tag's onclick event handler calls the `goPage()` function we'll create later that takes the user to the page for that menu item, for example the `OakWood.htm` page.

You'll also notice something rather strange in the `<TD>` tag's definition: `RollOver` and `RollOut`. You're probably thinking that the `<TD>` tag does not have those attributes, so what are they doing there? Surely this is not valid HTML?

Well you'd be right. The <TD> tag does not have these attributes – I just made them up. However, there is some logic to it. As far as the HTML goes, the RollOver and RollOut attributes will be ignored. IE will take one look at them when creating the page, not recognize them as valid HTML attributes, and ignore them as far as displaying HTML goes. However, it does not completely ignore them, as when IE is creating the objects representing those <TD> tags, it will add RollOver and RollOut as properties of the Td object – properties we can use in our JavaScript. For our code, we're not interested in whether the attributes have values, but simply whether they exist, but why should we care whether they exist?

The RollOver and RollOut properties mark out those <TD> tags as being tags that we want to change the style of. More precisely, when the user's mouse pointer rolls over them, we want to change their style, and when the user's mouse pointer rolls out of them, we want to change their style back again. If it's a <TD> tag and does not contain those properties, there is no need to change the style when the user rolls over/rolls out with their mouse pointer.

The reason why we need to do this in the first place is that the code we'll be adding later to do the roll over and roll out style changes is actually in the document object's onmouseover and onmouseout event handlers. We'll be putting it there because it saves having to write an event handler for every <TD> menu tag in the page. Instead we'll let the onmouseover and onmouseout events bubble up from the <TD> tags and capture them in the document. If the <TD> tags have the RollOver and RollOut properties, then we'll change their style, otherwise we'll just ignore the event. We'll see in more detail how this works when we look at the code.

We've added only one menu item above, so let's now add the rest for the wood menu:

```
<DIV ID="WoodMenuDiv" CLASS="DivMenu"
    onmouseout="return hideMenu(this)">
<TABLE BORDER=0 CELLSPACING=1 CELLPADDING=1 ID="WoodTable">
    <TR>
        <TD ID="WoodOak" RollOver RollOut
            onclick="goPage('OakWood.htm')"
            CLASS="TDMenu">
                Oak Timber
        </TD>
    </TR>
    <TR>
        <TD ID="WoodTeak" RollOver RollOut
            onclick="goPage('TeakWood.htm')"
            CLASS="TDMenu">
                Teak Timber
        </TD>
    </TR>
    <TR>
        <TD ID="WoodPine" RollOver RollOut
            onclick="goPage('PineWood.htm')"
            CLASS="TDMenu">
                Pine Timber
        </TD>
    </TR>
    <TR>
        <TD ID="WoodYew" RollOver RollOut
            onclick="goPage('YewWood.htm')"
            CLASS="TDMenu">
```

```
                    Yew Timber
            </TD>
        </TR>
    </TABLE>
    </DIV>
```

Hopefully you can see a pattern emerging as all the `<TR>` and `<TD>` tags are identical except for their ID values and, in the case of the `<TD>` tags, the page that they go to when clicked. That's all of the dynamic part of the HTML created, so let's look at the style sheets.

The Style Sheets

You will have seen in the above code that two style classes, `DivMenu` and `TDMenu`, have been used.

```
<STYLE>
    .DivMenu {
        position:absolute;
        left:-200px;
        top:-1000px;
        width:180px;
        z-index:100;
        background-color: darkorange;
        border: 4px groove lightgrey;
    }

    .TDMenu {
        color:darkblue;
        font-family:verdana;
        font-size:70%;
        width:100%;
        cursor:default;
    }
</STYLE>
```

We talked about style sheets and classes in the first section of this chapter. Using classes like this helps make page maintenance easier, as changing properties for a class of tags, such as our menu items, only requires changes to be made in the style sheet and not in every tag.

The first class, `DivMenu`, is applied above to our `<DIV>` menu tags. The style it defines is that the position of the `<DIV>` should be `absolute`, that it should be at `left` position of `-200` and top of `-1000`. This means that when the page is first loaded, the `<DIV>` will be off screen and therefore invisible. Then we've set its `z-index` style attribute to 100. The `z-index` style attribute specifies how 'high up' in the page the tag will be. By this I mean that if certain tags are positioned on top of each other, the higher the `z-index` attribute, the more likely it is that the tag will be in front of the other tags. The value 100 has been selected arbitrarily as a value high enough that it's unlikely that anything else on our page will have a `z-index` higher. Thus, it is unlikely that the `<DIV>` will be covered over by any other tag on the page. Finally we've set the background `color` to dark orange and added a 4 pixel wide light gray grooved border.

The `TDMenu` class is applied to each `<TD>` used for a menu item in our menus. It defines the color of any text to be dark blue, its font to be Verdana, and its size to be 70% of the normal font size. We've made sure that the `<TD>` is 100% of the width of the table and that when the cursor rolls over the `<TD>` it remains the default cursor, normally a pointer. Without this last attribute you'll find the mouse cursor would be a single line when over a `<TD>` tag.

Showing and Hiding the Menus

To show and hide the menus, we use the showMenu() and hideMenu() functions. As we have seen, the showMenu() function is connected to the onmouseover event handler of the menu image, and the hideMenu() function is connected to the onmouseout event handlers of both the menu image and the menu <DIV>. First let's see the finished showMenu():

```
function showMenu(menuToShow)
{
    var srcElement = event.srcElement;
    var xPos = parseInt(srcElement.offsetLeft);
    var yPos = parseInt(srcElement.offsetTop);

    menuToShow.style.left = xPos + (srcElement.width)
    menuToShow.style.top = yPos;
}
```

As you can see, it's surprisingly short and simple. On the first line we declare a new variable, srcElement, and set it to reference the srcElement property of the event object. Whenever an event fires, this global event object is populated with various bits of information. The srcElement property, as we saw earlier, contains a reference to the object of the tag that caused the event to fire. Here we are using this reference to the tag that fired the event to get the position of that tag on the page. We want to position our menu next to the element that 'asked' for the menu to be shown.

Next we set the xPos and yPos variables to the left and top position values of the element that fired the event by using the offsetLeft and offsetTop properties of the srcElement, our <IMG> tag's object. These tell us where the left of the image is and where the top of the image is. In fact, it actually tells us how far from the edge of the parent tag the image is offset. As the images are not inside any tags, the parent tag is the <BODY> or the document itself, so the offsetLeft and offsetTop properties in this case are simply the screen co-ordinates of the tags inside the document.

The only parameter of the showMenu() function is the object of the <DIV> containing the menu we want to show. We use this parameter to move the <DIV> from its place off screen to a position on screen at the same height as the image that 'asked' for it to be shown, but directly to the right. The horizontal position is simply the xPos position of the image plus its width, which we can get from our variable srcElement using the width property.

Next we have our hideMenu() function – again it's short and sweet:

```
function hideMenu(menuToHide)
{
    if (event.toElement != menuToHide &&
        menuToHide.contains(event.toElement) == false)
    {
        menuToHide.style.left = -200;
        menuToHide.style.top = -1000;
    }
}
```

The `hideMenu()` function may be called by either the image's `onmouseout` event handler or the `onmouseout` event handler of the `<DIV>` for each menu. Basically, we want to hide the menu in two situations:

- ❑ The mouse pointer moves off the image, but not onto the `<DIV>`
- ❑ The mouse pointer moves off the `<DIV>`, but not onto a tag inside the `<DIV>`

It is easy to handle the first part of these situations – if the mouse is moving off the image or `<DIV>`. This is handled as a simple consequence of the `hideMenu()` function being called by the `onmouseout` event handlers for the image and the `<DIV>`. The hard part is checking the second two conditions: that we are not moving to the `<DIV>` and we are not moving to a tag inside the `<DIV>`.

The parameter of the function, `menuToHide`, is the object of the `<DIV>` tag we may want to hide. Then the function checks whether it should hide the menu or not in an `if` statement. The condition of this statement has two parts. The first part checks that the mouse pointer is not going to the `<DIV>` tag. Remember that `event.toElement` gives the object of the element that the mouse is moving to when the event occurs. The second part of the `condition` uses the `contains()` method of a tag's object, which returns `true` if an element contains another element and `false` otherwise. If it's `false` that the `menuToHide` object contains the element the mouse pointer is moving to, then the mouse pointer is certainly not going to any of our menu item elements inside the `<DIV>`.

If the condition of the `if` statement evaluates to `true`, the function hides the `<DIV>` by setting its `style` object's `left` and `top` properties to a position off screen.

Menu Rollover and Rollout Style Changes

We've seen how the menus are created and why they appear and disappear when the user runs their mouse pointer over or away from them. How do we create the effect of highlighting the text and background of a menu item when the user's mouse pointer runs over it?

The key to this is our capture of the `document` object's events with the event handlers `onmouseover` and `onmouseout`. The `document` object is not defined by any particular tag, so we can't use our normal method of connecting to events by setting the particular tag's attributes. Instead we need to specify that the `document` object's `onmouseover` and `onmouseout` properties are set to our functions to handle these events – in this case we'll be calling the functions `document_onmouseover()` and `document_onmouseout()`:

```
document.onmouseover = document_onmouseover;
document.onmouseout = document_onmouseout;
```

Here the `document_onmouseover()` function is connected to the `onmouseover` event of the `document` object, and the `document_onmouseout()` function is connected to the `onmouseout` event of the `document` object. We'll be putting these two lines of code in a script block outside of any function so that they're called when the page loads.

We'll look at the `document_onmouseover()` function first:

```
function document_onmouseover()
{
    var srcElement = event.srcElement;
```

```
        if (srcElement.tagName == "TD" &&
            typeof(srcElement.RollOver) != "undefined")
        {
            srcElement.style.color = "white";
            srcElement.style.backgroundColor ="darkblue";
        }
    }
```

Rather than capture the onmouseover event on every <TD> tag, we've decided to create a generic event handler that captures any onmouseover events of the document object. As the document is at the top of the BOM hierarchy, it means any events that occur at the lower levels, such as with <TD> tags inside <TR> tags, themselves inside <TABLE> blocks, which in our case are inside <DIV> tags, will bubble up to the document. We then just need to check that the source of the event, that is the srcElement property, was a <TD> tag and confirm that it's one of our menu item <TD> tags rather than from another unrelated table in the page. The srcElement.tagName property tells us what type of tag was at the center of events. If it's TD then we know it's a <TD> tag.

Although this page has no other <TD> tags except for menu ones, it's quite likely that when used in reality we would have various other tables with <TD> tags, which we don't want effected by highlighting. How can we determine whether the <TD> is one of the menu item tags?

Well, remember when the <TD> tags were defined, that we added two attributes, RollOver and RollOut, that we can now use to check to see if this is one of our menu tags. If the srcElement has a property named RollOver whose type is not undefined, then we know that this is one of our menu item tags that requires a style change if the user rolls over it. We set the color of the text to white and the background color to darkblue.

The document_onmouseout() function works nearly identically to the document_onmouseover() function. The only difference is the style being changed. This time we want to revert back to the default menu colors of darkblue and darkorange.

```
function document_onmouseout()
{
    var srcElement = event.srcElement;

    if (srcElement.tagName == "TD" && typeof(srcElement.RollOut) != "undefined")
    {
        srcElement.style.color = "darkblue";
        srcElement.style.backgroundColor = "darkorange";
    }
}
```

Clicking a Menu Item

The final part of the simple version of the DHTML menu system that we need to explain is the onclick event that every menu item responds to. Each <TD> tag has its onclick event handler connected to the goPage() function. This navigates the page to a new source, using the href property of the location object.

```
function goPage(src)
{
    window.location.href = src;
}
```

Putting it Together : Simple DHTML Menu Example

OK, we've seen the components of the simple menus example. Let's now create the whole page:

```
<HTML>
<HEAD>
<SCRIPT LANGUAGE=JavaScript>

function showMenu(menuToShow)
{
   var srcElement = event.srcElement;
   var xPos = parseInt(srcElement.offsetLeft);
   var yPos = parseInt(srcElement.offsetTop);

   menuToShow.style.left = xPos + (srcElement.width)
   menuToShow.style.top = yPos;
}

function hideMenu(menuToHide)
{
   if (event.toElement != menuToHide &&
      menuToHide.contains(event.toElement) == false)
   {
      menuToHide.style.left = -200;
      menuToHide.style.top = -1000;
   }
}

function document_onmouseover()
{
   var srcElement = event.srcElement;

   if (srcElement.tagName == "TD" && typeof(srcElement.RollOver) != "undefined")
   {
      srcElement.style.color = "white";
      srcElement.style.backgroundColor ="darkblue";
   }
}

function document_onmouseout()
{
   var srcElement = event.srcElement;
   if (srcElement.tagName == "TD" && typeof(srcElement.RollOut) != "undefined")
   {
      srcElement.style.color = "darkblue";
      srcElement.style.backgroundColor = "darkorange";
   }
}

function goPage(src)
{
   window.location.href = src;
}
```

479

```
document.onmouseover = document_onmouseover;
document.onmouseout = document_onmouseout;
</SCRIPT>

<STYLE>
   .DivMenu {position:absolute;
      left:-200;
      top:-1000;
      width:180;
      z-index:100;
      background-color:darkorange;
      border: 4px groove lightgrey;
   }

   .TDMenu {
      color:darkblue;
      font-family:verdana;
      font-size:70%;
      width:100%;
      cursor:default;
   }
</STYLE>
</HEAD>

<BODY>
<DIV ID="WoodMenuDiv" CLASS="DivMenu"
   onmouseout="return hideMenu(this)">
<TABLE BORDER=0 CELLSPACING=1 CELLPADDING=1 ID="WoodTable">
   <TR>
      <TD ID="WoodOak" RollOver RollOut
         onclick="goPage('OakWood.htm')"
         CLASS="TDMenu">
            Oak Timber
      </TD>
   </TR>
   <TR>
      <TD ID="WoodTeak" RollOver RollOut
         onclick="goPage('TeakWood.htm')"
         CLASS="TDMenu">
            Teak Timber
      </TD>
   </TR>
   <TR>
      <TD ID="WoodPine" RollOver RollOut
         onclick="goPage('PineWood.htm')"
         CLASS="TDMenu">
            Pine Timber
      </TD>
   </TR>
   <TR>
      <TD ID="WoodYew" RollOver RollOut
         onclick="goPage('YewWood.htm')"
         CLASS="TDMenu">
            Yew Timber
```

```
            </TD>
        </TR>
    </TABLE>
    </DIV>

    <IMG ID="WoodMenuImage"
        SRC="WoodButton.gif"
        STYLE="position:absolute;left:10;top:75"
        onmouseover="return showMenu(WoodMenuDiv)"
        onmouseout="return hideMenu(WoodMenuDiv)">
    </BODY>
    </HTML>
```

Save this as IEMenus.htm. You will also need an image, WoodButton.gif, for this example. Load it into your browser and roll your mouse pointer over the image and menu that appears. We've not created the pages for each menu item, so if you click a menu item you'll get a 'page not found' error.

The Full IE DHTML Menu Example

We've successfully completed all the DHTML functionality for our example. What we will do now is adapt the page, so that instead of writing the HTML for each menu <DIV> by hand, we'll instead create a function that will, based on information in an array, create all the <DIV> and its <TABLE>, <TR>, and <TD> tags for us, and write the information to the page using document.write().

You might think, "Why bother?" Surely the example works just fine as it is, so let's just add the metal and bricks menus and get off home.

Well yes, it does work fine, but we could make life easier for ourselves later if adding, removing, or editing a menu item could be done by simply changing the text in an array. If we want to add a menu item we simply add a few lines to an array. If we want to remove an item we simply delete a few lines. To edit a menu just involves changing the details stored in the array. It also takes up less space, so it'll be quicker to download and easier to read. Once you've read the chapters on server-side scripting and databases (Chapters 15 and 16) you could even store the menus in a database and create them using server-side script.

DHTML Code

It's time to type in the code necessary for the full menu system. The good news is that the changes, although long, are fairly simple to understand. The first change is an addition to the script block in the head of the page:

```
<HEAD>
<SCRIPT LANGUAGE=JavaScript>
```

```
var woodMenuItems = new Array();
woodMenuItems[0] = new Array();

woodMenuItems[0][0] = "Oak";
woodMenuItems[0][1] = "OakWood.htm";
woodMenuItems[0][2] = "Oak Timber";
```

```
woodMenuItems[1] = new Array();
woodMenuItems[1][0] = "Teak";
woodMenuItems[1][1] = "TeakWood.htm";
woodMenuItems[1][2] = "Teak Timber";

woodMenuItems[2] = new Array();
woodMenuItems[2][0] = "Pine";
woodMenuItems[2][1] = "PineWood.htm";
woodMenuItems[2][2] = "Pine Timber";

woodMenuItems[3] = new Array();
woodMenuItems[3][0] = "Yew";
woodMenuItems[3][1] = "YewWood.htm";
woodMenuItems[3][2] = "Yew Timber";

// Second menu
var metalMenuItems = new Array();
metalMenuItems[0] = new Array();

metalMenuItems[0][0] = "Steel";
metalMenuItems[0][1] = "SteelMetal.htm";
metalMenuItems[0][2] = "Steel Girders";

metalMenuItems[1] = new Array();
metalMenuItems[1][0] = "Copper";
metalMenuItems[1][1] = "CopperMetal.htm";
metalMenuItems[1][2] = "Copper Pipes";

metalMenuItems[2] = new Array();
metalMenuItems[2][0] = "Gold";
metalMenuItems[2][1] = "GoldMetal.htm";
metalMenuItems[2][2] = "Gold Ingots";

var bricksMenuItems = new Array();
bricksMenuItems[0] = new Array();

bricksMenuItems[0][0] = "StdHouse";
bricksMenuItems[0][1] = "StdHousebricks.htm";
bricksMenuItems[0][2] = "Standard House Brick";

bricksMenuItems[1] = new Array();
bricksMenuItems[1][0] = "LargeHouseBrick";
bricksMenuItems[1][1] = "LargeHousebricks.htm";
bricksMenuItems[1][2] = "Large House Bricks";

bricksMenuItems[2] = new Array();
bricksMenuItems[2][0] = "BreezeBlock";
bricksMenuItems[2][1] = "BreezeBlock.htm";
bricksMenuItems[2][2] = "Breeze Block";

function createMenu(menuName, menuItems)
{
    var divHTML = '<DIV ID="' + menuName + 'MenuDiv" CLASS="DivMenu"';
    divHTML = divHTML + ' onmouseout="return hideMenu(this)">';
```

```
      var tableHTML = '<TABLE BORDER=0 CELLSPACING=1 CELLPADDING=1 ID="'
        + menuName + 'Table">';
      var tableRowHTML = "";
      var rowCount;
      var totalNoRows = menuItems.length;
      for (rowCount = 0; rowCount < totalNoRows; rowCount++)
      {
         tableRowHTML = tableRowHTML + '<TR><TD ID="' +
            menuName + menuItems[rowCount][0] +
            '" RollOver RollOut';
         tableRowHTML = tableRowHTML + ' onclick="goPage(\''
            + menuItems[rowCount][1] + '\')"';
         tableRowHTML = tableRowHTML
            + 'CLASS="TDMenu">' + menuItems[rowCount][2]
            + '</TD></TR>';
      }

      return divHTML + tableHTML + tableRowHTML + '</TABLE></DIV>';
}

function showMenu(menuToShow)
{
```

The other changes are within the body of the page:

```
<BODY>
<SCRIPT LANGUAGE=JavaScript>
   document.write(createMenu('Wood', woodMenuItems))
   document.write(createMenu('Metal', metalMenuItems))
   document.write(createMenu('Bricks', bricksMenuItems))
</SCRIPT>

<IMG ID="WoodMenuImage"
   SRC="WoodButton.gif"
   STYLE="position:absolute;left:10;top:75"
   onmouseover="return showMenu(WoodMenuDiv)"
   onmouseout="return hideMenu(WoodMenuDiv)">

<IMG ID="MetalMenuImage"
   SRC="MetalButton.gif"
   STYLE="position:absolute;left:10;top:115"
   onmouseover="return showMenu(MetalMenuDiv)"
   onmouseout="return hideMenu(MetalMenuDiv)">

<IMG ID="BricksMenuImage"
   SRC="BricksButton.gif"
   STYLE="position:absolute;left:10;top:155"
   onmouseover="return showMenu(BricksMenuDiv)"
   onmouseout="return hideMenu(BricksMenuDiv)">
</BODY>
```

Re-save the page. Also note that three images are needed for this example: WoodButton.gif, MetalButton.gif, and BricksMenu.gif. You need to create these, or alternatively retrieve them from the code download for the book.

483

Load the page into your browser. Rolling the mouse pointer over any of the images causes a menu to popup with various menu options. When you pass the mouse pointer over these menu options, notice that the background and text change color. If you select a menu option it will take you to the relevant page, though as we've not created any other pages you'll just get a 'page not found' error message.

How It Works

The first thing we notice about the above code is that the tags we talked about above, such as the <DIV>, <TABLE>, <TR>, and <TD> tags, are nowhere to be found in the page. Instead we've used a function, createMenu(), which takes information from an array and uses this to create the necessary HTML for the menu, which is written out to the page using document.write(). This way we don't have to do quite as much typing.

Let's start our look at the code by looking at the menu arrays. These appear at the top of the first script block within the head of the page.

For each menu we have a separate array. Each array follows the same pattern and principles, so we'll just look at the first menu array, woodMenuItems[].

We first declare the variable woodMenuItems and set it to reference a new Array object:

```
var woodMenuItems = new Array();
```

Now, this array is going to be a multidimensional array. Therefore every element woodMenuItems[x] will also be declared as an array. Each of these inner arrays will hold information for a particular menu item.

We start this process with the array element of index 0:

```
woodMenuItems[0] = new Array();
```

Now we can use the elements of this array, namely woodMenuItems[0][0], woodMenuItems[0][1], and woodMenuItems[0][2], to hold information about the first menu item. That information will be the name of the menu item, the page to be loaded if the menu item is clicked, and finally the text to be displayed in the menu. So we see below that:

```
woodMenuItems[0][0] = "Oak";
```

holds the name of the menu,

```
woodMenuItems[0][1] = "OakWood.htm";
```

holds the page to be loaded, and

```
woodMenuItems[0][2] = "Oak Timber";
```

holds the text to be displayed in the menu.

The remainder of the menu items for the Wood menu choice follow the same pattern of defining a new Array object and inserting it in the first dimension, then making the second dimension of the array hold the name, the page to load the if item is clicked, and text to display for that menu choice.

```
woodMenuItems[1] = new Array();
woodMenuItems[1][0] = "Teak";
woodMenuItems[1][1] = "TeakWood.htm";
woodMenuItems[1][2] = "Teak Timber";

woodMenuItems[2] = new Array();
woodMenuItems[2][0] = "Pine";
woodMenuItems[2][1] = "PineWood.htm";
woodMenuItems[2][2] = "Pine Timber";

woodMenuItems[3] = new Array();
woodMenuItems[3][0] = "Yew";
woodMenuItems[3][1] = "YewWood.htm";
woodMenuItems[3][2] = "Yew Timber";
```

Although not shown here, the remainder of the menus for `metalMenuItems` and `bricksMenuItems` follow the same principles.

The function that makes use of the arrays to create the menus is the aptly named `createMenu()` function. This comes next in the first script block in the head of the page. This function creates the same HTML we saw above when discussing the principles of the menu system, but by using arrays and a function like this we make it much easier to create new menus or change existing menus. All that is involved in creating a new menu is to create the `<IMG>` tag for the menu, then add the menu details to a new array and finally call the `createMenu()` function.

The `createMenu()` function starts by building up the HTML for the start tag for the `<DIV>` and `<TABLE>` inside the `divHTML` and `tableHTML` variables. We use the `menuName` parameter passed to the function to create a unique `ID` values for the `<DIV>` and `<TABLE>` HTML:

```
function createMenu(menuName, menuItems)
{
   var divHTML = '<DIV ID="' + menuName + 'MenuDiv" CLASS="DivMenu"';
   divHTML = divHTML + ' onmouseout="return hideMenu(this)">';

   var tableHTML = '<TABLE BORDER=0 CELLSPACING=1 CELLPADDING=1 ID="'
      + menuName + 'Table">';
```

Next we loop through the items in the `menuItems` array, passed as the function's second parameter, which will be one of the three arrays created above. We create the `<TR>` and `<TD>` tags necessary for each menu item:

```
   var tableRowHTML = "";
   var rowCount;
   var totalNoRows = menuItems.length;
   for (rowCount = 0; rowCount < totalNoRows; rowCount++)
   {
      tableRowHTML = tableRowHTML + '<TR><TD ID="' +
         menuName + menuItems[rowCount][0] +
         '" RollOver RollOut';
      tableRowHTML = tableRowHTML + ' onclick="goPage(\''
         + menuItems[rowCount][1] + '\')"';
```

```
        tableRowHTML = tableRowHTML
           + 'CLASS="TDMenu">' + menuItems[rowCount][2]
           + '</TD></TR>';
    }
```

Finally we join the start tags for the `<DIV>` and `<TABLE>`, the `<TR>` and `<TD>` tags created for the menu items, and the close tags for the `<TABLE>` and `<DIV>`, and return these to the code that called the function:

```
    return divHTML + tableHTML + tableRowHTML + '</TABLE></DIV>';
}
```

Next, within a script block at the top of the body of the page, we write the menus out to the page using `document.write()`, which calls `createMenu()` to provide the HTML. This will insert exactly the same DHTML as we saw in the earlier simple version of this example. The DHTML consisting of a `<DIV>` for each menu, that is wood, metal, and bricks, with each `<DIV>` containing a table, with each row containing a menu item. The only change is that now we have the HTML for the metal and bricks menus too.

```
<SCRIPT LANGUAGE=JavaScript>
    document.write(createMenu('Wood', woodMenuItems))
    document.write(createMenu('Metal', metalMenuItems))
    document.write(createMenu('Bricks', bricksMenuItems))
</SCRIPT>
```

Following this, we also define an `<IMG>` tag for each of our menu buttons. The wood one was there before, but we've now added one for the metal menu and one for the bricks menu, using exactly the same principles.

Dynamic HTML in Netscape Navigator 4.x

As we said at the beginning of the chapter, the DHTML supported by Netscape Navigator (NN) 4.x is very, very different from that supported in IE 4.0+, due to the differences between the BOMs for the browsers. There are still some similarities, such as the use of style sheets, and using the ID in HTML tags to identify tags, but the programming is quite different. NN 4.x supports style sheets that allow the attributes of tags to be defined as the page loads, but, generally speaking, its ability to change the page after loading is more limited than what is possible with IE. Also, where IE makes every tag on a page available to us as a particular object type with its own specific properties, methods, and events (for example the `<DIV>` tag has the `Div` object, the `<P>` tag with the `P` object), NN 4.x only makes some tags available in this way. Most tags are instead represented by just one object type, the `Layer` object. This object is key to NN 4.x DHTML.

The <LAYER> Tag and Layer Object

First introduced in NN 4.0 and deprecated in NN 6, the `<LAYER>` tag, represented in scripting as the `Layer` object, is the key to dynamically changing content on a page once it has been loaded.

The easiest way to think of layers is as separate windows in the page, even to the extent of having their own `document` objects that we can use.

Creating Layers

There are a number of ways of creating a `Layer` object. Here we'll concentrate on three of them. The first two ways are explicit creation using the `<LAYER>` and `<ILAYER>` tags. The third way is by positioning the element as absolute or relative with style sheets, in which case NN reflects the element into JavaScript as a `Layer` object whose properties, such as `left`, `top`, `visibility`, and `content`, we can change.

The `Layer` objects in a page can be referenced in the `document` object's `layers` array property, by index or `ID` value.

`<LAYER>` and `<ILAYER>` Tags

The simplest way to create a `Layer` object is by using either the `<LAYER>` or the `<ILAYER>` tag. The `<LAYER>` tag produces an invisible rectangle of screen space in 'front' of other non-layer content in the page. It is positioned absolutely, and can be repositioned, as well as written to, after the page has loaded. The `<ILAYER>` tag creates an inline layer, which is positioned relatively and can be repositioned. However, changing content inside its `document` is very difficult and usually best avoided.

Both `<LAYER>` and `<ILAYER>` tags can contain other tags and help group things together.

We would define a normal `<LAYER>` like this:

```
<LAYER ID="myLayer1" LEFT="100" TOP="250">
   <H3>Content within the layer</H3>
   <P>a paragraph in a layer</P>
</LAYER>
```

For an inline layer, it is a nearly identical definition. What changes is that `LEFT` is not absolute left, but relative to the previous tag. The same applies to the `TOP` attribute.

```
<ILAYER ID="myILayer1" LEFT="100" TOP="250">
   <H3>Content within the ilayer</H3>
   <P>a paragraph in an ilayer</P>
</ILAYER>
```

To reference either of the two layers above from JavaScript, we just use its `ID` via the `document` object. For example, to move the `<LAYER>` tag with `ID` of `myLayer1`, we would use:

```
document.myLayer1.left = 200;
```

and to change the background color of the `<ILAYER>` tag with `ID` of `myILayer1`, we would use:

```
document.myILayer1.bgColor = "red";
```

Implicit Layer Creation

To implicitly create a `layer` object for any tag, we need to use style sheets to specify that it be positioned absolutely or relatively. We saw how to do this at the beginning of the chapter. If we do this, then NN will automatically create a `Layer` object for the tag, although we need to remember to give it an `ID` value to make it easier to reference later. Even without an `ID`, it's possible to access a `Layer` object in a page via the `document` object's `layers` array property, but using `ID` values makes identifying which tag the code is acting on that much easier.

For example, if we defined a <DIV> tag with absolute positioning, like this:

```
<DIV STYLE="position:absolute;left:0px;top:100px;" ID="div1">
<P>
    My absolute positioned div containing a paragraph
</P>
</DIV>
```

we can access the Layer object implicitly created by using the unique ID:

```
document.div1.left = 200;
```

An alternative method of specifying the style is to use the <STYLE> tag to create style classes, and then use a tag's CLASS attribute to set its style to a predefined class, as we saw at the beginning of the chapter.

Although we've used a <DIV> in the example, it is possible to use many of the HTML tags available. However, while it's possible, it's not generally a good idea to do so due to bugs in Netscape, particularly the earlier versions of NN 4. The <DIV> and <SPAN> tags work fine as far as positioning goes, but other tags can prove more risky – they might work or you might find all sorts of problems.

Moving Layers

The Layer object has two properties that allow us to re-position a layer after the page has loaded; these are top and left. They take values, in pixels, which re-position the layer.

For example, if our <LAYER> tag was defined like this:

```
<LAYER ID="myLayer1" LEFT="100" TOP="250">
    <H3>Content within the layer</H3>
    <P>a paragraph in a layer</P>
</LAYER>
```

we could re-position it (absolutely, since the <LAYER> tag is automatically positioned absolutely) using the script below:

```
document.myLayer.left = 500;
document.myLayer.top = 100;
```

Additionally, the Layer object has the moveTo() and moveBy() methods in which we can specify the horizontal and vertical movement of the Layer in one go. The method moveTo() moves to a point on the screen specified by the parameters, and moveBy() moves the tag along and down by the parameters passed. They work with both absolutely and relatively positioned layers, though the moveTo() method will use the coordinate system of the containing tag rather than the page if it is for a relatively positioned layer.

For example, if we want to reposition our layer at 200 pixels across the screen and at 150 pixels down the screen we could write:

```
myLayer1.MoveTo(200,150);
```

If we want to move our layer by a certain number of pixels, for example if the layer is at 100 along by 200 down and we want to move it along 10 pixels and up 5 pixels we'd write:

```
myLayerMoveBy(10,-5);
```

Note how a negative value moves the layer up the screen.

What would happen if two layers were placed on top of each other?

Well, the order of the layers is determined by their Z-INDEX attribute. The higher the value of this attribute, the further into the foreground the layer becomes. We can define this when we create the tag, for example:

```
<LAYER ID="myLayer1" LEFT="100" TOP="250" Z-INDEX="1">
    <H3>Content within the layer</H3>
    <P>a paragraph in a layer</P>
</LAYER>
```

This layer will be positioned above any layers with a Z-INDEX of 0. As it happens, 0 is the default value if we don't specify the Z-INDEX attribute, and so this element will be positioned above all elements without a defined Z-INDEX attribute.

We can change the Z-INDEX attribute value after the page has loaded via script. We can either specify the Z-INDEX directly using the zIndex property of the Layer object (note the omission of the hyphen), or we can use the moveAbove() and moveBelow() methods of the Layer object. Both methods take as a parameter the ID of the Layer object we want to move above or below.

Try It Out – The z-index

Let's look at this in the simple example shown below where we have two partially overlapping <DIV> tags each with a different z-index style attributes. As each <DIV> is positioned absolutely using style sheets, a Layer object will be created for each <DIV>, accessible via the unique ID attribute specified in each <DIV> tag's HTML.

```
<HTML>
<HEAD>
<STYLE>
    DIV { position: absolute; left : 100; }
</STYLE>
</HEAD>

<BODY>
<DIV ID="layer1" STYLE="background-color: red; top: 100;z-index: 2">
HHHHHHHH
<BR>
HHHHHHHH
<BR>
HHHHHHHH
</DIV>
<DIV ID="layer2" STYLE="background-color: blue; top: 120; z-index: 1">
XXXXXXXX
<BR>
```

```
XXXXXXXX
<BR>
XXXXXXXX
</DIV>
<FORM>
<INPUT TYPE="button" VALUE="Red Div Above" onclick="layer1.moveAbove(layer2)"
   NAME=button1>
<INPUT TYPE="button" VALUE="Red Div Below" onclick="layer1.moveBelow(layer2)"
   NAME=button2>
</BODY>
</HTML>
```

Save this as `zindex_NN.htm`, and load it into a NN 4.x browser. You should get a page similar to the following. Note that the red `<DIV>` (with the H values) is uppermost.

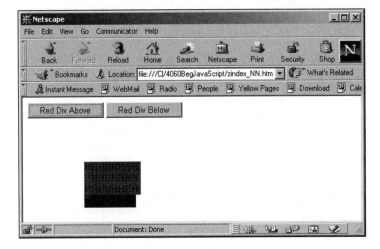

If you press the **Red Div Below** button, the page will change to the following.

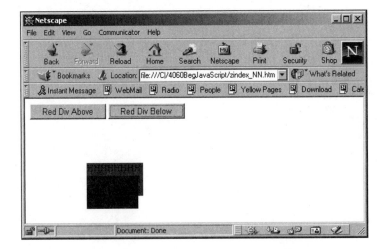

The uppermost <DIV> is now blue (containing X values). Click the **Red Div Above** button, and the page will change back to how it was before.

How It Works

In the body of the page we define two <DIV> tags, each positioned absolutely using a style class. The first <DIV> has a red background, has a z-index of 2, and is filled with HHHHHHH. The second has a blue background, has a z-index of 1, and is filled with XXXXXXX. Initially, as the blue <DIV> has a lower z-index number, it is partially hidden by the red <DIV>. However, the code in the **Red Div Below** button's onclick event handler:

```
layer1.moveBelow(layer2);
```

causes the red layer, layer1, to move below layer2, which we pass as a parameter to the moveBelow() method. Hit the **Red Div Above** button and this time its onclick event handler contains:

```
layer1.moveAbove(layer2);
```

which moves the red <DIV> above the blue <DIV>.

Try It Out – Moving Netscape Paragraphs

Let's look at another example. We'll re-write the MovingTags_IE.htm example we created for IE, so that it will work with NN 4.x.

The code for the NN moving paragraphs is almost identical to the IE version, so load MovingTags_IE.htm into your web page editor and make the four line alterations necessary:

```
<HTML>
<HEAD>
<SCRIPT LANGUAGE=JavaScript>

var paraOneLeft = 100;
var paraTwoLeft = 400;
var switchDirection = false;

function window_onload()
{
    window.setInterval("moveParas()",50);
}

function moveParas()
{
    if (switchDirection == false)
    {
        paraOneLeft++;
        paraTwoLeft--;
        if (paraOneLeft == 400)
        {
            switchDirection = true;
        }
```

```
        }
        else
        {
            paraOneLeft--;
            paraTwoLeft++;

            if (paraOneLeft == 100)
            {
                switchDirection = false;
            }
        }

        document.para1.left = paraOneLeft;
        document.para2.left = paraTwoLeft;
    }

</SCRIPT>
</HEAD>
<BODY LANGUAGE=JavaScript onload="return window_onload()">

<DIV ID="para1" STYLE="position:absolute;left:100;top:30"><P>Para 1</P></DIV>
<DIV ID="para2" STYLE="position:absolute;left:400;top:10"><P>Para 2</P></DIV>

</BODY>
</HTML>
```

Save the page as `MovingTags_NN.htm`.

How It Works

The page is identical to `MovingTags_IE.htm` apart from four lines. First there are the two lines of HTML defining the paragraphs:

```
<DIV ID="para1" STYLE="position:absolute;left:100;top:30"><P>Para 1</P></DIV>
<DIV ID="para2" STYLE="position:absolute;left:400;top:10"><P>Para 2</P></DIV>
```

We've moved the paragraphs inside `<DIV>` tags, which we have given the same ID values and properties that the paragraph tags had in the IE version. The big question is, of course, why?

Well, as mentioned earlier, while we can in theory position most tags with style sheets and then move them about with their `Layer` object, this can be rather risky due to bugs in the Netscape browser, bugs that vary with operating system and version of Netscape. Sometimes it will work and we'll get away with it, and other times it leads to disaster. We'd probably get away with doing this with the `<P>` tag, but trying to move tables, table cells, lists, and so on could prove a bad move and is best avoided. So for safety reasons I've used `<DIV>` tags in the examples.

The second two lines that have changed are those that assign the left positions of the paragraphs with the revised values:

```
document.para1.left = paraOneLeft;
document.para2.left = paraTwoLeft;
```

With NN we specify the `document` object, but don't need to specify the `style` object as we did in the IE version. For comparison in the IE version, these two lines were:

```
para1.style.left = paraOneLeft;
para2.style.left = paraTwoLeft;
```

Although the code is very similar it hides big differences underneath. With IE we are referencing the `style` object of the tag itself. With NN we are not actually accessing the tag, but instead the `Layer` object that was created for the tag and placed in the `layers[]` array property of the `document` object.

Changing Content Within a Layer

We mentioned above that it's best to think of layers as windows in the page, and this is particularly relevant when changing the content inside a layer. Every `Layer` object has the `document` property, which gives access to that layer's document, just as the `document` property of the `window` object gives access to the page within a window. We can do many of the things to a `Layer`'s document that we can do to a `window`'s document. For example we can use the `document.write()` method to re-write HTML to the `Layer`'s document.

For example, if we had an `<DIV>` tag defined like this:

```
<DIV ID=myDIV STYLE="position:absolute;left:10;top:10"
<H2>
    A Heading
</H2>
</DIV>
```

then to change the content inside the `<DIV>` and remove the `<H2>` tag, we first open the `<DIV>` tag's `Layer` object's `document`:

```
document.myDiv.document.open();
```

Then we just use `document.write()` method:

```
document.myDiv.document.write("<P>Now it's a paragraph</P>");
```

We close the document once we've finished adding content, otherwise any later `document.write()`'s will add to and not replace the HTML inside the `Layer`.

```
document.myDiv.document.close();
```

We're not restricted as to what HTML we insert, as long as it's valid and we make sure the appropriate close tags are used.

Layer Events

Unfortunately, although IE provides every tag with many new events, under NN 4.x we're generally left with the standard HTML events made available in version 3 browsers. The `Layer` object has events including `onmouseover`, `onmouseout`, `onmouseup`, `onload`, `onfocus`, and `onblur`.

With a `Layer` object created by a `<LAYER>` tag or an `<ILAYER>` tag, we can use our standard method of attaching code to the event handler as an attribute of the tag.

For example, if we have a `Layer` object defined using the `<LAYER>` tag and we want to connect the function `myLayer_onmouseover()` to the `onmouseover` event handler, we just add the `onmouseover` attribute to the tag's definition:

```
<LAYER ID="myLayer" LEFT=10 TOP=10 onmouseover="myLayer_onmouseOver()">
   Layer HTML
</LAYER>
```

However, if it's an implicitly created `Layer` object, as with absolutely or relatively positioned tags, then we can't simply add the event name to the tag's HTML definition. For example, if we have a `<DIV>` which, due to being positioned absolutely, has a `Layer` object defined for it and we want to connect that `Layer` object's `onmouseover` event handler to the function `myDiv_onmouseover()`, then we need to write the following:

```
<DIV ID="myDiv" STYLE="position:absolute;left:10;top:10">
   <P>A paragraph inside the div</P>
</DIV>

<SCRIPT LANGUAGE="JavaScript">
   document.myDiv.onMouseOver = myDiv_onmouseover();
</SCRIPT>
```

We need to have defined the function `myDiv_onmouseover()` earlier in the page, prior to trying to connect it to the `onmouseover` event handler.

Try It Out – Roll Over Heading

In the earlier section on IE DHTML, we had an example where the color of a paragraph changed when the user's mouse pointer rolled over it, and then reverted back when it rolled out. Let's try the same in NN:

```
<HTML>
<BODY>
<DIV ID=RollOverDiv STYLE="position:absolute;left:10;top:10">
   <P STYLE='color:black'>Roll your mouse over me</P>
</DIV>

<SCRIPT LANGUAGE=JavaScript>
function RollOverDiv_mouseOver()
{
   document.RollOverDiv.document.open();
   document.RollOverDiv.document.write("<P STYLE='color:red'>" +
      "Wow that feels good</P>");
   document.RollOverDiv.document.close();
}

function RollOverDiv_mouseOut()
{
```

```
      document.RollOverDiv.document.open();
      document.RollOverDiv.document.write("<P STYLE='color:black'>" +
        "Roll your mouse over me</P>");
      document.RollOverDiv.document.close();
  }

  document.RollOverDiv.onMouseOver = RollOverDiv_mouseOver
  document.RollOverDiv.onMouseOut = RollOverDiv_mouseOut
  </SCRIPT>

  </BODY>
  </HTML>
```

Save the page as `RollOverHeading_NN.htm` and load it in your browser. When the mouse pointer rolls over the text, the text changes and turns red.

How It Works

At the top of the page we define our `<DIV>` tag:

```
<DIV ID=RollOverDiv STYLE="position:absolute;left:10;top:10">
  <P STYLE='color:black'>Roll your mouse over me</P>
</DIV>
```

As it has been positioned absolutely through its `STYLE` attribute, a `Layer` object will be created for it, which we can access to make the rollover changes.

In the following script block we define two functions, which will be the ones connected to the `onmouseover` and `onmouseout` events of the `<DIV>`.

```
function RollOverDiv_mouseOver()
{
    document.RollOverDiv.document.open();
    document.RollOverDiv.document.write("<P STYLE='color:red'>" +
        "Wow that feels good</P>");
    document.RollOverDiv.document.close();
}

function RollOverDiv_mouseOut()
{
    document.RollOverDiv.document.open();
    document.RollOverDiv.document.write("<P STYLE='color:black'>" +
        "Roll your mouse over me</P>");
    document.RollOverDiv.document.close();
}
```

In both functions we access the `<DIV>` tag's `Layer` object's document using:

```
document.RollOverDiv.document
```

We substitute new HTML inside the layer's document using document.write(). When the mouse pointer rolls over the <DIV>, we write a different paragraph and make its color red. When it rolls out of the heading, we write the original text and color into the document. In both cases we make sure that we close the document using the document.close() method. If we don't do this we'll find that instead of replacing the HTML in the document the next time we roll over or roll out of the header with our mouse pointer, we'll keep adding to it instead.

The final thing to do in the script block is to connect the onmouseover and onmouseout events of the Layer object for the paragraph tag to our functions:

```
document.RollOverDiv.onMouseOver = RollOverDiv_mouseOver
document.RollOverDiv.onMouseOut = RollOverDiv_mouseOut
```

The NN event Object

NN, like IE, also supports an event object, which, like the IE version, contains properties that help us find out more about the event that fired. However the name and purpose is almost all that the two objects have in common.

An event object is created automatically for us whenever an event occurs. Unlike IE, it's not available globally, but instead only in the event handler's code. This means that if we want to access the event object, for example from a function called by an event handler, then we need to pass the event object to the function as a parameter when we define our event handler.

For example, below we have an <A> tag whose onclick event handler is connected to a function, mylink_onclick(), that we've written:

```
<SCRIPT LANGUAGE=JavaScript>
function mylink_onclick ()
{
// Event Code
}
</SCRIPT>

<A HREF="#" ID=myLink onclick="myLink_onclick()">My Link</A>
```

To make use of the event object, we need to change the definition of the <A> tag so that the event object, which is available only in the event connection code, is passed to the mylink_onclick() function:

```
<SCRIPT LANGUAGE=JavaScript>
function mylink_onclick(theEventObject)
{
    alert(theEventObject.type);
}
</SCRIPT>

<A HREF="#" ID=myLink onclick="myLink_onclick(event)">My Link</A>
```

In the above code, the alert box will display the event object's type property, which is the type of event that was fired, such as click, mouseout, mouseover, and so on.

Alternatively, if we're connecting an event handler directly to a function as a property rather than an attribute, for example:

```
document.onclick = myFunction()
```

then we just define a parameter in the definition of the event handling function, `myFuntion()`, which will automatically be set to the relevant `event` object by JavaScript:

```
function myEventHandler(eventObject)
{
    alert(eventObject.type);
}
```

The parameter `eventObject` will automatically reference the `event` object without us needing to do a thing – we can simply use it.

Try It Out – The NN event Object

In the example below we demonstrate some of the `event` object's properties.

```
<HTML>
<HEAD>
<SCRIPT LANGUAGE=JavaScript>

function document_onclick(evtObj)
{
    if (evtObj.which == 1)
    {
        document.xLayer.left = evtObj.x;
        document.xLayer.top = evtObj.y;
    }
}

document.onclick = document_onclick;

</SCRIPT>
</HEAD>

<BODY>

<LAYER ID="xLayer" TOP=-100 LEFT=0>
    <H3>X</H3>
</LAYER>

</BODY>
</HTML>
```

Save this code as `EventObject_NN.htm`, and load into your NN 4.x browser. When the document in the browser is clicked with the left mouse button, an X is placed at that point in the page.

While this is not that useful as it is, we could alter the example so that instead of an X, a popup menu appears with a list of options the user can choose from.

497

How It Works

First we define the <LAYER> tag that will hold the X. We could have defined a <DIV> tag and used the Layer object created automatically – this just demonstrates a variation. It's this Layer that will be moved to the position of the latest mouse click giving the effect that an X has been placed on the spot the user just clicked on. By setting the TOP attribute of the <LAYER> to -100 we can be sure that the layer will start off being displayed off screen – we only want the user to see the X the first time they actually click the page.

```
<LAYER ID="xLayer" TOP=-100 LEFT=0>
    <H3>X</H3>
</LAYER>
```

The code works by connecting the document object's onclick event handler to our function document_onclick().

```
document.onclick = document_onclick();
```

We've connected to the event in this way, because there is no tag defining the document that we can add the onclick event handler to as an attribute.

The function itself makes use of the event object, which is automatically passed as the first parameter when we connect as we have above.

```
function document_onclick(evtObj)
{
    if (evtObj.which == 1)
    {
        document.xLayer.left = evtObj.x;
        document.xLayer.top = evtObj.y;
    }
}
```

The first property of the event object we use is the which property in the if statement. The which property contains either 1 for the left mouse button, 2 for the middle button, or 3 for the right button. If a key was pressed, then instead the which property contains the ASCII value of the key pressed. Note that some ASCII characters are unavailable because they are hotkeys, like *F1*, and *Ctrl-A*.

If the left mouse button was pressed, then we move the layer, xLayer, to the current mouse position, which is contained in the event object's x and y properties.

That completes the brief tour of DHTML under NN. Our final task is to create the same dynamic menus that we created under IE.

Dynamic Menus in NN 4.x

For the NN 4.x version of the DHTML menus, we'll be using a number of the same principles we used in the IE 4.0+ version. Firstly we'll be creating the menus themselves using information in an array that is virtually identical to the IE array, except that we've added an extra bit of information. We'll also be using the same idea of hiding the menus off screen until the user's mouse rolls over the image. The key difference between the versions of the code is that we're using layers for our menus rather than tables and <DIV> tags. The NN version is shown in the screenshots opposite:

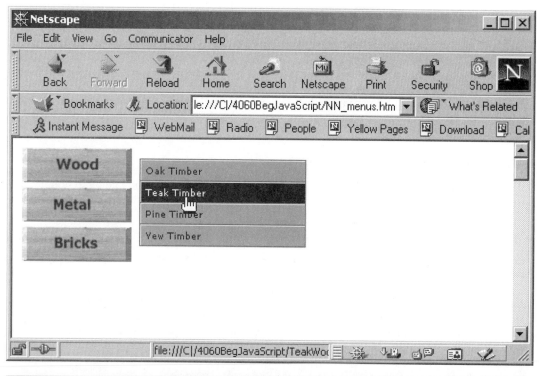

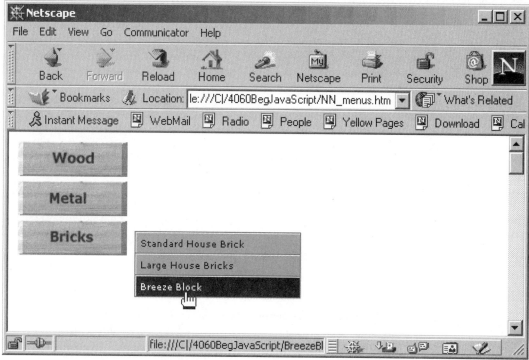

Just like the IE version, when you roll the mouse pointer over the menu images another sub-menu pops out with options you can choose from. Again as the mouse pointer rolls over a menu item it changes background and text color to give a visual indication of the menu item currently selected.

As with the IE version we'll first look at the principles behind the menu system, then we will look at the HTML, style sheets, and code necessary to create a simplified version of the menu system. Then we'll make changes to this simpler version so that all the dynamic HTML is written into the page using `document.write()`, gaining its information from arrays, as with the IE version. Finally we'll wrap up by explaining the new code.

THE NN DHTML Menu System Principles

If you were happy with the principles behind the IE menu system then you're going to find the Netscape version almost identical, in principle at least. The main changes are the tags used and the code used to manipulate those tags. You'll find the `<DIV>` tags of the IE version have mostly been replaced by `<LAYER>` tags.

Let's briefly run down the high-level principles of the Netscape system. Once we've done that we'll take a detailed look at all the tags and code necessary.

As with the IE version we have an `<IMG>` tag – when the user runs their mouse pointer over it, a menu appears just to the right of the image. With the IE version, the menu was contained in a `<DIV>` tag containing the various menu items. With the NN version the menu items are now stored in a `<LAYER>` tag. As with the IE version, the `<LAYER>` tag for the menu starts life off screen. When we want to display it we simply move it onto the screen at the correct position. When the mouse pointer leaves the image or the menu layer, we hide the menu `<LAYER>` off screen.

With IE we found that the `<DIV>` tag's `onmouseout` event handler was called not just if the mouse pointer left the `<DIV>` but also if it went "inside" the `<DIV>` and over elements in there. With the `<LAYER>` tag this does not happen – the `onmouseout` event handler only fires when the mouse pointer leaves the `<LAYER>` altogether, not when it goes inside the `<LAYER>`. This makes it easier for our coding.

In the IE version each menu item was contained inside a table row and table cell inside the menu `<DIV>`. When the user rolled their mouse pointer from one row to another we changed the `style` object of the table cell to indicate which menu the user was selecting. In the NN version, we still give the appearance of highlighting a menu item when the mouse pointer rolls over it, but the HTML and code is very different. In the NN version each menu item is contained inside its own `<LAYER>` tag. Initially each menu item is simply plain blue text on an orange background. When the user's mouse pointer rolls over the tag, we write HTML to the menu item `Layer`'s document, the HTML being simply a hyperlink, but with style sheets providing the change of appearance by making the hyperlink text white and removing the underlining. We also change the `Layer` object's background to blue. If the hyperlink is clicked then the user is taken to the page specific to that menu item and specified in the `<A>` tag's `HREF` attribute. When the mouse pointer rolls off the menu item `Layer`, we rewrite the plain text to its document.

DHTML Menus Simple Version

As with the IE version, in this simple NN version we'll only create the wood menu – we'll add the metal and bricks menus when we build the final version. We'll create all the code and HTML except the parts that build up our page with `document.write()` and arrays.

The DHTML

First we have the image over which the user rolls their mouse pointer to display the menu:

```
<LAYER ID=WoodMenuImgLayer
    onmouseover="showNNMenu(event)"
    onmouseout="hideNNMenu(event)"
    LEFT=10
    TOP=10>
        <IMG SRC="WoodButton.gif" BORDER=0>
</LAYER>
```

The image is inside a <LAYER> tag with a unique ID, which is positioned absolutely using the <LAYER> tag's LEFT and TOP attributes. We use the associated Layer object to capture the onmouseover and onmouseout events and also to calculate where the menu layers needs to be positioned. We've set the onmouseover event handler to call showNNMenu() and pass the event object as a parameter. The event handler onmouseout calls the function hideNNMenu() and again passes the event object.

Each menu is also contained in a <LAYER> tag:

```
<LAYER ID="WoodMenuLayer" LEFT=120 TOP=-1400 Z-INDEX=99
    onmouseout="this.top = -1400;">
</LAYER>
```

We've given the tag a unique ID and used the <LAYER> tag's LEFT and TOP attributes to set it off screen. The Z-INDEX attribute is set to 99 just to make sure it appears in front of any other layers on the screen. (A word of warning – while the menu will appear in front of most content, the way Netscape handles forms means that the menu layer will appear behind a form and there's little we can do about this.) Finally we've added an event handler for the onmouseout event that causes the menu to hide itself by setting the top style attribute to -1400 – well and truly off screen – if the mouse pointer moves off the menu. This differs from the IE version where we called the hide menu function in this event handler's code.

So far what we have is an empty menu layer, so lets add the first menu item, that representing Oak Timber:

```
<LAYER ID="WoodMenuLayer" LEFT=120 TOP=-1400 Z-INDEX=99
    onmouseout="this.top = -1400;">
        <LAYER ID="WoodOak" TOP=0 LEFT=0
            CLASS="LayerItemMenu"
            WIDTH=175 HEIGHT=20
            BGCOLOR="orange"
            onmouseover="showOverMenu(this,'Oak Timber','OakWood.htm')"
            onmouseout="showOutMenu(this,'Oak Timber')">
            Oak Timber
        </LAYER>
</LAYER>
```

Each menu item is represented by its own <LAYER> tag. We've given it a unique ID, WoodOak, and set its TOP and LEFT attributes to zero so that it appears at the top left of the inside of the <LAYER> tag with ID WoodMenuLayer. We've applied the style class LayerOutMenu that gives it its appearance – we'll see the style defined later. The <LAYER> tag has the BGCOLOR attribute, which here we've defined as orange. Style sheets can be used to define the background, but in Netscape using style sheets tends to mean that the background is given a border, letting the page beneath show through.

When the user's mouse pointer rolls over the menu item, we want to change the menu item layer's style. When it rolls out again, we want to change the style back. To do this we've added the `onmouseover` and `onmouseout` event handlers, which call `showOverMenu()` and `showOutMenu()` functions respectively. We'll create and look at these functions later.

All the other menu items follow exactly the same pattern, the differences being the unique ID for the layer, the TOP attribute that specifies the position of the `<LAYER>` within the outer menu `<LAYER>`, and the values passed to the `showOverMenu()` and `showOutMenu()` functions. Let's add all the other menu items:

```
<LAYER ID="WoodMenuLayer" LEFT=120 TOP=-1400 Z-INDEX=99
    onmouseout="this.top = -1400;">
    <LAYER ID="WoodOak" TOP=0 LEFT=0
        CLASS="LayerItemMenu"
        WIDTH=175 HEIGHT=20
        BGCOLOR="orange"
        onmouseover="showOverMenu(this,'Oak Timber','OakWood.htm')"
        onmouseout="showOutMenu(this,'Oak Timber')">
            Oak Timber
    </LAYER>
    <LAYER ID="WoodTeak" TOP=22 LEFT=0
        CLASS="LayerItemMenu"
        WIDTH=175 height=20
        BGCOLOR="orange"
        onmouseover="showOverMenu(this,'Teak Timber','TeakWood.htm')"
        onmouseout="showOutMenu(this,'Teak Timber')">Teak Timber
    </LAYER>
    <LAYER ID="WoodPine" TOP=44 LEFT=0
        CLASS="LayerItemMenu"
        WIDTH=175 height=20
        BGCOLOR="orange"
        onmouseover="showOverMenu(this,'Pine Timber','PineWood.htm')"
        onmouseout="showOutMenu(this,'Pine Timber')">Pine Timber
    </LAYER>
    <LAYER ID="WoodYew" TOP=66 LEFT=0
        CLASS="LayerItemMenu"
        WIDTH=175 height=20
        BGCOLOR="orange"
        onmouseover="showOverMenu(this,'Yew Timber','YewWood.htm')"
        onmouseout="showOutMenu(this,'Yew Timber')">Yew Timber
    </LAYER>
</LAYER>
```

The Style Sheets

Our HTML makes use of a number of style classes, so let's look at them in turn.

First we want to avoid any borders round our images or layers, as they tend to mess up the appearance and cause problems with `onmouseover` and `onmouseout` events. For example, if there's a border then even though to the user it looks like their mouse pointer has moved outside the image, the `onmouseout` event does not fire since their mouse pointer is on the invisible border. Note that Netscape adds its own 3 pixel border around all elements anyway. So, the first thing we do in our style sheet is limit borders by specifying a style that will apply to all `<LAYER>` and `<IMG>` tags:

```
<STYLE>
   LAYER { border : none 0px;}
   IMG { border : none 0px;}
```

Next we need to specify the appearance of menu items:

```
.LayerItemMenu
{
   font-family:verdana;
   font-size:60%;
   margin:0;
   padding:0;
   border: 3px groove lightgrey;
}
```

We've seen this class used for the menu item <LAYER> tags above. As well as specifying font-family and size, we've also tried to limit any possible padding or margins around our elements as we want the menu items to sit as close as possible to each other. Finally, we specify a 3 pixel wide grooved border in light gray. (Note, for some odd reason, the British English spelling of gray with an e. This only happens with lightgrey and not with gray!)

The final style class we need is for the links inside the menu items when they are rolled over by the mouse pointer. We'll see this in use when we see the showOverMenu() function.

```
.textLink { color: white; text-decoration: none;}
</STYLE>
```

Showing and Hiding the Menus

Let's start with the function that displays the menu when the mouse pointer rolls over a menu image, the showNNMenu() function:

```
function showNNMenu(evt)
{
   var srcLayer = evt.target;
   var menuLayerId = new String(srcLayer.name).replace("ImgLayer","Layer");
   document.layers[menuLayerId].top = srcLayer.pageY;
   document.layers[menuLayerId].left = parseInt(srcLayer.pageX +
      srcLayer.clip.width + 4);
}
```

The function has just one parameter, evt, which is the event object that we pass in the onmouseover event handler connected to the <LAYER> round the image. Remember the event object is something the browser creates for us automatically and populates with various useful pieces of information about the event that fired.

The first line of the function uses the event object's target property, which passes us a reference to the object element that is at the center of the event, in this case the Layer object of the <LAYER> tag we put our <IMG> inside.

We know which layer was rolled over, but we don't know which menu layer we need to display. However, we can find out easily, because of the naming convention we've used. All <LAYER> tags around menu images are named WoodMenuImgLayer or MetalMenuImgLayer or BrickMenuImgLayer. You can see that what they have in common is they all start with the name of the menu to be displayed and all end with the words MenuImgLayer. Now all our menu item <LAYER> tags also follow a similar convention being named WoodMenuLayer, MetalMenuLayer, and BricksMenuLayer. Again they start with the name of the menu and end with MenuLayer. Given this information we know that if WoodMenuImgLayer has been rolled over, then we need to display the WoodMenuLayer layer. How can we deal with this in code? Easy – we just replace the ImgLayer part with Layer and, hey presto, we have the unique ID of the menu layer we need to display. This is exactly what the second line of the function does.

Now we know what layer we need to move onto the screen, we can do so on the third and fourth lines. We use document.layers[] to access the layers array property of the document object, which gives us a reference to the Layer object whose ID we pass inside the square brackets. In our case, it's the ID inside variable menuLayerId, the ID of the Layer holding the menu items. First we set the top property of this Layer object to the same level as the srcLayer, that is the layer around the image that was rolled over. Then in the final line we set the left property of the menu Layer object to be the left property of the Layer object round the image, plus the width of the image. We add 4 on as well, just to make sure the layer round the image and the menu layer don't overlap – otherwise the onmouseout and onmouseover events won't fire correctly.

We've seen how to show the menu layer, so now let's look at the function that hides it when the mouse pointer leaves the image. This is connected to the onmouseout event handler of the layer around the image.

```
function hideNNMenu(evt)
{
   var srcLayer = evt.target;
   if (evt.pageX < srcLayer.clip.right)
   {
      var menuLayerId = new String(srcLayer.name).replace("ImgLayer","Layer");
      document.layers[menuLayerId].top = -1400;
   }
}
```

If the user moves their mouse pointer off the layer around the image, above, below or to the left of it, then we want to hide the menu again. However, if the mouse pointer moves to the right off the image, it will pass over to the menu's layer, so we do not want to hide it.

The event object, passed as a parameter evt to the function, contains all the information we need to find out where the mouse pointer has moved. Again we declare and set variable srcLayer to the target of the event, namely the Layer object of the <LAYER> tag around the <IMG> tag. Then if evt.pageX, the current horizontal position of the mouse pointer on the page, is less than the right edge of the layer round the image, we hide the menu by setting it off screen. The right edge of the image is available through the clip.right property of the Layer object.

As with the showNNMenu() function, we find out which menu layer we need to hide from the ID of the Layer round the image. Using that, we just need to replace the ImgLayer part with Layer and we have the ID that we can use to get a reference to the Layer to hide, using the document.layers array. We can then set this menu Layer off screen by setting its top property to an appropriate value.

Menu Rollover and Rollout Style Changes

Let's look at the `showOverMenu()` function, the function that changes the style of a menu item when we roll over it. This function is connected to the `onmouseover` event handler for each `<LAYER>` containing a menu item:

```
function showOverMenu(menuLayer, menuText, menuPage)
{
    menuLayer.bgColor = "blue";
    menuLayer.document.open();
    menuLayer.document.write('<DIV CLASS="LayerItemMenu">');
    menuLayer.document.write('<A HREF="' + menuPage + '" CLASS="textLink">'
        + menuText + '</A>');
    menuLayer.document.write('</DIV>')
    menuLayer.document.close();
}
```

The function has three parameters. The first is the `Layer` object for the menu item layer we want to change. The second parameter is the text of the menu we want to display, such as `Oak Timber`, and the third is the source for the hyperlink that takes the user to the page for that menu item, for example the `OakWood.htm` page for the Oak Timber menu item.

In the first line we use the `Layer` object referenced in `menuLayer` to set the background color to blue. Then we open the layer's document for writing and write a `<DIV>`, inside which is a hyperlink (`<A>`) that if clicked will take the user to the page relevant for that menu item. Note we're using the style classes defined earlier in the style sheet for the `<DIV>` and `<A>` tags. Apart from applying style to the tags, the class for the `<A>` tag also makes sure that the link has white text and is not underlined like a link would normally be.

Finally we close the `document.write()` – next time we use `document.write()` it will clear the current contents.

The `showOutMenu()` function works in a similar way to the `showOverMenu()` in that it uses `document.write()` to change the contents of the HTML inside the menu item layer so it's back to a non rolled over look. It is called by the `onmouseout` event handler for each `<LAYER>` containing a menu item.

```
function showOutMenu(menuLayer, menuText)
{
    menuLayer.bgColor = "orange";
    menuLayer.document.open();
    menuLayer.document.write('<DIV CLASS="LayerItemMenu">' +
        menuText + '</DIV>');
    menuLayer.document.close();
}
```

This time there are just two parameters, the `Layer` object of the menu item that needs to be acted upon, and the text to be displayed. As no hyperlink will be created (after all how can the user click on a link if they are not over it?), there is no need for the final hyperlink `source` parameter of the previous function.

In the first line, we set the background color of the menu item back to orange. Then, we start the document writing with an `open()` method and just write out our `<DIV>` and the text to be displayed inside it. Finally we close the layer's `document`.

Putting it Together : Simple DHTML Menu Example

Well, that's all the HTML and code we need for our simple version, so let's create that in a full page:

```
<HTML>
<HEAD>

<STYLE>
   LAYER { border : none 0px;}
   IMG { border : none 0px;}
   .LayerItemMenu {
      font-family:verdana;
      font-size:60%;
      margin:0;
      padding:0;
      border: 3px groove lightgrey;
   }
   .textLink { color: white; text-decoration: none;}
</STYLE>

<SCRIPT LANGUAGE=JavaScript>
function showNNMenu(evt)
{
   var srcLayer = evt.target;
   var menuLayerId = new String(srcLayer.name).replace("ImgLayer","Layer");
   document.layers[menuLayerId].top = srcLayer.pageY + 10;
   document.layers[menuLayerId].left = parseInt(srcLayer.pageX
      + srcLayer.clip.width + 4);
}

function hideNNMenu(evt)
{
   var srcLayer = evt.target;
   if (evt.pageX < srcLayer.clip.right)
   {
      var menuLayerId = new String(srcLayer.name).replace("ImgLayer","Layer");
      document.layers[menuLayerId].top = -1400;
   }
}

function showOverMenu(menuLayer, menuText, menuPage)
{
   menuLayer.bgColor = "blue";
   menuLayer.document.open();
   menuLayer.document.write('<DIV CLASS="LayerItemMenu">');
   menuLayer.document.write('<A HREF="' + menuPage
      + '" CLASS="textLink">' + menuText + '</A>');
   menuLayer.document.write('</DIV>')
   menuLayer.document.close();
}

function showOutMenu(menuLayer, menuText)
{
   menuLayer.bgColor = "orange";
   menuLayer.document.open();
```

```
        menuLayer.document.write('<DIV CLASS="LayerItemMenu">'
            + menuText + '</DIV>');
        menuLayer.document.close();
}

</SCRIPT>
</HEAD>

<BODY>

<LAYER ID=WoodMenuImgLayer
    onmouseover="showNNMenu(event)"
    onmouseout="hideNNMenu(event)"
    LEFT=10
    TOP=10>
        <IMG SRC="WoodButton.gif" BORDER=0>
</LAYER>

<LAYER ID="WoodMenuLayer" LEFT=120 TOP=-1400 ZINDEX=99
    onmouseout="this.top = -1400;">
        <LAYER ID="WoodOak" TOP=0 LEFT=0
            CLASS="LayerItemMenu"
            WIDTH=175 HEIGHT=20
            BGCOLOR="orange"
            onmouseover="showOverMenu(this,'Oak Timber','OakWood.htm')"
            onmouseout="showOutMenu(this,'Oak Timber')">
                Oak Timber
        </LAYER>
        <LAYER ID="WoodTeak" TOP=22 LEFT=0
            CLASS="LayerItemMenu"
            WIDTH=175 height=20
            BGCOLOR="orange"
            onmouseover="showOverMenu(this,'Teak Timber','TeakWood.htm')"
            onmouseout="showOutMenu(this,'Teak Timber')">Teak Timber
        </LAYER>
        <LAYER ID="WoodPine" TOP=44 LEFT=0
            CLASS="LayerItemMenu"
            WIDTH=175 height=20
            BGCOLOR="orange"
            onmouseover="showOverMenu(this,'Pine Timber','PineWood.htm')"
            onmouseout="showOutMenu(this,'Pine Timber')">Pine Timber
        </LAYER>
        <LAYER ID="WoodYew" TOP=66 LEFT=0
            CLASS="LayerItemMenu"
            WIDTH=175 height=20
            BGCOLOR="orange"
            onmouseover="showOverMenu(this,'Yew Timber','YewWood.htm')"
            onmouseout="showOutMenu(this,'Yew Timber')">Yew Timber
        </LAYER>
</LAYER>

</BODY>
</HTML>
```

507

Save the page as NNMenus.htm and then load it into Netscape 4.x browser. The menus look and work in a very similar way to the IE ones, though perhaps a little less effectively as they have a tendency to close before you get a chance to roll over them. If this was for a real-world situation we might consider adding a timer so that the menus stay visible for a second before closing.

The Full NN DHTML Menu Example

We now take a look at the full code for this example. This makes use of arrays to store the menu information, and creates the HTML for the menus dynamically from this.

The first change is to the script block in the head of the page where we define the arrays and the function that will be used to dynamically create the HTML for the menus:

```
<SCRIPT LANGUAGE=JavaScript>
```

```
var woodMenuItems = new Array();
woodMenuItems[0] = new Array();

woodMenuItems[0][0] = "Oak";
woodMenuItems[0][1] = "OakWood.htm";
woodMenuItems[0][2] = "Oak Timber";
woodMenuItems[0][3] = 0;

woodMenuItems[1] = new Array();
woodMenuItems[1][0] = "Teak";
woodMenuItems[1][1] = "TeakWood.htm";
woodMenuItems[1][2] = "Teak Timber";
woodMenuItems[1][3] = 22;

woodMenuItems[2] = new Array();
woodMenuItems[2][0] = "Pine";
woodMenuItems[2][1] = "PineWood.htm";
woodMenuItems[2][2] = "Pine Timber";
woodMenuItems[2][3] = 44;

woodMenuItems[3] = new Array();
woodMenuItems[3][0] = "Yew";
woodMenuItems[3][1] = "YewWood.htm";
woodMenuItems[3][2] = "Yew Timber";
woodMenuItems[3][3] = 66;

var metalMenuItems = new Array();
metalMenuItems[0] = new Array();

metalMenuItems[0][0] = "Steel";
metalMenuItems[0][1] = "SteelMetal.htm";
metalMenuItems[0][2] = "Steel Girders";
metalMenuItems[0][3] = 0;

metalMenuItems[1] = new Array();
metalMenuItems[1][0] = "Copper";
metalMenuItems[1][1] = "CopperMetal.htm";
metalMenuItems[1][2] = "Copper Pipes";
metalMenuItems[1][3] = 22;
```

```
metalMenuItems[2] = new Array();
metalMenuItems[2][0] = "Gold";
metalMenuItems[2][1] = "GoldMetal.htm";
metalMenuItems[2][2] = "Gold Ingots";
metalMenuItems[2][3] = 44;

var bricksMenuItems = new Array();
bricksMenuItems[0] = new Array();

bricksMenuItems[0][0] = "StdHouse";
bricksMenuItems[0][1] = "StdHousebricks.htm";
bricksMenuItems[0][2] = "Standard House Brick";
bricksMenuItems[0][3] = 0;

bricksMenuItems[1] = new Array();
bricksMenuItems[1][0] = "LargeHouseBrick";
bricksMenuItems[1][1] = "LargeHousebricks.htm";
bricksMenuItems[1][2] = "Large House Bricks";
bricksMenuItems[1][3] = 22;

bricksMenuItems[2] = new Array();
bricksMenuItems[2][0] = "BreezeBlock";
bricksMenuItems[2][1] = "BreezeBlock.htm";
bricksMenuItems[2][2] = "Breeze Block";
bricksMenuItems[2][3] = 44;

function createMenu(menuName, menuItems)
{
   var outerLayerHTML = '<LAYER ID="' + menuName + 'MenuLayer" '
   outerLayerHTML = outerLayerHTML +
      ' onmouseout="this.top = -1400;" LEFT=120 TOP=-1400 Z-INDEX=99>'

   var totalLayers = menuItems.length;
   var layerCount;
   var innerLayerHTML = "";
   var layerName = "";
   for (layerCount = 0; layerCount < totalLayers; layerCount++)
   {
      layerName = menuName + menuItems[layerCount][0];
      innerLayerHTML = innerLayerHTML + '<LAYER ID="' + layerName + '" '
      innerLayerHTML = innerLayerHTML + ' TOP=' + menuItems[layerCount][3]
         + ' LEFT=0 '
      innerLayerHTML = innerLayerHTML + ' CLASS="LayerItemMenu" '
      innerLayerHTML = innerLayerHTML + ' WIDTH=175 HEIGHT=20 BGCOLOR="orange" '
      innerLayerHTML = innerLayerHTML + ' onmouseover="showOverMenu(this,\''
         + menuItems[layerCount][2] + '\''
      innerLayerHTML = innerLayerHTML + ',\''
         + menuItems[layerCount][1] + '\')" '
      innerLayerHTML = innerLayerHTML + ' onmouseout="showOutMenu(this,\''
         + menuItems[layerCount][2] + '\')">'
      innerLayerHTML = innerLayerHTML + menuItems[layerCount][2] + '</LAYER>';
   }

   return outerLayerHTML + innerLayerHTML + '</LAYER>';
}

function showNNMenu(evt)
{
```

The next change is within the body of the page. We add the layers containing the images for the other two menus, and instead of the layers for the menus themselves, insert a script block that calls the `createMenu()` function we defined above:

```
<BODY>
<LAYER ID=WoodMenuImgLayer
    onmouseover="showNNMenu(event)"
    onmouseout="hideNNMenu(event)"
    LEFT=10
    TOP=10>
        <IMG SRC="WoodButton.gif" BORDER=0>
</LAYER>
<LAYER ID=MetalMenuImgLayer
    onmouseover="showNNMenu(event)"
    onmouseout="hideNNMenu(event)"
    TOP=50
    LEFT=10>
    <IMG SRC="MetalButton.gif" BORDER=0>
</LAYER>
<LAYER ID=BricksMenuImgLayer
    onmouseover="showNNMenu(event)"
    onmouseout="hideNNMenu(event)"
    TOP=90
    LEFT=10>
        <IMG SRC="BricksButton.gif" BORDER=0>
</LAYER>

<SCRIPT LANGUAGE=JavaScript>
    document.write(createMenu("Wood",woodMenuItems));
    document.write(createMenu("Metal",metalMenuItems));
    document.write(createMenu("Bricks",bricksMenuItems));
</SCRIPT>

</BODY>
```

Re-save this page as `NNMenus.htm`. You will also need the three images that were used in the `IEMenus.htm` example.

Load the page into your NN 4.x browser to test it.

How It Works

As with the IE version, the information for creating the menus is in arrays. The array structure and use is identical to the IE version, except that there is an additional element at the index 3 of the second dimension of the array. This gives the `top` value for each menu item layer within the enclosing menu layer.

So, each array element contains the following information:

- ❑ `menuItems[X][0]` – name of the menu item
- ❑ `menuItems[X][1]` – page to go to if menu item is clicked
- ❑ `menuItems[X][2]` – text to display for menu item
- ❑ `menuItems[X][3]` – top position of menu item inside outer menu layer

The menus themselves are created in a very similar fashion to the IE version, using the `createMenu()` function. The function's purpose is to re-create, based on the menu arrays, the HTML that we discussed in the DHTML principles behind the menus above.

Let's have a look at the `createMenu()` function. We start by actually defining the function. We can see the function takes two parameters, `menuName` and `menuItems`. Parameter `menuName` will be used to generate the unique ID values for our `<LAYER>` tags. The `menuItems` parameter is actually a multi-dimensional array. The first dimension is for each menu item and the second, as detailed above holds the details for each menu item such as name, page to go to, text to display and position of the top of the menu items `<LAYER>` inside the main menu `<LAYER>`.

```
function createMenu(menuName, menuItems)
{
```

We then build up the start tag of the outer `<LAYER>` tag for the menu in the `outerLayerHTML` variable using the `menuName` parameter passed to the function to create the ID:

```
var outerLayerHTML = '<LAYER ID="' + menuName + 'MenuLayer" '
outerLayerHTML = outerLayerHTML +
    ' onmouseout="this.top = -1400;" LEFT=120 TOP=-1400 Z-INDEX=99>'
```

Next we declare and initialize a number of variables that we'll need to create the `<LAYER>` tags for each menu item:

```
var totalLayers = menuItems.length;
var layerCount;
var innerLayerHTML = "";
var layerName = "";
```

The variable `totalLayers` holds the length of `menuItems`, our array. As the name suggests, this tells us how many menu items need creating. The variable `layerCount` will be used to count through each array item, and `innerLayerHTML` will be used to store all the inner `<LAYER>` tags inside our main menu `<LAYER>`. Finally, the variable `layerName` will hold a unique ID for each menu item layer.

Our next task is to loop through each of the items in the menu array and build up the `<LAYER>` tags for each menu item. We can find out how many items there are in the menu from the `totalLayers` variable defined above, and then loop that number of times through the array:

```
for (layerCount = 0; layerCount < totalLayers; layerCount++)
{
```

The next few lines are fairly straightforward – we are simply concatenating strings to create the HTML for a menu item layer's HTML:

```
layerName = menuName + menuItems[layerCount][0];
innerLayerHTML = innerLayerHTML + '<LAYER ID="' + layerName + '" '
innerLayerHTML = innerLayerHTML + ' TOP=' + menuItems[layerCount][3]
    + ' LEFT=0 '
innerLayerHTML = innerLayerHTML + ' CLASS="LayerItemMenu" '
innerLayerHTML = innerLayerHTML + ' WIDTH=175 HEIGHT=20 BGCOLOR="orange" '
```

511

The remaining lines of the `for` loop do look a little confusing at first:

```
        innerLayerHTML = innerLayerHTML + ' onmouseover="showOverMenu(this,\''
            + menuItems[layerCount][2] + '\''
        innerLayerHTML = innerLayerHTML + ',\''
            + menuItems[layerCount][1] + '\')" '
        innerLayerHTML = innerLayerHTML + ' onmouseout="showOutMenu(this,\''
            + menuItems[layerCount][2] + '\')">'
        innerLayerHTML = innerLayerHTML + menuItems[layerCount][2] + '</LAYER>';
    }
```

The reason for the forward slashes is that we are indicating escape characters – in this case the single quote. We need to put them as escape characters, otherwise JavaScript is going to think we mean the end of the string rather than what we really mean, which is a single quote *inside* a string.

Once one item layer has been created we loop around again and create the next one, and the next one, and so on until we come to the end of our array's elements.

In our final lines of code in the function, we join the `outerLayerHTML` containing the main menu `<LAYER>` tag, the `innerLayerHTML` containing the `<LAYER>` tags for all the menu items, and add the closing `</LAYER>` tag for the outer layer:

```
    return outerLayerHTML + innerLayerHTML + '</LAYER>';
    }
```

All this is returned to the code that called the function, this code being given in the body of the page:

```
<SCRIPT LANGUAGE=JavaScript>
    document.write(createMenu("Wood",woodMenuItems));
    document.write(createMenu("Metal",metalMenuItems));
    document.write(createMenu("Bricks",bricksMenuItems));
</SCRIPT>
```

Each line calls the `createMenu()` function and writes the HTML returned into the page using `document.write()`.

That completes our look at the NN 4.x version of dynamic menus.

Cross Browser IE 4.0+ and NN 4.x DHTML

With a little ingenuity we can rework simple DHTML to work with both IE 4.0+ and NN 4.x browsers.

Small Changes Within Pages

If the tags required for the IE and NN versions of a piece of code are the same and it's just some of the properties or methods in our code that'll need changing, then it's fairly easy to accommodate IE and NN browsers in one page. The easiest way to achieve this is by testing for certain properties of a browser object that you know are only supported by a specific browser.

For example, we can use the `all` collection property of the `document` to test for IE 4+ and we can use the `layers` array property of the `document` to test for just NN 4.x. If the property does exist, then JavaScript treats it as `true`. If the property does not exist, undefined is returned, which JavaScript treats as `false`. It may seem strange that when a property of an object does not exist, then undefined is returned rather than an error occurring, but that's simply the way JavaScript objects work. In our case this is a bonus:

```
if (document.all)
{
    alert("Use IE 4+ code here");
}
else if (document.layers)
{
    alert("Use NN 4.x code here")
}
else
{
    alert("Put your other code here");
}
```

This is an ideal method for simple code differences. For example, say we have a `<DIV>` with ID `myDiv`, which we've positioned absolutely (so that an implicit `Layer` object is created for it in NN 4.x) and we want to change its background color. In IE the code to do this is:

```
myDiv.style.backgroundColor = "blue";
```

In NN 4.x, however, the same thing is achieved by:

```
document.myDiv.bgColor = "blue";
```

Such small changes are easily accommodated in a single page.

It also raises another important point, and that is, while NN 4.x supports the `<LAYER>` and `<ILAYER>` tags, they are in fact best avoided in favor of a relative or absolute positioned `<DIV>` tag if possible. If you know that the page you'll be creating will be very different between IE 4+ and NN 4.x browsers then a separate page will be needed for each browser and avoiding use of the `<LAYER>` tag is much less important. However, if the differences won't need a separate page, then use of the `<DIV>` is likely to make coding much easier and has the advantage that the `<DIV>` tag is supported by IE 4+, NN 4, and NN 6. The `<LAYER>` tag is strictly NN 4.x only.

Try It Out – Moving Tags Again

Let's see how this might work in practice by changing the moving tags examples that we created for IE and NN. Originally both versions were strictly for one or other browser, but with just a few minor changes we can make it work with both.

We'll use the Netscape version and need to make only very simple changes for it to work under IE. The general rule anything NN 4 can do IE 4+ can do too, but some things that IE 4 can do NN 4 cannot. For example, while NN 4 supports moving of `<P>` tags positioned with style sheets, bugs in Netscape mean this can be unreliable. The NN 4 version moved a `<DIV>` with a paragraph inside and this will work fine on IE 4+ with the following changes to the code.

Open up `NNMovingTags.htm` and make the following changes:

```
function moveParas()
{
    if (switchDirection == false)
    {
        paraOneLeft++;
        paraTwoLeft--;
        if (paraOneLeft == 400)
        {
            switchDirection = true;
        }
    }
    else
    {
        paraOneLeft--;
        paraTwoLeft++;
        if (paraOneLeft == 100)
        {
            switchDirection = false;
        }
    }

    var para1Style;
    var para2Style;

    if (document.all)
    {
        para1Style = para1.style;
        para2Style = para2.style;
    }
    else if (document.layers)
    {
        para1Style = document.para1;
        para2Style = document.para2;
    }
    else
    {
        para1Style = document.getElementById("para1").style;
        para2Style = document.getElementById("para2").style;
    }

    para1Style.left = paraOneLeft;
    para2Style.left = paraTwoLeft;
}
```

Save this page as `MovingTags_NN_IE.htm` and load it into IE 4+, NN 4.x, or NN 6 – it'll work fine with all of them.

How It Works

In this example the other thing that differs is the object for which we need to set the `left` property – how do we get to this object?

In IE 4+ and Netscape 6, it's the `Div` object's `style` property that has the `left` property we need to change. With NN 4.x, it's the `left` property of the `Layer` object that is created for the style sheet positioned `<DIV>` tag. Our goal is to set the variables `para1Style` and `para2Style` to reference the objects with the `left` property that needs changing.

First we check to see if the browser supports `document.all`:

```
if (document.all)
{
    para1Style = para1.style;
    para2Style = para2.style;
}
```

Only IE 4+ support this property, so if it is IE 4+ then the `if` statement's condition will be `true` and the variables `para1Style` and `para2Style` will be set to the `style` objects of the relevant `<DIV>` tags.

Next we check to see if the `layers` array property of the `document` object is supported:

```
else if (document.layers)
{
    para1Style = document.para1;
    para2Style = document.para2;
}
```

Only Netscape 4.x supports this property, so only if it's NN 4.x will the code inside the curly braces be executed. This code sets our `para1Style` and `para2Style` variables to reference the `Layer` object that was created for the `<DIV>` tags.

Finally in the `else` statement at the end we have our NN 6 compatible code:

```
else
{
    para1Style = document.getElementById("para1").style;
    para2Style = document.getElementById("para2").style;
}
```

This retrieves references to the `<DIV>` tags we're moving using the `getElementById()` method of the `document` object. This is only supported by NN 6 and IE 5+ and is part of the W3C Document Object Model (DOM). Don't worry too much about it now – we'll be seeing it in a lot more detail in the next chapter when we look at DOM compliant code.

Finally, we can set the `left` property of whatever object is referenced in the `para1Style` and `para2Style` variables:

```
para1Style.left = paraOneLeft;
para2Style.left = paraTwoLeft;
```

While this code will work fine on any DHTML browser, basically IE 4+ and NN 4+, we still need to re-direct users with older browsers to a nice simple static page. We'll look at how to do this next.

Redirecting the browser

There are times when what one browser can achieve simply can't be achieved by other browsers. Or it could be that it can be achieved, but the code and tags required for each version are so radically different, as in our menu systems, that attempting to have more than one version on a single page would be either impossible or exceptionally difficult. If this is the case then the best thing is to have a different page for each and re-direct to the correct page after doing the sort of browser version checking we discussed in Chapter 5.

We can use either the methods above, using `document.all` or `document.layers`, or those we discussed in Chapter 5 on the Browser Object Model to check which browser has loaded the page. With that information we can re-direct the user to the appropriate page using the `location` objects `replace()` method.

Let's see how we could add this to our dynamic menu systems so that if a NN 4.x browser has loaded the IE version, or an IE 4+ browser has loaded the NN 4.x version, then they re-direct to the correct version.

Starting with the `IEMenus.htm` version, this needs to be added at the very top of the first script block:

```
if (!(document.all))
{
    if (document.layers)
    {
        window.location.replace("NNMenus.htm");
    }
    else
    {
        window.location.replace("NoMenus.htm");
    }
}
```

The first `if` statement's condition says that if `document.all` is not `true` then execute the code in the block. The exclamation mark outside the parentheses containing the `document.all` reverses the logic to give us our *not*.

So if a browser that does not support `document.all` (remember only IE 4+ supports this) has loaded this page, then the code inside the `if` statement's curly braces will execute. This code checks to see if the browser supports layers, that is whether it is NN 4.x. If it does then we replace the page loaded with the `NNMenus.htm` page. If not true then we replace the page with a `NoMenus.htm` page, which we'd need to create.

The code that needs to be inserted at the top of the first script block in `NNMenus.htm` is shown below:

```
if (!(document.layers))
{
    if (document.all)
    {
        window.location.replace("IEMenus.htm");
    }
    else
    {
        window.location.replace("NoMenus.htm");
    }
}
```

This is very similar in principle to the IE version, except we are checking that the browser does not support layers, that is it is not NN 4.x. If it does not, then we check to see if it supports the document.all property, that is whether it is IE 4+. If it is, we replace this page with the IEMenus.htm page. Otherwise, we load a NoMenus.htm page.

Summary

DHTML is a large topic, and we've only been able to touch upon the basic foundations in this chapter. However, with this knowledge you can explore DHTML in greater detail and create more complex user interface tricks.

The main points this chapter covered were:

❑ Style sheets can be used to set the style for various types of tags, or individual tags. We can also define style classes that we can apply to certain tags using the CLASS attribute. Styles include the font, color, and position of a tag.

❑ DHTML allows us to change and add to page content even after a page has loaded. Netscape Navigator and Internet Explorer have very, very different implementations of DHTML due to their differing Browser Object Models, and ones that are generally incompatible.

❑ IE 4.0+ makes every tag in the page accessible and open to change after loading, by associating an object with it. To be able to access this object we must give the tag a unique ID attribute.

   ❑ To change the appearance of tags after they have loaded, we can use the style object property of the object associated with a tag. We can use this to change any style for the tag.

   ❑ Using the properties innerText, innerHTML, and outerHTML of a tag's object, we can alter the content inside a tag; the latter two for any HTML changes are re-rendered automatically.

   ❑ Totally new content can also be inserted with the insertAdjacentText() and insertAdjacentHTML() methods of the tag's object. These allow us to insert new content before a tag's start, after its start, before its end tag, or just after its end tag.

   ❑ IE supports a special global object, the event object. This is populated with useful information regarding the circumstances of an event. For example, what were the x and y positions of the mouse pointer at the time of the event, what, if any, key did the user press, and which tags' objects are involved in the event.

   ❑ We then created a dynamic menu system for IE based on the DHTML looked at in the chapter. When a user rolled their mouse pointer over an image representing a menu option a list of menu items appeared from which the user could pick. If they rolled off the menu without choosing an option, then we hid the menu.

❑ NN 4.x takes a very different approach and bases much of its DHTML programming on the Layer object. We access most tags via the Layer object, which is created for them if they are positioned using style sheets. We can also create a Layer object directly using the <LAYER> and <ILAYER> tags. The bad news is that Netscape 6 is not backwards compatible with NN 4.x, so use of layers will not work on NN 6.

❑   Using the Layer object, we can move the content around the page after it has loaded. Moving a layer around involves the top and left properties, or the moveTo() and moveBy() methods. The order in which layers are stacked in a page is determined by the Layer object's zIndex property or moveAbove() and moveBelow() methods.

     ❑   Layers are like mini windows on the page and, like a window object, they have a document property very much like the document object of a normal window. To change the content inside a layer we first use document.open() and then can use the document.write() method to insert new content. Once we have inserted new content, we must use the document.close() method, otherwise any further document.write()s will add to and not replace content.

     ❑   NN also has an event object, which is generated each time an event occurs, with the same purpose of allowing us to gather information about the event any and associated user input as the IE event object. However, it has a very different set of properties. The event object is only available in the event connection code, so care needs to be taken when connecting an event handler to a function that needs the event object.

     ❑   Finally we created a very similar DHTML menu system but in NN. We saw that the main change was that layers were central to its functioning.

❑   We ended the chapter by looking at ways in which we can write cross-browser compatible pages. This can either be achieved in a single page by checking for an object's property that is supported in one browser but not another, or by redirecting the user to different pages depending on their browser.

In the next chapter, we will take a closer look at what can be achieved in IE 5.0+ and NN6 browsers, which support the W3C Document Object Model (DOM) to varying extents.

Exercise Questions

Suggested solutions to these questions can be found in Appendix A.

Question 1

Create a series of images, each of which is a button linking to a different page on your web site. When the mouse pointer rolls over an image display some text somewhere on the page that describes what the user would find if they followed the link. For example, an image saying "What's New" might have the description, "Find out what has been added to the web site since your last visit". When the mouse pointer rolls off then the descriptive text should disappear. Your page must work with IE 4+ and NN 4.x.

Question 2

Create an image that says "Welcome" and which floats round the page. When the user's mouse pointer rolls over the image change it so it displays "Click For What's New". When clicked it should take the user to a page detailing new additions to the web site. The solution must work with both IE 4+ and with NN 4.x.

Online discussion at http://p2p.wrox.com

Understanding the Document Object Model

One of the most misunderstood sections in the W3C Web standards is the Document Object Model or DOM for short. The DOM gives us a way of representing everything on a web page so that it is accessible via a common set of properties and methods in JavaScript, or indeed any other object-based programming language. By everything, we mean everything – the graphics, the tables, the forms, and even the text itself should be changeable by just altering a relevant property in script.

The DOM should not to be confused with the Browser Object Model (BOM) that we introduced in Chapter 5 and used extensively in the last chapter. We'll look at the differences between the two in detail shortly. For now though, think of the BOM as a browser-dependent representation of every feature of the browser – from the browser buttons, URL address line, title bar, to the browser window controls, as well as parts of the web page too. The DOM, however, *only* deals with the contents of the browser window or web page, in other words the HTML document. It makes the document available in such a way that any browser can use exactly the same code to access and manipulate the content of the document. To summarize, the BOM gives access to the browser and some of the document, while the DOM give access to all of the document, but *only* the document.

The great thing about the DOM is that it is browser and platform independent. This means that we can finally consider the possibility of being able to write a piece of JavaScript code that dynamically updates the page as we saw in the last chapter, and will work on any DOM compliant browser without any tweaking. We should not need to code for different browsers or take excessive care when coding.

The DOM does this by representing the contents of the page as a generic tree structure. Whereas in the BOM, you might expect to access something by looking up a property relevant to that part of the browser and adjusting this, the DOM requires you to navigate through its representation of the page via nodes and non-browser–specific properties. We'll explore this structure a little later.

However, in order to use the DOM standard, ultimately we require browsers that completely implement the standard. Unfortunately, IE 5.5 still doesn't support many aspects of the standard. Even NN 6, which at least aims to support the standard, still falls short in some ways. So while crossbrowser coding is much simpler than for NN 4 and IE 4, it is still not as simple as it could be.

This makes the DOM sound like an impossible ideal, yet the DOM doesn't exist purely as a standard. Features of the DOM standard have been implemented in browsers as far back as NN 2. However, in NN versions 2, 3, and 4, many HTML page elements and their properties were not scriptable at all, while, as we have seen, IE 4 made nearly all page elements and their properties scriptable. Unfortunately, the way in which NN 4 provides scripting access to some elements is often incompatible with the way in which IE 4 makes those elements available. Thus a Document Object Model standard was developed. The latest versions of both IE and NN browsers now support many features outlined in the standard.

To give you a true perspective of how the DOM fits in, we need to briefly outline its relationship with some of the other currently existing web standards. We also need to explain why there is more than one version of the DOM standard, and within the standard itself, why there are different sections. (Microsoft, in particular, added a number of extensions to the W3C DOM.) Then we can look at using JavaScript to navigate the DOM and to dynamically change content on our web pages, in a way that previously with just pure DHTML was impossible in more than one browser. The items on the agenda are:

❑   The HTML, ECMAScript, XML, and XHTML Web Standards

❑   The DOM standards

❑   The DOM tree structure

❑   Writing Cross Browser DHTML

Remember that the examples within this chapter only are targetted at the DOM and therefore will only be supported by IE 5.0/5.5. and NN 6.

Why Do We Need Web Standards?

When Tim Berners-Lee created HTML in 1991, he probably had little idea that this technology for marking up scientific papers via a set of tags for his own global hypertext project, known as the World Wide Web, would within a matter of years become a battleground between the two giants of the software business of the mid nineties. HTML was a simple derivation from the meta-language SGML (Standard Generalized Markup Language) that had been kicking around academic institutions for decades before. It's purpose was to preserve the structure of the documents created with it. HTML depends on a protocol, HTTP (HyperText Transfer Protocol) to transmit the documents back and forth between the resource and the viewer (for example, the server and the client computer). These two technologies formed the foundation of the Web, and it became quickly obvious in the early 1990s that there needed to be some sort of policing of both specifications to ensure a common implementation of both HTML and HTTP, meaning that communications could be conducted worldwide.

In 1994, Tim founded the W3C (the World Wide Web Consortium), a body which aimed to oversee the technical evolution of the Web. It has three main aims:

❑   To provide universal access, so that anybody can use it

❑   To develop a software environment to allow users to make use of the Web

❑   To guide the development of the Web, taking into consideration the legal, social and commercial issues that are raised

Each new version of a specification of a web technology has to be carefully vetted by W3C before it can become a standard. The HTML and HTTP specifications are subject to this process, and each new set of updates to these specifications yields a new version of the standard. Each standard has to go through a working draft, a candidate recommendation, and a proposed recommendation stage before it can be considered as a fully operational standard. At each stage of the process, members of the W3C consortium vote on what amendments to make, or even whether to cancel the standard completely and send it back to square one.

It sounds a very painful and laborious method of creating a standard format, and not something you'd consider as spearheading the cutting edge of technical revolution. Indeed, the software companies in the mid 1990s found the processes involved too slow, so they set the tone by implementing new innovations themselves and then submitting them to the standards body for approval. Netscape started by introducing new tags in their browser, such as the <FONT> tag, which added presentational content to the web pages. This proved popular, so they added a whole raft of tags that enabled users to alter aspects of presentation and style on the web pages. Indeed, JavaScript itself was such an innovation from Netscape.

When Microsoft entered the fray, they were playing catch up for the first two iterations of their Internet Explorer browser. However, with Internet Explorer 3 in 1996, they established a roughly equal set of features to compete with Netscape, and so were able to add their own browser-specific tags. Very quickly the Web polarized between these two browsers, but the problem was that pages that were viewable on one browser, quite often wouldn't appear on another. One problem was that Microsoft had used its much stronger position in the market to give away its browser for free, while Netscape still needed to sell its own browser, as it couldn't afford to freely distribute its flagship product. To maintain a competitive position they needed to offer new features to make the user want to purchase their browser rather than use the free Microsoft browser.

Things came to head with both company's version 4 browsers, when they introduced dynamic page functionality. Unfortunately, as we saw in the last chapter, Netscape did this by the means of a <LAYER> tag, while Microsoft chose to implement it via scripting language properties and methods. The W3C consortium needed to take a firm hand here, since one of their three principal aims had been compromised – that of universal access. How could you guarantee this aim, if you needed a particular vendor's browser to be able to view a particular set of pages? They decided on a solution that used existing standard HTML tags and Cascading Style Sheets, both of which had been adopted as part of Microsoft's solution. As a result, Microsoft gained a dominant position in the browser "war". They haven't relinquished this position since, while the Netscape Navigator browser hasn't undergone a significant upgrade in over two years, until only very recently, when Netscape 6 was released. Current usage statistics hover between 70 vs. 30 percent and 90 vs. 10 percent in Microsoft's favor, depending on which browser statistics sites you visit.

With a relatively stable version of the HTML standard in place with version 4.01, boasting a set of features that will take a long time for any browser manufacturer to implement completely, attention was turned to other areas of the Web. A new set of standards was introduced in the late nineties governing the methods of presentation (style sheets) and the representation of the HTML document in script (the Document Object Model or DOM). Other standards emerged, such as XML (Extensible Markup Language), which offers a common format for representing data in a way that preserves its structure. We'll take a look now at the main standards that have been created, and say a bit about what each of the technologies does.

The Web Standards

If you go to the W3C web site, `http://www.w3.org`, you'll find a huge number of standards in varying stages of creation. Not all of these standards concern us, and not all of the ones that concern us can be found at this web site. However, the vast majority of standards that do concern us can be found there.

We're going to have brief look now at the technologies and standards that have an impact on JavaScript and give a little background information about each. Some of the technologies may be unfamiliar to you, but you need to be aware of their existence at the very least.

HTML

The HTML standard is maintained by W3C. This standard might seem fairly straightforward, given that each version should have introduced just a few new tags, but in reality the life of the standards body was vastly complicated by the browser wars. The versions 1.0 and 2.0 of HTML were simple enough small documents, but when W3C came to debate HTML version 3.0, they found that much of the new functionality they were discussing had already been superceded by new additions made to the version 3.0 browsers such as the `<APPLET>` and `<STYLE>` tags. Version 3.0 was discarded, and a new version 3.2 became the standard.

However, a lot of the features that went into HTML 3.2 had been introduced at the behest of the browser manufacturers and ran contrary to the spirit of HTML – it was intended to solely define structure. The new features, stemming right back to the `<FONT>` tag, just confused the issue and added un-necessary presentational features to HTML. These features really became redundant with the introduction of style sheets. So suddenly, in the version 3 browsers, there were three distinct ways to define the style of an item of text. Which was the correct way? And if all three ways were used, then which style did the text ultimately assume? The version 4.0 of the HTML standard was left with the job of unmuddling this chaotic mess, and marked a lot of tags up for deprecation (removal) in the next version of the standards. It was the largest version of the standard and included features that linked it to style sheets, the Document Object Model, and also added facilities for the visually impaired and other unfairly much neglected minority interest areas.

The current version of the HTML standard, 4.01, readies the standard for it's rewriting as an XML document. We will touch briefly on XML a little later in the chapter.

ECMAScript

JavaScript itself followed a similar trajectory to HTML. It was first used in Netscape Navigator and then added to Internet Explorer at a later date. The Internet Explorer version of JavaScript was christened JScript and wasn't far removed from the version of JavaScript found in Netscape Navigator. However, once again there were differences between the implementations of the two and so when writing script for both browsers a lot of care had to be taken.

Funnily enough, it was left to the European Computer Manufacturers Association (ECMA) to propose a standard specification of JavaScript. This didn't appear until a few versions of JavaScript had already been released. Unlike HTML, which had been developed right from the very start with the W3C consortium, JavaScript was a proprietary creation. This is the reason that it is governed by a different standards body. Microsoft and Netscape both agreed to use ECMA as the standards vehicle/debating forum, because of its reputation for fast-tracking standards and perhaps also because of its perceived neutrality. The name ECMAScript was chosen so as not to be biased to either vendor's creation and also because 'Java' of JavaScript was a trademark of Sun licensed to Netscape. The standard, named ECMA-262, laid down a specification that was roughly equivalent to the JavaScript 1.1 specification.

Having said that, the ECMAScript standard only covers core JavaScript features, such as the primitive data types of numbers, strings, and booleans, native objects like the `Date`, `Array`, and `Math` objects, and the procedural statements like `for` and `while` loops, and `if` and `else` conditionals. It makes no reference to client-side objects and collections, such as `window`, `document`, `forms`, `links`, and `images`. So, while the standard helps to make core programming tasks compatible when both JavaScript and JScript comply with it, it is of no use in making the scripting of client-side objects compatible between the main browsers. Some incompatibilities remain.

All current implementations of JavaScript are expected to conform to the current ECMAScript standard. While in the version 3 browsers there were quite a few irregularities between the Microsoft and Netscape dialects of JavaScript, they're now close enough together to be considered the same language. The Opera browser also supports and offers the same kind of support for the standard. This is a good example of how standards have provided a uniform language across browser implementations, although a feature war similar to HTML still applies to a lesser degree for JavaScript.

XML

Extensible Markup Language, or XML, is a standard for creating markup languages (such as HTML). XML itself has been designed to look as much like HTML as possible, but that's where the similarities end.

HTML is actually an application of the meta-language SGML, which is also a standard for generating markup languages. SGML has been used to create many markup languages, but HTML is the only one that enjoys universal familiarity and popularity. XML on the other hand is a direct subset of SGML. SGML is generally considered to be too complex for people to be able to accurately represent it on a computer, so XML is a simplified subset of SGML. XML is much easier to read than SGML as well.

XML's main purpose is for the creation of customized markup languages which are very similar in look and structure to HTML. One main use of XML is in the representation of data. Whereas a normal database can store information, databases don't allow individual stored items to contain information about their structure. XML can use the tag structure of markup languages to represent any kind of data, from mathematical and chemical notations to the entire works of Shakespeare, where information contained in the structure of the data might otherwise be lost. For instance, an XML document could be used to record that Mark Anthony doesn't appear until Scene II Act I of Shakespeare's play Julius Caesar, while a relational database would struggle to do this without a lot of extra fields. For example:

```
<play>
    <act1>
        <scene1>
            ...
        </scene1>
        <scene2>
            <mark_anthony>
                Caeser, my lord?
            </mark_anthony>
        </scene2>
        <scene3>
            ...
        </scene3>
    </act1>
    <act2>
        ...
    </act2>
    <act3>
        ...
    </act3>
    <act4>
        ...
    </act4>
    <act5>
        ...
    </act5>
</play>
```

XML is also completely cross-platform, since it contains just text. This means that an application on Windows can package up the data in this format, while a completely different application on UNIX should be able to unravel it and read the data.

XML is more complex than HTML, as you might imagine. Whereas your browser will take HTML code, interpret the relevant details and display the corresponding web page for you without any intervenion, XML requires several extra steps.

As you're creating the markup language yourself, you need to first create a set of rules via which the language will be run. This can be done in one of two ways, either by an **XML schema** or by a **DTD** (**Document Type Definition**). Both of these are used to draw up rules, such as which tags you can use in your markup language, what attributes these tags take, and what kind of data these attributes are expecting.

Secondly, once you've written your XML document in your new language, it must be checked against both the syntax rules laid down for XML documents and the rules in the schema or the DTD to see if the code conforms.

Well Formed and Valid XML

Let's just break off here for a moment, as this is where we can connect with JavaScript and the DOM. An XML document has to undergo two checks at this stage of the process.

The first check is for well-formedness. An XML document is said to be **well-formed** if it matches the criteria laid down in the XML standard. The XML document is sent to an **XML parser** (these are built into the most recent versions of the browsers, but can exist outside a browser also) to check for this.

526

One criterion for an XML document is that all opening tags are also closed. This is similar to what happens in HTML also. However, while in the HTML standard, it *suggests* that all HTML tags must be completed by a closing tag, it's common practice for many tags to leave off the closing tag. The browser will still interpret it, and usually the page won't break (depending on which browser you are using and how tolerant it is). For example, the following code will be allowed by most browsers:

```
<P>
First Paragraph
<P>
Second Paragraph
```

when strictly speaking it should be:

```
<P>
First Paragraph
</P>
<P>
Second Paragraph
</P>
```

XML isn't tolerant of this. In fact this will cause errors to be thrown by the XML parser.

The main browsers' toleration of sloppy HTML will also usually allow you to be lax about nesting tags inside one another – you don't have to close one tag before you start another. So, yet again the following will be perfectly acceptable to a browser interpreting an HTML page:

```
<DIV>
First Paragraph
<P>
Second Paragraph
</DIV>
</P>
```

while in XML it will cause an error, as XML requires that you close your nested tags correctly.

Lastly, XML also requires all elements to be contained within a single (outermost) root element, rather similar to HTML's <HTML> tag, although the root element doesn't have to be any particular element. Only then can an XML document be well formed.

Now this is where the DOM comes in. When you use the DOM through JavaScript, it dynamically generates HTML, but the HTML it generates must also be well-formed. This is because each separate DOM object on the page has a one-to-one correspondence with a set of HTML tags, and the content they contain. If you don't close or nest the HTML tags correctly, then you can't create the corresponding DOM objects correctly. We will be looking at DOM objects shortly.

If we generate HTML using these rules, which are specifically laid out in the XML standard, then the HTML document will have a strict hierarchical structure, which is much easier to represent with an object model. You might wonder why we've switch from talking about XML to HTML here – the reason is that the rules for generating well-formed documents are the same in *both* languages, they're just not strictly enforced in HTML by the browsers. You should be able to deduce from this that both XML and HTML can have Document Object Models if the documents are well formed.

The second test done in XML is for **validity**. This is where the XML document is checked against the rules specified in the XML schema or DTD. For example, the rules might say that a set of <CAR> tags are valid, with a set of tags inside these that reflect different features such as a the <CHASSIS>, <ROOF>, and <WHEELS>. Your document will have to be checked to see that these rules haven't been abused, such as the setting of a sunroof attribute for a convertible car, or a numberOfGears attribute for an automatic (that is, setting impossible values for attributes that presumably the schema or DTD won't allow).

Once again, checking for validity can also be done in HTML, with the much forgotten <!DOCTYPE> element. However, none of the browsers, except NN 6, currently supply the means for checking your HTML against a valid DTD, even though HTML actually has a DTD defined by the W3C. If you specify the 'strict' DTD for HTML in NN 6, the browser will demand that the page be well-formed and valid, that is it won't be at all forgiving of any unclosed tags or incorrectly nested tags. You would do well to check your documents via this as it could be a requirement in all future browsers with the introduction of XHTML, as we will see shortly.

Generating the Output

Lastly, with XML there's no place for the browser to interpret what your tags mean, so any rules for how the XML should be displayed have to be implemented by yourself. Typically this can either done by a third party language, such as Java or more commonly by a set of display rules specified in a style sheet.

In HTML this is done automatically for you – if you specify a <B> tag or an <I> tag, then the browser will know to display the corresponding text in bold or italics. With XML you will have to use a style sheet or program to create the styles yourself.

While XML itself has been around for a few years, it's only been adopted relatively recently by the standards committee W3C. Currently, we're only at version 1.0 of the standard, although a second edition of the 1.0 standard has just been ratified, which amends some bugs in the first edition of 1.0. The reason why we're talking about XML is that while the DOM works with HTML, it was principally designed for working with XML. It just so happens that many of the features that work with XML can be used with an HTML document or HTML code.

While we're not going to be using any XML in this chapter, you will come across it very briefly later in the book. More importantly, the principles for navigating XML and HTML documents are the same, as are the properties and methods used.

XHTML

XHTML is where the XML and HTML standards meet. XHTML is just a re-specifying of the HTML 4.01 standard as an XML application. The advantages of this allow XHTML to get around some of the problems caused by a browser's particular interpretation of HTML, and more importantly to provide a specification that allows the Web to be used by clients other than browsers, such as those provided on handheld computers, mobile phones, or any software device that might be connected to the Internet (perhaps even your refrigerator!).

It also offers a common method for specifying your own tags, rather than just adding them randomly. You can specify new tags via a common method using an XML DTD and an XML **namespace** (this is a way of identifying one set of tags uniquely from any other set of tags). This is particularly useful for the new markup languages such as WML (Wireless Markup Language), which are geared towards mobile technology and require a different set of tags to be able to display on the much reduced ability interfaces.

Having said that, anyone familiar with HTML should be able to look at an XHTML page and understand what's going on. There are differences, but not ones that add new tags or attributes.

The main differences between XHTML and HTML are that:

❏   XHTML requires an XML declaration at the top of the file: `<?xml version='1.0'?>`

❏   You also have to provide a DTD declaration at the top of the file referencing the version of the DTD standard you are using.

❏   You have to include a reference to the XML namespace within the HTML tag.

❏   You need to supply all XHTML tag names in lower case, as XML is case-sensitive.

❏   The `<head>` and `<body>` elements must always be included in an XHTML document.

❏   Tags must always be closed and also nested correctly. In the cases where only one tag is required, such as line breaks, the tag is closed with a /, for example `<br/>`

❏   Attribute values must always be denoted by quotation marks.

This set of rules makes it possible to keep a strict hierarchical structure to the tags, which in turn makes it possible for the Document Object Model to work correctly. This is the route that HTML is currently taking, and all future HTML standards will be XHTML standards. This also provides a way of standardizing markup languages across all device types, so that the next version of WML (the markup language of mobile devices), will also be compliant with the XHTML standard. You should now be creating your HTML documents according to the rules specified above. If you do so, you will find the job of writing JavaScript that manipulates the page via the DOM, and works in the way it was intended, much, much easier.

If you wish to know more about the future plans for HTML and XHTML, then this is covered in the Wrox Press book *Beginning XHTML* with ISBN 1-861003-43-9.

It's now time for us to consider the Document Object Model itself.

The Document Object Model (DOM)

The Document Object Model is, as we've mentioned, a way of representing the document in a browser-independent way. It allows a user to access the document via a common set of objects, properties, methods, and events, and alter the contents of the web page dynamically, using script.

As you're well aware, there are several types of script languages available, such as JavaScript and VBScript. Each requires a slightly different syntax and therefore a different approach when programming. Even when using a language common to all browsers, such as JavaScript, there are usually some small variations added by the vendor to the language. So, to guarantee that you don't fall foul of a particular implementation, the W3C has provided a generic set of objects, properties and methods that should be available in all scripting languages, in the form of the DOM standard.

The DOM Standard

We've avoided talking about the DOM standard so far, and that's for a particular reason – it's not the easiest standard to follow. Supporting a generic set of properties and methods has proved a very complex task, and the DOM standard has been broken down into separate levels and sections to deal with the different areas. The different levels of the standard are all at differing stages of completion.

Level 0

Level 0 is a bit of a misnomer, as there wasn't really a level 0 of the standard. Level 0 in fact refers to the "old way" of doing things. By the "old way" we mean the methods implemented by the browser vendors before the DOM standard. If you come across someone mentioning level 0 properties, they're referring to a more linear notation of accessing properties and methods. For example, typically you'd reference items on a form by the following code:

```
document.forms[0].elements[1].value = "button1";
```

We're not going to cover such properties and methods in this chapter, as they have been superceded by newer methods.

Level 1 of the Standard

Level 1 of the standard is the first version of the standard and the only one that is actually complete. It is split into two sections – one is defined as core (objects, properties, and methods that can apply to both XML and HTML) and the other as HTML (HTML–specific objects, properties and methods). The first section deals with how you'd go about navigating and manipulating the structure of the document. The objects, properties, and methods in this section are very abstract. The second section deals with HTML only and offers a set of objects corresponding to all of the HTML elements. This chapter mainly deals with the second section of level 1 of the standard.

Recently level 1 has been revamped and corrected. You can see the corrected version of level 1, referred to as the second edition, on the W3C web site.

Level 2 of the Standard

Level 2 of the standard is currently a candidate recommendation, but given that many of the properties, methods, and events have already been implemented by both main browsers, it is unlikely to change significantly before it is finally approved. It has sections that add specifications for events and style sheets to the specifications for core and HTML–specific properties and events. It also provides sections on views and traversal ranges, neither of which we will be covering in this book, but you can find more information at http://www.w3.org/TR/2000/PR-DOM-Level-2-Views-20000927/ and http://www.w3.org/TR/2000/PR-DOM-Level-2-Traversal-Range-20000927/ respectively. We will be making use of some of the features of the event and style sections of this level of the DOM later in this chapter, as they have been implemented in the latest version of both browsers.

Level 3 of the Standard

Level 3 of the standard is still early in its infancy, as it is currently a working draft. It attempts to resolve a lot of the complications that still exist in the event model in level 2 of the standard, and adds support for XML features, such as contents models and being able to save the DOM as an XML document. As of writing, much of this level hadn't been implemented, so we won't be considering any of the new features in this level of the standard.

Browser Compliance with the Standards

Almost no browser has 100% compliance to *any* standard, although some, such as NN 6, come pretty close with the DOM. You, therefore, have no guarentee that all of the objects, properties, and methods of the DOM standard will be available in a given version of a browser, although a few level 1 and level 2 objects, properties, and methods have been available in both browsers since version 4, and in Netscape's case, as far back as version 2. However, IE 5.5. and NN 6 offer by far the closest compliance so far.

While in previous chapters we've aimed at supporting version 4 and later browsers, in this chapter it isn't possible. Much of material in the DOM standards has only recently been clarified, and a lot of DOM features and support have only been added to the latest browser versions. For this reason, examples in this chapter will only be guaranteed to work on the *latest* IE and NN versions. While crossbrowser scripting is much more realistic, backwards support isn't at all.

While the standards might still not be fully implemented, they do provide a guideline as to how a particular property or method should be implemented, and a guideline for all browser manufacturers to agree to work towards in later versions of their browsers. The DOM doesn't introduce any new HTML tags or style sheet properties to achieve its ends. The idea of the DOM is to make use of the existing technologies, and quite often the existing properties and methods of one or other of the browsers.

Differences Between the DOM and the BOM

We've already hinted strongly at the two main differences between the Document Object Model and the Browser Object Models. However, this difference is often confused since a BOM is sometimes refered to under the name DOM. Look out for this in any literature you see on the subject.

Firstly, the DOM only covers the document of the web page, while the BOM offers scripting access to all areas of the browsers, from buttons to the title bar, including some parts of the page.

Secondly, the BOM is unique to a particular browser. This makes sense if you think about it – you can't expect to standardize browsers, as they have to offer competitive features over each other. Therefore you're going to need a different set of properties and methods and even objects to be able to manipulate them with JavaScript.

Representing the HTML Document as a Tree Structure

As HTML is standardized so that web pages can only contain standard features supported in the language, such as forms, tables, images, and the like, there needs to be a common method of accessing these features. This is where the DOM comes in. The way that the DOM works is to have a uniform representation of the HTML document. This is achieved by representing the entire HTML document/web page as a **tree structure**.

Only the more recent browser versions (5 and upwards) allow you to access all parts of the web page via such a tree structure. Up until then, they would only partially represent web pages in this tree structure, and leave bits, such as the text, beyond reach and inaccessible to script.

In fact it is possible to represent *any* HTML document (in fact, any XML document) as a tree structure. The only pre-condition is that the HTML document should be well-formed. We've already mentioned earlier why this is such a desirable attribute, but it doesn't hurt to emphasize it again. While different browsers might be tolerant, to a greater or lesser extent, of quirks such as unclosed tags, or HTML form controls not being enclosed within a set of <FORM> tags, for the structure of the HTML document to be accurately depicted you need to be able to always predict the structure of the document. Abuses of the structure, such as unclosed tags, stop you from depicting the structure as a true hierarchy, and therefore cannot be allowed. Accessing elements via the DOM depends on the ability to represent the page as a hierarchy.

What is a Tree Structure?

If you're not familiar with the concept of trees, don't worry. They're just a diagrammatic way of representing a hierarchical structure.

Let's consider the example of a book, which has several sets of chapters. If I told you to go and find the third line on page 543, then you'd be able to find it after a little searching. If an updated edition of the book was printed with extra chapters, more likely than not you'd completely fail to find the same point given those same instructions. However, if the instructions were changed to, say, find the chapter on still life painting, and the section on using water colors, and the paragraph on positioning light sources, then you'd still be able to find it even in a reprinted edition with extra pages and chapters, albeit with perhaps a little more effort than by using the first method.

Books aren't particularly dynamic examples, but given something like a web page, where the information could be changed daily, or even hourly, can you see why it would be of more use to give the second set of directions rather than the first? The same principle applies with the DOM. Navigating the DOM in a hierarchical fashion, rather than a strictly linear way, makes much more sense. When you treat the DOM as a tree, it becomes easy to navigate the page in this fashion. Consider how you locate files on Windows using Windows Explorer, which creates a tree view of folders through which you can drill down. Instead of looking for a file alphabetically, you locate it by going into a particular folder.

The rules for creating trees are simple. You start at the top of the tree with the document and the element that contains all other elements in the page. The document is the **root node**. A **node** is just a point on the tree representing a particular element or attribute of an element or even the text that an element contains. The root node contains all other nodes, such as the DTD declaration, the XML declaration, and the root element (the HTML or XML element that contains all other elements). This is typically (it should always be) the <HTML> tag in an HTML document. Underneath the root element, come the HTML elements that the root element contains. Typically an HTML page will have <HEAD> and <BODY> elements inside the <HTML> element. These elements are represented as nodes underneath the root element's node, which itself is underneath the root node at the top of the tree:

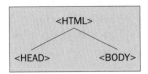

The two nodes representing the <HEAD> and <BODY> elements are examples of **child nodes** and the <HTML> element's node above them is a **parent node**. Since the <HEAD> and <BODY> elements are both child nodes of the <HTML> element, they both go on the same level underneath the parent node/<HTML> element. The <HEAD> and <BODY> elements in turn contain other child nodes/HTML elements which will appear at a level underneath their nodes. So, child nodes can also be parent nodes. Each time you encounter a set of HTML elements within another element, they each form a separate node at the same level on the tree. The easiest way of explaining this clearly is with an example.

An Example HTML Page

Let's consider a basic HTML page such as this:

```
<HTML>
<HEAD>
</HEAD>
<BODY>
<H1>My Heading</H1>
<P>This is some text in a paragraph</P>
</BODY>
</HTML>
```

The <HTML> element contains <HEAD> and <BODY> elements. Only the <BODY> element actually contains anything. It contains an <H1> element and a <P> element. The <H1> element contains the text "My Heading". When we reach an item such as text or an image, or an element that contains no others, then the tree-structure will terminate at that node. Such a node is termed a **leaf node**. We then continue to the <P> node, which contains some text, which is also a node in the document. We can depict this as the following tree structure:

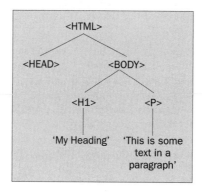

Simple, eh? This example is almost too straightforward, so let's move on to a slightly more complex one now, which involves a table as well:

```
<HTML>
<HEAD>
<TITLE>This is a test page</TITLE>
</HEAD>
<BODY>
<SPAN>Below is a table...</SPAN>
<TABLE BORDER=1>
<TR>
    <TD>Row 1 Cell 1</TD>
    <TD>Row 1 Cell 2</TD>
</TR>
<TR>
    <TD>Row 2 Cell 1</TD>
    <TD>Row 2 Cell 2</TD>
</TR>
</TABLE>
</BODY>
</HTML>
```

There is nothing out of the ordinary here. The document just contains a table with two rows, and two cells in each row. We can once again represent the hierarchical structure of our page (for example, the fact that the <HTML> tag contains a <HEAD> and a <BODY>, tag and that the <HEAD> tag contains a <TITLE> tag, and so on) using our tree structure:

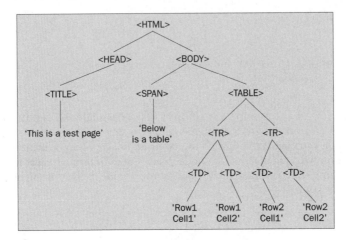

The top level of the tree is simple enough – the <HTML> element contains <HEAD> and <BODY> elements. The <HEAD> element in turn contains a <TITLE> element and the <TITLE> element itself contains some text. This text node is a child node that terminates the branch (a leaf node). We can then go back to the next node, the <BODY> element node, and go down that branch. Here we have two elements contained within the <BODY> element, the <SPAN> and <TABLE> elements. While the <SPAN> element contains only text and terminates there, the <TABLE> element contains two rows <TR>, and the two <TR> elements contain two table cell <TD> elements. Only then do we get to the bottom of the tree with the the text contained in each table cell. Our tree is now a complete representation of our HTML code.

The DOM Objects

What we have seen so far has been highly theoretical, so let's get a little more practical now.

The DOM provides us with a concrete set of objects, properties and methods accesible via JavaScript to navigate the tree structure of the DOM. Let's start with the set of objects within the DOM that are used to represent the nodes (elements, attributes, or text) on our tree.

Base DOM Objects

There are three objects that are known as the base DOM objects. These are as follows:

Object	Description
Node	Each node in the document has its own Node object.
NodeList	This is a list of all Node objects.
NamedNodeMap	This provides access by name to all of the Node objects, rather than just by index.

This is where we differ from the BOM quite extensively. In the BOM you're probably used to objects that have names that relate to a specific part of the browser, such as the `window` object, or the `forms` and `images` arrays. We've already explained that to be able to navigate in the web page as though it was a tree, we have to do it on a more abstract basis. You can have no prior knowledge of the structure of the page – everything ultimately is just a node. To move around from HTML element to element, or element to attribute, you have to go from node to node. This also means we can add, replace, or remove parts of our web page without affecting the structure as a whole, as we're just changing nodes. This is why we have three rather obscure sounding objects that represent our tree structure.

We've already mentioned that the top of our tree structure is the root node, and that the root node contains the XML declaration, the DTD and the root element. You can probably deduce that therefore we need more than just these three objects to represent our document. In fact there are different objects to represent the different types of nodes on the tree.

High Level DOM objects

As we have seen, nodes come in a variety of types. Is it an element, an attribute, or just plain text? The `Node` object has different objects to represent each possible type of node. The following is a complete list of all the different node type objects that can be accessed via the DOM. A lot of them won't concern us in this book as they are concerned only with XML documents and not HTML documents, but you should notice that our three main types of node, namely element, attribute, and text are all covered.

Object	Description
Document	The root node of the document
DocumentType	The DTD or schema type of the XML document
DocumentFragment	A temporary storage space for parts of the document
EntityReference	A reference to an entity in the XML document
Element	An element in the document
Attr	An attribute of an element in the document
ProcessingInstruction	A processing instruction
Comment	A comment in an XML document
Text	Text that must form a child node of a element
CDATASection	A CDATA Section within the XML document
Entity	An unparsed entity in the DTD
Notation	A notation declared within a DTD

We're not going to cover most of these objects in this chapter, but should you need to navigate the DOM of an XML document, then you will find yourself having to use them.

Each of these objects inherits all the properties and methods of the `Node` object, but also has some properties and methods of its own. We will be looking at some examples of these in the next section.

DOM Properties and Methods

If we tried to look at the properties and methods of all the above objects in the DOM, we would find that this took up half the book. Instead we're only going to actively consider three of the objects, namely the node object, the element object, and the document object itself. This is all we'll need to be able to create, amend, and navigate our tree structure. Also we're not going to spend ages trawling through each of the properties and methods of these objects, but rather we'll cherry pick some of the most useful properties and methods and use them to achieve specific ends. We'll start with two of the most useful methods of the document object itself.

Methods of the document Object (Returning an Element or Elements)

Let's begin at the most basic level. You have your HTML web page, so how do you go about getting back a particular element on the page in script? We're going to ignore the way used in IE 4 and IE 5 (the document.all collection) and the NN4 way of doing this (for example, with the document.layers collection), and instead concentrate on the two crossbrowser ways of doing this in IE 5.5 and NN 6.

Methods of the document Object	Description
getElementById(*idvalue*)	Returns a reference (a node) to an element, when supplied with the value of the ID attribute of that element
getElementsByTagName(*tag name*)	Returns a reference (a node list) to a set of elements that have the same tag as the one supplied in the argument

The first of the two methods, getElementById(), requires us to ensure that every element we want to access in the page uses an ID attribute, otherwise a null value (a word indicating a missing or unknown value) will be returned by our method. Let's go back to our first example and add some ID attributes to our elements:

```
<HTML>
<HEAD></HEAD>
<BODY>
<H1 ID="Heading1">My Heading</H1>
<P ID="Paragraph1">This is some text in a paragraph</P>
</BODY>
</HTML>
```

Now we can use the getElementById() method to return a reference to any of the HTML elements with ID attributes on our page. For example, if you add the following code to the above, we can reference the <H1> element:

```
<HTML>
<HEAD>
</HEAD>
<BODY>
<H1 ID="Heading1">My Heading</H1>
<P ID="Paragraph1">This is some text in a paragraph</P>
<SCRIPT LANGUAGE="Javascript">
alert(document.getElementById("Heading1"));
</SCRIPT>
</BODY>
</HTML>
```

This will display the following:

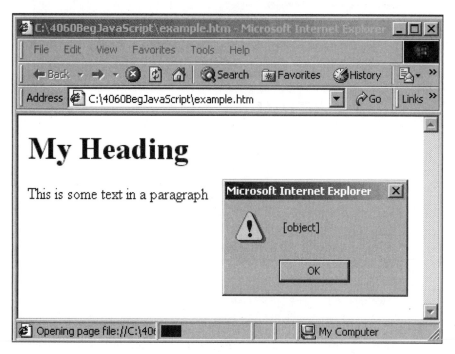

You might have been expecting it to return something along the lines of `<H1>` or
`<H1 ID="Heading1">`, but all it's actually returning is a reference to the `<H1>` element. This is more useful though, as you can use this to alter attributes of the `<H1>` element, such as to change the color or size. We can do this via the `style` object, quickly just to demonstrate:

```
<HTML>
<HEAD>
</HEAD>
<BODY>
<H1 ID="Heading1">My Heading</H1>
<P ID="Paragraph1">This is some text in a paragraph</P>
<SCRIPT LANGUAGE="Javascript">
var H1Element = document.getElementById("Heading1");
H1Element.style.fontFamily = "Arial";
</SCRIPT>
</BODY>
</HTML>
```

If we display this in the browser, then we see that we can directly influence the attributes of the `<H1>` element in script, as we have done here by changing its font type to Arial:

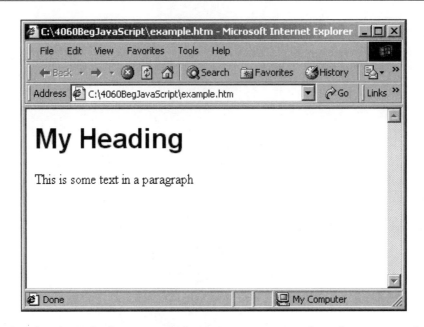

The second of the two methods, getElementsByTagName(), works in the same way, but, as its name implies, it can return more than one element. If we were to go back to our second example with the table and use this method to return the table cells <TD> in our code, then we would get a total of four table cells returned to our object. We'd still only have one object returned, but this object would be a collection of elements. To reference a particular element in the collection, you would therefore have to be more precise. You need to specify an index number which we do using the item() method:

```
<HTML>
<HEAD>
<TITLE>This is a test page</TITLE>
</HEAD>
<BODY>
<SPAN>Below is a table...    </SPAN>
<TABLE BORDER=1>
<TR>
    <TD>Row 1 Cell 1</TD>
    <TD>Row 1 Cell 2</TD>
</TR>
<TR>
    <TD>Row 2 Cell 1</TD>
    <TD>Row 2 Cell 2</TD>
</TR>
</TABLE>
<SCRIPT LANGUAGE="Javascript">
var TDElement = document.getElementsByTagName("TD").item(0);
TDElement.style.fontFamily = "arial";
</SCRIPT>
</BODY>
</HTML>
```

Like arrays, collections are zero-based and so the first element in the table would correspond to the index number zero. If we ran this example, once again using the `style` object, it would alter the style of the contents of the first table cell only in the table:

Once again, all of the attributes of each element are available to the DOM. We can use these to alter any aspect of the element, from presentation to the actual links contained. If you wanted to reference all of the cells in this way, you would have to mention each one explicitly in the code, and assign a new variable for each element as follows:

```
<SCRIPT LANGUAGE="Javascript">
var TDElement0 = document.getElementsByTagName("TD").item(0);
var TDElement1 = document.getElementsByTagName("TD").item(1);
var TDElement2 = document.getElementsByTagName("TD").item(2);
var TDElement3 = document.getElementsByTagName("TD").item(3);
TDElement0.style.fontFamily = "arial";
TDElement1.style.fontFamily = "arial";
TDElement2.style.fontFamily = "arial";
TDElement3.style.fontFamily = "arial";
</SCRIPT>
```

One thing to note about the `getElementsByTagName()` method is that it takes the element names within quotation marks and without the angle brackets `<>` that normally surround tags. The tag name should also be in upper case.

Where the DOM and BOM Overlap

One quick point to consider here is that in the previous set of examples we've used a feature that we introduced in the previous chapter under the heading of the Browser Object Model to access the style properties of an element, namely the `style` object. However, we're still using part of the DOM. This is a common point of confusion, as while the DOM only concerns itself with the contents of the browser window, the BOM does concern itself with some features inside the browser window as well as the different parts of the actual browser. This overlap inside the browser window where both object models can be used is where things aren't quite so clear. This is down to the fact that browsers have had object models for the contents of the document long before there were standards outlining them. Style is one major point where both browsers have supported changing style via scripting properties and methods, which is definitely part of the document, but currently still browser-dependent.

539

Given this information, the style object (discussed in Chapter 12) might appear to be part of the Browser Object Model and not the Document Object Model, as it is browser-dependent. However, while the style object isn't addressed in level 1 of the DOM, it isn't because the style object is non-standard. The style object isn't covered in the standard, because the first version of the standard wasn't able to address all things, and it left styles to the second level. They're not totally resolved there either, and it will probably be the third version before they get properly sorted. While being browser dependent, the style object actually works well in both browsers and supplies a very similar set of properties in both IE 5.5 and NN 6, which is why we chose it for this example. You could also use the DOM method setAttribute() (which we will look at shortly) to set the STYLE attributes, but this is a lot more messy and currently only works in NN 6. Even NN 6 won't allow you to set the attribute to a variable name (as opposed to a text string).

Properties of the document Object (Returning a Reference to the Topmost Element)

We've now got a reference to individual elements on the page, but what of the tree structure we've discussed? The tree structure encompasses all of the elements on the page and gives them a hierarchical structure. If you want to reference that, then you need a particular property of the document object that returns the outermost element of your document. In HTML, this should always be the <HTML> element. The property that does this is documentElement.

Property of the document Object	Description
documentElement	Returns a reference to the outermost element of the document (the root element, for example <HTML>)

You can use documentElement as follows. If we go back to our previous example code, we can transfer our entire DOM into one variable as follows:

```
<HTML>
<HEAD>
</HEAD>
<BODY>
<H1 ID="Heading1">My Heading</H1>
<P ID="Paragraph1">This is some text in a paragraph</P>
<SCRIPT LANGUAGE="Javascript">
var Container = document.documentElement;
</SCRIPT>
</BODY>
</HTML>
```

The variable Container now contains the root element, which is <HTML>. The documentElement property has returned a reference to this element in the form of an object, an Element object to be precise. The Element object has its own set of properties and methods. If we want to use them, we can just refer to them by using the variable name, followed by the method or property name:

```
Container.elementobjectproperty
```

Fortunately, the Element object only has one property.

Property of the Element Object

The property of the `Element` object is a reference to the tag name of the element.

Property of the Element Object	Description
`tagName`	Can either set or return the element tag name

In our previous example you had to take my word for it that the variable `Container` contained the `<HTML>` element, but using this property we can demonstrate it. Add the following line, which makes use of the `tagName` property:

```
<HTML>
<HEAD>
</HEAD>
<BODY>
<H1 ID="Heading1">My Heading</H1>
<P ID="Paragraph1">This is some text in a paragraph</P>
<SCRIPT LANGUAGE="Javascript">
var Container = document.documentElement;
alert(Container.tagName);
</SCRIPT>
</BODY>
</HTML>
```

This code will now return proof that our variable `Container` holds the outermost element, and by implication all other elements within:

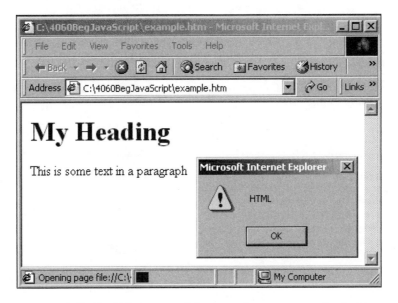

Now we can return any individual element, and the root element, we can look at how we can start navigating our tree structure.

Properties of the Node Object (Navigating the Document)

We've now got back our element or elements from the web page, but what happens if we want to move through our page systematically, from element to element, or from attribute to attribute? This is where we need to step back to a higher level. To move between elements, attributes, and text, we have to move between nodes in our tree structure. It doesn't matter what is contained within the node, or rather what sort of node it is. This is why we need to go back to one of the objects we called base objects. Our whole tree structure is made up of these base-level Node objects.

Here's a list of some common properties of the Node object provide information about the node, whether it be an element, attribute, or text, and allow us to move from one node to another:

Properties of the Node Object	Description of Property
firstChild	Returns the first child node of an element
lastChild	Returns the last child node of an element
previousSibling	Returns the previous child node of an element at the same level as the current child node
nextSibling	Returns the next child node of an element at the same level as the current child node
ownerDocument	Returns the root node of the document that contains the node
parentNode	Returns the element that contains the current node in the tree structure
nodeName	Returns the name of the node
nodeType	Returns the type of the node as a number
nodeValue	Sets the value of the node in plain text format

Let's take a quick look at how some of these properties work. Consider once more our first example:

```
<HTML>
<HEAD>
</HEAD>
<BODY>
<H1 ID="Heading1">My Heading</H1>
<P ID="Paragraph1">This is some text in a paragraph</P>
<SCRIPT LANGUAGE="Javascript">
var H1Element = document.getElementById("Heading1");
H1Element.style.fontFamily = "Arial";
</SCRIPT>
</BODY>
</HTML>
```

We can now use `H1Element` to navigate our tree structure, access the contents of the text, and change it. If we add the following lines:

```
<HTML>
<HEAD>
</HEAD>
<BODY>
<H1 ID="Heading1">My Heading</H1>
<P ID="Paragraph1">This is some text in a paragraph</P>
<SCRIPT LANGUAGE="Javascript">
var H1Element = document.getElementById("Heading1");
H1Element.style.fontFamily = "Arial";
var PElement = H1Element.nextSibling;
PElement.style.fontFamily = "Arial";
</SCRIPT>
</BODY>
</HTML>
```

we are setting the reference in the variable `PElement` to the next element along in the tree structure on the same level. In effect we are navigating along the tree structure like so:

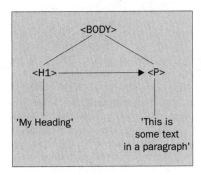

The same principles also work in reverse. We can go back and add yet more code to our example that navigates back to the previous node and changes the text of our previous element as follows:

```
<HTML>
<HEAD>
</HEAD>
<BODY>
<H1 ID="Heading1">My Heading</H1>
<P ID="Paragraph1">This is some text in a paragraph</P>
<SCRIPT LANGUAGE="Javascript">
var H1Element = document.getElementById("Heading1");
H1Element.style.fontFamily = "Arial";
var PElement = H1Element.nextSibling;
PElement.style.fontFamily = "Arial";
H1Element = PElement.previousSibling;
H1Element.style.fontFamily = "Courier";
</SCRIPT>
</BODY>
</HTML>
```

What we're doing here is setting the first <H1> element to the font Arial; we're then navigating across to the next sibling, which is the next child node of our <BODY> element. The first child is the <H1> element, the second one is the <P> element. We set the font to be Arial here as well. Our new two lines of code then use the previousSibling property to jump back to our <H1> element, and then we again change the fontFamily style, but this time we change it to Courier. So the sum effect of our program is to change the <H1> element to Courier, and the <P> element to Arial.

Try It Out – Navigating Our HTML Document Using the DOM

I've now got a confession to make. Up until now we've been "cheating", in that we haven't truly navigated our HTML document, we've just used document.getElementById() to return an element and navigated to differnt nodes from there. Now let's use the documentElement property of the document object and do this properly. We'll start at the top of our tree and move down through the child nodes, to get at those elements, then we'll navigate through our child nodes and change the properties the same way as before.

Type the following into your text editor:

```
<HTML>
<HEAD>
</HEAD>
<BODY>
<H1 ID="Heading1">My Heading</H1>
<P ID="Paragraph1">This is some text in a paragraph</P>

<SCRIPT LANGUAGE="Javascript">
var HTMLElement;        // HTMLElement stores reference to <HTML>
var HeadingElement;     // HeadingElement stores refrence to <HEAD>
var BodyElement;        // BodyElement stores refrence to <BODY>
var H1Element;          // H1Element stores reference to <H1>
var PElement;           // PElement stores reference to <P>

HTMLElement = document.documentElement;

HeadingElement = HTMLElement.firstChild;
alert(HeadingElement.tagName);

if(HeadingElement.nextSibling.nodeType==3)
{
    BodyElement = HeadingElement.nextSibling.nextSibling;
}
else
{
    BodyElement = HeadingElement.nextSibling;
}
alert(BodyElement.tagName);

if(BodyElement.firstChild.nodeType==3)
{
    H1Element = BodyElement.firstChild.nextSibling;
}
else
```

```
{
     H1Element = BodyElement.firstChild;
}
alert(H1Element.tagName);
H1Element.style.fontFamily = "Arial";

if(H1Element.nextSibling.nodeType==3)
{
     PElement = H1Element.nextSibling.nextSibling;
}
else
{
     PElement = H1Element.nextSibling;
}
alert(PElement.tagName);
PElement.style.fontFamily = "Arial";

if(PElement.previousSibling.nodeType==3)
{
     H1Element = PElement.previousSibling.previousSibling
}
else
{
     H1Element = PElement.previousSibling
}
H1Element.style.fontFamily = "Courier"
</SCRIPT>
</BODY>
</HTML>
```

Save this as `navlast.htm`. Then open the page in your browser, clicking on **OK** through each of the message boxes until you see this page:

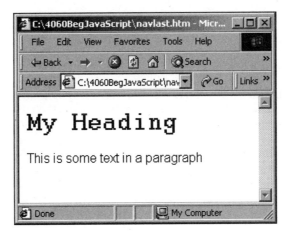

How It Works

We've hopefully made this example very transparent by the addition of several alerts to demonstrate where we are along each section of the tree. We've also named the variables with their various different elements, to give a clearer idea of what is stored in each variable. We could just as easily have named them a, b, c, d, and e, so don't think you need to be bound by this naming convention.

We start at the top of the script block by retrieving our whole document using the documentElement property:

```
var HTMLElement = document.documentElement;
```

The root element is the <HTML> element, hence the name of our first variable. Now if you refer back to our tree, you'll see that the HTML element must have two child nodes, one containing the <HEAD> element and the other containing the <BODY> element. We start by moving to the <HEAD> element as follows:

```
var HeadingElement = HTMLElement.firstChild;
```

We get there using the firstChild property of our Node object, which contains our <HTML> element. We use our first alert to demonstrate that this is true:

```
alert(HeadingElement.tagName);
```

Our <BODY> element is our next sibling across from the <HEAD> element, so we navigate across by creating a variable that is the next sibling from the <HEAD> element:

```
if(HeadingElement.nextSibling.nodeType==3)
{
    BodyElement = HeadingElement.nextSibling.nextSibling;
}
else
{
    BodyElement = HeadingElement.nextSibling;
}
alert(BodyElement.tagName);
```

Here we check to see what the nodeType of the nextSibling of HeadingElement is. If it returns 3, then we set BodyElement to be the nextSibling of the nextSibling of HeadingElement, otherwise we just set it to the nextSibling of HeadingElement. Why do we do this? The answer lies with the implementation of the DOM in NN 6. We would think that the next sibling of the <HEAD> element in the tree would be the <BODY> element, and indeed it is in IE 5.5. However, NN 6 adds text nodes to every element in the tree, whether the element contains text or not, because of the way Netscape has interpreted the DOM. This is explained more fully later in the chapter. To navigate through the tree in a way that works both in IE 5.5 and NN 6, we check to see whether the next sibling has a nodeType of 3. If it has, then it is a text node, and we need to move along the next node.

We use an alert to prove that we are now at the <BODY> element:

```
alert(BodyElement.tagName);
```

The <BODY> element in this page also has two children, the <H1> and <P> elements. We move down to the <H1> element, using the firstChild property. Again we check for the extra text node that NN 6 might have added. We use alert again to show that we have arrived at <H1>:

```
if(BodyElement.firstChild.nodeType==3)
{
     H1Element = BodyElement.firstChild.nextSibling;
}
else
{
     H1Element = BodyElement.firstChild;
}
alert(H1Element.tagName);
```

After the third alert, the style will be altered on our first element, changing the font to Arial:

```
H1Element.style.fontFamily = "Arial";
```

We then navigate across to the <P> element using the nextSibling property, again checking for the extra text node:

```
if(H1Element.nextSibling.nodeType==3)
{
     PElement = H1Element.nextSibling.nextSibling;
}
else
{
     PElement = H1Element.nextSibling;
}
alert(PElement.tagName);
```

We change the <P> element's font to Arial also:

```
PElement.style.fontFamily = "Arial";
```

Finally, we use the previousSibling property to move back in our tree to the <H1> element and this time change the font to Courier:

```
if(PElement.previousSibling.nodeType==3)
{
     H1Element = PElement.previousSibling.previousSibling
}
else
{
     H1Element = PElement.previousSibling
}
H1Element.style.fontFamily = "Courier"
```

It's hopefully a fairly easy to follow example, as we're just using the same tree structure we created with diagrams, but showing how the DOM effectively creates this hierarchy and that you can move about using script within this hierarchy.

Methods of the Node Object (Adding and Removing Elements from the Document)

So we can now move through our tree structure and alter the contents of elements as we go. We still can't fundamentally alter the structure of our HTML document though. Help is at hand though, as the Node object's methods let us do this.

Here's a list of methods that allow you to alter the structure of an HTML document by creating new nodes and adding them to our tree:

Methods of the Node Objects	Description
appendChild(*new node*)	Adds a new node object to the end of the list of child nodes
cloneNode(*child option*)	Creates a new node object that is identical to the node object supplied as an argument, optionally including all of the child nodes
hasChildNodes()	Returns true if a node has any child nodes
insertBefore(*new node, current node*)	Inserts a new node object into the list of child nodes, before the node stipulated in current node
removeChild(*child node*)	Removes a child node from a list of child nodes of the node object
replaceChild(*new child, old child*)	Replaces an old child node object with a new child node object

We'll look at how they work shortly.

Methods of the document Object (Adding and Removing Elements from the Document)

In addition to the above methods of the Node object, the document object itself boasts some methods for creating elements, attributes, and text.

Methods of the document Object	Description
createElement(*element name*)	Creates an element node with a specified name
createTextNode(*text*)	Creates a text node with the specified text
createAttribute(*attribute name*)	Creates an attribute node with a specified name

The best way to demonstrate both sets of methods for the Node object and the document object at once, is with an example.

Try It Out – Create HTML elements and text with DOM JavaScript

We'll create a web page with just a paragraph <P> and heading <H1> element, but instead of HTML we'll use the DOM properties and methods to place these elements on the web page. While the screenshot in the following example was taken in IE, you'll find that the example works equally well in NN 6, without any changes being required. Start up your preferred text editor and type in the following:

```
<HTML>
<HEAD>
</HEAD>
<BODY>
<SCRIPT LANGUAGE=JavaScript>
var newText;
var newElem;

newText = document.createTextNode("My Heading")
newElem = document.createElement("H1")
newElem.appendChild(newText)
document.body.appendChild(newElem)

newText = document.createTextNode("This is some text in a paragraph")
newElem = document.createElement("P")
newElem.appendChild(newText)
document.body.appendChild(newElem)

</SCRIPT>
</BODY>
</HTML>
```

Save this page as `create.htm` and open it in your browser:

How It Works

It all looks a bit dull and ordinary doesn't it? And yes, before you say it, we could have done this much more simply with HTML. That isn't the point though. The idea is that we use DOM properties and methods, accessed via JavaScript, to insert these features. The first two lines of the script block are just used to define the variables in our script, which will hold the text we want to insert into the page and the HTML element we wish to insert:

```
var newText;
var newElem;
```

We start at the bottom of our tree first, by creating a text node with the `createTextNode()` method:

```
newText = document.createTextNode("My Heading")
```

We then use the `createElement()` method to create an HTML heading:

```
newElem = document.createElement("H1")
```

At this point the two variables are entirely separate to each other. We have a text node, and we have an `<H1>` element, but they're not connected. The next line allows us to attach the text node to our HTML element. We reference the HTML element we have created with the variable name `newElem` and use the `appendChild()` method of our node, and supply the contents of the `newText` variable we created earlier as a parameter:

```
newElem.appendChild(newText);
```

Let's recap. We created a text node and stored it the `newText` variable. We created an `<H1>` element and stored it in the `newElem` variable. Then we appended the text node as a child node to the `<H1>` element. That still leaves us with a problem – we've created an element with a value, but it isn't part of our document. We need to attach the entirety of what we've created so far to the document body. We can do this again with the `appendChild()` method, but this time supplying it to the `document.body` object:

```
document.body.appendChild(newElem)
```

This completes the first part of our code. Now all we have to do is repeat the process for the `<P>` element:

```
newText = document.createTextNode("This is some text in a paragraph")
newElem = document.createElement("P")
newElem.appendChild(newText)
document.body.appendChild(newElem)
```

We create a text node first, then we create an element. We attach the text to the element and lastly we attach the element and text to the body of the document. This completes our creation of parts of the HTML document in script.

We've now created elements and changed text, but we've left out one of the important parts of the web page, namely attributes. We'll look at how we can do this now.

Methods of the Element Object (Getting and Setting Attributes)

While we mentioned that it is still acceptable to set the STYLE attributes via the style object, if you want to set any other element attributes, then you should use the DOM specific methods of the Element object.

The two methods we can use to return and alter the contents of an HTML element's attributes are getAttribute() and setAttribute().

Methods of the Element Object	Description
getAttribute(*attribute name*)	Returns the value of an attribute
setAttribute(*attribute name, value*)	Sets the value of an attribute
removeAttribute(*attribute name*)	Removes the value of an attribute and replaces it with the default value

Let's take a quick look at how they work now. In the previous example, you may have noticed that createElement() and createTextNode() were used to add HTML elements and text to our page, but that we didn't actually make use of createAttribute(). That's because there's a much easier method of creating attributes, using the setAttribute() and getAttribute() methods.

Try It Out – Creating Attributes

We're now going to take our last example and add some attributes to it which will effect the presentation and layout of our text. Make sure that you replicate the case of these lines when you type them in, as it could effect whether the example works or not as we shall see.

Open create.htm in your text editor and add the following highlighted lines:

```
<HTML>
<HEAD>
</HEAD>
<BODY>
<SCRIPT LANGUAGE=JavaScript>
var newText;
var newElem;

newText = document.createTextNode("My Heading")
newElem = document.createElement("H1")
newElem.setAttribute("align","center")
newElem.appendChild(newText)
document.body.appendChild(newElem)

newText = document.createTextNode("This is some text in a paragraph")
newElem = document.createElement("P")
alert(newElem.getAttribute("align"))
newElem.setAttribute("align","right")
alert(newElem.getAttribute("align"))
newElem.appendChild(newText)
document.body.appendChild(newElem)
</SCRIPT>
</BODY>
</HTML>
```

Save this as `attribute.htm` and open it in your browser:

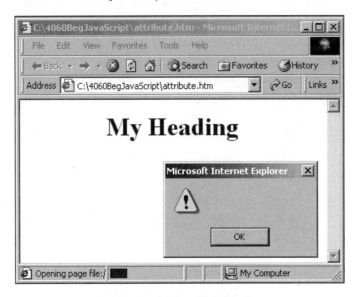

Click OK on the alert, and the second time it should display correctly:

Click on OK again and you will see the final screen:

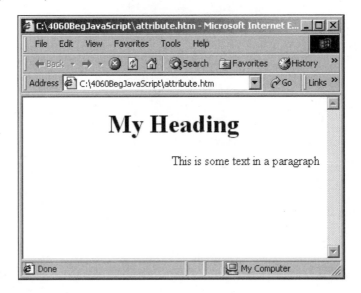

How It Works

We've only added four lines of code here to augment our existing document structure. The first takes our `<H1>` element and adds an `ALIGN` attribute to it:

```
newText = document.createTextNode("My Heading")
newElem = document.createElement("H1")
newElem.setAttribute("align","center")
```

You should note that in the `setAttribute()` method, `align`, is in lower-case as per the XHTML standards recommended earlier in this chapter. If it was in upper case:

```
newElem.setAttribute("ALIGN","CENTER")
```

the example would fail. The `setAttribute()` method takes any existing attribute, `ALIGN`, (by existing attribute, I mean one that is specified for that particular element in the HTML specifications) and supplies it the value `CENTER`. The result is to position our text in the center of the page.

> *Strictly speaking, the ALIGN attribute is deprecated under XHTML, but we have used it as it works, and it has one of the easily demonstrable visual effects on a web page.*

So `setAttribute()` takes the name of the attribute first and the value second. If you set the attribute name to be a non-existent attribute, then it will have no effect on the page. You can also set the attribute to a non-existent value, which is perfectly legal, but once again will have no effect on the page.

The second part of the code is very similar to the first:

```
newText = document.createTextNode("This is some text in a paragraph")
newElem = document.createElement("P")
alert(newElem.getAttribute("align"))
newElem.setAttribute("align","right")
alert(newElem.getAttribute("align"))
```

Once we've created our `<P>` element and accompanying text, we use `getAttribute()` to return the value of the `ALIGN` attribute. As `ALIGN` hasn't been set yet, it returns no value, not even the default. We then use the `setAttribute()` method to set the `ALIGN` attribute to `right`, and use `getAttribute()` to return the value. This time it returns `right`, as you'd expect. This is then reflected in the final display of the web page.

What have we seen so far? We started with a nearly empty DOM hierarchy. We then returned the HTML document to a variable, navigated through the different parts of it via DOM objects outside the hierarchy itself (the `Node` objects), changed the contents of objects and thus altered the content of the web page and then inserted DOM objects into the hierarchy and thus inserted new elements onto the page. This leaves just one area to cover in the DOM – the event model.

The DOM Event Model

The DOM event model is introduced in level 2 of the DOM standard. It's a way of both handling events and providing information about these events to the script. It provides guidelines for a standard way of determining what generated an event, what type of event it was, where the event occurred, and at what time.

All of this was, of course, trackable in IE 4, and to a lesser extent in NN 4, through the `event` object as we saw in the last chapter. However, the main problem was that the ways of accessing this object and the names of its properties were completely different between the two browsers.

The DOM event model doesn't look complete in some ways and might yet be tweaked in level 3 of the standard, but what it does do is introduce a basic set of objects, properties, and methods. It also makes some important distinctions.

First there is an `event` object, which provides information about the element that has generated an event and allows you to retrieve it in script. To make it available in script, it must be passed as a parameter to the function connected to the event handler, as we saw with NN 4.x in the previous chapter. It is not globally available, as the IE `event` object was/is.

The standard outlines several properties and methods of the `event` object that have long since been a source of dispute between IE and NN. We will only be using the properties, so we will just be considering them here:

Properties of the event Object	Description
`bubbles`	Indicates whether an event can bubble (pass control from one element to another) or not
`cancelable`	Indicates whether an event can have its default action canceled or not
`currentTarget`	Indicates which event is currently being processed
`eventPhase`	Indicates which phase of the event flow an event is in
`target` (Netscape Navigator 6 only)	Indicates which element caused the event; In the DOM event model, text nodes are the possible target of an event
`timeStamp` (Netscape Navigator 6 only)	Indicates at what time the event occurred
`type`	Indicates the name of the event

Secondly, the DOM introduces a `mouse` event object which deals with events generated specifically by the mouse. This is introduced because you might need more specific information about the event, such as the position in pixels of the cursor, or the element the mouse has come from.

Properties of the mouse Event Object	Description
altKey	Indicates whether the *Alt* key was pressed when the event was generated
button	Indicates which button on the mouse was pressed
clientX	Indicates where in the browser window, in horizontal coordinates, the mouse pointer was when the event was generated
clientY	Indicates where in the browser window, in vertical coordinates, the mouse pointer was when the event was generated
ctrlKey	Indicates whether the *Ctrl* key was pressed when the event was generated
metaKey	Indicates whether the meta key was pressed when the event was generated
relatedTarget (Netscape Navigator 6 only)	In the DOM event model text nodes are the (possible) target of mouseover event
screenX	Indicates where in the browser window, in horizontal coordinates relative to the origin in the screen coordinates, the mouse pointer was when the event was generated
screenY	Indicates where in the browser window, in vertical coordinates relative to the origin in the screen coordinates, the mouse pointer was when the event was generated
shiftKey	Indicates whether the *shift* key was pressed when the event was generated

While any event might create an event object, only a select set of events can generate a mouse object. On the occurrence of a mouse event, you'd be able to access properties from both the event object and the mouse object, while with a non-mouse event, none of the above mouse object properties would be available. The mouse events that can create a mouse event object are:

❑ onclick: occurs when a mouse button is clicked (pressed and released) with the pointer over an element or text

❑ onmousedown: occurs when a mouse button is pressed with the pointer over an element or text

❑ onmouseup: occurs when a mouse button is released with the pointer over an element or text

❑ onmouseover: occurs when a mouse button is moved onto an element or text

❑ onmousemove: occurs when a mouse button is moved and it is already on top of an element or text

❑ onmouseout: occurs when a mouse button is moved out and away from an element or text

To get at an event using the DOM, all you have to do is query the event object that is created by the individual element that has raised the event. For example, in the following code the <P> element will raise a ondblclick event:

```
<P ondblclick="handlekey(event)">Paragraph</P>

<SCRIPT LANGUAGE="JavaScript">
function handlekey(e)
{
    alert(e.type);
}
</SCRIPT>
```

We have to pass the `event` object that is created by the `<P>` element as an argument in the function call to be able to use it within the function. You can then use the parameter passed as the `event` object and use its general properties made available through the DOM.

However, this is where the browsers get shaky. The DOM level 2 standard has only recently been agreed and that means that IE 5.5 doesn't support a lot of the DOM properties mentioned in the table, although it does support the `type` property. Instead, it has its own set of IE-specific properties, which we won't be discussing in a chapter on the DOM as they are not part of the DOM.

If you ran the previous example, it would just tell you what kind of event raised our event-handling function. This might seem self-evident in the above example, but if you had included the following extra lines of code:

```
<P ondblclick="handlekey(event)">Paragraph</P>
<H1 onclick="handle(event)">Heading 1</H1>
<SPAN onmouseover="handle(event)">Special Text</SPAN>

<SCRIPT LANGUAGE="JavaScript">
function handlekey(e)
{
    alert(e.type);
}
</SCRIPT>
```

then any one of three elements could have raised the function, and so the code becomes much more useful. In general you will use relatively few event handlers to deal with any number of events, and you can use the event properties as a filter to determine what type of event happened and what HTML element triggered it, so that you can treat each event differently.

For example:

```
<P ondblclick="handlekey(event)">Paragraph</P>
<H1 onclick="handlekey(event)">Heading 1</H1>
<SPAN onmouseover="handlekey(event)">Special Text</SPAN>
...
<SCRIPT LANGUAGE="JavaScript">
function handlekey(e)
{
    if (e.type == "onmouseover")
    {
        alert("You moved over the Special Text");
    }
}
</SCRIPT>
```

Depending on what type of event was returned, you could take a different course of action.

Let's take a quick look at an example now, which creates a mouse event object when the user clicks anywhere on the screen and returns to the user the x and y coordinates of the position on the screen of the mouse pointer when the mouse button was clicked. This example will work in both IE 5+ and NN 6 browsers.

Open your text editor and type in the following:

```
<HTML>
<HEAD>
</HEAD>
<BODY onclick="handleClick(event)">
Click anywhere on the screen...
<SCRIPT LANGUAGE="JavaScript">
function handleClick(e)
{
    alert("You clicked on the screen at X" + e.clientX +" and Y" + e.clientY);
}
</SCRIPT>
</BODY>
</HTML>
```

Save this as mouseevent.htm and run it in your browser:

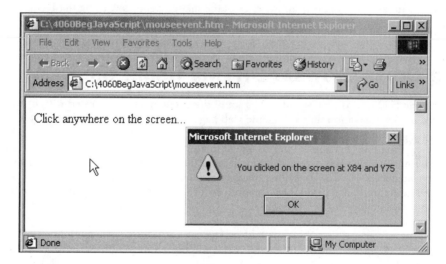

Now click OK, move the pointer in the browser window and click again. A different result appears.

How It Works

This example is consistent with the event-handling behavior – the browser waits for an event, and every time a specific event occurs, it will raise the corresponding function. It will continue to wait for the event until you exit the browser or that particular web page. In this example, we use the <BODY> element to raise an onclick event:

```
<BODY onclick="handleClick(event)">
```

Whenever that function is encountered, the `handleClick()` function is raised and a new `mouse` event object is generated. Remember that `mouse` event objects also give you access to `event` object properties as well as `mouse` event object properties, even though we don't use them in this example.

The function takes the `mouse` event object and assigns it the reference `e`:

```
function handleClick(e)
{
    alert("You clicked on the screen at X" + e.clientX +" and Y" + e.clientY);
}
```

Inside the function we use the `alert()` statement to display the contents of the `clientX` and `clientY` properties of the `mouse` event object on the screen. This `mouse` event object is overwritten and recreated every time you generate an event, so the next time you click on the mouse pointer, it returns new co-ordinates for the X and Y positions.

As described earlier one problem that precludes greater discussion of the DOM event model is the fact that only one browser supports it in any detail. We will see in a later example that we are still in a position of having to dual-code for both browsers when it comes to returning information about events via properties, but this should give you a little taster for how they should work, and how they will work in future browsers. We won't go into any further detail here about events, but we will be returning to the DOM event object model in an example later in the chapter, when we discuss how to cross-code for both browsers. In fact let's get down to the crux of the matter right now, using the DOM to create web pages that work in both browsers.

Writing Cross-Browser DHTML Using the DOM

When Dynamic HTML was first introduced, a lot of the excitement it generated with its new features was eclipsed by the realization that a dynamic web page in NN 4 wouldn't work in IE 4 and vice versa. A lot of finger-pointing and blame-apportioning went on. This was aimed at the two main browser vendors for creating their versions of the language in advance/defiance of the standards, at the book publishers for encouraging this diversity by explaining the two methods of Dynamic HTML as almost two separate languages, at W3C for failing to agree a standard method before the browsers were released, and at the web page developers themselves for daring to use two separate sets of code. It isn't really fair to blame anyone for this though.

The heart of the matter was that Netscape had created a `<LAYER>` tag as a method of implementing dynamic content. Allegedly, they had initially received positive sounds from the W3C standards committee that their method of Dynamic HTML would be adopted as the standard. Unfortunately, as the rumor goes, their method was ditched when the standards authority found out that in fact the method proposed by Microsoft was deemed easier, more intuitive, and more workable. By then Netscape had almost completed their browser and were irreversibly committed to releasing it.

Whether you choose to blame one particular side or the other is irrelevant, as ultimately Dynamic HTML became a browserspecific language, and the Microsoft method became the de facto way of using it. This isn't to say that Microsoft's implementation was perfect, and Netscape's latest browser, NN 6, written under the direction of the Open Source group, Mozilla, by an army of volunteers, goes a long way towards reversing the browser-specific pitfalls that has dogged Dynamic HTML for a long time. In short it brings NN up to date with the standards, and in some cases surpasses IE's compliance with them.

As described, the DOM is a standard that provides a generic set of properties, methods, and events for any language and therefore any browser to address the HTML document and manipulate it. What we're now going to do is go back to some previous examples from the last chapter and demonstrate how to translate them, firstly into something that uses only DOM standards and methods, and secondly, if this isn't possible, into something that provides a functioning dynamic page that can be viewed on two browsers, without requiring two completely separate sets of code.

This isn't intended to be an entirely exhaustive guide as to how to get your page working in both browsers, but by examining four varying examples, we hope to cover a lot of the common ground between the two.

Animated Text Example

Our first example takes the animated text example from the last chapter. In fact, we saw three versions of this example in the last chapter – one that worked on IE 4+, one that worked on NN 4.x, and one that worked on both IE 4+ and NN 4+. The last example made use of browser-specific code to accommodate the different browser types. Here we will rewrite the example for DOM-compliant browsers, with no browser-specific code necessary.

Try It Out – Animating Text

Start up your text editor and type in the following:

```
<HTML>
<HEAD>
<SCRIPT LANGUAGE=JavaScript>

var paraOneLeft = 100;
var paraTwoLeft = 400;
var switchDirection = false;

function window_onload()
{
    window.setInterval("moveParas()",50);
}

function moveParas()
{
    var paraOne = document.getElementById("paraOneID");
    var paraTwo = document.getElementById("paraTwoID");

    if (switchDirection == false)
    {
        paraOneLeft++;
        paraTwoLeft--;

        if (paraOneLeft == 400)
        {
            switchDirection = true;
        }
    }
    else
    {
        paraOneLeft--;
        paraTwoLeft++;
```

```
        if (paraOneLeft == 100)
        {
            switchDirection = false;
        }
    }

    paraOne.style.left = paraOneLeft + 'px';
    paraTwo.style.left = paraTwoLeft + 'px';
}

</SCRIPT>
</HEAD>
<BODY LANGUAGE=JavaScript onload="return window_onload()">

<P STYLE="position:absolute;left:100px;top:30px" ID="paraOneID">Para 1</P>
<P STYLE="position:absolute;left:400px;top:10px" ID="paraTwoID">Para 2</P>

</BODY>
</HTML>
```

Save this as `animate.htm`. Then open this up in your browser and observe the animated text:

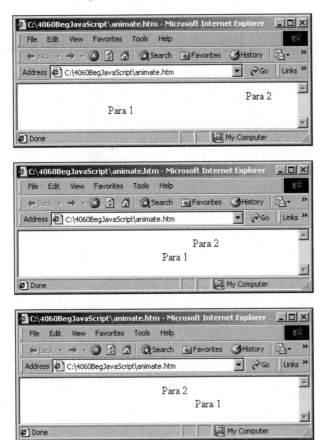

How It Works

The code relies on two functions to make it work. The first `window_onload()` function has not changed from our previous examples. It is connected to the `onload` event handler given in the `<BODY>` tag, which fires when the window is opened. It is used to start a timer, which calls the second function, `moveParas()`, at intervals of 50 milliseconds.

Before we call the `window_onload()` function, we set three global variables, two of which initialize the starting positions of our moving text, and the other of which sets a variable that will be used to decide on the direction of scrolling:

```
var paraOneLeft = 100;
var paraTwoLeft = 400;
var switchDirection = false;
function window_onload()
{
    window.setInterval("moveParas()",50);
}
```

The second function is the one that does the animation, and which we have made changes to in this example. We start by using the `getElementById()` method of the `document` object to return a reference to both paragraph elements on the screen. This is the main difference between this example and the ones we saw before.

```
function moveParas()
{
    var paraOne = document.getElementById("paraOneID");
    var paraTwo = document.getElementById("paraTwoID");
```

The next part of the function should be familiar to you. If we have no need to reverse the direction of the scrolling (that is, the pieces of text haven't reached the boundaries we set of 100 and 400), we can add one to the variable that contains the left position of the first piece of text, and subtract one from the variable that contains the left position of the second piece of text. Note that this doesn't amend the style properties themselves as yet, just updates the variable they will be referencing.

```
    if (switchDirection == false)
    {
        paraOneLeft++;
        paraTwoLeft--;
```

If we've reached 400 pixels with the first paragraph, then we need to set our `switchDirection` variable to reflect this – it ensures we will switch the scrolling direction on the next call of the function:

```
        if (paraOneLeft == 400)
        {
            switchDirection = true;
        }
    }
```

If we've switched direction, then the `else` statement comes into play. We subtract one from our left position variable for our first piece of text, and add one to the second piece of text's left position variable.

```
    else
    {
        paraOneLeft--;
        paraTwoLeft++;
    }
```

We then again run a check to see if the paragraphs have reached the boundaries we imposed, and if so we reverse direction again:

```
    if (paraOneLeft == 100)
    {
        switchDirection = false;
    }
}
```

It's left to the last two lines to actually animate the text by assigning the current value of whatever's in the `paraOneLeft` and `paraTwoLeft` variables, which will have been recently incremented and decremented by one, to alter the `style.left` properties:

```
    paraOne.style.left = paraOneLeft + 'px';
    paraTwo.style.left = paraTwoLeft + 'px';
}
```

Thus our example becomes an infinite loop, as the paragraphs are shuttled back and forth across the screen, within the specified limits, which they can't go beyond.

Adding and Deleting Text Example

The next example is also adapted from one in the previous chapter. Recall the `innertext_IE.htm` example where we supplied the user with a text box and two buttons that allowed the user to retrieve or change the text written in the page. The example we give here is slightly more complex than that example, and needs extra coding to ensure that it is DOM compliant.

Try It Out – Adding and Deleting Text (nodes) on a Page

Start up your text editor of choice and type in the following:

```
<HTML>
<HEAD>
<SCRIPT LANGUAGE=JavaScript>

function bttnAdd_onClick()
{
    var elemPara = document.getElementById("Para1");
    var elemTxtBox = document.getElementById("textarea1");

    var oldTxtNode = elemPara.firstChild;
    var oldText = oldTxtNode.nodeValue;
    var newText = oldText + elemTxtBox.value;
    var newTxtNode = document.createTextNode(newText);
```

```
      elemPara.replaceChild(newTxtNode, oldTxtNode);
   }

   function bttnNew_onClick()
   {
      var elemPara = document.getElementById("Para1");
      var elemTxtBox = document.getElementById("textarea1");

      var newText = elemTxtBox.value;
      var newTxtNode = document.createTextNode(newText);

      var elemNew = document.createElement("P");
      elemNew.appendChild(newTxtNode);

      document.body.insertBefore(elemNew, elemTxtBox);
   }

   function bttnRem_onClick()
   {
      var elemTxtBox = document.getElementById("textarea1");
      var elemLastPara = elemTxtBox.previousSibling;
      document.body.removeChild(elemLastPara);
   }
   </SCRIPT>
   </HEAD>

   <BODY>
   <P ID="Para1">
      Some text...
   </P>
   <TEXTAREA COLS=30 ID="textarea1" ROWS=3></TEXTAREA>
   <BR>
   <INPUT TYPE="button" VALUE="Add Text" NAME="bttnAdd"
      onclick="bttnAdd_onClick()">
   <INPUT TYPE="button" VALUE="New Paragraph" NAME="bttnNew"
      onclick="bttnNew_onClick()">
   <INPUT TYPE="button" VALUE="Remove Paragraph" NAME="bttnRem"
      onclick="bttnRem_onClick()">

   </BODY>
   </HTML>
```

Save this as `textnode.htm` and open it in your browser. Type some text into the text area:

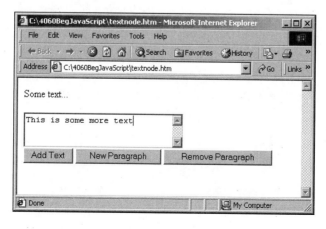

Click on the Add Text button, and see your text added to Some text... in the page. Then click on the New Paragraph button and see your text appear as a new paragraph:

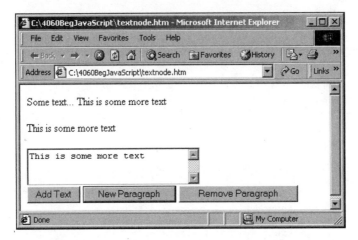

Click on the Remove Paragraph button and the second occurence of your text disappears again:

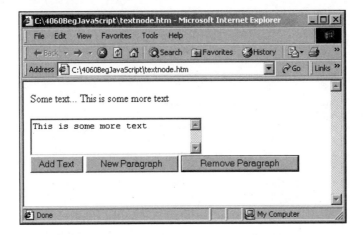

Note with this example that errors will occur if you try to remove or add text to a paragraph that has previously already been removed.

How It Works

In this example we have three functions that do all the work, each connected to one of the three buttons in the form. The first function is activated if we click on the Add Text button:

```
function bttnAdd_onClick()
{
    var elemPara = document.getElementById("Para1");
    var elemTxtBox = document.getElementById("textarea1");
```

```
        var oldTxtNode = elemPara.firstChild;
        var oldText = oldTxtNode.nodeValue;

        var newText = oldText + elemTxtBox.value;
        var newTxtNode = document.createTextNode(newText);

        elemPara.replaceChild(newTxtNode, oldTxtNode);
    }
```

It starts by creating two variables elemPara and elemTxtBox, which contain references to the <P> element and the <TEXTAREA> control element. Next we create two new variables, oldTxtNode and oldText, which store a reference to the text node that is a child of the paragraph node, and the text itself. This is so that when we add the new text, we don't delete the old. The next two lines create our new text, first by adding the old text to the contents of the <TEXTAREA> control, and then by creating a new text node with this new text.

On its own this does nothing – we still have to connect the new text node back to our tree structure. We do this with the replaceChild() method of the paragraph node object, which takes two arguments, one a reference to the old text node and the other the text node we want to replace it with.

The second function is activated when somebody clicks on the **New Paragraph** button:

```
function bttnNew_onClick()
{
    var elemPara = document.getElementById("Para1");
    var elemTxtBox = document.getElementById("textarea1");

    var newText = elemTxtBox.value;
    var newTxtNode = document.createTextNode(newText);

    var elemNew = document.createElement("P");
    elemNew.appendChild(newTxtNode);

    document.body.insertBefore(elemNew, elemTxtBox);
}
```

It works in a similar way to the first function. First it creates variables that store references to the <P> element and the <TEXTAREA> control. This time we don't have to worry about the existing contents of the <P> element, as we are creating a new element. We create two new variables, newText, which stores the value supplied by the user in the <TEXTAREA> control and newTxtNode into which we create a new text node, with the contents of the <TEXTAREA> control.

Next we create a new <P> element using the document object's createElement() method. We append the new text node to it using the appendChild() method, which just takes one argument, a reference to our new text node. Finally, we use the insertBefore() method to insert our <P> element onto the web page. The insertBefore() method takes two arguments, the first being the element we wish to insert, a new <P> element, while the second is the <TEXTAREA> control. It inserts a new child node before the node stipulated in the second argument of the method. This way the new <P> element is inserted after the first <P> element at the top, and before the <TEXTAREA> control.

The last function is the one that removes the latest paragraph on the web page and is activated when someone clicks the Remove Paragraph button. It is a lot simpler than the previous two functions:

```
function bttnRem_onClick()
{
    var elemTxtBox = document.getElementById("textarea1");
    var elemLastPara = elemTxtBox.previousSibling;
    document.body.removeChild(elemLastPara);
}
```

We only need to identify one element, the <TEXTAREA> control. We store the reference to it in the elemTxtBox variable. We then use the previousSibling property in the next line of code to navigate back one in our tree struture to the previous element. If we haven't added any paragraphs to the page, this will be the first one created in the HTML page. We store a reference to this node in the variable elemLastPara. We then supply this variable to the removeChild() method, which removes the child node from the web page.

Mouse Rollover Example

The next example we will consider is, again, one we have already looked at in the last chapter. This is where a piece of text has its content and color changed as the mouse pointer rolls over it. We'll recreate the example, but using DOM methods and properties.

Try It Out - Roll Mouse Pointer Over Text to Dynamically Change it

Will your text editor to life once more and type in the following:

```
<HTML>
<HEAD>
<SCRIPT LANGUAGE=JavaScript>

function myPara_onmouseout()
{
    var myPara = document.getElementById("DynamicText");
    myPara.firstChild.nodeValue = "Roll your mouse over my text";
    myPara.style.color = "Black"
}

function myPara_onmouseover()
{
    var myPara = document.getElementById("DynamicText");
    myPara.firstChild.nodeValue = "Wow that feels good!!!";
    myPara.style.color = "Red"
}

</SCRIPT>
</HEAD>
<BODY>

<P ID="DynamicText" onmouseout="return myPara_onmouseout()"
onmouseover="return myPara_onmouseover()">
    Roll your mouse over my text
</P>

</BODY>
</HTML>
```

Save this as `rollover.htm` and start the page up in your browser:

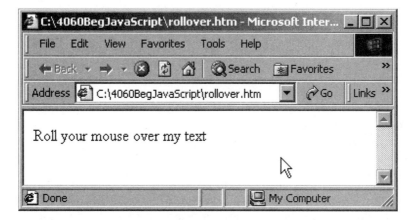

Move your mouse cursor over the text:

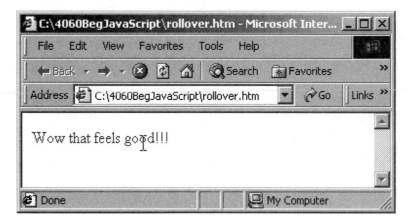

How It Works

This example is very straight forward. If the `onmouseover` event handler is fired, meaning that the mouse pointer has moved over the text, then we set the `<P>` element's child node's node value (in other words the text of the `<P>` element) to equal "Wow that feels good", and change the paragraph's `style.color` to be red:

```
function myPara_onmouseover()
{
    var myPara = document.getElementById(DynamicText)
    myPara.firstChild.nodeValue = "Wow that feels good!!!";
    myPara.style.color = "Red"
}
```

When the mouse pointer rolls outside the target text, we set the `<P>` element's child node's node value to be equal to "Roll your mouse over my text" and the paragraph's `style.color` to be black:

```
function myPara_onmouseout()
{
    var myPara = document.getElementById(DynamicText)
    myPara.firstChild.nodeValue = "Roll your mouse over my text";
    myPara.style.color = "Black"
}
```

That's all there is to this example.

Dynamic Menu Example

We have left the most ambitious of our examples until last. This is where we provide a dynamic menu system that works in both Internet Explorer 5.5 and Netscape Navigator 6. Up until now, all of the examples in this chapter have worked on both IE and Netscape Navigator without requiring any separate coding. This is where it changes. Previously, this example had been coded with a view to using *only* IE's capabilities or *only* NN 4.x's capabilities. However, now that NN 6 and IE 5.5 support much of the DOM, a cross-browser version is possible – but it does still require some amendments to be made first.

Cross Coding Issues

Everything that the dynamic menu example does in the IE and NN specific versions, is theoretically achievable by using only properties and methods specified in the DOM. In fact we're doing nothing special or out of the ordinary in this example.

However, it isn't all plain sailing. Just because both browsers now broadly support the DOM, doesn't mean that they both support it to the letter. There are places where one browser supports a set of methods or properties created in an earlier version of the browser that haven't been included in the DOM, or places where they both support a particular feature of the DOM, but offer slightly different ways of doing it. What we've done is tried to create a version of this example that:

❑   uses as few as lines of browser-dependent code as possible

❑   offers identical functionality in both browsers

❑   uses the DOM way of accessing elements on the page

When translating the code, we came across five main areas in the program that needed fixing to get the example to work on both browsers. Let's look at them now before we create the example.

The ID and NAME attributes

As we have seen, the ID attribute is the preferred way in the DOM of identifying a particular occurrence of an element on the page. However, IE makes the actual object available directly via its ID attribute, while Netscape Navigator doesn't. This means that to get access to the elements, we have to use our old friend, the getElementById() method of the document object, once more. This method is available to both IE and NN 6 and is used in preference to IE's ability to directly reference the ID attribute in script, which we saw in the last chapter.

> *There is also a non-DOM specified* getElementByName() *method, which works in the same way as the* getElementById() *method, that can be used in IE 5 only. However, since you are meant to identify elements with the ID attribute and not the NAME attribute in the DOM, we won't be using this. We mention it for reference use only.*

Passing Event Arguments Explicitly

IE is a lot more relaxed about making the `event` object available globally. When connecting an event handler to a function, you don't have to pass the `event` object as an argument – it's already available to that function as though it was globally created. In Netscape, and indeed the DOM level 2 standard, to be able to make use of the properties and methods of the `event` object, you have to pass the `event` object as an argument to the function.

In the IE-specific version of this example, we can use the `event` object within a function, without any extra code. It works as follows without any arguments and will return IMG in the `alert()` statement:

```
<IMG ID="Picture 1" SRC="link.jpg" onmouseover="menudisplay()">

<SCRIPT LANGUAGE=JavaScript>
function menudisplay()
{
    alert(event.tagName);
}
</SCRIPT>
```

However, this code wouldn't pass any parameters to the function in Netscape Navigator, and consequently the `alert()` statement wouldn't display any value. We have to pass the `event` object explicitly. The following code assigns an `onmouseover` event handler to an `<IMG>` tag and also passes the `event` object as an argument to the function. Then we can make use of the properties and methods within the function as follows:

```
<IMG ID="Picture 1" SRC="link.jpg" onmouseover="menudisplay(event)">

<SCRIPT LANGUAGE=JavaScript>
function menudisplay(e)
{
    alert(e.tagName);
}
</SCRIPT>
```

There are quite a few examples of this in our dynamic menu example, so we will have to translate each occurrence, as above.

The srcElement and toElement Properties

A lot of what made the event handling facilities in IE 4 superior to those in NN 4 was down to the fact they were simpler to use, due to the reasons given above. However other problems arose due to the `event` object having different properties.

In NN 4 and the DOM standards, to get at which element on a web page had generated an event, you have to use the `target` property of the `event` object. However, in IE, once an event has been generated, the same element can be retrieved by checking the contents of the `srcElement` property of the `event` object.

If a mouse pointer crosses elements, and you want to discover the element that the mouse pointer is moving into, then with IE you need to use the `toElement` property of the `event` object. Once again this property isn't specified in the DOM standards, and the DOM and NN 6 require you to use the `relatedTarget` property instead.

Fortunately, both sets of properties (`target` and `srcElement`, and `relatedTarget` and `toElement`) work in the same way, despite their different names. This makes the job of writing separate lines of code for each browser fairly straightforward. For once it's IE that is at fault, as it doesn't support the methods outlined in the DOM. It is safe to assume that the next full version of IE, probably IE 6, will support these properties.

To get around this problem and to create a dual browser version of the code, we need to perform a check every time one of these properties needs to be used. If the browser running the page is IE, then no changes to our previous IE version of the page are needed. If, on the other hand, it's NN 6 that is browsing the code, we need to use the `target` or `relatedTarget` property instead.

Text Nodes and HTML tags

One disappointment about IE's DHTML implementation was the fact that while everything was theoretically open to a scripting language, the actual text on a page wasn't considered a separate entity or object in the way the different elements were. You could access it and change it using the `innerHTML` and `innerText` properties. (Actually, the `innerHTML` property is also now supported in NN 6, although it isn't strictly in the DOM.) However, the text wasn't recognized in the script as an object.

NN 6 rectifies this and follows the DOM's wording by adding text nodes to the object model. This means that every element that contains a piece of text, as we noted earlier, should make the text available as a text node. IE 4 doesn't do this, and although IE 5+ does add text nodes to the object model, there are still differences between the implementations of the two browsers. As we saw earlier in the chapter, NN 6 seems to add a text node for every element, even if it doesn't contain any text, whereas IE only adds a text node for elements with text.

There are also differences between how some of the event properties return information. In IE only HTML elements can raise an event, but in NN6 text nodes can also raise an event. This causes a problem in our example. If you use the `onmouseover` event to generate an event over a piece of text, in IE it will still return the name of the element that contains the text, while NN 6 may return the text node.

In our example, when we generate an `onmouseover` event, in NN 6 we have to move up our tree structure to the parent node (the element that contains the text). This is because we can change the style of an element node, but not of a text node. We use the `parentNode` property to go back up the tree here.

Dynamically Generating "Correct" Code

One last quirk with this example is that when we create a menu by placing a `<DIV>` tag containing a table on the page, we create the `<DIV>`, `<TABLE>`, `<TR>`, and `<TD>` tags dynamically using Javascript. However, according to the HTML 4.01 standard, tables should also contain headers (`<THEAD>`) and bodies (`<TBODY>`) and footers (`<TFOOT>`) in a similar way to that in which a HTML document is divided up into `<HEAD>` and `<BODY>` tags. Ordinarily this shouldn't cause us any problems, but this one time in our example it does.

The HTML 4.01 standard proposes that when we create a table, we should create it as so:

```
<TABLE>
<THEAD>
</THEAD>
<TBODY>
<TR>
   <TD>Cell Number 1</TD>
```

```
    </TR>
    <TR>
        <TD>Cell Number 2</TD>
    </TR>
    </TBODY>
    <TFOOT>
    </TFOOT>
    </TABLE>
```

even though creating it as follows will have exactly the same effect:

```
    <TABLE>
    <TR>
        <TD>Cell Number 1</TD>
    </TR>
    <TR>
        <TD>Cell Number 2</TD>
    </TR>
    </TABLE>
```

It's back to the well-formed HTML document requirement that we described earlier. When we dynamically create our tables without the header, body and footer sections, NN 6, because it requires a well-formed HTML document, takes the liberty of effectively adding these tags to the code for us. This can be demonstrated if you add an alert() statement to the code returning the tag name of the element the mouse pointer is currently over. If you move over the image, it returns IMG. If you move over the menu, it returns TABLE. As we have a border around the table, this forms part of the <TBODY> section, and when we move our mouse pointer over it, it will show TBODY.

Now, you might remember from the previous chapter that the way we detect whether we need to display the menu is by checking to see whether we're over an image, or inside the <DIV>. This can cause problems in IE since the onmouseout event of the <DIV> can be raised when the mouse pointer passes inside the <DIV> and over the contained table elements. The way in which we got around this in the previous IE version of the page can not be replicated using the DOM, so we have to come up with a new strategy.

As you will see later, the new strategy depends on being able to check whether the element the mouse pointer is over and the <DIV> to be hidden have similar ID attributes. We do this by setting the start of the ID attributes for the elements of the table to all be the same. As the ID attributes are set by hand in the program, when NN 6 adds its own <TBODY> element, it doesn't add any ID attributes. This has the effect that whenever we move over a part of the menu that returns a <TBODY> element, it makes the menu disappear.

This means we have had to add some extra script to make our <TABLE> well-formed, by adding the <TBODY> element and also adding an ID attribute that starts in the same way as the other table element's ID values, so that JavaScript doesn't think the <TBODY> element is outside the menu!

These are the five areas that needed changing to make our dynamic menu work across browsers. Now let's get on with it.

Try It Out - Dynamic menus

Start up your preferred web page editor and type in the following:

```
<HTML>
<HEAD>
<SCRIPT LANGUAGE=JavaScript>
var ns = (navigator.appName.indexOf('Netscape')>-1);
var ie = (navigator.appName.indexOf('Microsoft Internet Explorer')>-1);
var woodMenuItems = new Array(
    ["Oak", "OakWood.htm", "Oak Timber"],
    ["Teak", "TeakWood.htm", "Teak Timber"],
    ["Pine", "PineWood.htm", "Pine Timber"],
    ["Yew", "YewWood.htm", "Yew Timber"]);
var metalMenuItems = new Array(
    ["Steel", "SteelMetal.htm", "Steel Girders"],
    ["Copper", "CopperMetal.htm", "Copper Pipes"],
    ["Gold", "GoldMetal.htm", "Gold Ingots"]);
var bricksMenuItems = new Array(
    ["StdHouse", "StdHousebricks.htm", "Standard House Brick"],
    ["LargeHouseBrick", "LargeHousebricks.htm", "Large House Bricks"],
    ["BreezeBlock", "BreezeBlock.htm", "Breeze Block"]);

function createMenu(menuName, menuItems)
{
    var divHTML = '<DIV ID="' + menuName + 'MenuDiv" CLASS="DivMenu"';
    divHTML = divHTML + 'onmouseout="return hideMenu(this, ' + menuName.length +
',event)">';

    var tableHTML = '<TABLE BORDER=0 CELLSPACING=1 CELLPADDING=1 ID="' +
        menuName + 'Table"><TBODY ID="' + menuName + 'TableBody">';
    var tableRowHTML = "";
    var rowCount;
    var totalNoRows = menuItems.length;
    for (rowCount = 0; rowCount < totalNoRows; rowCount++)
    {
        tableRowHTML = tableRowHTML + '<TR ID="' + menuName +
            menuItems[rowCount][0] + 'TR"><TD ID="' + menuName +
            menuItems[rowCount][0];
        tableRowHTML = tableRowHTML + '" onclick="goPage(\'' +
            menuItems[rowCount][1] + '\')"';
        tableRowHTML = tableRowHTML + 'CLASS="TDMenu">' + menuItems[rowCount][2] +
            '</TD></TR>';
    }

    return divHTML + tableHTML + tableRowHTML + '</TBODY></TABLE></DIV>';
}

function showMenu(menuToShow, e)
{
    if (ns)
    {
        var srcElement = e.target;
    }
```

```
      else
      {
         var srcElement = event.srcElement;
      }
      var xPos = parseInt(srcElement.style.left);
      var yPos = parseInt(srcElement.style.top);
      menuToShow.style.left = xPos + (srcElement.width)
      menuToShow.style.top = yPos;
}

function hideMenu(menuToHide, menuIDLength, e)
{
   var toElementID;
   if (ns)
   {
      var mouseLastIn = e.relatedTarget;
   }
   else
   {
      var mouseLastIn =  event.toElement;
   }
   if (mouseLastIn != null)
   {
      if (mouseLastIn.nodeType == 3)
      {
         mouseLastIn = mouseLastIn.parentNode;
      }
      toElementID = mouseLastIn.id;
   }
   else
   {
       return false;
   }

   if (typeof(toElementID) == "undefined")
   {
      toElementID = "UNDEF";
   }
   toElementID = toElementID.substr(0,menuIDLength);
   var divMenuID = menuToHide.id;
   divMenuID = divMenuID.substr(0,menuIDLength);
   if (toElementID != divMenuID)
   {
      menuToHide.style.left = -200 + 'px';
      menuToHide.style.top = -1000 + 'px';
   }
}

function document_onmouseover(e)
{
   if (ns)
   {
      var srcElement = e.target;
   }
   else
   {
      var srcElement = event.srcElement;
   }
```

```
    if (srcElement.nodeType == 3)
    {
        srcElement = srcElement.parentNode;
    }

    if (srcElement.tagName=="TD")
    {
        srcElement.style.color = "white";
        srcElement.style.backgroundColor = "darkblue"
    }
}

function document_onmouseout(e)
{
    if (ns)
    {
        var srcElement = e.target;
    }
    else
    {
        var srcElement = event.srcElement;
    }

    if (srcElement.nodeType == 3)
    {
        srcElement = srcElement.parentNode;
    }
    if (srcElement.tagName == "TD")
    {
        srcElement.style.color ="darkblue";
        srcElement.style.backgroundColor = "darkorange";
    }
}

function goPage(src)
{
    window.location.href = src;
}
</SCRIPT>
<STYLE>
    .DivMenu {position:absolute;
        left:-200;
        top:-1000;
        width:180;
        z-index:100;
        background-color:darkorange;
        border: 4px groove lightgrey;
    }

    .TDMenu {
        color:darkblue;
        font-family:verdana;
        font-size:70%;
        width:100%;
        cursor:default;
    }
</STYLE>
</HEAD>
```

```
<BODY onmouseover="document_onmouseover(event)"
   onmouseout="document_onmouseout(event)">
<SCRIPT LANGUAGE=JavaScript>
   document.write(createMenu('Wood', woodMenuItems))
   document.write(createMenu('Metal', metalMenuItems))
   document.write(createMenu('Bricks', bricksMenuItems))
</SCRIPT>

<IMG id="WoodMenuImage"
   SRC="WoodButton.gif"
   style="position:absolute;left:10;top:75"
   onmouseover="return showMenu(document.getElementById('WoodMenuDiv'), event)"
   onmouseout="return hideMenu(document.getElementById('WoodMenuDiv'),4,event)">

<IMG id="MetalMenuImage"
   SRC="MetalButton.gif"
   style="position:absolute;left:10;top:115"
   onmouseover="return showMenu(document.getElementById('MetalMenuDiv'),event)"
   onmouseout="return hideMenu(document.getElementById('MetalMenuDiv'),5,event)">

<IMG id="BricksMenuImage"
   SRC="BricksButton.gif"
   style="position:absolute;left:10;top:155"
   onmouseover="return showMenu(document.getElementById('BricksMenuDiv'),event)"
   onmouseout="return hideMenu(document.getElementById('BricksMenuDiv'),6,event)">
</BODY>
</HTML>
```

If the image files aren't available, the page won't work in NN6 (although it does in IE 5.5). NN6
won't display anything at all, not even a broken link symbol. You can get the images from the code
download for the book.

Save this as IE_NN_Menus.htm and open up this example in both IE 5+ and NN 6:

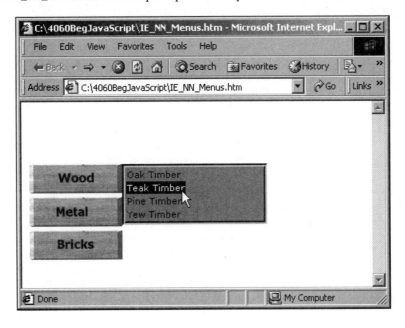

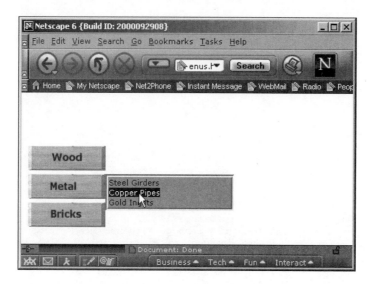

Move the mouse pointer over the buttons and you should find that they both generate menus dynamically in an identical fashion.

How It Works

We've not changed the fundamental workings of this example in any way. All we've done is translated the troublesome browser-specific properties into something DOM-specific. Where this hasn't been possible, we've used a little browser sniffing code to determine which browser it is that we're using and then pursued an appropriate course of action for that browser.

Indeed the first two lines of code check for the type of browser we're using:

```
var ns = (navigator.appName.indexOf('Netscape')>-1);
var ie = (navigator.appName.indexOf('Microsoft Internet Explorer')>-1);
```

We generate two variables, one called ns that will only contain a true value if our browser is a Netscape browser, while the second variable, ie, conversely will only contain a true value if the browser is Internet Explorer. However, this is all we need to change in our first section.

The array of menu elements is generated in virtually the same way as before. The only difference is in the shortcut way of writing out the system of array elements.

Let's skip this and jump to the createMenu() function. Only two things have changed here.

In the <DIV> tag we have an onmouseout event handler to hide the menu when the user moves outside the <DIV> tag. We have added two parameters to the function called here. The first parameter is the length of the menu name. We will investigate the need for this later. Also, as we're going to want to check the event object after we've moved outside the <DIV> tag, we need to pass the event object explicitly, and so have added this as another parameter.

The second thing we have changed is that the function now dynamically generates a <TBODY> tag to ensure that our document is well-formed, and adds ID attributes to this and the <TR> tags:

```
function createMenu(menuName, menuItems)
{
    var divHTML = '<DIV ID="' + menuName + 'MenuDiv" CLASS="DivMenu"';
    divHTML = divHTML + 'onmouseout="return hideMenu(this, ' + menuName.length +
        ',event)">';

    var tableHTML = '<TABLE BORDER=0 CELLSPACING=1 CELLPADDING=1 ID="' +
        menuName + 'Table"><TBODY ID="' + menuName + 'TableBody">';
    var tableRowHTML = "";
    var rowCount;
    var totalNoRows = menuItems.length;
    for (rowCount = 0; rowCount < totalNoRows; rowCount++)
    {
        tableRowHTML = tableRowHTML + '<TR ID="' + menuName +
            menuItems[rowCount][0] +  'TR"><TD ID="' + menuName +
            menuItems[rowCount][0];
        tableRowHTML = tableRowHTML + '" onclick="goPage(\'' +
            menuItems[rowCount][1] + '\')"';
        tableRowHTML = tableRowHTML + 'CLASS="TDMenu">' + menuItems[rowCount][2] +
            '</TD></TR>';
    }

    return divHTML + tableHTML + tableRowHTML + '</TBODY></TABLE></DIV>';
}
```

The `showMenu()` function comes next and has to be changed as it previously made use of the IE-only property `srcElement` of the `event` object to return the element which generated an event. According to DOM level 2, you should use the `target` property to do this. However, while Netscape supports this property, IE doesn't. The `ie` and `ns` variables we created globally at the beginning of the script come into play, as we now need to make use of them. The function creates a variable called `srcElement` that contains the name of the HTML element that generated the event. The way that this variable is set depends on the browser being used.

The only other change to the `showMenu()` function, is that the `event` object is passed as a parameter instead of being globally available as it was with the IE only version:

```
function showMenu(menuToShow, e)
{
    if (ns)
    {
        var srcElement = e.target;
    }
    else
    {
        var srcElement = event.srcElement;
    }
    var xPos = parseInt(srcElement.style.left);
    var yPos = parseInt(srcElement.style.top);
    menuToShow.style.left = xPos + (srcElement.width)
    menuToShow.style.top = yPos;
    return false;
}
```

577

The `hideMenu()` function needs more drastic changes. It too, like the `showMenu()` function, suffers from the `event` object properties affliction, except that the problem is with the IE-specific property `toElement`, which records the element the mouse pointer has just moved into. The DOM-compliant equivalent that is supported in NN 6 is `relatedTarget`. Once again we have to supply conditional code that will check the `ns` variable and create a `mouseLastIn` variable that holds one or other of the properties:

```
function hideMenu(menuToHide, menuIDLength, e)
{
    var toElementID;
    if (ns)
    {
        var mouseLastIn = e.relatedTarget;
    }
    else
    {
        var mouseLastIn =  event.toElement;
    }
```

The second problem that has to be dealt with here is one we mentioned earlier. The `relatedTarget` property in NN can return text nodes whereas the `toElement` property in IE can only return element nodes. The menu code here has to check the `ID` of the element that the mouse pointer is going to, but `ID` values are only applicable to elements and not text nodes. As a result, if `mouseLastIn` is a text node, then our code needs to go up the node hierarchy to the containing element of the text. The DOM allows that with the `parentNode` property of every node.

To make sure this happens, we check the `nodeType` property of `mouseLastIn`. If it returns a value 3, we know `onmouseout` has returned a text node. We then move back up the tree structure to the HTML element that contains the text node and use that instead.

We then store the `ID` attribute's value for the `mouseLastIn` node in the variable `toElementID`.

```
    if (mouseLastIn != null)
    {
        if (mouseLastIn.nodeType == 3)
        {
            mouseLastIn = mouseLastIn.parentNode;
        }
        toElementID = mouseLastIn.id;
    }
    else
    {
        return false;
    }
```

Finally, we have to check whether the start of the `ID` attribute of the `mouseLastIn` node matches the start of the `<DIV>` tag's `ID`. If so, we know that the mouse pointer has just moved onto a tag inside the `<DIV>` rather than outside the `<DIV>`, so we don't hide the menu.

We perform this check by first cutting out the first part of the `ID` of `mouseLastIn` stored in variable `toElementID`. We know how much of the `ID` we have to cut out due to the second parameter of the function, which gives the length of the menu name. We then do the same thing for the `ID` attribute of the `<DIV>` tag, stored in variable `menuToHide`, which was passed as the first parameter of the function. Finally we compare the two values obtained, and if they do not match we set the `left` and `top` style properties of the `<DIV>` so that it is placed off screen and hidden.

```
        if (typeof(toElementID) == "undefined")
        {
            toElementID = "UNDEF";
        }
        toElementID = toElementID.substr(0,menuIDLength);
        var divMenuID = menuToHide.id;
        divMenuID = divMenuID.substr(0,menuIDLength);
        if (toElementID != divMenuID)
        {
            menuToHide.style.left = -200 + 'px';
            menuToHide.style.top = -1000 + 'px';
        }
    }
```

Let's now look at the document_onmouseover() function. Once again the IE-specific srcElement property is used in IE 5+, while NN 6 uses the DOM-compliant property target. We've just added a conditional if statement checking the contents of the ns variable and setting the srcElement variable correspondingly. We also have to check to see that our onmouseover event has generated an HTML element, rather than text node, and we do this by checking the nodeType property again. If it does equal 3, we hop one up the tree structure to the HTML element and use that instead:

```
function document_onmouseover(e)
{
    if (ns)
    {
        var srcElement = e.target;
    }
    else
    {
        var srcElement = event.srcElement;
    }

    if (srcElement.nodeType == 3)
    {
        srcElement = srcElement.parentNode;
    }

    if (srcElement.tagName=="TD")
    {
        srcElement.style.color = "white";
        srcElement.style.backgroundColor = "darkblue"
    }
}
```

Lastly the document_onmouseout() function has to be changed in this way also:

```
function document_onmouseout(e)
{
    if (ns)
    {
        var srcElement = e.target;
    }
    else
    {
        var srcElement = event.srcElement;
    }
```

```
    if (srcElement.nodeType == 3)
    {
        srcElement = srcElement.parentNode;
    }
    if (srcElement.tagName == "TD")
    {
        srcElement.style.color ="darkblue";
        srcElement.style.backgroundColor = "darkorange";
    }
}
```

Note that in these two functions we check to see whether the tag the mouse pointer is over is a <TD> tag and if so we change the style of the tag's contents. In previous version of the example, we performed more vigorous checks to make sure that the <TD> tag was contained in our menu rather than in any other content on the page.

While the example has been very large, we've not had to adjust that much code within it and consequently it hasn't really grown in size. In fact, there are only really the two problems that prompted many changes. The first was IE using `srcElement` and `toElement` properties instead of `target` and `relatedTarget` properties, and the second was that NN 6 can return text nodes from its `event` object's `target` and `relatedTarget` properties, whereas IE can only return element nodes from the corresponding `srcElement` and `toElement` properties. If you're aware of these problems, then the task of amending them really isn't too great. Hopefully, as you can see, we're miles away from the problems caused by IE 4 and NN 4 and having to using the `layers` collection. The task of upgrading, despite our earlier warnings, has been fairly painless.

Summary

This chapter has featured quite a few diversions and digressions, but these have been necessary to demonstrate the position and importance of the Document Object Model in JavaScript.

❑ We started by outlining four of the main standards, HTML, ECMAScript, XML, and XHTML and examined the relationships between them. We saw that a common aim was emerging from these standards that required stricter guidelines for coding HTML web pages, but that those guidelines in turn benefited the Document Object Model making it possible to access and manipulate any item on the web page using script, if web pages were coded according to these guidelines.

❑ We examined the Document Object Model and saw that it offered a browser and language independent method of accessing the items on a web page and resolved the problems that dogged version 4 of the browsers. We saw how the DOM represents the HTML document as a tree structure and how it is possible to navigate through the tree to different elements and use the properties and methods it exposes to access the different parts of the web page.

❑ While this provides the best method for manipulating the contents of the web page, none of the main browsers yet implements it in its entirety. We looked at the two most up to date examples, IE 5.5 and NN 6, and saw how they provided a strong basis for creating dynamic, inter-operable web pages due to their support of the DOM.

Exercises

Question 1

Here's some HTML code that creates a web page. Recreate this page, using JavaScript to generate the HTML with document.write(), and using only DOM objects, properties and methods. Test your code on both IE 5.5 and NN 6 to make sure it works on both if possible.

Hint: Comment each line as you write it to keep track of where you are in the tree structure and also create a new variable for every element on the page (for example, not just one for each of the TD cells, but 9).

```
<HTML>
<HEAD>
</HEAD>
<BODY>
<TABLE>
    <THEAD>
        <TR>
            <TD>Car</TD>
            <TD>Top Speed</TD>
            <TD>Price</TD>
        </TR>
    </THEAD>
    <TBODY>
        <TR>
            <TD>Chevrolet</TD>
            <TD>120mph</TD>
            <TD>$10,000</TD>
        </TR>
        <TR>
            <TD>Pontiac</TD>
            <TD>140mph</TD>
            <TD>$20,000</TD>
        </TR>
    </TBODY>
</TABLE>
</BODY>
</HTML>
```

Question 2

Augment your DOM web page so that the table has a border and so that the headings only of the table (that is, not the column headings) are center aligned. Again test your code on both IE 5.5 and NN 6 if possible.

Hint: Add any extra code to the end of the script code you have already written.

581

Online discussion at http://p2p.wrox.com

Using ActiveX and Plug-ins with JavaScript

While browsers like Internet Explorer and Netscape Navigator provide a lot of built in functionality, there are many things that they can't do unaided. Examples include playing video clips or sound bites – functionality that is becoming more and more common on the Internet. To get around this problem, browsers can have their functionality extended by using plug-ins.

Plug-ins, as their name suggests, are downloaded and "plugged into" the browser. There are literally hundreds of different plug-ins available, though the more common ones include Macromedia's Flash, which plays Flash movies, and RealNetworks' Real Audio and video player, which plays real audio and media files.

Essentially, plug-ins are objects that encapsulate all the functionality they need to perform their tasks, such as playing audio files, in a way that hides the complexity from the programmer. They are usually written in languages such as C++ and Java.

Plug-ins usually, but not always, have some sort of user interface. For example, the Real Audio plug-in has a user interface that displays buttons to play, pause, and stop the playing of an audio file.

Some plug-ins make objects with various methods and properties available to us. We can access these through JavaScript, in a similar manner to how we access the methods and properties of the `window` object or the `Math` object. For example, the Real Audio player plug-in makes available the `DoPlay()` method that we can use to start the playing of a sound clip.

I guess you're not going to be shocked to find out that IE and NN do things differently.

Netscape has supported plug-ins since NN 3.0. (Currently, Netscape 6 has some problems with plug-ins, so the code in this chapter may not work on this browser.)

IE does not support plug-ins very well, but IE 4.0+ does support ActiveX controls, which provide the same functionality as plug-ins.

Fortunately, as we'll see, using ActiveX controls and Netscape plug-ins is similar, and with a few tweaks can be done with almost the same code. The main difference is actually making sure that the plug-in or ActiveX control is available for use and ready to run in the user's browser in the first place. We'll cover this problem in more detail for NN and IE, before going on to discuss using the plug-ins and ActiveX controls.

Checking for and Embedding Plug-ins on Netscape Navigator

It's all very well creating script to use a 'WizzoUltra3D' plug-in for the web page experience of a lifetime, but unless the visitor to your web page also has the 'WizzoUltra3D' plug-in installed on their computer, their experience of the web page is going to be one full of bugs and error messages. It's therefore important that we not only correctly add the HTML required to use the plug-in in our page, but also use JavaScript to check to see if the user's browser has the plug-in that our page makes use of installed. We look at both these topics in this section.

Adding a Plug-in to the Page

In order to make use of a plug-in that is installed in the user's browser, we need to use HTML to tell the browser where and when in our page we want to use it. This process is called **embedding** the plug-in.

In Netscape Navigator 3 and 4 the key to embedding plug-ins is the <EMBED> tag. This inserts the visible interface, if any, of the plug-in at that point in the page. The <EMBED> tag supports a number of general attributes applicable to all plug-ins, such as HEIGHT, WIDTH, PLUGINSPAGE, SRC, and TYPE. We'll look at the last two of these attributes, SRC and TYPE, in more detail here. We will also look at the PLUGINSPAGE attribute in the next section.

Most plug-ins display content that is stored on a web server. For example, a plug-in for sound, such as Real Audio, will play music from a file with the .ra extension, and the Flash plug-in will play Flash movies, that is files with the .swf extension. The <EMBED> tag's SRC attribute allows us to specify the initial file for the plug-in to load and play. This will be a URL pointing to the file, usually hosted on the same web server as the HTML page. It's from this file that the browser works out what sort of plug-in is required. For example, if the SRC was www.myserver.com/myflashmovie.swf, then by checking the type of the file, the browser can see that a Flash player plug-in needs to be used.

However, not all plug-ins require data from an external source, and therefore a value for the SRC attribute. In such situations, how can the browser tell what plug-in to load? Well, that's where the <EMBED> tag's TYPE attribute comes in. The actual value for the TYPE attribute will be specific to the plug-in. We can find out this information by opening up NN 4.x and selecting the About Plug-ins option from the Help menu:

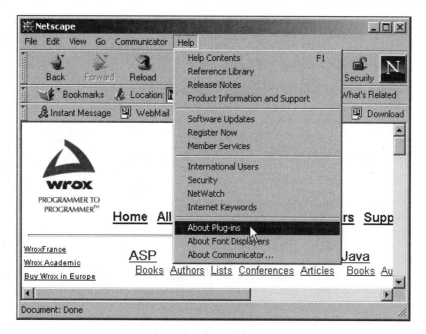

This will show a list of all the plug-ins installed on our browser. The value required for the TYPE attribute is listed as the **Mime Type**, which stands for Multipurpose Internet Mail Extensions and specifies a type of content such as a web page, an image, or a Flash file. For example, for Flash the **Mime Type** is:

```
application/x-shockwave-flash
```

As well as a number of attributes common to all plug-ins, we can also use the <EMBED> tag to specify properties specific to a particular plug-in.

For example, the Flash plug-in supports the QUALITY attribute, which determines the image quality of the flash movie. To set this attribute in the <EMBED> tag, we just add it to the list of attributes set. For example:

```
<EMBED ID="FlashPlugIn1"
    SRC="topmenu.swf"
    BORDER=0
    HEIGHT=100
    WIDTH=500
    QUALITY=high
    TYPE="application/x-shockwave-flash"
</EMBED>
```

Checking for and Installing Plug-ins

After working out what type of plug-in we want to embed into the page, what happens if the browser finds that particular plug-in does not exist on the user's computer?

To solve this problem we can set the PLUGINSPAGE attribute of the <EMBED> tag to point to a URL on the plug-in creator's page. If the plug-in is not on the user's computer, then a link to the URL specified in the PLUGINSPAGE attribute will be displayed within the web page. The user can click on the link, and load the plug-in, so that our web page will function properly.

For example, with Flash the PLUGINSPAGE attribute needed is:

```
PLUGINSPAGE="http://www.macromedia.com/shockwave/download/index.cgi?P1_Prod_Versio
n=ShockwaveFlash">
```

However, if the user doesn't have the plug-in installed, we might prefer to send them to a version of our web site that doesn't rely on that plug-in. How do we know whether a plug-in is installed?

The navigator object, which we introduced in Chapter 5, has a property called plugins, which is an array of Plugin objects, one for each plug-in installed on that browser. We can access a Plugin object in the plugins array either by using an index value that indexes all the plug-ins installed on the user's browser, or by using the name of the plug-in application.

Each Plugin object has four properties, description, filename, length, and name. We can find these values by looking at the About Plug-ins option on the Help menu in Netscape.

Let's use Flash as an example. Click the About plug-ins option on the Help menu, which will show a list of the plug-ins installed on your browser. In the screenshot below, we can see that Flash has Shockwave Flash as its name property. The filename and description properties have quite obvious meanings. The length property gives the number of Mime Types supported by the plug-in.

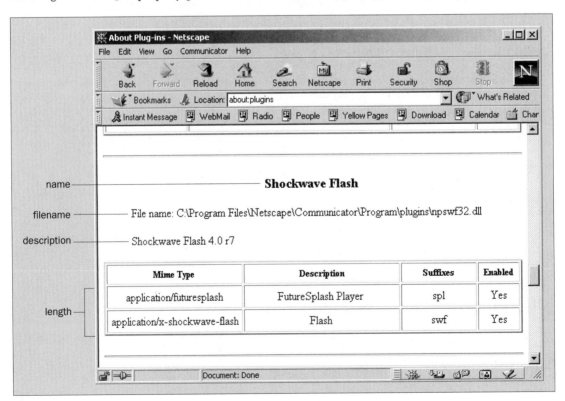

As we said above, the `name` property can be used to reference the `Plugin` object in the `plugins` array. So, in NN:

```
var shockWavePlugIn = navigator.plugins["Shockwave Flash"];
```

will set the variable `shockWavePlugin` to the `Plugin` object for Flash, if it's installed. If it's not, then `navigator.plugins["Flash"]` will return as undefined.

We can use this to re-direct users on browsers that do not have the plug-in we need installed:

```
if (navigator.plugins["Shockwave Flash"])
{
    window.location.replace("my_flash_enabled_page.htm");
}
else
{
    window.location.replace("my_non_flash_page.htm");
}
```

If the Flash plug-in is not installed, then `navigator.plugins["Shockwave Flash"]` will be undefined, which JavaScript considers to be `false`, thereby causing the `else` statement to execute. If Flash is installed, then `navigator.plugins["Shockwave Flash"]` will return the Flash `Plugin` object, which JavaScript treats as `true`, and the main `if` statement will execute.

The problem with this method of detection is that the name given to a plug-in may vary from operating system to operating system. For example, the name of the Windows 98 version of the plug-in may vary from the name of the Apple Mac's version, which in turn may vary from the name of the Linux version. Some plug-ins, such as RealPlayer, will not work reliably at all with this detection method, because the name is not simply RealPlayer but something that contains the word "RealPlayer". For example, on my Windows 2000 system with Netscape 4.73, the name is "RealPlayer(tm) G2 LiveConnect-Enabled Plug-In (32bit)" – something of a mouthful. This varies not only with the browser version and operating system, but also with the RealPlayer version.

An alternative method for checking that a plug-in is installed is to loop through the `plugins[]` array and check each `name` for certain key words. If they are found, then we assume that the control is installed. For example, to check for RealPlayer we may use the following:

```
var plugInCounter;

for (plugInCounter = 0; plugInCounter < navigator.plugins.length;
    plugInCounter++)
{
    if (navigator.plugins[plugInCounter].name.indexOf("RealPlayer") >= 0)
    {
        alert("RealPlayer is installed");
        break;
    }
}
```

The `for` loop goes through the `navigator.plugins` array, starting from index 0 and continuing up to the last element. Each plug-in in the array has its `name` property checked to see if it contains the text "RealPlayer". If it has, then we know RealPlayer is installed and we break out of the loop; if not then RealPlayer is clearly not installed.

587

An alternative to using `navigator` object's `plugins[]` array is the `navigator` object's `mimeTypes[]` array, which contains an array of `mimeType` objects, representing the MIME types supported by the browser. We can use this to check whether the browser supports a specific type of media, such as Flash movies.

We have already come across MIME types before – the `TYPE` attribute of the `<EMBED>` tag can be used to specify a MIME type so that the browser knows which plug-in to embed. Again, using the About plug-ins option on the Help menu, we can find out the MIME types for a particular plug-in. In fact, one plug-in may well support more than one MIME type. When we check for a particular MIME type, we are checking that the browser supports a particular type of file format rather than necessarily a particular plug-in.

For example, we may use the `mimeTypes` array to check for the Flash plug-in:

```
if (navigator.mimeTypes["application/x-shockwave-flash"] &&
    navigator.mimeTypes['application/x-shockwave-flash'].enabledPlugin)
{
   window.location.replace("my_flash_enabled_page.htm");
}
else
{
   window.location.replace("my_non_flash_page.htm");
}
```

The `if` statement is the important thing here. Its condition has two parts separated by the AND operator `&&`.

The first part checks that the specified MIME type is supported by trying to access a specific `mimeType` object in the `mimeTypes` array. If there is no such object, then null is returned which as far as an `if` statement goes, works the same as if `false` is returned.

The second part checks to see that not only is the MIME type supported, but that a plug-in to handle this MIME type is enabled. Although unusual, it is possible for a MIME type to be supported, or recognized, by the browser, but no plug-in to be installed. For example, if the user has Microsoft Word installed, then the MIME type `"application/msword"` would be valid, but that does not mean a plug-in exists to display it in a NN browser! The `enabledPlugin` property of the `mimeType` object actually returns a `Plugin` object, but again if it does not exist, null will be returned and this will be considered as `false` by the `if` statement.

What happens if someone browses to our page with a browser that has no support at all for plug-ins?

Well, basically the `<EMBED>` tags will be ignored and, if the browser does support script, then errors will occur if we access the plug-in through our script. To get round this, NN supports the `<NOEMBED>` tag. Anything in between the opening `<NOEMBED>` tag and the closing `</NOEMBED>` tag is ignored by any version of NN that supports the `<EMBED>` tag, so we can put a message in there telling users that the page requires a browser that supports plug-ins.

```
<NOEMBED>
   <H2> This page requires a browser that supports plug-ins </H2>
</NOEMBED>
```

Checking for and Embedding ActiveX Controls on Internet Explorer

Although IE does support plug-ins to a certain extent, its support for ActiveX controls is more complete. The main difference between an ActiveX control and a plug-in is how they are embedded into a page and how they are installed. Once they are embedded and installed, their use as far as scripting goes will be very similar to that for plug-ins.

ActiveX controls are a little like mini programs, usually created in languages like C++ or Visual Basic. Unlike a normal program, like Notepad or Microsoft Word, ActiveX controls cannot run on their own; they need to be sited in a container program. Not all programs can act as containers for ActiveX controls, only those specifically designed to do so, such as Microsoft Access and, of course, Internet Explorer. When the creator of the ActiveX control compiles their code, they also assign it a unique identification string that allows programmers like us to specify exactly which control we want to embed in our IE ActiveX container.

Adding an ActiveX Control to the Page

Adding an ActiveX control to a page for an IE browser requires the use of the <OBJECT> tag. There are two very important attributes of the <OBJECT> tag that are common to all controls, namely CLASSID and CODEBASE. The CLASSID attribute is the unique ID that the creator of the control gave to it when it was compiled. The CODEBASE attribute gives a URL where the ActiveX control can be found – we'll look at this attribute in more detail in the next section.

How can we find out the CLASSID? Well, one way to do this is by checking the documentation that came with the control or is available on the control creator's web site. If we have the control installed, then another way to do this is via IE itself, which will tell us which controls are installed on the computer and available to IE, and also give us additional information such as CLASSID, though it won't inform us about any controls that were installed with the operating system. For example, Flash 3 is installed with Windows 98, and so won't appear.

To get this information we need to open up IE, then select Internet Options from the Tools menu:

This will open up the console shown below. In the **Temporary Internet** files area, click the **Settings** button:

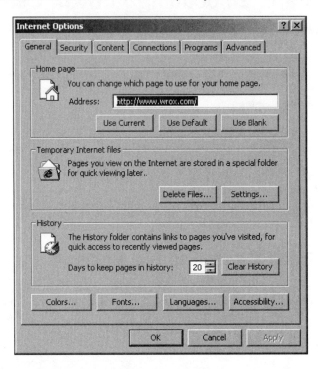

In the next console that opens, click the **View Objects** button:

This will display a list of all the ActiveX controls IE has installed from the Internet. The list shown below will most likely be different from that on your own computer.

We can see lots of information about each control, such as when it was created and its version number. However, to find out the CLASSID we need to right-click on the name of the control we're interested in and select Properties from the menu that pops up.

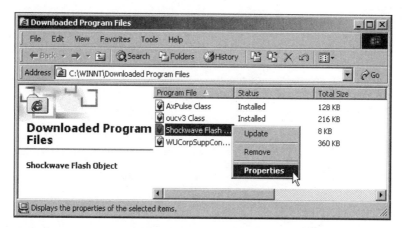

The following information is displayed, though this may be slightly different on your system:

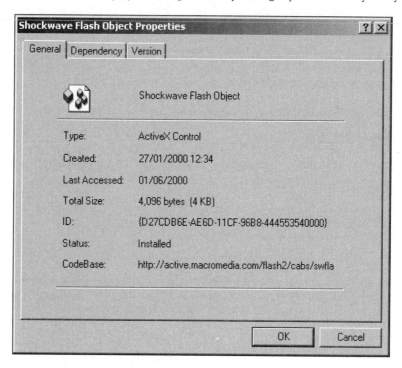

We can see that the CLASSID attribute, listed as just ID, and the CODEBASE attribute, listed as CodeBase, are both displayed, although for CODEBASE you may need to click on the line and then scroll using the arrow keys to see all the information.

From this information, we see that to insert a Flash ActiveX control in our web page we need to add the following <OBJECT> tag:

```
<OBJECT CLASSID="clsid:D27CDB6E-AE6D-11cf-96B8-444553540000"
    ID=flashPlayer1
    WIDTH=500
    HEIGHT=100>
</OBJECT>
```

We can also set attribute or parameter values for the control itself. For example, with Flash we need to set the SRC attribute to point to the .swf file we want loaded, and we may also want to set the QUALITY attribute, which determines the quality of appearance of the Flash movie. However, to set parameters of the ActiveX control such as these, as opposed to the attributes of the <OBJECT> tag, we need to insert <PARAM> tags in between the start <OBJECT> tag and the close </OBJECT> tag.

In each <PARAM> tag we need to specify the name of the parameter we want to set and the value we want it set to. For example, if we wanted to set the SRC attribute to myFlashMovie.swf, we need to add a <PARAM> tag like this:

```
<PARAM NAME=SRC VALUE="myFlashMovie.swf">
```

Let's add this to the full <OBJECT> tag definition, and also define the QUALITY attribute at the same time.

```
<OBJECT CLASSID="clsid:D27CDB6E-AE6D-11cf-96B8-444553540000"
    ID=flashPlayer1
    WIDTH=500
    HEIGHT=100>
        <PARAM NAME=SRC VALUE="myFlashMovie.swf">
        <PARAM NAME=QUALITY VALUE=high>
</OBJECT>
```

Installing an ActiveX control

We've seen how to insert an ActiveX control into our page, but what happens if the user doesn't have that control installed on their computer?

This is where the CODEBASE attribute of the <OBJECT> tag comes in. If the browser finds that the ActiveX control is not installed on the user's computer, then it will try to download and install the control from the URL pointed to by the CODEBASE attribute.

The creator of the ActiveX control will usually have a URL that we can use as a value for the CODEBASE attribute. The information under the Internet Options option of the Tools menu we saw earlier provides the CODEBASE for the control that was installed on your computer, though this may not necessarily be the best URL to use, particularly if it's not a link to the creator of the control.

For Flash, the CODEBASE is http://active.macromedia.com/flash2/cabs/swflash.cab, so our <OBJECT> tag will look like this:

```
<OBJECT CLASSID="clsid:D27CDB6E-AE6D-11cf-96B8-444553540000"
    CODEBASE="http://active.macromedia.com/flash2/cabs/swflash.cab"
    ID=flashPlayer1
    WIDTH=500
    HEIGHT=100 >
        <PARAM NAME=SRC VALUE="myFlashMovie.swf">
        <PARAM NAME=QUALITY VALUE=high>
</OBJECT>
```

Subject to license agreements, you may be able to download the .cab file that installs the control to your own server and point the CODEBASE attribute to that.

Unfortunately, there is no easy foolproof way of checking which ActiveX controls are installed on the user's computer. However, the Object object of the <OBJECT> tag does have the readyState property. This returns 0, 1, or 4 indicating the object's operational status. The possible values are:

❑   0 – Control un-initialized and not ready for use

❑   1 – Control is still loading

❑   4 – Control loaded and is ready for use

We need to give the control time to load before checking its readyState property, so any checking is best left until the window's onload event handler or even the document object's onreadystatechange event handler has fired.

To redirect the user to another page that doesn't need the control, we need to write:

```
if (myControl.readyState == 0)
{
    window.location.replace("NoControlPage.htm");
}
```

and attach this code to the window's onload event handler.

We saw that the <NOEMBED> tag allows us to display a message for users with browsers not supporting plug-ins. This tag works in exactly the same way with IE. Alternatively you can place text in between the <OBJECT> and </OBJECT> tags, in which case it will only be displayed if the browser is not able to display the ActiveX control.

Using Plug-ins and ActiveX Controls

Once we've got the plug-in or ActiveX control embedded into the page, their actual use is very similar. To make life easier for us, most developers of plug-ins and controls make the properties, methods, and events supported by the plug-in and ActiveX control, similar. However it's important to check the developer's documentation, as it's likely that there will be some differences.

Inside the <EMBED> or <OBJECT> tag, we give our plug-in or control a unique ID value. We can then access the corresponding object's methods, properties and events just as we would for any other tag. The actual properties, methods and events supported by a plug-in or control will be specific to that control, but let's look at one of the more commonly available controls, RealNetworks' RealPlayer, which comes in both plug-in form for NN and ActiveX control form for IE. You can find more information on this control from http://www.realnetworks.com/devzone/index.html, and there is a free version (Real Player Basic)that can be downloaded from http://www.realnetworks.com. Note that a version you can pay for with more features is provided, but if you search their web site a no charge basic version is available.

First we need to embed the control in a web page. Type the following into a text editor:

```
<HTML>
<HEAD>
<OBJECT CLASSID="clsid:CFCDAA03-8BE4-11CF-B84B-0020AFBBCCFA" ID="real1">
    <PARAM NAME="HEIGHT" VALUE="0">
    <PARAM NAME="WIDTH" VALUE="0">
    <EMBED NAME="real1"
        ID="real1"
        BORDER="0"
        CONTROLS="play"
        HEIGHT=0
        WIDTH=0
        TYPE="audio/x-pn-realaudio-plugin">
</OBJECT>
</HEAD>

<BODY>
<NOEMBED>
    <H2>This Page requires a browser supporting Plug-ins or ActiveX controls</H2>
</NOEMBED>
</BODY>
</HTML>
```

Save this code as realplayer.htm.

The first thing to note is that the <EMBED> tag for the NN plug-in has been inserted in between the opening <OBJECT> tag and closing </OBJECT> tag. The reason for this is that NN will ignore the <OBJECT> tags and just display the plug-in defined in the <EMBED> tag. IE, on the other hand, will ignore the <EMBED> tag inside the <OBJECT> tags, but will display the ActiveX control.

IE does support the <EMBED> tag, though its use is discouraged. This means that if we placed the <EMBED> tag outside the <OBJECT> tags, then IE would recognize both the <OBJECT> and <EMBED> tags and get confused, particularly over the ID values as both have the same ID of real1.

We've placed the <EMBED> and <OBJECT> tags inside the <HEAD>. Why?

Well, for this example we don't want to display the graphical interface of the control itself, but just want to use its ability to play sounds. By placing it inside the head of the document it becomes invisible to the user.

Finally, we've put a <NOEMBED> tag inside the body of the page for users of browsers that don't support plug-ins or ActiveX controls. This will display a message to such users telling them why they are staring at a blank page!

We want to make sure that users without the RealPlayer plug-in or control don't see error messages when we start scripting the controls. So let's re-direct them to another page if they do not have the right plug-in or control. We'll do this by adding a function to check for the availability of the plug-in or control and attaching this to the window object's onload event handler in the <BODY> tag:

```
</OBJECT>

<SCRIPT LANGUAGE=JavaScript>

function window_onload()
{
    var plugInInstalled = false;

    if (navigator.appName.indexOf("Microsoft") == -1)
    {
        var plugInCounter;

        for (plugInCounter = 0; plugInCounter < navigator.plugins.length;
            plugInCounter++)
        {
            if (navigator.plugins[plugInCounter].name.indexOf("RealPlayer") >= 0)
            {
                plugInInstalled = true;
                break;
            }
        }
    }
    else
    {
        if (real1.readyState == 4)
        {
            plugInInstalled = true;
        }
    }

    if (plugInInstalled == false)    {
        window.location.replace("NoRealPlayerPage.htm");
    }
}

</SCRIPT>
</HEAD>
<BODY onload="return window_onload()">
<NOEMBED>
```

In the window_onload() function, we first define a variable plugInInstalled and initialize it to false.

Next, as checking for plug-ins or controls is very browser-dependant, we check to see if this is a Microsoft browser. If not, we assume it's Netscape Navigator, though for a real-life example we might want to do more detailed checks.

If the browser is Netscape Navigator, then we use a `for` loop to go through the `navigator` object's `plugins` array, checking each installed plug-in's name for the word "RealPlayer". If this word is found, then we set the variable `plugInInstalled` to `true` and break out of the `for` loop.

If we found that this was a Microsoft browser, then we use the `readyState` property of the `<OBJECT>` tag's `Object` object to see if the ActiveX control is loaded, initialized successfully, and is now ready for action. If its value is 4, then we know that all systems are go and we can use the control, so we set the variable `plugInInstalled` to `true`.

Finally, the last `if` statement in the function checks to see if `plugInInstalled` is `true` or `false`. If `false`, the user is re-directed to another page called `NoRealPlayerPage.htm` where we can either provide alternative ways of displaying the content or provide a link to load the RealPlayer control. Let's create a simple page to do this:

```
<HTML>
<HEAD>
<TITLE>No Real Player Installed</TITLE>
</HEAD>
<BODY>

<H2>You don't have the required RealPlayer plug-in</H2>
```

```
<P>
You can download the plug-in from
<A HREF="http://www.real.com">Real Player</A>
</P>
</BODY>
</HTML>
```

This needs to be saved as `NoRealPlayerPage.htm`.

Finally, back in the `realplayer.htm` page, let's enable the user to select a sound file and start and stop playing it. We add the following code to the top of the script block:

```
<SCRIPT LANGUAGE=JavaScript>

var fileName = "";

function butPlay_onclick()
{
    document.real1.SetSource("file://" + fileName);
    document.real1.DoPlay();
}

function butStop_onclick()
{
    document.real1.DoStop();
}

function file1_onblur()
{
    fileName = document.form1.file1.value;
}

function window_onload()
{
```

We also add a form with buttons for starting, stopping, and choosing a sound file to the body of the page:

```
   </NOEMBED>
<FORM ID=form1 NAME=form1>
<INPUT TYPE="button" VALUE="Play Sound" ID=butPlay NAME=butPlay
   LANGUAGE=JavaScript onclick="return butPlay_onclick()">
<INPUT TYPE="button" VALUE="Stop Sound" ID=butStop NAME=butStop
   LANGUAGE=JavaScript onclick="return butStop_onclick()">
<INPUT TYPE="file" ID=file1 NAME=file1
   LANGUAGE=JavaScript onblur="return file1_onblur()">
</FORM>
</BODY>
</HTML>
```

We've completed our page, so now re-save it. Load `realplayer.htm` into your browser and, as long as your browser supports plug-ins or ActiveX controls and the RealPlayer plug-in is installed, you should see something like the following:

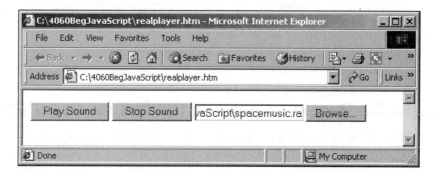

Click the **Browse** button and browse to a sound file with extension `.ra` (`spacemusic.ra` is provided with the code download, or you can create your own with Real Producer Basic, also available from `www.realnetworks.com`). Click the **Play Sound** and **Stop Sound** buttons to play and stop the sound.

So how does this work?

The form in the body of the page contains three form elements. The first two of these are just standard buttons, but the last is a `<INPUT>` element of `TYPE="file"`. This means that a text box and a button are displayed. When the button is clicked, a **Choose File** dialog box is opened, allowing you to choose the `.ra` file you want to hear. When chosen, this file's name appears in the text box.

We've connected the two buttons' `onclick` event handlers and the file control's `onblur` event handler to three functions, `butPlay_onclick()`, `butStop_onclick()`, and `file1_onblur()`, which are defined in the script block in the head of the page.

In the function `file1_onblur()` we set a global variable, `fileName`, to the value of the file control. In other words, `fileName` will contain the name and path of the file the user has chosen to play. The `onblur` event will fire whenever the user moves focus from the file control to another control or area of the page. In reality we would perform checks to see whether the file type selected by the user is actually a valid sound file.

In the other two functions, we access the RealPlayer plug-in or control that we embedded in the page. We use one function to load the file the user selected and play it, and the other function to stop play.

In both functions, we access the RealPlayer control by using its name prefixed with `document`. The script will work with IE and NN, though under IE it's accessing the ActiveX control defined in `<OBJECT>` and in NN it's accessing the plug-in defined in the `<EMBED>` tag.

In the `butPlay_onclick()` function, we use the `SetSource()` method of the RealPlayer object. This method takes one parameter – the file that we want the RealPlayer plug-in to load. So, in the line:

```
document.real1.SetSource("file://" + fileName);
```

we load the file the user specified. Next we use the `DoPlay()` method of the RealPlayer object, which starts the playing of the source file:

```
document.real1.DoPlay();
```

In function `butStop_onclick()`, we stop the playing of the clip using the `DoStop()` method of the RealPlayer object:

```
document.real1.DoStop();
```

Testing your No Plug-in or ActiveX Control Re-direction Script

It's quite likely that if you plan to use an ActiveX control or plug-in then you're going to make sure it's installed in your computer. The problem is that while that's great for testing pages to see they work when there is a control installed, it does make it very difficult to check re-direction scripts for users without that control. You have a number of possible options:

1. Have a second computer with a clean install of an operating system and browser, then load your pages on that computer. This is the way I do it, as it's the only 100% way of checking your pages.

2. Uninstall the plug-in. Depending on how the plug-in/control was installed, there may be an uninstall program for it, or for Windows users there is the Add/Remove programs option in the Control Panel.

3. For Netscape browsers, install a different version of the browser. For example, if you have Netscape 4.73 installed, try installing an older version, say Netscape 3.0 or even 2.0 if you can find it. The plug-ins currently installed are not normally available to a browser installed later, though this may not be true all of the time.

4. With IE, you can only have one version of the browser installed at once. However, IE does make it quite easy to remove ActiveX controls. In IE 5, choose Internet Options form the Tools menu. Click the Settings button under Temporary Internet files, followed by the View Objects button. From here you need to right-click on the name of the control you want removed and select Remove from the popup menu.

Potential Problems

Plug-ins and ActiveX controls provide a great way to extend a browser's functionality, but they do so at a price – compatibility problems. Some of the problems that might be faced include the following.

Similar, but Not the Same – Differences Between Browsers

Although a plug-in for NN and the equivalent ActiveX control for IE may support many similar properties and methods, you will often find significant, and sometimes subtle, differences.

For example, both the plug-in and ActiveX control version of RealPlayer support the `SetSource()` method. However, while:

```
document.real1.SetSource("D:\MyDir\MyFile.ra")
```

will work with IE, it will cause problems will NN. To work with NN we must specify the protocol by which the file will be loaded. If it is URL, we need to specify `http://`, but for a file on a user's local hard drive we need to add `file://`.

To make the code work for both IE and NN, we must type:

```
document.real1.SetSource("file://D:\MyDir\MyFile.ra")
```

Differences Between Plug-ins

When scripting the RealPlayer plug-in for NN, we embedded it like this:

```
<EMBED NAME="real1" ID="real1"
    BORDER="0"
    CONTROLS="play"
    HEIGHT=0 WIDTH=0 TYPE="audio/x-pn-realaudio-plugin">
```

We then accessed it via script just by typing this:

```
document.real1.DoPlay()
```

However, if we are scripting a Flash player, we need to add the attribute:

```
SWLIVECONNECT=true
```

to the `<EMBED>` definition in the HTML, otherwise any attempts to access the plug-in will result in errors.

```
<EMBED NAME="map"
    SWLIVECONNECT=true
    SRC="topmenu.swf"
    WIDTH=300 HEIGHT=200
    PLUGINSPAGE="http://www.macromedia.com/shockwave/download/index.cgi?P1_Prod_
    VERSION=ShockwaveFlash">
```

It's very important to study any available documentation that comes with a plug-in to check that there are no subtle problems like this.

Differences Between Operating Systems

Support for ActiveX controls varies greatly between different operating systems. IE for Windows 3.1 does not support ActiveX controls. IE for the Apple Mac does, but not as well as with Win32 operating systems, such as Windows 95, 98, and 2000.

Also, we need to be aware that an ActiveX control written for Win32 will not work on the Apple Mac: we need to make sure a Mac-specific control is downloaded.

IE on the Mac supports plug-ins as well as ActiveX controls, so for example Flash is a plug-in on the Mac and an ActiveX control on Win32. Clearly, if we want to support both Mac and Windows users, we need to write more complex code.

It's very important to check which operating system the user is running (for example, using the scripts given at the end of Chapter 5) and deal with any problems that may arise.

Differences Between Different Versions of the Same Plug-in or ActiveX Control

Creators of plug-ins and controls will often periodically release new versions with new features. If we make use of these new features, then we need to make sure that the user not only has the right plug-in or ActiveX control loaded, but that it's also the right version.

ActiveX Controls

With ActiveX controls, we can add version information in the CODEBASE attribute of the <OBJECT> tag.

```
<OBJECT CLASSID=clsid:AAA03-8BE4-11CF-B84B-0020AFBBCCFA
    ID=myControl
    CODEBASE="http://myserver/mycontrol.cab#version=3,0,0,0">
</OBJECT>
```

Now, not only will the browser check that the control is installed on the user's system, but it'll also check that the installed version is version 3 or greater.

What about if we want to check the version, and then re-direct to a different page if it's a version earlier than our page requires?

With ActiveX controls there's no easy way of using JavaScript code to check the ActiveX control version. One way is to find a property that the new control supports, but older versions don't, and then compare that to null. For example, imagine we have a control whose latest version introduces the property BgColor. To check if the installed version is the version we want, we type:

```
if (document.myControl.BgColor == null)
{
    alert("This is an old version");
}
```

It's also possible that the ActiveX creator has added a version property of some sort to their control's object that we can check against, but this will vary from control to control.

Plug-ins

With plug-ins we need to make use of the `Plugin` objects in the `navigator` object's `plugins[]` array property. Each `plugin` object in the array has a `name`, `filename`, and `description` property, which may provide version information. However, this will vary between plug-ins.

For example, for Flash Player 4 on Win32 the description given by:

```
navigator.plugins["Flash"].description
```

is Flash 4.0 r7.

Using regular expressions, which we introduced in Chapter 8, we could extract the version number from this string:

```
var myRegExp = /\d{1,}.\d{1,}/;
var flashVersion = navigator.plugins["Flash"].description;
flashVersion = parseFloat(flashVersion.match(myRegExp)[0]);
```

In the first line of code we define a regular expression that will match one or more numbers, followed by a dot, and then one or more numbers. Next we store the description of the Flash plug-in in the variable `flashVersion`. Finally we search the variable for the regular expression, returning an array of all the matches made. We then use the `parseFloat()` function on the contents of the element in the array at index 0 (in other words, the first element in the array).

Summary

We looked in this chapter at how we can use plug-ins and ActiveX controls to extend a browser's functionality.

We saw that:

❑   Internet Explorer supports ActiveX controls and to some extent plug-ins. Netscape Navigator has good support for plug-ins, but does not support ActiveX controls.

❑   Most creators of plug-ins also provide an ActiveX control equivalent. Internet Explorer and Netscape Navigator are incompatible as far as the installation of plug-ins and ActiveX controls goes.

❑   Plug-ins are embedded in a web page using the <EMBED> tag. We let NN know which plug-in is to be embedded by either specifying a source file or by specifying a MIME type using the SRC and TYPE attributes of the <EMBED> tag. If we define a value for the <EMBED> tag's PLUGINSPAGE attribute, then users who don't have that plug-in installed will be able to click a link and install it.

❑   We can find detailed information about what plug-ins are installed on our NN browser, their names, descriptions, and types, by using the About Plug-ins option on the Help menu.

❑ To use script to check if a user has a certain plug-in, we can use the `navigator` object's `plugins[]` array property. For each plug-in installed there will be a `Plugin` object defined in this array. Each `Plugin` object has the properties `name`, `description`, `filename`, and `type`, which we can use to determine if a plug-in exists on the user's computer. We can also use the `navigator` object's `mimeTypes[]` array property to check if a certain type of file is supported.

❑ Internet Explorer supports ActiveX controls as an alternative to plug-ins. These are embedded into a web page using the `<OBJECT>` tag. We specify which ActiveX control we want using the `CLASSID` attribute. If we want the user without a particular control installed to have it installed automatically, then we need to specify the `CODEBASE` attribute.

❑ Any parameters particular to the control are specified using the `<PARAM>` tag, which is inserted in between the opening and closing `<OBJECT>` tags.

❑ We can check if a control has loaded successfully using the `readyState` property of the `Object` object, which returns a number; 0 for control not installed, 1 for it's still loading, and 4 for it's installed and ready for use.

❑ Virtually every different type of plug-in and ActiveX control has its own interface, for which the control's documentation will provide the details. We looked briefly at the RealPlayer control by RealNetworks.

❑ We also saw that while plug-ins and controls are great for extending functionality they are subject to potential pitfalls. These include differences in the way plug-ins and ActiveX controls are scripted, differences in operating system and differences between versions of the same plug-in or control.

In the next chapter we change direction slightly to look at how script can be used on the web server rather than the browser. We'll look at how to set up your own web server, and how we can use JavaScript to control the web server and dynamically create pages on the fly.

Exercises

A suggested solution to this question can be found in Appendix A.

Question 1

Using the RealPlayer plug-in/ActiveX control, create a page with three images, so that when the mouse pointer rolls over them a sound is played. The page should work with NN 4.x and IE 4+. However, any other browsers should be able to view the page and roll over the images without errors appearing.

Online discussion at http://p2p.wrox.com

15

Server-Side Scripting with ASP

Up to now, we've been looking at JavaScript that runs in the user's browser and we've been loading our pages directly from our local hard drive. However, in reality our web pages usually sit on a **web server** that is connected to the Internet or a local intranet. While we could just treat a web server as a dumb file server that does nothing more then pass web pages back to users' browsers, we'll see in this chapter that the web server can process and change pages "on the fly", before they are passed to a user. Server-side scripting, especially when coupled with database access, can take our web site to a completely new dimension of sophistication, way beyond what can be achieved with client-side scripting. For example, e-commerce is mostly made possible with server-side processing.

In this chapter, we'll first look at what server-side scripting is and how it works. Then I'll show you how to set up your own web server – using Personal Web Server, a simple web server that's freely available for the Windows platform, as an example. While this server is not powerful enough to run a big e-commerce web site from, it's certainly good enough while you are learning and for simple intranet (corporate network) web sites.

We'll then look in more detail at how we insert server-side script into a web page using ASP (Active Server Pages) and what server-side techniques are available to add extra power to our web site. We'll finish off by adding server-side processing to the Trivia Quiz, in readiness for the next chapter where we will use a database to store the trivia questions.

What is Server-Side Scripting?

In web applications, there are usually at least two computers involved: a client computer that requests a particular web page, and a server computer that processes that request and serves the page back to the client.

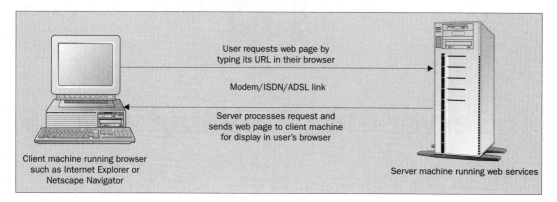

User requests web page by typing its URL in their browser

Modem/ISDN/ADSL link

Server processes request and sends web page to client machine for display in user's browser

Client machine running browser such as Internet Explorer or Netscape Navigator

Server machine running web services

In the diagram above, we can see the process of requesting a web page. Recall that we looked at this briefly in Chapter 1. It starts on the client machine with our web site visitor entering or choosing a URL (Universal Resource Locator) in their browser. The URL tells the browser which server machine on the Internet to request the web page from, together with a path for the server directory that the web page is located in and of course the file name of the web page. If we just supply a server name, or a server name and path to a directory, then the default page, if there is one, for that directory will be passed back from the server.

The browser then sends a request for the page to the server indicated in the URL. The server machine receives the request, and then goes and finds this page before sending it back to the client computer. The client computer receives the page and passes it to the browser, which then displays it, executing any JavaScript code embedded inside the page.

So far in this book, we have been dealing with **client-side JavaScript**. This is simply JavaScript code that executes in the browser running on the client computer. However, server machines are not just dumb computers that simply find a file and pass it back to the client. They can also do their own processing before passing the page to the client. Any processing done by the server machine before the web page is sent back to the client is referred to as **server-side processing**.

Server-side processing can involve a variety of tasks, such as processing information sent by the user in a web page's form, accessing a database to retrieve or store information, running a program on the server to check credit card details before telling another computer to send goods to a customer, and even sending e-mails. With the right components installed, a server can undertake a vast range of tasks.

So where does JavaScript fit into all this? Well, most web servers support the embedding of script into a web page that is then processed by the server itself, before the page is sent to the client computer. One of the scripting languages that can be embedded in pages on a Microsoft web server is JavaScript. However, Microsoft web servers are not the only web servers we can use – there are many, many different web servers available from companies such as IBM, Sun, and Netscape to name just a few. One of the most popular web servers is Apache on the Linux operating system. Many of these web servers have their own scripting languages, such as PHP, which provide similar functionality to JavaScript. Some also support JavaScript itself, such as Netscape's Enterprise Server, and others, such as Apache, can have JavaScript support installed.

We know that JavaScript is just a programming language and that it needs an environment to run in for it to be useful. When we were writing JavaScript client-side code, that environment was the web browser and the Browser Object Model (BOM) it makes available. Server-side scripting also needs to run in an environment – this time one provided by the server itself. On Microsoft servers, this environment is called Active Server Pages (ASP). Just as the browser made the page available via objects such as the `window` object and `document` object, ASP also enables interaction with the server via objects. The good news is that the knowledge you'll gain here about ASP and server-side scripting can also be used on other web servers, such as those that run on Unix and Linux operating systems.

Before we start looking at the ASP objects, we need to install a server. Normally the web server and user's browser would be on different machines, but there's no reason they can't be on the same machine. In fact, this is very handy for development purposes.

Personal Web Server (PWS)

The good news is that if you're running Windows, with the exception of Windows 3.1 and earlier versions, you can install Microsoft's Personal Web Server (PWS) for free. The downside is that, while PWS is fine for internal intranet web sites, it's definitely not suitable for high-use Internet web sites as it's not robust enough or secure enough. However, it is great for developing server-side script before deploying it to the full Windows web server called Internet Information Services (IIS) – this is supplied with Windows NT Server and Windows 2000 editions.

The steps needed to install a web server on Windows depend on which operating system is being used. Windows 2000 Server and Advanced Server users will already have IIS installed. If you're running Windows 2000 Professional, then note that IIS comes with it, but is not installed by default. Instead, you'll need to go to Control Panel, Add/Remove programs and select Add/Remove Windows Components, under which you'll find the option to install Internet Information Services (IIS).

Windows NT 4 Server and Workstation users will need to install NT Option pack. For Server users, this installs the full IIS server version. Workstation users will have the PWS version installed. The NT Option pack can be obtained both on CD and from the Microsoft web site at:

```
http://www.microsoft.com/ntserver/nts/downloads/recommended/NT4OptPk/default.asp
```

If you're running Windows 95, then you can download PWS from the Microsoft web site at:

```
http://www.microsoft.com/Windows/ie/pws/default.htm
```

Finally, Windows 98 and 98SE users will find PWS on the Windows disk.

We'll look next at all the steps necessary to install PWS on a Windows 98 machine. You should find that most of the steps are similar to other versions of Windows, with just a few minor variations.

Installing PWS on Windows 98

The set up files for PWS are on the Windows 98 CD in the directory \add-ons\pws\.

We need to copy these files from the PWS directory on the CD to the local hard drive – the C:\Temp directory would be a good place.

Due to changes in Windows operating system one of the files, MtsSetup.dll, is out of date and needs to be replaced with one downloaded from the Microsoft web site. This file can be downloaded from:

http://download.microsoft.com/download/transaction/Patch/1/W95/EN-US/Mtssetup.exe

Save the executable file to your hard drive in the C:\Temp directory, and then run it. First, the license agreement will appear. Read it, and if you agree, click Yes to start the install.

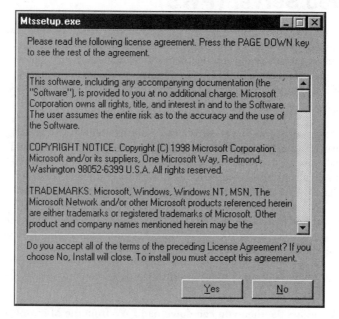

Next, in the text box that appears, either enter or browse to the directory into which the PWS directory was copied from the CD, then click OK.

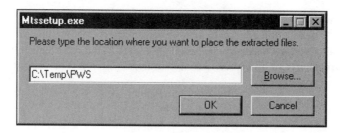

When the box shown below pops up asking if you want to overwrite the existing `Mtssetup.dll` file with the new one you just downloaded, click Yes.

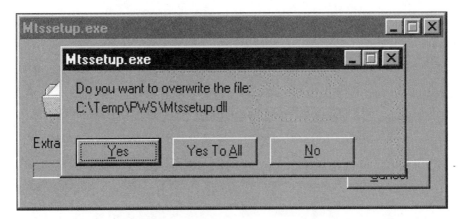

That completes the update. Now we can start the PWS installation process by running `setup.exe` in `C:\Temp\PWS` from Run on the Start menu.

We should then see the following screen:

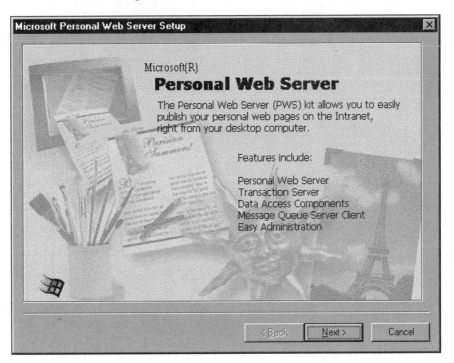

Click the Next button and we'll be given a choice of whether we want a Minimum, Typical, or Custom install. Unless hard drive space is at a premium (that is, you have less than 50Mb free) then go for the Typical install, which requires about 32 Mb of hard drive space.

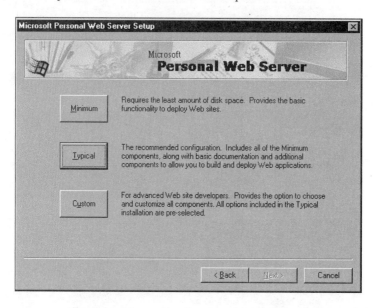

In the next screen, we are allowed to choose the directory where the web directories and web pages for the server will be stored. The default directory is fine unless you have limited space on your C: drive, in which case any hard drive is acceptable. We're not given the option of selecting an FTP or application directory, since the Windows 98 PWS does not support either of these. Once the directory is selected, click Next and the PWS installation will commence.

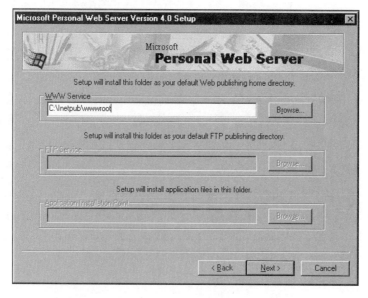

Once the installation has finished, click Finish and re-start the computer.

Managing PWS under Windows 98

Web servers are a little different from a normal program. Normally, you load or start a program by clicking its icon. When you've stopped using it, you close it down. However, web servers usually start when the operating system starts, unless you specify otherwise. They run in the background, and are termed a service rather than a normal program.

PWS comes with its own basic console, which gives us control over the web service. For example, if we want to stop the service we use the console's Stop button. To start it running again, we need to start it using the Start button in the console. Note that when the service is stopped, any attempts to load web pages from the server will fail. The console also gives us the ability to create new web directories and check usage statistics, such as how many visitors per day have visited our site.

After PWS has installed, the PWS tray icon, shown here, will be placed in the Windows task bar at the bottom of your desktop.

Double clicking this will open up the PWS console. Alternatively, you can also access the console from an option on the Start menu. Windows 2000 users can find the Personal Web Manager under Administrative Tools in the Control Panel. NT 4 users will find it under Start, Windows NT 4.0 Option Pack, Microsoft Internet Information Server, Internet Service Manager. Note that this may vary with your operating system.

Open up the PWS console now:

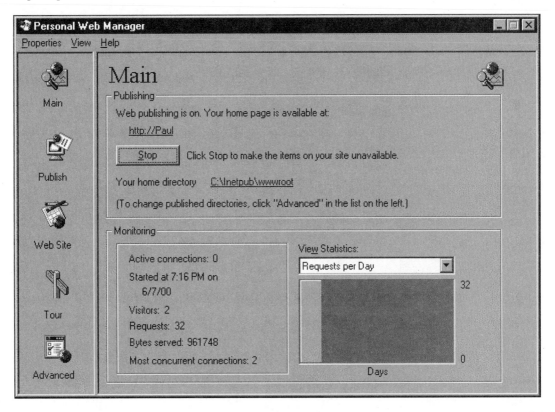

From the main section of the console, we can glean a lot of information. First, below the line "Web publishing is on. Your home page is available at:" we can see the name given to the server. In my case, the name is set automatically as http://Paul. If you click on this http://myservername link, where myservername is the server name for your web server, it will open up your default browser with the current home page for the server.

Underneath this, we are told what the physical path for the root directory (labeled home directory) of our server is. If you selected the default options when PWS was installed, then, like mine shown above, yours will be C:\Inetpub\wwwroot.

If we put a file in the root directory of our server called myPage.htm, then typing:

```
http://myservername/myPage.htm
```

into our browser will load the myPage.htm page. If we create a new directory under our root directory, C:\Inetpub\wwwroot, called myDir and put a file called myPage2.htm in there, then typing:

```
http://myservername/myDir/myPage2.htm
```

into our web browser will cause myPage2.htm in myDir to be loaded.

In addition, if the web server is on the same machine as the browser, then you can type http://localhost instead of http://myservername.

At the bottom of the console, grouped under Monitoring, we have various web site usage statistics, such as visitors per day, which records the number of people who visited your web site, and total requests, which lists how many pages have been requested.

Now let's open the advanced section of the console by clicking on the Advanced icon in the bottom left of the console:

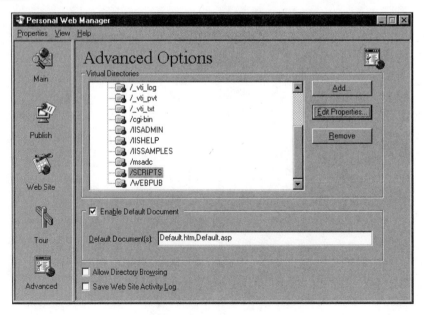

This part of the console deals mainly with virtual directories. What are virtual directories?

Without virtual directories, any document that can be browsed to needs to be in a folder under the web server's root directory. However, **virtual directories** allow us to give a physical directory on the hard drive an alias name, and then allow this physical directory to be accessible to users through the web server, without it being physically placed under the web server's root directory. This process is also called **aliasing**. The virtual directories are not real – they are just a way of referencing a physical directory.

Say, for example, that we want to create a directory `C:\MyWeb sites\MyExampleDirectory` and allow people to access its contents by typing:

```
http://myservername/AWalkOnTheServerSide
```

or

```
http://localhost/AWalkOnTheServerSide
```

To do this we create a new virtual directory called `AWalkOnTheServerSide`. There are actually two ways of creating a virtual directory. One way is to use the PWS console, and the other way is from Windows Explorer. Let's see how each works.

First, the PWS console method. Load the console by double-clicking the PWS tray icon, and then click the **Advanced icon**. Now make sure the **<Home>** directory is selected as shown below:

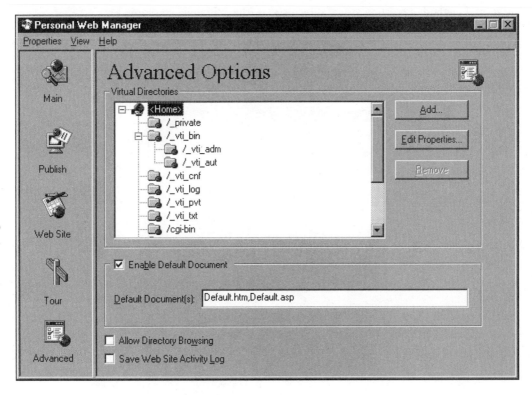

Now click the Add button and you'll see the dialog box below, where I've already typed in the name of an existing physical directory and the name I want as its alias – that is its name when accessed via the web server.

There are also three check boxes to choose from, which specify the type of access that the directory will have on the web server. Read enables user's to view the web pages by browsing to your web site, Execute allows users to run programs in that directory, and Script enables server-side scripts to run. For security reasons, it's normally best not to enable Execute permissions, as on most occasions we don't want people browsing our web site to be able to run any programs in our directory.

Click OK and the virtual directory AWalkOnTheServerSide will be created and mapped to the physical directory C:\MyWeb sites\MyExampleDirectory. We refer to the physical directory as being **web shared** – it's now viewable with a web browser by people on other computers on the network.

The second method of creating virtual directories is from Windows Explorer.

Open Windows Explorer, then select the directory to be web shared. For example, I'm going to web share my directory C:\MyWeb sites. Right-click on it and select Properties from the menu that pops up.

From the dialog box that pops up select the Web Sharing tab:

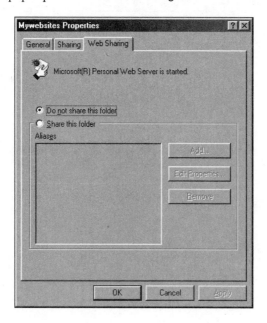

In the form, change the radio button from Do not share this folder to Share this folder – the same dialog box we saw before will appear, allowing you to set the directory's alias or virtual name, and the permissions as under the PWS console. By default the name of the directory you right-clicked is shown as a suggested virtual directory name, as shown below. To use another name such as AWalkOnTheServerSide just type that in instead.

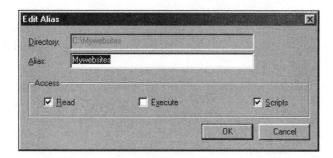

That completes our look at PWS. It's time to start putting it to use with some server-side scripting.

Introduction to Active Server Pages

In this section, we'll be taking a short tour of using JavaScript server-side within the Active Server Pages (ASP) environment. We'll see how to build up pages dynamically as they are being loaded by the user, look at the various objects supported by ASP, and finally see how we can retrieve information posted to the server by a form on a web page.

Pages that contain server-side script stored on a Microsoft web server must be saved with the file extension .asp. The Microsoft servers (PWS and IIS) only check pages with .asp extension for server-side script, so if we put server-side script in a standard .htm or .html file, it will be ignored.

If it is an .asp page, then the web server goes through each line in the page before it's sent back to the browser, and executes any JavaScript marked for server-side execution. If it's just an .htm or .html file, then the page is simply sent back to the browser with no checks for any script that should be run server-side. If we have a page that contains no server-side script, then it's best to save it with an .htm or .html extension rather than an .asp extension, otherwise the server will spend valuable processing time checking for server-side script that is not there.

Although ASP files have a different file extension, as far as web browsers are concerned they are just standard HTML pages containing HTML and client-side JavaScript. They are compatible with all web browsers, so there are no browser compatibility problems. In fact, ASP scripting can help us with browser compatibility problems as it allows us to build up pages dynamically, and then send them to the browser as standard HTML without the problems of dynamic HTML browser support. For example, using ASP we can make sure that a different banner advert image is shown every time a page is viewed by the user and, because we're doing it server-side, it doesn't matter if the browser supports JavaScript and image replacement.

Let's take our first step by looking at how we can insert server-side script into a web page.

Inserting Server-Side Script

When we inserted client-side JavaScript, we didn't need to specify that the script language was JavaScript (although it is always good coding practice to do so); the browser's scripting language default was JavaScript. If we wanted to insert script in a different language, such as VBScript, we would have needed to specify that VBScript was the language we were using.

However, in server-side scripting in ASP, the default language is VBScript. If we don't specify the language, then the server will process the script as VBScript and, of course, our JavaScript will cause errors.

Therefore, whenever we insert script server-side, we must specify that the language is JavaScript (although, in fact, it's JScript, the Microsoft version of JavaScript). We can insert script and specify the language in one of two ways, which we will look at now.

<SCRIPT> Tags

The first way of inserting server-side script is using the same `<SCRIPT>` tags we used for client-side JavaScript. However, we now need to specify the language using the `LANGUAGE` attribute and specify that the script is to be run at the server-side using the `RUNAT` attribute.

```
<SCRIPT LANGUAGE="JavaScript" RUNAT=SERVER>
    // Your server-side JavaScript here
</SCRIPT>
```

<% and %> Delimiters

The second and preferred method of inserting server-side script is to tell the server what language is to be used for all server-side script on the current page by adding:

```
<%@ LANGUAGE = JavaScript%>
```

to the very first line of the page. Then any server-script we add later in that page will be treated as JavaScript. (Note that this only counts for the current page – any other pages loaded must have their own language specification.)

The `<%@   %>` code is unusual as it's actually designed to contain server **directives**. These are commands issued to the server itself. In this case, our directive to the server is that it treats all server-side code on the page as written in JavaScript, not VBScript. The directive must be on just one line by itself and at the top of the page.

Now, to add server-side script to the page we simply enclose it in `<%` and `%>`, which are called **script delimiters**:

```
<%
    // Your Server-side JavaScript here
%>
```

One benefit of this second method of inserting server-side script is being able to write directly to the page by adding an equals sign to the first `<%` tag like this: `<%=`. For example, if we want to write the contents of a variable named `myVariable` to the page we just write:

```
<%= myVariable %>
```

Differences between Server-Side and Client-Side Script

The core JavaScript language, that is its syntax and its native objects, remains the same server-side as we saw client-side. For example, we have the same `if` statement, the `for` loop, the `Math` object, the `String` object, and so on.

However, the client-side script was being hosted (in other words, run) in a browser. This meant that we had access to the various objects that are made available in the BOM and are relevant to the browser. For example, we had the `window` object, the `document` object, and so on.

Server-side script is not being hosted in a browser, but is now being run by the server and its environment. For this reason, instead of browser-related objects and the BOM, we have server-related objects and the ASP object model. Thus, when we are writing server-side script, we can't use the `window` object or the `document` object or, indeed, any of the BOM objects that a browser makes available. We'll see shortly what the new ASP object model contains and how we use that.

A second important point to make is that server-side script runs on one "machine", the web server, and client-side script runs on a different "machine", the one with the browser running. Any script created server-side is not accessible to client-side script, and vice versa. For example, if we declared a variable or created a function in client-side script, we won't be able to access that variable or function in server-side script. It can get confusing when you're running the browser and the server on the same computer, but they are still considered as separate machines and no access is possible between the server and client sides. We will see later how we can pass information from client-side script to server-side script and back again, but it's not achieved using the normal JavaScript variables.

Writing Server-Side Script

We've seen how we can insert server-side script, so now let's use this to create our first server-side script program.

Try It Out – Random Banner Advert

Let's create a page that loads a random banner advert image, from a choice of three, each time the user browses to it. In Chapter 9, we used three banner advert images called `AdvertImage1.jpg`, `AdvertImage2.jpg`, and `AdvertImage3.jpg`, so we may as well use these again:

```
<%@ LANGUAGE = JavaScript%>
<HTML>
<HEAD>
<%
    var randomAdvertNumber = parseInt(Math.random() * 3) + 1;
    var imgName = 'AdvertImage' + randomAdvertNumber + '.jpg';
%>
</HEAD>
<BODY>

<IMG SRC="<%= imgName %>">

</BODY>
</HTML>
```

617

Save the file as `BannerAdvert.asp`. The file needs to be saved with a `.asp` extension, because we want the server-side script to be processed. Also, it needs to be placed either under the root directory of the server or in a directory which has been made into a virtual directory.

Here, I have placed the file in the physical directory `C:\MyWeb sites\MyExampleDirectory` that has the associated `AWalkOnTheServerSide` virtual directory, which I created in the previous section. I can then browse to the page using the URL:

```
http://localhost/AWalkOnTheServerSide/BannerAdvert.asp
```

When loaded, the page randomly selects one of our three images as seen below:

Refresh the page a few times to see the random selection of the image.

How It Works

At the very top of our page's code we have placed:

```
<%@ LANGUAGE = JavaScript%>
```

As we have seen, this tells the server that the language used for any scripts in this page is JavaScript. It's very important that this line is always the very first in the file and is on its own line with nothing else, because it's a server directive.

Next, we have inserted two lines of JavaScript inside the head of the page. We've used `<%` to mark the start of the server-side script block and `%>` to mark its end. We can do this because we have already told the server that the language we are using for server-side script is JavaScript.

```
<HEAD>
<%
    var randomAdvertNumber = parseInt(Math.random() * 3) + 1;
    var imgName = 'AdvertImage' + randomAdvertNumber + '.jpg';
%>
</HEAD>
```

The code itself generates a random whole number between 1 and 3, and stores that in variable randomAdvertNumber. Then it creates the name of the image, stored in the variable imgName, by appending the text AdvertImage to the start of the randomly created number, and the file extension, .jpg, to the end.

Finally, inside the body of the document, we define an <IMG> tag:

```
<IMG SRC="<%= imgName %>">
```

We can see that the SRC attribute of the <IMG> tag contains not the file name of an image, but some server-side script, the results of which will be inserted at that point in the page. The opening <% and closing %> mark out the script block, and the equals sign = added to the <% causes the contents of the server-side JavaScript to be written out to the page. In this case, we are inserting the value of the variable imgName.

View the source for the page in the browser. To do this in Internet Explorer, choose **Source** from the **View** menu, and on Navigator choose **Page Source** from the **View** menu. You should see something similar to the following:

```
<HTML>
<HEAD>

</HEAD>
<BODY>

<IMG SRC="AdvertImage1.jpg">

</BODY>
</HTML>
```

Note that all server-side script has disappeared. You'll also notice that it doesn't say:

```
<IMG SRC="<%= imgName %>">
```

but rather it contains the file name of the randomly selected image, in this case:

```
<IMG SRC="AdvertImage1.jpg">
```

This is because all the script processing is done server-side. What is sent to the client's browser is the result of that processing, so the browser never gets to see our server-side JavaScript. This is something of a bonus if we don't want our script code to be shared with the world.

if Statements and Loops, and Their Effect on Page HTML

In server-side scripting, we can include HTML between JavaScript statements. For example, an if statement may start in one block of server-side JavaScript, but actually be closed in the following block of script, the script blocks being separated by HTML. Any HTML between the blocks will be affected by the if statement.

We can see this more clearly in the example below, which writes a heading to the page, which says whether a number contained in the variable myNumber is 101 or not.

```
<%
    var myNumber = 101;

    if (myNumber == 101)
    {
%>

<H2>My Number was 101</H2>

<%
    }
    else
    {
%>

<H2>My number was not 101</H2>

<%
    }
%>
```

At the top of the first script block, we've set myNumber to 101, so we know the outcome of the code already. However, what's important is that the HTML:

```
<H2>My Number was 101</H2>
```

which is between the open curly brace of the if statement in the first block of JavaScript and its closing curly brace in the second block of JavaScript, will only appear in the code sent to the client machine if the condition of the if statement is true. In this case, the condition is myNumber == 101, so the heading will appear in the code.

The HTML between the open and close braces of the else statement won't be written out to the page, because the condition in the if statement was true. This is very different from client-side JavaScript where each script block must contain whole statements only.

This ability to use conditions to decide which blocks of HTML should be written to the final page and which should not is very powerful. We'll see later how we can detect what browser and operating system the user has. With this information, we could use an if statement to only write HTML to the page that is compatible with the user's browser.

In a similar way, loops, such as for and while, cause not only any JavaScript statements to be repeated, but also any HTML that might be inside the loop. In the example below, we repeatedly write out a sentence containing a number that increments from 1 to 10:

```
<%
    var myNumber;

    for (myNumber = 1; myNumber <= 10; myNumber++)
    {
%>
```

```
    <P>
        <STRONG>The Number this time is <%=myNumber%></STRONG>
    </P>

<%
    }
%>
```

Just as with the `if` statement, it's not only any JavaScript between the `for` loop's opening and closing braces that is run, but also the enclosed HTML that is repeated each time the loop is repeated.

ASP Objects

When we looked at client-side JavaScript, we saw that on its own it can't actually do that much; it's simply a programming language. It's only when it is used to manipulate the Browser Object Model (BOM) that we find out how powerful it can be. With server-side scripting, we have a new set of objects to learn about, which we can manipulate to create the results we want. The good news is that the server-side object model available to ASP is much smaller and easier to learn than the client-side BOM.

In this section, we'll look at some of the ASP objects available, including the `Request`, `Response`, `Server`, `Session`, and `Application` objects. We'll see how they enable us to obtain information submitted to the page in a form, find out which browser the user has, and re-direct users to different pages. We'll also see how we can keep track of users as they move around our web site and how we can store information on the server.

Requests and Responses

Before we start looking at ASP objects in detail, we'll briefly look at two important concepts that once understood help explain why two of the ASP objects we'll see shortly exist and what their purpose is.

We talked earlier in the chapter about how browsing to a web page on the Internet or on a web server running on a local network is a two stage process. First, the user requests a web page from a server by typing in the name of the server, the directory, and the file name of the web page they want. The request might have also been made by clicking a link in a web page or by submitting a form in a page. The web server receives the request along with some additional information about the client computer, the browser, and any information contained inside a form if the request was a result of a form being submitted.

When the ASP object model was being designed by Microsoft, they had to decide on the name of the object that would represent a request and, yes, you guessed it, they decided to name it the `Request` object. Anything that has anything to do with an incoming request, such as form data being passed or even cookies being sent, can be accessed in our server-side JavaScript code using the `Request` object.

We know that the request is only half the equation – once we have the request we need to deal with the response side of things. The page that was requested is automatically sent back to the requesting browser, so what is the programmer's part in the response? Well, we can set cookies which are sent back to the browser, we can change the HTML in the page before it's sent back, and we can even redirect the user so that a different page to the one requested is sent back.

With much imagination, it was decided that the ASP object to represent the response side of things would be called ... the Response object. Bet you didn't see that coming!

Both the Response and Request objects are like the BOM objects that a browser makes available in that we don't need to create them – they are created for us and are ready to use. The difference is that it's now the server that creates them for us, and not a browser. This applies to all of the ASP objects.

It's time now to look in much more detail at the Request and Response objects, and also some of the other objects that ASP makes available to us.

Request Object – Getting Information from the User

The Request object's purpose is to help us find out details about the last request made by the user for a page on our server.

When the user makes a request for a web page, for example by clicking on a link in a web page, or typing a URL into the browser's location box, the details of the request are carried to the server via HTTP (HyperText Transport Protocol). This protocol simply specifies, at a low level, how the request should be made, what information should be passed to the server, and the way that the sent information must be structured. The HTTP request contains a header and possibly a body. The header contains information about the request, such as which browser the user has, which page (if any) made the request, what cookies there are for that server, and so on. The body contains information sent with the request, such as information entered in the form that posted the request. Luckily enough, we don't need to worry about these details or how the HTTP protocol works, as using the Request object makes getting all this information very easy.

We'll start by looking at how we can get information submitted from a form.

Getting Information Posted by a Form

In Chapter 6, we saw how to create a form in a web page and how we can access that information client-side, using the objects associated with the different form elements.

There were two attributes of the <FORM> tag that we briefly mentioned, but did not use since they were only applicable to server-side script. The METHOD attribute determines how the information is sent to the server. The most common value for this attribute is POST, although sometimes GET is used. For the moment, we'll concentrate on how to retrieve information that has been sent via the POST method.

The other attribute of the <FORM> tag that is now relevant is the ACTION attribute. This specifies the page to which the information in the form should be sent.

Let's look at an example. Say we have a form in the page MyFormPage.htm and that the form has just two text boxes and a submit button:

```
<FORM ACTION="ProcessFormPage.asp" METHOD=POST NAME=form1>
    <INPUT TYPE="text" NAME="txtName">
    <BR>
    <INPUT TYPE="text" NAME="txtAge">
    <BR>
    <INPUT TYPE="submit" VALUE="Post This Form" NAME=submit1>
</FORM>
```

When the user hits the submit button, all the information in the form elements, that is the values entered in the text boxes at the time of the form submission, will be sent to the server. Where to? In this case, our form will be submitted to the page `ProcessFormPage.asp`. We must specify an `.asp` page, otherwise we won't be able to do any server-side processing and make use of the form information. You can think of the form posting as a little like the user clicking a hyperlink in that they are directed to a new page. The main difference is that any form data is passed, along with the direction to a new page.

Once the form is submitted to the page specified in the `ACTION` attribute of the `<FORM>` tag, we can then read the values sent with the form. In our form above, the page receiving the request will be the `ProcessFormPage.asp` and it's here that we can write the JavaScript to read and process the form information before sending the page `ProcessFormPage.asp` back to the user. The key to getting form information is the `Form` collection property of the `Request` object. A **collection property** is very similar to an array property, and is accessed in a similar way.

The page that contains the form being submitted will submit the form's content information, along with the `NAME` attribute value of each control that the information relates to. Note that it's the `NAME` attribute and not the `ID` attribute that's important here. In our example, our page contained a form with two text controls, one named `txtName` and the other `txtAge`. To get that information we could write something like this in our `ProcessFormPage.asp`:

```
var postedName = Request.Form("txtName")
var postedAge = Request.Form("txtAge")
```

This will result in our variables `postedName` and `postedAge` containing the values contained by `txtName` and `txtAge` when the form was submitted by the user.

Try It Out – A Simple Form Post

In this simple example, we'll create a form that asks the user for their first and last names, and then submits this information to another page, which displays it back to the user. We'll first create the page with a form on it, with just two text boxes and a submit button:

```
<HTML>
<BODY>
<FORM ACTION="ReceiveSimpleForm.asp" METHOD=POST ID=form1 NAME=form1>
    <P>
        First Name : <INPUT ID=txtFirstName NAME=txtFirstName>
    </P>
    <P>
        Last Name : <INPUT ID=txtLastName NAME=txtLastName>
    </P>
    <P>
        <INPUT ID=submit1 NAME=submit1 TYPE=submit VALUE="Post me to the server">
    </P>
</FORM>
</BODY>
</HTML>
```

Save it as `SimpleForm.htm` in the physical directory `C:\MyWeb sites\MyExampleDirectory` of the `AWalkOnTheServerSide` virtual directory.

Now create the ASP file that the form is to be posted to:

```
<%@ LANGUAGE = JavaScript%>
<HTML>
<HEAD>
<%
    var lastName = Request.Form("txtLastName");
%>
</HEAD>
<BODY>
    <P>The value you entered for your first name was
    <%= Request.Form("txtFirstName") %></P>
    <P>The value you entered for your last name was
    <%= lastName %></P>
</BODY>
</HTML>
```

Save this as `ReceiveSimpleForm.asp` in the same directory as `SimpleForm.htm`.

You need to browse to the `SimpleForm.htm` page on your local server by using either your server name or `localhost`. For example, type:

```
http://localhost/AWalkOnTheServerSide/SimpleForm.htm
```

into your browser. Now enter some information in the text boxes, and click the Post me to the server button.

You'll see that the page posted to, our `ReceiveSimpleForm.asp` page, displays the information we entered in the text boxes.

How It Works

The `SimpleForm.htm` page is easy enough to follow, just a form containing two text boxes and a submit button.

```
<FORM ACTION="ReceiveSimpleForm.asp" METHOD=POST ID=form1 NAME=form1>
```

Notice that the form's definition specifies how the form is to be posted using the METHOD attribute, set here as POST. In addition, the ACTION attribute specifies which page is to receive and handle the form data that is posted, which in our case is `ReceiveSimpleForm.asp`.

We'll now turn to the `ReceiveSimpleForm.asp` page. At the very top of the page, we've specified that the scripting language for that page is JavaScript:

```
<%@ LANGUAGE = JavaScript%>
```

In between the <HEAD> tags, we have our first server-side JavaScript. We mark the start of the server-side script using <% and the end with %>. Inside our server-side script block we have just one line:

```
    var lastName = Request.Form("txtLastName");
```

We declare a variable called `lastName` and set its value to the value of the form element `txtLastName`. The variable is declared outside of any function, so it will be global to this page and available to any server-side script later in the page. Remember, this is server-side script so the variable is only available during the server-side processing and will be lost once the page is received at the user's browser.

Then, in the body of the page, we get the information contained within the form element `txtFirstName`, again using the `Request.Form` collection property and the name of the element:

```
<P>The value you entered for your first name was
<%= Request.Form("txtFirstName") %></P>
```

We write the information out to the page by enclosing the script in `<%=` and `%>` tags; the equals sign after the opening tag causes whatever value is returned by the script to be written to the page at that point.

Finally, we write out the value of variable `lastName` that we declared earlier to the page:

```
<P>The Value you entered for your last name was
<%= lastName %></P>
```

Dealing with More Complex Forms

While accessing the values of text boxes is quite easy, what about controls like lists, drop-down list boxes, radio buttons, and finally the text area element? Actually, all of these are accessed in the same way as the text box.

Select Elements and Radio Buttons

When we define select elements and radio buttons, we give each item in the select list or each radio button in a group a `VALUE` attribute. Whichever item in the select list, or radio button in the group, has been selected by the user will have its value sent to the server; all the values of the other select items and radio buttons are ignored.

For example, let's imagine that we have the form elements shown below in a form that has been posted to the server:

```
<INPUT TYPE="radio" NAME=radio1 VALUE="FirstRadioButton">
<INPUT TYPE="radio" NAME=radio1 VALUE="SecondRadioButton">
<INPUT TYPE="radio" NAME=radio1 VALUE="ThirdRadioButton">

<SELECT NAME=selYear SIZE=1>
   <OPTION VALUE=1999>1999</OPTION>
   <OPTION VALUE=2000>2000</OPTION>
   <OPTION VALUE=2001>2001</OPTION>
</SELECT>
```

If, at the time when the form was submitted, the user had selected the second radio button and the third item in the select element, then what would be contained in the variables below?

```
var radioValue = Request.Form("radio1");
var selectValue = Request.Form("selYear");
```

The answer is that the server-side variable radioValue would contain the string "SecondRadioButton" and the selectValue variable would contain the string "2001". Although, when client-side, the radio button group and the select option array contain more than one value, when they are posted to an ASP page and processed server-side, we only get the value of the radio button or option that the user selected prior to submitting the form.

Checkboxes

With a checkbox, if it's checked when the form is submitted to the server, then its value is sent to the server. If it's not checked, then no value is sent to the server.

If the checkbox didn't have a VALUE attribute when the checkbox was defined in the form, then a checked checkbox will have "on" as its value.

You can define two or more checkboxes with the same name in a form, in which case the value of each ticked checkbox will be passed. For example, if our form is this:

```
<FORM ACTION="test.asp" METHOD=POST ID=form1 NAME=form1>
  <INPUT TYPE="checkbox" NAME=checkbox1 VALUE="Hello">
  <INPUT TYPE="checkbox" NAME=checkbox1 VALUE="GoodBye">
  <INPUT TYPE="submit" NAME=submit1 VALUE="Submit">
</FORM>
```

and just the first checkbox was ticked, then the value of the checkboxValue variable:

```
var checkboxValue = Request.Form("checkbox1");
```

would be just the string "Hello".

If the user had ticked both checkboxes, then the value of checkboxValue variable would be "Hello, GoodBye".

Text areas

The TEXTAREA form element sends its value just like a text box, but with one important difference: it has multiple lines, carriage returns and line feeds. When we looked at this control in Chapter 6, we mentioned the WRAP attribute. There are three possible values to this attribute: off, soft, and hard. If the WRAP attribute is off, which is the default if the attribute is not set, then any text in the control will be on the same line, unless the user hits the return key. If the WRAP attribute is set to soft, then when the text reaches the end of the line it will wrap automatically on to the next line, much as your word processor does. However, any new lines caused by this wrapping won't be sent along with the text when it is posted to the server. If WRAP is set to hard, then text will wrap at the end of a line *and* the new line characters will be sent along with the text when posted to the server.

Different operating systems may use different characters for new lines, as we saw in Chapter 6, so it's important to be aware of the new line characters for each operating system your visitors might have. You might be surprised at the differences! It's best to test your ASP pages with all the platforms that you expect your visitors to be using.

Try It Out – Suggestion Form

Let's create a more complex form – this time it's a suggestion form. The user enters their name and e-mail details, gender, age, whether they expect a response to their suggestion, and finally their suggestion. We do some basic validation of the form client-side and only post the form if it's actually filled in. If the form passes this validation, it is posted to another page, which displays the values to the user.

First let's create the form page:

```
<HTML>
<HEAD>
<SCRIPT LANGUAGE=JavaScript>

function form1_onsubmit()
{
    var returnValue = false;

    if (document.form1.txtName.value == "")
    {
        alert("Please enter your name");
        document.form1.txtName.focus();
    }
    else if (document.form1.txtEmail.value == "")
    {
        alert("Please enter your e-mail address");
        document.form1.txtEmail.focus();
    }
    else if (document.form1.txtaSuggestion.value == "")
    {
        alert("Please enter your suggestion");
        document.form1.txtaSuggestion.focus();
    }
    else
    {
        returnValue = true;
    }

    return returnValue;
}

</SCRIPT>
</HEAD>
<BODY>
<FORM ACTION="ReceiveComplexForm.asp"
    METHOD=post
    NAME=form1
    onsubmit="return form1_onsubmit()">
        <P>Name : <INPUT NAME=txtName></P>
        <P>E-mail : <INPUT NAME=txtEmail></P>
        Gender : <BR>
        Female <INPUT TYPE="radio" CHECKED NAME=radGender VALUE=Female>
        Male <INPUT TYPE="radio" NAME=radGender VALUE=Male>
        <BR><BR>
```

```
      Your age range
      <SELECT NAME=selAgeRange SIZE=1>
          <OPTION VALUE=0_18 SELECTED>Under 18</OPTION>
          <OPTION VALUE=19_40>19 - 40</OPTION>
          <OPTION VALUE=41_70>41 - 70</OPTION>
          <OPTION VALUE=70+>70+</OPTION>
      </SELECT>
      <BR><BR>
      Tick if you want a response
      <INPUT NAME=chkResponse TYPE=checkbox VALUE=SendResponse>
      <BR><BR>
      Your suggestion <BR>
      <TEXTAREA COLS=20 ROWS=10 NAME=txtaSuggestion WRAP=hard></TEXTAREA>
      <BR><BR>
      <P>
      <INPUT NAME=submit1 TYPE=submit VALUE="Send Suggestion">
      </P>
    </FORM>
  </BODY>
</HTML>
```

Save this as `ComplexForm.htm` in a directory that can be browsed to via your web site, for example the physical directory of the `AWalkOnTheServerSide` virtual directory or your web server's `wwwRoot` directory.

Next, we have the page that receives the post from the form:

```
<%@ LANGUAGE = JavaScript%>
<HTML>
<BODY>
    <P>Name is <%= Request.Form("txtName") %></P>
    <P>E-mail is <%= Request.Form("txtEmail") %></P>
    <P>Gender is <%= Request.Form("radGender") %></P>
    <P>Response is <%= Request.Form("chkResponse") %></P>
    <P>Age Range is <%= Request.Form("selAgeRange") %></P>
    <PRE>
        <P>Suggestion is <%= Request.Form("txtaSuggestion") %></P>
    </PRE>
</BODY>
</HTML>
```

Save this in the same directory as the `ComplexForm.asp` with the name `ReceiveComplexForm.asp`.

Load the `ComplexForm.htm` page into your web browser, for example by typing:

```
http://localhost/AWalkOnTheServerSide/ComplexForm.htm
```

You'll see a form like that opposite above, which you need to fill in (I've filled in my details). Client-side script checks that you have entered your name, e-mail, and suggestion and won't let you submit the form unless you have.

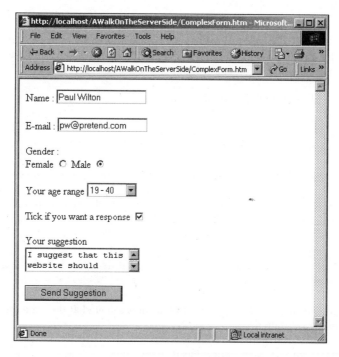

With the form completed, click on the Send Suggestion button and the form is posted to the
`ReceiveComplexForm.asp` page, which displays the details that were entered in the form submitted:

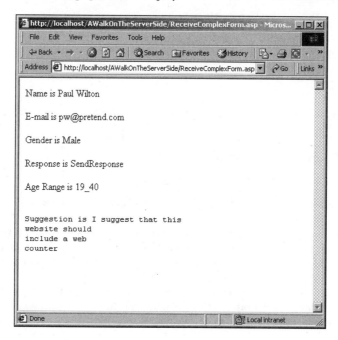

Try submitting the form with different values. In particular, see what happens when the check box is not
ticked as opposed when it is ticked.

How It Works

Within the body of `ComplexForm.htm` we have a form with the name `form1`. As well as text boxes, the form also includes a radio button group, a select control, a check box, and a text area. This allows us to demonstrate what information each control passes back to the server.

First, we have two text boxes for the name and e-mail address of the user:

```
<P>Name : <INPUT NAME=txtName></P>
<P>E-mail : <INPUT NAME=txtEmail></P>
```

As we saw in the last example, the value sent to the server for these controls is the value entered by the user.

For each control other than the text boxes and the text area, we have a value specified by the VALUE attribute. The radio buttons:

```
Gender : <BR>
Female <INPUT TYPE="radio" CHECKED NAME=radGender VALUE=Female>
Male <INPUT TYPE="radio" NAME=radGender VALUE=Male>
```

have values `Female` and `Male`. Whichever radio button is selected at the time the form is posted is the one whose value will be submitted.

In the case of the select control, each option has its own value:

```
Your age range
<SELECT NAME=selAgeRange SIZE=1>
    <OPTION VALUE=0_18 SELECTED>Under 18</OPTION>
    <OPTION VALUE=19_40>19 - 40</OPTION>
    <OPTION VALUE=41_70>41 - 70</OPTION>
    <OPTION VALUE=70+>70+</OPTION>
</SELECT>
```

Again, whichever item is selected in the select control when the form is submitted, will be the one whose value is posted.

The checkbox is also given a VALUE attribute:

```
Tick if you want a response
<INPUT NAME=chkResponse TYPE=checkbox VALUE=SendResponse>
```

However, this differs from the situations above in that the value is posted only if the checkbox is checked, otherwise no value is posted to the server. If we want to discover whether the checkbox was ticked, we simply need to see if its value is `SendResponse` or whether it has no value.

Within the TEXTAREA control, we've set its WRAP attribute to `hard`. That way when the user's text comes to the end of a line, it will wrap over to the next, and this formatting will be passed to the server when the form is posted.

```
Your suggestion <BR>
<TEXTAREA COLS=20 ROWS=10 NAME=txtaSuggestion WRAP=hard></TEXTAREA>
```

Also, notice that we've not left any spaces between the open and close <TEXTAREA> tags and that they are on the same line. This is because the value of the text area is the string contained between its opening and closing tags. If we don't do this, then if the user does not enter any input into the text area, the value of the text area won't be an empty string, but either a space or a new line character. This makes it more difficult to check whether the user has entered a suggestion.

The last item in the form is a submit button for the form:

```
<INPUT NAME=submit1 TYPE=submit VALUE="Send Suggestion">
```

In the simple form example we gave earlier in the chapter, we didn't do any form validation client-side before posting the form. We simply had a submit button, which when clicked automatically posted the form without the need for further JavaScript.

This time however, when we define the <FORM>, we capture the Form object's onsubmit event handler, and connect it to the form1_onsubmit() function, which we defined in the head of the page. Notice that the onsubmit attribute of the <FORM> tag returns the value from the function form1_onsubmit(). If false is returned, the form submission is canceled; if true is returned then the form submission goes ahead:

```
<FORM ACTION="ReceiveComplexForm.asp"
    METHOD=post
    NAME=form1
    onsubmit="return form1_onsubmit()">
```

Also, note from the definition of the <FORM>, that the method for submission of the form is post, and the form is to be submitted to the page ReceiveComplexForm.asp. We will look at this page shortly.

First we will take a closer look at the form1_onsubmit() function, defined in the head of the ComplexForm.htm page. This starts by defining the variable returnValue and initializing it to false.

```
function form1_onsubmit()
{
    var returnValue = false;
```

The function then checks whether the text box with name txtName has a value. If it doesn't, then the user is alerted to this fact, and the focus of the page is sent back to this control:

```
if (document.form1.txtName.value == "")
{
    alert("Please enter your name");
    document.form1.txtName.focus();
}
```

This check is then repeated for the text box controls called txtEmail, and the text area control called txtaSuggestion:

```
else if (document.form1.txtEmail.value == "")
{
    alert("Please enter your e-mail address");
    document.form1.txtEmail.focus();
}
else if (document.form1.txtaSuggestion.value == "")
{
    alert("Please enter your suggestion");
    document.form1.txtaSuggestion.focus();
}
```

Finally, if none of the conditions is true, meaning that everything we want filled in is filled in, then the final `else` statement sets `returnValue` to `true`:

```
else
{
    returnValue = true;
}
```

The variable `returnValue` is returned at the end of the function. As explained above, if it contains `false` then the form submission is canceled, otherwise it goes ahead as normal:

```
    return returnValue;
}
```

That's enough checks for our simple test web site, but if our page was accessible from the Internet we'd need to thoroughly check that every form element both exists and has a value, in order to defeat evil hackers who try to crash our ASP page by sending it erroneous form data.

We'll now turn to the `ReceiveComplexForm.asp` page, to which the form in `ComplexForm.htm` is posted. Recall that now we're operating server-side, so if we want to use JavaScript we always need to specify the language for the page as JavaScript:

```
<%@ LANGUAGE = JavaScript%>
```

Then inside the body of the page we print out the values of the text boxes, the radio button, the check box, and the select list:

```
<P>Name is <%= Request.Form("txtName") %></P>
<P>E-mail is <%= Request.Form("txtEmail") %></P>
<P>Gender is <%= Request.Form("radGender") %></P>
<P>Response is <%= Request.Form("chkResponse") %></P>
<P>Age Range is <%= Request.Form("selAgeRange") %></P>
```

Finally, we've put the response from the text area box inside `<PRE>` tags. That way it will show the text in the box exactly as it's submitted, line breaks and all. If the text in the textarea box is on different lines, then that will be reflected here:

```
<PRE>
    <P>Suggestion is <%= Request.Form("txtaSuggestion") %></P>
</PRE>
```

If we change the text area box's definition in the `ComplexForm.htm` page so that its `WRAP` attribute is `soft` rather than `hard`, we'll find that all the text submitted will be on one line unless the user has explicitly put the text on another line by hitting return.

Getting Information Passed in a URL

As well as passing values using a form submission, we can also attach values to the URL of the page we want the values to be sent to. You may well have seen web sites where, for example, the URLs for searches look something like:

```
http://www.someserver.com/search_web site.asp?SearchFor=SomeInfo&AndSomeOtherInfo
```

We can pass information like this from a web page to the server in various ways:

- ❑ We can add the information to a hyperlink manually
- ❑ We can use script to navigate to a URL with data added to the end
- ❑ We can use a form, but change the METHOD attribute to GET rather than POST

Here, we'll just look at how to add data to the end of a URL using the first two methods, rather than using a form. The form POST method is usually preferable to the form GET method, since it's easier to use and can handle much larger amounts of data.

We'll start by looking at how we build up a URL that has values attached. Let's imagine that we want to pass a name and someone's age via a URL.

First, we have the URL of the page that will receive the data. If it's on our local server, it might be something like:

```
http://localhost/MyGetInfopage.asp
```

To add data to the end of the URL, we first need to tell the browser where the URL ends and the data starts. We do this using a question mark:

```
http://localhost/MyGetInfopage.asp?
```

Now, let's add the name data by first adding the key name for the data. This can be anything you like, but it must only include characters and numbers, not punctuation or spaces. Let's use a key name of Name:

```
http://localhost/MyGetInfopage.asp?Name
```

Now we need to say what Name is equal to, that is what data we are passing. To do this, we simply add an equals sign, then the data itself. In the example shown below, I'm passing Paul as the data:

```
http://localhost/MyGetInfopage.asp?Name=Paul
```

It's important to note that only characters and numbers can be passed like this in NN. To pass punctuation, spaces or special characters, we need to make some extra steps – we need to encode them with their ASCII hexadecimal value, in front of which we put a % sign. (See Appendix D for details.) For example, for a space you should use %20. So, to pass the data Paul Wilton we need:

```
http://localhost/MyGetInfopage.asp?Name=Paul%20Wilton
```

633

However, if we are using JavaScript to navigate the page to a different location, for example:

```
window.location.href = "http://localhost/MyGetInfopage.asp?Name=Paul%20Wilton"
```

then we can use the escape() function, which does any necessary encoding for us. For example:

```
var myURLData = escape("Paul Wilton");
window.location.href = " http://localhost/MyGetInfopage.asp?Name=" +
    myURLData;
```

What do we do if we want to pass more than one item of data?

In this case, we simply need to separate the items of data with ampersands (&). For example, to pass a Name and Age we use:

```
http://localhost/MyGetInfopage.asp?Name=Paul&Age=31
```

As mentioned, the escape() function is only strictly necessary for NN, but we can use it with IE. It won't cause any problems, and saves checking for the browser type.

Now that we know how to send the data, how do we extract it using server-side script?

To extract the data from the ASP page that has been navigated to, we use the Request object's QueryString collection property. This contains all the data passed in the URL, which can be retrieved by name.

For example, to retrieve the Name and Age data sent in the above URL, we would write:

```
Request.QueryString("Name")
```

and:

```
Request.QueryString("Age")
```

Try It Out – Passing and Retrieving Data in a URL

In this example, we'll create a simple page that will pass information in a URL to another page, which will then display it. We illustrate two methods of attaching the data to the URL: by writing out the URL as we have done above, and by using script to add the data to the end of the URL.

```
<HTML>
<HEAD>

<SCRIPT LANGUAGE=JavaScript>

function butNavigate_onclick()
{
    var urlData = "Name=" + escape("Paul Wilton") + "&Age=31";
    window.location.href = "GetInfo.asp?" + urlData;
```

```
        }
    </SCRIPT>
    </HEAD>
    <BODY>

    <A HREF="GetInfo.asp?Name=Paul%20Wilton&Age=31">Get Info</A>
    <FORM NAME=form1 ID=form1>
        <INPUT TYPE="button"
            VALUE="Send Data"
            NAME=butNavigate
```

```
            onclick="return butNavigate_onclick()">
    </FORM>
    </BODY>
    </HTML>
```

Save this page as `PostInfo.htm` into the physical directory of the `AWalkOnTheServerSide` virtual directory on your web server.

Next, we have the page that extracts the data:

```
    <%@ LANGUAGE = JavaScript%>
    <HTML>
    <BODY>

    <P>The info posted by the URL was</P>
    Name : <%= Request.QueryString("Name") %>
    <BR>
    Age : <%= Request.QueryString("Age") %>

    </BODY>
    </HTML>
```

Save this page as `GetInfo.asp` in the same directory as the `PostInfo.htm` file.

Browse to the `PostInfo.htm` page on your web server using the following URL:

    http://localhost/AWalkOnTheServerSide/PostInfo.htm

and you'll see a page with a link and a button:

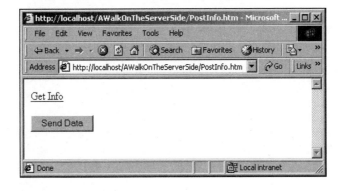

Here we are giving the user two methods, either clicking the link or clicking the button, to send the data that we were looking at above to the GetInfo.asp page. This data will be captured and displayed on that page:

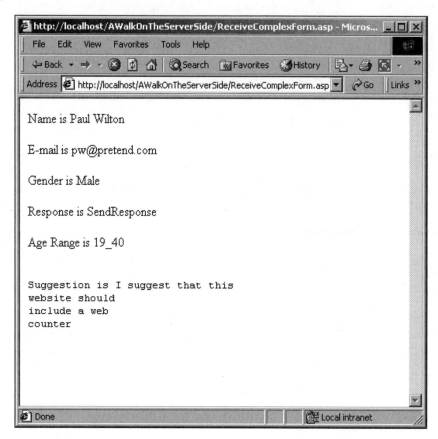

How It Works

In PostInfo.htm, the first method for sending the data to GetInfo.asp is through a hyperlink. The hyperlink has the data added to the end, as we've already seen:

```
<A HREF="GetInfo.asp?Name=Paul%20Wilton&Age=31">Get Info</A>
```

Note how we've manually replaced the space between Paul and Wilton with %20, the hexadecimal character equivalent.

The second method for sending the data is through clicking on a button:

```
<INPUT TYPE="button"
   VALUE="Send Data"
   NAME=butNavigate
   onclick="return butNavigate_onclick()">
```

The button's `onclick` event handler is connected to the `butNavigate_onclick()` function, which is contained in the head of the page:

```
function butNavigate_onclick()
{
    var urlData = "Name=" + escape("Paul Wilton") + "&Age=31";
    window.location.href = "GetInfo.asp?" + urlData;
}
```

In this function, the variable `urlData` to initialized to the data string to be attached to the end of the URL. We need to use the `escape()` function to convert Paul Wilton into a form that can be sent with the URL. We don't need to escape the age data, as that is acceptable as it is. In addition, we mustn't escape the names of the data or the equals sign, as that must be sent as it is. The `escape()` function would convert the = to its hexadecimal character equivalent, which we don't want.

Finally, the `urlData` variable is concatenated to the end of the URL, and used to navigate the page to the `GetInfo.asp` page where we extract the data.

Turning to the `GetInfo.asp` page, we start with the code:

```
<%@ LANGUAGE = JavaScript%>
```

to tell the server that we are using the JavaScript language for our scripting. Then, within the body of the page:

```
Name : <%= Request.QueryString("Name") %>
```

retrieves the `Name` value from the URL and writes it to the page. The code:

```
Age : <%= Request.QueryString("Age") %>
```

does the same for the `Age` data.

Reading Cookies on the User's Computer

We saw in Chapter 11 that we can create something called a cookie. A cookie can hold small amounts of information and is stored on the user's computer. Normally any variables stored in a web page disappear when we leave the web page. However, using cookies we can store information and specify when it should expire, that is when it should cease to exist. For example, we can set a cookie to last until six months time, and until it expires, we can read and write its information, even if a different page has been navigated to or the browser has been closed by the user.

We also saw that cookies are particular to a web site, that is to say to a particular domain. Cookies on a page in www.somedomain.com cannot be read by a page in www.someotherdomain.com. In fact, all the cookies for a domain are passed to the server when you request a page in that domain. For example, if I write client-side code that sets a cookie called `UserName` with the value `"Paul"` in a page in www.mydomain.com, then when I next request a page from the same web site, the cookie name and its value will be sent along with the rest of the request. This means that we are actually able to read cookies server-side that have been set on the client-side. The important thing to remember is that although we can read the cookies server-side, their data is actually always physically stored on the client computer – there is no cookies file on the server.

637

We will see later how we can create and modify cookies server-side, but again this is done by the server sending the cookie and its information as part of the response. The browser picks up the cookie information from the response, and then creates the cookie on the client machine.

The information regarding cookies that was given in Chapter 11, for example about expiry dates, path names, and so on, applies also to cookies accessed on the server.

To read a cookie we use the `Request` object's `Cookies` collection property. As with the `Form` collection, we use the name given to a cookie to read its value.

For example, to retrieve a cookie called `BakedFreshToday` we just write:

```
var myCookieValue = Request.Cookies("BakedFreshToday");
```

We can use this technique to read cookies that have been set either server-side or client-side.

Finding out More about the User's Computer, OS, and Browser

As we have said before, the request sent to a server usually contains extra information about the client computer and browser. When the request arrives at a server, the server takes this information and stores it in various **server variables**. These variables are read only – we can read their values, but we can't set their values. This can only be done by the server when it receives a request. The variables give us information such as the user's browser, their operating system, the name of the server, the actual physical path of the file, and much more.

The `Request` object allows direct access to the server variables. Again, like the `Form` and `Cookie` collection properties, there is a `ServerVariables` collection property of the `Request` object. For example, to get information contained in a server variable called `NameOfServerVariable` we just type:

```
Request.ServerVariables("NameOfServerVariable")
```

Of course, there is not really a server variable called `NameOfServerVariable`. The server variables have fixed names, since they are set by the server. Here, we'll just look at one of the server variables, `HTTP_USER-AGENT`. The value returned by the code:

```
Request.ServerVariables("HTTP_USER-AGENT")
```

is the same as the client-side `navigator` object's `userAgent` property, which we saw in Chapter 5.

Try It Out – Server-Side Browser Detection

We've previously looked at the `userAgent` property of the `navigator` object, using it to create some JavaScript functions that detected the browser name, version, and operating system. In this example, we'll create server-side versions of those functions:

```
<%@ LANGUAGE = JavaScript%>
<HTML>
<BODY>

<%= Request.ServerVariables("HTTP_USER-AGENT") %>
```

```
<%
function getBrowserName()
{
   var lsBrowser = new String(Request.ServerVariables("HTTP_USER-AGENT"));
   if (lsBrowser.indexOf("MSIE") >= 0)
   {
      lsBrowser = "MSIE";
   }
   else if (lsBrowser.indexOf("Mozilla") >= 0)
   {
      lsBrowser = "NETSCAPE";
   }
   else
   {
      lsBrowser = "UNKNOWN";
   }

   return lsBrowser;
}

function getOS()
{
   var userPlat = "unknown";
   var navInfo = new String(Request.ServerVariables("HTTP_USER-AGENT"));

   if ((navInfo.indexOf("Windows NT") != -1)
       || (navInfo.indexOf("Windows 95") != -1 )
       || (navInfo.indexOf("Windows 98") != -1 )
       || (navInfo.indexOf("WinNT") != -1 )
       || (navInfo.indexOf("Win95") != -1 )
       || (navInfo.indexOf("Win98") != -1 ))
   {
      userPlat = "Win32";
   }
   else if(navInfo.indexOf("Win16") != -1)
   {
      userPlat = "Win16";
   }
   else if(navInfo.indexOf("Macintosh") != -1)
   {
      userPlat = "PPC";
   }
   else if(navInfo.indexOf("68K") != -1)
   {
      userPlat = "68K";
   }
   return userPlat;
}

function getBrowserVersion()
{
   var findIndex;
   var browserVersion;
```

```
      var browser = getBrowserName();
      browserVersion = new String(Request.ServerVariables("HTTP_USER-AGENT"));

      if (browser == "MSIE")
      {
         findIndex = browserVersion.indexOf("MSIE") + 5;
         browserVersion = parseFloat(browserVersion.substring(findIndex,
            findIndex + 4));
      }
      else if (browser == "NETSCAPE")
      {
         findIndex = browserVersion.indexOf("Mozilla") + 8;
         browserVersion = parseFloat(browserVersion.substring(findIndex,
            findIndex + 4));
      }
      else if (browser == "UNKNOWN")
      {
         browserversion = 0;
      }

      return browserVersion;
   }

%>
<P>
Browser is <%=getBrowserName()%>
<BR>
Operating system is <%=getOS()%>
<BR>
Browser Version is <%=getBrowserVersion()%>
</P>
</BODY>
</HTML>
```

Save the file as `ServerBrowserDetect.asp` in the physical directory of the virtual directory `AWalkOnTheServerSide`. Load it into various different browsers to see what sort of results you get.

Here are some of the results you're likely to see.

First is Internet Explorer 5 running under Windows 2000:

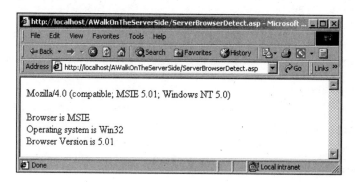

Next, we have Netscape 4.7 running under Windows 2000:

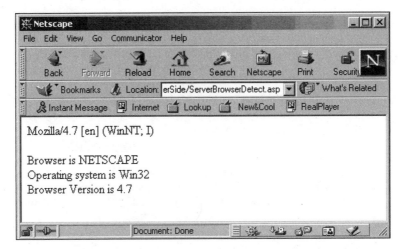

Note that on Netscape 3.03 running under Windows 98, the HTTP_USER-AGENT variable says Win95 rather than Win98. This is because Windows 98 came out after NN 3.03.

The detection routines in the code give us the ability to check whether the browser is Netscape or IE, whether the browser is running on Windows32, and what the browser version is. If we require more sophisticated checking, then either we need to modify the code or we can use the browser capabilities component that is available with PWS and which we'll look at later.

How It Works

This code is essentially very similar to the client-side version. At the top of the page, the code:

```
<%= Request.ServerVariables("HTTP_USER-AGENT") %>
```

writes out the contents of the HTTP_USER_AGENT server variable to the page. Then, near the bottom of the page, the code:

```
Browser is <%=getBrowserName()%>
<BR>
Operating system is <%=getOS()%>
<BR>
Browser Version is <%=getBrowserVersion()%>
```

writes the return values of three functions, getBrowserName(), getOS(), and getBrowserVersion(), to the page. We'll look at each of these functions in turn.

For detecting the browser name we have the getBrowserName() function. First, we obtain the value of the server variable HTTP_USER-AGENT. The reference Request.ServerVariables("HTTP_USER-AGENT") actually returns an object, an item in the ServerVariables collection, so we need to create a new String object based on its value. That way we can use String methods such as indexOf().

```
function getBrowserName()
{
    var lsBrowser = new String(Request.ServerVariables("HTTP_USER-AGENT"));
```

Then in the `if` statement, we check using `indexOf()` whether `MSIE` is contained in the `lsBrowser` string. If it is, then we know that the browser is Internet Explorer and set the variable `lsBrowser` to `MSIE`:

```
if (lsBrowser.indexOf("MSIE") >= 0)
{
    lsBrowser = "MSIE";
}
```

Otherwise, we check in an `else if` statement for `Mozilla`. If that's present, then we make the assumption that the browser is Netscape or at least a Netscape-compatible browser, and set the variable `lsBrowser` to `NETSCAPE`. This is sufficient most of the time, but there may be some unusual browsers that fail to work with this.

```
else if (lsBrowser.indexOf("Mozilla") >= 0)
{
    lsBrowser = "NETSCAPE";
}
```

Finally, if `Mozilla` is not found, then we set the variable `lsBrowser` to `UNKNOWN` in the final `else` statement.

```
else
{
    lsBrowser = "UNKNOWN";
}
```

The variable `lsBrowser` is then returned by the function:

```
    return lsBrowser;
}
```

The operating system detection function, `getOS()`, is virtually identical to the corresponding client-side version. In fact, the only difference is that the variable `navInfo` is not the `navigator` object's `userAgent` property, but the `HTTP_USER-AGENT` server variable, which happens to be the same thing.

```
function getOS()
{
    var userPlat = "unknown";
    var navInfo = new String(Request.ServerVariables("HTTP_USER-AGENT"));
```

We then simply search the value of `navInfo` for different variations of operating system. A series of `if` and `else if` statements use the `String` object's `indexOf()` method to search for the various names of operating systems. If the name is found, then we set the `userPlat` variable to store a generic name for those operating systems. For example, for Windows 95, 98, NT, and 2000, we set the `userPlat` variable to `Win32`.

The first `if` statement is the most complex as its condition is a series of `indexOf()` methods. If any of these don't return -1, then the condition is treated as `true` by the `if` statement – remember that when using an OR operator only one of the conditions needs to be `true` for the whole condition to be `true`.

```
if ((navInfo.indexOf("Windows NT") != -1)
    || (navInfo.indexOf("Windows 95") != -1 )
    || (navInfo.indexOf("Windows 98") != -1 )
    || (navInfo.indexOf("WinNT") != -1 )
    || (navInfo.indexOf("Win95") != -1 )
    || (navInfo.indexOf("Win98") != -1 ))
{
    userPlat = "Win32";
}
```

The other conditions checking for other operating systems are simpler:

```
else if(navInfo.indexOf("Win16") != -1)
{
    userPlat = "Win16";
}
else if(navInfo.indexOf("Macintosh") != -1)
{
    userPlat = "PPC";
}
else if(navInfo.indexOf("68K") != -1)
{
    userPlat = "68K";
}
```

Finally, the variable `userPlat` is returned by the function:

```
    return userPlat;
}
```

We'll finally look at the function that returns the browser version – `getBrowserVersion()`. This function is again similar to the client-side version. We first find out which browser we're dealing with, by setting the variable `browser` to the return value of the `getBrowserName()` function. Then we store `Request.ServerVariables("HTTP_USER-AGENT")` as a new `String` object in the `browserVersion` variable:

```
function getBrowserVersion()
{
    var findIndex;
    var browserVersion;
    var browser = getBrowserName();
    browserVersion = new String(Request.ServerVariables("HTTP_USER-AGENT"));
```

With Internet Explorer, the version number is always straight after the characters MSIE in the HTTP_USER_AGENT string. So, in the `if` statement, we check whether the variable `browser` has value MSIE and if it does, we search for MSIE in `browserVersion`, add 5 onto its index in the string, and store this in the variable `findIndex`. To get the version number, we cut out the substring from an index of `findIndex`, to an index of `findIndex + 4`, from the string `browserVersion`, and then resave this as `browserVersion`.

```
if (browser == "MSIE")
{
    findIndex = browserVersion.indexOf("MSIE") + 5;
    browserVersion = parseFloat(browserVersion.substring(findIndex,
        findIndex + 4));
}
```

With Netscape, the version number appears straight after the characters Mozilla/ in the HTTP_USER_AGENT string. So, in the else if statement, we use the same method as for the Internet Explorer version to get the browser version stored in the variable browserVersion:

```
else if (browser == "NETSCAPE")
{
    findIndex = browserVersion.indexOf("Mozilla") + 8;
    browserVersion = parseFloat(browserVersion.substring(findIndex,
        findIndex + 4));
}
```

In the final else if statement, we check whether the variable browser has value UNKNOWN, in which case we set browserVersion to 0:

```
else if (browser == "UNKNOWN")
{
    browserversion = 0;
}
```

The variable browserVersion is then returned by the function:

```
    return browserVersion;
}
```

This method of browser detection works fine in most cases, but as we'll see later that it's possible to do more sophisticated browser capability checking.

Response Object – Sending Information to the Client

We'll now move on from the Request object to the Response object. This object deals with the out going side of things on the server. It allows us to write information to the page sent to the user's browser, to create cookies, and to re-direct the user's browser to a different page from the one they requested. We'll now look at how each of these is achieved.

Writing Information to a Page

We've already been writing content to the page using the <%= and %> notation.

However, this is actually a shorthand for Response.Write(), where Write() is a method of the Response object. For example, to write "Hello World" to the page using Response.Write(), we type:

```
<% Response.Write("Hello World"); %>
```

While the `<%= %>` notation is often convenient, there are times where it's not suitable for use. For example, it is not suitable where the text we want to write to the page is built up with a number of lines of JavaScript in a block, perhaps including a number of loops and `if` statements.

Let's look at an example. Imagine that we want to calculate the cost of shipping an item, the cost of which is dependent on the country the item is being shipped to.

First let's see how this could be done with `Response.Write()`:

```
<%
var shippingcost = 0;
var custCountry = Request.Form("txtCountry");

if (custCountry != "Rest Of World")
{
    if (custCountry == "USA")
    {
        shippingCost == 4.95;
    }
    else if (custCountry == "Canada")
    {
        shippingCost == 5.95;
    }

    Response.Write("<P>Shipping will cost $" + shippingCost + "</P>");
}
else
{
    Response.Write("Sorry we don't currently ship to that country");
}
%>
```

Now let's see it done using the `<%= %>` notation:

```
<%
var shippingcost = 0;
var custCountry = Request.Form("txtCountry");

if (custCountry != "Rest Of World")
{
    if (custCountry == "USA")
    {
        shippingCost == 4.95;
    }
    else if (custCountry == "Canada")
    {
        shippingCost == 5.95;
    }
%>

<P>Shipping to your country will cost $" + <%= shippingCost %></P>
```

```
<%
}
else
{
%>
<P>Sorry we don't currently ship to that country</P>
<%
}
%>
```

There are two main problems with the second approach using the `<%= %>` notation.

The first is that the `Response.Write()` method allowed us to do all our server-side scripting in just one server-side script block, that is all the code was contained in one set of `<%` and `%>`. This makes it easier for the server to find and process our code, and therefore reduces the load on the server and speeds up our page. In comparison the second method, with `<%=` and `%>` needs four server-side script blocks, making life harder on the server as it has to search out each individual block. When we're creating client-side code containing many script blocks, this is not a problem as even the most modest processor can cope with this load. However, a server machine might have to cope with thousands, or maybe tens or hundreds of thousands, of users requesting a page at the same time, that is **concurrently**. In this case, a very small amount of extra required processing is multiplied many times, and could cause loading problems.

The second disadvantage of the `<%= %>` notation is that, in this case, it has made the code's flow less clean and easy to read. This may not be a problem in a short piece of code like this, but can make life tricky if it's a big page with many separate script blocks.

Creating Cookies

We saw earlier how the `Request` object allows us to read cookies stored on the client machine. Let's now look at how we can create them with the `Response` object.

Just as with client-side cookie creation, we can use the `Response` object to specify the cookie's name, its value, and also, optionally, the date it should expire, the domain on which it's valid, the path on which it's valid, and whether it should only be sent via secure means over an HTTPS connection. We do this using the `Cookies` collection property of the `Response` object.

For example, to create a cookie named `UserName` with the value `Paul` that expires on 1 Jan 2010, we type:

```
Response.Cookies("UserName") = "Paul";
Response.Cookies("UserName").Expires = "Jan 1, 2010"
```

As we saw before, to read this back we simply use the `Cookies` collection property of the `Request` object. We can now use `Response.Write()` method to write the value of the cookie to the page:

```
var myUserName = Request.Cookies("UserName");
Response.Write(myUserName);
```

As you can see, creating and reading cookies is actually a lot easier server-side than it is client-side.

Redirecting the User

The ability to re-direct the user to a page other than the requested one is very useful. For example, we could re-direct users to a page that is compatible with their browser. Also, if we have incorporated some sort of security into our site, such as a logon system for access to part of our web site, then we can quickly re-direct invalid users.

To re-direct the user, we simply use the `Response` object's `Redirect()` method, which we pass the URL of the page we want to re-direct to as a parameter. For example, to re-direct a user to `http://locahost/AWalkOnTheServerSide/IllegalUser.htm` we write:

```
Response.Redirect("http://locahost/AWalkOnTheServerSide/IllegalUser.htm");
```

Try It Out – A Simple Logon System

Let's use some of the knowledge we've gathered so far on cookies and re-direction to create a simple logon system that restricts certain parts of a web site to valid users. It's not the sort of security that is suitable for keeping credit card details safe on an e-commerce web site, but it would be sufficient for slightly sensitive pages on an intranet.

We'll create three pages. The first allows the user to log on, the second tests whether the user is a valid user, and the third is the private page that should only be reached by a valid user.

First, let's create the page that will let the user log onto the system:

```
<HTML>
<HEAD>
<SCRIPT LANGUAGE=JavaScript>

function form1_onsubmit()
{
   var form = document.form1;
   var returnValue = false;

   if (form.txtUsername.value == "")
   {
      alert("Please enter your username");
      form.txtUsername.focus();
   }
   else if (form.txtPassword.value == "")
   {
      alert("Please enter your password");
      form.txtPassword.focus();
   }
   else
   {
      returnValue = true;
   }

   return returnValue;
}
```

```
</SCRIPT>
</HEAD>

<BODY>
<P>
To access this web site please enter your username and password in the boxes below
</P>

<FORM ACTION="CheckLogOn.asp"
    METHOD=POST
    ID=form1 NAME=form1
    onsubmit="return form1_onsubmit()">

<P>Username : <INPUT ID=txtUsername NAME=txtUsername TYPE=text></P>
<P>Password : <INPUT ID=txtPassword NAME=txtPassword TYPE=password></P>

<P>
<INPUT ID=reset1 NAME=reset1 TYPE=reset VALUE=Reset> 
<INPUT ID=submit1 NAME=submit1 TYPE=submit VALUE="Log On">
</P>

</FORM>

</BODY>
</HTML>
```

Save this as `Logon.htm` in the physical directory of the `AWalkOnTheServerSide` virtual directory on your web server.

Next, we have the page that actually checks the validity of the logon information:

```
<%@ LANGUAGE = JavaScript%>

<%
if (Request.Form("txtUsername") == "SecureUser" &&
    Request.Form("txtPassword") == "letmethrough")
{
    Response.Cookies("IsValid") = "Yes";
    Response.Redirect("SecureHome.asp");
}
else
{
    Response.Redirect("Logon.htm")
}

%>
```

Save this page as `CheckLogOn.asp` in the same directory as `Logon.htm`.

Finally, let's create a simple, secure page that's only accessible if the user is valid:

```
<%@ LANGUAGE = JavaScript%>

<%

if (Request.Cookies("IsValid") != "Yes")
{
    Response.Redirect("Logon.htm")
}

%>
<HTML>
<BODY>

<P ALIGN=center>
<FONT SIZE=5>This page is for valid users only</FONT>
</P>

</BODY>
</HTML>
```

Save this as SecureHome.asp, again in the same directory as Logon.htm.

Now browse to the Logon.htm page, for example using the URL:

```
http://localhost/AWalkOnTheServerSide/Logon.htm
```

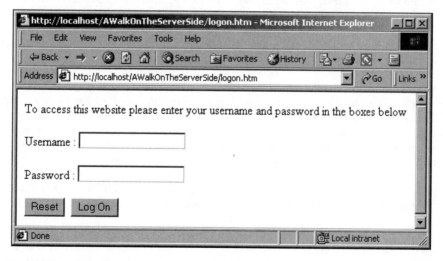

The valid username is SecureUser and the password is letmethrough. Enter these valid values and click the Log On button – you will be taken to the secure home page SecureHome.asp, displaying the text **This page is for valid users only**. However, if you enter an invalid value and click the Log On button, you will find yourself back at the logon page.

Note that the Reset button on the logon page is there for the user's convenience. It allows them to clear the username and password by just clicking the button rather than having to delete each character in both boxes if they've entered the wrong username or password.

Close the browser, then try navigating to `SecureHome.asp` directly, avoiding the logon page.

```
http://localhost/AWalkOnTheServerSide/SecureHome.asp
```

You'll find that you're redirected to the logon page.

How It Works

The logon page simply consists of a text box and a password box, a submit button and a reset button. When the submit button is clicked, the code connected to the form's `onsubmit` event handler in the `<FORM>` tag's definition shown below, is executed. In other words, the `form1_onsubmit()` function, which we defined in the head of the page, is executed. This performs some validity checking on the form data.

```
<FORM ACTION="CheckLogOn.asp"
    METHOD=POST
    ID=form1 NAME=form1
    onsubmit="return form1_onsubmit()">
```

The function `form1_onsubmit()` simply checks that the user has entered values for both the username and password. The function uses two `if` statements to check that the `value` properties of the objects associated with the `txtUserName` and `txtPassword` input boxes are not empty strings. If they are we alert the user and stop the form from being posted by returning `false`. Remember that if we return `true` to the `onsubmit` event handler, the form submission continues; if we return `false` it is canceled and no post to a new page occurs.

But why do this? Surely, we could let the form be submitted to the server where the empty input boxes will be spotted as invalid and the user will be returned to this page.

Well, to start with, our aim should usually be to limit the amount of processing the server has to do. On web sites with few visitors, it won't be such an issue, but if one day we find ourselves writing for servers with tens of thousands of concurrent users, we'll be glad we got into the practice of easing pressure on the server. The amount of processing required to check for empty values is very small and certainly no great burden on the client computer. However, if it's done on a high load server, this burden might be multiplied by tens of thousands or more, and our server would struggle.

A second advantage of doing this validation client-side is that we can tell the user there and then that there is a problem with the data they are submitting, rather than letting them submit the form and then telling them.

However, if this was a live web site and the access was to vital information, then we'd be advised to have similar server-side checks in addition to the client-side checks just to stop malicious hackers trying to post to the `CheckLogon.asp` page from their own version of `Logon.htm`, circumventing our client-side checks. However, for this example what we have is fine.

Let's turn our attention to `CheckLogon.asp`. This is the page that the form data is posted to and which checks whether the username and password are valid.

As always, at the top of the page we tell the server that we'll be using JavaScript for all our scripting on this page.

```
<%@ LANGUAGE = JavaScript%>
```

Then we validate the values the user entered on the `Logon.htm` form. Here we simply see if the username is `SecureUser` and the password is `letmethrough`. In reality, we'd use a system that allows many usernames and passwords to be checked, such as a database or a directory service that also contains user validation details.

In the first `if` statement we check whether the username and password are valid. If they are, we set the cookie `IsValid` to `Yes`. We can use this cookie on each secure page to check whether the user has logged on and is valid, just in case they have tried to access a page directly without logging on. We've not set an expiry date for the cookie, so it will expire as soon as the user closes the browser. Finally, we redirect the user to the `SecureHome.asp` page, so in effect they never actually see the `CheckLogon.asp` page; it's just a page they pass through.

```
<%
if (Request.Form("txtUsername") == "SecureUser" &&
    Request.Form("txtPassword") == "letmethrough")
{
    Response.Cookies("IsValid") = "Yes";
    Response.Redirect("SecureHome.asp");
}
```

In the `else` statement, which is executed if the user details are not valid, we redirect the user back to the `Logon.htm` page to give them another chance to enter the correct username and password:

```
else
{
    Response.Redirect("Logon.htm");
}
%>
```

Finally, let's look at the `SecureHome.asp` page, which the user is redirected to from `CheckLogon.asp` if they entered the correct user details.

Again, the page starts by setting the language for the script:

```
<%@ LANGUAGE = JavaScript%>
```

The page then checks to see if the cookie `IsValid` has the value `Yes`. If not, the user is re-directed away from this page and to the `Logon.htm` page:

```
<%
if (Request.Cookies("IsValid") != "Yes")
{
    Response.Redirect("Logon.htm");
}
%>
```

Finally, we have the body of the page containing the 'secure' information. Obviously, in a real application this would contain information for which there was a need for user validation.

```
<HTML>
<BODY>
<P ALIGN=center>
    <FONT SIZE=5>This page is for valid users only</FONT>
</P>
</BODY>
</HTML>
```

Server Object – Using it to Run Components

The Server object, as its name suggests, represents the server itself. We're going to look at how it can be used to create **components** that run on the server; but what do we mean by components?

Think of components as a little like plug-ins for a server. They are small programs written in languages such as C++ and Visual Basic, which we can create as objects in our server-side code and use to perform functions beyond what a basic web server can do. For example, a credit card component might validate credit card numbers, and an e-mail component may allow web pages to send and receive e-mails. PWS comes with a number of components already installed, such as a file access component that allows us to create new files and directories on the server, a page hit counter component, and a component that checks the capabilities of browsers, which we'll be looking at shortly.

To create an object based on a component installed on the server, we need the Server object's CreateObject() method. To tell the server which component we want to create an object for, we need to pass this method the programmatic Id (ProgID) for the component, something that we'll need to find out from the component's documentation.

A single component may actually be able to create a number of different objects, each with a different function and each represented by a different ProgID.

As said above, Personal Web Server includes the browser capability component. Let's now look at how we can make use of it.

Browser Capability Component

The browser capability component uses information sent in the HTTP request header to work out not only information such as the browser name and version number, but also details such as whether the browser supports JavaScript, cookies, HTML frames, and much more. However, it won't tell you if the user has switched off or disabled some of these features. How does the browser capability component work out all this information?

The key to the component's knowledge is a text information file, which contains details about various browsers. The file is called browscap.ini and is usually found in the windows\system32\inetserv folder. Of course, new browsers come out all the time so it's important to update this file, either by altering it yourself or even better by downloading a new one. More information is available from http://www.microsoft.com/ISN/faq /latest_browscapini_file.asp.

The Microsoft web site also has full details of browscap.ini at http://msdn.microsoft.com /library/psdk/iisref/comp1g11.htm.

To get an idea of what sort of properties the browser capability component supports, take a look at the browscap.ini file on your own system, which divides into sections for various browsers with each browsers' properties listed. Shown below is just a very small bit of the browscap.ini file on my computer:

```
;;;;;;;;;;;;;;;;;;;;;;;;;;;;;;;;;;;;;;;; IE 5.0
[IE 5.0]
browser=IE
Version=5.0
majorver=5
minorver=0
frames=True
tables=True
cookies=True
backgroundsounds=True
vbscript=True
javaapplets=True
javascript=True
ActiveXControls=True
Win16=False
beta=True
AK=False
SK=False
AOL=False
Update=False

[Mozilla/4.0 (compatible; MSIE 5.*; Windows 95*)]
parent=IE 5.0
platform=Win95
beta=True

[Mozilla/4.0 (compatible; MSIE 5.*; Windows 98*)]
parent=IE 5.0
platform=Win98
beta=True

[Mozilla/4.0 (compatible; MSIE 5.*; Windows NT*)]
parent=IE 5.0
platform=WinNT
beta=True

[Mozilla/4.0 (compatible; MSIE 5.*; Windows 2000*)]
parent=IE 5.0
platform=Win2000
beta=True

[Mozilla/4.0 (compatible; MSIE 5.*)]
parent=IE 5.0
```

Try It Out – Browser Capabilities

In this example, we'll create a page that uses the browser capability component to list some of the more useful properties of the browser that the user is using.

```
<%@ LANGUAGE = JavaScript%>
<HTML>
<BODY>
<P>Your Browser's details</P>
<%
var BrowsCapComponent = Server.CreateObject("MSWC.BrowserType");
%>

Browser Name : <%= BrowsCapComponent.browser %>
<BR>
Browser Version : <%= BrowsCapComponent.version %>
<BR>
Supports JavaScript : <%= BrowsCapComponent.javascript %>
<BR>
Supports Frames : <%= BrowsCapComponent.frames %>
<BR>
Supports Cookies : <%= BrowsCapComponent.cookies %>

<%
BrowsCapComponent = null;
%>

</BODY>
</HTML>
```

Save this file as `BrowserCapability.asp` in the physical directory of the `AWAlkOnTheServerSide` virtual directory of your server. Then browse to it with your browser using the URL:

```
http://localhost/AWalkOnTheServerSide/BrowserCapability.asp
```

When you load the page into your browser you should see information like that shown below. This was from Internet Explorer 5.

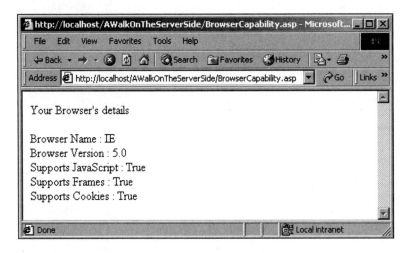

If, on the other hand, you get information like that shown below, then it suggests you need to update your `browscap.ini` file because your browser and/or operating system were released at a later date than the `browscap.ini` file was created. The `browscap.ini` file can only tell you about browsers and operating systems that exist at the time the file was created. You may find that even an up-to-date `browscap.ini` seems to not correctly identify particular browsers, quite often even common browsers. In this case, you need to alter the `browscap.ini` file, or use a different browser detection component, or use the browser detection scripts we created previously.

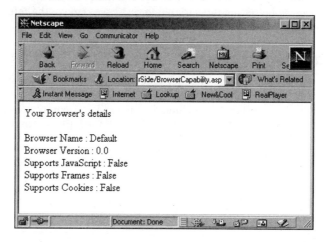

How It Works

We start the page as usual by defining the language to be used in the script:

```
<%@ LANGUAGE = JavaScript%>
```

We then create an object for the browser capability component on the server using the `Server` object's `CreateObject()` method:

```
var BrowsCapComponent = Server.CreateObject("MSWC.BrowserType");
```

`MSWC.BrowserType` is the browser capability component's `ProgID`.

Now, with the component's object created, we can access its properties as we would any object. In the lines that follow, we find out the browser's name, version, and whether the browser supports JavaScript, frames, or cookies. Here we just write out the results to the page, but in practice, we could make use of this information to redirect a browser to a page with content it supports or by only writing content to the current page if the browser supports it.

```
Browser Name : <%= BrowsCapComponent.browser %>
<BR>
Browser Version : <%= BrowsCapComponent.version %>
<BR>
Supports JavaScript : <%= BrowsCapComponent.javascript %>
<BR>
Supports Frames : <%= BrowsCapComponent.frames %>
<BR>
Supports Cookies : <%= BrowsCapComponent.cookies %>
```

On the final line, we set the variable `BrowsCapComponent`, which holds the reference to the created component, to `null`.

```
BrowsCapComponent = null;
```

But why do this? Well, as long as the reference to the component held by a variable remains in scope, that is available for scripting, it will remain in memory. We want to limit the load on the server and in particular, memory usage, so by setting the variable to `null` we remove the reference and the server can unload the component and free up spare memory on the server.

Server-Side Include (SSI) Directives

The first question is, what is a server-side include? A server-side include is simply a means of including one file inside another. Before the server starts any processing of your web page's server-side code, it does a pre-processing check for server-side include directives. This is simply an instruction made by us to insert the contents of an `.asp` page, `.htm` page or any valid text file inside the current page. We do this with the `#include` directive.

OK, let's say we have two files, `MyWebPage.asp` and `MyOtherPage.inc`. `MyWebPage.asp` looks like this:

```
<HTML>
<BODY>
<H2>My Main Page</H2>
      <!-- #include file="MyOtherPage.inc" -->
</BODY>
</HTML>
```

You can see that we've used `#include` to insert the file `MyOtherPage.inc` and the contents of that file will be replace the `#include` line. The `file=""` must be set to a filename and file path. If this file is in the same directory as the `MyWebPage.asp` file, then there's no need to use the path. If it's not then we must include the whole path, for example:

```
      <!-- #include file="C:\MyIncludeFiles\MyOtherPage.inc" -->
```

Now, if our `MyOtherPage.inc` file looks like this:

```
<H2>My Include File</H2>
<P>This is included in another page</P>
<P>Included with the include directive</P>
```

Then the `#include` file directive will make the server include all of this file at the point of the `#include`, and send this page to the client:

```
<HTML>
<BODY>
<H2>My Main Page</H2>
<H2>My Include File</H2>
<P>This is included in another page</P>
<P>Included with the include directive</P>
</BODY>
</HTML>
```

Although this is the page that's sent to the user's browser, it's all done in the server's memory. No changes are made to either `MyWebPage.asp` or `MyOtherPage.inc`. The use of the suffix `.inc` in the included file's name is not mandatory, but helps us to keep track of what the file is used for.

If we want, either or both of the including and included pages can include server-side or client-side script. The only proviso is that the page that is sent to the user's browser, with all of its server-side includes, must be a valid page in terms of HTML and script. For example, if `MyOtherPage.inc` was this:

```
<H2>My Heading</H2>
</BODY>
</HTML>
```

then this would not be valid as the page that its being inserted into already has a `</BODY>` and `</HTML>` tag and only one set of these is allowed per page.

Server-side includes are useful for the situation where you have the same bit of code or same bit of HTML used in more than one page on your web site. Take for example our client-side cookie functions – we may well use those in many pages on a web site. Now we could use frames and put the cookie code in there, but what about if we don't want frames? Well, we can just include the code wherever we want it with server-side includes. It also reduces the size of our pages on the server if we are using the same script functions or HTML repeatedly, as we only have to store this information once.

Using server-side includes also means that we can make our pages more modularized, by separating script from content. This means that if we want to update our code, we can just update the include file and all of our pages will automatically be changed to reflect our updates.

Just remember that any included script must be contained in the correct script tags. For example, if `MyOtherPage.inc` looked like this it would be fine:

```
<%
// My server-side JavaScript
%>
```

or for client-side JavaScript:

```
<SCRIPT>
// My client-side JavaScript
</SCRIPT>
```

But just including some script would not be fine. You just need to imagine what the final page will look like after all the `#inserts` have been processed. Will it be valid HTML or valid script? If it won't, then the page will fail.

Session Object – Keeping Track of Users

The next ASP object we'll be looking at is the `Session` object. This object enables us to keep track of users, and to store information temporarily on the server, which we can use from any page during the user's visit to our web site.

For example, if we have a section of our web site that requires a user to logon before viewing the pages, then we would force the user to logon. However, having logged on once during a visit to our web site, we don't want them to have to enter their username and password again and again every time they go to a different secure page. The solution is that we log them on once and store this information using the `Session` object. We can then use this logon information when they go to a different page.

What are Sessions?

A `Session` object embodies the idea of a user session, that is a user's visit to our web site. A user session starts when a user first browses to an ASP page on our web site and ends twenty minutes after the user last requests a page (although it is possible to set this time lapse differently). The only problem with the time delay is that it could be that the user didn't actually leave the web site, but simply spent longer than twenty minutes looking at a single page. In this case, as soon as they move to another page a new session will be created.

Also, note that sessions are specific to a particular virtual directory, so if the user starts by loading a page in `AWalkOnTheServerSide`, and then loads a page in `AnotherVirtualDirectory`, this will start a new session.

Every session is automatically assigned a session ID that is unique to that user for that session; it will be different if they return later and create a new session. We can retrieve this session id using the `Session` object's `SessionID` property:

```
var thisSessionID = Session.SessionID
```

The server actually uses cookies to keep track of `SessionID` values, so if the user's browser doesn't support cookies or they are turned off, then the `SessionID` can't be stored, nor can the session itself be properly created.

Adding Code to the Start and End of Sessions

The `Session` object is one of the few ASP objects that actually have events as well as properties and methods. There are two events, `Session_OnStart` and `Session_OnEnd`. These events have names that differ in syntax form the BOM events we have looked at so far, and as we will see shortly, they are dealt with differently in code.

The names of the events give away when they fire; they fire automatically when the user first requests an ASP page and when twenty minutes has elapsed since they last requested a page. In other words, they fire at the start and end of a user's session. We can see the order of events in the diagram below:

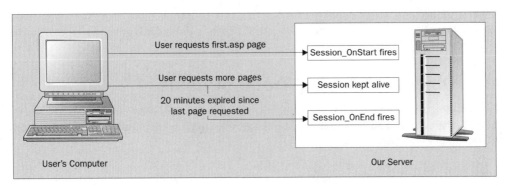

As the `Session_OnStart` and `Session_OnEnd` events could fire on any page in our web application, we need to connect them to code in a special file not linked with any particular page. This file is named `global.asa` – we must use exactly this name and can't make up our own name.

To connect code to these events, we write:

```
function Session_OnStart()
{
    // Code that executes when the session starts
}
function Session_OnEnd()
{
    // Code that executes when the session ends
}
```

When we have previously used events, we needed to connect an event handler to the function that we wanted to execute on the occurrence of a specific event. However, in the case of these events, that is not necessary. The server automatically knows when these functions should be executed.

It's important to note that the `Session_OnStart` and `Session_OnEnd` events only fire when the first ASP page is requested; they don't fire if it's a static HTML page, that is any page saved with the `.htm` or `.html` extension. Also important to note is that browsers that don't support cookies or those with cookies disabled won't properly support sessions. In this case, every time the user requests an ASP page, the `Session_OnStart` event will fire.

There can only be one `global.asa` file for each root directory or root of a virtual directory, so we'll find one in `wwwRoot` and we can put one in each physical directory corresponding to a virtual directory we define. The contents of the `global.asa` file are accessed automatically by the web server when a new session starts or times out.

We can't write information out to a page from the `global.asa`, but we can initialize session variables to be used later in our pages, so let's look at creating and using session variables.

Session Variables

The `Session` object allows us to store information on the server for the life of the session in **session variables**. We can use this information throughout the session regardless of which page the user is on. For example, imagine we requested the user to logon with a username and password. If we store this information in session variables, then later on if we need that information, say for looking up more information in a database, we don't need to ask the user for their details again.

To create a session variable we simply give it a name and value. For example:

```
Session("MySessionVariableName") = "MyVariableValue"
```

will store the value `MyVariableValue` in the session variable `MySessionVariableName`. We can store numbers, strings, and even objects, such as a `Date` object, in session variables.

To get the information out again we just write:

```
var MySessionVariableValue = Session("MySessionVariableName")
```

which will store the value of the `MySessionVariableName` session variable in the variable `MySessionVariableValue`.

If we wish, we can initialize session variables in the `Session_OnStart` event code, within the `global.asa` page. For example:

```
function Session_OnStart()
{
    Session("MySessionVariableName") = "InitialValue"
}
```

We need to stress that session variables are not cookies and, unlike cookies, they are stored in the memory of the server and not on the client computer. In addition, we can't read or write them directly from client-side script, though of course form information passed from the client-side to the server could then be stored in a session variable.

However, as sessions require cookies, we'll find that session variables are also limited to cookie-enabled browsers. If we want to make use of sessions, then we need to either inform the user that cookies are required or direct them to a page not requiring sessions and cookies. An alternative to using session variables is to either pass the information in a URL or create a form with hidden input boxes and post the information to the next page in this way.

We also need to avoid going crazy with the amount of data we store in session variables since all this information takes up precious memory on the server. If we have large numbers of sessions going at one time and we're using up a lot of memory for each session, we'll find at best, the server goes very slow, and at worst, it's brought to a virtual standstill. So, be judicious with your use of session variables. Always ask yourself whether you really need to keep track of this information, or whether there is a more convenient way of keeping track of the information without overloading the server.

Application Object

The last of the ASP objects which we will look at is the `Application` object. This represents our web site as a whole. It might perhaps have made more sense to call it the `"Web site"` object as, generally speaking, that's what it is.

All that we have seen so far on passing information from a client-side form to an ASP page on the server, of setting and reading cookies, and of passing information in URLs, has been either page-specific or specific to just the individual user browsing the web site. Even sessions and session variables are specific to one user. There is no way that we can share information between users. We have variables with global *page* scope, but no variables with global *web site* scope, or at least we don't unless we use the `Application` object.

The main purpose of the `Application` object is to allow us to define information that we can access server-side on any page for any user. Just as we can define session variables by writing the name and assigning a value, so too we can use the `Application` object to store variables called **application variables** whose scope is the entire web site, or at least the virtual directory.

For example, to set an application variable called `MyAppVariable` and with the value `"ABC"`, we'd write:

```
Application("MyAppVariable") = "ABC";
```

To read it back, we just write:

```
var myVar = Application("MyAppVariable");
```

Just as the `Session` object has the `Session_OnStart` and `Session_OnEnd` events, the `Application` object also has its start and stop events, `Application_OnStart` and `Application_OnEnd`. Again, these are created in the `global.asa` file.

`Application_OnStart` fires when the web server is first started and the first web page is requested. For example, it fires after the operating system has been re-booted, or if you manually stopped and then re-started the web server using the server console. As you can imagine, the `Application_OnEnd` event occurs when the web server is stopped, again because either the operating system is being re-booted or you have manually stopped the web server.

For example, if we want to initialize the application variable `MyAppVariable` to `"XYZ"` as soon as the server starts, we'd add this to the `global.asa` file of the virtual directory we want affected:

```
function Application_OnStart()
{
    Application("MyAppVariable") = "XYZ";
}
```

Trivia Quiz goes Server-Side

Let's use some of the knowledge just gained about sessions and session variables to alter the trivia quiz, so that it remembers user selections.

Shown overleaf is the start page for the trivia quiz, where the user selects how many questions they want to answer and in what time limit. If the user changes the default values, completes the quiz, and then asks to re-start the quiz, we want to return to this page with the same options selected as the user selected previously – at present the default values are shown each time. The user can change their previous selections if they wish, and if they do so, then these changes will be noted for the next time they re-start the quiz. Although not a major innovation of interface design, it does make the quiz just that little bit more user friendly.

To accomplish the changes, we will do the following:

1. Create a virtual directory for our trivia quiz web site.

2. Create a `global.asa` file for our new virtual directory and use the `Session_OnStart` event to initialize session variables.

3. Change the `QuizPage.htm` to `QuizPage.asp` so that we can add server-side JavaScript. This page will be altered to show the user's selected time limit and number of questions as selected in the select lists.

4. We'll also be creating a new page, `NoteUserSelections.asp`, that will be posted to at the start of the quiz from `QuizPage.asp` and will store the user's selected number of questions and time limit in session variables.

5. Finally as `QuizPage.htm` has become `QuizPage.asp`, we need to update any links or references to it. In fact, it's just `TriviaQuiz.htm` and `GlobalFunctions.htm` that need changing.

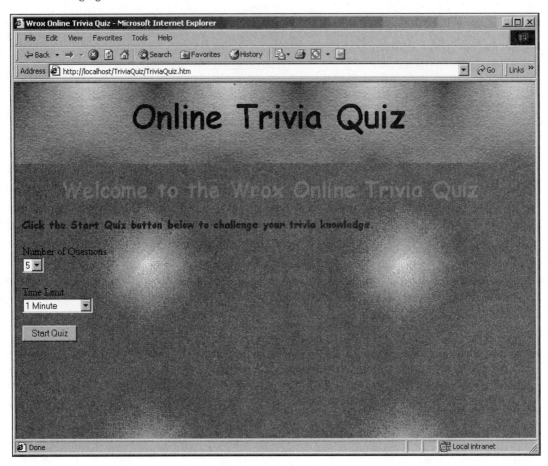

Before we make any changes to the trivia quiz's code, we first need to make the directory containing the trivia quiz web shared, so that visitors to our web server can view it. The easiest way to do this is to make the directory containing the trivia quiz a virtual directory and give it the alias `TriviaQuiz`. We can either do this from Windows Explorer by right-clicking the directory and selecting **Properties**, then **web sharing**, or we can use the **Advanced** tab in the PWS console (see the earlier part of this chapter for details on how to do this).

Now that we've set up the virtual directory, we can create a `global.asa` file using any text editor, containing the code below. Save this into the `TriviaQuiz` directory.

```
<SCRIPT RUNAT=Server LANGUAGE=JavaScript>

function Session_OnStart()
{
    Session("NoQsToAsk") = 3;
    Session("TimeLimit") = -1;
}

</SCRIPT>
```

We have connected some code to the `Session_OnStart` event. We create two session variables, `NoQsToAsk` and `TimeLimit`, and give them initial values of 3 and -1. These two session variables will be used to determine the number of questions option and time limit option that are selected in the drop-down lists on the `QuizPage.htm` page shown above.

We next need to change `QuizPage.htm` from a static HTML file to an ASP file so that we can insert server-side scripting. Load the page into Notepad or whatever HTML editor you're using, and then re-save it with the `.asp` extension.

We then need to set the default server-side scripting language for the page by adding a directive to the very top line of the page:

```
<%@ LANGUAGE = JavaScript%>
<HTML>
<HEAD>
<META HTTP-EQUIV="expires" CONTENT="Mon, 1 Jan 1980 00:00:00 GMT">
<SCRIPT LANGUAGE=JavaScript>
```

Note that we have also added a `<META>` tag. This is because we want to make sure that `QuizPage.asp` is reloaded from the server each time it is navigated to, rather than being reloaded from the browser's cache. If the browser did reload from its cache, the server-side script would not be run and the select lists would not be updated.

Our next task is to alter the `<FORM>` tag's attributes and the definition of the select controls:

```
<FORM NAME="frmQuiz" METHOD="post" ACTION="NoteUserSelections.asp">
<P>
Number of Questions <BR>
<SELECT NAME=cboNoQuestions SIZE=1>
    <OPTION VALUE=3>3
    <OPTION VALUE=5
  <%
      if (Session("NoQsToAsk") == 5)
      {
          Response.Write(" SELECTED ");
      }
  %>
```

```
    >5
</SELECT>
</P>
<P>
Time Limit <BR>
<SELECT NAME=cboTimeLimit SIZE=1>
    <OPTION VALUE=-1>No Time Limit
    <OPTION VALUE=60
    <%
        if (Session("TimeLimit") == 60)
        {
            Response.Write(" SELECTED ");
        }
    %>
    >1 Minute
    <OPTION VALUE=180
    <%
        if (Session("TimeLimit") == 180)
        {
            Response.Write(" SELECTED ");
        }
    %>
    >3 Minutes
    <OPTION VALUE=300
    <%
        if (Session("TimeLimit") == 300)
        {
            Response.Write(" SELECTED ");
        }
    %>
    >5 Minutes
</SELECT>
```

We've altered the <FORM> by adding a METHOD attribute, which determines how information from the form is sent to the server. Additionally, the ACTION attribute has been added, which determines where the form will be submitted. We want it submitted to the NoteUserSelections.asp page, which we will need to create shortly.

Within the form, to alter which option is selected in the select controls, we need to insert a SELECTED attribute into the relevant <OPTION> tag. We use server-side script to do this.

For the second <OPTION> tag of the cboNoQuestions control, we insert a server-side if statement that checks the value of the session variable NoQsToAsk. If it's 5, we write out a SELECTED attribute to the <OPTION> tag, so that when the page is sent to the client browser it reads <OPTION VALUE=5 SELECTED>, causing the browser to make this option the default selected one rather than the first <OPTION> in the list, which is the normal default.

We do the same thing for the cboTimeLimit select control. In each of the <OPTION> tags, except the first since this is selected by default, we check the value of the TimeLimit session variable using an if statement. If it is the same as the value of that <OPTION> tag, then we write the SELECTED attribute to the page.

Before we leave the page, we need to alter the function `cmdStartQuiz_onclick()`, which is connected to the **Start Quiz** button in the `QuizPage.asp` page.

```
function cmdStartQuiz_onclick()
{
    var cboNoQuestions = document.frmQuiz.cboNoQuestions;
    var noQuestions = cboNoQuestions.options[cboNoQuestions.selectedIndex].value
    var cboTimeLimit = document.frmQuiz.cboTimeLimit;
    var timeLimit = cboTimeLimit.options[cboTimeLimit.selectedIndex].value
    window.top.fraTopFrame.fraGlobalFunctions.resetQuiz(noQuestions,timeLimit);

    document.frmQuiz.submit();
}
```

We've deleted the line

```
window.location.href = "AskQuestion.htm";
```

and instead added `document.frmQuiz.submit();`. This submits the form – the form submission now kicks off the start of the quiz.

That completes the changes for this page, so make sure you re-save it.

We now need to create the page `NoteUserSelections.asp`, to which the values of the `frmQuiz` form in `QuizPage.asp` are submitted. These values are used to update the session variables `NoQsToAsk` and `TimeLimit`.

```
<%@ LANGUAGE = JavaScript%>

<%
    Session("NoQsToAsk") = parseInt(Request.Form("cboNoQuestions"));
    Session("TimeLimit") = parseInt(Request.Form("cboTimeLimit"));
    Response.Redirect("AskQuestion.htm");
%>
```

Save the page as `NoteUserSelections.asp` in the same directory as the other trivia quiz pages.

In this page, we first define the default script language for the page as JavaScript. Then we set the session variables `NoQsToAsk` and `TimeLimit` to the values passed by the form submitted. Finally, we re-direct the user to the `AskQuestion.htm` page so that the quiz can start.

The remaining changes that we need to make to the quiz are merely to reflect the change in the `QuizPage`'s extension from `.htm` to `.asp`.

First, the main `TriviaQuiz.htm` page needs to have the `SRC` attribute for the `fraQuizPage` frame changed.

```
<HTML>
<HEAD>
<TITLE>Wrox Online Trivia Quiz</TITLE>
</HEAD>
<FRAMESET ROWS="120,*" BORDER="0">
<FRAME SRC="TopFrame.htm" NAME="fraTopFrame">
<FRAME SRC="QuizPage.asp" NAME="fraQuizPage">
</FRAMESET>
</HTML>
```

Save the page, then load the `GlobalFunctions.htm` page. This also has one change necessary, within the `getQuestion()` function. The change is to the code at the very end of the function, just before the return value is given. If your HTML editor supports 'find and replace', then it's easier to just do a 'find' on `QuizPage.htm` and replace with `QuizPage.asp`.

```
        questionHTML = questionHTML + "<BR>This brings your average todate to " +
            currentAvgScore + "%"
        questionHTML = questionHTML + "<P><INPUT TYPE=button " +
            "VALUE='Reset Stats' " +
            "onclick=\"window.top.fraTopFrame.fraGlobalFunctions.setCookie" +
            "('previousNoAsked', 0,'','1 Jan 1970')\" " +
            "NAME=buttonReset>"
        questionHTML = questionHTML + "<P><INPUT TYPE=button " +
            "VALUE='Restart Quiz' " +
            "onclick=\"window.location.replace('quizpage.asp')\" " +
            "NAME=buttonRestart>"

    }

    return questionHTML;
}
```

Re-save the page.

That completes the changes to the trivia quiz for this chapter. Try it out by running the quiz with non-default settings. When you restart the quiz, these settings should be displayed in the select lists as selected options.

In the next chapter, we'll store the questions in a database, and then see how easy it is to access the database with server-side script and build our HTML based on its information.

Summary

We've covered a lot of ground in this chapter and have really just scratched the surface of server-side scripting.

In this chapter, we saw that:

❑ Client-side script is script that runs in the client's browser. Server-side script is script that runs on the server after the page is requested, but before it's sent to the browser.

❑ We looked at Personal Web Server (PWS), a free Internet server available for use with Microsoft Windows. It is essentially a cut down version of Windows NT4 Server's Internet Information Server (IIS). We looked at where we could obtain PWS and how to install it.

❑ The server-side scripting environment with PWS and IIS is called Active Server Pages. By saving a normal HTML page with the .asp extension, we can then insert script inside the page that will run server-side. Only .asp pages can include server-side processing.

❑ Inserting server-side script can be done via a normal <SCRIPT> tag or by using the <% and %> delimiters. The default server-side script language on PWS is VBScript. Therefore, the <SCRIPT> tag must specify the LANGUAGE attribute as JavaScript, and that the script is to be run at the server using the RUNAT attribute. If we use the <% and %> syntax, we must specify the language of the whole page using the directive <%@ LANGUAGE = JavaScript%> on the page's very top line.

❑ Server-side script works very much as client-side script, though we saw that any HTML inside an if statement or a loop was controlled by the JavaScript.

❑ Whereas client-side scripting uses the Browser Object Model (BOM) to get things done, server-side scripting uses ASP objects, which enable us to get information from the user, write information to pages, and manipulate the server itself.

❑ The ASP Request object deals with information surrounding a user's request for a page. This includes the browser details, information posted in forms, information sent via a URL, and cookies.

❑ The Response object allows us to determine the response the user will get. This includes writing information to a page, sending cookies and even re-directing the user to a different page altogether.

❑ We looked at the Server object and saw how it allows us to run components on the server. Components are a little like plug-ins for the browser, in that they are code modules installed on the server, which extend its functionality. They may perform tasks like enabling database access, checking browser capabilities, or more complex tasks, like sending e-mails and checking credit cards.

❑ We looked at the idea of a session and how this was objectified in the web server by the Session object. Sessions start with the first request of an ASP page by a user and end twenty minutes after the last page request by the user.

❑ We can capture the session start and end points in the Session_OnStart and Session_OnEnd events, which need to be placed in the global.asa file.

❑ The Session object also provides an easy method of storing information for the duration of a session in session variables.

❑ Finally, we looked briefly at the Application object which is used to control the actual web site. This is similar to the Session object, in that it has Application_OnStart and Application_OnEnd events, and can be used to store information on the server using application variables.

Try experimenting with the knowledge you've gained in this chapter. In the next chapter we take server-side scripting even further and look at how we can access databases from a web page. The ability to access a database will enable us to take our web site to a completely new dimension.

Exercises

Suggested solutions to these questions can be found in Appendix A.

Question 1

Alter the logon example from this chapter, so that if a user enters an invalid value more than three times they are not taken back to the logon page, but to another page telling them that they are not valid users.

Question 2

In Question 2 of Chapter 6 and continuing with Question 1 of Chapter 7, we created a form that allowed the user to select their dream computer system and to see the price alter as different components were selected. Our task for this question is to enable the user to purchase the system they have selected. This involves:

❑ When the user clicks to buy the system, you need to obtain all the information necessary for an e-commerce purchase, for example name, address, and credit card details.

❑ With all the information obtained, show a final summary page that displays the system selected, its price, and the user's details. There should be a confirm order button and a cancel order button on the page.

❑ If the user clicks on the confirm order button then the system is purchased: simply take them to a page saying, "Thanks for your order". If they cancel the order, then wipe their details and return them to the home page.

Databases

Databases are very important to web development, as they are the main way of storing large quantities of easily accessible and updateable data. For example, online order systems need somewhere to permanently store customer and order details, and even a simple message board needs somewhere to store and retrieve messages.

You may ask, "Why not store data in plain text files rather than a database?" This would be possible, but not very efficient. Databases don't just *store* data – they also organize it, sort it and make it very easy for us to find and retrieve just the data we want. For example, an online bookseller such as Amazon may have a million or more books, and want to allow customers to search for specific books by either the author name, year of publication, book title, or publisher. If we had one, or even many, text files holding all the book information, it would prove a massive undertaking to try to find all the books published by Wrox Press between the years 1998 and 2000. A database makes a task such as this very easy, since ways of sorting and retrieving the data are built into its structure. Of course, we still need to design the database correctly, but if we get that right we find data retrieval is fast and easy.

In this chapter, we'll look at the theory behind relational databases, and how to create our own database, using Microsoft Access as an example. However, building the database is only half the problem – we want to access it from our web pages too.

The solution to this problem is made very easy, as Microsoft supplies components called ActiveX Data Objects that make searching for and storing information using server-side JavaScript and ASP very easy. The components are either present on your Windows operating system or installed when you install PWS (Personal Web Server, which we saw in the last chapter) or IIS (Microsoft's Internet Information Server).

We'll look at how to use these components to access a database using server-side script later in the chapter. Since we are using server-side script, the database must be in a place that the server, PWS or IIS in this case, has access to. We won't be looking at database access from client-side JavaScript, which though possible is nowhere near as easy, and is too advanced for this book. Needing to access a database client-side is fairly unusual anyway – most of the time it's server-side access that's required.

A Brief Guide to Databases

Databases are another of those big topics that you could fill a library with books on. In this section we'll just be taking the briefest of tours, giving you enough to get started with. We will cover databases themselves, how to define and design them, as well as a brief summary of SQL, the language used to talk to databases. However, if you are already familiar with these topics, you may want to go straight on to the next section where we start to talk about accessing databases from web pages.

We'll be using Microsoft's Access database for our examples, though much of what we'll be talking about applies to any relational database. I'm using Access 2000, but Access 95 or 97 will work just as well. Access is a good database for individual use and for intranet web sites that don't expect high numbers of concurrent users. However, it would not be suitable for a big e-commerce web site on the Internet; it does not cope well with large numbers of users and doesn't have the security of something like MS SQL Server 7.

How Information is Organized in Databases

The aim of a database is to store information. However, as we said above, some logical way of organizing the structure of this information is also needed. This can be achieved through a series of **tables**, each containing data that logically fits together. Such databases are called **relational databases** and are the most common form of database found in use.

Tables themselves contain data separated into **records**, each record being a set of related data. For example, my hospital medical record is all the medical information relating to me. It might contain my name, age, address, illnesses I've had, operations I've had, and so on. The important thing is that it all relates to me. You will have your own separate medical record, storing the same bits of information, that is name, age, and so on, but obviously it'll be your age and name information, not mine. Each item of information stored inside a record, for example name, age, address, is called a **field**. We have a name field, an age field, an address field, and so on.

To re-cap, a database contains tables, tables contain records, and records are made up of fields.

When we design our database, we create our own tables and specify the field names that they will contain. Let's use an example to explore these concepts. Imagine we're creating a database for a big computer parts supplier called CompBitsCo. This database may contain one table with information about the stock that the company has, another table containing information about their customers, and yet another containing information about the orders made by the customers.

In our example of the CompBitsCo company database, what information might be stored in the stock information table?

The information may be things like the item description, cost of the item, and the number in stock. There's probably lots more information that could be stored, but we'll keep things simple for our example.

Each piece of information, for example the description, cost, or number in stock, is represented by a field in the database table. We need to specify a unique name for each field inside the table and specify what sort of data it will be storing. For example, it might be storing text, such as the item's description, or it might be storing numbers, such as the stock number, or currency, such as the cost of an item, or dates, such as the date the next delivery of stock is due. There is a wide range of types of data that can be stored, though some are more common than others. A list of some the main data types available in an Access database is shown in the table:

Data Type	Description
Text	Can store up to 255 characters
Memo	Can store up to 64,000 characters
Number	Numerical data
Date/Time	Stores dates and times
Currency	Store monetary values
Yes/No	Can store values which are Yes/No or True/False

Different databases will support different data types. Although all of them support common ones like text and number, they may have a different name and be able to store different amounts of data.

Let's define some fields for the stock table in our example.

First we have the item description. We'll give this field a logical descriptive name like the ItemDescription field. It's going to be holding text so its data type is clearly Text.

The next field is the number of items available for a particular product. Let's call this the NumberInStock field. It will hold numerical data, so its field type will be Number.

Finally we have the cost information, for which the field name ItemCost seems fairly logical and descriptive. We could use the number for the format of the field's data, but as it's money data, the Currency data type seems more logical in this circumstance.

So now we have the collection of fields shown in the table below:

Field Name	Data Type
ItemDescription	Text
NumberInStock	Number
ItemCost	Currency

It is important to note that even relatively small databases could have hundreds of fields. If they were not grouped in some logical way, trying to make sense of it all could prove challenging, to say the least. This is why databases often contain multiple tables, with fields being logically grouped together into one table of another. For example, the CompBitsCo database will contain another table of customer information, which contains fields such as customer name and customer address.

We mentioned earlier the concept of a record, which consists of data corresponding to a group of fields. For example, if we had an item called a Widget, with 10 in stock, and they cost $10.99, then our ItemDescription field would hold Widget, NumberInStock would hold 10, and ItemCost would hold $10.99. Collectively this data is called a record. A table can have many, many records. For example, a second record might be where ItemDescription is BigWidget, NumberInStock is 7 and ItemCost is $16.99.

Creating a Database

Let's create a new Access 2000 database and add the stock table discussed above.

First open up Access. Once it's opened, you'll be presented with the following dialog box:

Create a new database by selecting the **Blank Access database** radio button, then clicking **OK**.

The dialog box shown below then allows you to pick a filename and location for the new database. It enters db1.mdb as a suggested name for the database – change this to CompBitsCo.mdb and click **Create**:

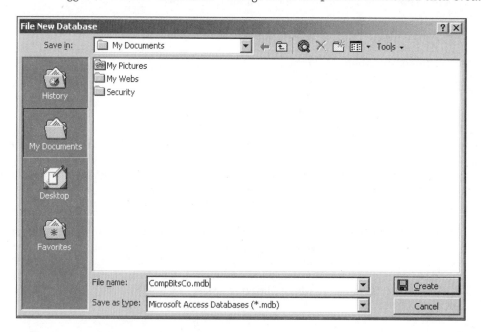

We've now got our database. Let's create our first table, which we'll call the Stock table.

In the view as shown below, make sure that **Tables** is selected under **Objects**, then double-click **Create table in Design view**:

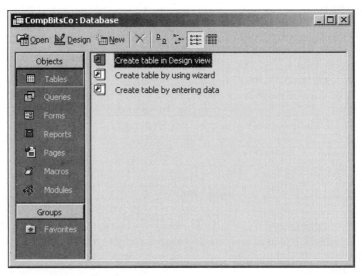

We're now in table design view and have a blank table in front of us that needs to have its fields defined as we defined them above. The screenshot below shows how it should look after all the fields have been defined. Type the field names into the appropriate **Field Name** boxes. On clicking on each **Data Type** box, a drop-down list will appear allowing you to choose the data type for that field.

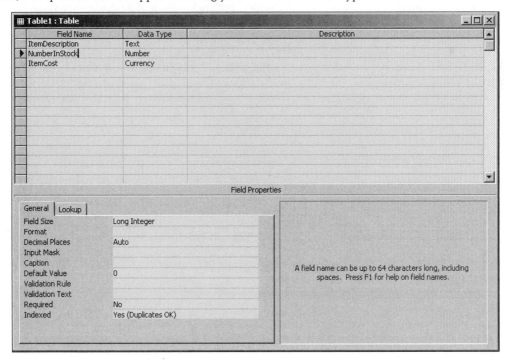

Although each field has a data type, this data type itself has various properties, which are shown under the General tab in the bottom left of the screen. Where these properties need to be changed I'll point it out, otherwise you can leave them at their default values.

The ItemDescription field has the Text data type, which itself has the Field Size property, the default for this being 50. This simply sets aside how much space might be required for this field, in terms of the number of characters it can hold. We can set it to any value from 1 to 255.

The NumberInStock field has the Number data type, which also has the Field Size property. However, this time we're given a choice from a drop-down list, which appears when you click on the Field Size input box. For our purposes the default value of Long Integer is fine, but it's worth noting that this field defines what type of numbers can be stored in the field. It goes from the smallest, a Byte, which can only hold a whole number from 0 to 255, right up to a Double, which is a floating point number holding a very large range of values. The Replication ID value of Field Size is a number, but for specialist purposes outside the scope of this book.

Why not just pick the Field Size that can hold the biggest number? Or choose the maximum number of characters for a field?

On a small scale using this strategy may just be acceptable, but imagine the effect on a large database with a hundred thousand customers, where even small wastages could have big consequences. When deciding the data type, we need to choose the smallest possible field size that will do the job and perhaps allow a little flexibility. For example, with the NumberInStock field we've chosen the Long Integer type, which will allow whole numbers up to 2,147,483,647. However, we might be able to cut the size of storage space of the field in half and use an Integer Field Size, which allows whole numbers up to 32,767. Whether we did this would depend on how much stock we expect to be held at any one time. If there's even a remote possibility that in the future the stock held would be more than 32,767, then we should choose Long Integer. If, on the other hand, the largest stock level ever recorded was 2,000 and it's not expected to get much larger, then we could choose the Integer field size. There's no hard and fast rule – just use your own good judgment.

With all the fields complete, you can close the table, making sure you save it first. Choose the name Stock for the table when asked. When you save the table a dialog box like that shown below will appear asking if you want to create a primary key – click No. We'll look at primary keys later and create one then.

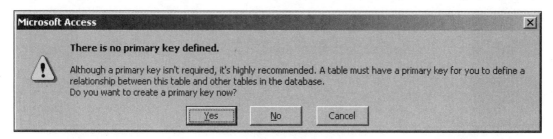

Before we add some data to the database, we'll create the tables necessary to store customers and customer order data.

Database Design – Adding More Fields and Tables

To complete our information storage for CompBitsCo, let's see what fields we might need to store customer information and order information.

For customers, we'll probably want to store their name, address, and telephone number. For orders, we'll want to store an order number, an order date, which customer ordered the goods, and what and how many goods were ordered.

Our fields will look something like those shown:

Field Name	Data Type
CustomerName	Text
CustomerAddress	Text
TelNumber	Text
OrderNo	Number
OrderDate	Date
GoodsOrdered	Text
QtyOrdered	Number

We now need to split the fields into tables. The important points to remember when splitting fields into tables is that firstly we need some sort of sensible split, secondly we need to allow data to be retrieved efficiently at a later date, and thirdly we want to avoid **data replication**, that is the unnecessary repetition of data.

We could lump the whole lot into one table, say the CustomerAndOrders table. This would work, but it would be very bad design, because it would be wasteful of storage space; we'd be duplicating data. Let's see what data would look like if it was stored in one table and we'll see why it's wasteful.

Assume that we need to store information for a customer called Mr. Big who has ordered three items. The data in the table would look like:

CustomerName	CustomerAddress	TelNumber	OrderNo	OrderDate	Goods Ordered	Qty Ordered
Mr Big	Some place, somewhere	1234 5678	112	1 Jan 2000	SomeBit	2
Mr Big	Some place, somewhere	1234 5678	112	1 Jan 2000	AnotherBit	7
Mr Big	Some place, somewhere	1234 5678	112	1 Jan 2000	ALittleBit	1

From the data above we can see that we've stored the customer's name, address, phone number, order number, and order date three times, when just once would do. The only things that are unique from row to row are the goods ordered and their quantity. This suggests that the goods ordered and their quantity need to go in a table on their own. We should have two tables, a `CustomerOrder` table and an `OrderItem` table. The `CustomerOrder` table will contain the fields `CustomerName`, `CustomerAddress`, `TelNumber`, `OrderNo`, and `OrderDate`. The `OrderItem` table will contain `GoodsOrdered`, `QtyOrdered`, and `OrderNo`. If we don't include the `OrderNo` field then we'll have no way of telling which order the goods relate to. By using it, for any row in the `OrderItems` table we just look up the `OrderNo` in the `CustomerOrder` table to see who ordered it.

Currently this leaves the `CustomerOrder` table looking like this:

Field Name	Data Type (Field Size)
CustomerName	Text (50)
CustomerAddress	Text (255)
TelNumber	Text (25)
OrderNo	Number (Long Integer)
OrderDate	Date

and the `OrderItem` table looking like this:

Field Name	Data Type (Field Size)
OrderNo	Number (Long Integer)
GoodsOrdered	Text (255)
QtyOrdered	Number (Integer)

However, another change we will make is that within the `CustomerOrder` table; instead of creating the `OrderNo` field as a number we'll create it as an `AutoNumber` field, a special type of number field that automatically populates a new record with a unique number, usually the next highest number available for that field. We'll look at this field in more detail later.

Let's create these tables in Access as we did for the `Stock` table. Within Access, make sure that **Tables** is selected under **Objects**, as shown opposite above.

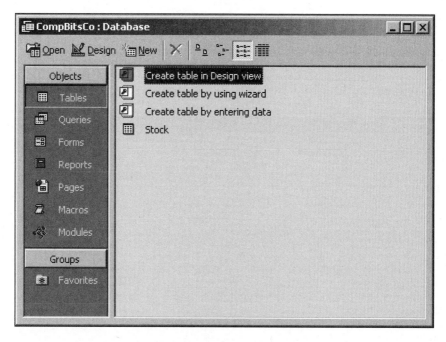

We'll first create the CustomerOrder table, so double-click **Create table in Design** view, and then create the fields as shown below. Note again that the properties of each field under the general tab can be left at their default values except CustomerAddress, which needs a Field Size of 255, and TelNumber, which needs a **Field Size** of 25.

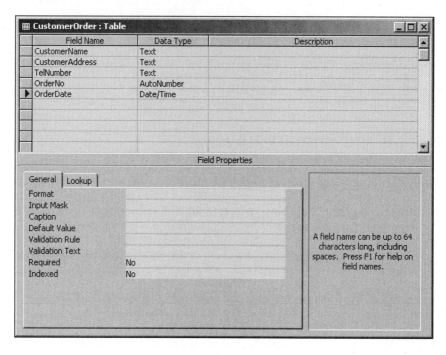

Make sure you save the table as `CustomerOrder` before closing it. When offered the opportunity to create a Primary Key, click **No**.

Now repeat the above steps to create the `OrderItem` table, again leaving the field properties at their default values. The completed fields are shown below. Save the table as `OrderItem`, and again don't select a primary key.

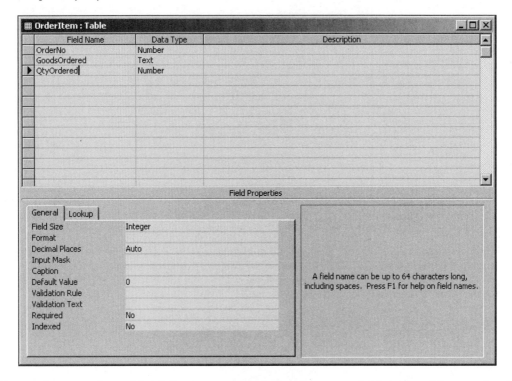

Now we have our three tables defined, we need to look at how some fields in the tables are related to one another.

Relationships and Primary Keys

Before we can populate our tables with data, we still have a few issues that need resolving with our database design. Firstly, although we have a `Stock` table containing all the things customers can buy and an `OrderItem` table containing all the things customers have bought, there's no relationship between them. For example, we could have an item in the `OrderItem` table that does not appear in the `Stock` table. This would be very strange. How can a customer have bought an item that CompBitsCo don't even sell, and if they did buy it, how much did it cost? Cost information is in the `Stock` table. Also if a customer buys something, we need to look up in the `Stock` table how much an item costs. Then when it has been purchased, we would want to change the amount of Stock held. Therefore we need two things:

❑   A way of matching items in the `OrderItem` table to items in the `Stock` table

❏   A way of ensuring that the `OrderItem` table can never contain items that don't exist in the `Stock` table

Currently we have a `GoodsOrdered` field containing the name of the item ordered. We could use this to match the same item in the `Stock` table. This helps us with the first requirement above, that is matching items in the two tables, but it doesn't help with the second requirement, ensuring items in the `OrderItem` table are in the `Stock` table. Also using a text field with the name of the item is very wasteful of both storage space and computer processing. Say our item is called a GruntMaster 7000. That's using approximately 10 bytes for necessary information about the field and then 32 bytes of memory for the actual characters and given there may be lots of customer orders for a GruntMaster 7000, it means this waste is repeated again and again. Also when doing a comparison between the `GoodsOrdered` field in the `OrderItems` table and the `ItemDescription` field in the `Stock` table the computer has to compare 32 bytes before being sure the two rows are the same. So what's the alternative?

The alternative is to use numbers, giving each item in the `Stock` table its own unique ID. We simply need to add an extra field to the `Stock` table, call it something like `StockId` and make it a `Long Integer` field size. Then in the `OrderItem` table instead of including the item's name we just include its `StockId`. Using a long integer only requires 4 bytes of memory, which makes for a big saving on storage space and makes comparisons between tables quicker. This process is called **normalization**.

Let's start by adding a `StockId` field to the `Stock` table.

From the table view, right-click the `Stock` table and select **Design View**, as I've done below. You can also select the **Design** icon from the tool bar.

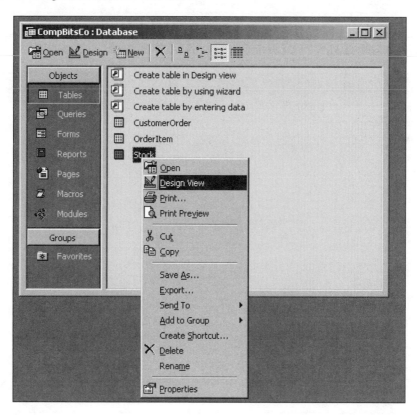

Now we're in design view, right-click on the `ItemDescription` field and select **Insert Rows**:

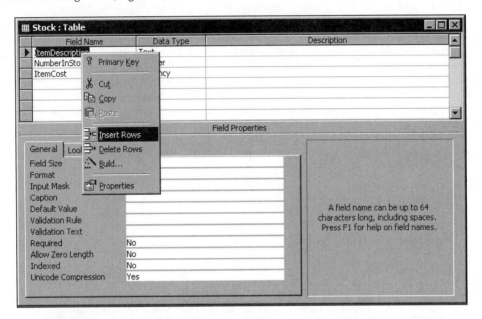

Complete the field definition as shown below, with the field name being `StockId` and the type as `Number` with a **Field Size** of `Long Integer`:

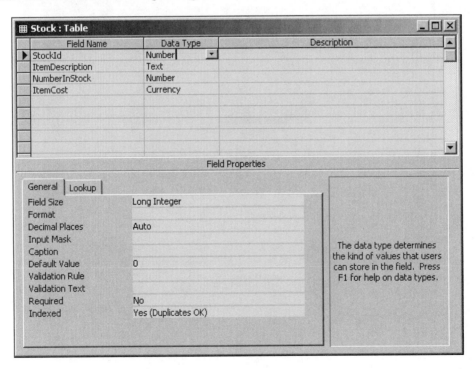

The primary way of looking up information in the `Stock` table is the `StockId` field that we just created. We can speed up the look-up of data in key fields such as `StockId` by making it the **primary key**. What this really means is that the field is indexed internally by Access so that it can do data lookups a lot faster. By saying it's the primary key, we're saying it's the most important index. We can define other indexes, but only one primary index or primary key, although as we'll see later, the primary key can be made up of more than one field. To make `StockId` the primary key in Access, we simply right-click the `StockId` field and select **Primary Key** from the menu that appears. It's as simple as that.

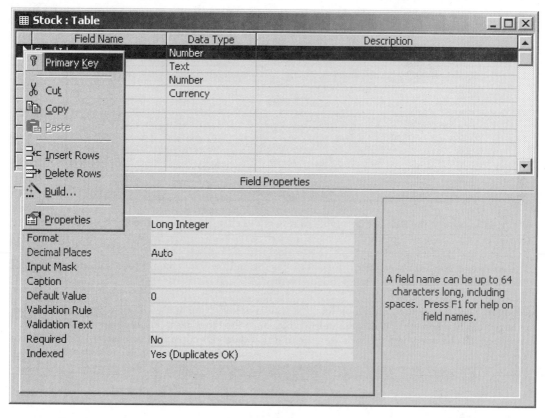

Once the field has been defined as the primary key field, we'll see a little key symbol next to the row defining the field. Also notice that the Indexed property changes from Yes (Duplicates OK) to Yes (No Duplicates). This is because primary key fields must contain unique data so that Access can quickly sort and find data.

The `StockId` field is simply a made up number we're using to enable items to be uniquely identified and represented in the `OrderItems` table. The number given for that field is not important, so long as it's unique for that table. To save us having to think up a unique number for each `StockId` we can use Access's `AutoNumber` data type. To change the data type of the `StockId` field, simply click the Data Type box and choose AutoNumber from the drop-down list. Now whenever we add information about a stock item, the `StockId` field will automatically be given a number. In fact we aren't able to edit the value in an auto number field.

Save the changes to the Stock table. However, before we leave it, let's add some stock data. To add data, it is easiest to switch from table design view to the data sheet view. We can either select the data sheet icon, shown here, or select **Datasheet View** from the **View** menu.

Now enter some example stock items. Each row represents one record, that is the information provided by the fields for one stock item. Some example values are shown below. Remember that the auto number field populates itself so don't try entering a value for the StockId. Once you've finished close the table. There is no need to save it since values are stored each time you move from one record (that is one row), to another.

Stock : Table

StockID	ItemDescription	NumberInStock	ItemCost
1	GruntMaster 7000	10	$1,000.00
2	GruntMaster 9000 Upgrade	2	$200.00
3	GruntMaster 9000	5	$1,400.00
4	SomeBit	50	$2.99
5	BigBit	25	$9.99
6	ALittleBit	1000	$0.99
(AutoNumber)		0	$0.00

Record: 7 of 7

We need to change the OrderItem table to reflect the changes made in the Stock table. View the OrderItem table in design view. We need to change the name of the GoodsOrdered field to StockId and its data type from Text to Number with a field size of Long Integer. Why Long Integer and not AutoNumber? Information for this field will be taken from the StockId field of the Stock table and will not be created independently of it.

When finished, the table should look like that shown below. Note that while field data types can be changed easily when there is no data in the table, once the table has been populated with data we should avoid changing data types or we may find that data gets corrupted or changed.

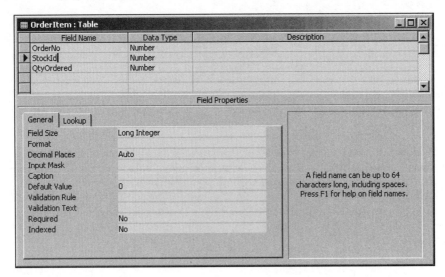

Should we go further and make `StockId` a primary key field? In this table it's not actually the `StockId` that's primary to looking up a record. In fact, to uniquely identify a record we need to look up both the `OrderNo` and `StockId` fields, so they must both be indexed as primary fields. Although we can only have one primary key index it can consist of more than one field. To do this we need to click on the gray box to the left of each field. First click on the `OrderNo` field, and then holding down the *Ctrl* key, click on the `StockId` field, so that both fields are blacked out. Now click the primary key icon in the tool bar and both fields will be indexed as primary keys.

Remember to save the table before closing it.

Defining Relationships between Tables

One of the issues we mentioned regarding the `Stock` and `OrderItem` tables is ensuring that there are no products in the `OrderItem` table that don't exist in the `Stock` table. We could say that there is a relationship between the two tables, in particular regarding the `StockId` field. This relationship is that for each item of stock in the `Stock` table there may be zero or more occurrences of that item in the `OrderItem` table. So, while there is only one definition in the `Stock` table of say the GruntMaster 7000, we may have lots of orders where a GruntMaster 7000 was sold and hence many occurrences of it in the `OrderItem` table. We call this a **one-to-many relationship** between the tables. There are also one-to-one relationships and many-to-many relationships. The one-to-many relationship is probably the most common.

Databases allow us to define these relationships, but why would we want to do so?

An important aspect of relationships is enforcing **data integrity**. We've already said that it's illogical to have orders for items that CompBitsCo don't sell. In terms of the database, this means that we shouldn't have items in the `OrderItem` table for which the `StockId` does not exist in the `Stock` table. Hopefully careful programming should prevent us from ever entering illogical data like this, but there's nothing to stop someone adding values to the database directly, and it's always possible that a bug in our program could allow invalid data to creep in. Once a database contains some invalid data, it can be an awful job cleaning it up.

If, however, we specify a relationship rule in the database itself that says we can only insert a `StockId` into the `OrderItem` table if it exists in the `Stock` table, then we are enforcing this rule regardless of whether data is entered by directly typing it in or by programming. With relationships we can guarantee the validity of our data.

So how do we go about defining a relationship in Access?

Let's create a one-to-many relationship between the `OrderItem` table and `Stock` table based on the `StockId` field.

First we need to choose Relationships from the Tools menu:

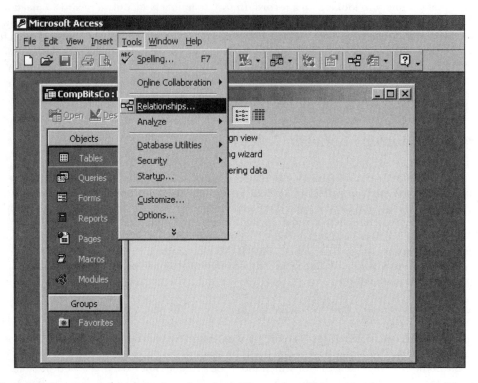

As this is the first time we've opened up the relationship tool, we'll be given the option of adding tables from our database onto the relationship diagram in the Show Table window. Double-clicking each of the tables in turn will add it to the diagram. Once all three tables have been added to the diagram click Close.

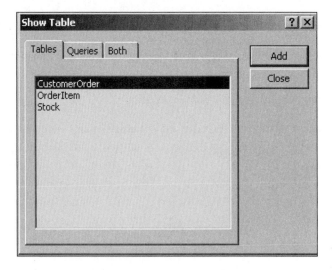

In the Relationships window, click on the StockID field in the OrderItem table and, keeping your mouse button down, drag over to the StockId field in the Stock table, before releasing your mouse button; the Edit Relationships dialog box will appear. We want to ensure that the relationship is enforced, so make sure the Enforce Referential Integrity box is checked. Once you've done this, click the Create button and the new relationship will be defined and data integrity enforced.

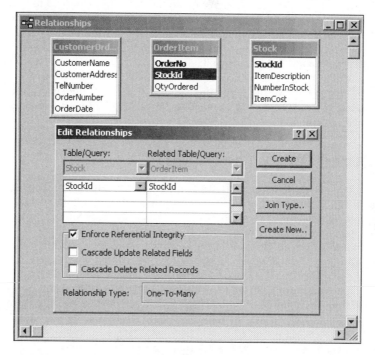

The relationship is displayed on the diagram via a line connecting the related fields in each table. It also indicates the type of relationship, such as one-to-one, one-to-many or many-to-many. We can see that Access has put a 1 next to the StockId field in the Stock table and has put an infinity symbol (∞) next to the OrderItem table indicating that there can be as many of the same StockId values in this table as we wish.

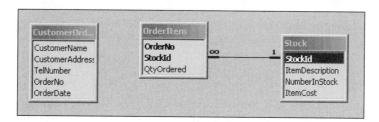

If we want to examine any relationship, we just double-click the relationship lines between tables. If we want to delete a relationship, we just right-click the line and choose Delete.

Before closing the Relationships diagram, be sure to click the Save icon to store the relationships defined to the database.

That completes our very brief look at creating a database, which is now at an acceptable stage for an example database. If we were to use it in a live situation, we would probably want to refine even further its structure and add more relationships.

For example we could add an Order table, and move the OrderNo and OrderDate fields from the CustomerOrder table to the Order table. We could then add an extra field to both tables to relate the two tables together. Why would we do this? Currently if the same customer places an order on two or more occasions, then we are creating duplicate information – we store their name and address more than once in the CustomerOrder table. Once you've read this chapter you might want to look again at this database and see how you could improve it.

Our next task is to look at how we can query the database to find out information stored inside it, then add, update, or delete records. To do this we need to use Structured Query Language (SQL), which is the topic of the next section.

SQL (Structured Query Language)

To access data inside a database we need to use a special data manipulation language called Structured Query Language (SQL, pronounced 'sequel'). The vast majority of relational databases support SQL, including Microsoft Access.

We'll be concentrating on just a small part of the language, enough to perform essential functions such as getting information out of the database, updating records, adding new records, and deleting records.

Pieces of SQL code are normally referred to as **queries**. Initially we'll be using Access to run our SQL queries to see how they work, but later in the chapter we'll see how we can run the queries from JavaScript in a web page.

Let's start by looking at how we can retrieve information from the database.

Selecting Records

SQL provides the SELECT statement, which enables us to specify which fields we want to retrieve information for. Note the capitalization: for good programming, all SQL command key words are written in capitals, though in fact the SQL language itself is case insensitive.

For example, if we want to retrieve records with just the fields StockId, ItemDescription, and NumberInStock, then our query would start:

```
SELECT StockId, ItemDescription, NumberInStock
```

We then need to specify which table the fields are selected from. StockId appears in two tables, Stock and OrderItems, so there could be some confusion if no table was specified. To specify the table, we write FROM then the name of the table (or tables) the fields are being selected from:

```
SELECT StockId, ItemDescription, NumberInStock
FROM Stock
```

Let's try this out in Access and see the results. In our CompBitsCo Access database, click on Queries under the Objects tab:

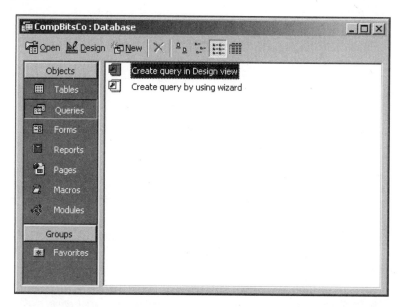

Now double-click Create query in Design view and the design dialog box will appear:

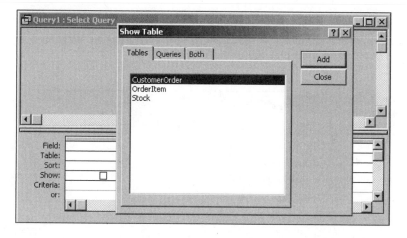

Since we're learning about SQL, we want to create the SQL ourselves rather than have Access do it for us. To switch to the SQL view, we first need to click the Close button in the Show Table window. Next click the SQL icon in the toolbar, illustrated here, and we'll be taken to the SQL view, with just the word SELECT; inside the SQL editing box.

SQL

Change the SQL inside the text box to our query:

```
SELECT StockId, ItemDescription, NumberInStock
FROM Stock
```

Note that, like JavaScript, the end of a SQL statement is indicated by a semi-colon, and again like JavaScript, most of the time leaving it off won't cause problems.

To run the query we need to either click the Run icon (shown here) from the toolbar, or select **Run** from the **Query** menu, or select **Datasheet View** from the **View** menu. Access will process our query and display the results in a grid:

StockId	ItemDescription	NumberInStock
1	GruntMaster 7000	10
2	GruntMaster 9000 Upgrade	2
3	GruntMaster 9000	5
4	SomeBit	50
5	BigBit	25
6	ALittleBit	1000
(AutoNumber)		0

Record: 1 of 6

To return to the SQL view, choose **SQL View** from the **View** menu.

As well as specifying which fields we want to view, we can also select which records are displayed by using a WHERE clause which we add to our SELECT statement. For example, if we wanted just those records where the number of items in stock was less than ten we would write:

```
SELECT StockId, ItemDescription, NumberInStock
FROM Stock
WHERE NumberInStock < 10
```

As the field we are searching on is a numerical field we don't place 10 in quotes. However, if it is a text field, then we must put the 10 in quotes, just as we do with JavaScript strings.

Alter the SQL in our Access query to read as above then re-run it. This time only records matching our WHERE clause's criteria are returned to the set of records:

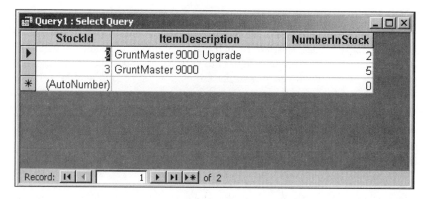

If we want to specify more than one criterion in the WHERE clause, then we can use Boolean operators, such as AND and OR. For example, if we wanted all records where the NumberInStock was less then 10 *and* the StockId was 2, we'd change our SQL to

```
SELECT StockId, ItemDescription, NumberInStock
FROM Stock
WHERE NumberInStock < 10 AND StockId = 2
```

Before we leave the SELECT statement, we'll look at how we can order the records returned using the ORDER BY clause.

Let's say we wanted to order our results by the field NumberInStock. To do this we add the ORDER BY clause to the end of the query, after any WHERE clause we might have, and specify the fields that will determine the resulting set's order.

```
SELECT StockId, ItemDescription, NumberInStock
FROM Stock
WHERE NumberInStock < 10
ORDER BY NumberInStock
```

This will return results in ascending order, that is from lowest to highest. If we want it in descending order from highest to lowest, we type DESC after the fields being ordered:

```
SELECT StockId, ItemDescription, NumberInStock
FROM Stock
WHERE NumberInStock < 10
ORDER BY NumberInStock DESC
```

If we wanted to order the data by more than one field, then we just add the fields to be ordered in a list separated by commas. The first field will be ordered first, then if there are two matching items, the order will be decided by the next field. If they are still the same, then they will be ordered by the next field, and so on. So to order by `NumberInStock` then `StockID`, we'd write:

```
SELECT StockId, ItemDescription, NumberInStock
FROM Stock
WHERE NumberInStock < 10
ORDER BY NumberInStock, StockID
```

Updating Records

To change the value of existing records in the database, SQL has the UPDATE statement. We can use this to update records en masse or just for an individual record. It allows us to specify what fields in a table are to be updated and what value they are to be updated with. An essential part of the UPDATE statement is the WHERE clause; if we don't specify a WHERE clause then every record in a table will be updated.

For example, if we wanted to update the stock levels for the GruntMaster 9000 Upgrade to 5, we would create the following SQL:

```
UPDATE Stock
SET NumberInStock = 5
WHERE StockId = 2
```

First we tell the database what we want to do, that is we want to UPDATE the table named Stock. Then we specify which fields are to be SET to new values and what the values are. Here we've just set one field; if we wanted to update more than one field we would just add a comma then the field name and value. For example:

```
SET NumberInStock = 5, ItemCost = 150
```

Finally, we have our WHERE clause, where we have a criterion that specifies the records that are to be affected by the update. Here, by specifying the StockId, which is unique for each record, we ensure that just one record is updated.

You can try this query in Access as we did for the SELECT query by selecting **Queries** from the **Objects** tab, clicking **Create query** in Design view, and then switching to the SQL view. When you run the query, Access will tell you how many records will be updated and give you the chance to cancel the query. Click **Yes** if you want the update to go ahead.

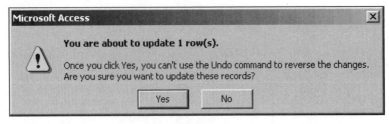

As well as updating with actual values that we specify, we can also update by selecting information from the database itself. For example, let's increase our prices by 10% by running the query below:

```
UPDATE Stock
SET ItemCost = ItemCost * 1.1
```

Inserting New Records

To insert a new record into the database, SQL has the aptly named INSERT statement. To use INSERT we need to tell it the name of the table, the fields in that table that we want to insert data in, and the values we wish to insert.

For example, to insert a new stock item called an UltraPC, which costs $5000 and for which we have none in stock, our SQL we be:

```
INSERT
INTO Stock (ItemDescription, NumberInStock, ItemCost)
VALUES ('UltraPC',0,5000)
```

First we told the database what we want to do, we wanted to INSERT a record. Then we stated that the table INTO which the new record would be going was the Stock table. We then specified in parentheses which fields we were putting new data into. Finally we specified the VALUES that would be inserted into each field.

If you type the SQL into Access and run it, your Stock table should now contain the following data:

	StockID	ItemDescription	NumberInStock	ItemCost
	1	GruntMaster 7000	10	$1,100.00
	2	GruntMaster 9000 Upgrade	5	$220.00
	3	GruntMaster 9000	5	$1,540.00
	4	SomeBit	50	$3.29
	5	BigBit	25	$10.99
	6	ALittleBit	1000	$1.09
	7	UltraPC	0	$5,000.00
*	(AutoNumber)		0	$0.00

Record: 1 of 7

Deleting Records

Deleting records is very easy; we use the DELETE statement, specify the table FROM which records are to be deleted, and use a WHERE clause to specify the criteria for determining the records to be removed. If we don't specify a WHERE clause, then all the records from that table will be deleted, something to be very careful of.

For example, to remove all items costing under $5, we would require the following SQL:

```
DELETE FROM Stock WHERE ItemCost < 5
```

Run this query in Access. It will remove the items SomeBit and ALittleBit, leaving our table with the following records:

	StockID	ItemDescription	NumberInStock	ItemCost
	1	GruntMaster 7000	10	$1,100.00
	2	GruntMaster 9000 Upgrade	5	$220.00
	3	GruntMaster 9000	5	$1,540.00
	5	BigBit	25	$10.99
	7	UltraPC	0	$5,000.00
*	(AutoNumber)		0	$0.00

Record: 1 of 5

The IN and NOT IN statements

The final SQL statements we will look at are the IN and NOT IN statements. These allow us to search for a list of items. Lets say we wanted to search for all items whose NumberInStock is 5, 10, or 20. Rather than writing:

```
SELECT StockId, NumberInStock
FROM Stock
WHERE NumberInStock = 5 OR NumberInStock = 10 OR NumberInStock = 20
```

we can use IN and write:

```
SELECT StockId, NumberInStock
FROM Stock
WHERE NumberInStock IN (5, 10, 20)
```

Basically, in plain English this is saying "where NumberInStock is equal to any of the values in the list 5, 10, 20".

The opposite of IN is NOT IN. For example, if we wanted all stock where NumberInStock is not 5, 10 or 20, we'd change our WHERE to:

```
SELECT StockId, NumberInStock
FROM Stock
WHERE NumberInStock NOT IN (5, 10, 20)
```

That completes our whirlwind tour of SQL in which we looked at just the basics of the language. However, it has given us enough knowledge to start creating SQL queries in web pages, the topic of the next section.

Accessing Databases from a Web Page

Now we've seen how to create a database, we'll turn our attention to connecting to a database using JavaScript and executing our SQL queries against it. We'll be looking solely at accessing a database that's located on the same computer as the web server. That means we'll be using server-side scripting inside ASP pages. It's likely that while learning about database access, you'll be using the same machine for your web server, your database and as the client computer browsing the web site. Just keep in mind that when your web site goes live to the outside world, the client computer will usually be completely separate from the computer with the database and web server.

What is it that enables us to access a database in script?

In the previous chapter on server-side scripting we looked at the Server object's CreateObject() method. We saw that by installing components onto the web server, we could extend its functionality beyond that available to the basic web server, a bit like plug-ins extend a browser's functionality beyond what it can normally achieve. We saw that Personal Web Server (PWS) comes with a number of components, such as a Browser Capability component, that extend the server's functionality. PWS also comes with something called **ActiveX Data Objects** (ADO), which is another component we can access via Server.CreateObject(), and it's this component that provides the server with the ability to access databases.

The ADO component provides extensive database access functionality, and has lots of objects we can create and use to connect to databases, execute queries, return sets of records, and do almost anything else you might care to do with a database. The full object hierarchy is fairly big, so we'll concentrate just on the objects that provide the essential tools for accessing and manipulating database data. We'll be looking at two ADO objects in particular, the Connection object and the Recordset object.

As the names suggest, the Connection object encapsulates things relating to connecting to a database and the Recordset object deals with a set of records returned from the database by a SELECT query. However, it's slightly less clear-cut than that, as the Connection object also allows us to execute SQL directly, and the Recordset object can connect to a database and return records without the need for a Connection object. We'll be looking at these objects in more detail shortly.

Let's start by talking about the first thing we must always do before running a query. That is, actually connecting to the database!

Making a Connection

Before we can query a database, we need to connect to it.

Connecting to a database requires a **connection string** that contains various pieces of information such as which database we want to connect to and how we are connecting to it. If we are connecting to a database with security restrictions, then the connection string will also include information such as user name and password. For now we'll just look at how we create a connection string – later we'll actually use it to connect to a database.

So what methods are there for connecting to the database that we can specify in the connection string?

Although ADO provides objects that represent connections, such as the Connection object, these are not the actual components that do the connecting, just our interface to them. There are two underlying technologies that can be used to connect to databases, Open Database Connectivity (ODBC) and Microsoft's OLE DB.

The aim of both ODBC and OLE DB is to provide an interface through which programmers can connect to databases. We don't actually use these technologies directly, but instead via ADO objects. Which of ODBC and OLE DB we choose, does, however impact on the connection string we need to use.

Of course the big question is which should we use, ODBC or OLE DB?

ODBC has become something of an industry standard and we'll find that almost all database companies create an ODBC driver necessary to connect to their database. OLE DB is a newer technology, so we might find that more exotic databases are not supported, although this will change over time. OLE DB connects directly to the database and should therefore be faster, though this is not always the case in practice.

ODBC requires that an **ODBC data source** is set up on the computer accessing the database. (We'll see how to do this in the next section.) After this has been done, we simply specify the data source name in our connection string. The advantage with this is that in theory we can easily switch the location of a database or even the type of database, say from Access to SQL Server, with no changes to the connection string necessary. All that's needed is that the data source is changed on each server accessing it.

OLE DB is less flexible in this sense, because we enter the location and type of database in the connection string. If we want to change the database, we must change our code.

Before we go on to look at database connection strings in more detail, let's look at how we set up an ODBC data source.

Setting Up an ODBC Data Source

First we need to open up the Control Panel on our Windows 98, 95, or NT computer by using the Start, Settings menu:

Next double-click the ODBC icon, which opens up the ODBC window. If you're using Windows 2000, then you'll find ODBC under Administrative Tools in the control panel.

In the ODBC window, make sure you select the System DSN tab. We want to add a data source for the machine, not a data source specific to a user.

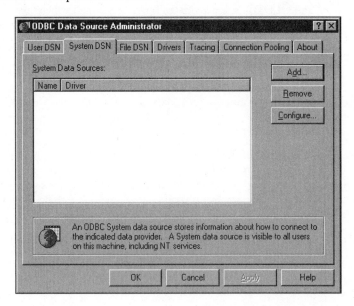

To add a new data source, click the Add button and the Create New Data Source dialog box will appear. We want to add a data source that connects to an MS Access database, so make sure that Microsoft Access Driver (*.mdb) is selected, and then click the Finish button:

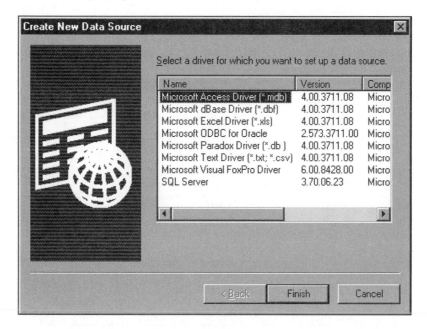

We're now given the opportunity to give our data source a name and select the .mdb file that contains our database:

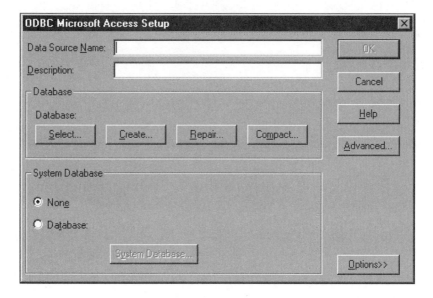

In the **Data Source Name** text box, enter `CompBitsCoDB`. Then click the **Select** button, browse to where you've placed the `CompBitsCo.mdb` file and select it, and then click **OK**. You can also enter a description of the data source in the **Description** box. This is optional, but may help you remember later what the data source is used for.

Once you've finished, your data source box should look something like that below. Click on the **OK** button to finish the set up.

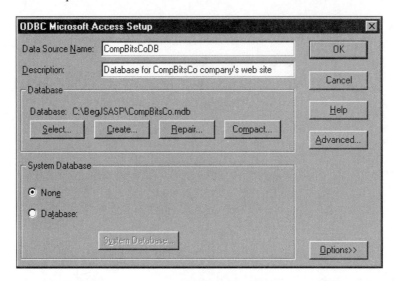

The new data source we've created will now be listed in the ODBC window. If you need to alter it, for example if the location of your database changes, then just click the **Configure** button. If we switch to another database type, such as SQL Server or Oracle, we just delete the data source (by clicking the **Remove** button) and then set up a new one with the same name.

The Connection String

Our connection string will depend on the database parameters, such as the location of the database, any user logging in details (username and password), and whether we're using ODBC or OLE DB.

For example, to connect to the ODBC connection we just made for our `CompBitsCo` Access database, the connection string would just need to specify the data source name (DSN):

```
"DSN=CompBitsCoDB"
```

Connecting using OLE DB requires slightly more detail.

First we need to specify which OLE DB driver, know as a Provider, will provide the connection. In our case it's an Access database, so the provider will be Microsoft.Jet.OLEDB.4.0.

We also need to specify the data source, which is where the database's `.mdb` file is located. Remember that in JavaScript the \ character is a special escape character. Since we need to use it to specify directory paths, we need to escape the escape character, by putting an extra \ in front of it, so that it is treated as an actual backslash.

I've put my `CompBitsCo.mdb` in the directory `C:\temp`, so my data source will be:

```
"Data Source=C:\temp\\CompBitsCo.mdb"
```

Putting this information together, our OLE DB connection string will be:

```
Provider=Microsoft.Jet.OLEDB.4.0;Data Source=C:\\temp\\CompBitsCo.mdb
```

Creating a Connection Object and Opening a Connection

A `Connection` object allows us to open up a reusable connection to a database that we can access again and again within the same page. To do this we first need to create a `Connection` object, and then use it to open the connection to the database.

We create a new `Connection` object using the `Server` object's `CreateObject()` method. The name of the library containing the ADO objects is `ADODB`. The parameter to pass to the `CreateObject()` method is this library name, `ADODB`, followed by a dot and then the name of the ADO object, here the `Connection` object, that we want to create.

So, to create a `Connection` object we write:

```
var adoConnection = Server.CreateObject("ADODB.Connection");
```

Next we use the `Connection` object's `Open()` method to open a connection to a database. The `Open()` method takes a connection string as the first parameter. For the examples we use here, we'll use the ODBC data source we created earlier, and so the ODBC version of the connection string. Therefore, to open a connection to the CompBitsCoDB ODBC data source we require:

```
adoConnection.Open("DSN=CompBitsCoDB");
```

Now we have our connection to the database. We'll see shortly how to use it, but for now let's see how having made use of the connection, we then close it and release the object we created so as to enable memory to be freed up:

```
adoConnection.Close() ;
adoConnection = null;
```

First, we close the connection using the `Close()` method of the `Connection` object. Then, by setting the variable containing the `Connection` object to `null`, we let it be known that we have finished with the variable and it can be removed from memory.

The `Connection` object is not the only way of connecting to a database. We'll see later how we can create a temporary connection with the `Recordset` object.

However, now that we have our connection, let's look at how we can use it.

Returning Information from a Database

To get records from the database, we must first make a connection to the database, as we have done above, and then run a SQL query against the database. This query returns a `Recordset` object containing the results of the query.

First we need to make a connection to the database:

```
var adoConnection = Server.CreateObject("ADODB.Connection");
adoConnection.Open("DSN=CompBitsCoDB");
```

Then we need to define a variable to hold the `Recordset` object that will be returned from our query:

```
var adoRecordSet;
```

Finally, we use the `Connection` object's `Execute()` method to execute a SQL `SELECT` statement, which will return the records we want. The `Execute()` method returns a `Recordset` object which we store in our `adoRecordSet` variable.

```
adoRecordSet = adoConnection.Execute("SELECT StockId, ItemDescription,
    NumberInStock FROM Stock");
```

That's got us a nicely populated `Recordset` object containing the columns and rows of data in a similar way to when we executed a query in Access. How do we access the rows of this recordset to get the information we want?

When we saw a `SELECT` statement executed in Access itself, we saw it returned results something like this:

StockId	ItemDescription	NumberInStock
1	GruntMaster 7000	10
2	GruntMaster 9000 Upgrade	2
3	GruntMaster 9000	5
4	SomeBit	50
5	BigBit	25
6	ALittleBit	1000
(AutoNumber)		0

Record: 1 of 6

Executing the same query in a web page using ADO produces the same recordset, with our current position being the first record in the recordset, that is the GruntMaster 7000 record.

To get the information in a particular field on the current record, we just use its field name and specify that we want the value. In the code below we put the contents of the `ItemDescription` field of our returned `Recordset` object into the variable called `description`:

```
var description = adoRecordSet("ItemDescription").Value;
```

This means that "GruntMaster 7000" is stored in description.

Having got this information, how do we go to the next record? In Access we could just move the cursor to the next row. In ADO we do exactly the same thing, except in code using the Recordset object's MoveNext() method.

If we type:

```
adoRecordSet.MoveNext();
```

then the 'cursor' will move to the next row, and now:

```
adoRecordSet("ItemDescription").Value
```

returns the value "GruntMaster 9000 Upgrade".

We can keep on using MoveNext() until we've reached the end of the recordset. In Access we can see where that is, but how do we know we're at the end of a recordset in ADO?

The ADO Recordset object has the Eof property (which stands for End Of File). If this property is true, then we've gone past the last record in the recordset. It's important to note the distinction that Eof does not mean we're on the last record, but that we've actually moved past the last record and come to the end of the information.

The Recordset object also has the Bof property, which indicates that we're at the beginning of the recordset. Again, Bof being true actually means we're before the first record. When the recordset is first populated, if there are records returned by the query then we will start on the first record, and Bof will be false – we're at the first record and not before the first record. This can be a little confusing.

There will be situations where a query will not return any values. For example, if there were no records in the database or if the WHERE clause in our SELECT statement excluded all records, then there would be no returned values. To check if what we have is an empty recordset, we can use the Bof and Eof properties together. If Bof and Eof are both true then it means we are before the first record and past the last record. This may sound illogical and so it is, unless the recordset is empty. So:

```
if (adoRecordSet.Bof == true &&  adoRecordSet.Eof == true)
{
    // Recordset empty
}
```

checks whether we have an empty recordset. This is something we should always do if an empty recordset is even a slight possibility.

Try It Out – Returning a List of Stock

Let's put what we have learnt into action and create a web page that returns all the records in our CompBitsCo database's Stock table. We'll return the values in an HTML table for formatting reasons. For each item, we'll also add a hyperlink that links to a page that enables the purchase of that item, although this page won't be created until a later example.

```
<%@ LANGUAGE = JavaScript%>
<HTML>
<BODY>
<TABLE BORDER=1>
<THEAD>
    <TR>
    <TH>Product</TH>
    <TH>Quantity In Stock</TH>
    <TH>Cost per Item</TH>
    <TH></TH>
    </TR>
</THEAD>

<%
// Open connection to database, then populate a recordset with list of stock
    var adoConnection = Server.CreateObject("ADODB.Connection");
    var adoRecordSet;
    var mySQL;
    adoConnection.Open("DSN=CompBitsCoDB");
    var mySQL = "SELECT StockId, ItemDescription, NumberInStock, ItemCost" +
        " FROM Stock";
    adoRecordSet = adoConnection.Execute(mySQL);

// Loop through recordset and write stock details out to page
    while ( adoRecordSet.Eof == false )
    {
%>
<TR>
    <TD><%=adoRecordSet("ItemDescription").Value%></TD>
    <TD><%=adoRecordSet("NumberInStock").Value%></TD>
    <TD><%=adoRecordSet("ItemCost").Value%></TD>
    <TD><A HREF="buyitem.asp?StockId=<%=adoRecordSet("StockId").Value%>">
        Buy this</A></TD>
</TR>
<%
    adoRecordSet.MoveNext();
    }

// Close Recordset and connections
// and release memory used by Recordset and Connection objects
    adoRecordSet.Close();
    adoRecordSet = null;
    adoConnection.Close();
    adoConnection = null;
%>
</TABLE>
</BODY>
</HTML>
```

Save this page as `DisplayStock.asp` into the physical directory of the virtual directory `AWalkOnTheServerSide` that we created in the previous chapter.

Browse to the page in your browser by typing:

```
http://localhost/AWalkOnTheWildSide/DisplayStock.asp
```

You should see a screen similar to that shown below:

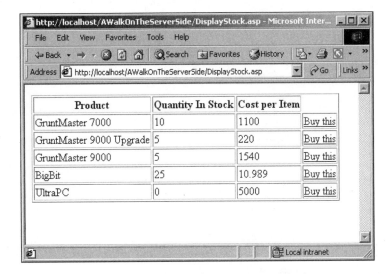

You'll notice that the BigBit price is shown as 10.989, whereas in the database it's shown as 10.99. The reason for this is that Access formats its display of data – in the case of currency it only displays the first two digits after the decimal point and does any rounding necessary. However, the data itself is still 10.989. Remember that originally BigBit cost 9.99, and we then executed a query that added 10% on to this price, which made it 10.989. Access 2000 has the ROUND function we can use to limit the number of decimal places – this would be best used with the original SQL that updated the database and added 10% to stock prices.

We could also write a JavaScript function that fixes the number of decimal places to two, as we saw in Chapter 4. However, if this was a real online shopping application we'd actually not be charging the correct price – the correct price is 10.989 as far as the database is concerned – so it's the database that needs changing. As this is just an example we'll leave it as it is.

How It Works

We start by making the default server-side script language for the page JavaScript:

```
<%@ LANGUAGE = JavaScript%>
```

Then in the body of the page we define our <TABLE> and its <THEAD>, containing four table headings. The first three of these are Product, Quantity In Stock, and Cost Per Item, but the last heading is empty. The rows of the table will contain the stock data and will be created dynamically later in the page.

```
<TABLE BORDER=1>
<THEAD>
    <TR>
    <TH>Product</TH>
    <TH>Quantity In Stock</TH>
    <TH>Cost per Item</TH>
    <TH></TH>
    </TR>
</THEAD>
```

Next we have the first server-side script block, the start of which is shown below:

```
<%
    var adoConnection = Server.CreateObject("ADODB.Connection");
    var adoRecordSet;
    var mySQL;
    adoConnection.Open("DSN=CompBitsCoDB");
```

In this script we first create a `Connection` object and declare two variables, `mySQL` in which we will build up our SQL query, and `adoRecordset`, which will hold the resulting recordset. We then open a connection to our `CompBitsCo` database.

In the next two lines of script shown below, we first declare our SQL query, which will return information about the products in our `Stock` database table. We then run this query against the database using the `Connection` object's `Execute()` method. This returns a `Recordset` object, which we store in the variable adoRecordSet.

```
    var mySQL = "SELECT StockId, ItemDescription, NumberInStock, ItemCost" +
        "FROM Stock";
    adoRecordSet = adoConnection.Execute(mySQL);
```

Our next code loops through the recordset stored in variable `adoRecordset`, starting with the first record and moving to the next, then the next and so on until we are at the end of the recordset. We use each record to write out HTML to the page displaying stock information.

The last column in the table is actually a link saying Buy this. When clicked, the link will take us to the page `buyitem.asp`, which we will create in a later example. In the URL for the link, we also pass the `StockId` value for that record, which can be retrieved in the `buyitem.asp` page. Using this value, we will be able to work out what the customer wants to buy.

```
    while ( adoRecordSet.Eof == false )
    {
%>
<TR>
    <TD><%=adoRecordSet("ItemDescription").Value%></TD>
    <TD><%=adoRecordSet("NumberInStock").Value%></TD>
    <TD><%=adoRecordSet("ItemCost").Value%></TD>
    <TD><A HREF="buyitem.asp?StockId=<%=adoRecordSet("StockId").Value%>">
        Buy this</A></TD>
</TR>
<%
    adoRecordSet.MoveNext();
    }
```

Having created a row in the HTML table based on a row in the recordset, we then move to the next row in the recordset using the `MoveNext()` method. Note that it is very easy to forgot to put this statement in and end up with an infinite loop that causes the web page to time out.

Finally, with all the data extracted, we close the `Recordset` and `Connection` objects and let the server know we've finished with the objects by setting the variables pointing to them to `null`. It's important that we do things in the right order – we must close the `Recordset` first, then set the variable `adoRecordset` to `null` to allow the memory to be made available. We must not set this variable to `null`, and then try to close it. Having closed the recordset, we can then close the connection and release that variable, again in that order.

```
    adoRecordSet.Close();
    adoRecordSet = null;
    adoConnection.Close();
    adoConnection = null;
%>
```

Opening Recordsets without a Connection Object

If we plan on opening a number of different recordsets within a page from a database, by running SQL commands against it, then it's worth using a `Connection` object as we have done above. It means a connection to the database only needs to be made once in the page and speeds up the page's processing.

If, however, we only want to retrieve one recordset in a page, then we can use the `Recordset` object without a `Connection` object. In fact, the `Recordset` object does create a `Connection` object for its own use, but it's destroyed immediately after it's used for retrieving the recordset and is not available for our own use.

The `Recordset` object has the `Open()` method, which opens not a new connection, but instead a new recordset. The minimum parameters we must pass to the `Open()` method are the SQL containing the `SELECT` statement that will return the records, and a connection string like the connection sting we would pass to a `Connection` object's `Open()` method.

First we need to create a new `Recordset` object:

```
var adoRecordset = Server.CreateObject("ADODB.Recordset");
```

Then we open the `Recordset`, passing first the SQL, then the connection string:

```
var mySQL = "SELECT StockId, ItemDescription, NumberInStock, ItemCost" +
    "FROM Stock";
adoRecordset.Open(mySQL, "DSN=CompBitsCoDB");
```

So far we have only seen recordsets that we can use the `MoveNext()` method to proceed through, starting from the first record and moving towards the last. An additional benefit of opening recordsets in the way we have here is the ability to move forwards, backwards and even jump to the beginning or end of the recordset. The downside of this type of flexibility is that greater resources are consumed and more load placed on our web server.

To open a `Recordset` object that we can move forwards and backwards in, we need to pass an additional parameter to the `Open()` method, the `CursorType` parameter. When we open a `Recordset` with no `CursorType` parameter, we are opening a **forward only cursor type** recordset. As the name suggests, this only allows `MoveNext()` type movement and retrieves records as we move through the records. If we want to open what's called a **static cursor type** recordset, we need to pass the number 3 as the `CursorType` parameter. A static cursor type recordset contains all the records returned by a query and can be moved forward and backward through with the following commands:

- ❑   `MoveFirst()` – moves to beginning of a recordset

- ❑   `MoveLast()` – moves to end of a recordset

- ❑   `MoveNext()` – moves to next record

- ❑   `MovePrevious()` – moves to previous record

For example, to open a static cursor type recordset, we would use the following code:

```
var adoRecordset = Server.CreateObject("ADODB.Recordset");
var mySQL = "SELECT StockId, ItemDescription, NumberInStock, ItemCost" +
   "FROM Stock";
adoRecordset.Open(mySQL, "DSN=CompBitsCoDB", 3);
```

This is identical to the previous example, except that we pass 3 as a third parameter for the `Open()` method of the `Recordset` object.

To move through the recordset we would type commands from the following list:

```
adoRecordset.MoveLast();
adoRecordset.MoveFirst();
adoRecordset.MoveNext();
adoRecordset.MovePrevious();
```

Remember that static cursors take up more of our limited server resources, so don't use them unless you actually need the ability to move in any direction through a recordset.

Changing Information in a Database

We'll now look at changing information in a database, such as adding, deleting, and updating records. We'll be using the sort of SQL queries we saw earlier such as INSERT, UPDATE, and DELETE to make the changes. To execute these queries against the database we can use the `Connection` object's `Execute()` method in which we pass the SQL that changes the data, just as we did with SELECT statements. However, with these type of queries there are no recordsets returned, and so no need for a `Recordset` object.

Whether we are inserting, updating, or deleting records, the JavaScript is the same, it's just the SQL being executed that changes.

The following statements show the `Execute()` method in action updating, inserting and deleting records:

```
var adoConnection = Server.CreateObject("ADODB.Connection");
adoConnection.Open("DSN=CompBitsCoDB");

adoConnection.Execute("UPDATE Stock SET NumberInStock = 5 WHERE StockId = 2");
adoConnection.Execute("DELETE FROM Stock WHERE ItemCost < 5");
adoConnection.Execute("INSERT INTO Stock (ItemDescription, NumberInStock,
   ItemCost) VALUES ('UltraPC',0,5000)");
```

In each case we can see it's simply the SQL statement passed to the `Execute()` method that varies and decides on the action.

Try It Out – Inserting Data

In a previous example we displayed a list of stock, which allowed the customer to buy an item by clicking a link to the `BuyItem.asp` page. We'll now create this `BuyItem.asp` page, within which we create a form asking for the user's details. This form is then submitted to another ASP page where we update the `CustomerOrder` and `OrderItem` database tables.

```
<%@ LANGUAGE = JavaScript%>
<HTML>
<HEAD>
<SCRIPT>

function form1_onsubmit()
{
    var form = document.form1
    var controlCounter;
    var returnValue = true;
    var formControl;

// Check that all text boxes on form have not been left empty by user
// Cancel form post if form is not complete by returning false
    for (controlCounter = 0; controlCounter < form.length; controlCounter++)
    {
        formControl = form.elements[controlCounter];
        if (formControl.type == "text" && formControl.value == "")
        {
            alert("Please complete all of the form");
            formControl.focus();
            returnValue = false;
            break;
        }
    }

    return returnValue;
}

</SCRIPT>
</HEAD>
<BODY>
Please enter your customer details
<BR>
<FORM ACTION="AddOrderDetails.asp" METHOD=POST NAME=form1 LANGUAGE=JavaScript
    onsubmit="return form1_onsubmit()">
<INPUT TYPE="hidden" NAME=txtStockId
    VALUE="<%=Request.QueryString("StockId")%>">
Name
<BR>
<INPUT TYPE="text" NAME=txtCustomerName MAXLENGTH=50>
<BR>
Address
<BR>
<INPUT TYPE="text" NAME=txtCustomerAddress MAXLENGTH=255>
<BR>
```

```
Telephone Number
<BR>
<INPUT TYPE="text" NAME=txtTelNumber MAXLENGTH=25>
<BR>
<INPUT TYPE="submit" VALUE="Send Order" ID=submit1 NAME=submit1>
</FORM>

</BODY>
</HTML>
```

Save this page as `BuyItem.asp` in the same directory as `DisplayStock.asp` from the previous example. This page enables the user to enter their name, address and telephone number. When they have done this, they submit their details, which are posted to the next page, `AddOrderDetails.asp`, shown below:

```
<%@ LANGUAGE = JavaScript%>
<HTML>
<HEAD>
</HEAD>
<BODY>
<%
    // Array to hold names of months
    // used for creating date in format day month year
    var month = new Array("Jan","Feb","Mar","Apr","May","Jun","Jul",
        "Aug","Sep","Oct","Nov","Dec");
    var nowDate = new Date();
    var nowDate = nowDate.getDate() + " " + month[nowDate.getMonth()] + " " +
        nowDate.getFullYear();
    var orderNo;

    // Connect to database
    var adoConnection = Server.CreateObject("ADODB.Connection");
    adoConnection.Open("DSN=CompBitsCoDB");
    var adoRecordset;

    // Create SQL to insert new order into CustomerOrder table
    var mySQL = "INSERT INTO CustomerOrder " +
        "(CustomerName, CustomerAddress, TelNumber, OrderDate)";
    mySQL = mySQL + " VALUES ('" + Request.Form("txtCustomerName") + "','";
    mySQL = mySQL + Request.Form("txtCustomerAddress") + "','";
    mySQL = mySQL + Request.Form("txtTelNumber") + "','";
    mySQL = mySQL + nowDate + "')";

    // Execute SQL to add new order
    adoConnection.Execute(mySQL);

    // Create SQL to get autonumber generated OrderNo from CustomerOrder table
    // for order just added
    mySQL = "SELECT Max(OrderNo) AS MaxOrderNo FROM CustomerOrder WHERE ";
    mySQL = mySQL + " OrderDate = #" + nowDate + "# AND ";
    mySQL = mySQL + " CustomerName = '" + Request.Form("txtCustomerName") + "'";
    // Populate recordset with SQL to get OrderNo
    adoRecordset = adoConnection.Execute(mySQL);

    orderNo = adoRecordset("MaxOrderNo").Value;

    // Recordset not needed after this so close it and allow release of memory
    adoRecordset.Close();
    adoRecordset = null;
```

```
      // Create SQL to insert item ordered into OrderItem table
      var mySQL = "INSERT INTO OrderItem (OrderNo, StockId, QtyOrdered)"
      mySQL = mySQL + " VALUES (" + orderNo + ","
      mySQL = mySQL + Request.Form("txtStockId") + ","
      mySQL = mySQL + "1)"

      // Execute SQL to insert details of order item purchased
      adoConnection.Execute(mySQL);

      // No more database access
      // so close connection and indicate memory no longer needed
      adoConnection.Close();
      adoConnection = null;

      Response.Write("<H2><CENTER>Your order was completed successfully" +
        "</CENTER></H2>");
  %>
  </BODY>
  </HTML>
```

Save this page as `AddOrderDetails.asp`, again in the same directory as `DisplayStock.asp`.

Start by browsing to the `DisplayStock.asp` page on your web server, using the URL:

```
http://localhost/AWalkOnTheServerSide/DisplayStock.asp
```

Click on any of the Buy this links to buy that item. You'll be taken to the customer form where you can enter your details. Notice that the `StockId` in the database for the item you clicked is added to the URL so that the page knows what item you clicked.

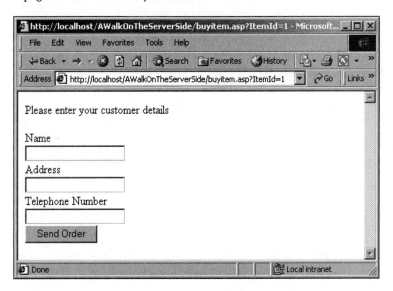

Then, when the Send Order button is clicked, the order is posted to another page, `AddOrderDetails.asp`, which enters the customer and order details into the relevant database tables, and displays a confirmation message to the user:

Check the database tables to see that your details have been added to both the `CustomerOrder` and `Order` tables.

How It Works

The way the code in the `BuyItem.asp` page works should be fairly familiar to us. The page starts with the familiar line, specifying that the script within the page is written in JavaScript:

```
<%@ LANGUAGE = JavaScript%>
```

Then within the head of the page, we define the `form1_onsubmit()` function. We will discuss this shortly.

Within the body of the page we have a form. The first control within this form is a hidden field. We saw how these worked in Chapter 6. It is identical to a text box, except that the `TYPE` attribute is set to `hidden` and therefore is not visible to the user on the browser. It allows us to store values in it and these values are then submitted along with the rest of the form when the user hits the submit button.

```
<INPUT TYPE="hidden" NAME=txtStockId
    VALUE="<%=Request.QueryString("StockId")%>">
```

This hidden field is used to transfer the `StockId` of the item the customer is buying to the current page and also to send this value to the next page. We include the `StockId` in a hidden field on the form so that when the form is posted, the `StockId` is posted as well. The `StockId` itself was included in the URL by being placed at the end of the hyperlink as an item of data with name `StockId`. We can see this from the code snippet from `DisplayStock.asp` that created the URL:

```
<A HREF="buyitem.asp?StockId=<%=adoRecordSet("StockId").Value%>">
```

We use the `Request` object's `QueryString` property to extract the value from the URL.

The form also contains three text boxes, which the user is asked to fill with their name, address, and telephone number. The final control in the form is a submit button, which tries to submit the form when clicked.

However, within the definition of the `<FORM>` element, the `onsubmit` event handler is connected to the `form1_onsubmit()` function, which we will take a closer look at now.

The `form1_onsubmit()` function does a basic validation that checks that all the text fields in the form are filled in. We start by defining four variables:

```
function form1_onsubmit()
{
    var form = document.form1
    var controlCounter;
    var returnValue = true;
    var formControl;
```

Next, as we can see from the code below, we use the `elements` array property of the `Form` object and a `for` loop to go through each control in the form in turn. Within the `for` loop, we first check whether the control is a text control and whether its value is empty. If any text control is found to be empty, we alert the user, set the focus of the page to the empty control, and set the `returnValue` to `false` to prevent the form being posted:

```
    for (controlCounter = 0; controlCounter < form.length; controlCounter++)
    {
        formControl = form.elements[controlCounter];
        if (formControl.type == "text" && formControl.value == "")
        {
            alert("Please complete all of the form");
            formControl.focus();
            returnValue = false;
            break;
        }
    }

    return returnValue;
}
```

We'll now turn to the `AddOrderDetails.asp` page, to which the form in `BuyItem.asp` is posted and where all the database action can be found. As usual, we start the page with the JavaScript language declaration.

In the `AddOrderDetails.asp` page we want to insert the customer and order details into the relevant tables in the database, based on the values posted from the form.

Within the body of the page, we start by getting today's date that will be inserted into the `OrderDate` field of the `CustomerOrder` table:

```
    var month = new Array("Jan","Feb","Mar","Apr","May","Jun","Jul",
        "Aug","Sep","Oct","Nov","Dec");
    var nowDate = new Date();
    var nowDate = nowDate.getDate() + " " + month[nowDate.getMonth()] + " " +
        nowDate.getFullYear();
```

We want to insert a date in the `OrderDate` field in the form 1 Jan 2000, the reason being that this avoids any issues of date format. For example in the USA 1/11/2000 is 11 Jan 2000, but a server in the UK would see this as 1 Nov 2000. Since the `Date` object's `getMonth()` method returns only numbers from 0 to 11 for the month, we need to convert this value to a three letter month. By defining an array of month names in order, then using the result of the `getMonth()` function as the array index, we get the name of the current month.

Next we declare another variable, and then create an ADO `Connection` object and make a connection, using ODBC, to our database. We also declare a variable to hold the `adoRecordset` object we'll be using shortly:

```
var orderNo;

var adoConnection = Server.CreateObject("ADODB.Connection");
adoConnection.Open("DSN=CompBitsCoDB");
var adoRecordset;
```

Our next block of code shown below inserts the new customer order record into the `CustomerOrder` table:

```
var mySQL = "INSERT INTO CustomerOrder " +
    "(CustomerName, CustomerAddress, TelNumber, OrderDate)";
mySQL = mySQL + " VALUES ('" + Request.Form("txtCustomerName") + "','";
mySQL = mySQL + Request.Form("txtCustomerAddress") + "','";
mySQL = mySQL + Request.Form("txtTelNumber") + "','";
mySQL = mySQL + nowDate + "')";

adoConnection.Execute(mySQL);
```

We use the variable `mySQL` to build up our SQL string, namely an `INSERT` statement with the inserted values being those passed by the form post. The posted values are retrieved using the `Request.Form()` collection property, which was introduced in Chapter 15. The completed SQL would look something like:

```
INSERT INTO CustomerOrder (CustomerName, CustomerAddress, TelNumber, OrderDate)
VALUES ('Paul','Some Town','1234 56789','6 Jun 2000')
```

This SQL query is then executed against the database using the `Connection` object's `Execute()` method.

Inserting details of the item ordered into the `OrderItem` table is a little more difficult. We first need to know the `OrderNo` for the record, which was generated automatically when we inserted the new record into the `CustomerOrder` table.

The auto numbering of the `OrderNo` is sequential, so by selecting the highest (`Max`) `OrderNo` number for the relevant customer name on today's date in the `CustomerOrder` table, we can be fairly sure of getting the `OrderNo` just created for this customer. Therefore we build up the following SQL code:

```
mySQL = "SELECT Max(OrderNo) AS MaxOrderNo FROM CustomerOrder WHERE ";
mySQL = mySQL + " OrderDate = #" + nowDate + "# AND ";
mySQL = mySQL + " CustomerName = '" + Request.Form("txtCustomerName") + "'";
```

However, while this is OK for our example, it would not be acceptable for a real online ordering system where there were thousands of concurrent users adding orders. The chance of someone with the same name making an order at the same time is slim, but possible.

The SQL created in `mySQL` will be something like:

```
SELECT Max(OrderNo) AS MaxOrderNo FROM CustomerOrder WHERE OrderDate = #6 Jun
2000# AND CustomerName = 'Paul'
```

The SQL `Max()` function returns the highest number in a recordset. The `AS MaxOrderNo` part of the statement simply gives the value returned by `Max(OrderNo)` an alias which allow us to access the value and store it in variable `orderNo`. Note also that Access is unusual in that it wants dates delimited by the `#` character rather than quotes as in JavaScript.

We now run this SQL query using the `Execute()` method of the `Connection` object, storing the resulting `Recordset` object in the variable `adoRecordset`. In the following line we extract the value that we require, and store it in the variable `orderNo`. Finally, we close the `Recordset` object, and set the variable `adoRecordset` to `null`, freeing up the memory space:

```
adoRecordset = adoConnection.Execute(mySQL);

orderNo = adoRecordset("MaxOrderNo").Value;

adoRecordset.Close();
adoRecordset = null;
```

Finally, we add the details of the item ordered to the `OrderItem` table. We first build up our SQL statement:

```
var mySQL = "INSERT INTO OrderItem (OrderNo, StockId, QtyOrdered)";
mySQL = mySQL + " VALUES (" + orderNo + ",";
mySQL = mySQL + Request.Form("txtStockId") + ",";
mySQL = mySQL + "1)";
```

The SQL that we build up will be something resembling:

```
INSERT INTO OrderItem (OrderNo, StockId, QtyOrdered) VALUES (20,5,1)
```

We then run the query against the database using the `Execute()` method. No `Recordset` object is returned since we are inserting data.

```
adoConnection.Execute(mySQL);
```

Finally we close the database connection and allow the `Connection` object to be released from memory:

```
adoConnection.Close();
adoConnection = null;

Response.Write("<H2><CENTER>Your order was completed successfully" +
   "</CENTER></H2>");
```

We've also added a `Response.Write()` to send a message informing the user of their successful order.

Although our example has many limitations, it does show the basics of how online ordering might work. Clearly a lot more needs to be added to make it a robust and complete system. At the moment we only allow one quantity of one particular item to be ordered. Also we take no payment details, so this would be the biggest loss making e-shop ever and that's saying something! Finally, we don't even deduct the item purchased from our stock.

It's time now to return one last time to the trivia quiz.

Trivia Quiz

Our final change to the trivia quiz is to use a database to supply the questions, rather than client-side arrays. We'll be using many of the principles of the client-side version of the quiz, so, while there are a lot of changes to make, the actual logic remains mostly the same. It's just the location of the information for the questions that's altered.

Of course, our first job is to create a database to hold the questions.

Trivia Quiz Database

In the previous chapter we made our first use of server-side scripting in the trivia quiz. In this chapter we build on that and use server-side script to access a database that contains all the questions and answers for our quiz, data that previously we kept client-side in arrays. Arrays are fine up to a point, but can you imagine how big our pages would be if we had 1000 or more questions in the quiz? Also, the code starts to become unmanageable; trying to add or edit questions involves modifying vast lines of code. Additionally, if the information is in a database it makes it possible for people without JavaScript skills to add, delete, and modify questions. We could even write a web page that provide that functionality wrapped up in an easy to use interface, so they would not even need to understand databases.

Creating the TriviaQuestions Database

We'll be using Microsoft Access again for our database. This time we are connecting using OLE DB and specifying the file location, rather than creating an ODBC data source and specifying that.

Before we create the database, let's first look at the table structure. The database will be nice and simple, just two tables.

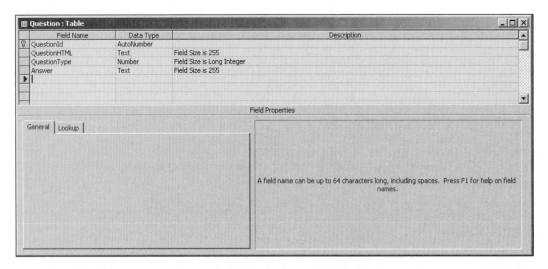

The first table is the Question table, shown above. This contains all the questions and answers for our quiz. It'll consist of four fields, QuestionId, QuestionHTML, QuestionType, and Answer. The QuestionId is an AutoNumber field and will allow us to uniquely identify a question, which will be useful when we come to look up the answer. QuestionHTML contains the text of the question such as "What is Homer Simpson's favorite food?"

Some questions require just a text answer typed into a text box. Others, such as Homer's favorite food question, are multi-choice questions. The field `QuestionType` will contain a number indicating the type of question, such as plain text or multi-choice, which that record deals with.

Finally in the `Answer` field, we either store a letter for the correct multi-choice answer, or a regular expression, which should match the correct text-based answer.

If the question is a multi-choice question, then we'll include each of the options given to the user in a second table, the `QuestionOptions` table shown below:

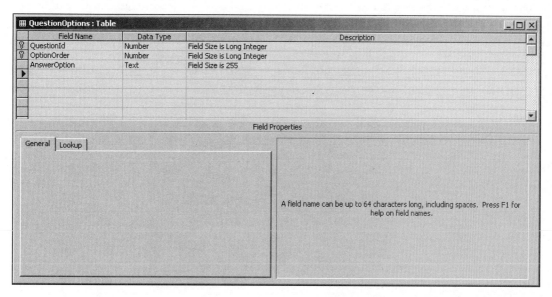

Each answer option for a multi-choice question has its own record in the `QuestionOptions` table. For example, if in the `Question` table we have "What is Homer's favorite food", records in the `QuestionOptions` table might include doughnuts, apples, fresh salad, and so on.

We can see that the first field in this table is the `QuestionId`. The value in this field for a particular record will be the same as the value in the `QuestionId` field of the question record in the `Question` table that this option is a possible answer for.

We've used the `OptionOrder` field of the `QuestionOptions` table to specify the order for the options for any particular question. Finally, the text displayed to the user for each option is given in the `AnswerOption` field.

The big question is, "Why not have just one table and put all the options in there?"

We could define extra fields in the `Question` table, for example an `Option1` field, `Option2` field and so on, and then store all the possible multi-choice options in these fields. However, there are problems with this. Firstly, text-based questions don't have options, so the extra fields would be wasted for these questions. Secondly, how many option fields should we define? Three? Four? Five?

If, for some strange reason, we decide later that we want to have some questions with eight options, then we have to go back to the database and add extra fields, which for most of the time are not used.

715

By including the options as rows in another table, we help reduce redundant fields and we can choose to have as many or few options for each question as we like. After all, options are just rows or records in the QuestionOptions table. We'll also see later that having a separate table for the options makes the programming a little easier. We can create the options in the page by just looping through a recordset from the QuestionOptions table until we hit Eof, rather than having to find some way of guessing how many fields are used and how many are redundant.

Having looked at the table structure, let's make a start on creating the database and its tables.

Our first task is to open up Access. At the initial start up dialog box select the Blank Access database option and click OK:

In the next dialog box we're given the option to name and save the database. Call it TriviaQuestions.mdb. I've saved mine in the C:\Temp directory, but any directory is fine. Remember where you save the database, as its location will be used in the web pages later. Click Create when you've finished:

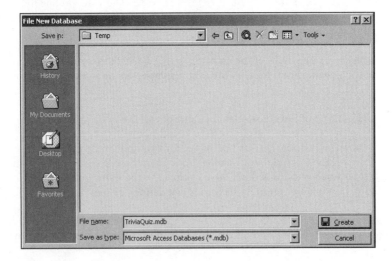

This takes us to the main database view with the **Tables** tab selected under **Objects**:

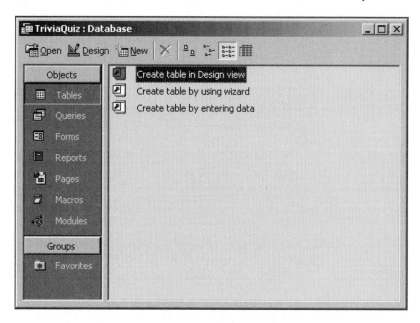

We'll create both of our tables by double-clicking the **Create table in Design view** option.

Create the `Question` table first. The fields are shown below along with suggested field sizes, which you need to change under the **General** tab:

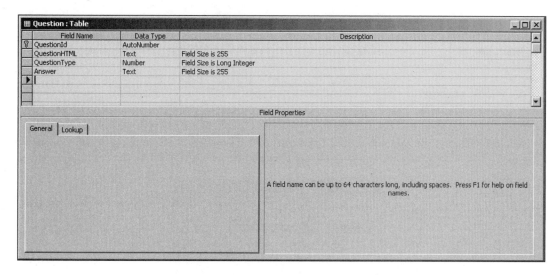

Make the `QuestionId` field a primary key by clicking on the field, then clicking the primary key icon in the tool bar (the yellow key icon). Finally, save the table and close it.

Now create the `QuestionOptions` table in the same way. Its fields are shown below:

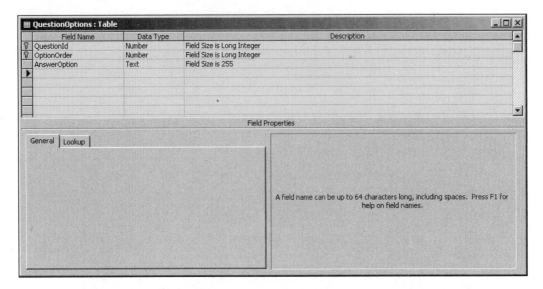

This time we'll make two fields into a primary key. Click the gray box to the very left of the `QuestionId` field, then keeping the *Ctrl* key pressed down, click the gray box next to the `OptionOrder` field; both rows should be blocked in black. Now click the primary key icon in the tool bar and both fields should become part of a primary key, each with a key icon next to them as above.

Why do we need to make both fields part of the primary key? Why not just the `QuestionId` field?

We'll be storing a number of options for each question, so the same `QuestionId` will appear in a number of records. Primary keys must be unique, so the `QuestionId` field on its own can't be a primary key. However, `QuestionId` and `OptionOrder` combined do provide the uniqueness we need to define a primary key.

Save the table, and then close it.

Our next task is to define the relationships between the two tables.

Select the **Relationships** option from the **Tools** menu. As it's the first time we've opened the diagram we'll be given the chance to add our two tables to the diagram. Add both tables then click the **Close** button:

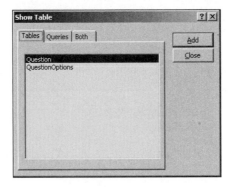

With the **Relationships** diagram now open and our two tables displayed, click on the `QuestionId` field in the `Question` table and, holding the mouse button down, drag over to the `QuestionId` field in the `QuestionOptions` table, then let go. The **Edit Relationships** dialog box should appear as below. Make sure you tick the **Enforce Referential Integrity** box. Doing so will prevent there ever being question option records in the `QuestionOptions` table for which there are no questions.

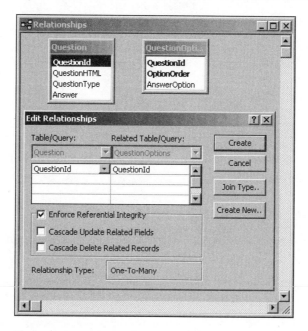

Finally click the **Create** button to create the new relationship. Save the diagram and close it to return to the table objects view.

All that's left is to put some questions in the database.

Open the `Question` table in datasheet view by double-clicking the Question table and enter the questions as shown below. The questions are identical to those in the `questions[]` array that we have used in previous versions of the trivia quiz. Be careful entering the answers, since they only need to be one character out for whatever the user answers to be wrong.

	QuestionId	QuestionHTML	QuestionType	Answer
⊞	1	What is Homer Simpson's favorite food?	1	2
⊞	2	The Beatles were	1	1
⊞	3	Lisa Simpson plays which musical instrument	1	3
⊞	4	In the Simpsons, Bleeding Gums Murphy played which instrument	2	^ ?sax(ophone)?\b
▶ ⊞	5	Which American President was involved in the Watergate Scandal?	2	^ *((Richard |R\.? ?)(Milhous |M\.?)?)?Nixon\b
*	(AutoNumber)		0	

Finally, add the data for the QuestionOptions table:

QuestionId	OptionOrder	AnswerOption
1	1	Fresh Salad
1	2	Doughnuts
1	3	Bread and Water
1	4	Apples
2	1	A sixties rock group from Liverpool
2	2	Four musically gifted insects
2	3	I don't know - can I have the questions on baseball
3	1	Clarinet
3	2	Oboe
3	3	Saxophone
3	4	Tubular Bells
0	0	

That completes the database's creation and population with questions. Now it's time to look at the changes to the trivia quiz's web pages.

Changes to the Trivia Quiz Logic

Although most of the logic for the Trivia Quiz has stayed the same, the screen flow and methods of passing data will be changed.

The frameset structure will remain the same as it has been since Chapter 7, but new pages will be added that load into the fraQuizPage frame.

Let's look at what happens when a user first clicks to start a quiz and answers the first question:

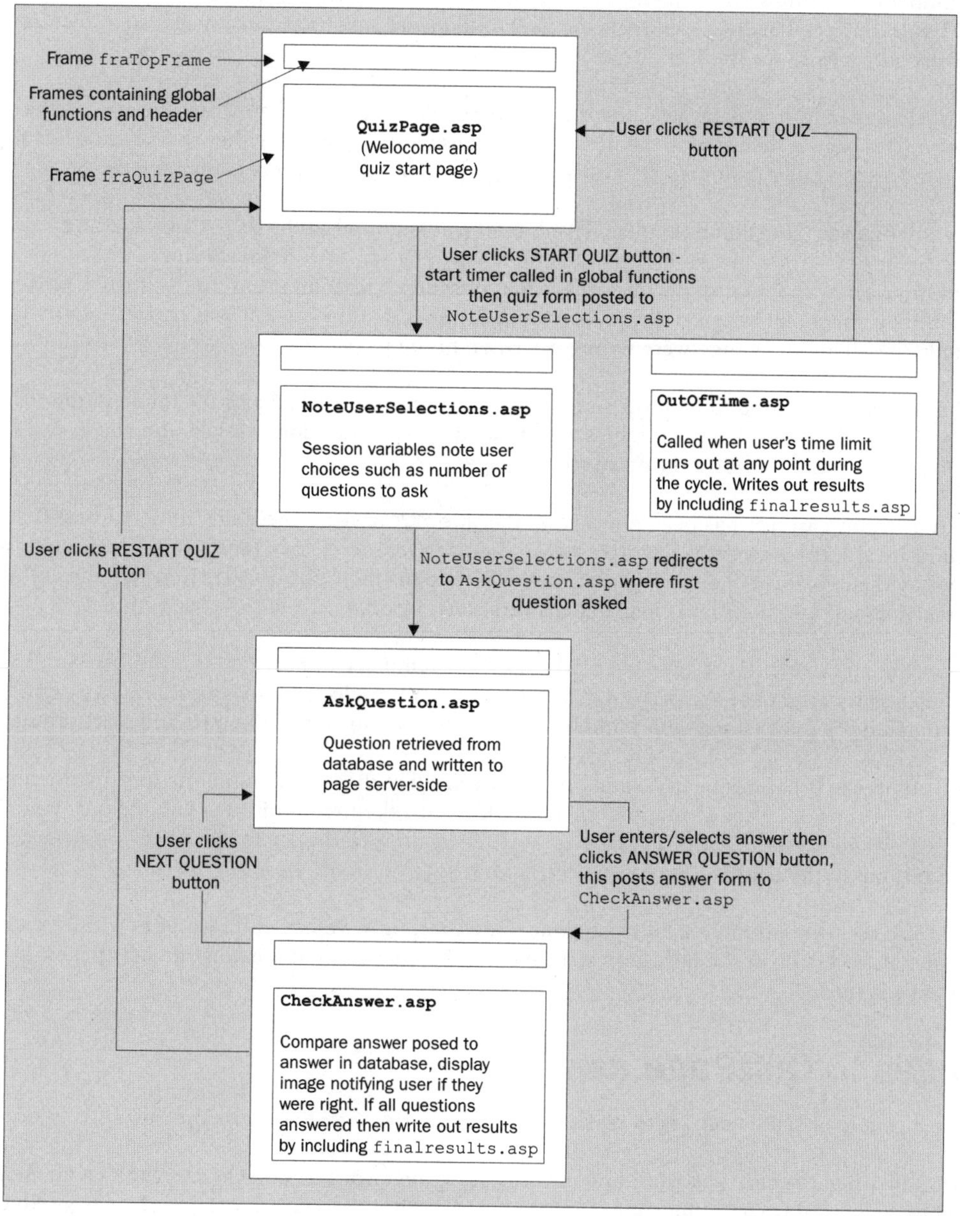

Let's look at each stage in the diagram. First the user browses to the `TriviaQuiz.htm` page on our web site. In the `QuizPage.asp` page loaded into the `fraQuizPage` frame, they select the options for the quiz, such as how many questions they want to answer and in what time limit, from the drop-down lists. Then they click the **Start Quiz** button, which starts a timer going by calling a function in the `Globalfunctions.htm` page in the top frame. Next, the form containing the quiz options is submitted to the `NoteUserSelections.asp` page for processing.

The `NoteUserSelections.asp` page simply resets any session variables holding quiz data, such as the number of questions asked, then notes the user's quiz choices posted by the form in `TriviaQuiz.htm`. Finally, it redirects the user to the `AskQuestion.asp` page, so in fact the user never actually gets to see the `NoteUserSelections.asp` page.

The `AskQuestion.asp` page gets a question from the database, and then writes this out, server-side, to the page. This page is then sent to the user and includes a form in which either radio buttons or a text box enable the user to enter their answer. The form includes a hidden text box containing the `QuestionId`.

When the **Answer Question** button is clicked, the form is posted to the page `CheckAnswer.asp`. Using the `QuestionId` posted in the hidden text box, the server-side JavaScript in `CheckAnswer.asp` looks up the answer for that question and compares it to the answer posted in the form. If they match, an image is displayed telling the user that the answer was correct, otherwise an image letting them know they were wrong is written to the page.

Session variables are used to hold the number of questions to be asked and the total number of questions already asked. These variables are updated as each question is asked and checked within the `AskQuestion.asp` and `CheckAnswer.asp` pages.

After a question's answer has been checked in the `CheckAnswer.asp` page, if there are still more questions to ask, then a button is written out to the page by server-side JavaScript. The button, when clicked by the user, fires client-side JavaScript, which loads the `AskQuestion.asp` page and the whole process of asking questions and checking answers starts again.

If, however, all the questions have been asked, then a summary of how the user did is created by server-side JavaScript in the page `FinalResults.asp` (which is included into `CheckAnswer.asp`) and is written out to the page, along with buttons allowing the user to restart the quiz and reset the statistics.

All this time, the timer has been running that was started at the beginning of the quiz by the function in `GlobalFunctions.htm`. If at any time during the quiz, the time limit runs out, the quiz page is replaced by another page, `OutOfTime.asp`, which again includes `FinalResults.asp` that will write the results out to the page.

As you can see, there is quite a lot to be done. However, now we have an idea of how things will work with the latest version of the quiz, let's start making the changes and creating the new pages, looking at each page in turn.

Changes to QuizPage.asp

We've a couple of small changes to make to the `QuizPage.asp` that starts the quiz off.

Previously, when the quiz was started by the user using the `cmdStartQuiz_onclick()` function, we called a client-side JavaScript function `resetQuiz()` in the `GlobalFunctions.htm` page. In this function, we reset various global client-side variables. However, in this version of the quiz we are moving virtually all of our global client-side variables to the server-side and storing them as session variables.

Because of this, we no longer need to reset client-side variables in the `GlobalFunctions.htm` page so the `resetQuiz()` function can be deleted from there, as we'll do shortly.

Our `cmdStartQuiz_onclick()` function only needs to call the `startTimer()` function in `GlobalFunctions.htm` to start a timer going if the user has selected a time limit, and then submit the quiz start values, that is the number of questions to answer, to an ASP page which will process them server-side.

Change `cmdStartQuiz_onclick()` function inside the page's header so it is as shown below:

```
<HTML>
<HEAD>
<META HTTP-EQUIV="expires" CONTENT="Mon, 1 Jan 1980 00:00:00 GMT">
<SCRIPT LANGUAGE=JavaScript>

function cmdStartQuiz_onclick()
{
    var timeLimit =
document.frmQuiz.cboTimeLimit.options[document.frmQuiz.cboTimeLimit.selectedIndex]
.value
    window.top.fraTopFrame.fraGlobalFunctions.startTimer(timeLimit);
    document.frmQuiz.submit();
}

</SCRIPT>
</HEAD>
```

The first line of our new `cmdStartQuiz_onclick()` function gets the value of the time limit selected by the user from the drop-down list element named `cboTimeLimit`. Remember it's the option that was selected by the user whose value we need. We find out which option is selected using the select control's `selectedIndex` property, the value of which we use to access the selected option in the `options` array.

In the second line we call the `startTimer()` function in the `GlobalFunctions.htm` page, passing the time limit that the user selected as a parameter.

Finally we submit the `frmQuiz` form to the server. In this case our `<FORM>` tag's `ACTION` attribute is `NoteUserSelections.asp` and it's this page that will deal with the quiz startup values.

We've completed the changes to `QuizPage.asp`, so you can save it and close it.

Changes to GlobalFunctions.htm

While we're thinking about the changes to `QuizPage.asp`, we may as well make the knock-on changes to the `GlobalFunctions.htm` page. It is mostly a matter of deleting the majority of the functions, with a few exceptions. We remove all the code defining the questions, along with the `answercorrect()`, `getquestion()`, and `resetquiz()` functions. We add two new functions, `stopTimer()` and `startTimer()`, and make a small change to the `UpdateTimeLeft()` function. Finally we remove the `getCookieValue()` function, and leave the `setCookie()` function unchanged. Here is the new `GlobalFunctions.htm` page in full:

```
<HTML>
<HEAD>
<SCRIPT LANGUAGE=JavaScript>

var timeLeft =-1;
var quizTimerId = 0;
```

```
function stopTimer()
{
   window.clearInterval(quizTimerId)
}

function startTimer(timeLimit)
{
   timeLeft = timeLimit;

   if (timeLimit == -1)
   {
      window.status = "No Time Limit";
   }
   else
   {
      quizTimerId = window.setInterval("updateTimeLeft()",1000);
   }
}

function updateTimeLeft()
{
   timeLeft--;

   if (timeLeft == 0)
   {
      alert("Time's Up");
      window.top.fraQuizPage.location.href = "OutOfTime.asp";
   }
   else
   {
      var minutes = Math.floor(timeLeft / 60);
      var seconds = timeLeft - (60 * minutes);

      if (minutes < 10)
      {
         minutes = "0" + minutes;
      }
      if (seconds < 10)
      {
         seconds = "0" + seconds;
      }
      window.status = "Time left is " + minutes + ":" + seconds;
   }
}

function setCookie(cookieName,cookieValue, cookiePath, cookieExpires)
{
   cookieValue = escape(cookieValue);
   if (cookieExpires == "")
   {
      var nowDate = new Date();
      nowDate.setMonth(nowDate.getMonth() + 3);
      cookieExpires = nowDate.toGMTString();
   }
```

```
    if (cookiePath != "")
    {
        cookiePath = ";Path=" + cookiePath;
    }
    document.cookie = cookieName + "=" + cookieValue +
        ";expires=" + cookieExpires + cookiePath;
}

</SCRIPT>
</HTML>
```

Let's look at the two new functions, stopTimer() and startTimer(); the names give away what they actually do.

The function stopTimer() uses the clearInterval() method of the window object to stop the firing of the quiz timer every second. This function is called either when the time limit is up or when the user has completed the quiz. It is called by a new page that we'll be creating shortly, which deals with the end of the quiz.

The function startTimer() is based on code in the resetQuiz() function, which has now been removed, so you can cut and paste it from there. The function's only parameter is the time limit, in seconds, that the user selected to complete the quiz in. The code checks to see what this time limit is. If it's -1, which indicates that no time limit has been selected, we write "No Time Limit" to the status bar. If a time limit has been selected, then we start the timer going by using the window object's setInterval() method so that every second the updateTimer() function is called.

Our next change is to the upDateTimeLeft() function and is just a one line change. When the time limit expires, we re-direct the user to the page OutOfTime.asp, where server-side script will create a summary of the user's results and display a button allowing them to restart the quiz. We'll be creating OutOfTime.asp shortly. Recall that, previously, we redirected the user to AskQuestion.htm, and the results-displaying functionality was bound up in the getQuestion() function in GlobalFunctions.htm which was called from there.

Save the GlobalFunctions.htm page and close it; we have no more changes to make to it.

Changes to NoteUserSelections.asp

The final change as far as the quiz starting goes is to the page NoteUserSelections.asp, which we created in Chapter 15:

```
<%@ LANGUAGE = JavaScript%>

<%
    Session("NoQsToAsk") = parseInt(Request.Form("cboNoQuestions"));
    Session("TimeLimit") = parseInt(Request.Form("cboTimeLimit"));
    Session("totalQuestionsAsked") = 0;
    Session("AskedQuestions") = "0";
    Session("numberOfQuestionsCorrect") = 0;

    Response.Redirect("AskQuestion.asp");
%>
```

All the data previously held client-side in the GlobalFunctions.htm page, such as how many questions to ask, how many have been asked, how many the user has got right and so on, are initialized and stored server-side in this page. We've used session variables, stored in the Session object, to keep track of these essential quiz variables.

Once the global quiz data has been stored, we redirect, using Response.Redirect(), to the AskQuestion.asp page, which we'll look at next.

Asking a Question – Changing AskQuestion.htm

Previously, questions were posed in the AskQuestion.htm page. Being an .htm page, we're not able to do any server-side processing inside it. Now that we need to access the questions from a server-side database, we need to change the AskQuestion page's file extension to .asp so that our web server will read through it before sending it to the client and process any server-side script.

Having re-saved the page as AskQuestion.asp, let's look at the changes we need to make to the page:

```
<%@ LANGUAGE = JavaScript%>
<HTML>
<HEAD>
<META HTTP-EQUIV="Expires" CONTENT="1 Jan 1980">
</HEAD>

<BODY BACKGROUND="bluewashqs.jpg">
<TABLE ALIGN=center BORDER="2" WIDTH="70%">
<TR>
<TD BGCOLOR=RoyalBlue>
<FORM NAME="QuestionForm" METHOD=post ACTION="CheckAnswer.asp">

<%
    Session("totalQuestionsAsked")= parseInt(Session("totalQuestionsAsked")) + 1;
    var questionId;
    var mySQL;
    var adoConnection = Server.CreateObject("ADODB.Connection")
    adoConnection.Open("Provider=Microsoft.Jet.OLEDB.4.0;Data" +
        " Source=C:\\Temp\\TriviaQuestions.mdb")

    mySQL = "SELECT TOP 1 QuestionId, QuestionHTML, QuestionType FROM Question ";
    mySQL = mySQL + " WHERE QuestionId NOT IN (" +
        Session("AskedQuestions") + ")";
    var adoRecordset = adoConnection.Execute(mySQL);

    questionId = adoRecordset("QuestionId").Value;
    Session("AskedQuestions") = Session("AskedQuestions") + "," + questionId;

    if (adoRecordset("QuestionType").Value == 1)
    {
        mySQL = "SELECT OptionOrder, AnswerOption FROM QuestionOptions ";
        mySQL = mySQL + " WHERE QuestionId = " + questionId;
        mySQL = mySQL + " ORDER BY OptionOrder"
        var adoOptionsRecordset = adoConnection.Execute(mySQL);
    }
```

```
                Response.Write("<H4>Question " + Session("totalQuestionsAsked") + "</H4>");

                Response.Write("<INPUT TYPE=hidden NAME=txtQuestionId" +
                   "VALUE=" + adoRecordset("QuestionId").Value + ">");

                // Check QuestionType field - if 2 then text based question
                if (adoRecordset("QuestionType").Value == 2)
                {
                    Response.Write("<P>" + adoRecordset("QuestionHTML").Value + "</P>");
                    Response.Write("<P><INPUT TYPE=text NAME=txtAnswer");
                    Response.Write(" MAXLENGTH=100 SIZE=35></P>");
                }
                else
                {
                    Response.Write("<P>" + adoRecordset("QuestionHTML").Value + "</P>");
                    while (adoOptionsRecordset.Eof == false)
                    {
                        Response.Write("<INPUT TYPE=radio NAME=radQuestionChoice");
                        if (adoOptionsRecordset("OptionOrder").Value == 1)
                        {
                            Response.Write(" CHECKED");
                        }
                        Response.Write(" VALUE=" + adoOptionsRecordset("OptionOrder").Value);
                        Response.Write(">" + adoOptionsRecordset("AnswerOption"));
                        Response.Write("<BR>");
                        adoOptionsRecordset.MoveNext();
                    }

                    adoOptionsRecordset.Close()
                    adoOptionsRecordset = null;
                }

                adoRecordset.Close();
                adoRecordset = null;
                adoConnection.Close();
                adoConnection == null;
        %>
        <BR>
        <INPUT TYPE="submit" VALUE="Answer Question" ID=submit1 NAME=submit1>
        </FORM>
        </TD>
        </TR>
        </TABLE>
        </BODY>
        </HTML>
```

As we can see, it's pretty much a whole new page bearing little resemblance to its previous client-side only incarnation. However, we'll see that much of its logic and code is actually borrowed from the now defunct client-side getQuestion() function, that we just deleted from the GlobalFunctions.htm page.

In the previous incarnation of the page, the body of the page held a form, inside which the getQuestion() function was called, which wrote the trivia quiz question to the page. In the new page, the body still contains a form, but the form contains a block of server-side script, which accesses our database, and writes the quiz question to the page.

727

We add two attributes to the <FORM> definition – method that we give the value post, and action that we give the value CheckAnswer.asp. Thus, when the form is submitted, it will be posted to CheckAnswer.asp, which will check the user's answer to the question. We will look at this in more detail in the next section.

```
<FORM NAME="QuestionForm" METHOD=post ACTION="CheckAnswer.asp">
```

Now let's look at the server-side script block contained within the form:

```
<%
    Session("totalQuestionsAsked") =
        parseInt(Session("totalQuestionsAsked")) + 1;
```

As shown above, we start the script block by incrementing the Session variable totalQuestionsAsked, which is used to keep track of the number of questions that the user has answered.

```
    var questionId;
    var mySQL;
    var adoConnection = Server.CreateObject("ADODB.Connection")
    adoConnection.Open("Provider=Microsoft.Jet.OLEDB.4.0;" +
        "Data Source=C:\\Temp\\TriviaQuestions.mdb")
```

Next, after declaring two variables, we create an ADO Connection object, which will be used to connect to our TriviaQuestions database. We then open a connection using the Open() method of the Connection object.

Note that here we are using OLE DB rather than ODBC to connect to the database. This means we don't need to create an ODBC data source as we did in previous examples. In practice, an ODBC data source would be fine – I just want to demonstrate the OLE DB way. If you've put your database in a directory other than C:\Temp, then you'll need to change the last line shown to point to the relevant directory. Note that we use two back slashes rather than one when specifying the directory path. Remember that in strings a single back slash is a special character, an escape character, which allows unprintable characters to be embedded in a string. So to tell JavaScript that the escape character is in fact an actual back slash we need to use the first back slash as an escape character and the second to indicate the special character being inserted is a back slash.

In the next two lines we create the SQL we want to execute against the database, then use the Connection object's Execute() method to run it.

```
    mySQL = "SELECT TOP 1 QuestionId, QuestionHTML, QuestionType FROM Question ";
    mySQL = mySQL + " WHERE QuestionId NOT IN (" +
        Session("AskedQuestions") + ")";
    var adoRecordset = adoConnection.Execute(mySQL);
```

The SQL statement itself simply returns a question from the database. We only want one question, so we've used the TOP SQL statement, which tells the database we just want the TOP, or first, record from the recordset. Note that this means that we get the questions in the same order every time we run the quiz, unlike the random order of the client-side version. However, once you've completed the chapter you might want to go back and write code that gets a random question.

To avoid getting the same question twice, we use a WHERE clause and the SQL NOT IN statement. The NOT IN statement simply compares the values of the QuestionId field in the Question table to a list of values and only picks records whose QuestionId is not in that list. For example:

```
SELECT TOP 1 QuestionId, QuestionHTML, QuestionType FROM Question ";
WHERE QuestionId NOT IN (1,2,3)
```

will not return any records whose QuestionId is 1 or 2 or 3.

Each time we ask a question we make a note of it in the session variable AskedQuestions and it's this that provides the list for the NOT IN statement.

When the SQL is run against the database, the record returned by our SELECT query is returned inside a Recordset object whose value we store in the adoRecordset variable.

It's the next two lines of code that retrieve the QuestionId from the recordset and update the session variable AskedQuestions:

```
questionId = adoRecordset("QuestionId").Value;
Session("AskedQuestions") = Session("AskedQuestions") + "," + questionId;
```

If the question returned by our SQL query is a multi-choice type of question, that is the QuestionType field has value 1, then we need to get the multi-choice options for this question from the QuestionOptions table. We do this in the next lines, shown below:

```
if (adoRecordset("QuestionType").Value == 1)
{
   mySQL = "SELECT OptionOrder, AnswerOption FROM QuestionOptions ";
   mySQL = mySQL + " WHERE QuestionId = " + questionId;
   mySQL = mySQL + " ORDER BY OptionOrder"
   var adoOptionsRecordset = adoConnection.Execute(mySQL);
}
```

As you can see, we create another SQL SELECT query, which gets all the possible options for a multi-choice question, and execute that against the database, this time storing the returned recordset in the variable adoOptionsRecordset.

Now we've got all the information we need from the database, it's time to write our question to the page.

We start by writing out the question number, which is contained in totalQuestionsAsked session variable. Recall that this was updated at the very start of the server-side script block. We also write out a hidden form element with the QuestionId in it. This will be used by the CheckAnswer.asp page when the form is posted to it to look up the actual answer to the question, so that the user's answer can be checked against it.

```
Response.Write("<H4>Question " + Session("totalQuestionsAsked") + "</H4>");

Response.Write("<INPUT TYPE=hidden NAME=txtQuestionId" +
   "VALUE=" + adoRecordset("QuestionId").Value + ">");
```

We next need to write out the question to the page. There are two types of question: ones requiring a text-based answer via a text box and ones where the user selects an answer from a list of possible answers. These can be distinguished by the value for the `QuestionType` field. We deal with text box questions first:

```
if (adoRecordset("QuestionType").Value == 2)
{
    Response.Write("<P>" + adoRecordset("QuestionHTML").Value + "</P>");
    Response.Write("<P><INPUT TYPE=text NAME=txtAnswer");
    Response.Write("MAXLENGTH=100 SIZE=35></P>");
}
```

If the `QuestionType` field is 2, then we know it is a text box answer. We write the question itself to the page based on the `QuestionHTML` field in the recordset, and then we write out the text box.

We next come on to multi-choice questions, which are a bit more complex. If it was a multi-choice type of question, that is if the `QuestionType` field is 1, then we need to first write out the question using the `QuestionHTML` field in the recordset:

```
else
{
    Response.Write("<P>" + adoRecordset("QuestionHTML").Value + "</P>");
```

Then, using the records in the `adoOptionsRecordset`, we need to write out each of the possible options with a radio button enabling the user to select what they think is the right answer. We don't know how many options there might be, so we simply loop through the `adoOptionsRecordset` recordset with a `while` loop, using `MoveNext()` to go to the next record or option:

```
while (adoOptionsRecordset.Eof == false)
{
    Response.Write("<INPUT TYPE=radio NAME=radQuestionChoice");
    if (adoOptionsRecordset("OptionOrder").Value == 1)
    {
        Response.Write(" CHECKED");
    }
    Response.Write(" VALUE=" + adoOptionsRecordset("OptionOrder").Value);
    Response.Write(">" + adoOptionsRecordset("AnswerOption"));
    Response.Write("<BR>");
    adoOptionsRecordset.MoveNext();
}
```

Inside the `while` loop we use `Response.Write()` to write each radio button, represented by `<INPUT TYPE=radio>` to the page. If it's the first radio button, that is if the `OptionOrder` field returned by the recordset is 1, then we add `CHECKED` to the HTML for the radio button thereby ensuring that the first radio button is selected by default when the page is loaded in the user's browser.

Next we complete the radio button's HTML by adding the `VALUE` attribute to its definition, with the value being the `OptionOrder` field from the recordset, which will provide the answer when the form is submitted. Finally we add some text to be displayed after the radio button, which indicates what answer the radio button signifies. For example, for "What is Homer Simpson's favorite food?" we write out "Fresh Salad" for the first radio button, "Doughnuts" for the second, and so on.

730

Finally in the `while` loop, we add an HTML `<BR>` tag so that each radio button goes on a separate line. Also, very importantly, we move to the next record in the `adoOptionsRecordset`. Forget this and the loop will never end, as it will stay on the same record and never actually reach the end of file (`Eof`).

When we've finished looping the `options` recordset, we make sure we close it and set the variable to null to allow the object to be released from memory:

```
    adoOptionsRecordset.Close()
    adoOptionsRecordset = null;
}
```

Finally we close off the `adoRecordset` and also the `Connection` object and set them to `null`:

```
    adoRecordset.Close();
    adoRecordset = null;
    adoConnection.Close();
    adoConnection == null;
%>
```

This ends the server-side script block. At the bottom of the form we have the **Answer Question** button, which submits the answer for checking to `CheckAnswer.asp`. We'll create this page next.

```
<INPUT TYPE="submit" VALUE="Answer Question" ID=submit1 NAME=submit1>
```

We've completed the changes to `AskQuestion.asp` so save and close it in your editor.

Checking the Answer – CheckAnswer.asp

`CheckAnswer.asp` is a completely new page that needs to be created. As its name suggests, it checks the answer submitted by the user in the `AskQuestion.asp` page. It retrieves the answer given in that page, then opens a connection to the database and retrieves the actual answer we have stored there. If they match, the user got the question right and we write an `<IMG>` tag to the page, which displays an image saying they got the answer correct. If the answers don't match, then we write a different `<IMG>` tag to the page and display an image letting the user know they got the answer wrong. You can either use the images in the code download available on the Wrox web site or create them yourself using a paint package.

Let's create the page, and then we'll look at how it works:

```
<%@ LANGUAGE = JavaScript%>
<% Response.Buffer = "True" %>
<HTML>
<HEAD>
</HEAD>
<BODY BACKGROUND="bluewash.jpg">
<%
    var answer;
    var mySQL;
    mySQL = "SELECT QuestionType, Answer FROM Question ";
    mySQL = mySQL + " WHERE QuestionId = " + Request.Form("txtQuestionId");
```

```
    var adoRecordset = Server.CreateObject("ADODB.Recordset");

    adoRecordset.Open(mySQL, "Provider=Microsoft.Jet.OLEDB.4.0;Data" +
                " Source=C:\\Temp\\TriviaQuestions.mdb");

    if (adoRecordset("QuestionType").Value == 2)
    {
        answer = new String(Request.Form("txtAnswer"));
    }
    else
    {
        answer = new String(Request.Form("radQuestionChoice"));
    }

    var answerRegExp = new RegExp(adoRecordset("Answer").Value,"i");

    adoRecordset.Close();
    adoRecordset = null;

    if (answer.search(answerRegExp) != -1)
    {
        Session("numberOfQuestionsCorrect") =
                parseInt(Session("numberOfQuestionsCorrect")) + 1;
%>
        <CENTER><IMG SRC="Correct.gif"></CENTER>
<%
    }
    else
    {
%>
        <CENTER><IMG SRC="Incorrect.gif"></CENTER>
<%
    }

    if (Session("totalQuestionsAsked") != Session("NoQsToAsk"))
    {
%>
        <FORM NAME="quizForm" ACTION="" METHOD="post">
        <INPUT TYPE="button" VALUE="Next Question" NAME=butNext
            onclick="window.location.replace('AskQuestion.asp')">
        </FORM>
<%
    }
    else
    {
%>
        <!-- #include file="FinalResults.asp" -->
<%
    }
%>

</FONT>
</BODY>
</HTML>
```

Once you have finished typing in the code, save it as `CheckAnswer.asp`.

The page starts with the usual declaration of server-side code being written in JavaScript:

```
<%@ LANGUAGE = JavaScript%>
```

Note also the use of the following line:

```
<% Response.Buffer = "True" %>
```

This sets the `Response` object's `Buffer` property to `True`. We need to do this because this page makes use of cookies (in the file `FinalResults.asp`, which is included into this page with a `#include` directive) that must be set in the header of the page. Buffering means that the server composes the whole page before it is sent to the user's browser. In ASP 3.0, buffering is set by default to `True`, but in ASP 2.0 it is set to `False`. If the page isn't buffered, then the header would have already be sent by the time the server was reading the code that sets the cookies and we would encounter errors. So, to make sure that our code will work on all Microsoft servers, we include this line.

Then, within the body of the page, we have a block of server-side script. The first task of this script is to open the database, look in the `Question` table, and get the correct answer to the question just asked. We know the `QuestionId` of the current question since that is passed inside the form just submitted.

```
<%
    var answer;
    var mySQL;
    mySQL = "SELECT QuestionType, Answer FROM Question ";
    mySQL = mySQL + " WHERE QuestionId = " + Request.Form("txtQuestionId");

    var adoRecordset = Server.CreateObject("ADODB.Recordset");
    adoRecordset.Open(mySQL, "Provider=Microsoft.Jet.OLEDB.4.0;Data" +
        " Source=C:\\temp\\TriviaQuestions.mdb")
```

We build up our SQL needed to obtain the answer from the database. In our query we select two fields, the `QuestionType` and the answer to the question. Our `WHERE` statement makes sure that we get the answer for the right question, the `QuestionId` being contained in a hidden text field passed along with the form data.

We don't create a `Connection` object this time, as we only need to connect to the database once. Instead we just use a `Recordset` object to connect to the database and open the recordset with the SQL we just created in `mySQL`.

We now need to retrieve the answer that the user gave for the question. This answer was posted to the `CheckAnswer.asp` page from the form in the `AskQuestion.asp` page. However, the name of the control containing the answer depends on the type of question, text or multi-choice, that was asked. A text answer will have been posted from a `txtAnswer` text box; a multi-choice answer is contained in the value of the `radQuestionChoice` radio button.

If the answer was a text answer, that is, the `QuestionType` field of the `Question` table has value 2, the answer is extracted from the `txtAnswer` text box and placed in the variable called `answer`:

```
    if (adoRecordset("QuestionType").Value == 2)
    {
        answer = new String(Request.Form("txtAnswer"));
    }
```

If the QuestionType field does not have value 2, that is the question is a multi-choice question, the answer is extracted from the radQuestionChoice radio button, and again placed in the variable answer:

```
    else
    {
        answer = new String(Request.Form("radQuestionChoice"));
    }
```

We've now got the answer that the user gave stored in the variable answer. Let's get the correct answer from the Recordset object. Remember that the answer we put in the database is actually a regular expression, so we use the answer in the database as the constructor for a new RegExp object:

```
    var answerRegExp = new RegExp(adoRecordset("Answer").Value,"i");
```

We've finished with our Recordset so let's close it now and remove the reference to the Recordset object, allowing the system to reclaim the memory used:

```
    adoRecordset.Close();
    adoRecordset = null;
```

We now need to check the answer that the user gave, which we've stored in variable answer, against the correct answer that we retrieved from the database and used to create a RegExp object. The method of checking the answer has not changed from when it was client-side in the answerCorrect() function in the GlobalFunctions.htm page.

In the case of multi-choice answers, the regular expression is a simple 1, 2, 3, or 4 for the option number that was correct. For text-based answers, it's a full regular expression.

In the condition of the following if statement, we search the answer variable containing the answer given by the user to see if it matches the correct answer given in answerRegExp. If it does, we write an image to the page, which tells the user that they got the question right and we also update a Session variable keeping note of how many questions have been answered correctly so far. If the answers don't match, we use the else statement to write a different image to the page, telling the user that they got the question wrong:

```
    if (answer.search(answerRegExp) != -1)
    {
        Session("numberOfQuestionsCorrect") =
            parseInt(Session("numberOfQuestionsCorrect")) + 1;
%>
        <CENTER><IMG SRC="Correct.gif"></CENTER>
<%
    }
    else
    {
```

```
%>
        <CENTER><IMG SRC="Incorrect.gif"></CENTER>
<%
    }
```

The final part of our server-side script checks whether the number of questions that have been asked is the same as the total number of questions the user opted to answer at the beginning of the quiz. If more questions need to be asked, we write a button to the page, which will take the user to the AskQuestion.asp page. If there are no more questions to ask, the quiz is over so we write out the results table listing how well the user did on the quiz this time and what their average score is. The code for this table is not contained in this page, but instead is inside the file FinalResults.asp, which we include inside this page using the #include directive we saw in the last chapter.

Why not just include it directly in this page? Well, we'll be reusing the FinalResults.asp page in another page, so to save repetition we create the results code just once, then #include it into the different pages.

```
    if (Session("totalQuestionsAsked") != Session("NoQsToAsk"))
    {
%>
        <FORM NAME="quizForm" ACTION="" METHOD="post">
        <INPUT TYPE="button" VALUE="Next Question" NAME=butNext
            onclick="window.location.replace('AskQuestion.asp')">
        </FORM>
<%
    }
    else
    {
%>
        <!-- #include file="FinalResults.asp" -->
<%
    }
%>
```

We'll look at the FinalResults.asp included file next.

Displaying a Summary of Results

The server-side code and HTML that displays a summary of results at the end of the quiz is contained inside a file called FinalResults.asp. We never actually load this file as a page on its own, but instead include it, using the #include directive, into the CheckAnswer.asp page, which we discussed above, and the OutOfTime.asp page we'll be creating shortly.

Creating FinalResults.asp

Here is the complete FinalResults.asp page. As mentioned in the previous chapter we can use any valid extension for the include file, for example .inc would be fine. However, many HTML editors will recognize .asp as a server-side web file and color-code its syntax among other things. For example, Microsoft Visual InterDev, which I'm using, even gives hints as to the methods and properties of BOM objects like the window object or server-side objects like Response. If it's a .inc file, then no help is given. Also, the .asp extension tells us what to expect inside the code – that it's a web page with server-side code.

Note that you can either use the `quizcomplete.gif` image from the code download or create your own with a paint package.

```
<FORM NAME="quizForm" ACTION="" METHOD="post">

<SCRIPT LANGUAGE=JavaScript>
    window.top.fraTopFrame.fraGlobalFunctions.stopTimer();
</SCRIPT>

<FONT COLOR=darkslateblue FACE="Comic Sans MS">
<P><IMG SRC="quizcomplete.gif"></P>
You got <%=Session("numberOfQuestionsCorrect")%>
questions correct out of <%= Session("NoQsToAsk") %>
<BR><BR>Your trivia rating is

<%
    var numberOfQuestionsCorrect = parseInt(Session("numberOfQuestionsCorrect"));
    var numberOfQuestionsAsked = parseInt(Session("NoQsToAsk"));
    switch(Math.round(((numberOfQuestionsCorrect / numberOfQuestionsAsked)
        * 10)))
    {
        case 0:
        case 1:
        case 2:
        case 3:
            Response.Write("Beyond embarrasing");
            break;
        case 4:
        case 5:
        case 6:
        case 7:
            Response.Write("Average");
            break;
        default:
            Response.Write("Excellent");
    }

    var previousNoCorrect = Math.floor(Request.Cookies("previousNoCorrect"));
    var previousNoAsked = Math.floor(Request.Cookies("previousNoAsked"));
    var currentAvgScore = Math.round(numberOfQuestionsCorrect /
        numberOfQuestionsAsked * 100);

    Response.Write("<BR>The percentage you've " +
        " answered correctly in this quiz is " + currentAvgScore + "%");

    if (previousNoAsked == 0)
    {
        previousNoCorrect = 0;
    }

    previousNoCorrect = previousNoCorrect + numberOfQuestionsCorrect;
    previousNoAsked = previousNoAsked + numberOfQuestionsAsked;

    currentAvgScore = Math.round(previousNoCorrect / previousNoAsked * 100);
```

```
        var nowDate = new Date();
        nowDate.setMonth(nowDate.getMonth() + 3);
        cookieExpires = nowDate.toGMTString();
        cookieExpires = cookieExpires.slice(5,cookieExpires.length - 4);

        Response.Cookies("previousNoAsked") = previousNoAsked;
        Response.Cookies("previousNoAsked").Expires = cookieExpires;

        Response.Cookies("previousNoCorrect") =  previousNoCorrect;
        Response.Cookies("previousNoCorrect").Expires = cookieExpires;

        Response.Cookies("AverageScore") = currentAvgScore;
        Response.Cookies("AverageScore").Expires = cookieExpires;

        Response.Write("<BR>This brings your average todate to " +
            currentAvgScore + "%");

%>

<P>
<INPUT TYPE=button VALUE='Reset Stats' NAME=buttonReset
    onclick="window.top.fraTopFrame.fraGlobalFunctions
        .setCookie('previousNoAsked', 0,'','Mon, 1 Jan 1970')" >

<P>
<INPUT TYPE=button VALUE='Restart Quiz' NAME=buttonRestart
    onclick="window.location.replace('quizpage.asp')" >
</FORM>
```

Save the page as `FinalResults.asp`. This code should look familiar to you. It is simply the same results-displaying code that was in the client-side version of the quiz – it was in the function `getQuestion()` in the `GlobalFunctions.htm` page – but converted to server-side code.

The main changes are that instead of global client-side variables being used to determine how many questions the user has got right out of how many answered, we're instead using session variables on the server. Also, instead of writing the code to the page client-side using `document.write()` we've used `Response.Write()`. We still use cookies to store and access average scores, but now we're using `Response.Cookies` and `Request.Cookies` to store and retrieve the `AverageScore` cookie.

As the logic is identical to what we've already discussed in Chapter 11, we'll just take a brief look at the code.

The first thing to point out is something that's not there, namely the language directive:

```
<%@ LANGUAGE = JavaScript %>
```

The reason is that this file is never loaded on its own, but instead included inside other ASP pages, which do have the language directive.

At the top of the page is some client-side script that calls the `stopTimer()` function in the `GlobalFunctions.htm` page. This causes the time limit counter to stop counting down.

```
<SCRIPT>
    window.top.fraTopFrame.fraGlobalFunctions.stopTimer();
</SCRIPT>
```

Next we display the number of questions the user got right and how many they answered, their values being retrieved from where we stored them in session variables:

```
You got <%=Session("numberOfQuestionsCorrect")%>
questions correct out of <%= Session("NoQsToAsk") %>
```

In the next section of code, this time server-side script, we write out to the page our opinion of how the user did. This is virtually the same code as was in client-side function `getQuestion()` in the `GlobalFunctions.htm` page of the previous version of the quiz. The main difference is the use of `Response.Write()`:

```
<BR><BR>Your trivia rating is

<%
    var numberOfQuestionsCorrect = parseInt(Session("numberOfQuestionsCorrect"));
    var numberOfQuestionsAsked = parseInt(Session("NoQsToAsk"));
    switch(Math.round(((numberOfQuestionsCorrect / numberOfQuestionsAsked)
        * 10)))
    {
        case 0:
        case 1:
        case 2:
        case 3:
            Response.Write("Beyond embarrasing");
            break;
        case 4:
        case 5:
        case 6:
        case 7:
            Response.Write("Average");
            break;
        default:
            Response.Write("Excellent");
    }
```

The final bit of server-side code is again a virtual copy of the client-side version in the `getQuestion()` function. In the code we calculate the percentage score for this quiz and also the average over all quizzes answered so far, or at least since the last time the Reset button was clicked:

```
    var previousNoCorrect = Math.floor(Request.Cookies("previousNoCorrect"));
    var previousNoAsked = Math.floor(Request.Cookies("previousNoAsked"));
    var currentAvgScore = Math.round(numberOfQuestionsCorrect /
        numberOfQuestionsAsked * 100);

    Response.Write("<BR>The percentage you've " +
        " answered correctly in this quiz is " + currentAvgScore + "%");
```

```
    if (previousNoAsked == 0)
    {
        previousNoCorrect = 0;
    }

    previousNoCorrect = previousNoCorrect + numberOfQuestionsCorrect;
    previousNoAsked = previousNoAsked + numberOfQuestionsAsked;

    currentAvgScore = Math.round(previousNoCorrect / previousNoAsked * 100);

    var nowDate = new Date();
    nowDate.setMonth(nowDate.getMonth() + 3);
    cookieExpires = nowDate.toGMTString();
    cookieExpires = cookieExpires.slice(5,cookieExpires.length - 4);

    Response.Cookies("previousNoAsked") = previousNoAsked;
    Response.Cookies("previousNoAsked").Expires = cookieExpires;

    Response.Cookies("previousNoCorrect") =  previousNoCorrect;
    Response.Cookies("previousNoCorrect").Expires = cookieExpires;

    Response.Cookies("AverageScore") = currentAvgScore;
    Response.Cookies("AverageScore").Expires = cookieExpires;

    Response.Write("<BR>This brings your average todate to " +
        currentAvgScore + "%");

%>
```

You can see that the main changes are that we are using `Response.Write()` to write HTML into the page and in the way we read and set our cookies. Previously we were doing this client-side with our `getCookieValue()` and `setCookie()` functions in `GlobalFunctions.htm`. However, now we can use the `Response` object's `Cookies()` collection to set cookie values and `Request` object's `Cookies()` collection to read them.

Finally, instead of writing the controls to the page to reset the quiz stats and restart the quiz we can simply include them directly in the page. Previously the same page was used to write new questions out and also write out the results summary, so we had to use an `if` statement to only write out the controls if this was the final page. However, `FinalResults.asp` only does one thing and that's write a final summary of the results, so we always need to include the controls:

```
<P>
<INPUT TYPE=button VALUE='Reset Stats' NAME=buttonReset
    onclick="window.top.fraTopFrame.fraGlobalFunctions" +
        ".setCookie('previousNoAsked', 0,'','Mon, 1 Jan 1970')" >

<P>
<INPUT TYPE=button VALUE='Restart Quiz' NAME=buttonRestart
    onclick="window.location.replace('quizpage.asp')" >
```

Creating OutOfTime.asp

We have just one final page to create, which you need to save as `OutOfTime.asp`:

```
<%@ LANGUAGE = JavaScript%>
<% Response.Buffer = "True" %>
<HTML>
<BODY BACKGROUND="bluewash.jpg">

<!-- #include file="FinalResults.asp" -->

</BODY>
</HTML>
```

As you can see, there's not a lot to it. Most of the code is in the file `FinalResults.asp` that we just looked at, which is added to this page using `#include`. Note again that we have set buffering to `True`.

`OutOfTime.asp` is browsed to by the client-side `updateTimeLeft()` function in the `GlobalFunctions.htm` page when the client-side timer reaches zero. At that point, we notify the user that their time is up, and then we load the `OutOfTime.asp` page, which displays the results of their efforts and stops the quiz.

Summary

We've covered a lot of ground in this chapter and yet barely touched upon the subject of databases and ActiveX Data Objects (ADO). However, we have learned enough to create an effective database. We've also learned enough about the database language SQL to retrieve data from a database, insert data into it, change data in it, and delete data from it. We've also now got enough knowledge of ADO to be able to access a server-side database from a web page.

- ❑ We learned that databases consist of one or more tables and that each table consists of one or more rows called records.

- ❑ A record consists of one or more fields. Each field holds information and has a particular data type such as numbers, text, or dates.

- ❑ When designing tables, we need to ensure that we don't duplicate information. A table should contain fields that have some sort of logical relationship between them. For example, store customer data in one table, and order data in another.

- ❑ Some fields have data that is unique to that record. We can use these fields to search for a particular record. We can define fields that are unique and likely to be used for searching as primary keys. Defining a primary key indexes the field and helps speed up data retrieval.

- ❑ Relationships allow us to specify that the data in one table is reliant on the existence of data in another. For example, it shouldn't be possible to have orders in the orders table for stock that does not exist in the stock table.

- ❑ We took a brief tour of Structured Query Language (SQL), which provides a means of retrieving, inserting, updating, and deleting data in a database.

❑   To retrieve a record or group of records we use SQL's SELECT statement. This allows us to specify which fields we require. It also allows us to define criteria for defining which records we want using the WHERE clause.

❑   The SQL UPDATE statement allows a record or group of records already existing in a database to have their field values changed. Adding new records involves the INSERT statement, and deleting records the DELETE statement.

❑   We looked at how to access a server-side database using script running server-side. To do this requires the use of components installed on the server. We looked at one such group of components called ActiveX Data Objects.

❑   A connection to the database needs to be made inside the web page before we can start selecting or changing data.

❑   Two technologies provide the means to connect to a database, ODBC and OLE DB. With OLE DB we just need to specify the OLE driver and the location of the database. Before we can use ODBC, we need to set up an ODBC data source on the server-computer.

❑   The ADO Connection object provides a means of connecting to a database. Once a connection is made it can be reused again and again within the same page; doing so speeds up database access.

❑   The ADO Connection object provides the Execute() method, which enables SQL to be run against the database. If we are executing a query that inserts, deletes, or updates data then we need only call the Execute() method passing the SQL.

❑   If our SQL is a SELECT query that returns records, then we need to use an ADO Recordset object to hold the results of the Execute() method. Alternatively if we are only making one database access in a page, then we can use the Open() method of a Recordset object to both connect to the database and retrieve records.

❑   Finally we changed the trivia quiz to generate the questions and check the answers by using information stored in a database

In the next chapter, we finish the book by looking at other areas in which you can put to good use the JavaScript skills you've learned in this book. We see that the power of JavaScript is not just in web pages, but also in creating scripts to administer your computer and to access and modify the sophisticated Windows 2000 Active directory.

Exercises

Suggested solutions to these questions can be found in Appendix A.

Question 1

In Chapter 15 we saw how to create a logon screen that redirects the user to one page if there password is valid or asks them to re-enter their password if invalid. The logon name and password were set in the code. Create a database, which holds user names and corresponding passwords, and use this to validate the user.

Question 2

Create a message board application. It should display a list of message subjects, with the names of the poster and the date posted for each message in the database. When a message subject is clicked, it should display the full message body. Add a button to the page that allows new messages to be created and added to the database online.

Online discussion at http://p2p.wrox.com

A Few Final Words

In this book, we've concentrated on using JavaScript within our web pages, whether this script is run client-side or server-side. We've seen how JavaScript enables us to change the page, interact with the user, build pages dynamically on the fly before the user sees them, and finally how we can access databases.

JavaScript is very good at what it was originally intended for, which is as a scripting language within a web page, doing user interaction and various BOM manipulation tricks. However, there are areas where, although JavaScript can be used, an alternative programming language may be more sensible. The first section in this chapter will look at the limitations of JavaScript, and help you decide when you should and when you shouldn't be using it.

However, on a more positive note, there is a huge range of different uses to which JavaScript can be put, and in the latter part of this final chapter we'll take a look at some of these. Unfortunately, the topics are too big to describe in full in one chapter. Many deserve a chapter or even a book of their own, so we'll not be looking at how to program them, but rather we'll concentrate on discussing what they are and what they can do for us.

JavaScript Limitations

We've seen how good JavaScript is and the multitude of uses to which it can be put, but are there limits? Are there things that it can do, but which can be done better by other means?

In essence there are three main problems with JavaScript. The first is speed, which is how fast the JavaScript executes on the computer, whether it's on the server-side or on the client-side. The second is the limitations on what JavaScript can actually do, that is how powerful it is. The third is the language and its development environment. Let's look at each of these problems in turn.

Speed

Recall from Chapter 1 that JavaScript is an interpreted language, rather than a compiled language. By this we mean that the computer reads through the JavaScript code and interprets it every time the code is run. For compiled languages, such as C++ and Visual Basic, the computer compiles (converts to machine code) the code just once, before it is actually run.

Browsers, such as Internet Explorer and Netscape Navigator, come with JavaScript interpreters, but you'll also find them elsewhere. Windows itself comes with an administration facility called Windows Script Host, which also includes a JavaScript interpreter. We'll discuss this a little more later on in the chapter.

So why should we care whether a language is interpreted or compiled? Speed and scalability, that's why.

Imagine we have three people, an English-speaking person, a French-speaking person, and someone who speaks both French and English. Now the only way the French speaking and English speaking people can communicate is via the bilingual third person who will act as the interpreter, much as our JavaScript needs an interpreter to translate it to machine code, the only language the computer understands. Clearly, communication between the English and French speaking people is going to be much slower than if they could talk directly to each other. The same applies to the JavaScript/machine code situation. Additionally there may be words, concepts, or phrases in one language for which there is no direct easy interpretation. Instead the interpreter has to work out different words to explain the phrase that needs translating. So it is with JavaScript and machine code. This in itself slows things down. For example, to display a popup box with a message is just one line in JavaScript, namely `alert()`. In machine code, this will be many thousands of lines involving all sorts of different functions.

Given the speed and power of modern desktop computers, this difference in speed is negligible, at least on the client-side. The fact that pure machine code could display a popup box in a tenth of a millisecond, whereas JavaScript takes more like one millisecond, makes no difference to our client-side interface – the user will simply never notice. However, on the server-side a popular web site, such as Amazon, may have hundreds of thousands of concurrent users at peak times. Suddenly that minuscule speed difference becomes magnified a hundred thousand times and is noticeable to the user, maybe to the point of the server appearing to be 'down'.

The upshot of all this is that while the speed of JavaScript is just fine client-side, it may not be fine server-side. However, if we have some fairly simple processing done by JavaScript server-side, then this will probably be fine on even a high use web site. We may also find that complex server-side JavaScript is fine on a low usage web site, though if we find we need to scale up to larger usage we'll be in trouble. This is not to say we shouldn't use server-side JavaScript, but rather we should use it in moderation and consider other options. Indeed, often speed is simply not paramount, but where it is, JavaScript may not be the best choice.

The alternatives to server-side processing in JavaScript are to write special server-side components in languages such as C++ and Visual Basic, which are then compiled to machine code. These will run much faster than JavaScript, and help maximize the number of users our web site can handle.

Power

Perhaps the biggest limitation of JavaScript when in a web browser is the access, or rather total lack of access, to the local file system of the computer that the browser is running on. JavaScript, when running in a web browser, generally has no method of loading, saving, or deleting such files, or even seeing what files exist.

In fact, JavaScript in web pages has very little ability to interact with the user's operating system, such as Microsoft's Windows. You can't access the inner depths of the operating system, such as the user details, the registry, or computer hardware.

Often this deliberate limitation of what power JavaScript has over a user's computer is good. If JavaScript gave every web site a free for all over any computer connecting to it, then most users would quite rightly disable JavaScript.

However, there are certain circumstances where there are legitimate reasons for accessing files on a user's computer, perhaps connecting to a client-side database. In these circumstances we find JavaScript alone is not enough. We need to find other means such as creating our own plug-ins or ActiveX controls in languages such as Visual Basic and C++.

Language and Programming Environment

One advantage that JavaScript has is that you can write it using just Notepad and nothing else. There are, of course, lots of tools out there for helping make our JavaScript creation easier, but there are few fully integrated environments that can match that of, say, Visual Basic's IDE (Integrated Development Environment). This does mean that the development of complex coding is much easier in languages such as Visual Basic than it is in JavaScript, and since programmer time is so expensive it makes sense for as many ways as possible to be found to speed up development.

A second problem is the JavaScript language itself. In some ways JavaScript makes life easy for us. It doesn't require variables to be declared and we can put any type of data in our variables we like, with no need to declare its type first. There is a downside with this though, as it allows errors to creep in undetected and makes it more difficult to remove bugs.

Other languages, such as C++, Java, and to a lesser extent Visual Basic, support language features that make programming easier, less prone to bugs, and more reusable. In particular, such languages may have language features that make Object Oriented Programming (OOP) possible. JavaScript does not really have the language features to achieve this, and is simply an object-based language. By this I mean that it can use objects, but we can't use it to define our own class of objects.

Other Uses for JavaScript

While JavaScript has its origins in web page scripting, it has really taken off as a programming tool and is now used in many different areas. We'll look at a few of these areas individually, and also point you in the direction of where you can find out more information.

Windows Script Host (WSH)

Windows Script Host (WSH) allows us to automate certain administrative tasks we might need to do on our Windows operating system computer. It is particularly useful for systems' administrators, who often have to perform the same basic steps when performing tasks, such as creating new user accounts.

We've seen that the browser provides an environment for client-side JavaScript. It provides, via the BOM, ways and means of accessing the browser and the web page inside it. We've seen the same situation for server-side scripting, but this time it's hosted by a web server and the object model made available is ASP. Well, WSH works in the same way – it's another hosting environment and provides its own objects to enable us to do something useful with our JavaScript.

A good example of WSH in practice would be the development of a sophisticated e-commerce web site. Let's imagine that the development team has completed its work in a development environment, but now needs the web application to go live by being created on an external web server connected to the Internet. A big project may consist of a number of components that need to be installed, user accounts that need creating, a database that needs creating and populating with tables and data, and system settings that need creating, such as virtual directories and ODBC data sources, before the whole project will work. The steps in setting up the new web site could be very numerous, and a mistake at any point would most likely cause the whole project not to work. However, WSH script files, written in JavaScript, can perform all of these tasks. All the administrator needs to do is run the WSH code provided by the developers. There's very little that WSH can't do within the Windows environment.

If you're running Windows 98, NT, or 2000, then WSH is already installed on your system. Users of other Windows versions need to download WSH from the Microsoft web site, with the URL:

```
http://msdn.microsoft.com/scripting/default.htm?/scripting/windowshost
/doc/wsAboutWSH20.htm.
```

Let's look at a very simple example of WSH programming with JavaScript.

Type the following code into a plain text editor, for example Windows NotePad. Save the file in the C:\Temp directory of your computer as WSHCreateURLShortCuts.js. Note the extension, .js, is very important.

```
var objShell = WScript.CreateObject("WScript.Shell");
var desktopDirectory = objShell.SpecialFolders("Desktop");

var urllink = objShell.CreateShortcut(desktopDirectory + "\\Wrox Press.url");
urllink.TargetPath = "http://www.wrox.com";
urllink.Save();

WScript.Echo("Shortcuts added successfully")
```

To run this code either go to the Start | Run menu, type:

```
wscript.exe c:\temp\WSHCreateURLShortCuts.js
```

and then hit return, or browse to the C:\Temp directory using Windows Explorer and double-click on the file.

What the code does is create a new shortcut to your desktop for the URL www.wrox.com. It then displays a message box informing us that Shortcuts added successfully. You should see a shortcut appear on your desktop like this:

WSH is a fairly involved topic, requiring at least a chapter to explain even the basics, but let's take a broad overview of what the code is doing.

First, we declare a variable objShell and use the built in WSH WScript object to create another object called WScript.Shell or simply the Windows Shell object. Remember when we were writing server-side pages we used the Server object's CreateObject() method to, for example, create an ADODB.Connection object. Well, this line is doing something very similar, just using a different object model:

```
var objShell = WScript.CreateObject("WScript.Shell");
```

We then use the Shell object we just created to find out where the file directory is for all desktop shortcuts. This can vary between different versions of Windows, and even for different users. However, with the Shell object's SpecialFolders property we can always find out where it is:

```
var desktopDirectory = objShell.SpecialFolders("Desktop");
```

Next we create a ShortCut object that we'll use to create our desktop shortcut to a URL, in this case www.wrox.com. We pass the file location of the desktop directory and also the filename we want to give to the shortcut:

```
var urllink = objShell.CreateShortcut(desktopDirectory + "\\Wrox Press.url");
```

Then in the next two lines we define the shortcut's target path, that is where the shortcut is a shortcut to. In our case it's a URL, however it could be a file on the computer or an application such as MS Word. Then in the second line we save the shortcut and it's added to the desktop:

```
urllink.TargetPath = "http://www.beginning-javascript.com";
urllink.Save();
```

In the following three lines, we create another shortcut in the same way. This time it points to the Wrox Press web site at www.wrox.com:

```
urllink = objShell.CreateShortcut(desktopDirectory + "\\Wrox Press.url");
urllink.TargetPath = "http://www.wrox.com";
urllink.Save();
```

Finally we display a message stating that the short cuts were created successfully:

```
WScript.Echo("Shortcuts added successfully");
```

While this example is nowhere near enough to tell you how to program in WSH, hopefully it gives you an idea of how WSH works. You can see that it has much in common with the JavaScript we've already seen. The difference is really the WSH object model that needs to be learnt, just as we learnt the Browser Object Model for the browser and the ASP object model on the server. Once you have understood the JavaScript language itself, your task is mostly just to learn more object models and new concepts.

Find Out More

There are a lot of web sites and books that cover Windows Script Host.

Some interesting links include:

```
http://www.windows-script.com/
http://msdn.microsoft.com/scripting/default.htm
http://www.devguru.com/index.asp?page=/Technologies/wsh/quickref/wsh_intro.html
```

For books try:

- ❑ *Windows Script Host Programmer's Reference* published by Wrox Press ISBN 1-861002-65-3

- ❑ *Sams Teach Yourself Windows Script Host in 21 Days* published by MacMillan Publishing Company

Extensible Markup Language (XML)

We have come across XML already in this book, most notably in Chapter 13 where we discussed it alongside the W3C DOM standards.

Recall that XML is used to define markup languages. Although this means that we are free to make up tag names of our own, our documents must adhere to a very strict syntax. For a document to be considered to be well-formed XML it must satisfy the following:

- ❑ It must contain an XML identifier.

- ❑ All content must be contained in one root tag.

- ❑ All tags must have an accompanying closing tag, for example `<p>` and `</p>`, or the tag must open and close itself, for example `<br/>`.

- ❑ Tags must be nested properly. For example if we open an `<a>` tag and then a `<b>` tag, we must close the `<b>` tag before closing the `</a>` tag.

- ❑ All attribute values must be enclosed in quote marks.

Initially XML was the subject of much hype, with talk of it replacing HTML as the dominant standard for creating web pages. However, where XML really scores is in the transfer and communication of data from disparate sources due to its excellent data description abilities and its lack of presentation information to cloud the real information.

In an ideal world, all our data would be kept in compatible sources, whether it is our Excel spreadsheets, our word processing files, or our SQL Server and Oracle databases. However, it's not an ideal world, or I'd be a millionaire living on an exotic island! In reality, data is stored in different formats. The next best alternative to compatible data sources is to find a source-independent way of transferring and retrieving data, and this is where XML comes in.

All we need is a way of converting data from whatever format it's in into XML. Then the data can be sent to wherever it's needed, before being converted into another document format or converted into the necessary format for storing.

So where does JavaScript come into all this? Well, browsers such as IE 5 and NN 6 support XML, and enable XML files to be read and used for creating web pages. The reading or parsing of the XML can be done using JavaScript to extract the data we want and make use of it.

We can also use XML on the web server in our ASP pages. Again, using JavaScript we can parse XML data sources and build up web pages from the extracted data.

Find Out More

You can find out more about XML in:

- ❏ *XML IE5 Programmer's Reference* from Wrox Press ISBN 1-861001-57-6
- ❏ *Beginning XML* from Wrox Press ISBN 1-861003-41-2

Just two of the many web sites with information on XML are:

```
http://www.xml-zone.com/
http://www.webdeveloper.com/xml/
```

Remote Scripting

Remote Scripting is a Microsoft technology that enables us to run code located in functions on a server-side script page from client-side script, without ever needing to actually navigate to the server-side page. Why would we want to do this?

Well, let's imagine an e-commerce transaction where the customer is buying a product. At some point in the transaction we'll want to get the delivery address that the customer wants the item posted to. Now, rather than getting the user to fill in the whole address, we could instead get them to enter their house number and zip or postal code, and use this to look up their full address. We can't get the information about the full address client-side, so normally we'd have to do a form post and get the information via the server. However, with Remote Scripting we could add a button to the web page that calls a server-side function, passing the zip code given by the user, and returning the full address. We can then populate the address input boxes with this information and allow the user to make any necessary changes, all without the need to navigate to another page.

Find Out More

To install and learn more about Remote Scripting, see the Microsoft web site. The direct URL is:

```
http://msdn.microsoft.com/scripting/default.htm?/scripting/RemoteScrip
ting/default.htm
```

You can also find out more from the links below:

```
http://www.learnasp.com/learn/remotescripting.asp
http://www.elementkjournals.com/asp/0005/asp0051.htm
```

Active Directory Service Interfaces (ADSI)

ADSI is a very powerful programming interface, which is available with Windows NT 4 and Windows 2000 Server. It enables network operations, both LAN (Local Area Network) and Internet, to be manipulated either from a web page or a Windows program. For example, we saw in Chapter 15 how to use the PWS console to create a virtual directory, set its permissions and location. With ADSI we can do this programmatically from an ASP page using JavaScript. In fact, we can do a whole lot more, including setting up domains, users, validating users, and sharing resources.

What sort of web applications might involve the use of ADSI?

One example might be controlling access to a pay-per-view web site. A user signs up for the service, hands over their credit card details, and provides a username and password. Using ADSI, we can write code to automatically create a new user account with those details, which gives them instant access to our protected web site, with no need for a systems administrator to have to manually create the user account.

You might ask why we don't use a database to store the details, and a web page for the logon and security. Using Windows NT or Windows 2000 built-in security has a number of advantages. First, the processing required to do a check on an NT username and password is a lot less than that required to do lookups in a database, so our system will be faster and more **scalable**, that is it will be able to handle more users at any one time. Secondly, it'll be more secure; getting past the security would involve getting past NT's security.

Find Out More

ADSI is a fairly involved subject, which you can find out more about from the Microsoft web site, with URL:

```
http://msdn.microsoft.com/library/default.asp?URL=/library/psdk/adsi/a
dsistartpage_7wrp.htm
```

Books on this subject include:

- ❑ *ADSI ASP Programmer's Reference* from Wrox Press ISBN 1-861001-69-X

- ❑ *Professional ADSI Programming - Active Directory Services Interface* from Wrox Press ISBN 1-861002-26-2

Summary

In this chapter, we learned that while JavaScript is great client-side and useful server-side, there are times when it's not the right tool for the job. For example, it doesn't have the speed of some languages, which may prove a problem in server-side processing where we have many users accessing the web site simultaneously.

We've also seen in this chapter that, as well as improving our existing JavaScript through practice, we can also use it in new areas such as with XML, Remote Scripting, Windows Script Host, and ADSI. Which of these you'll actually need rather depends on your task at hand. However, XML is starting to become more and more central to web-based systems, especially where there is a requirement to use data from disparate sources.

With your knowledge gained from reading this book, the information given in this chapter, and the additional resources in Appendix I, you can now go out and further explore what's possible with the JavaScript language.

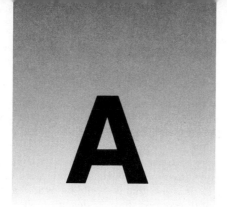

Exercise Solutions

In this appendix you'll find some suggested solutions to the exercise questions that were posed at the end of most of the chapters throughout the book.

Chapter 2

In this chapter we looked at how JavaScript stores and manipulates data, such as numbers and text.

Question 1

Write a JavaScript program to convert degrees centigrade into degrees Fahrenheit and write the result to the page in a descriptive sentence. The JavaScript equation for Fahrenheit to centigrade is:

$degFahren = 9 / 5 * degCent + 32$

Solution

```
<HTML>
<BODY>

<SCRIPT LANGUAGE=JavaScript>

var degCent = prompt("Enter the degrees in centigrade",0);
var degFahren = 9 / 5 * degCent + 32;

document.write(degCent + " degrees centigrade is " + degFahren +
   " degrees Fahrenheit");

</SCRIPT>

</BODY>
</HTML>
```

Save this as ch02_q1.htm.

We get the degrees centigrade the user wants to convert by using the `prompt()` function, and store it inside the `degCent` variable.

We then do our calculation, which uses the data stored in `degCent` and converts it to Fahrenheit. The result is assigned to the `degFahren` variable.

Finally, we write the results to the web page, building it up in a sentence using the concatenation operator +. Note how JavaScript knows in the calculation that `degCent` is to be treated as a number, but in the `document.write()` it knows that it should be treated as text for concatenation. So how does it know? Simple, it looks at the context. In the calculation, `degCent` is surrounded by numbers and numerical only operators, such as * and /. In the `document.write()`, `degCent` is surrounded by strings, hence JavaScript assumes the + means concatenate.

Question 2

The following code uses the `prompt()` function to get two numbers from the user. It then adds those two numbers together and writes the result to the page:

```
<HTML>
<BODY>
<SCRIPT LANGUAGE=JavaScript>

var firstNumber = prompt("Enter the first number","");
var secondNumber = prompt("Enter the second number","");
var theTotal = firstNumber + secondNumber;
document.write(firstNumber + " added to " + secondNumber + " equals " + theTotal);

</SCRIPT>
</BODY>
</HTML>
```

However if you try the code out you'll spot that it doesn't work. Why not?

Change the code so that it does work.

Solution

The data that the `prompt()` actually obtains is a string. So both `firstNumber` and `secondNumber` contain text that happens to be number characters. When we use the + symbol to add the two variables together, JavaScript assumes that as it's string data we must want to concatenate the two together and not sum them.

To make it explicit to JavaScript that we want to add the numbers together we need to convert the data to numbers using the `parseFloat()` function:

```
<HTML>
<BODY>
<SCRIPT LANGUAGE=JavaScript>

var firstNumber = parseFloat(prompt("Enter the first number",""));
var secondNumber = parseFloat(prompt("Enter the second number",""));
```

```
    var theTotal = firstNumber + secondNumber;
    document.write(firstNumber + " added to " + secondNumber + " equals " +
        theTotal);

</SCRIPT>
</BODY>
</HTML>
```

Save this as ch02_q2.htm.

Now the data returned by the prompt() function is converted to a floating point number before being stored in the firstNumber and secondNumber variables. Then, when we do the addition that is stored in theTotal, JavaScript makes the correct assumption that, as both the variables are numbers, we must mean to add them up and not concatenate them.

The general rule is that where we have expressions with only numerical data, the + operator means "do addition". If there is any string data then the + will mean concatenate.

Chapter 3

In this chapter we looked at how JavaScript can make decisions based on conditions. We also looked at loops and functions.

Question 1

A junior programmer comes to you with some code that appears not to work. Can you spot where they have gone wrong? Give them a hand and correct the mistakes.

```
var userAge = prompt("Please enter your age");

if (userAge = 0);
{
    alert("So you're a baby!");
}
else if ( userAge < 0 | userAge > 200)
    alert("I think you may be lying about your age");
else
{
    alert("That's a good age");
}
```

Solution

Oh dear, our junior programmer is having a bad day! There are two mistakes on the line:

```
if (userAge = 0);
```

Firstly, they have only one equals sign instead of two in the `if`'s condition, which means `userAge` will be assigned the value of zero rather than `userAge` being compared to zero. The second fault is the semi-colon at the end of the line – statements such as `if` and loops such as `for` and `while` don't require semi-colons. The general rule is that if the statement has an associated block (that is, code in curly braces) then no semi-colon is needed. So the line should be:

```
if (userAge == 0)
```

The next two faults are with these lines:

```
else if ( userAge < 0 | userAge > 200)
    alert("I think you may be lying about your age");
else
```

The junior programmer's condition is asking if `userAge` is less than zero OR `userAge` is greater than 200. The correct operator for a Boolean OR is `||`, but the programmer has only used one `|`. Secondly, the `alert()` function needs to be inside a block, which we indicate with curly braces. If there was no `else` statement, this would have been acceptable, though poor programming, but with the `else` statement JavaScript insists on the block. So the code should read:

```
else if ( userAge < 0 || userAge > 200)
{
    alert("I think you may be lying about your age");
}
else
```

Question 2

Write JavaScript code that displays, using `document.write()`, the results of the 12 times table. Its output should be the results of the calculations:

```
12 * 1 = 12
12 * 2 = 24
12 * 3 = 36
.....
12 * 11 = 132
12 * 12 = 144
```

Solution:

```
<HTML>
<BODY>
<SCRIPT LANGUAGE=JavaScript>
var timesTable = 12;
var timesBy;

for (timesBy = 1; timesBy < 13; timesBy++)
{
    document.write(timesTable + " * " + timesBy + " = " + timesBy * timesTable +
        "<BR>");
}
</SCRIPT>
</BODY>
</HTML>
```

Save this as ch03_q2.htm.

We use a `for` loop to calculate from 1 * 12 up to 12 * 12. The results are written to the page with `document.write()`. What's important to note here is the effect of the order of precedence; the concatenation operator, the +, has a lower order of precedence than the multiplication operator, *. This means that the `timesBy * timesTable` is done before the concatenation, the result we want. If this were not the case we'd have had to put the calculation in parentheses to raise its order of precedence.

Question 3

Change the code of Question 2 so that it's a function that takes as its parameters the times table required and what values it should start and end at. For example, we might want the 4 times table displayed starting with 4 * 4 and ending at 4 * 9.

Solution:

```
<HTML>
<BODY>
<SCRIPT LANGUAGE=JavaScript>
function writeTimesTable(timesTable, timesByStart, timesByEnd)
{
    for (;timesByStart <= timesByEnd; timesByStart++)
    {
        document.write(timesTable + " * " + timesByStart + " = " +
            timesByStart * timesTable + "<BR>");
    }
}

writeTimesTable(4,4,9);
</SCRIPT>
</BODY>
</HTML>
```

Save this as ch03_q3.htm.

We've declared our function, calling it `writeTimesTable()`, and given it three parameters. The first is the times table we want to write, the second the start point, and the third the number it should go up to.

We've modified our `for` loop. First we don't need to initialize any variables, so the initialization part is left blank – we still need to put a semi-colon in, but there's no code before it. The `for` loop continues while the `timesByStart` parameter is less than or equal to the `timesByEnd` parameter. You can see that, as with a variable, we can modify parameters – in this case `timesByStart` is incremented by one for each iteration through the loop.

The code to display the times table is much the same. For the function's code to be executed we now actually need to call it, which we do in the line:

```
writeTimesTable(4,4,9);
```

This will write the four times table starting at four times four and ending at nine times four.

Question 4

Modify the code of Question 3 to request the times table to be displayed from the user. The code should continue to request and display times tables until the user enters -1. Additionally, do a check to make sure that the user is entering a valid number; if it's not valid, ask them to re-enter it.

Solution:

```
<HTML>
<BODY>
<SCRIPT LANGUAGE=JavaScript>

function writeTimesTable(timesTable, timesByStart, timesByEnd)
{
   for (;timesByStart <= timesByEnd; timesByStart++)
   {
       document.write(timesTable + " * " + timesByStart + " = " +
          timesByStart * timesTable + "<BR>");
   }
}

var timesTable;

while ( (timesTable = prompt("Enter the times table",-1)) != -1)
{
   while (isNaN(timesTable) == true)
   {
    timesTable = prompt(timesTable + " is not a valid number, please retry",-1);
   }

   if (timesTable == -1)
   {
      break;
   }

   document.write("<BR>The " + timesTable + " times table<BR>");
   writeTimesTable(timesTable,1,12);

}
</SCRIPT>
</BODY>
</HTML>
```

Save this as ch03_q4.htm.

The function remains the same, so let's look at the new code. The first change from Question 3 is that we declare a variable, timesTable, and then initialize it in the condition of the first while loop. This may seem a strange thing to do at first, but it does work. The code in parentheses inside the while loop's condition:

```
(timesTable = prompt("Enter the times table",-1))
```

is executed first as its order of precedence has been raised by the parentheses. This will return a value and it is this value that is compared to -1. If it's not -1 then the `while` condition is `true` and the body of the loop executes, otherwise it's skipped over and nothing else happens in this page.

In a second `while` loop, nested inside the first, we check to see that the value the user has entered is actually a number using the function `isNaN()`. If it's not, then we prompt the user to try again and this will continue until a valid number is entered.

If the user had entered an invalid value initially, then in the second `while` loop they may have entered -1 so following the `while` is an `if` statement which checks to see if -1 has been entered. If it has then we `break` out of the `while` loop, otherwise the `writeTimesTable()` function is called.

Chapter 4

In this chapter we saw that JavaScript is an object-based language, and how we can use some of the native JavaScript objects, such as the `Date` and `Math` objects.

Question 1

Using the `Date` object, calculate the date 12 months from now and write this into a web page.

Solution

```
<HTML>
<BODY>
<SCRIPT LANGUAGE=JavaScript>

var months = new Array("Jan","Feb","Mar","Apr","May","Jun","Jul","Aug",
                       "Sep","Oct","Nov","Dec");
var nowDate = new Date();

nowDate.setMonth(nowDate.getMonth() + 12);
document.write("Date 12 months ahead is " + nowDate.getDay());
document.write(" " + months[nowDate.getMonth()]);
document.write(" " + nowDate.getFullYear());

</SCRIPT>
</BODY>
</HTML>
```

Save this as ch04_q1.htm.

Because the `getMonth()` method returns a number between 0 and 11 for the month rather than its name, an array called `months` has been created that stores the name of each month. We can use `getMonth()` to get the array index for the correct month name.

Variable `nowDate` is initialized to a new `Date` object. As no initial value is specified, the new `Date` object will contain today's date.

To add 12 months onto the current date we simply use `setMonth()`. We get the current month value with `getMonth()`, and then add 12 to it.

Finally we write the result out to the page.

Question 2

Obtain a list of names from the user, storing each name entered in an array. Keep getting another name until the user enters nothing. Sort the names into ascending order then write them out to the page, each name being on its own line.

Solution

```
<HTML>
<BODY>
<SCRIPT LANGUAGE=JavaScript>

var inputName = "";
var namesArray = new Array();

while ( (inputName = prompt("Enter a name","")) != "" )
{
    namesArray[namesArray.length] = inputName;
}

namesArray.sort();

var namesList = namesArray.join("<BR>")
document.write(namesList);

</SCRIPT>
</BODY>
</HTML>
```

Save this as ch04_q2.htm.

First we declare two variables: inputName, which will hold the name entered by the user, and namesArray, which holds an Array object that stores each of the names entered.

We use a while loop to keep getting another name from the user so long as they haven't left the prompt box blank. Note that the use of parentheses in the while condition is essential. By placing:

```
(inputName = prompt("Enter a name",""))
```

inside parentheses, we ensure that this is executed first and that a name is obtained from the user and stored in inputName variable. Then we compare the value returned inside the parentheses, whatever was entered by the user, with an empty string (denoted by ""). If they are not equal, that is if the user did enter a value, we loop round again.

Now, to sort the array into order we use the sort() method of the Array object:

```
namesArray.sort();
```

Finally, to create a string containing all values contained in the array elements with each being on a new line, we use the HTML <BR> tag and we write:

```
var namesList = namesArray.join("<BR>")
document.write(namesList);
```

The code namesArray.join("<BR>") creates the string of array elements with a <BR> between each. Finally, we write the string into the page with document.write().

Question 3

We saw in Chapter 4 when looking at the pow() method that we could use it inventively to fix a number to a certain number of decimal places. However, there is a flaw in the function we created. A proper fix() function should return 2.1 fixed to three decimal places as:

    2.100

However, our fix() function instead returns it as:

    2.1

Change the fix() function so that the additional zeros are added where necessary.

Solution

```
<HTML>
<HEAD>
<SCRIPT LANGUAGE=JavaScript>

function fix(fixNumber, decimalPlaces)
{
    var div = Math.pow(10,decimalPlaces);
    fixNumber = new String(Math.round(fixNumber * div) / div);

    var zerosRequired = decimalPlaces -
            (fixNumber.length - fixNumber.lastIndexOf(".") - 1);

    for (; zerosRequired > 0; zerosRequired--)
    {
        fixNumber = fixNumber + "0";
    }
    return fixNumber;
}
</SCRIPT>
</HEAD>
<BODY>
<SCRIPT LANGUAGE=JavaScript>

var number1 = prompt("Enter the number with decimal places you want to fix","");
var number2 = prompt("How many decimal places do you want?","");

document.write(number1 + " fixed to " + number2 + " decimal places is: ");
document.write(fix(number1,number2));

</SCRIPT>
</BODY>
</HTML>
```

Save this as ch04_q3.htm.

The function declaration and the first line remain the same as the fix() function we saw earlier in the chapter. However, things change after that.

We create the fixed number as before, using `Math.round(fixNumber * div) / div`. What is new is that we pass the result of this as the parameter to the `String()` constructor that creates a new `String` object, storing it back in `fixNumber`.

Now we have our number fixed to the number of decimal places required, but it will still be in the form 2.1 rather than 2.100 as required. Our next task is therefore to add the extra zeros required. To do this we need to subtract the number of digits after the decimal point from the number of digits required after the decimal point as specified in `decimalPlaces`. First, to find out how many digits are after the decimal point we write:

```
(fixNumber.length - fixNumber.lastIndexOf(".") - 1)
```

For our number of 2.1, `fixNumber.length` will be 3. `fixNumber.lastIndexOf(".")` will return 1; remember that the first character is 0, the second 1 and so on. So `fixNumber.length - fixNumber.lastIndexOf(".")` will be 2. Then we subtract 1 at the end leaving a result of 1, which is the number of digits after the decimal place.

The full line is:

```
var zerosRequired = decimalPlaces -
            (fixNumber.length - fixNumber.lastIndexOf(".") - 1);
```

We know the last bit (`fixNumber.length - fixNumber.lastIndexOf(".") - 1`) is 1 and that the `decimalPlaces` parameter passed is three, 3 – 1 leaves 2 zeros required to be added.

Now we know how many extra zeros are required, let's add them:

```
for (; zerosRequired > 0; zerosRequired--)
{
    fixNumber = fixNumber + "0";
}
```

Now we just need to return the result from the function to the calling code:

```
    return fixNumber;
```

Chapter 5

This chapter dealt with how JavaScript uses the objects, methods, properties, and events made available by the Browser Object Model (BOM) of the user's browser.

Question 1

Create a page with a number of links. Then write code that fires on the window `onload` event, displaying the `href`'s of each of the links on the page.

Solution

```
<HTML>
<HEAD>
<SCRIPT LANGUAGE=JavaScript>
function displayLinks()
{
   var linksCounter

   for (linksCounter = 0; linksCounter < document.links.length; linksCounter++)
   {
       alert(document.links[linksCounter].href);
   }

}
</SCRIPT>
</HEAD>
<BODY onload="displayLinks()">

<A HREF="link0.htm" >Link 0</A>
<A HREF="link1.htm">Link 2</A>
<A HREF="link2.htm">Link 2</A>

</BODY>
</HTML>
```

Save this as ch05_q1.htm.

We connect to the window object's onload event handler by adding an attribute to the <BODY> tag:

```
<BODY onload="displayLinks()">
```

On the onload event firing, this will run the script in quotes calling the displayLinks() function.

In this function we use a for loop to cycle through each A object in the document object's links array:

```
function displayLinks()
{
   var linksCounter

   for (linksCounter = 0; linksCounter < document.links.length; linksCounter++)
   {
       alert(document.links[linksCounter].href);
   }

}
```

We used the length property of the links array in our condition to determine how many times we need to loop. Then, using an alert box we display each A object's href property. We can't use document.write() in the onload event, because it occurs when the page has finished loading.

Question 2

Create two pages, one called `IEOnly.htm` and the other called `NNOnly.htm`. Each page should have a heading telling you what page is loaded, for example:

```
<H2>Welcome to the Internet Explorer only page</H2>
```

Using the functions for checking browser type, connect to the `window` object's `onload` event handler and detect what browser the user has. Then if it's the wrong page for that browser, redirect to the other page.

Solution

The `NNOnly.htm` page:

```html
<HTML>
<HEAD>
<SCRIPT LANGUAGE=JavaScript>

function getBrowserName()
{
   var lsBrowser = navigator.appName;
   if (lsBrowser.indexOf("Microsoft") >= 0)
   {
      lsBrowser = "MSIE";
   }
   else if (lsBrowser.indexOf("Netscape") >= 0)
   {
      lsBrowser = "NETSCAPE";
   }
   else
   {
      lsBrowser = "UNKNOWN";
   }
   return lsBrowser;
}


function checkBrowser()
{
   if (getBrowserName() == "MSIE")
   {
      window.location.replace("IEOnly.htm");
   }
}

</SCRIPT>
</HEAD>
<BODY onload="checkBrowser()">

<H2>Welcome to the Netscape Navigator only page</H2>

</BODY>
</HTML>
```

The `IEOnly.htm` page is very similar:

```
<HTML>
<HEAD>
<SCRIPT LANGUAGE=JavaScript>

function getBrowserName()
{
    var lsBrowser = navigator.appName;
    if (lsBrowser.indexOf("Microsoft") >= 0)
    {
        lsBrowser = "MSIE";
    }
    else if (lsBrowser.indexOf("Netscape") >= 0)
    {
        lsBrowser = "NETSCAPE";
    }
    else
    {
        lsBrowser = "UNKNOWN";
    }
    return lsBrowser;
}


function checkBrowser()
{
    if (getBrowserName() == "NETSCAPE")
    {
        window.location.replace("NNOnly.htm");
    }
}

</SCRIPT>
</HEAD>
<BODY onload="checkBrowser()">

<H2>Welcome to the Internet Explorer only page</H2>

</BODY>
</HTML>
```

Starting with the `IEOnly.htm` page, first we add an `onload` event handler, so that on loading the page our `checkBrowser()` function is called:

```
<BODY ONLOAD="checkBrowser()">
```

Then in `checkBrowser()` we use our `getBrowserName()` function to tell us which browser the user has. If it's Netscape then we `replace` the page loaded with the `NNOnly.htm` page. Note that we use `replace()` rather than `href`, as we don't want the user being able to hit the browser back button. This way the fact a new page is being loaded is less easy to spot.

```
function checkBrowser()
{
    if (getBrowserName() == "NETSCAPE")
    {
        window.location.replace("NNOnly.htm");
    }
}
```

The NNOnly.htm page is identical, except that in our if statement we check for MSIE and re-direct to IEOnly.htm if it is MSIE:

```
function checkBrowser()
{
    if (getBrowserName() == "MSIE")
    {
        window.location.replace("IEOnly.htm");
    }
}
```

Question 3

Insert an image in the page with the <IMG> tag. When the mouse pointer rolls over the image it should switch to a different image. When it rolls out, that is leaves the image, it should swap back again. You'll need to wrap the images inside <A> tags, as IMG objects don't have the onmouseover and onmouseout events in NN 3 and 4.

Solution

```
<HTML>
<HEAD>
<SCRIPT LANGUAGE=JavaScript>

function mouseOver()
{
    document.images["myImage"].src = "Img2.jpg";
}

function mouseOut()
{
    document.images["myImage"].src = "Img1.jpg";
}
</SCRIPT>
</HEAD>
<BODY>

<A STYLE="cursor : default" HREF="" onclick="return false" NAME="link1"
    onmouseover="mouseOver()" onmouseout="mouseOut()">
        <IMG SRC="Img1.jpg" NAME="myImage">
</A>

</BODY>
</HTML>
```

Save this as ch05_q3.htm.

At the top of the page we define our two functions to handle the onmouseover and onmouseout events:

```
function mouseOver()
{
    document.images["myImage"].src = "Img2.jpg";
}

function mouseOut()
{
    document.images["myImage"].src = "Img1.jpg";
}
```

The function names give away what event they will be handling. We access the IMG object for our <IMG> tag using the document.images array and putting the name in square brackets. In the onmouseover event we change the src property of the image to Img2.jpg and in the onmouseout event we change it back to img1.jpg, the image we specified when the page was loaded.

In the page itself we have our <IMG> tag inside an <A> tag:

```
<A STYLE="cursor : default" HREF="" onclick="return false" NAME="link1"
    onmouseover="mouseOver()" onmouseout="mouseOut()">
        <IMG SRC="Img1.jpg" NAME="myImage">
</A>
```

We need to do it this way so that our pages work with NN 3 and 4. Only IE 4 and 5 and NN 6 support the onmouseover and onmouseout events for an IMG object. However, NN 4 does support these events for the <A> tag's A object, so we use this workaround to get the result we want.

Note that I've also added onclick="return false", why? By returning false the click event is canceled; remember this link is here for its events only and not as a hyperlink. Why not leave the HREF="" out altogether? Well, while this will work fine in IE, it won't in NN, which ignores events if no HREF is included. Finally, for IE only, I've set the cursor style when the mouse pointer is over the link to the default cursor rather than a hyperlink mouse cursor:

```
STYLE="cursor : default"
```

Chapter 6

In this chapter, we saw how we could add functionality to our web pages with HTML forms and elements, such as checkboxes, text areas, and radio buttons, with JavaScript.

Question 1

Using the code from the temperature converter example we saw in Chapter 2, create a user interface for it and connect it to the existing code so that the user can enter a value in degrees Fahrenheit and convert it to centigrade.

Solution

```
<HTML>
<HEAD>
<SCRIPT LANGUAGE=JavaScript>
function convertToCentigrade(degFahren)
{
    var degCent;
    degCent = degCent = 5/9 * (degFahren - 32);

    return degCent;
}

function butToCent_onclick()
{
    var CalcBox = document.form1.txtCalcBox;

    if (isNaN(CalcBox.value) == true || CalcBox.value == "")
    {
        CalcBox.value = "Error Invalid Value";
    }
    else
    {
        CalcBox.value = convertToCentigrade(CalcBox.value);
    }
}
</SCRIPT>
</HEAD>
<BODY>

<FORM NAME=form1>
<P>
    <INPUT TYPE="text" NAME=txtCalcBox VALUE="0.0">
</P>
    <INPUT TYPE="button"
           VALUE="Convert to centigrade"
           NAME=butToCent
           onclick="butToCent_onclick()">
</FORM>
</BODY>
</HTML>
```

Save this as ch06_q1.htm.

The interface part is simply a form containing a textbox into which the user enters the Fahrenheit value and a button they click to convert that value to centigrade. The button has its onclick event handler set to call a function butToCent_onclick().

The first line of butToCent_onclick() declares a variable and sets it to reference the object representing the textbox:

```
    var CalcBox = document.form1.txtCalcBox;
```

Why do this? Well, in our code when we want to use `document.form1.txtCalcBox`, we can now just use the much shorter `CalcBox`; it saves typing and keeps our code shorter and easier to read.

So,

```
alert(document.form1.txtCalcBox.value);
```

is the same as:

```
alert(CalcBox.value);
```

In the remaining part of the function we do a sanity check – if what the user has entered is a number (that is, it is not NotANumber) and the text box does contain a value, then we use the Fahrenheit to centigrade conversion function we saw in Chapter 3 to do the conversion, the results of which are used to set the text box's value.

Question 2

Create a user interface that allows the user to pick the computer system of their dreams, similar in principle to the e-commerce sites selling computers over the Internet. For example, they could be given a choice of processor type, speed, memory, hard drive size, and the option to add additional components like DVD-ROM drives, sound cards, and so on. As the user changes the selection, the price of the system should update automatically and notify the user of the cost of the system as they have specified it either by using an alert box or updating the contents of a text box.

Solution

```
<HTML>
<HTML>
<HEAD>

<SCRIPT LANGUAGE=JavaScript>
var CompItems = new Array();
CompItems[100] = 1000;
CompItems[101] = 1250;
CompItems[102] = 1500;

CompItems[200] = 35;
CompItems[201] = 65;
CompItems[202] = 95;

CompItems[300] = 50;
CompItems[301] = 75;
CompItems[302] = 100;

CompItems[400] = 10;
CompItems[401] = 15;
CompItems[402] = 25;
```

```
function updateOrderDetails()
{
    var total = 0;
    var orderDetails = "";
    var formElement;
    formElement =
        document.form1.cboProcessor[document.form1.cboProcessor.selectedIndex];
    total = parseFloat(CompItems[formElement.value]);
    orderDetails = "Processor : " + formElement.text;
    orderDetails = orderDetails + " $" + CompItems[formElement.value] + "\n";

    formElement =
        document.form1.cboHardDrive[document.form1.cboHardDrive.selectedIndex];
    total = total + parseFloat(CompItems[formElement.value]);
    orderDetails = orderDetails + "Hard Drive : " + formElement.text;
    orderDetails = orderDetails + " $" + CompItems[formElement.value] + "\n";

    formElement = document.form1.chkCDROM
    if (formElement.checked == true)
    {
        orderDetails = orderDetails + "CD-ROM : $" +
            CompItems[formElement.value] + "\n";
        total = total + parseFloat(CompItems[formElement.value]);
    }

    formElement = document.form1.chkDVD
    if (formElement.checked == true)
    {
        orderDetails = orderDetails + "DVD-ROM : $" +
            CompItems[formElement.value] + "\n";
        total = total + parseFloat(CompItems[formElement.value]);
    }

    formElement = document.form1.chkScanner
    if (formElement.checked == true)
    {
        orderDetails = orderDetails + "Scanner : $" +
            CompItems[formElement.value] + "\n";
        total = total + parseFloat(CompItems[formElement.value]);
    }

    formElement = document.form1.radCase
    if (formElement[0].checked == true)
    {
        orderDetails = orderDetails + "Desktop Case : $" +
            CompItems[formElement[0].value];
        total = total + parseFloat(CompItems[formElement[0].value]);
    }
    else if (formElement[1].checked == true)
    {
        orderDetails = orderDetails + "Mini Tower Case : $" +
            CompItems[formElement[1].value];
        total = total + parseFloat(CompItems[formElement[1].value]);
    }
```

```
      else
      {
         orderDetails = orderDetails + "Full Tower Case : $" +
            CompItems[formElement[2].value]
         total = total + parseFloat(CompItems[formElement[2].value]);
      }

      orderDetails = orderDetails + "\n\nTotal Order Cost is $" + total;

      document.form1.txtOrder.value = orderDetails;
}

</SCRIPT>
</HEAD>

<BODY>
<FORM NAME=form1>
<TABLE>
<TR>
<TD WIDTH=300>
Processor
<BR>
<SELECT NAME=cboProcessor>
   <OPTION VALUE=100>MegaPro 1ghz</OPTION>
   <OPTION VALUE=101>MegaPro 1.2</OPTION>
   <OPTION VALUE=102>MegaPro 1.5ghz</OPTION>
</SELECT>
<BR><BR>
Hard drive
<BR>
<SELECT NAME=cboHardDrive>
   <OPTION VALUE=200>30gb</OPTION>
   <OPTION VALUE=201>40gb</OPTION>
   <OPTION VALUE=202>60gb</OPTION>
</SELECT>
<BR><BR>
CD-ROM
<INPUT TYPE="checkbox" NAME=chkCDROM VALUE="300">
<BR>
DVD-ROM
<INPUT TYPE="checkbox" NAME=chkDVD VALUE="301">
<BR>
Scanner
<INPUT TYPE="checkbox" NAME=chkScanner VALUE="302">
<BR><BR>
Desktop Case
<INPUT TYPE="radio" NAME=radCase CHECKED VALUE="400">
<BR>
Mini Tower
<INPUT TYPE="radio" NAME=radCase VALUE="401">
<BR>
Full Tower
<INPUT TYPE="radio" NAME=radCase VALUE="402">
<P>
```

```
<INPUT TYPE="button" VALUE="Update" NAME=butUpdate onclick="updateOrderDetails()">
</P>
</TD>
<TD>
<TEXTAREA ROWS=20 COLS=35 ID=txtOrder NAME=txtOrder>
</TEXTAREA>
</TD>
</TABLE>
</FORM>
</BODY>
</HTML>
```

Save this as ch06_q2.htm.

There are lots of ways of tackling this question and this is just one – you may well have thought of a better way.

I've decided to display the results of the user's selection as text in a TEXTAREA box, with each item and its cost displayed on separate lines with a final total at the end.

Each form element has a value that I've set to hold a stock id number. For example, a full tower case is stock ID 402. The actual cost of the item is held in arrays defined at the beginning of the page. Why have I not just stored the price in the VALUE attribute of each form element? Well, this way is more flexible. Currently our array just holds price details for each item, but we could modify that so it holds more data, for example price, description, number in stock, and so on. Also if this form was posted to a server then the values passed will be stock IDs, which we could then use for a lookup in a stock database. If the values were set to prices and the form was posted we'd have no way of telling what the customer has ordered – all we'd know is how much it all cost.

I've chosen to have an **Update** button which, when clicked, updates the order details in the TEXTAREA box. However, you may want to add event handlers to each form element and update when anything changes.

Turning to the function that actually displays the order summary, updateOrderDetails(), we can see there is a lot of code and although it looks complex, it's actually fairly simple. A lot of it is repeated with slight modification.

To save on typing and make the code a little more readable I've declared a variable, formElement, which will be set to each element on the form in turn and used to extract the stock ID and, from that, the price. After the variable's declaration, we then find out which processor has been selected, calculate the cost and add the details to the TEXTAREA:

```
formElement =
    document.form1.cboProcessor[document.form1.cboProcessor.selectedIndex];
total = parseFloat(CompItems[formElement.value]);
orderDetails = "Processor : " + formElement.text;
orderDetails = orderDetails + " $" + CompItems[formElement.value] + "\n";
```

The selectedIndex property tells us which Option object inside the select control has been selected by the user and we set our formElement variable to reference that.

The same principle applies when we find the hard drive size selected, so let's turn next to the checkboxes for the optional extra items, looking first at the CD-ROM checkbox:

```
formElement = document.form1.chkCDROM
if (formElement.checked == true)
{
    orderDetails = orderDetails + "CD-ROM : $" +
        CompItems[formElement.value] + "\n";
    total = total + parseFloat(CompItems[formElement.value]);
}
```

Again, we set `formElement` variable to now reference the `chkCDROM` checkbox object. Then if the checkbox is checked, we add a CD-ROM to the order details and update the running total. The same principle applies for the DVD and scanner checkboxes.

Finally, we have the case type. As only one case type out of the options can be selected, we've used a radio button group. Unfortunately, there is no `selectedIndex` for radio buttons as there is for checkboxes, so we have to go through each radio button in turn and find out if it has been selected:

```
formElement = document.form1.radCase
if (formElement[0].checked == true)
{
    orderDetails = orderDetails + "Desktop Case : $" +
        CompItems[formElement[0].value];
    total = total + parseFloat(CompItems[formElement[0].value]);
}
    else if (formElement[1].checked == true)
{
    orderDetails = orderDetails + "Mini Tower Case : $" +
        CompItems[formElement[1].value];
    total = total + parseFloat(CompItems[formElement[1].value]);
}
else
{
    orderDetails = orderDetails + "Full Tower Case : $" +
        CompItems[formElement[2].value]
    total = total + parseFloat(CompItems[formElement[2].value]);
}
```

We check to see which radio button has been selected and add its details to the TEXTAREA and its price to the total. If our array of stock defined at the beginning of the code block had further details such as description as well as price, then we could have looped through the radio button array and added the details based on the CompItems array.

Finally, we set the TEXTAREA to the details of the system the user has selected:

```
orderDetails = orderDetails + "\n\nTotal Order Cost is " + total;
document.form1.txtOrder.value = orderDetails;
```

Chapter 7

In this chapter, we looked at how we could put frames into our web pages, and how to write JavaScript code that scripted between frames. We also looked at how to open and modify new browser windows using script.

Question 1

In the previous chapter's exercise questions we created a form that allowed the user to pick a computer system. They could view the details of their system and its total cost by clicking a button that wrote the details to a text area. Change the example so that it's a frames-based web page – instead of writing to a text area, the details should be written to another frame.

Solution

The solution I have created involves a frameset that divides the page into two frames, left and right. In the left we have the form that allows the user to pick their system. In the right frame the system chosen is summarized when the user clicks an Update button.

The first page is the top frameset defining page and is the one that needs to be loaded into the browser first:

```
<HTML>
<HEAD>
</HEAD>
<FRAMESET COLS="55%,*">
    <FRAME SRC="PickSystem.htm" NAME="pickSystem">
    <FRAME SRC="blank.htm" NAME="systemSummary">
</FRAMESET>

</HTML>
```

Save this as ch7Q1TopFrame.htm

Next we need to create a blank page for the right frame. Until the user clicks an **Update** button, that frame is blank, but if we don't put an HTML page into that frame, Netscape throws an error, though IE is happy with SRC="".

```
<HTML>
<BODY>
</BODY>
</HTML>
```

Save this as blank.htm

Finally, we come to the page that's loaded into the left frame and allows the user to choose their computer system and its components. This is very similar to the solution to Question 2 in the previous chapter, so I'll just concentrate on what's been changed here. All the changes are within the updateOrderDetails() function.

```
function updateOrderDetails()
{
    var total = 0;
    var orderDetails = "<H3>Your selected system</H3>";
    var formElement;
    formElement =
        document.form1.cboProcessor[document.form1.cboProcessor.selectedIndex];
    total = parseFloat(CompItems[formElement.value]);
    orderDetails = orderDetails + "Processor : " + formElement.text
    orderDetails = orderDetails + " $" + CompItems[formElement.value] + "<BR>";

    formElement =
        document.form1.cboHardDrive[document.form1.cboHardDrive.selectedIndex];
    total = total + parseFloat(CompItems[formElement.value]);
    orderDetails = orderDetails + "Hard Drive : " + formElement.text
    orderDetails = orderDetails + " $" + CompItems[formElement.value] + "<BR>";

    formElement = document.form1.chkCDROM
    if (formElement.checked == true)
    {
        orderDetails = orderDetails + "CD-ROM : $" +
            CompItems[formElement.value] + "<BR>";
        total = total + parseFloat(CompItems[formElement.value]);
    }

    formElement = document.form1.chkDVD
    if (formElement.checked == true)
    {
        orderDetails = orderDetails + "DVD-ROM : $" +
            CompItems[formElement.value] + "<BR>";
        total = total + parseFloat(CompItems[formElement.value]);
    }

    formElement = document.form1.chkScanner
    if (formElement.checked == true)
    {
        orderDetails = orderDetails + "Scanner : $" +
            CompItems[formElement.value] + "<BR>";
        total = total + parseFloat(CompItems[formElement.value]);
    }

    formElement = document.form1.radCase
    if (formElement[0].checked == true)
    {
        orderDetails = orderDetails + "Desktop Case : $" +
            CompItems[formElement[0].value] + "<BR>";
        total = total + parseFloat(CompItems[formElement[0].value]);
    }
    else if (formElement[1].checked == true)
    {
        orderDetails = orderDetails + "Mini Tower Case : $" +
            CompItems[formElement[1].value] + "<BR>";
        total = total + parseFloat(CompItems[formElement[1].value]);
    }
```

```
        else
        {
            orderDetails = orderDetails + "Full Tower Case : $" +
                CompItems[formElement[2].value]
            total = total + parseFloat(CompItems[formElement[2].value]);
        }

            orderDetails = orderDetails + "<P>Total Order Cost is $" + total + "</P>";

        window.parent.systemSummary.document.open();
        window.parent.systemSummary.document.write(orderDetails);
        window.parent.systemSummary.document.close();
    }
```

Save this as `PickSystem.htm`, and load `ch7Q1TopFrame.htm` into your browser to try out the code.

The first difference between this and the code from Question 2 in the last chapter is that when creating the text summarizing the system we are creating HTML rather than plain text, so rather than \n for new lines we use the <BR> tag.

The main change, however, is the following three lines:

```
        window.parent.systemSummary.document.open();
        window.parent.systemSummary.document.write(orderDetails);
        window.parent.systemSummary.close();
```

Instead of setting the value of a text area box as we did in the solution to Question 2 in the last chapter, this time we are writing the order summary to an HTML page, the page contained in the right-hand frame, `systemSummary`. First we open the document for writing, then write out our string, and finally close the document indicating that we have completed our writing to the page.

Question 2

In the first example in Chapter 7, we had a page with images of books, where clicking on a book's image brought up information about that book in a popup window. Amend this so that the popup window also has a button or link that when clicked adds the item to the users shopping basket. Also on the main page, give the user some way of opening up a shopping basket window with details of all the items the user has purchased so far, and give them a way of deleting items from this basket.

Solution

For this exercise I have created four pages, two that display the book's details, very similar to the pages we created in the example, a third that displays the book's images and opens the new windows, and a fourth totally new page, which will hold the shopping basket.

Let's look at the main page to be loaded, which I've called `online_books.htm`:

```
<HTML>
<HEAD>
<TITLE>Online Books</TITLE>
<SCRIPT LANGUAGE="JavaScript">
```

```
var detailsWindow;
var basketWindow;

var stockItems = new Array();

stockItems[100] = new Array();
stockItems[100][0] = "Beginning Active Server Pages";
stockItems[100][1] = "$39.99";
stockItems[100][2] = 0;

stockItems[101] = new Array();
stockItems[101][0] = "Professonal JavaScript";
stockItems[101][1] = "$46.99";
stockItems[101][2] = 0;

function removeItem(stockId)
{
    stockItems[stockId][2] = 0;
    alert("Item Removed");
    showBasket();
    return false;
}

function showDetails(bookURL)
{
    detailsWindow = window.open(bookURL,"bookDetails","width=400,height=500");
    detailsWindow.focus();
    return false;
}

function addBookToBasket(stockId)
{
    stockItems[stockId][2] = 1;
    alert("Item added successfully");
    detailsWindow.close();
}

function showBasket()
{
    basketWindow =
        window.open('ShoppingBasket.htm','shoppingBasket','width=400,height=350');
    basketWindow.document.open();
    var basketItem;
    var containsItems = false;
    basketWindow.document.write("<H4>Your shopping basket contains :</H4>");

    for (basketItem in stockItems)
    {
        if (stockItems[basketItem][2] > 0)
        {
            basketWindow.document.write(stockItems[basketItem][0] + " at ");
            basketWindow.document.write(stockItems[basketItem][1]);
            basketWindow.document.write("    ");
            basketWindow.document.write("<A href='' onclick='return " + "
            window.opener.removeItem(" + basketItem + ")'>");
```

```
            basketWindow.document.write("Remove Item</A><BR>");
            containsItems = true;
        }
    }

    if (containsItems == false)
    {
        basketWindow.document.write("<H4>No items</H4>");
    }
    basketWindow.document.close();
    basketWindow.focus();
}

</SCRIPT>
</HEAD>
<BODY>
<H2 ALIGN=center>Online Book Buyer</H2>
<FORM NAME=form1>
<INPUT TYPE="button" VALUE="Show Shopping Basket" onclick="showBasket()"
NAME=butShowBasket>
</FORM>
<P>
Click any of the images below for more details
</P>
<STRONG>Beginning Active Server Pages 3</STRONG>
<BR>
<A NAME="begASPLink" HREF="" onclick="return showDetails('beg_asp3_details.htm')">
<IMG SRC="beg_asp3.gif" BORDER=0>
</A>
<BR><BR>
<STRONG>Professional JavaScript</STRONG>
<BR>
<A NAME="profJSLink" HREF=""
onclick="return showDetails('prof_js_details.htm')">
<IMG SRC="prof_js.gif" border=0>
</A>
</BODY>
</HTML>
```

The details of the books are stored in the stockItems array, which we've made a multi-dimensional array. The second dimension stores the book's title, its price and finally the quantity the customer has in their basket.

So, in the first element, we have:

```
stockItems[100] = new Array();
stockItems[100][0] = "Beginning Active Server Pages";
stockItems[100][1] = "$39.99";
stockItems[100][2] = 0;
```

[100][0] is the title, [100][1] the price, and finally [100][2] the quantity required, which starts as zero. In fact, though there is the potential to have the customer order more than one of a certain book the code does not facilitate that.

The first function defined in the code is `removeItem()`:

```
function removeItem(stockId)
{
    stockItems[stockId][2] = 0;
    alert("Item Removed");
    showBasket();
    return false;
}
```

This removes a book from the shopping basket. The parameter `stockId` is simply the array element index of that book which we then use to set the quantity element of the second dimension to 0.

Next, we have the function that adds a book to the shopping basket:

```
function addBookToBasket(stockId)
{
    stockItems[stockId][2] = 1;
    alert("Item added successfully");
    detailsWindow.close();
}
```

The final function displays the contents of the shopping basket in a new window:

```
function showBasket()
{
    basketWindow =
        window.open('ShoppingBasket.htm','shoppingBasket','width=400,height=350');
    basketWindow.document.open();
    var basketItem;
    var containsItems = false;
    basketWindow.document.write("<H4>Your shopping basket contains :</H4>");

    for (basketItem in stockItems)
    {
        if (stockItems[basketItem][2] > 0)
        {
            basketWindow.document.write(stockItems[basketItem][0] + " at ");
            basketWindow.document.write(stockItems[basketItem][1]);
            basketWindow.document.write("    ");
            basketWindow.document.write("<A href='' onclick='return " +
            " window.opener.removeItem(" + basketItem + ")'>");
            basketWindow.document.write("Remove Item</A><BR>");
            containsItems = true;
        }
    }

    if (containsItems == false)
    {
        basketWindow.document.write("<H4>No items</H4>");
    }
    basketWindow.document.close();
    basketWindow.focus();
}
```

A new window is opened up and its `window` object reference stored in `basketWindow`. We then write to the new window's `document`, first a heading, then we loop through each item in the `stockItems` array and check the quantity element of the second dimension, that is `stockItems[basketItem][2]`. If it is greater than zero, we write the book's details to the shopping list window. We also write out a link to the shopping basket, which when clicked calls our `removeItem()` function.

Let's create the shopping basket page:

```
<HTML>
<HEAD>
<TITLE>Shopping Basket</TITLE>
</HEAD>
<BODY>
</BODY>
</HTML>
```

Save this as `ShoppingBasket.htm`. There's no code, but if we don't create the page and load it into the shopping basket window then we wouldn't be able to `document.write()` to it.

Finally, we need to create the book description pages. First we have `prof_js_details.htm`. This is identical to the version we created for the example, except the addition of the form and button inside. When clicked, the button calls the `addToBasket()` function in the window that opened this window, that is our `online_books.htm` page.

```
<HTML>
<HEAD>
<TITLE>Professional JavaScript</TITLE>
</HEAD>
<BODY><STRONG>Professional JavaScript</STRONG>
<BR>
<FORM NAME=form1>
<INPUT TYPE="button" VALUE="Add to basket" NAME=butAddBook
onclick="window.opener.addBookToBasket(101)">
</FORM>

<STRONG>Subjects</STRONG>
    ECMAScript<BR>
    Internet<BR>JavaScript
    <BR>XML and Scripting<BR>

<HR COLOR=#cc3333>
<P>This book covers the broad spectrum of programming JavaScript - from the core
language to browser applications and server-side use to stand-alone and embedded
JavaScript.
</P>
<P>
It includes a guide to the language - when where and how to get the
most out of JavaScript - together with practical case studies demonstrating
JavaScript in action. Coverage is bang up-to-date, with discussion of
compatability issues and version differences, and the book concludes with a
comprehensive reference section. </P>

</BODY>
</HTML>
```

Finally, we have our `beg_asp3_details.htm` page. Again, it is identical to the version created in the example with a form and button to add the book to the shopping basket, like the page above:

```
<HTML>
<HEAD>
<TITLE>Beginning Active Server Pages 3.0</TITLE>
</HEAD>
<BODY>
<STRONG>Beginning Active Server Pages 3.0</STRONG>
<FORM NAME=form1>
<INPUT TYPE="button" VALUE="Add to basket" NAME=butAddBook
onclick="window.opener.addBookToBasket(100)">
</FORM>

<BR>
Subjects
<BR>
ASP
<BR>
Internet
<BR>

<HR COLOR=#cc3333>

<P>ASP 3.0 is the most recent version of ASP, and is released with version 5.0
of Microsoft's <B>Internet Information Server</B> (IIS 5.0) web server, with
<B>Windows 2000</B>. It is also ported for use on UNIX.
</P>
<P>ASP is an easy way to control content - giving us the
flexibility to handle complex professional commercial sites. If you want to
program a web page, pure HTML is fine, however this book shows how to add
dynamism to web site generation and will utilize components, objects and
Databases to achieve that.
</P>

</BODY>
</HTML>
```

Chapter 8

In this chapter we looked at string manipulation using the `String` object and the use of the `RegExp` object to match patterns of characters within strings

Question 1

What problem does the code below solve?

```
var myString = "This sentence has has a fault and and we need to fix it."
var myRegExp = /(\b\w+\b) \1/g;
myString = myString.replace(myRegExp,"$1");
```

If we now change our code, so that we create our `RegExp` object like this:

```
var myRegExp = new RegExp("(\b\w+\b) \1");
```

Why would this not work, and how could we rectify the problem?

Solution

The problem is the sentence has "has has" and "and and" inside it, clearly a mistake. A lot of word processors have an auto correct that fixes common mistakes like this and what our regular expression does is mimic this feature.

So the erroneous `myString`:

"This sentence has has a fault and and we need to fix it."

will become:

"This sentence has a fault and we need to fix it."

Let's look at how the code works, starting with the regular expression:

```
/(\b\w+\b) \1/g;
```

By using parentheses we have defined a group, so `(\b\w+\b)` is group 1. The pattern this group matches is a word boundary followed by one or more alphanumeric characters, that is a-z, A-Z, 0-9, and _, followed by a word boundary. Following the group we have a space then `\1`. What `\1` means is match exactly the same characters as were matched in pattern group 1. So, for example, if group 1 matched "has" then `\1` will match "has" as well. It's important to note that `\1` will match the exact previous match by group 1. So when group 1 then matches the "and", the `\1` now matches "and" and not the "has" that was previously matched.

We use the group again in our `replace()` method, this time the group is specified using the $ symbol, so $1 matches group 1. It's this that causes the two matched "has" and "and" to be replaced by just one.

Turning to the second part of the question, how do we need to change the following code so that it works:

```
var myRegExp = new RegExp("(\b\w+\b) \1");
```

Easy; now we are using a string passed to the `RegExp` object's constructor, we need to use two \ rather than one when we mean a regular expression syntax character, like this:

```
var myRegExp = new RegExp("(\\b\\w+\\b) \\1","g");
```

Notice we've also passed a g to the second parameter to make it a global match.

Question 2

Write a regular expression that finds all of the occurrences of the word "a" in the following sentence, and replaces them with "the":

"a dog walked in off a street and ordered a finest beer"

So the sentence becomes:

"the dog walked in off the street and ordered the finest beer"

Solution

```
<HTML>
<BODY>
<SCRIPT LANGUAGE=JavaScript>
var myString = "a dog walked in off a street and ordered a finest beer";
var myRegExp = /\ba\b/gi;
myString = myString.replace(myRegExp,"the");
alert(myString)
</SCRIPT>
</BODY>
</HTML>
```

Save this as ch08_q2.htm

With regular expressions it's often not just what you want to match, but also what you don't want to match that is a problem. Here we want to match the letter a, so why not just write:

```
var myRegExp = /a/gi;
```

Well that would work, but it would also replace the "a" in "walked", which we don't want. We want to replace the letter "a" but only where it's a word on its own and not inside another word. So when does a letter become a word? The answer is when it's between two word boundaries. The word boundary is represented by the regular expression special character \b so the regular expression becomes:

```
var myRegExp = /\ba\b/gi;
```

The gi at the end ensures a global, case insensitive search.

Now with our regular expression created we can use it in the replace() method's first parameter:

```
myString = myString.replace(myRegExp,"the");
```

Question 3

Imagine you have a web site with a message board. Write a regular expression that would remove barred words (I'll let you make up your own words!!!)

Solution

```
<HTML>
<BODY>
<SCRIPT LANGUAGE=JavaScript>
    var myRegExp = /(sugar )?candy|choc(olate|oholic)?/gi
    var myString = "Mmm, I love chocolate, I'm a chocoholic. " +
        "I love candy too, sweet, sugar candy";
    myString = myString.replace(myRegExp,"salad");
    alert(myString)
</SCRIPT>
</BODY>
</HTML>
```

Save this as `ch08_q3.htm`

For my example, we'll pretend we're creating script for a board on a dieting site where text relating to candy is barred, and will be replaced with a much healthier option, salad.

My barred words are:

chocolate
choc
chocoholic
sugar candy
candy

Let's see how I built up the regular expression to remove the offending words.

I started with the two basic words, so to match choc or candy I use:

```
candy|choc
```

Next I added the matching for sugar candy. As the "sugar" bit is optional we group it by placing it in parentheses and adding the "?" after it. This means match the group zero times or one time.

```
(sugar )?candy|choc
```

Finally we need to add the optional "olate" and "oholic" end bits. We add these as a group after the choc word and again make the group optional. We can match either of the endings in the group by using the | character:

```
(sugar )?candy|choc(olate|oholic)?/gi
```

Finally, we declare it as:

```
var myRegExp = /(sugar )?candy|choc(olate|oholic)?/gi
```

The `gi` at the end means the regular expression will find and replace words on a global, case insensitive basis.

So, to sum up:

```
/(sugar )?candy|choc(olate|oholic)?/gi
```

reads as:

Either match zero or one occurrence of sugar followed by candy. Or alternatively match choc followed by either one or zero occurrence of olate or match choc followed by zero or one occurrence of oholic.

Finally:

```
myString = myString.replace(myRegExp,"salad");
```

Replaces the offending words with "salad" and sets `myString` to the new clean version:

Mmm, I love salad, I'm a salad. I love salad too, sweet, salad.

Chapter 9

In this chapter we looked in more detail at the `Date` object, particularly with respect to world time and local time. We also looked at how to create timers to trigger code on a web page

Question 1

Create a web page with an advertisement image at the top. When the page loads, select a random image for that advertisement. Every four seconds change the advertisement to a different image making sure a different advertisement is selected until all the advertisement images have been seen.

Solution

```
<HTML>
<HEAD>
<SCRIPT LANGUAGE=JavaScript>

var imagesSelected = new Array(false,false,false);
var noOfImages = 3;
var totalImagesSelected = 0;

function window_onload()
{
```

```
        setInterval("switchImage()",4000);
}

function switchImage()
{

    var imageIndex;

    if (totalImagesSelected == noOfImages)
    {
        for (imageIndex = 0; imageIndex < noOfImages; imageIndex++)
        {
            imagesSelected[imageIndex] = false;
        }

        totalImagesSelected = 0;
    }

var selectedImage = Math.floor(Math.random() * noOfImages) + 1;
while (imagesSelected[selectedImage - 1] == true)
{
        selectedImage = Math.floor(Math.random() * noOfImages) + 1;
    }
    totalImagesSelected++;
    imagesSelected[selectedImage - 1] = true;
    document.imgAdvert.src = "AdvertImage" + selectedImage + ".jpg";

}

</SCRIPT>
</HEAD>
<BODY ONLOAD="window_onload()">
<IMG SRC="AdvertImage1.jpg" NAME="imgAdvert">
</BODY>
</HTML>
```

Save this as ch09_q1.htm.

This solution is based on the example in the chapter, Adverts.htm, where we displayed three images at set intervals one after the other. The first difference is that we select a random image each time, rather than the images in sequence. Secondly, we make sure we don't select the same image twice in one sequence by having an array, imagesSelected, with each element of that array being true or false depending on whether the image has been selected before. Once we've shown each image, then we reset the array and start the sequence of selecting images randomly again.

The final difference between this solution and the example in the chapter is that we set the timer going continuously with setInterval(). So, until the user moves to another page our random display of images will continue.

Question 2

Create a form that gets the user's date of birth. Then, using that information, tell them what day they were born on.

Solution:

```
<HTML>
<HEAD>
<SCRIPT LANGUAGE=JavaScript>

var days = new Array();
days[0] = "Sunday";
days[1] = "Monday";
days[2] = "Tuesday";
days[3] = "Wednesday";
days[4] = "Thursday";
days[5] = "Friday";
days[6] = "Saturday";

function dayOfWeek()
{

   var form = document.form1;
   var date = parseInt(form.txtDate.value)
   var year = parseInt(form.txtYear.value)

   if (isNaN(date) || isNaN(year))
   {
      alert("Please enter a valid whole number");
   }
   else
   {
      if (date < 1 || date > 31)
      {
         alert("Day of the month must be between 1 and 31");
      }
      else
      {
         userDate = date + " ";
         userDate = userDate +
form.selMonth.options[form.selMonth.selectedIndex].value;
         userDate = userDate + " " + year;
         var dateThen = new Date(userDate);
         alert(days[dateThen.getDay()]);
      }
   }
}
</SCRIPT>
</HEAD>
<BODY>
```

```
<P>Find the day of your birth</P>
<P>
<FORM NAME=form1>
<INPUT TYPE=text NAME=txtDate SIZE=2 MAXLENGTH=2>
<SELECT NAME=selMonth>
    <OPTION selected value="Jan">Jan</OPTION>
    <OPTION selected value="Feb">Feb</OPTION>
    <OPTION selected value="Mar">Mar</OPTION>
    <OPTION selected value="Apr">Apr</OPTION>
    <OPTION selected value="May">May</OPTION>
    <OPTION selected value="Jun">Jun</OPTION>
    <OPTION selected value="Jul">Jul</OPTION>
    <OPTION selected value="Aug">Aug</OPTION>
    <OPTION selected value="Sept">Sept</OPTION>
    <OPTION selected value="Oct">Oct</OPTION>
    <OPTION selected value="Nov">Nov</OPTION>
    <OPTION selected value="Dec">Dec</OPTION>
</SELECT>
<INPUT TYPE=text NAME=txtYear SIZE=4 MAXLENGTH=4>
<BR>
<INPUT TYPE="button" VALUE="Day of the week"
        onclick="dayOfWeek()" NAME=button1>
</FORM>
</P>

</BODY>
</HTML>
```

Save this as ch09_q2.htm

The solution is surprisingly simple. We create a new Date object based on the date entered by the user. Then we get the day of the week using the Date object's getDay() method. This returns a number, but by defining an array of days of the week to match this number we can use the value of getDay() as the index to our days array.

We also do some basic sanity checking to check that the user has entered numbers and that in the case of the date it's between 1 and 31. We could have defined a select element as the method of getting the date and only having number from 1 to 31. Of course either way we don't check that invalid dates are entered, for example the 31st February. You might want to try this as an additional exercise.

Hint: to get the last day of the month get the first day of the next month then subtract 1.

Chapter 10

In this chapter we looked at some common mistakes in JavaScript code, debugging code using the Microsoft script debugger, and ways of handling errors using the try...catch clause and the throw statement.

Question 1

The example `debug_timestable2.htm` has a deliberate bug. For each times table it only creates the values from 1 to 11 as you can see from the output for the two times table shown below:

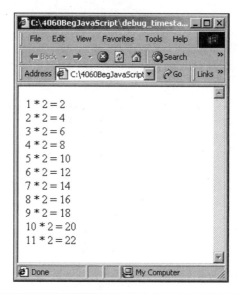

Use the script debugger to work out why this is happening, and then correct the bug.

Solution

The problem is one of our code's logic rather than syntax. Logic errors are much harder to spot and deal with because unlike syntax errors the browser won't inform you that there's such and such error at line so and so but instead just fails to work as expected. The error is with this line:

```
for (counter = 1; counter < 12; counter++)
```

We want our loop to go from 1 to 12 inclusive. Our `counter < 12` statement will be `true` up to and including 11 but will be `false` when counter reaches 12, hence 12 gets missed off. To correct this we could change our code to:

```
for (counter = 1; counter <= 12; counter++)
```

Question 2

There are a number of common errors in the following code, see if you can spot them:

```
<HTML>
<HEAD>
</HEAD>
<BODY>
```

```
<SCRIPT LANGUAGE=JavaScript>

function checkForm(theForm)
{
    var formValid = true;
    var elementCount  = 0;

    while(elementCount =< theForm.length)
    {
        if (theForm.elements[elementcount].type == "text")
        {

            if (theForm.elements[elementCount].value() = "")
                alert("Please complete all form elements")
                theForm.elements[elementCount].focus;
                formValid = false;
                break;

        }
    }

    return formValid;

}

</SCRIPT>

<FORM NAME=form1 onsubmit="return checkForm(document.form1)">
    <INPUT TYPE="text" ID=text1 NAME=text1>
    <BR>
    CheckBox 1<INPUT TYPE="checkbox" ID=checkbox2 NAME=checkbox2>
    <BR>
    CheckBox 1<INPUT TYPE="checkbox" ID=checkbox1 NAME=checkbox1>
    <BR>
    <INPUT TYPE="text" ID=text2 NAME=text2>
    <P>
    <INPUT TYPE="submit" VALUE="Submit" ID=submit1 NAME=submit1>
    </P>
</FORM>

</BODY>
</HTML>
```

Solution

The bug free version looks like this:

```
<HTML>
<HEAD>
</HEAD>
<BODY>

<SCRIPT LANGUAGE=JavaScript>
```

```
function checkForm(theForm)
{
    var formValid = true;
    var elementCount  = 0;

    while(elementCount < theForm.length)
    {
        if (theForm.elements[elementCount].type == "text")
        {
            if (theForm.elements[elementCount].value == "")
            {
                alert("Please complete all form elements")
                theForm.elements[elementCount].focus();
                formValid = false;
                break;
            }
        }

        elementCount++;
    }

    return formValid;

}

</SCRIPT>

<FORM NAME=form1 onsubmit="return checkForm(document.form1)">
    <INPUT TYPE="text" ID=text1 NAME=text1>
    <BR>
    CheckBox 1<INPUT TYPE="checkbox" ID=checkbox2 NAME=checkbox2>
    <BR>
    CheckBox 1<INPUT TYPE="checkbox" ID=checkbox1 NAME=checkbox1>
    <BR>
    <INPUT TYPE="text" ID=text2 NAME=text2>
    <P>
    <INPUT TYPE="submit" VALUE="Submit" ID=submit1 NAME=submit1>
    </P>
</FORM>

</BODY>
</HTML>
```

Let's look at each error in turn.

The first error is a logic error:

```
while(elementCount =< theForm.length)
```

Arrays start at zero so the first Form object is at index array 0, the second at 1 and so on. The last Form object has an index value of 4. However, theForm.length will return 5, as there are 5 elements in the form. So the while loop will continue until elementCount is less than or equal to 5, but as the last element has index of 4 this is one past the limit. We should either write:

```
    while(elementCount < theForm.length)
```

or:

```
    while(elementCount =< theForm.length - 1)
```

Either is fine, though the first is shorter.

We come to our second error in:

```
    if (theForm.elements[elementcount].type == "text")
```

On a quick glance it looks fine, but it's JavaScript's strictness on case sensitivity that has caused our downfall. The variable name is elementCount, not elementcount with a lower case c. So this line should read:

```
    if (theForm.elements[elementCount].type == "text")
```

The next line with an error is this:

```
    if (theForm.elements[elementCount].value() = "")
```

This has two errors. Firstly, value is a property and not a method, so there is no need for parentheses after it. Secondly, we have the all-time classic error of one equals sign and not two. Remember one equals sign means make it equal to, two equal signs means check if it is equal to. So with the changes the line is:

```
    if (theForm.elements[elementCount].value == "")
```

The next error is our failure to put our block of if code in curly braces. JavaScript won't throw an error as the syntax is fine, but the logic is not and we won't get the results we expect. With the braces, the if statement should be:

```
    if (theForm.elements[elementCount].value == "")
    {
        alert("Please complete all form elements")
        theForm.elements[elementCount].focus;
        formValid = false;
        break;
    }
```

The penultimate error is in:

```
    theForm.elements[elementCount].focus;
```

This time we have a method but with no parentheses after it. Even methods that have no parameters must have the empty parentheses after them. So, corrected, the line is:

```
    theForm.elements[elementCount].focus();
```

Now, we're almost done, there is just one more error. This time not something that is wrong with what's there, but rather something very important that should be there but is missing. What is it? It's:

```
elementCount++;
```

which should be in our `while` loop, otherwise `elementCount` will never go above 0 and the `while` loop's condition will always be `true`, resulting in the loop continuing for ever; a classic infinite loop.

Chapter 11

In this chapter we looked at storing small amounts of information, called cookies, on the user's computer and using that information to customize our web site for the user.

Question 1

Create a page that keeps track of how many times the page has been visited by the user in the last month.

Solution

```
<HTML>
<HEAD>
<SCRIPT LANGUAGE=JavaScript>

function getCookieValue(cookieName)
{
    var cookieValue = document.cookie;
    var cookieStartsAt = cookieValue.indexOf(" " + cookieName + "=");

   if (cookieStartsAt == -1)
   {
       cookieStartsAt = cookieValue.indexOf(cookieName + "=");
   }

   if (cookieStartsAt == -1)
   {
       cookieValue = null;
   }
   else
   {

       cookieStartsAt = cookieValue.indexOf("=", cookieStartsAt) + 1;
       var cookieEndsAt = cookieValue.indexOf(";", cookieStartsAt);
       if (cookieEndsAt == -1)
       {
           cookieEndsAt = cookieValue.length;
       }
       cookieValue = unescape(cookieValue.substring(cookieStartsAt,
           cookieEndsAt));
```

```
      }

   return cookieValue;
}

function setCookie(cookieName,cookieValue, cookiePath, cookieExpires)
{
   cookieValue = escape(cookieValue);
   if (cookieExpires == "")
   {
      var nowDate = new Date();
      nowDate.setMonth(nowDate.getMonth() + 6);
      cookieExpires = nowDate.toGMTString();
   }

   if (cookiePath != "")
   {
      cookiePath = ";Path=" + cookiePath;
   }
   document.cookie = cookieName + "=" + cookieValue + ";Expires=" +
      cookieExpires + cookiePath;
}

var pageViewCount = getCookieValue("pageViewCount");
var pageFirstVisited = getCookieValue("pageFirstVisited");

if (pageViewCount == null)
{
   pageViewCount = 1;
   pageFirstVisited = new Date();
   pageFirstVisited.setMonth(pageFirstVisited.getMonth());
   pageFirstVisited = pageFirstVisited.toGMTString();
   setCookie("pageFirstVisited",pageFirstVisited,"",pageFirstVisited)
}
else
{
   pageViewCount = Math.floor(pageViewCount) + 1;
}

setCookie("pageViewCount",pageViewCount,"",pageFirstVisited)

</SCRIPT>
</HEAD>
<BODY>
<SCRIPT>
var pageHTML = "You've visited this page " + pageViewCount;
pageHTML = pageHTML + " times since " + pageFirstVisited;
document.write(pageHTML);
</SCRIPT>
</BODY>
</HTML>
```

Save this as ch11_q1.htm.

We discussed the cookie functions in Chapter 11, so let's turn straight to the new code.

In the first two lines we get two cookies and store them in variables. The first cookie holds the number of visits, the second the date the page was first visited:

```
var pageViewCount = getCookieValue("pageViewCount");
var pageFirstVisited = getCookieValue("pageFirstVisited");
```

If the pageViewCount cookie does not exist, it's either because the cookie expired (remember we are counting visits in the last month) or because they have never visited our site before. Either way we need to set the pageViewCount to 1 and store the date the page was first visited plus one month in the pageFirstVisited variable. We'll need this value later when we want to set the expires value for the pageViewCount cookie we'll create as there is no way of using code to find out an existing cookie's expiry date.

```
if (pageViewCount == null)
{
   pageViewCount = 1;
   pageFirstVisited = new Date();
   pageFirstVisited.setMonth(pageFirstVisited.getMonth() + 1)
   pageFirstVisited = pageFirstVisited.toGMTString();
   setCookie("pageFirstVisited",pageFirstVisited,"",pageFirstVisited)
}
```

In the else statement we increase the value of pageViewCount:

```
else
{
   pageViewCount = Math.floor(pageViewCount) + 1;
}
```

We then set the cookie keeping track of the number of page visits by the user:

```
setCookie("pageViewCount",pageViewCount,"",pageFirstVisited)
```

Finally, later on in the page we write out the number of page visits and the date since the counter was re-set:

```
var pageHTML = "You've visited this page " + pageViewCount;
pageHTML = pageHTML + " times since " + pageFirstVisited;
document.write(pageHTML);
```

Question 2

Use cookies to load a different advert every time a user visits a web page.

Solution

```
<HTML>
<HEAD>
<SCRIPT LANGUAGE=JavaScript>

function getCookieValue(cookieName)
{
   var cookieValue = document.cookie;
   var cookieStartsAt = cookieValue.indexOf(" " + cookieName + "=");

  if (cookieStartsAt == -1)
  {
     cookieStartsAt = cookieValue.indexOf(cookieName + "=");
  }

  if (cookieStartsAt == -1)
  {
     cookieValue = null;
  }
  else
  {

     cookieStartsAt = cookieValue.indexOf("=", cookieStartsAt) + 1;
     var cookieEndsAt = cookieValue.indexOf(";", cookieStartsAt);
     if (cookieEndsAt == -1)
     {
        cookieEndsAt = cookieValue.length;
     }
     cookieValue = unescape(cookieValue.substring(cookieStartsAt, cookieEndsAt));

  }

  return cookieValue;
}

function setCookie(cookieName,cookieValue, cookiePath, cookieExpires)
{
   cookieValue = escape(cookieValue);
   if (cookieExpires == "")
   {
      var nowDate = new Date();
      nowDate.setMonth(nowDate.getMonth() + 6);
      cookieExpires = nowDate.toGMTString();
   }

   if (cookiePath != "")
   {
      cookiePath = ";Path=" + cookiePath;
   }
```

```
        document.cookie = cookieName + "=" + cookieValue + ";Expires=" +
            cookieExpires + cookiePath;
    }

</SCRIPT>
</HEAD>
<BODY>
<IMG SRC="AdvertImage1.jpg" NAME="imgAdvert">
<SCRIPT>

var imageNumber = getCookieValue("displayedImages");
var totalImages = 3;

if (imageNumber == null)
{
    imageNumber = "1";
}
else
{
    imageNumber = Math.floor(imageNumber) + 1;
}

if (totalImages == imageNumber)
{
    setCookie("displayedImages","","","Mon, 1 Jan 1970 00:00:00");
}
else
{
    setCookie("displayedImages",imageNumber,"","");
}

document.imgAdvert.src = "AdvertImage" + imageNumber + ".jpg";
</SCRIPT>
</BODY>
</HTML>
```

Save this as ch11_q2.htm.

This solution is based on similar questions in previous chapters, such as Chapter 9 where we displayed a randomly selected image. In this case we display a different image in the page each time the user visits it, as far as our selection of images allows.

We've seen the cookie setting and reading functions before in the chapter, so let's look at the new code.

We store the number of the previously displayed image in a cookie named displayedImages. The next image we display is that image number + 1. Once all of our images have been displayed then we start again at 1. If the user has never been to the web site, then no cookie will exist so null will be returned from getCookieValue(), in which case we set imageNumber to 1.

Most of the code is fairly self-explanatory, except perhaps this line:

```
if (totalImages == imageNumber)
{
    setCookie("displayedImages","","","Mon, 1 Jan 1970 00:00:00")
}
```

What this bit of code does is delete the cookie by setting the cookie's expiry date to a date that has already gone.

Chapter 12

In this chapter, we looked at Dynamic HTML (DHTML), in which we use scripting languages, like JavaScript, to open up the page to manipulation after the page has loaded, to enhance user interaction.

Question 1

Create a series of images, each of which is a button linking to a different page on your web site. When the mouse pointer rolls over an image display some text somewhere on the page that describes what the user would find if they followed the link. For example, an image saying, "What's New" might have the description, "Find out what has been added to the web site since your last visit". When the mouse pointer rolls off then the descriptive text should disappear. Your page must work with IE 4+ and NN 4.x.

Solution

```
<HTML>
<HEAD>
<SCRIPT LANGUAGE=JavaScript>

var descriptions = new Array();
descriptions[0] = "<P>See what's been added to the website since your last
        visit</P>";
descriptions[1] = "<P>Find out more about me and this website</P>";
descriptions[2] = "<P>Check out the interesting and useful links on this
        page</P>";

function showDescription(descriptionIndex)
{
    if (document.all)
    {
        DescriptionDiv.style.visibility = "visible";
        DescriptionDiv.innerHTML = descriptions[descriptionIndex];
    }
    else
    {
        document.DescriptionDiv.visibility = "visible";
        document.DescriptionDiv.document.open();
        document.DescriptionDiv.document.write("<DIV
            class='DescriptionDivStyle'>");
        document.DescriptionDiv.document.write(descriptions[descriptionIndex]);
        document.DescriptionDiv.document.write("</DIV>");
        document.DescriptionDiv.document.close();
    }
}

function clearDescription()
{
    if (document.all)
    {
        DescriptionDiv.style.visibility = "hidden";
    }
    else
    {
```

```
                document.DescriptionDiv.visibility = "hidden";
        }
}
</SCRIPT>
<STYLE>

    DIV
        {
            border-width: thin;
            border-style: ridge;
            border-color: red;
            width: 250px;
            height: 70px;
            visibility: hidden;
        }

        .DescriptionDiv
        {
            position: absolute;
            left: 120px;
            top: 50px;


        }
</STYLE>

</HEAD>
<BODY>

<A HREF="WhatsNew.htm"
    onmouseover="showDescription(0)"
    onmouseout="clearDescription()">
    <IMG SRC="WhatsNew.jpg" BORDER=0></A>
<BR>
<A HREF="AboutMe.htm"
    onmouseover="showDescription(1)"
    onmouseout="clearDescription()">
    <IMG SRC="AboutMeButton.jpg" BORDER=0></A>
<BR>
<A HREF="InterestingLinks.htm"
    onmouseover="showDescription(2)"
    onmouseout="clearDescription()">
    <IMG SRC="InterestingLinks.jpg" BORDER=0></A>

<DIV ID=DescriptionDiv NAME=DescriptionDiv CLASS="DescriptionDiv">
</DIV>

</BODY>
</HTML>
```

Let's look at this page in more detail, starting with the style sheet definition where we define border styles, dimensions, positioning, and visibility. The first style defines style for all <DIV> tags on the page; the second defines a style class called DescriptionDiv.

As <IMG> tags don't support the onmouseover and onmouseout events in NN 4, we've use the mouse events of the <A> tag:

```
<A HREF="WhatsNew.htm"
    onmouseover="showDescription(0)"
    onmouseout="clearDescription()">
    <IMG SRC="WhatsNew.jpg" BORDER=0></A>
```

Finally we have a <DIV> that will contain the text we wish to display:

```
<DIV ID=DescriptionDiv NAME=DescriptionDiv CLASS="DescriptionDiv">
</DIV>
```

At the top of the script block we define a new array called descriptions that holds the descriptions we'll display when the user rolls the pointer over a menu button. As it's declared outside of any function it has global scope and will be accessible from all functions in the page.

```
var descriptions = new Array();
descriptions[0] = "<P>See what's been added to the website since your last
        visit</P>";
descriptions[1] = "<P>Find out more about me and this website</P>";
descriptions[2] = "<P>Check out the interesting and useful links on this
        page</P>";
```

The first function declared is showDescription(), called by the onmouseover event handler of the <A> tag surrounding the image. It takes just one parameter, descriptionIndex, which is the index value for the description in the descriptions array.

How we actually insert HTML after the page has loaded differs between IE 4+ and NN 4, so we check to see if document.all returns a value. If it does this must be IE 4+ as only IE 4+ supports the all property of the document object. For IE, we simply make the <DIV> visible, then set its innerHTML to the string contained inside our descriptions array, which replaces any previous HTML in there.

If this is NN 4 then we again make the <DIV> visible and then write our HTML to the document object contained inside the Layer object that represents our Div. The document.open() clears any previous HTML in there.

Although the IE and NN versions may look similar in that they both appear to be accessing the Div object of the <DIV> tag they are in fact very different. NN 4 does not have a Div object but instead represents any absolutely positioned tags with a Layer object, regardless of their actual tag type. So document.DescriptionDiv.visibility is actually changing the visibility property for the Layer object created for that <DIV>.

The final function, clearDescription(), called by the onmouseout event handler of the <A> tag surrounding the image, works in a similar way. We first check if this is IE or NN. If it's IE we hide the Div using its style property, and if it's NN we access the Layer object representing the <DIV> and set its visibility property to hidden.

Question 2

Create an image that says "Welcome" and which floats round the page. When the user's mouse pointer rolls over the image change it so it displays "Click For What's New". When clicked it should take the user to a page detailing new additions to the web site. The solution must work with both IE 4+ and with NN 4.x.

Solution

```
<HTML>
<HEAD>
<SCRIPT LANGUAGE=JavaScript>

var isIE;

var floatingDivHeight = 65;
var floatingDivWidth = 265;
var timerId;
var screenWidth;
var screenHeight;
var horizontalMovement = Math.ceil(Math.random() * 6);
var verticalMovement = Math.ceil(Math.random() * 3);

function startTimer()
{
   timerId = window.setInterval("moveDiv()",100);

   if (document.all)
   {
      floatingDiv.style.left = "6px";
      floatingDiv.style.top = "6px";

      screenWidth = document.body.clientWidth;
      screenHeight = document.body.clientHeight;

      isIE = true;
   }
   else
   {
      screenWidth = window.innerWidth;
      screenHeight = window.innerHeight;
      isIE = false;
   }
}

function moveDiv()
{

   var currentLeft;
   var currentTop;

   if (isIE)
   {
      // IE4+ Code
```

```
            currentLeft = parseInt(floatingDiv.style.left);
            currentTop = parseInt(floatingDiv.style.top);
    }
    else
    {
        // NN4 Code
        currentLeft = parseInt(document.floatingDiv.left);
        currentTop = parseInt(document.floatingDiv.top);
    }

    if (currentTop < 6)
    {
        verticalMovement = Math.ceil(Math.random() * 5);
    }
    else if ( ( currentTop + floatingDivHeight) > screenHeight )
    {
        verticalMovement = -(Math.ceil(Math.random() * 5));
    }

    if (currentLeft < 6)
    {
        horizontalMovement = Math.ceil(Math.random() * 5);
    }
    else if ( ( currentLeft + floatingDivWidth) > screenWidth )
    {
        horizontalMovement = -(Math.ceil(Math.random() * 5));
    }

    currentLeft = currentLeft + horizontalMovement;
    currentTop = currentTop + verticalMovement;

    if (isIE)
    {
        // IE4+ Code
        floatingDiv.style.left = currentLeft;
        floatingDiv.style.top = currentTop;
    }
    else
    {
        // NN4 Code
        document.floatingDiv.left = currentLeft;
        document.floatingDiv.top = currentTop;
    }
}

</SCRIPT>
<STYLE>

    .FloatingDiv {
                position: absolute;
                left: 6px;
                top: 6px;
                width : 410px;
                height : 260px;
                }
```

```
    </STYLE>

    </HEAD>
    <BODY onload="startTimer()">
    <H3>Hello World</H3>
    <DIV ID=floatingDiv NAME=floatingDiv CLASS="FloatingDiv">
        <A HREF="WhatsNew.htm"
                onmouseover="document.FloatingImage.src = 'clickforwhatsnew.jpg'"
                onmouseout="document.FloatingImage.src = 'Welcome.jpg'">
            <IMG NAME="FloatingImage" ID="FloatingImage" SRC="Welcome.jpg" BORDER=0>
        </A>
    </DIV>

    </BODY>
    </HTML>
```

Let's see how the page works. When the page is loaded, the window's `onload` event handler calls the function `startTimer()`. This starts a timer going at regular 100 millisecond intervals. Each time the timer fires it calls the function `moveDiv()`, which moves a `<DIV>` containing our image about the page.

Let's look at the page in more detail.

Before we look at the code we'll look at the style sheet definition in the head of the page. This defines just one style sheets class, `FloatingDiv`, which defines attributes that make the positioning absolute, set the left to 6 pixels, top to 6 pixels, the width as 410 pixels, and height as 260 pixels. If you use a different size image then change these values to be as large as or just slightly larger than your image. Our `<DIV>` tag that is used to hold an image and a hyperlink has this style class applied:

```
<DIV ID=floatingDiv NAME=floatingDiv CLASS="FloatingDiv">
    <A HREF="WhatsNew.htm"
            onmouseover="document.FloatingImage.src = 'clickforwhatsnew.jpg'"
            onmouseout="document.FloatingImage.src = 'Welcome.jpg'">
        <IMG NAME="FloatingImage" ID="FloatingImage" SRC="Welcome.jpg" BORDER=0>
    </A>
</DIV>
```

Notice that we wrap our image inside an `<A>` tag and use its `onmouseover` and `onmouseout` events to switch the image loaded by changing the `IMG` object's `src` property.

Now let's look at the code. At the top of the script block we define some global, page-level variables. These are accessible from any JavaScript function on the page. Variable `isIE` will be populated with `true` or `false` depending on whether the browser is IE 4+. We then set two variables to hold the width and height of the `Div`; these will be used later for determining whether the bottom right corner of the `Div` has hit the end of the screen. Variables `horizontalMovement` and `verticalMovement` contain random numbers. These are between between 1 and 6 for `horizontalMovement` and 1 and 3 for the `verticalMovement` variable. These hold the amount of movement that the `Div` should be moved each time the timer fires. Initially the `Div` will be moving between 1 and 6 pixels along and between 1 and 3 pixels down the page. We'll see how this works when we look at the `moveDiv()` function.

```
var isIE;

var floatingDivHeight = 65;
var floatingDivWidth = 265;
var timerId;
var screenWidth;
var screenHeight;
var horizontalMovement = Math.ceil(Math.random() * 6);
var verticalMovement = Math.ceil(Math.random() * 3);
```

The function startTimer() is called by the window's onload event handler. As the name suggests it starts a timer going at the interval of 100 milliseconds, each time calling moveDiv(). Next comes an if statement, which checks to see if document.all returns any value. If it does then this must be IE 4 or later. If this is the case we have some IE 4+ specific code that sets the screenWidth and screenHeight variables to the size of the current window, in pixels. Just before that we set the floatingDiv's left and top properties to 6. We need to do this even though we set it using a style sheet so that we can read the values later in divMove(). It's a quirk of IE that if we don't do this then reading the values will return nothing. We also set isIE to true.

The NN 4 part of the code does exactly the same thing as the IE section, except there's no need with Netscape to set style properties with code before reading them with code. Whereas clientWidth and clientHeight give us the browser window's size in IE, in Netscape we need window object's innerWidth and innerHeight. We also set isIE to false.

```
function startTimer()
{
    timerId = window.setInterval("moveDiv()",100);

    if (document.all)
    {
        floatingDiv.style.left = "6px";
        floatingDiv.style.top = "6px";

        screenWidth = document.body.clientWidth;
        screenHeight = document.body.clientHeight;

        isIE = true;
    }
    else
    {
        screenWidth = window.innerWidth;
        screenHeight = window.innerHeight;
        isIE = false;
    }
}
```

Finally we come to the moveDiv() function, which is called every 100 milliseconds by the timer we set going in the window onload event.

Starting from the top our first task is to find out whereabouts on the page the `Div` is currently positioned. How we do this in IE differs from NN so we need to use the `isIE` variable we set earlier to find out which browser this is and run the correct code. In IE the `Div` object's `style` property object's `left` and `top` properties tell us the current position. In NN we use the `Layer` object created implicitly for the `<DIV>` tag when we set the `Div`'s position to absolute. It's the layer's `left` and `top` properties that provide the current position.

```
function moveDiv()
{

    var currentLeft;
    var currentTop;

    if (isIE)
    {
        // IE4+ Code
        currentLeft = parseInt(floatingDiv.style.left);
        currentTop = parseInt(floatingDiv.style.top);
    }
    else
    {
        // NN4 Code
        currentLeft = parseInt(document.floatingDiv.left);
        currentTop = parseInt(document.floatingDiv.top);
    }
```

Our next task is to work out where we should move the `Div` to next.

Our first `if` statement checks to see if the `Div` has reached either the top or the bottom of the page. If the top of the `Div` has reached the top of the page, that is if `currentTop` is less than 6, then we need to start the `Div` moving downwards again. Why 6 and not 0 for the top of the page? Well, we are moving our `Div` in jumps of up to 5 pixels at a time. If the top is currently at position 2 then if we don't start moving downward then the next position could be 2 – 5 making –3 which leaves part of the `Div` off the top of the page. If we move down when it reaches less than 6 then we avoid this. The variable `verticalMovement` contains the number of pixels up or down a page our `<DIV>` is moved. We set this to a positive randomly selected number between 1 and 5.

If the bottom of the page has been reached by the `Div`'s bottom then we need to start moving the `Div` back up the page each time the timer fires so we set `verticalMovement` to be a negative random number between 1 and 5. So if the position is currently 594 and verticalMovement is –5 then next time the timer is called it'll be 589, then 584 and so on giving the impression of floating up the page.

```
    if (currentTop < 6)
    {
        verticalMovement = Math.ceil(Math.random() * 5);
    }
    else if ( ( currentTop + floatingDivHeight) > screenHeight )
    {
        verticalMovement = -(Math.ceil(Math.random() * 5));
    }
```

We've checked vertical movement up or down the page, so next we check to see that the Div is not at the left or right edges of the page. The principles are the same as with the vertical movement; if we're at the left we start moving right by setting the horizontalMovement variable to a random positive number and if at the right we start moving left by setting horizontalMovement to a random negative number:

```
if (currentLeft < 6)
{
    horizontalMovement = Math.ceil(Math.random() * 5);
}
else if ( ( currentLeft + floatingDivWidth) > screenWidth )
{
    horizontalMovement = -(Math.ceil(Math.random() * 5));
}
```

Finally, we calculate the required new position, by adding the amount of movement needed to the current position. The variables horizontalMovement and verticalMovement either have the values allocated to them in the previous if...else statements, or the random values allocated to them at the top of the page.

```
currentLeft = currentLeft + horizontalMovement;
currentTop = currentTop + verticalMovement;
```

Again, setting the left and top positions is different for IE and NN so we need to use different code for each:

```
if (isIE)
{
    // IE4+ Code
    floatingDiv.style.left = currentLeft;
    floatingDiv.style.top = currentTop;
}
else
{
    // NN4 Code
    document.floatingDiv.left = currentLeft;
    document.floatingDiv.top = currentTop;
}
```

Chapter 13

In this chapter we looked at the DOM and how the standard method for accessing objects on the HTML document can be applied in JavaScript and used to create web pages that will work in both major browsers.

Question 1

Here's some HTML code that creates a web page. Recreate this page, using JavaScript to generate the HTML with document.write(), and using only DOM objects, properties, and methods. Test your code on both IE 5.5 and NN 6 to make sure it works on both if possible.

Hint: Comment each line as you write it to keep track of where you are in the tree structure and also create a new variable for every element on the page (for example, not just one for each of the TD cells, but 9).

```
<HTML>
<HEAD>
</HEAD>
<BODY>
<TABLE>
    <THEAD>
        <TR>
            <TD>Car</TD>
            <TD>Top Speed</TD>
            <TD>Price</TD>
        </TR>
    </THEAD>
    <TBODY>
        <TR>
            <TD>Chevrolet</TD>
            <TD>120mph</TD>
            <TD>$10,000</TD>
        </TR>
        <TR>
            <TD>Pontiac</TD>
            <TD>140mph</TD>
            <TD>$20,000</TD>
            </TR>
            </TBODY>
</TABLE>
</BODY>
</HTML>
```

Solution

It seems a rather daunting example, but rather than being difficult it is just a conjunction of two areas, one building a tree structure and the other navigating the tree structure. You start by navigating to the <BODY> element and then create a <TABLE> element, navigate to the new <TABLE> element you've created and then create a new <THEAD> element and carry on from there. It's a lengthy and repetitious process, so that's why it's a good idea to comment your code to keep track of where you are.

```
<HTML>
<HEAD>
</HEAD>
<BODY>
<SCRIPT LANGUAGE="JavaScript">
var TableElem = document.createElement("TABLE")
var THElem = document.createElement("THEAD")
var TRElem1 = document.createElement("TR")
var TRElem2 = document.createElement("TR")
var TRElem3 = document.createElement("TR")
var TDElem1 = document.createElement("TD")
var TDElem2 = document.createElement("TD")
var TDElem3 = document.createElement("TD")
```

```
var TDElem4 = document.createElement("TD")
var TDElem5 = document.createElement("TD")
var TDElem6 = document.createElement("TD")
var TDElem7 = document.createElement("TD")
var TDElem8 = document.createElement("TD")
var TDElem9 = document.createElement("TD")
var TBODYElem = document.createElement("TBODY")
var TextNodeA1 = document.createTextNode("Car")
var TextNodeA2 = document.createTextNode("Top Speed")
var TextNodeA3 = document.createTextNode("Price")
var TextNodeB1 = document.createTextNode("Chevrolet")
var TextNodeB2 = document.createTextNode("120mph")
var TextNodeB3 = document.createTextNode("$10,000")
var TextNodeC1 = document.createTextNode("Pontiac")
var TextNodeC2 = document.createTextNode("140mph")
var TextNodeC3 = document.createTextNode("$14,000")

docNavigate = document.documentElement;   //Starts with HTML document
docNavigate = docNavigate.lastChild;       //Moves to BODY element
docNavigate.appendChild(TableElem);        //Adds the TABLE element
docNavigate = docNavigate.lastChild;       //Moves to the TABLE element
docNavigate.appendChild(THElem);           //Adds the THEAD element
docNavigate = docNavigate.firstChild;      //Moves to the THEAD element
docNavigate.appendChild(TRElem1);          //Adds the TR element
docNavigate = docNavigate.firstChild;      //Moves the TR element
docNavigate.appendChild(TDElem1);          //Adds the first TD element in the
                                           // heading
docNavigate.appendChild(TDElem2);          //Adds the second TD element in the
                                           // heading
docNavigate.appendChild(TDElem3);          //Adds the third TD element in the
                                           // heading
docNavigate = docNavigate.firstChild;      //Moves to the first TD element
docNavigate.appendChild(TextNodeA1);       //Adds the second text node
docNavigate = docNavigate.nextSibling;     //Moves to the next TD element
docNavigate.appendChild(TextNodeA2);       //Adds the second text node
docNavigate = docNavigate.nextSibling;     //Moves to the next TD element
docNavigate.appendChild(TextNodeA3);       //Adds the third text node

docNavigate = docNavigate.parentNode;      //Moves back to the TR element
docNavigate = docNavigate.parentNode;      //Moves back to the THEAD element
docNavigate = docNavigate.parentNode;      //Moves back to the TABLE element
docNavigate.appendChild(TBODYElem);        //Adds the TBODY element
docNavigate = docNavigate.lastChild;       //Moves to the TBODY element
docNavigate.appendChild(TRElem2);          //Adds the second TR element
docNavigate = docNavigate.lastChild;       //Moves to the second TR element
docNavigate.appendChild(TDElem4);          //Adds the TD element
docNavigate.appendChild(TDElem5);          //Adds the TD element
docNavigate.appendChild(TDElem6);          //Adds the TD element
docNavigate = docNavigate.firstChild;      //Moves to the first TD element
docNavigate.appendChild(TextNodeB1);       //Adds the first text node
docNavigate = docNavigate.nextSibling;     //Moves to the next TD element
docNavigate.appendChild(TextNodeB2);       //Adds the second text node
docNavigate = docNavigate.nextSibling;     //Moves to the next TD element
docNavigate.appendChild(TextNodeB3);       //Adds the third text node
```

```
docNavigate = docNavigate.parentNode;          //Moves back to the TR element
docNavigate = docNavigate.parentNode;          //Moves back to the TBODY element
docNavigate.appendChild(TRElem3);              //Adds the TR element
docNavigate = docNavigate.lastChild;           //Moves to the TR element
docNavigate.appendChild(TDElem7);              //Adds the TD element
docNavigate.appendChild(TDElem8);              //Adds the TD element
docNavigate.appendChild(TDElem9);              //Adds the TD element
docNavigate = docNavigate.firstChild;          //Moves to the TD element
docNavigate.appendChild(TextNodeC1);           //Adds the first text node
docNavigate = docNavigate.nextSibling;         //Moves to the next TD element
docNavigate.appendChild(TextNodeC2);           //Adds the second text node
docNavigate = docNavigate.nextSibling;         //Moves to the next TD element
docNavigate.appendChild(TextNodeC3);           //Adds the third text node
</SCRIPT>
</BODY>
</HTML>
```

Question 2

Augment your DOM web page so that the table has a border and so that the headings only of the table (that is, not the column headings) are center aligned. Again test your code on both IE 5.5 and NN 6 if possible.

Hint: Add any extra code to the end of the script code you have already written.

Solution

Add these lines to the bottom of the script code to add a border:

```
docAttr = document.getElementsByTagName("TABLE").item(0)
docAttr.setAttribute("border","1")
```

Add these lines to the bottom of the script code to center-align headings:

```
docNewAttr = document.getElementsByTagName("THEAD").item(0)
docNewAttr.setAttribute("align","center")
```

Chapter 14

In this chapter, we saw how we could extend the functionality of our browser by using plug-ins and ActiveX controls, and how we could use these plug-ins within our web pages.

Question 1

Using the RealPlayer plug-in/ActiveX control, create a page with three images so that when the mouse pointer rolls over them a sound is played. The page should work with NN 4.x and IE 4+. However, any other browsers should be able to view the page and click the images without errors appearing.

Solution

```
<HTML>
<HEAD>

<SCRIPT LANGUAGE=JavaScript>

function play(fileName)
{
   document.real1.SetSource(fileName);
   document.real1.DoPlay();
}


function window_onload()
{
   var plugInInstalled = false;

   if (navigator.appName.indexOf("Microsoft") == -1)
   {
      var plugInCounter;

      for (plugInCounter = 0; plugInCounter < navigator.plugins.length;
plugInCounter++)
      {
         if (navigator.plugins[plugInCounter].name.indexOf("RealPlayer") >= 0)
         {
            plugInInstalled = true
            break;
         }
      }
   }
   else
   {
      if (real1.readyState == 4)
         plugInInstalled = true;
   }

   if (plugInInstalled == false)
      window.location.replace("NoRealAudioPage.htm");
}

</SCRIPT>

<OBJECT classid="clsid:CFCDAA03-8BE4-11CF-B84B-0020AFBBCCFA"
   id="real1" VIEWASTEXT>
   <PARAM NAME="HEIGHT" VALUE="0">
   <PARAM NAME="WIDTH" VALUE="0">
<EMBED name="real1" id="real1"
   BORDER="0"
   CONTROLS="play"
   HEIGHT=0 WIDTH=0 TYPE="audio/x-pn-realaudio-plugin">
</OBJECT>
```

```
    </HEAD>
    <BODY onload="window_onload()">
    <A onmouseover="play('Evil_Laugh.ra')"
        onmouseout=document.real1.DoStop();
        href="#">
        <IMG src="AdvertImage1.jpg" border=0>
    </A>
    <A onmouseover="play('Whoosh.ra')"
        onmouseout=document.real1.DoStop();
        href="#">
        <IMG src="AdvertImage2.jpg" border=0>
    </A>
    <A onmouseover="play('Explosion.ra')"
        onmouseout=document.real1.DoStop();
        href="#">
        <IMG src="AdvertImage3.jpg" border=0>
    </A>
    </BODY>
    </HTML>
```

Save this as ch14_q1.htm.

This solution is based on our RealPlayer example in the chapter. Note that the three sound files, Evil_Laugh.ra, Whoosh.ra, and Explosion.ra can be found in the code download for this book.

We verify that the user has the ability to play Real Audio files in the window onload event handler which calls the window_onload() function.

Just as the IE and NN support of plug-ins is different, so therefore are the means of checking for a plug-in. For NN we go through the navigator object's plugins array and check each installed plug-in for the name RealPlayer; if it's found we know they have the RealAudio player installed.

With IE we simply use the real1 ActiveX control's readyState property to see if it's installed and initialized correctly.

To play the sounds we've defined a function called play() whose parameter is the name of the .ra (or .rm) sound file to be played:

```
function play(fileName)
{
    document.real1.SetSource(fileName);
    document.real1.DoPlay();
}
```

The function makes use of the RealAudio player's setSource() method to set the sound file to be played and the DoPlay() method to actually start playing the clip. We have used different sounds for each image by simply specifying a different filename as the parameter for the play() function.

We need to use the onmouseover and onmouseout events to start playing the sound when the mouse pointer is over the image and stop it when the mouse pointer moves out of the image. However, in NN 4 the IMG object does not have these event handlers so we need to wrap the image inside an <A> tag, which does have them. The onmouseout event starts playing the audio clip by calling our play() function, and the onmouseout event stops the playing by calling the RealPlayer's DoStop() method.

```
<A onmouseover="play('audiosig.ra')"
   onmouseout=document.real1.DoStop();
   href="#">
   <IMG src="RedImage.jpg" border=0>
</A>
```

Chapter 15

In this chapter, we looked at running our scripts server-side, how running scripts sever-side differed from running them client-side, and using ASP objects.

Question 1

Alter the logon example, so that if a user enters an invalid value more than three times they are not taken back to the logon page, but to another page telling them that they are not valid users.

Solution

```
<%@ LANGUAGE = JavaScript %>
<HTML>
<HEAD>
<SCRIPT LANGUAGE=JavaScript>

function form1_onsubmit()
{
   var form = document.form1;
   var returnValue = false;

   if (form.txtUsername.value == "")
   {
      alert("Please enter your username");
      form.txtUsername.focus();
   }

   else if (form.txtPassword.value == "")
   {
      alert("Please enter your password");
      form.txtPassword.focus();
   }
   else
   {
      returnValue = true;
   }

   return returnValue;
}

</SCRIPT>
</HEAD>
<BODY>
<%
```

```
if (Request.Form.Count != 0)
{
   if (Request.Form("txtUsername") == "SecureUser" &&
       Request.Form("txtPassword") == "letmethrough")
   {
      Response.Cookies("IsValid") = "Yes";
      Response.Redirect("SecureHome.asp");
   }
   else
   {
      Session("LogonTrys") = parseInt(Session("LogonTrys")) + 1;
      Response.Redirect("logon.asp")
   }
}

var invalidTrys = Session("LogonTrys");
if (isNaN(invalidTrys))
{
   invalidTrys = 1;
   Session("LogonTrys") = invalidTrys;
}
else
{
   invalidTrys = parseInt(invalidTrys);
}

if ( invalidTrys != 1 )
{
   Response.Write("<P><FONT color=red size=+2>"+ "Sorry the username/password" +
      " you entered were invalid</FONT></P>")
   if ( invalidTrys <= 3)
   {
      Response.Write("<P><FONT color=black size=+2>"+
                     "Please re-enter your details" +
                     "</FONT></P>")
   }
}

if ( invalidTrys <= 3)
{
%>
<P> To access this website please enter your username and password in the boxes
below</P>

<FORM ACTION="LogOn.asp" METHOD=POST ID=form1 NAME=form1
      onsubmit="return form1_onsubmit()">

<P>Username : <INPUT ID=txtUsername NAME=txtUsername></P>
<P>Password : <INPUT ID=txtPassword NAME=txtPassword TYPE=password></P>

<P>
<INPUT ID=reset1 NAME=reset1 TYPE=reset VALUE=Reset> 
<INPUT ID=submit1 NAME=submit1 TYPE=submit VALUE="Log On">
</P>
```

```
</FORM>
<%
}
%>
</BODY>
</HTML>
```

Save this as `LogOn.asp`.

What I've done with the example in the chapter is modify it so it limits the user to three attempts and it is now just one page `LogOn.asp`, rather than two pages `LogOn.htm` and `CheckLogon.asp`. `LogOn.asp` contains both the form, which posts to itself, and the check for logon validity.

The first change is that the page's file extension is `.asp` rather than `.htm`; this is to allow us to insert script that runs on the server-side. We then add:

```
<%@ LANGUAGE = JavaScript %>
```

This is to instruct the server to run the server-side scripts on that page in the JavaScript language. Remember that by default it's VBScript.

The client-side scripting remains unchanged from the earlier example – the next change is the addition of a big server-side script block after the <BODY> tag, so let's look at it step by step.

The first part checks the logon details submitted. We need to check if this page is being loaded due to a form submission (remember this page has a form, which submits to this same page). The `Request.Form.Count` lists the number of form elements whose values have been submitted. If it's zero it means either a form with no elements was submitted or, as in this case, that the page has not been loaded as a result of a form submission. If it's not zero then this page has been loaded by a form submission and therefore we need to check the user logon details. If they are a valid user, then we redirect them to the `SecureHome.asp` page. If not, then we increase the variable, `LogonTrys`, which stores the number of attempts that the user has made to log in and let the page continue loading.

```
<%
if (Request.Form.Count != 0)
{
    if (Request.Form("txtUsername") == "SecureUser" && Request.Form("txtPassword")
== "letmethrough")
    {
        Response.Cookies("IsValid") = "Yes";
        Response.Redirect("SecureHome.asp");
    }
    else
    {
        Session("LogonTrys") = parseInt(Session("LogonTrys")) + 1;
    }
}
```

Our next bit of server-side code deals with the number of logon attempts the user has made in this session. If this is the first time this session they have loaded the page then `Session("LogonTrys")` won't contain any value so we assign it the value of 1. Otherwise we retrieve its value and store it as an integer in variable `invalidTrys`.

```
    var invalidTrys = Session("LogonTrys");
    if (isNaN(invalidTrys))
    {
        invalidTrys = 1;
        Session("LogonTrys") = invalidTrys;
    }
    else
    {
        invalidTrys = parseInt(invalidTrys);
    }
```

Then we come to the server-side code that displays a message telling them their logon/username was invalid. If this is the first time they have been to this page then clearly they've not yet had chance to enter logon details, valid or otherwise. If it's not their first time here they can only have arrived back because they have submitted an invalid username or password. So if `invalidTrys` is not 1 it's not their first time here this session and so we display the invalid logon message. If the number of retries is less than 3 then we also display a message telling them to re-enter their details and try again.

```
    if ( invalidTrys != 1 )
    {
        Response.Write("<P><FONT COLOR=red SIZE=+2>"+
                       "Sorry the username/password" +
                       " you entered were invalid</FONT></P>")
        if ( invalidTrys <= 3)
        {
            Response.Write("<P><FONT color=black size=+2>"+
                           "Please re-enter your details" +
                           "</FONT></P>")
        }
    }
```

The final bit of server-side code is wrapped around some HTML, in particular the form that allows the user to enter a username and password. If they have made 3 attempts or less then the `if` statement will let the form HTML be written to the page and displayed to the user. If they've already got it wrong three times then no form is displayed this session for a fourth attempt and only by closing their browser and navigating to the page's URL again will they be able to try again.

```
    if ( invalidTrys <= 3)
    {
%>
<P> To access this website please enter your username and password in the boxes
below</P>

<FORM ACTION="LogOn.asp" METHOD=POST ID=form1 NAME=form1
      onsubmit="return form1_onsubmit()">

<P>Username : <INPUT ID=txtUsername NAME=txtUsername></P>
<P>Password : <INPUT ID=txtPassword NAME=txtPassword TYPE=password></P>

<P>
<INPUT ID=reset1 NAME=reset1 TYPE=reset VALUE=Reset> 
<INPUT ID=submit1 NAME=submit1 TYPE=submit VALUE="Log On">
</P>

</FORM>
<%
    }
```

Question 2

In Question 2 of Chapter 6 and continuing with Question 1 of Chapter 7, we created a form that allowed the user to select their dream computer system and to see the price alter as different components were selected. Our task for this question is to enable the user to purchase the system they have selected. This involves:

❑ When the user clicks to buy the system, you need to obtain all the information necessary for an e-commerce purchase, for example name, address, and credit card details.

❑ With all the information obtained, show a final summary page that displays the system selected, its price, and the user's details. There should be a confirm order button and a cancel order button on the page.

❑ If the user clicks on the confirm order button then the system is purchased: simply take them to a page saying, "Thanks for your order". If they cancel the order, then wipe their details and return them to the home page.

Solution

I'm re-using the exercise answers from Chapter 7. Firstly we need a top frameset page, identical to the one used in Chapter 7, Question 1. This time I've called it ch15Q2_TopFrame.htm.

```
<HTML>
<HEAD>
</HEAD>
<FRAMESET COLS="55%,*">
    <FRAME SRC="ch15Q2_PickSystem.htm" NAME="pickSystem">
    <FRAME SRC="blank.htm" NAME="systemSummary">
</FRAMESET>
</HTML>
```

You'll also need a blank HTML file, blank.htm, like so:

```
<HTML>
<BODY>
</BODY>
</HTML>
```

Then we have the page that allows the user to pick the system, ch15Q2_PickSystem.htm. This is virtually identical to the version of PickSystem.htm in Chapter 7, apart from in two places. Firstly at the top of the updateOrderDetails() function:

```
function updateOrderDetails()
{
    var total = 0;
    var orderDetails = "<H3>Your selected system</H3>";
    var orderForm = "";
    var formElement;
```

and secondly towards the end of the function:

```
    else
    {
        orderDetails = orderDetails + "Full Tower Case : $" +
CompItems[formElement[2].value]
        total = total + parseFloat(CompItems[formElement[2].value]);
    }

    orderForm = orderForm + "<FORM ACTION='ch15Q2_BuySystem.asp' METHOD=post "
                + "NAME=form1 TARGET=_top><INPUT TYPE='submit' "
                + "value='Buy System'>"
                + "<INPUT TYPE='hidden' NAME='txtCost' "
                + " VALUE='" + total + "'>"
                + "<INPUT TYPE='hidden' NAME='txtDescription' "
                + "VALUE='" + orderDetails + "'></FORM>"

    orderDetails = orderDetails + "<P>Total Order Cost is $" + total + "</P>";

    window.parent.systemSummary.document.open();
    window.parent.systemSummary.document.write(orderDetails + orderForm);
    window.parent.systemSummary.document.close();
}
```

Save this as ch15Q2_PickSystem.htm

Next we have our first new page, the one that is loaded when the **Buy System** button is clicked:

```
<%@ LANGUAGE=JavaScript %>
<HTML>
<HEAD>
<TITLE>Buy System</TITLE>

<SCRIPT LANGUAGE=JavaScript>

function checkForm()
{
    var regExp = /[^\d ]/
    var formValid = true;
    var theForm = document.form1;
    var elementIndex;
    var element;
    var nowDate = new Date();
    var expMonth = parseInt(theForm.selMonth.value)
    var expYear = parseInt(theForm.selYear.value)

    for (elementIndex = 0; elementIndex < theForm.length; elementIndex++)
    {
        element = theForm[elementIndex];
        if (element.type == "text")
        {
            if (element.value == "")
            {
```

```
                  formValid = false;
                  element.focus();
                  alert("Please complete all of the boxes");
                  break;
               }
            }
         }

   if (formValid == true && expYear <= parseInt(nowDate.getFullYear()) &&
parseInt(nowDate.getMonth()) > expMonth)
      {
         formValid = false;
         theForm.selMonth.focus();
         alert("The credit card expiry date you selected has expired")
      }
   else if (regExp.test(theForm.txtCCNumber.value) == true)
      {
         formValid = false;
         alert("Please enter a valid credit card number");
         theForm.txtCCNumber.focus();
         theForm.txtCCNumber.select();
      }

   return formValid;
}

</SCRIPT>

</HEAD>
<BODY>
<H2>Purchase System</H2>
<P>Please enter you name, address and credit card details below</P>
<FORM ACTION="ch15Q2_FinalStage.asp" METHOD=POST NAME=form1 onsubmit="return
checkForm()">
<P>
Your Full Name:
<BR>
<INPUT TYPE="text" NAME=txtName>
</P>
<P>
House Name/Number
<BR>
<INPUT TYPE="text" NAME=txtHouse>
</P>
<P>
Street:
<BR>
<INPUT TYPE="text" NAME=txtStreet>
</P>
<P>
City:
<BR>
<INPUT TYPE="text" NAME=txtCity>
</P>
<P>
```

```
<P>
Credit Card Number:
<BR>
<INPUT TYPE="text" NAME=txtCCNumber>
<P>
Expiry Date
<BR>
<SELECT NAME=selMonth>
<OPTION VALUE="01">01</OPTION>
<OPTION VALUE ="02">02</OPTION>
<OPTION VALUE ="03">03</OPTION>
<OPTION VALUE ="04">04</OPTION>
<OPTION VALUE ="05">05</OPTION>
<OPTION VALUE ="06">06</OPTION>
<OPTION VALUE ="07">07</OPTION>
<OPTION VALUE ="08">08</OPTION>
<OPTION VALUE ="09">09</OPTION>
<OPTION VALUE ="10">10</OPTION>
<OPTION VALUE ="11">11</OPTION>
<OPTION VALUE ="12">12</OPTION>
</SELECT>
<SELECT NAME=selYear>
<%

var yearCount;
var nowYear = new Date();
nowYear = parseInt(nowYear.getFullYear());

for (yearCount = nowYear; yearCount < nowYear + 5; yearCount++)
{
    Response.Write("<OPTION value='" + yearCount + "'>")
    Response.Write(yearCount + "</OPTION>");
}

%>

</SELECT>

<INPUT TYPE="hidden" NAME="txtCost" VALUE="<%=Request.Form("txtCost")%>">

<INPUT TYPE="hidden" NAME="txtDescription"
       VALUE="<%=Request.Form("txtDescription")%>">
<P>
<INPUT TYPE="submit" VALUE="Submit" NAME=submit1>
</P>
</FORM>
</BODY>
</HTML>
```

Save this as ch15Q2_BuySystem.asp.

Next we have the `ch15Q2_FinalStage.asp` page, which displays a summary of the user's order and order details and gives them the chance to purchase or cancel the order:

```
<%@ LANGUAGE = JavaScript %>
<HTML>
<HEAD>
<TITLE>Final Summary</TITLE>
</HEAD>
<BODY>

<H3>Order Summary</H3>

<%

var description = Request.Form("txtDescription").item;
var cost = Request.Form("txtCost").Item
var name = Request.Form("txtName").Item
var houseNo = Request.Form("txtHouse").Item
var street = Request.Form("txtStreet").Item
var city = Request.Form("txtCity").Item
var ccNumber = Request.Form("txtCCNumber").Item

var expiryDate = Request.Form("selMonth") + "/" +Request.Form("selYear")

Response.Write ("<P>" + description + "</P>")
Response.Write ("<P>Will be delivered to </P>")
Response.Write ("<P>Name : " + name + "</P>")
Response.Write ("<P>At address</P>")
Response.Write ("<P>" + houseNo + " " + street + "<BR>")
Response.Write (city)
Response.Write ("<P>Your credit card " + ccNumber)
Response.Write (" expiry date " + expiryDate)
Response.Write (" will be debited by $" + cost)

%>

<FORM action="ch15Q2_PurchaseOrder.asp" method=POST name=form1>
<INPUT TYPE="hidden" NAME="txtName" VALUE ="<%=name%>">
<INPUT TYPE="hidden" NAME="txtDescription" VALUE ="<%=description%>">
<INPUT TYPE="hidden" NAME="txtCost" VALUE ="<%=cost%>">
<INPUT TYPE="hidden" NAME="txtHouseNo" VALUE ="<%=houseNo%>">
<INPUT TYPE="hidden" NAME="txtStreet" VALUE ="<%=street%>">
<INPUT TYPE="hidden" NAME="txtCity" VALUE ="<%=city%>">
<INPUT TYPE="hidden" NAME="txtCCNumber" VALUE ="<%=ccNumber%>">
<INPUT TYPE="hidden" NAME="txtExpiryDate" VALUE ="<%=expiryDate%>">
<INPUT TYPE="submit" VALUE ="Purchase System" NAME=submit1>
<P>
<INPUT TYPE="button" value="Cancel Purchase" name=butCancel
            onclick="window.location.replace('Ch15Q2_TopFrame.htm')" >
</P>
</FORM>

</BODY>
</HTML>
```

Lastly we have the `ch15Q2_PurchaseOrder.asp` page that does the actual purchase of the system, or at least it would if this were not an example!

```
<%@ LANGUAGE=JavaScript %>
<HTML>
<HEAD>
<TITLE>Order Completed</TITLE>
</HEAD>
<BODY>

<H3>Thank you for your order <%=Request.Form("txtName")%>
<BR> it'll be with you shortly
</H3>

</BODY>
</HTML>
```

Save this page as `ch15Q2_PurchaseOrder.asp`.

Let's take a brief look at how it all works; I won't cover the bits we did in Chapters 6 and 7, just the additions.

First in `ch15Q2_PickSystem.htm` we added the code below:

```
orderForm = orderForm + "<FORM ACTION='Ch15Q2_BuySystem.asp' METHOD=post "
           + "NAME=form1 TARGET=_top><INPUT TYPE='submit' "
           + "value='Buy System'>"
           + "<INPUT TYPE='hidden' NAME='txtCost' "
           + " VALUE='" + total + "'>"
           + "<INPUT TYPE='hidden' NAME='txtDescription' "
           + "VALUE='" + orderDetails + "'></FORM>"
```

When the user clicks the update button to view the system they have chosen, not only is the HTML necessary to display the system written to the page, but now we also write an HTML form which contains a button saying **Buy System** and two hidden input boxes, which we discussed in Chapter 6, that contain details of the system the user wants and the cost. When the **Buy System** button is clicked the form will submit to the first of our new pages, `ch15Q2_BuySystem.asp`.

Let's start at the top of `ch15Q2_BuySystem.asp`.

First as we want to use JavaScript as our server-side scripting language we have:

```
<%@ LANGUAGE=JavaScript %>
```

Next we have a block of client-side script which contains the function `checkForm()`.

This function does some basic checks to see that all the input boxes have been filled in, a valid date has been selected for the credit card expiry date, and the credit card number only contains permitted characters, that is numbers and spaces

If any of these tests fails then we alert the user and stop the form submit from continuing by returning `false` from the function to the event handler it was called from.

Next we come to the form itself, where the user enters their details such as name, address, and credit card number. Most of the form should be fairly self-explanatory except this, the credit card expiry year select box:

```
<SELECT name=selYear>
<%

var yearCount;
var nowYear = new Date();
nowYear = parseInt(nowYear.getFullYear());

for (yearCount = nowYear; yearCount < nowYear + 5; yearCount++)
{
    Response.Write("<OPTION VALUE='" + yearCount + "'>")
    Response.Write(yearCount + "</OPTION>");
}

%>
</SELECT>
```

Rather than write in the years ourselves, we've used some server-side script to create the <OPTION> tags with a series of 5 years starting from the current year. The advantage of that is we don't need to change our page for it to be up-to-date. So even if you're reading this appendix in 2030 the years will still be valid, that is 2030, 2031, 3032, 2033 and 2034. The months select box I wrote in myself, and although it would save typing to have JavaScript create them it would add an extra and unnecessary load on the server for it to dynamically create them for each page load. If you're wondering why select rather than text input boxes have been chosen to get the expiry date then it's because this helps prevent validation errors. If we asked the user for the expiry date there is a danger they will enter it in an unexpected or invalid format and we'd have to write lots of code to check for this situation. With select boxes they have no choice but to get the format right.

Finally we have two hidden input boxes, their purpose being to hold the information posted from the last page, that is the system description and cost:

```
<INPUT TYPE="hidden" NAME="txtCost" VALUE="<%=Request.Form("txtCost")%>">
<INPUT TYPE="hidden" NAME="txtDescription"
   VALUE="<%=Request.Form("txtDescription")%>">
```

Hidden input boxes are a very useful way of transferring information from page to page when using form submits, as then you have no need for server variables or cookies.

Next we come to ch15Q2_FinalStage.asp where we display a summary of what the user has entered so they can check the order details before finally committing themselves to it.

First we have the server-side code that retrieves the posted form details and uses it to write a summary to the page before it's sent to the client browser:

```
<%

var description = Request.Form("txtDescription").item;
var cost = Request.Form("txtCost").Item
var name = Request.Form("txtName").Item
var houseNo = Request.Form("txtHouse").Item
```

```
    var street = Request.Form("txtStreet").Item
    var city = Request.Form("txtCity").Item
    var ccNumber = Request.Form("txtCCNumber").Item

    var expiryDate = Request.Form("selMonth") + "/" +Request.Form("selYear")

    Response.Write ("<P>" + description + "</P>")
    Response.Write ("<P>Will be delivered to </P>")
    Response.Write ("<P>Name : " + name + "</P>")
    Response.Write ("<P>At address</P>")
    Response.Write ("<P>" + houseNo + " " + street + "<BR>")
    Response.Write (city)
    Response.Write ("<P>Your credit card " + ccNumber)
    Response.Write (" expiry date " + expiryDate)
    Response.Write (" will be debited by $" + cost)

%>
```

Finally we have a form, most of which is hidden input boxes that contain all the order details received so far. When the user clicks the **Purchase** button all the information will be submitted in one go. It's much easier to deal with all the info for a transaction at once rather than try and do it in little stages, otherwise we'd need to deal with the situation where the user changes their mind half way through or where their computer, browser, or connection terminate unexpectedly.

```
<FORM action="Ch15Q2_PurchaseOrder.asp" method=POST name=form1>
<INPUT TYPE="hidden" NAME="txtName" VALUE ="<%=name%>">
<INPUT TYPE="hidden" NAME="txtDescription" VALUE ="<%=description%>">
<INPUT TYPE="hidden" NAME="txtCost" VALUE ="<%=cost%>">
<INPUT TYPE="hidden" NAME="txtHouseNo" VALUE ="<%=houseNo%>">
<INPUT TYPE="hidden" NAME="txtStreet" VALUE ="<%=street%>">
<INPUT TYPE="hidden" NAME="txtCity" VALUE ="<%=city%>">
<INPUT TYPE="hidden" NAME="txtCCNumber" VALUE ="<%=ccNumber%>">
<INPUT TYPE="hidden" NAME="txtExpiryDate" VALUE ="<%=expiryDate%>">
<INPUT TYPE="submit" VALUE ="Purchase System" NAME=submit1>
<P>
<INPUT TYPE="button" VALUE="Cancel Purchase" NAME=butCancel
            onclick="window.location.replace('Ch15Q2_TopFrame.htm')" >
</P>
</FORM>
```

The very last page is `ch15Q2_PurchaseOrder.asp` in which we simply say thank you for buying the system. In reality this is where all the order processing would be done, such as placing the order details in a database, processing the credit card, and ensuring that the orders department are told to send the system.

Chapter 16

In this chapter we looked at databases, and how to access them using server-side JavaScript.

Question 1

In Chapter 15 we saw how to create a logon screen that redirects the user to one page if their password is valid or asks them to re-enter their password if invalid. The logon name and password were set in the code. Create a database, which holds user names and corresponding passwords, and use this to validate the user.

Solution

This is a modified version of my solution to Chapter 15, Question 1. We can reuse the SecureHome.asp page from Chapter 15 as the secure page that the user is directed to if their name and password is correct. We need to create a database of user names and passwords, which I've called security.mdb and a log on page, which I've called Ch16_LogOn.asp. Make sure the pages are saved in a directory under your web server such as the virtual directory AWalkOnTheServerSide that we created in the chapter. The example only works if the pages are browsed to on a server and not if loaded as normal files.

```
<%@ LANGUAGE = JavaScript %>
<HTML>
<HEAD>
<SCRIPT LANGUAGE=JavaScript>
function form1_onsubmit()
{
    var form = document.form1;
    var returnValue = false;

    if (form.txtUsername.value == "")
    {
        alert("Please enter your username");
        form.txtUsername.focus();
    }
    else if (form.txtPassword.value == "")
    {
        alert("Please enter your password");
        form.txtPassword.focus();
    }
    else
    {
        returnValue = true;
    }

    return returnValue;

}
</SCRIPT>
</HEAD>
<BODY>
<%
```

```
if (Request.Form.Count != 0)
{

   var userNameInDatabase;
   var userName = new String(Request.Form("txtUsername")).toLowerCase();
   var password = new String(Request.Form("txtPassword")).toLowerCase();

   var mySQL = "SELECT UserName FROM User WHERE " +
               "UserName='" + userName +
               "' AND Password='" + password + "'";

   var adoRecordset = Server.CreateObject("ADODB.Recordset")
   adoRecordset.Open(mySQL,"DSN=SecureUsersDSN");

   if (adoRecordset.EOF == false )
   {
      var userNameInDatabase = adoRecordset("Username").Value;
      userNameInDatabase = userNameInDatabase.toLowerCase();
      if (userNameInDatabase == userName)
      {
         Response.Cookies("IsValid") = "Yes";
         Response.Redirect("SecureHome.asp");
      }
      else
      {
         Session("LogonTrys") = parseInt(Session("LogonTrys")) + 1;
      }
   }
   else
   {
      Session("LogonTrys") = parseInt(Session("LogonTrys")) + 1;
   }

   adoRecordset.Close();
   adoRecordset = null;
}

var invalidTrys = Session("LogonTrys");
if (isNaN(invalidTrys))
{
   invalidTrys = 1;
   Session("LogonTrys") = invalidTrys;
}
else
{
   invalidTrys = parseInt(invalidTrys);
}

if ( invalidTrys != 1 )
{
   Response.Write("<P><FONT color=red size=+2>"
               + "Sorry the username/password"
               + " you entered were invalid</FONT></P>")
   if ( invalidTrys <= 3)
   {
```

```
        Response.Write("<P><FONT color=black size=+2>"
                    + "Please re-enter your details"
                    + "</FONT></P>")
    }
}

if ( invalidTrys <= 3)
{
%>
    <P> To access this website please enter your
        username and password in the boxes below</P>

    <FORM ACTION="CH16_LogOn.asp" METHOD=POST
        ID=form1 NAME=form1
        ONSUBMIT="return form1_onsubmit()">

    <P>Username : <INPUT ID=txtUsername NAME=txtUsername></P>
    <P>Password : <INPUT ID=txtPassword NAME=txtPassword TYPE=password></P>

    <P><INPUT ID=reset1 NAME=reset1 TYPE=reset VALUE=Reset> 
        <INPUT ID=submit1 NAME=submit1 TYPE=submit VALUE="Log On">
    </P>

    </FORM>
<%
}
%>
</BODY>
</HTML>
```

Save this page as `Ch16_LogOn.asp`.

We now need to create the Access database to store usernames and passwords. Call it `Security.mdb` and create one table called `User` with two fields, `UserName` and `Password` as shown below. You can leave the fields' properties at their default values:

Field Name	Data Type
⚷ UserName	Text
⚷ Password	Text

You'll need to enter some user names and passwords into your database.

Finally you need to create an ODBC data source for your database called `SecureUsersDSN`.

Now let's look at how the code works.

At the very top of `Ch16_LogOn.asp` we have the all-important language direction telling the server our server-side code is JavaScript:

```
<%@ LANGUAGE = JavaScript %>
```

Next we have a block of client-side script containing the function `form1_onsubmit()` that will be called by the form's `onsubmit` event handler. Its purpose is to check that values have been entered by the user in the username and password text boxes. If they are empty we let the user know and prevent the form submission from going ahead by returning `false` from the function.

Next, we come to some server-side script, starting with an `if` statement in which we check to see if this page has any form elements submitted to it. Why do this? Well, this page both provides the means for the user to enter their username and password, and does the checking of that username and password when the form is submitted. We'll see shortly that the form on this page submits to the same page. So we must check if the user has loaded this page by navigating to this page with their browser, in which case we don't need to check their security details, or if it's been loaded due to the user submitting the form to have their security details checked:

```
<%

if (Request.Form.Count != 0)
{
```

If this page has been loaded by a form submission, then it's because the user has pressed the Submit button and wants their logon details checking and then to be taken to the secure home page or given another chance to enter their details. The next bit of code carries out that task:

```
var userNameInDatabase;
var userName = new String(Request.Form("txtUsername")).toLowerCase();
var password = new String(Request.Form("txtPassword")).toLowerCase();

var mySQL = "SELECT UserName FROM User WHERE " +
            "UserName='" + userName +
            "' AND Password='" + password + "'";

var adoRecordset = Server.CreateObject("ADODB.Recordset")
adoRecordset.Open(mySQL, "DSN=SecureUsersDSN");

if (adoRecordset.EOF == false )
{
    var userNameInDatabase = adoRecordset("Username").Value;
    userNameInDatabase = userNameInDatabase.toLowerCase();
    if (userNameInDatabase == userName)
    {
        Response.Cookies("IsValid") = "Yes";
        Response.Redirect("SecureHome.asp");
    }
    else
    {
        Session("LogonTrys") = parseInt(Session("LogonTrys")) + 1;
    }
}
else
{
    Session("LogonTrys") = parseInt(Session("LogonTrys")) + 1;
}

adoRecordset.Close();
adoRecordset = null;
}
```

The code above first retrieves the username and password submitted by the user and converts them to lower case. This is done so that the username and password are case insensitive, although we could leave this out if we wanted to make the username and password case sensitive.

Then the code creates a string of SQL (mySQL) that selects the username from the database where there is a matching username and password. We create a Recordset object and use the SQL string to open this recordset with the results of the SELECT query. We can then check that the recordset has records in it, by checking it's not at the EOF (end of file) position, then we compare the username value returned with the username submitted from the form. If they match we can be sure it's a valid user. If it is a valid user, we set a cookie and re-direct the user to the securehome.asp page. If it is an invalid user we add 1 to the session variable LogOnTrys in which we keep count of how many attempts to login the user has made. If it's more than 3 we don't give them another chance – this helps to stop malicious hackers writing code to submit to our form millions of different password/username combinations in the hope of getting one right.

It's inthe next bit of code that we actually use the LogOnTrys session variable. If this is the first time this session they have been to the page then the variable will contain no value so we give it the value 1. Then in the second if statement we check to see if the number of attempts is not 1. If it's not 1, then this is clearly not the first time this session they have been to the page and therefore they must have been returned here as a result of entering an invalid username or password. This being the case, we write out a message telling them they entered an invalid username/password. If they have got it wrong 3 or fewer times then we write out HTML asking them to try again.

```
var invalidTrys = Session("LogonTrys");
if (isNaN(invalidTrys))
{
   invalidTrys = 1;
   Session("LogonTrys") = invalidTrys;
}
else
{
   invalidTrys = parseInt(invalidTrys);
}

if ( invalidTrys != 1 )
{
   Response.Write("<P><FONT COLOR=red SIZE=+2>"
               + "Sorry the username/password"
               + " you entered were invalid</FONT></P>")
   if ( invalidTrys <= 3)
   {
   Response.Write("<P><FONT COLOR=black SIZE=+2>"
               + "Please re-enter your details"
               + "</FONT></P>")
   }
}
```

In the final part of the page we use a server-side if statement to check that the number of logon attempts is three or less. If it is, then the if statement allows the HTML to be written to the page displaying a form with textboxes for the user to attempt another logon. If this is more than their third attempt then no logon form appears in the browser and they get no fourth chance unless they close their browser down, and navigate back to the page. Note that the form's ACTION attribute is LogOn.asp meaning that the form submits to itself.

```
   if ( invalidTrys <= 3)
   {
%>
   <P> To access this website please enter your
       username and password in the boxes below</P>

   <FORM ACTION="LogOn.asp" METHOD=POST
       ID=form1 NAME=form1
       onsubmit="return form1_onsubmit()">

   <P>Username : <INPUT ID=txtUsername NAME=txtUsername></P>
   <P>Password : <INPUT ID=txtPassword NAME=txtPassword TYPE=password></P>

   <P><INPUT ID=reset1 NAME=reset1 TYPE=reset VALUE=Reset> 
      <INPUT ID=submit1 NAME=submit1 TYPE=submit VALUE="Log On">
   </P>

   </FORM>
<%
}
%>
</BODY>
</HTML>
```

Question 2

Create a message board application. It should display a list of message subjects, with the name of the person who posted the message and the date posted for each message in a database. When a message subject is clicked, it should display the full message body. Add a button to the page that allows new messages to be created and added to the database online.

Shown below is an example of what the main message screen might look like:

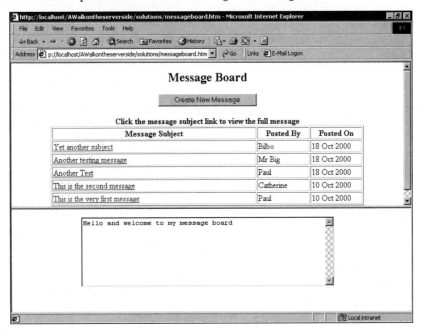

When one of the subject links is clicked the full message is displayed in the text box in the lower frame.

If the Create New Message button is clicked then the user should be taken to a form like that shown below, allowing them to enter a new message and click submit to send it to the database:

These interface suggestions are just that, suggestions. Use any interface design you wish so long as it displays and stores messages.

Solution

For my solution we need to create five pages. Make sure the pages are saved in a directory under your web server such as the virtual directory AWalkOnTheServerSide we created in the chapter. The example only works if the pages are browsed to on a server and not if they are loaded as normal files.

First is the page we load into the browser that creates the framesets loading the other pages; call this page Ch16_MessageBoard.htm:

```
<HTML>
<FRAMESET ROWS="*,200">
    <FRAME NAME="messages" SRC="Ch16_messages.asp">
    <FRAME NAME="messagebody" SRC="Ch16_messagebody.asp">
</FRAMESET>
</HTML>
```

Then we have the page that displays all the messages available; I've called this `Ch16_Messages.asp`:

```
<%@ LANGUAGE=JavaScript %>
<HTML>
<BODY>
<CENTER>
    <H2>Message Board</H2>
    <FORM   NAME="form1" METHOD=post ACTION="Ch16_NewMessage.asp" TARGET=_top>

        <INPUT TYPE="submit" VALUE="Create New Message" NAME=submit1>
    </FORM>
    <STRONG>
    Click the message subject link to
    view the full message
    </STRONG>

<TABLE BORDER=1>
<TR>
    <TH>Message Subject</TH>
    <TH>Posted By</TH>
    <TH>Posted On</TH>
</TR>
<%
var months = new Array("Jan","Feb","Mar","Apr","May","Jun",
                       "Jul","Aug","Sep","Oct","Nov","Dec");
var postedDate;
var lsSQL = "SELECT MessageId, UserName, MessageSubject, " +
            "DatePosted FROM Message " +
            "ORDER BY MessageId DESC"
var adoRS = Server.CreateObject("ADODB.Recordset")
adoRS.Open(lsSQL,"DSN=MessageBoardDSN")

while (adoRS.EOF == false)
{
   Response.Write("<TR><TD width=400>" +
                  "<A href='Ch16_MessageBody.asp?MessageId=" +
                  adoRS("MessageId") +
                  "' target=messagebody>" +
                  adoRS("MessageSubject") +
                  "</A></TD>")

   Response.Write("<TD width=100>" +adoRS("UserName") + "</TD>")

   postedDate = new Date(adoRS("DatePosted"))
   postedDate =postedDate.getDate() + " " + months[postedDate.getMonth()] +
               " " + postedDate.getFullYear();

   Response.Write("<TD width=100>" + postedDate + "</TD></TR>" )

   adoRS.MoveNext();
}

adoRS.Close()
adoRS = null;

%>

</TABLE>

</CENTER>
</BODY>
</HTML>
```

Next we have the page that displays the message's body when the user clicks on a link in the subject line; this page needs to be saved as Ch16_MessageBody.asp:

```
<%@ LANGUAGE=JavaScript%>
<HTML>
<BODY>
<CENTER>
<FORM>
<%
var lsMessageBody = "";
if (isNaN(Request.QueryString("MessageId")) == false)
{
    var lsSQL = "SELECT MessageBody FROM Message " +
                "WHERE MessageId = " + Request.QueryString("MessageId")
    var adoRS = Server.CreateObject("ADODB.Recordset")
    adoRS.Open(lsSQL,"DSN=MessageBoardDSN")
    lsMessageBody = adoRS("MessageBody").Value;

    adoRS.Close();
    adoRS = null;
}
%>
    <TEXTAREA ROWS=8 COLS=60 NAME=textarea1><%=lsMessageBody%></TEXTAREA>
</FORM>
</CENTER>
</BODY>
</HTML>
```

Now we have the page in which users can create a new message; save as Ch16_NewMessage.asp:

```
<HTML>
<HEAD>
<TITLE>Create New Message</TITLE>
<SCRIPT LANGUAGE=JavaScript>

function checkForm()
{
    var form = document.form1
    var controlCounter;
    var returnValue = true;
    var formControl;

    for (controlCounter = 0; controlCounter < form.length; controlCounter++)
    {
        formControl = form.elements[controlCounter]
        if ((formControl.type == "text" || formControl.type == "textarea")
            && formControl.value == "")
        {
            alert("Please complete all of the form");
            formControl.focus();
            returnValue = false;
            break;
        }
    }
```

```
        return returnValue;
    }

</SCRIPT>
</HEAD>
<BODY>
<H2>Add New Message</H2>
<FORM ACTION="Ch16_StoreMessage.asp"
      METHOD=POST NAME=form1
      onsubmit="return checkForm()">
<P>
Your Name:<BR>
<INPUT TYPE="text" NAME=txtUserName MAXLENGTH=50>
</P>
<P>
Message Subject:<BR>
<INPUT TYPE="text" MAXLENGTH=50 NAME=txtMessageSubject>
</P>
<P>
Message Body:<BR>
<TEXTAREA ROWS=8 COLS=60 NAME=txtMessageBody></TEXTAREA>
</P>
<P>
<INPUT TYPE="submit" VALUE="Submit" NAME=submit1>
</P>
</FORM>
</BODY>
</HTML>
```

Lastly, we have the page that stores new messages created by the user into the database; save this as
`Ch16_StoreMessage.asp`:

```
<%@ LANGUAGE=JavaScript %>
<HTML>
<HEAD>
<TITLE>Message Added</TITLE>
</HEAD>
<BODY>

<%

var months = new Array("Jan","Feb","Mar","Apr","May","Jun",
                       "Jul","Aug","Sep","Oct","Nov","Dec");

var messageSubject = Request.Form("txtMessageSubject");
var messageBody = Request.Form("txtMessageBody");
var userName = Request.Form("txtUserName");
var postedDate = new Date();
postedDate = postedDate.getDate() + " "
             + months[postedDate.getMonth()] + " "
             + postedDate.getFullYear();
```

```
if (messageSubject != "" && messageBody != "" && userName != "")
{
    var mySQL = "INSERT INTO Message " +
                "(UserName, MessageSubject, " +
                " MessageBody,DatePosted) " +
                "VALUES ('" + userName + "'," +
                "'" + messageSubject + "'," +
                "'" + messageBody + "'," +
                "#" + postedDate + "#)";

    var adoConnection = Server.CreateObject("ADODB.Connection");
    adoConnection.Open("DSN=MessageBoardDSN")
    adoConnection.Execute(mySQL);
    adoConnection.Close();
    adoConnection = null;
    Response.Write("<H2>Message Posted Successfully</H2>");
}

%>
<FORM NAME=form1>
    <INPUT TYPE="button" VALUE="Return to Message Board"
           onclick="window.location.href='CH16_MessageBoard.htm'"
           NAME=button1>
</FORM>
</BODY>
</HTML>
```

Now we need to create the database that holds the messages and set up an ODBC data source.

Create a new database in Access and call it Message.mdb. Now create one new table called Message with the fields and field types shown below. You can leave the sub-properties at their default values. Make MessageId the primary key field:

Field Name	Data Type
MessageId	AutoNumber
UserName	Text
MessageSubject	Text
MessageBody	Memo
DatePosted	Date/Time

You might want to add a few dummy values to start with, though you can also use the new message form page to enter your data.

Now close the database and create a new DSN named MessageBoardDSN and select the database just created.

Let's look at how it works, starting with the Ch16_Messages.asp page. Near the top we have a form with just a button in it, when clicked the button submits the form to the New Message page where a new message can be created. We don't actually pass any values and simply use the form post as a way of navigating to a new page using a button but without using code. An alternative would be adding code to the onclick event handler of the button.

```
<FORM NAME="form1" METHOD=post ACTION="NewMessage.asp" TARGET=_top>
   <INPUT TYPE="submit" VALUE="Create New Message" NAME=submit1>
</FORM>
```

The action is all happening in the block of server-side code we see below. It's this that actually accesses the database, retrieves the messages, and writes them out to the page:

```
<%
var months = new Array("Jan","Feb","Mar","Apr","May","Jun",
                       "Jul","Aug","Sep","Oct","Nov","Dec");
var postedDate;
var lsSQL = "SELECT MessageId, UserName, MessageSubject, " +
            "DatePosted FROM Message " +
            "ORDER BY MessageId DESC"
var adoRS = Server.CreateObject("ADODB.Recordset")
adoRS.Open(lsSQL,"DSN=MessageBoardDSN")

while (adoRS.EOF == false)
{
    Response.Write("<TR><TD width=400>" +
                   "<A href='Ch16_MessageBody.asp?MessageId=" +
                   adoRS("MessageId") +
                   "' target=messagebody>" +
                   adoRS("MessageSubject") +
                   "</A></TD>")

    Response.Write("<TD width=100>" +adoRS("UserName") + "</TD>")

    postedDate = new Date(adoRS("DatePosted"))
    postedDate =postedDate.getDate() + " " + months[postedDate.getMonth()] +
                " " + postedDate.getFullYear();

    Response.Write("<TD width=100>" + postedDate + "</TD></TR>" )

    adoRS.MoveNext();
}

adoRS.Close()
adoRS = null;
```

At the top of the code above an array containing the names of all the months of the year is created, which we use later to format the date that the message was posted before writing it to the page. Then we create our SQL query that selects the information we need from the database so that we can create the list of messages posted to our message board. Using this SQL we open a recordset and populate it with the data.

Then, in the `while` loop, we loop through the records in the recordset and write out a table row containing the message subject, message author, and date it was posted. Notice that the subject is wrapped inside a link that loads `Ch16_MessageBody.asp` into the `messagebody` frame at the bottom of the page. We add data to the URL with the name `MessageId` and give it the value of `MessageId` retrieved for that record. That way the message body page knows which message body it needs to get from the database and display.

Let's turn next to the `Ch16_Messagebody.asp` page. It's fairly simple; first we get the message ID we added above to the URL from the `Request.QueryString` property. We check that it contains a valid number. If it doesn't then the message body page has been loaded by the frameset and not because the user clicked a link to see it, so we need to access the database. We create our SQL to select the message body from the database before using it to open a recordset and store the body in `lsMessageBody` variable:

```
<%
var lsMessageBody = "";
if (isNaN(Request.QueryString("MessageId")) == false)
{
    var lsSQL = "SELECT MessageBody FROM Message " +
                "WHERE MessageId = " + Request.QueryString("MessageId")
    var adoRS = Server.CreateObject("ADODB.Recordset")
    adoRS.Open(lsSQL,"DSN=MessageBoardDSN")
    lsMessageBody = adoRS("MessageBody").Value;

    adoRS.Close();
    adoRS = null;
}
%>
```

Finally we display the body by putting `lsMessageBody` inside the `<TEXTAREA>` tags:

```
<TEXTAREA ROWS=8 COLS=60 NAME=textarea1><%=lsMessageBody%></TEXTAREA>
```

The `Ch16_NewMessage.asp` page is also straightforward. It simply consists of a form for the user to enter their message details. At the top of the page we have some client-side script, the `checkForm()` function, that's called by the form's `onsubmit` event handler. It goes through each text box and text area in turn and checks that they have been filled in by the user, if not `false` is returned to the calling event handler and the `onsubmit` canceled.

```
function checkForm()
{
    var form = document.form1
    var controlCounter;
    var returnValue = true;
    var formControl;

    for (controlCounter = 0; controlCounter < form.length; controlCounter++)
    {
        formControl = form.elements[controlCounter]
        if ((formControl.type == "text" || formControl.type == "textarea")
            && formControl.value == "")
        {
            alert("Please complete all of the form");
            formControl.focus();
            returnValue = false;
            break;
        }
    }

    return returnValue;
}
```

Finally if the form is complete then it is submitted to our final page `Ch16_StoreMessage.asp`. As the name suggests this inserts the new message as a new record in the database.

In the page's server-side script block we need to connect to the database and insert a new record based on what the user submitted as their message.

First we declare an array of months that we'll use in creating the date posted details. Then we retrieve the message subject, body, and user's name from the form submitted and store these in variables. Finally we generate a `postedDate` variable containing today's date. This gives us all the information we need to then move on and generate the SQL that will insert the record.

```
var months = new Array("Jan","Feb","Mar","Apr","May","Jun",
                       "Jul","Aug","Sep","Oct","Nov","Dec");

var messageSubject = Request.Form("txtMessageSubject");
var messageBody = Request.Form("txtMessageBody");
var userName = Request.Form("txtUserName");
var postedDate = new Date();
postedDate = postedDate.getDate() + " "
             + months[postedDate.getMonth()] + " "
             + postedDate.getFullYear();
```

In the remainder of the server-side script we first check that there actually has been a message subject, body, and username submitted. If any of these variables is empty then we don't put the information in the database. This helps make it slightly more difficult for hackers to post directly to your database without going through the proper form or indeed the situation where a user's browser doesn't support JavaScript and so our client-side check of the form `onsubmit` has not occurred.

Assuming the variables do contain values, then we generate our SQL and store it in variable `mySQL`. We use an `INSERT` statement to do this making sure that any text or memo fields are surrounded by single quotes and the date field by a #.

Then the code creates an ADO `Connection` object and uses it to open a connection to the database using our DSN, and finally executes our SQL `INSERT` statement and adds the message to the database.

```
if (messageSubject != "" && messageBody != "" && userName != "")
{
   var mySQL = "INSERT INTO Message " +
               "(UserName, MessageSubject, " +
               " MessageBody,DatePosted) " +
               "VALUES ('" + userName + "'," +
               "'" + messageSubject + "'," +
               "'" + messageBody + "'," +
               "#" + postedDate + "#)";

   var adoConnection = Server.CreateObject("ADODB.Connection");
   adoConnection.Open("DSN=MessageBoardDSN")
   adoConnection.Execute(mySQL);
   adoConnection.Close();
   adoConnection = null;
   Response.Write("<H2>Message Posted Successfully</H2>");
}
```

Online discussion at http://p2p.wrox.com

JavaScript Core Reference

This appendix outlines the syntax of all the JavaScript core language functions and objects with their properties and methods. If changes have occurred between versions, they have been noted.

Browser Reference

The Internet Explorer support for JavaScript (not JScript) is flaky, but works in most cases.

Language Version	Netscape Navigator Version	Internet Explorer Version
JavaScript 1.0, JScript 1.0	2.x	3.x
JavaScript 1.1	3.x	
JavaScript 1.2, JScript 3.0	4.0 - 4.05	4.x
JavaScript 1.3	4.06+	
JavaScript 1.4, JScript 5.0	5.0	5.x
JavaScript 1.5	6.0	

Reserved Words

There are various words and symbols that are reserved by JavaScript. These words cannot be used as variable names, nor can the symbols be used within them. They are listed below:

abstract	boolean	break
byte	case	catch
char	class	const
continue	debugger	default
delete	do	double
else	enum	export
extends	false	final
finally	float	for
function	goto	if
implements	import	in
instanceof	int	interface
long	native	new
null	package	private
protected	public	return
short	static	super
switch	synchronized	this
throw	throws	transient
true	try	typeof
var	void	volatile
while	with	
-	!	~
%	/	*
>	<	=
&	^	|
+	?	

Other Identifiers to avoid

It is best to avoid the use of these identifiers as variable names:

JavaScript 1.0

```
abs acos anchor asin atan atan2 big blink bold ceil charAt comment cos Date
E escape eval exp fixed floor fontcolor fontsize getDate getDay getHours
getMinutes getMonth getSeconds getTime getTimezoneOffset getYear indexOf
isNaN italics lastIndexOf link log LOG10E LOG2E LN10 LN2 Math max min
Object parse parseFloat parseInt PI pow random round setDate setHours
setMinutes setMonth setSeconds setTime setYear sin slice small sqrt SQRT1_2
SQRT2 strike String sub substr substring sup tan toGMTString toLocaleString
toLowerCase toUpperCase unescape UTC
```

JavaScript 1.1

```
caller className constructor java JavaArray JavaClass JavaObject
JavaPackage join length MAX_VALUE MIN_VALUE NaN NEGATIVE_INFINITY netscape
Number POSITIVE_INFINITY prototype reverse sort split sun toString valueOf
```

JavaScript 1.2

```
arity callee charCodeAt compile concat exec fromCharCode global ignoreCase
index input label lastIndex lastMatch lastParen leftContext match multiline
Number Packages pop push RegExp replace rightContext search shift slice
splice source String test unshift unwatch watch
```

JavaScript 1.3

```
apply call getFullYear getMilliseconds getUTCDate getUTCDay getUTCFullYear
getUTCHours getUTCMilliseconds getUTCMinutes getUTCMonth getUTCSeconds
Infinity isFinite NaN setFullYear setMilliseconds setUTCDate setUTCFullYear
setUTCHours setUTCMilliseconds setUTCMinutes setUTCMonth setUTCSeconds
toSource toUTCString undefined
```

JavaScript Operators

Assignment operators were introduced in JavaScript 1.0, JScript 1.0.

Name	Introduced	Example	Meaning
Assignment	JavaScript 1.0 JScript 1.0	v1 = v2	Sets variable v1 to the value of variable v2
Shorthand Addition *or* Shorthand Concatenation	JavaScript 1.0 JScript 1.0	v1 += v2	v1 = v1 + v2

Table continued on following page

843

Name	Introduced	Example	Meaning
Shorthand Subtraction	JavaScript 1.0 JScript 1.0	`v1 -= v2`	`v1 = v1 - v2`
Shorthand Multiplication	JavaScript 1.0 JScript 1.0	`v1 *= v2`	`v1 = v1 * v2`
Shorthand Division	JavaScript 1.0 JScript 1.0	`v1 /= v2`	`v1 = v1 / v2`
Shorthand Modulus	JavaScript 1.0 JScript 1.0	`v1 %= v2`	`v1 = v1 % v2`
Shorthand left shift	JavaScript 1.0 JScript 1.0	`v1 <<= v2`	`v1 = v1 << v2`
Shorthand right shift	JavaScript 1.0 JScript 1.0	`v1 >>= v2`	`v1 = v1 >> v2`
Shorthand zero fill right shift	JavaScript 1.0 JScript 1.0	`v1 >>>= v2`	`v1 = v1 >>> v2`
Shorthand AND	JavaScript 1.0 JScript 1.0	`v1 &= v2`	`v1 = v1 & v2`
Shorthand XOR	JavaScript 1.0 JScript 1.0	`v1 ^= v2`	`v1 = v1 ^ v2`
Shorthand OR	JavaScript 1.0 JScript 1.0	`v1 |= v2`	`v1 = v1 | v2`

Comparison operators were first introduced in JavaScript 1.0, though a few changes have been made as noted. If `v1=1` and `v2=2`, the following example statements are all true. Boolean literal values `true` and `false` are returned by the comparisons.

In JavaScript 1.4, `==` has been deprecated with respect to objects in favor of `JSObject.equals`. In JavaScript 1.2 only, neither `==` or `!==` attempted type conversion before returning a value.

Name	Introduced	Example	Meaning
Equal	JavaScript 1.0 JScript 1.0	`v1 == 1`	True if two operands are strictly equal or equal once cast to the same type.
Not Equal	JavaScript 1.0 JScript 1.0	`v1 != v2`	True if two operands are not strictly equal or not equal once cast to the same type.

Name	Introduced	Example	Meaning
Greater Than	JavaScript 1.0 JScript 1.0	`v2 > v1`	True if LHS operand is greater than RHS operand.
Greater Than Or Equal	JavaScript 1.0 JScript 1.0	`v2 >= v2`	True if LHS operand is greater than or equal to RHS operand.
Less Than	JavaScript 1.0 JScript 1.0	`v1 < v2`	True if LHS operand is less than RHS operand.
Less Than Or Equal	JavaScript 1.0 JScript 1.0	`v1 <= v1`	True if LHS operand is less than or equal to RHS operand.
Strictly Equal	JavaScript 1.3 JScript 1.0	`v2 === v2`	Not in ECMA-262. True if operands are equal and of same type.
Not Strictly Equal	JavaScript 1.3 JScript 1.0	`v1 !== v2`	Not in ECMA-262. True if operands are not strictly equal.

Arithmetic operators were first introduced in JavaScript 1.0 and JScript 1.0.

Name	Introduced	Example	Result
Addition	JavaScript 1.0 JScript 1.0	`v1 + v2`	Sum of `v1` and `v2` concatenation of `v1` and `v2`, if they are strings
Subtraction	JavaScript 1.0 JScript 1.0	`v1 - v2`	Difference of `v1` and `v2`.
Multiplication	JavaScript 1.0 JScript 1.0	`v1 * v2`	Product of `v1` and `v2`.
Division	JavaScript 1.0 JScript 1.0	`v1 / v2`	Quotient of `v2` into `v1`.
Modulus	JavaScript 1.0 JScript 1.0	`v1 % v2`	Integer remainder of dividing `v1` by `v2`.
Prefix Increment	JavaScript 1.0 JScript 1.0	`++v1 * v2`	`(v1 + 1) * v2`. Note: `v1` will be left as `v1 + 1`.

Table continued on following page

845

Name	Introduced	Example	Result
Postfix Increment	JavaScript 1.0 JScript 1.0	`v1++ * v2`	`(v1 * v2)`; v1 is then incremented by 1.
Prefix Decrement	JavaScript 1.0 JScript 1.0	`--v1 * v2`	`(v1 - 1) * v2`. Note: v1 is left as `v1 - 1`.
Postfix Decrement	JavaScript 1.0 JScript 1.0	`v1-- * v2`	`(v1 * v2)`. v1 is then decremented by 1.

Bitwise logical operators were first introduced in JavaScript 1.0 and JScript 1.0. They work by converting values in `v1` and `v2` to 32 bit binary numbers and then comparing the individual bits of these two binary numbers. The result is returned as a normal decimal number.

Name	Introduced	Example	Result
Bitwise AND	JavaScript 1.0 JScript 1.0	`v1 & v2`	ANDs each pair of corresponding bits.
Bitwise OR	JavaScript 1.0 JScript 1.0	`v1 | v2`	ORs each pair of corresponding bits.
Bitwise XOR	JavaScript 1.0 JScript 1.0	`v1 ^ v2`	XORs each pair of corresponding bits.
Bitwise NOT	JavaScript 1.0 JScript 1.0	`~v1`	Inverts all the bits in the number.

Bitwise shift operators were first introduced in JavaScript 1.0 and JScript 1.0. They work by converting values in `v1` to 32 bit binary numbers and then moving the bits in the number to the left or the right by the specified number of places.

Name	Introduced	Example	Result
Left Shift	JavaScript 1.0 JScript 1.0	`v1 << v2`	Shifts v1 to the left by v2 places, filling the new gaps in with zeros.
Right Shift	JavaScript 1.0 JScript 1.0	`v1 >> v2`	Shifts v1 to the right by v2 places, ignoring the bits shifted off the number.
Zero-fill Right Shift	JavaScript 1.0 JScript 1.0	`v1 >>> v2`	Shifts v1 to the right by v2 places, ignoring the bits shifted off the number and adding v2 zeros to the left of the number.

Logical operators were first introduced in JavaScript 1.0 and JScript 1.0. They should return one of the Boolean literals, `true` or `false`. However, this may not happen if either v1 or v2 is neither a Boolean value nor a value that easily converts to a Boolean value, such as 0, 1, `null`, the empty string, or `undefined`.

Name	Introduced	Example	Result
Logical AND	JavaScript 1.0 JScript 1.0	`v1 && v2`	Returns `true` if both v1 and v2 are `true`, `false` otherwise. Will not evaluate v2 if v1 is `false`.
Logical OR	JavaScript 1.0 JScript 1.0	`v1 || v2`	Returns `false` if both v1 and v2 are `false`, `true` otherwise. Will not evaluate v2 if v1 is `true`.
Logical NOT	JavaScript 1.0 JScript 1.0	`!v1`	Returns `false` if v1 is `true`, `true` otherwise.

Several operators have been introduced to JavaScript to deal with **objects**:

Name	Introduced	Example	Description
`delete`	JavaScript 1.2 JScript 3.0	`delete someObject` `delete someObject. property` `delete someArray[index]`	Deletes an object, one of its properties or the element of an array at the specified index.
`in`	JavaScript 1.4	`property in someObject`	Not in ECMA-262. Returns `true` if `someObject` has the named property. Not supported by Internet Explorer.
`instanceof`	JavaScript 1.4 JScript 5.0	`someObject instanceof objectType`	Not in ECMA-262. Returns true if `someObject` is of type `objectType`.
`new`	JavaScript 1.0 JScript 1.0	`someObject = new objectType (parameterList)`	Creates a new instance of an object with type `objectType`. The `parameterList` obeys a constructor function specified elsewhere.
`this`	JavaScript 1.0 JScript 1.0	`this` `this.property`	Refers to the current object.

There are several other miscellaneous operators in JavaScript:

Name	Introduced	Example	Description
Conditional Operator	JavaScript 1.0 JScript 1.0	`evalquery ? v1 : v2`	If `evalquery` is `true`, the operator returns `v1`, else it returns `v2`.
Comma Operator	JavaScript 1.0 JScript 1.0	`eval1, eval2`	Evaluates both `eval1` and `eval2` while treating the two as one expression.
`typeof`	JavaScript 1.1 JScript 1.0	`typeof v1` `typeof (v1)`	Returns a string holding the type of `v1`, which is not evaluated.
`void`	JavaScript 1.1 JScript 2.0	`void eval1` `void (eval1)`	Evaluates `eval1` but does not return a value.

Operator Precedence

Does `1 + 2 * 3 = 1 + (2 * 3) = 7` or does it equal `(1 + 2) * 3 = 9`?

The ECMAScript standard doesn't yet clearly document operator precedence. However, JavaScript closely follows Java, and Java closely follows C. The table shows precedence with the highest at the top, and like operators grouped together. The third column explains whether to read `1+2+3+4` as `((1+2)+3)+4` or `1+(2+(3+(4)))`.

Operator type	Operators	Evaluation order for like elements
postfix operators	`[] () . expr++ expr--`	left to right
unary operators	`++expr --expr +expr -expr ~ !`	right to left
object management or cast	`delete new typeof void`	right to left
multiplicative	`* / %`	left to right
additive	`+ -`	left to right
shift	`<< >> >>>`	left to right
relational	`< > <= >= in instanceof`	left to right
equality	`== != === !==`	left to right
bitwise AND	`&`	left to right
bitwise exclusive OR	`^`	left to right

Operator type	Operators	Evaluation order for like elements
bitwise inclusive OR	|	left to right
logical AND	&&	left to right
logical OR	||	left to right
conditional	? :	right to left
assignment	= += -= *= /= %= &= ^= |= <<= >>= >>>=	right to left
multiple evaluation	,	left to right

JavaScript Statements

The following tables describe core JavaScript statements.

Declarations

Statement	Introduced	Example	Description

var	JavaScript 1.0 JScript 1.0	`var Number;`
		`var Number = 6;`
		`var N1, N2, N3 = 6;`
			Used to declare a variable. Initializing it to a value is optional at the time of declaration.

function	JavaScript 1.0 JScript 1.0	`function doItNow() { statements }`
		
		`function doThis(p1, p2, p3) { statements }`
			Used to declare a function with the specified parameters, which can be strings, numbers, or objects. To return a value the function must use the return statement.

Loops

Statement	Introduced	Example	Description

do...while	JavaScript 1.2
	JScript 3.0
		```do```
		``` statements```
		``` --test;```
		```while (0 <=```
		```test);```
			Not in ECMA-262.
			
			Executes the statements specified until the test condition after the while evaluates to false. The statements are executed at least once because the test condition is evaluated last.

for	JavaScript 1.0
	JScript 1.0
		```for (var i=0;```
		```i<15; i++)```
		```{```
		``` var x += i;```
		``` doSomething(x)```
		```;```
		```}```
			Creates a loop controlled according to the three optional expressions enclosed in the parentheses after the for and separated by semicolons. The first of these three expressions is the initial-expression, the second is the test condition, and the third is the increment-expression.

for...in	JavaScript 1.0
	JScript 1.0
		```for (var i in```
		```obj)```
		```{```
		``` return obj[i];```
		```}```
			Used to iterate over all the properties of an object using a variable. For each property the specified statements within the loop are executed.

if...else	JavaScript 1.0
	JScript 1.0
		```if (x <= y)```
		```{```
		``` thing += x;```
		``` x++;```
		```}```
		```else```
		``` thing += y;```
			Executes a block of statements if the condition evaluates to true. If the condition evaluates to false, another block of statements can be executed.

while	JavaScript 1.0
	JScript 1.0
		```while(y < 3)```
		```{```
		``` doSomething();```
		```}```
			Executes a block of statements if a test condition evaluates to true. The loop then repeats, testing the condition with each repeat, ceasing if the condition evaluates to false.

Execution Control Statements

Statement	Introduced	Example	Description
break	JavaScript 1.0 JScript 1.0	```function loopWithBreak(b) { var x = 0; while (x < 20) { if (10 == x) break; x++; } return x*b; }```	Used within a while or for loop to terminate the loop and transfer program control to the statement following the loop. Can also be used with a label to break to a particular program position outside of the loop.
continue	JavaScript 1.0 JScript 1.0	```function loopWithContinue(c) { var count = 0; while (count < 16) { if (0 == (++count % 2)) continue; return count*c; } }```	Used to stop execution of the block of statements in the current iteration of a while or for loop; execution of the loop continues with the next iteration.
label	JavaScript 1.2 JScript 3.0	```function breakWithLabel(b) { var outer, inr = 0; myFirstLabel: while (++outer < 12) { for(inr=0;inr<12; inr++) { if(6 == outer) break myFirstLabel; return inr*outer; } } }```	An identifier that can be used with break or continue statements to indicate where the program should continue execution after the loop execution is stopped.

Table continued on following page

Statement	Introduced	Example	Description

return	JavaScript 1.0
	 JScript 1.0
		```function returnSthg(x, y)```
		 ```{```
		     ```return x/y;```
		 ```}```
			Used to specify the value to be returned by a function.

switch	JavaScript 1.2
	 JScript 3.0
		```switch(x)```
		 ```{```
		     ```case 0 :```
		         ```doSomething();```
		         ```break;```
		     ```case 1 :```
		         ```doSomethingElse();```
		         ```break;```
		     ```default :```
		         ```doThisInstead();```
		 ```}```
			Not in ECMA-262.
			
			 Specifies various blocks of statements to be executed depending on the value of the expression passed in as the argument. Similar to a Visual Basic `Select Case` statement.

with	JavaScript 1.0
	 JScript 1.0
		```with(myObject)```
		 ```{```
		     ```myProperty="New Value";```
		 ```}```
			Specifies the default object for a set of statements.

Exception Statements

These were introduced in JavaScript 1.4.

Statement	Introduced	Example	Description

throw	JavaScript 1.4
	 JScript 5.0
		```function```
		 ```ValidateDay(DayOfWk)```
		 ```{```
		 ```if (DayOfWk < 1 | DayOfWk > 7)```
		 ```{```
		 ```throw "Invalid day of week";```
		 ```}```
		 ```}```
			Not in ECMA-262.
			
			 Throws a custom exception defined by the user.

Statement	Introduced	Example	Description

try...catch ...finally	JavaScript 1.4 JScript 5.0	```
		function
		catchException()
		{
		    try
		    {
		        throw "Errors
		occurred";
		    }
		    catch(excptn)
		    {
		        alert(excptn);
		    }
		    finally
		    {
		        doSomething();
		    }
		}
		``
			Not in ECMA-262.
			
			Executes the statements in the try block; if any exceptions occur, these are handled in the catch block. The finally block allows us to stipulate statements that will be executed after both the try and catch statements.

Conditional Compile Statements

These are specific to JScript and are not supported by Netscape Navigator. Introduced in JScript 3.0. These statements allow JScript code to be compiled only if certain conditions are met. Conditional compilation also provides access to the conditional compilation variables, which provide information about the platform and version of Script in use. Conditional compilation statements should be placed inside comments, where they will be ignored by browsers that do not support conditional compilation.

Statement	Introduced	Example	Description
@cc_on	JScript 3.0	`/*@cc_on @*/`	Turns conditional compilation on.
@if...@elif ...@else... @end	JScript 3.0	``` /*@if (@_jscript_version==5) alert("Glad you've got the latest version of JScript!"); @elif (@_jscript_version>2) alert("It's not the latest version, but it'll do!"); @else @*/ alert("You're not using IE, or your browser's too old!"); /*@end @*/ ```	Compiles the following code only if the given condition equates to true. The @elif statement allows for another condition to be tested, and @else supplies a default if no conditions are met.

Table continued on following page

Statement	Introduced	Example	Description
@set	JScript 3.0	/*@set @v1=23 @*/	Allows variables to be created for use in conditionally compiled code. The variable must start with the character @.

Predefined Conditional Compilation Variables

These predefined variables return information about the system and platform on which the browser is running and can be accessed when conditional compilation is enabled.

Variable	Description
@_alpha	Returns true if the browser is running on a DEC Alpha machine, otherwise NaN.
@_jscript	Returns true if the browser supports JScript. This always returns true.
@_jscript_build	Returns the build number for the version of JScript in use.
@_jscript_version	Returns the version number for the version of JScript in use.
@_mac	Returns true if the browser is running on an Apple Macintosh machine, otherwise NaN.
@_mc680x0	Returns true if the browser is running on a Motorola 680x0 machine, otherwise NaN.
@_PowerPC	Returns true if the browser is running on a Motorola Power PC machine, otherwise NaN.
@_win16	Returns true if the browser is running on a Windows 16-bit platform, otherwise NaN.
@_win32	Returns true if the browser is running on a Windows 32-bit platform, otherwise NaN.
@_x86	Returns true if the browser is running on an IBM PC or compatible, otherwise NaN.

Other Statements

Statement	Introduced	Example	Description
comment	JavaScript 1.0 JScript 1.0	`// one-line comment` `/* multiple-line comment, of any length */`	Notes, which are ignored by the script engine, and which can be used to explain the code.
import	JavaScript 1.2	`import myObject.myProperty, myObject.myFunction`	Allows a script to import objects, and their properties and methods, which have been exported from another script. Not supported by Internet Explorer.
export	JavaScript 1.2	`export myProperty, myFunction`	Allows a signed script to export objects, and their properties and methods, so that they can be imported by other scripts. Not supported by Internet Explorer.

Top-Level Properties and Functions

These are core properties and functions, which are not associated with any lower-level object, although in the terminology used by ECMAScript and by JScript, they are described as properties and methods of the global object.

Top-Level Properties

These were introduced in JavaScript 1.3 and JScript 3.0, but in previous versions, `Infinity` and `NaN` existed as properties of the `Number` object.

Property	Introduced	Example	Description
Infinity	JavaScript 1.3 JScript 3.0	```function getNumber(x)
{
if (isFinite(x))
{
return x;
}
else
{
return Infinity;
}
}```	Returns infinity.

Table continued on following page

Property	Introduced	Example	Description
| NaN | JavaScript 1.3 <br> JScript 3.0 | ```javascript
function getNumber(x)
{
    if (isNaN(x))
    {
        return NaN;
    }
    else
    {
        return x;
    }
}
``` | Returns a value which is not a number. |
| undefined | JavaScript 1.3 | ```javascript
if (v1 == undefined)
{
    alert("Variable not defined");
}
else
{
    alert("Value is " + v1);
}
``` | Indicates that a value has not been assigned to a variable. Not supported by Internet Explorer. |

Top-Level Functions

Function	Introduced	Example	Description
| escape() | JavaScript 1.0 <br> JScript 1.0 | ```javascript
str1 = escape("&");
// str1 == "%26"
``` | Used to encode a string in the ISO Latin-1 character set, for example to add to a URL. |
| eval() | JavaScript 1.0 <br> JScript 1.0 | ```javascript
strOp = "*";
v1 = 10;
strCode = "v1 = v1" + strOp + "2";
eval (strCode);
alert(v1);
``` | Returns the result of the JavaScript code which is passed in as a parameter. |

Function	Introduced	Example	Description
isFinite()	JavaScript 1.3 JScript 3.0	```function getNumber(x)
{
if (isFinite(x))
{
return x;
}
else
{
return Infinity;
}
}```	Indicates whether the argument is a finite number.
isNaN()	JavaScript 1.0 (Unix only), 1.1 JScript 1.0	```function getNumber(x)
{
if (isNaN(x))
{
return NaN;
}
else
{
return x;
}
}```	Indicates if the argument is not a number.
Number()	JavaScript 1.2 JScript 2.0	```function getNumber(strNum)
{
return Number(strNum);
}```	Converts an object to a number.
parseFloat()	JavaScript 1.0 JScript 1.0	```x = parseFloat("21.99");
// x == 21.99```	Parses a string and returns it as a floating-point number.

Table continued on following page

Function	Introduced	Example	Description

parseInt()	JavaScript 1.0
	
	JScript 1.0
		`x = parseInt("21.99");`
		`//x == 21`
		`x = parseInt("FF", 16);`
		`//x == 255`
			Parses a string and returns it as an integer. An optional second parameter specifies the base of the number to be converted.

String()	JavaScript 1.2
	
	JScript 1.0
		`objDate = new Date(940000000000);`
		`strDate=String(objDate);`
		`/*strDate == "Fri Oct 15 16:06:40 UTC+0100 1999" */`
			Converts an object to a string.

unescape()	JavaScript 1.0 JScript 1.0	`str1 = unescape("%28");` `//str1 == "("`	Returns the ASCII string for the specified hexadecimal encoding value.

JavaScript Core Objects

The following tables describe the objects available in the JavaScript core language and their methods and properties.

ActiveXObject

The `ActiveXObject` object represents an ActiveX object when accessed from within JScript code. Introduced in JScript 3.0, it's not available in ECMAScript or Netscape JavaScript. Created with the `ActiveXObject` constructor; for example, to create a Microsoft Word document, we would write:

```
var objActiveX = new ActiveXObject("Word.Document");
```

The properties and methods of this object will be those of the ActiveX object thus created. For example, the following code opens a Word document and writes some text to it and to the HTML page:

```
var objActiveX = new ActiveXObject("Word.Document");
strText="This is being written both to the HTML page and to the Word document.";
objActiveX.application.selection.typeText(strText);
document.write(strText);
```

Array

The `Array` object represents an array of variables. It was introduced in JavaScript 1.1 and JScript 2.0. An `Array` object is created with the `Array` constructor:

```
var objArray = new Array(10)              // an array of 11 elements
var objArray = new Array("1", "2", "4")   // an array of 3 elements
```

Properties

Property	Introduced	Description
constructor	JavaScript 1.1 JScript 2.0	Used to reference the constructor function for the object.
index	JavaScript 1.2	Not in ECMA-262. The zero-based index indicating the position in the string that matches a regular expression. Not supported by Internet Explorer.
input	JavaScript 1.2	Not in ECMA-262. Returns the string against which a regular expression was matched. Not supported by Internet Explorer.
length	JavaScript 1.1 JScript 2.0	Returns the number of elements in the array.
prototype	JavaScript 1.1 JScript 2.0	Returns the prototype for the object, which can be used to extend the object's interface.

Methods

Method	Introduced	Description
concat()	JavaScript 1.2 JScript 3.0	Not in ECMA-262. Concatenates two arrays and returns the new array thus formed.
join()	JavaScript 1.1 JScript 2.0	Joins all the elements of an array into a single string.
pop()	JavaScript 1.2	Not in ECMA-262. Pops the last element from the end of the array and returns that element. Not supported by Internet Explorer.

Table continued on following page

Method	Introduced	Description
push()	JavaScript 1.2	Not in ECMA-262.
		Pushes one or more elements onto the end of the array and returns the new length of the array. (In JavaScript 1.2, the last element rather than the new length is returned.) Not supported by Internet Explorer.
reverse()	JavaScript 1.1	Reverses the order of the elements in the array, so that the first element becomes the last and the last becomes the first.
	JScript 2.0	
shift()	JavaScript 1.2	Not in ECMA-262.
		Removes the first element from the beginning of the array and returns that element. Not supported by Internet Explorer.
slice()	JavaScript 1.2	Not in ECMA-262.
	JScript 3.0	Returns a subarray from the array.
sort()	JavaScript 1.1	Sorts the elements of the array.
	JScript 2.0	
splice()	JavaScript 1.2	Not in ECMA-262.
		Adds, removes, or replaces elements in the array. Not supported by Internet Explorer.
toSource()	JavaScript 1.3	Not in ECMA-262.
		Returns a string containing the source code for the Array object. Not supported by Internet Explorer.
toString()	JavaScript 1.1	Converts the Array object into a string.
	JScript 2.0	
unshift()	JavaScript 1.2	Not in ECMA-262.
		Adds elements to the beginning of the array and returns the new length. Not supported by Internet Explorer.
valueOf()	JavaScript 1.1	Returns the primitive value of the array.
	JScript 2.0	

In Netscape JavaScript, this object also inherits the methods watch() and unwatch() from the Object object (not ECMAScript or IE).

Boolean

The `Boolean` object is used as a wrapper for a Boolean value. It was introduced in JavaScript 1.1 and JScript 2.0. It is created with the `Boolean` constructor, which takes as a parameter the initial value for the object (if this is not a Boolean value, it will be converted into one):

```
var objBoolean = new Boolean("true");
```

Properties

Property	Introduced	Description
constructor	JavaScript 1.1 JScript 2.0	Specifies the function that creates an object's prototype.
prototype	JavaScript 1.1 JScript 2.0	Returns the prototype for the object, which can be used to extend the object's interface.

Methods

Method	Introduced	Description
toSource()	JavaScript 1.3	Not in ECMA-262. Returns a string containing the source code for the `Boolean` object. Not supported by Internet Explorer.
toString()	JavaScript 1.1 JScript 2.0	Converts the `Boolean` object into a string.
valueOf()	JavaScript 1.1 JScript 2.0	Returns the primitive value of the `Boolean` object.

In Netscape JavaScript, this object also inherits the methods `watch()` and `unwatch()` from the `Object` object (not ECMAScript or IE).

Date

The `Date` object is used to represent a given date-time. It was introduced in JavaScript 1.0 and JScript 1.0. Created with the `Date` constructor:

```
objDate = new Date()                  // Current date-time
objDate = new Date(940000000000)      // milliseconds since Jan 1 1970 00:00:00
objDate = new Date("Jan 1, 1999");
objDate = new Date(1999,11,31,8,0)    // 31 Dec 1999 08:00:00
```

Properties

Property	Introduced	Description
constructor	JavaScript 1.1 JScript 2.0	Used to reference the constructor function for the object.
prototype	JavaScript 1.1 JScript 2.0	Returns the prototype for the object, which can be used to extend the object's interface.

Methods

Method	Introduced	Description
getDate()	JavaScript 1.0 JScript 1.0	Retrieves the date in the month from the Date object.
getDay()	JavaScript 1.0 JScript 1.0	Retrieves the day of the week from the Date object.
getFullYear()	JavaScript 1.3 JScript 3.0	Retrieves the full year from the Date object.
getHours()	JavaScript 1.0 JScript 1.0	Retrieves the hour of the day from the Date object.
getMilliseconds()	JavaScript 1.3 JScript 3.0	Retrieves the number of milliseconds from the Date object.
getMinutes()	JavaScript 1.0 JScript 1.0	Retrieves the number of minutes from the Date object.
getMonth()	JavaScript 1.0 JScript 1.0	Retrieves the month from the Date object.
getSeconds()	JavaScript 1.0 JScript 1.0	Retrieves the number of seconds from the Date object.
getTime()	JavaScript 1.0 JScript 1.0	Retrieves the number of milliseconds since January 1 1970 00:00:00 from the Date object.
getTimezoneOffset()	JavaScript 1.0 JScript 1.0	Retrieves the difference in minutes between the local time zone and UTC.

Method	Introduced	Description
getUTCDate()	JavaScript 1.3 JScript 3.0	Retrieves the date in the month from the Date object adjusted to universal time.
getUTCDay()	JavaScript 1.3 JScript 3.0	Retrieves the day of the week from the Date object adjusted to universal time.
getUTCFullYear()	JavaScript 1.3 JScript 3.0	Retrieves the year from the Date object adjusted to universal time.
getUTCHours()	JavaScript 1.3 JScript 3.0	Retrieves the hour of the day from the Date object adjusted to universal time.
getUTCMilliseconds()	JavaScript 1.3 JScript 3.0	Retrieves the number of milliseconds from the Date object adjusted to universal time.
getUTCMinutes()	JavaScript 1.3 JScript 3.0	Retrieves the number of minutes from the Date object adjusted to universal time.
getUTCMonth()	JavaScript 1.3 JScript 3.0	Retrieves the month from the Date object adjusted to universal time.
getUTCSeconds()	JavaScript 1.3 JScript 3.0	Retrieves the number of seconds from the Date object adjusted to universal time.
getVarDate()	JScript 3.0	Not in ECMA-262 or Netscape JavaScript. Returns the date in VT_DATE format (used for communicating with ActiveX objects).
getYear()	JavaScript 1.0 JScript 1.0	Retrieves the year from the Date object.
parse()	JavaScript 1.0 JScript 1.0	Retrieves the number of milliseconds in a date since January 1 1970 00:00:00, local time.
setDate()	JavaScript 1.0 JScript 1.0	Sets the date in the month for the Date object.
setFullYear()	JavaScript 1.3 JScript 3.0	Sets the full year for the Date object.
setHours()	JavaScript 1.0 JScript 1.0	Sets the hour of the day for the Date object.

Table continued on following page

Method	Introduced	Description
setMilliseconds()	JavaScript 1.3 JScript 3.0	Sets the number of milliseconds for the Date object.
setMinutes()	JavaScript 1.0 JScript 1.0	Sets the number of minutes for the Date object.
setMonth()	JavaScript 1.0 JScript 1.0	Sets the month for the Date object.
setSeconds()	JavaScript 1.0 JScript 1.0	Sets the number of seconds for the Date object.
setTime()	JavaScript 1.0 JScript 1.0	Sets the time for the Date object according to the number of milliseconds since January 1 1970 00:00:00.
setUTCDate()	JavaScript 1.3 JScript 3.0	Sets the date in the month for the Date object according to universal time.
setUTCFullYear()	JavaScript 1.3 JScript 3.0	Sets the full year for the Date object according to universal time.
setUTCHours()	JavaScript 1.3 JScript 3.0	Sets the hour of the day for the Date object according to universal time.
setUTCMilliseconds()	JavaScript 1.3 JScript 3.0	Sets the number of milliseconds for the Date object according to universal time.
setUTCMinutes()	JavaScript 1.3 JScript 3.0	Sets the number of minutes for the Date object according to universal time.
setUTCMonth()	JavaScript 1.3 JScript 3.0	Sets the month for the Date object according to universal time.
setUTCSeconds()	JavaScript 1.3 JScript 3.0	Sets the number of seconds for the Date object according to universal time.
setYear()	JavaScript 1.0 JScript 1.0	Sets the year for the Date object.
toGMTString()	JavaScript 1.0 JScript 1.0	Converts the Date object to a string according to Greenwich Mean Time. Replaced by toUTCString.

Method	Introduced	Description
toLocaleString()	JavaScript 1.0 JScript 1.0	Converts the Date object to a string according to the local time zone.
toSource()	JavaScript 1.3	Returns a string containing the source code for the Date object.
toString()	JavaScript 1.1	Converts the Date object into a string.
toUTCString()	JavaScript 1.3	Not in ECMA-262. Converts the Date object to a string according to universal time. Not supported by Internet Explorer.
UTC()	JavaScript 1.0 JScript 1.0	Retrieves the number of milliseconds in a date since January 1 1970 00:00:00, universal time.
valueOf()	JavaScript 1.1 JScript 2.0	Returns the primitive value of the Date object.

In Netscape JavaScript, this object also inherits the methods watch() and unwatch() from the Object object (not ECMAScript or IE).

Enumerator

The Enumerator object allows us to iterate through the items in a collection. Introduced in JScript 3.0; not ECMAScript or Netscape JavaScript. It is created through the Enumerator constructor; the collection to be enumerated is passed in as a parameter. For example, this code creates an Enumerator object for the forms collection in an HTML page:

```
<FORM NAME="form1">
   <INPUT TYPE=button VALUE="Click me!">
</FORM>

<FORM NAME="form1">
   <INPUT TYPE=button VALUE="No, click me instead!">
</FORM>

<SCRIPT>
var colForms = document.forms;
var objEnum = new Enumerator(colForms);
</SCRIPT>
```

Methods

Method	Introduced	Description
AtEnd()	JScript 3.0	Returns true if the Enumerator is at the end of the collection.
Item()	JScript 3.0	Returns the item at the current position in the collection.
MoveFirst()	JScript 3.0	Moves to the first item in the collection.
MoveNext()	JScript 3.0	Moves to the next item in the collection.

Function

Represents a block of JavaScript code that is to be compiled as a function. Introduced in JavaScript 1.1, JScript 2.0. A Function object is created with the Function constructor. For example, to create an object that represents the following function, which adds two values passed in as parameters:

```
function fnAddition(v1,v2)
{
    return v1+v2
}
```

We could create a Function object as follows; the names of the parameters for the function are passed in to the Function constructor, followed by the body of the function:

```
var fnAddition = new Function ("v1", "v2", "return v1+v2");
```

We can then call this as though it were a normal function:

```
var total = fnAddition(4,3);
```

Properties

Property	Introduced	Description
arguments	JavaScript 1.1 JScript 2.0	An array containing the parameters passed into the function (replaced in Netscape JavaScript by arguments as a local variable within the Function object).
arguments.callee	JavaScript 1.2	Returns the body of the current Function object (replaced by the callee property of the arguments local variable). Not supported by Internet Explorer.

Property	Introduced	Description
arguments.caller	JavaScript 1.1	Not in ECMA-262.
		Returns the name of the function that called the current Function object (replaced by the caller property of the arguments local variable). Not supported by Internet Explorer.
arguments.length	JavaScript 1.1 JScript 2.0	Returns the number of parameters passed into the function (replaced in Netscape JavaScript by the length property of the arguments local variable).
arity	JavaScript 1.2	Not in ECMA-262.
		Returns the number of parameters expected by the function. Replaced by the length property. Not supported by Internet Explorer.
caller	JScript 2.0	Not in ECMA-262 or Netscape JavaScript.
		Returns a reference to the function that called the current Function object.
constructor	JavaScript 1.1 JScript 2.0	Used to reference the constructor function for the object.
length	JavaScript 1.1	Returns the number of parameters expected by the function. This differs from arguments.length, which returns the number of parameters actually passed into the function. Not supported by Internet Explorer.
prototype	JavaScript 1.1 JScript 2.0	Returns the prototype for the object, which can be used to extend the object's interface.

Methods

Method	Introduced	Description
apply()	JavaScript 1.3	Not in ECMA-262.
		Applies a method of one object in the context of the object that calls the method. Not supported by Internet Explorer.
call()	JavaScript 1.3	Not in ECMA-262.
		Executes a method of one object in the context of the object that calls the method. Not supported by Internet Explorer.

Table continued on following page

Method	Introduced	Description
toSource()	JavaScript 1.3	Not in ECMA-262.
		Returns a string containing the source code for the Function object. Not supported by Internet Explorer.
toString()	JavaScript 1.1	Converts the Function object into a string.
	JScript 2.0	
valueOf()	JavaScript 1.1	Returns the primitive value of the Function object.
	JScript 2.0	

java

This is merely a synonym for Packages.java. Introduced in JavaScript 1.1, but not supported by ECMAScript or Internet Explorer.

JavaArray

Represents a Java array accessed from within JavaScript. Introduced in JavaScript 1.1; not supported by ECMAScript or Internet Explorer. Created by Java methods that return an array.

Properties

Property	Introduced	Description
length	JavaScript 1.1	Not in ECMA-262.
		The number of elements in the Java array.

Methods

Method	Introduced	Description
toString()	JavaScript 1.1	Not in ECMA-262.
		In JavaScript 1.4, this method is overridden by the toString method of the java.lang.Object superclass.
		In earlier versions, this method returns a string, which identifies the object as a JavaArray.

In JavaScript 1.4, the JavaArray object also inherits methods from the Java array superclass java.lang.Object.

JavaClass

Used to reference a Java class from within JavaScript. Introduced in JavaScript 1.1; not supported by ECMAScript or Internet Explorer. Created through the `Packages` object; for example, the following code gets a reference to the Java `Date` class provided by the `java.util` package:

```
var javaDate = Packages.java.util.Date;
```

Properties

The properties of a `JavaClass` object are the static fields of the Java class.

Methods

The methods of a `JavaClass` object are the static methods of the Java class.

JavaObject

Represents a Java object accessed from within JavaScript code. Introduced in JavaScript 1.1, it is not supported by ECMAScript or Internet Explorer. Created by any Java method that returns an object, or using the new keyword with the `Packages` object:

```
var javaDate = new Packages.java.util.Date;
```

Properties

Inherits the public properties of the Java class of which it is an instance. It also inherits the properties of any superclass of which the Java class is a member.

Methods

Inherits the public methods of the Java class of which it is an instance. It also inherits methods from `java.lang.Object` and from any other superclass of which the Java class is a member.

JavaPackage

Represents a Java package when accessed from within JavaScript code. Introduced in JavaScript 1.1, it is not supported by ECMAScript or Internet Explorer. Created through the `Packages` object:

```
var javaUtilPackage = Packages.java.util;
```

Properties

The properties of a `JavaPackage` are the `JavaClass` and `JavaPackage` objects that it contains.

Math

The Math object provides methods and properties used for mathematical calculations. Introduced in JavaScript 1.0, JScript 1.0. The Math object is a top-level object, which can be accessed without a constructor.

Properties

Property	Introduced	Description
E	JavaScript 1.0 JScript 1.0	Returns Euler's constant (the base of natural logarithms) (approximately 2.718).
LN10	JavaScript 1.0 JScript 1.0	Returns the natural logarithm of 10 (approximately 2.302).
LN2	JavaScript 1.0 JScript 1.0	Returns the natural logarithm of 2 (approximately 0.693).
LOG10E	JavaScript 1.0 JScript 1.0	Returns the base 10 logarithm of E (approximately 0.434).
LOG2E	JavaScript 1.0 JScript 1.0	Returns the base 2 logarithm of E (approximately 1.442).
PI	JavaScript 1.0 JScript 1.0	Returns PI, the ratio of the circumference of a circle to its diameter (approximately 3.142).
SQRT1_2	JavaScript 1.0 JScript 1.0	Returns the square root of 1/2 (approximately 0.707).
SQRT2	JavaScript 1.0 JScript 1.0	Returns the square root of 2 (approximately 1.414).

Methods

Method	Introduced	Description
abs()	JavaScript 1.0 JScript 1.0	Returns the absolute (positive) value of a number.
acos()	JavaScript 1.0 JScript 1.0	Returns the arccosine of a number (in radians).
asin()	JavaScript 1.0 JScript 1.0	Returns the arcsine of a number (in radians).

Method	Introduced	Description
atan()	JavaScript 1.0	Returns the arctangent of a number (in radians).
	JScript 1.0	
atan2()	JavaScript 1.0	Returns the angle (in radians) between the x-axis and the position represented by the y and x coordinates passed in as parameters.
	JScript 2.0	
ceil()	JavaScript 1.0	Returns the value of a number rounded up to the nearest integer.
	JScript 1.0	
cos()	JavaScript 1.0	Returns the cosine of a number.
	JScript 1.0	
exp()	JavaScript 1.0	Returns E to the power of the argument passed in.
	JScript 1.0	
floor()	JavaScript 1.0	Returns the value of a number rounded down to the nearest integer.
	JScript 1.0	
log()	JavaScript 1.0	Returns the natural logarithm (base E) of a number.
	JScript 1.0	
max()	JavaScript 1.0	Returns the greater of two numbers passed in as parameters.
	JScript 1.0	
min()	JavaScript 1.0	Returns the lesser of two numbers passed in as parameters.
	JScript 1.0	
pow()	JavaScript 1.0	Returns the first parameter raised to the power of the second.
	JScript 1.0	
random()	JavaScript 1.0 (Unix only), 1.1	Returns a pseudo-random number between 0 and 1.
	JScript 1.0	
round()	JavaScript 1.0	Returns the value of a number rounded up or down to the nearest integer.
	JScript 1.0	
sin()	JavaScript 1.0	Returns the sine of a number.
	JScript 1.0	
sqrt()	JavaScript 1.0	Returns the square root of a number.
	JScript 1.0	
tan()	JavaScript 1.0	Returns the tangent of a number.
	JScript 1.0	

In Netscape JavaScript, this object also inherits the methods watch() and unwatch() from the Object object (not ECMAScript or IE).

netscape

This is merely a synonym for `Packages.netscape`. Introduced in JavaScript 1.1, it is not available in ECMAScript or Internet Explorer.

Number

The `Number` object acts as a wrapper for primitive numeric values. Introduced in JavaScript 1.1, JScript 2.0. A `Number` object is created using the `Number` constructor with the initial value for the number passed in as a parameter:

```
var myNum = new Number(27);
```

Properties

Property	Introduced	Description
constructor	JavaScript 1.1 JScript 2.0	Used to reference the constructor function for the object.
MAX_VALUE	JavaScript 1.1 JScript 2.0	Returns the largest number that can be represented in JavaScript (approximately 1.79E+308).
MIN_VALUE	JavaScript 1.1 JScript 2.0	Returns the smallest number that can be represented in JavaScript (5E-324).
NaN	JavaScript 1.1 JScript 2.0	Returns a value that is "not a number".
NEGATIVE_INFINITY	JavaScript 1.1 JScript 2.0	Returns a value representing negative infinity.
POSITIVE_INFINITY	JavaScript 1.1 JScript 2.0	Returns a value representing (positive) infinity.
prototype	JavaScript 1.1 JScript 2.0	Returns the prototype for the object, which can be used to extend the object's interface.

Methods

Method	Introduced	Description
toSource()	JavaScript 1.3	Not in ECMA-262. Returns a string containing the source code for the Number object. Not supported by Internet Explorer.
toString()	JavaScript 1.1 JScript 2.0	Converts the Number object into a string.
valueOf()	JavaScript 1.1 JScript 2.0	Returns the primitive value of the Number object.

In Netscape JavaScript, this object also inherits the methods watch and unwatch from the Object object (not ECMAScript or IE).

Object

Object is the primitive type for JavaScript objects, from which all other objects are descended (that is, all other objects inherit the methods and properties of the Object object). Introduced in JavaScript 1.0, JScript 3.0. An Object object is created using the Object constructor:

```
var myObj = new Object();
```

Properties

Property	Introduced	Description
constructor	JavaScript 1.1 JScript 3.0	Used to reference the constructor function for the object.
prototype	JavaScript 1.1 JScript 3.0	Returns the prototype for the object, which can be used to extend the object's interface.

Methods

Method	Introduced	Description
eval()	JavaScript 1.0	Not in ECMA-262. Evaluates a string of JavaScript code in the context of the specified object. Not supported in Internet Explorer and no longer available in Netscape JavaScript: replaced by the top-level eval function.

Table continued on following page

Method	Introduced	Description
toSource()	JavaScript 1.3	Returns a string containing the source code for the Object object. Not supported by Internet Explorer.
toString()	JavaScript 1.0 JScript 3.0	Converts the Object object into a string.
unwatch()	JavaScript 1.2	Not in ECMA-262. Removes from the object's property a watchpoint that was added with the watch method. Not supported by Internet Explorer.
valueOf()	JavaScript 1.1 JScript 3.0	Returns the primitive value of the Object object.
watch()	JavaScript 1.2	Not in ECMA-262. Allows us to specify a function, which will be called when a value is assigned to the specified property of the object. Not supported by Internet Explorer.

Packages

Allows access to Java packages from within JavaScript code. Introduced in JavaScript 1.1, it is not supported by ECMAScript or Internet Explorer. This is a top-level object, which does not need to be created with a constructor. The Packages object takes as its properties the Java package that is to be accessed; for example, to get a reference to the Java package java.util, we would write:

```
var javaUtilPackage = Packages.java.util;
```

RegExp

The RegExp object is used to contain the pattern for a regular expression. Introduced in JavaScript 1.2 and JScript 3.0, it is not supported by ECMAScript. RegExp objects can be created in two ways: with the RegExp constructor, or using a text literal. For example, the following code creates a regular expression that performs a global match for "Smith" or "Smyth":

```
var objRegExp = new RegExp("Sm[iy]th", "g");
```

or:

```
var objRegExp = /Sm[iy]th/g;
```

The second argument may be omitted, or may be one or both of the following flags:

- ❏ g: global match
- ❏ i: ignore case

Properties

Some of these properties have both long and short names. The short names are derived from the Perl programming language.

Property	Introduced	Description
`$1, $2, ... $9`	JavaScript 1.2 JScript 3.0	Not in ECMA-262. Matches placed in parentheses and remembered. Not supported by Internet Explorer.
`$_`	JavaScript 1.2 JScript 3.0	See `input`.
`$*`	JavaScript 1.2	See `multiline`.
`$&`	JavaScript 1.2	See `lastMatch`.
`$+`	JavaScript 1.2	See `lastParen`.
`` $` ``	JavaScript 1.2	See `leftContext`.
`$'`	JavaScript 1.2	See `rightContext`.
`constructor`	JavaScript 1.2 JScript 3.0	Used to reference the constructor function for the object.
`global`	JavaScript 1.2	Not in ECMA-262. Indicates whether all possible matches in the string are to be made, or only the first. Corresponds to the g flag. Not supported by Internet Explorer.
`ignoreCase`	JavaScript 1.2	Not in ECMA-262. Indicates whether the match is to be case-insensitive. Corresponds to the i flag. Not supported by Internet Explorer.
`index`	JScript 3.0	Not in ECMA-262 or Netscape JavaScript. The position of the first match in the string.
`input`	JavaScript 1.2 JScript 3.0	Not in ECMA-262. The string against which the regular expression is matched.
`lastIndex`	JavaScript 1.2 JScript 3.0	Not in ECMA-262. The position in the string from which the next match is to be started.

Table continued on following page

Property	Introduced	Description
lastMatch	JavaScript 1.2	Not in ECMA-262.
		The last characters to be matched. Not supported by Internet Explorer.
lastParen	JavaScript 1.2	Not in ECMA-262.
		The last match placed in parentheses and remembered (if any occurred). Not supported by Internet Explorer.
leftContext	JavaScript 1.2	Not in ECMA-262.
		The substring preceding the most recent match. Not supported by Internet Explorer.
multiline	JavaScript 1.2	Not in ECMA-262.
		Indicates whether strings are to be searched across multiple lines. Not supported by Internet Explorer.
prototype	JavaScript 1.2 JScript 3.0	Returns the prototype for the object, which can be used to extend the object's interface.
rightContext	JavaScript 1.2	Not in ECMA-262.
		The substring following the most recent match. Not supported by Internet Explorer.
source	JavaScript 1.2 JScript 3.0	Not in ECMA-262.
		The text of the pattern for the regular expression.

Methods

Method	Introduced	Description
compile()	JavaScript 1.2 JScript 3.0	Not in ECMA-262.
		Compiles the RegExp object.
exec()	JavaScript 1.2 JScript 3.0	Not in ECMA-262.
		Executes a search for a match in the string parameter passed in.
test()	JavaScript 1.2 JScript 3.0	Not in ECMA-262.
		Tests for a match in the string parameter passed in.
toSource()	JavaScript 1.3	Not in ECMA-262.
		Returns a string containing the source code for the RegExp object. Not supported by Internet Explorer.

Method	Introduced	Description
toString()	JavaScript 1.2 JScript 3.0	Converts the RegExp object into a string.
valueOf()	JavaScript 1.2 JScript 3.0	Returns the primitive value of the RegExp object.

In Netscape JavaScript, this object also inherits the methods watch() and unwatch() from the Object object (not ECMAScript or IE).

The following table lists the special characters that may be used in regular expressions:

Character	Examples	Function
\	/n/ matches n /\n/ matches a linefeed character /^/ matches the start of a line /\^/ matches ^	For characters that are by default treated as normal characters, the backslash indicates that the next character is to be interpreted with a special value. For characters that are usually treated as special characters, the backslash indicates that the next character is to be interpreted as a normal character.
^	/^A/ matches the first but not the second A in "A man called Adam"	Matches the start of a line or of the input.
$	/r$/ matches only the last r in "horror"	Matches the end of a line or of the input.
*	/ro*/ matches r in "right", ro in "wrong" and "roo" in "room"	Matches the preceding character zero or more times.
+	/l+/ matches l in "life", ll in "still" and lll in "stilllife"	Matches the preceding character once or more. For example, /a+/ matches the 'a' in "candy" and all the a's in "caaaaaaandy."
?	/Smythe?/ matches "Smyth" and "Smythe"	Matches the preceding character once or zero times.
.	/.b/ matches the second but not the first b in "blob"	Matches any character apart from the newline character.

Table continued on following page

Character	Examples	Function
(x)	/(Smythe?)/ matches "Smyth" and "Smythe" in "John Smyth and Rob Smythe" and allows the substrings to be retrieved as RegExp.$1 and RegExp.$2 respectively.	Matches x and remembers the match. The matched substring can be retrieved from the elements of the array which results from the match, or from the RegExp object's properties $1, $2 ... $9 or lastParen.
x|y	/Smith|Smythe/ matches "Smith" and "Smythe"	Matches either x or y (where x and y are blocks of characters).
{n}	/1{2}/ matches 11 in "still" and the first two 1s in "stilllife"	Matches exactly n instances of the preceding character (where n is a positive integer).
{n, }	/1{2,}/ matches 11 in "still" and 111 in "stilllife"	Matches n or more instances of the preceding character (where n is a positive integer).
{n,m}	/1{1,2}/ matches 1 in "life", 11 in "still" and the first two 1s in "stilllife"	Matches between n and m instances of the preceding character (where n and m are positive integers).
[xyz]	[ab] matches a and b [a-c] matches a, b and c	Matches any one of the characters in the square brackets. A range of characters in the alphabet can be matched using a hyphen.
[^xyz]	[^aeiouy] matches s in "easy" [^a-y] matches z in "lazy"	Matches any character except for those enclosed in the square brackets. A range of characters in the alphabet can be specified using a hyphen.
[\b]		Matches a backspace.
\b	/t\b/ matches the first t in "about time"	Matches a word boundary (for example, a space or the end of a line).
\B	/t\Bi/ matches ti in "it is time"	Matches when there is no word boundary in this position.
\cX	/\cA/ matches ctrl-A	Matches a control character.
\d	/IE\d/ matches IE4, IE5, etc.	Matches a digit character. This is identical to [0-9].
\D	/\D/ matches the decimal point in "3.142"	Matches any character which is not a digit. This is identical to [^0-9].

Character	Examples	Function
\f		Matches a form-feed character.
\n		Matches a line-feed character.
\r		Matches a carriage return character.
\s	/\s/ matches the space in "not now"	Matches any white space character, including space, tab, line-feed, etc. This is identical to [\f\n\r\t\v].
\S	/\S/ matches a in " a "	Matches any character other than a whitespace character. This is identical to [^ \f\n\r\t\v].
\t		Matches a tab character.
\v		Matches a vertical tab character.
\w	/\w/ matches O in "O?!" and 1 in "$1"	Matches any alphanumeric character or the underscore. This is identical to [A-Za-z0-9_].
\W	/\W/ matches $ in "$10million" and @ in "j_smith@wrox"	Matches any non-alphanumeric character (excluding the underscore). This is identical to [^A-Za-z0-9_].
\n	/(Joh?n) and \1/ matches John and John in "John and John's friend" but does not match "John and Jon"	Matches the last substring that matched the nth match placed in parentheses and remembered (where n is a positive integer).
\octal \xhex	/\x25/ matches %	Matches the character corresponding to the specified octal or hexadecimal escape value.

String

The String object is used to contain a string of characters. Introduced in JavaScript 1.0 and JScript 1.0. This must be distinguished from a string literal, but the methods and properties of the String object can also be accessed by a string literal, since a temporary object will be created when they are called. Created with the String constructor:

```
var objString = new String("This is a string object.");
```

Properties

Property	Introduced	Description
constructor	JavaScript 1.1 JScript 2.0	Used to reference the constructor function for the object.
length	JavaScript 1.0 JScript 1.0	Returns the number of characters in the string.
prototype	JavaScript 1.1 JScript 2.0	Returns the prototype for the object, which can be used to extend the object's interface.

Methods

Method	Introduced	Description
anchor()	JavaScript 1.0	Not in ECMA-262.
	JScript 1.0	Returns an HTML anchor element. This can be used as a target for another link but cannot be used to link to another document or part of a document.
big()	JavaScript 1.0	Not in ECMA-262.
	JScript 1.0	Encloses the string in <BIG>...</BIG> tags.
blink()	JavaScript 1.0	Not in ECMA-262.
	JScript 1.0	Encloses the string in <BLINK>...</BLINK> tags.
bold()	JavaScript 1.0	Not in ECMA-262.
	JScript 1.0	Encloses the string in <B>...</B> tags.
charAt()	JavaScript 1.0 JScript 1.0	Returns the character at the specified position in the string.
charCodeAt()	JavaScript 1.2 JScript 3.0	Returns the Unicode value of the character at the specified position in the string.
concat()	JavaScript 1.2	Not in ECMA-262.
	JScript 3.0	Concatenates the strings supplied as arguments and returns the string thus formed.
fixed()	JavaScript 1.0	Not in ECMA-262.
	JScript 1.0	Encloses the string in <TT>...</TT> tags.

Method	Introduced	Description
`fontcolor()`	JavaScript 1.0	Not in ECMA-262.
	JScript 1.0	Encloses the string in `<FONT COLOR=string>`...`</FONT>` tags.
`fontsize()`	JavaScript 1.0	Not in ECMA-262.
	JScript 1.0	Encloses the string in `<FONT SIZE=string>`...`</FONT>` tags.
`fromCharCode()`	JavaScript 1.2	Returns the string formed from the concatenation of the characters represented by the supplied Unicode values.
	JScript 3.0	
`indexOf()`	JavaScript 1.0	Returns the position within the `String` object of the first match for the supplied substring. Returns -1 if the substring is not found.
	JScript 1.0	
`italics()`	JavaScript 1.0	Not in ECMA-262.
	JScript 1.0	Encloses the string in `<I>`...`</I>` tags.
`lastIndexOf()`	JavaScript 1.0	Returns the position within the `String` object of the last match for the supplied substring. Returns -1 if the substring is not found.
	JScript 1.0	
`link()`	JavaScript 1.0	Not in ECMA-262.
	JScript 1.0	Creates an HTML link element that can be used to link to another web page.
`match()`	JavaScript 1.2	Not in ECMA-262.
	JScript 3.0	Used to match a regular expression against a string.
`replace()`	JavaScript 1.2	Not in ECMA-262.
	JScript 3.0	Used to replace a substring that matches a regular expression with a new value.
`search()`	JavaScript 1.2	Not in ECMA-262.
	JScript 3.0	Searches for a match between a regular expression and the string.
`slice()`	JavaScript 1.0	Not in ECMA-262.
	JScript 3.0	Returns a substring of the `String` object.
`small()`	JavaScript 1.0	Not in ECMA-262.
	JScript 1.0	Encloses the string in `<SMALL>`...`</SMALL>` tags.

Table continued on following page

Method	Introduced	Description
split()	JavaScript 1.1 JScript 3.0	Splits a `String` object into an array of strings by separating the string into substrings.
strike()	JavaScript 1.0	Not in ECMA-262.
	JScript 1.0	Encloses the string in `<STRIKE>...</STRIKE>` tags.
sub()	JavaScript 1.0	Not in ECMA-262.
	JScript 1.0	Encloses the string in `<SUB>...</SUB>` tags.
substr()	JavaScript 1.0	Not in ECMA-262.
	JScript 3.0	Returns a substring of the characters from the given starting position and containing the specified number of characters.
substring()	JavaScript 1.0 JScript 1.0	Returns a substring of the characters between two positions in the string.
sup()	JavaScript 1.0	Not in ECMA-262.
	JScript 1.0	Encloses the string in `<SUP>...</SUP>` tags.
toLowerCase()	JavaScript 1.0 JScript 1.0	Returns the string converted to lower case.
toSource()	JavaScript 1.3	Not in ECMA-262.
		Returns a string containing the source code for the `String` object. Not supported by Internet Explorer.
toString()	JavaScript 1.1 JScript 2.0	Converts the `String` object into a string.
toUpperCase()	JavaScript 1.0 JScript 1.0	Returns the string converted to upper case.
valueOf()	JavaScript 1.1 JScript 2.0	Returns the primitive value of the `String` object.

In Netscape JavaScript, this object also inherits the methods `watch()` and `unwatch()` from the `Object` object (not ECMAScript or IE).

sun

A synonym for `Packages.sun`. Introduced in JavaScript 1.1, it is not supported by ECMAScript or Internet Explorer.

VBArray

The VBArray object represents in JScript an array created in Visual Basic or VBScript. Introduced in JScript 3.0, it is not supported by ECMAScript or Netscape JavaScript. A JScript VBArray object is created with the VBArray constructor, which takes a Visual Basic array as a parameter. The following code builds an array in VBScript and creates from that a JScript VBArray object:

```
<SCRIPT LANGUAGE=VBScript>
function getArray()
dim arrVB(1)
arrVB(0)=100
arrVB(1)=250
getArray=arrVB
End Function
</SCRIPT>

<SCRIPT LANGUAGE=JavaScript>
var vbArr = new VBArray(getArray());
</SCRIPT>
```

Methods

Method	Introduced	Description
dimensions()	JScript 3.0	Returns the number of dimensions in the VBArray.
getItem()	JScript 3.0	Retrieves the specified element from the VBArray.
lbound()	JScript 3.0	Retrieves the index position of the first element in the VBArray.
toArray()	JScript 3.0	Converts the VBArray into a normal JScript array.
ubound()	JScript 3.0	Retrieves the index position of the last element in the VBArray.

Online discussion at http://p2p.wrox.com

JavaScript Client Reference

The tables on the following pages represent the additional features of the JavaScript language that are available client-side.

Since ECMAScript supports only the core language, none of the features described in this appendix are compatible with ECMAScript.

The additions to the core language available in client-side JavaScript are concerned almost exclusively with the Browser Object Model. Since the Browser Object Models for Internet Explorers 4 and 5 and Netscape Navigator 4 are given in detail in Appendices E, F, and G (respectively), this appendix will confine itself to objects, methods and properties which are common to both models, and which can therefore be used for cross-browser scripting.

Operators

These are identical to those of the JavaScript core language, with the addition of the object operators `in` and `instanceof`, which were not introduced until JavaScript 1.4.

Statements

These are identical to those of the JavaScript core language, with the addition of the exception functions `throw` and `try...catch`, which were introduced in JavaScript 1.4.

Events

The following tables describe the event handlers available in client-side JavaScript. Note that the elements supporting these event handlers differ considerably in Netscape Navigator and Internet Explorer.

To handle an event, the event handler and the function to handle it must be specified in the HTML element for which the event applies:

```
<FORM>
    <INPUT TYPE="button" VALUE="Click here!" onclick=fnEventHandler()>
</FORM>

<SCRIPT LANGUAGE=JavaScript>
function fnEventHandler()
{
    // handle the event here
}
</SCRIPT>
```

Mouse Events

Event	Introduced	Description
onclick	JavaScript 1.0	Raised when the user clicks on an HTML control.
ondblclick	JavaScript 1.2	Raised when the user double-clicks on an HTML control.
onmousedown	JavaScript 1.2	Raised when the user presses a mouse button.
onmousemove	JavaScript 1.2	Raised when the user moves the mouse pointer.
onmouseout	JavaScript 1.1	Raised when the user moves the mouse pointer out from within an HTML control.
onmouseover	JavaScript 1.0	Raised when the user moves the mouse pointer over an HTML control.
onmouseup	JavaScript 1.2	Raised when the user releases the mouse button.

Keyboard Events

Event	Introduced	Description
onkeydown	JavaScript 1.2	Raised when the user presses a key on the keyboard.
onkeypress	JavaScript 1.2	Raised when the user presses a key on the keyboard. This event will be raised continually until the user releases the key.
onkeyup	JavaScript 1.2	Raised when the user releases a key which had been pressed.

HTML Control Events

Event	Introduced	Description
onblur	JavaScript 1.0	Raised when an HTML control loses focus.
onchange	JavaScript 1.0	Raised when an HTML control loses focus and its value has changed.
onfocus	JavaScript 1.0	Raised when focus is set to the HTML control.
onreset	JavaScript 1.1	Raised when the user resets a form.
onselect	JavaScript 1.0	Raised when the user selects text in an HTML control.
onsubmit	JavaScript 1.0	Raised when the user submits a form.

Window Events

Event	Introduced	Description
onload	JavaScript 1.0	Raised when the window has completed loading.
onresize	JavaScript 1.2	Raised when the user resizes the window.
onunload	JavaScript 1.0	Executes JavaScript code when the user exits a document.

Other Events

Event	Introduced	Description
onabort	JavaScript 1.1	Raised when the user aborts loading an image.
onerror	JavaScript 1.1	Raised when an error occurs loading the page.

Top-Level Functions

In addition to the core top-level functions, two extra functions are available in client-side JavaScript. These are only added here for sake of completeness, as it is unlikely that you would want to use them. These are not supported in Internet Explorer.

Function	Introduced	Example	Description
taint()	JavaScript 1.1 (removed 1.2)	v1=taint(v2)	Secures data and prevents it being passed to the server without the user's permission.
untaint()	JavaScript 1.1 (removed 1.2)	v1=untaint(v2)	Removes tainting from data and allows it to be passed to the server.

Objects

The following objects are supported in client-side JavaScript, in addition to the core objects.

The Anchor Object

An Anchor object represents an HTML <ANCHOR> element. Introduced in JavaScript 1.0. Anchor objects can be created either through HTML <A> tags or through the anchor() method of the String object. The following example shows how to create an Anchor object in HTML code and reference it in JavaScript:

```
<A NAME="myAnchor" HREF="http://www.wrox.com">Wrox Press</A>

<SCRIPT LANGUAGE="JavaScript">
var objAnchor=document.anchors[0];
</SCRIPT>
```

In Navigator, the anchor can be referred to by its NAME:

```
var objAnchor=document.anchors['myAnchor'];
```

However, this will not work in Internet Explorer; instead, we must use document.all if we wish to use the anchor's name:

```
var objAnchor=document.all['myAnchor'];
```

However, this will generate a message in Navigator, so the first method is to be recommended.

Properties

The only property shared by the Anchor object in NN and IE is name:

Property	Introduced	Description
name	JavaScript 1.2	Indicates the name of the anchor. Corresponds to the NAME attribute.

Methods

No methods are shared between the NN and IE Anchor objects.

The Applet Object

Represents a Java applet. Introduced in JavaScript 1.1, JScript 3.0. Applet objects are created with an HTML <APPLET> element and referenced through the applets collection of the document object:

```
<APPLET CODEBASE="http://mysite.com/applets/samples/" CODE="myapp.class"
        WIDTH=250 HEIGHT=150 NAME="myApp">
   <PARAM NAME="Quantity" VALUE="34372">
   <PARAM NAME="Color" VALUE="BrightPink">
</APPLET>

<SCRIPT LANGUAGE=JavaScript>
var objApplet=document.applets['myApp'];
</SCRIPT>
```

Properties

The Applet object inherits the public properties of the Java applet.

Methods

The Applet object inherits the public methods of the Java applet.

The Area Object

Area objects define an area of an image as an image map; they are a type of Link object. Introduced in JavaScript 1.1, JScript 3.0.

The Button Object

Represents an HTML button element. Introduced in JavaScript 1.0, JScript 1.0. To create a Button object, use the HTML <INPUT> tag with a TYPE attribute equal to "button":

```
<FORM NAME="myForm">
<INPUT TYPE=button VALUE="Click me!" NAME="myButton">
</FORM>

<SCRIPT LANGUAGE="JavaScript">
var objButton=document.forms['myForm'].elements['myButton'];
</SCRIPT>
```

The Button object, in both NN and IE, supports the following events:

❑ onblur

❑ onclick

❑ onfocus

❑ onmousedown

❑ onmouseup

Properties

Property	Introduced	Description
form	JavaScript 1.0	References the form to which the Button object belongs.
name	JavaScript 1.0	Indicates the name of the button. Corresponds to the NAME attribute.
type	JavaScript 1.1	Indicates the type of element, corresponding to the TYPE attribute. This will return "button".
value	JavaScript 1.0	Indicates the value of the element, corresponding to the VALUE attribute.

Methods

Method	Introduced	Description
blur()	JavaScript 1.0	Causes the element to lose focus.
click()	JavaScript 1.0	Simulates a mouse-click on the element and fires the onclick event.
focus()	JavaScript 1.0	Causes the element to receive focus.

This object also inherits the methods watch() and unwatch() from the Object object.

The Checkbox Object

The Checkbox object represents an HTML checkbox. Introduced in JavaScript 1.0, JScript 1.0. To create a Checkbox object, use the HTML <INPUT> element with the TYPE attribute set to "checkbox":

```
<FORM NAME="myForm">
<INPUT NAME="Check1" TYPE=checkbox>Check me!
</FORM>

<SCRIPT LANGUAGE="JavaScript">
var objCheck=document.forms['myForm'].elements['Check1'];
</SCRIPT>
```

The Checkbox object supports the following events:

❑   onblur

❑   onclick

❑   onfocus

Properties

Property	Introduced	Description
checked	JavaScript 1.0	Indicates whether the checkbox is currently checked.
defaultChecked	JavaScript 1.0	Indicates whether the checkbox is checked by default.
form	JavaScript 1.0	References the form to which the Checkbox object belongs.
name	JavaScript 1.0	Indicates the name of the checkbox. Corresponds to the NAME attribute.
type	JavaScript 1.1	Indicates the type of element, corresponding to the TYPE attribute. This will return "checkbox".
value	JavaScript 1.0	Indicates the value of the element, corresponding to the VALUE attribute.

Methods

Method	Introduced	Description
blur()	JavaScript 1.0	Causes the element to lose focus.
click()	JavaScript 1.0	Simulates a mouse-click on the element and fires the onclick event.
focus()	JavaScript 1.0	Causes the element to receive focus.

The document Object

Represents the current document. Introduced in JavaScript 1.0, JScript 1.0. Created with the HTML <BODY> tag and referenced with the document keyword:

```
<BODY>
    The body of the page goes here.
</BODY>
<SCRIPT LANGUAGE="JavaScript">
    var objDoc=document;
</SCRIPT>
```

The following events are supported by the document object. However, note that events placed in the <BODY> tag apply to the window rather than the document object:

- ❑ onclick
- ❑ ondblclick
- ❑ onkeydown
- ❑ onkeypress
- ❑ onkeyup
- ❑ onmousedown
- ❑ onmouseup

Properties

Property	Introduced	Description
alinkColor	JavaScript 1.0	Indicates the color of active links in the document, corresponding to the ALINK attribute.
anchors	JavaScript 1.0	Returns an array of the anchor elements in the document.
applets	JavaScript 1.1	Returns an array of the applet elements in the document.
bgColor	JavaScript 1.0	Indicates the background color for the document, corresponding to the BGCOLOR attribute.
cookie	JavaScript 1.0	Indicates the value of a cookie.
domain	JavaScript 1.1	Indicates the domain name of the server.
embeds	JavaScript 1.1	Returns an array of embedded objects in the document.
fgColor	JavaScript 1.0	Indicates the foreground color for text in the document, corresponding to the TEXT attribute.
form_name	JavaScript 1.1	References the named form.
forms	JavaScript 1.1	Returns an array of the forms in the document.
images	JavaScript 1.1	Returns an array of the images in the document.
lastModified	JavaScript 1.0	Indicates when the document was last modified.
linkColor	JavaScript 1.0	Indicates the default color for links in the document, corresponding to the LINK attribute.
links	JavaScript 1.0	Returns an array of the links in the document.
referrer	JavaScript 1.0	Returns the URL of the document that called the current document.
title	JavaScript 1.0	Indicates the title of the document, corresponding to the contents of the <TITLE> tag.
URL	JavaScript 1.0	Returns the URL of the document.
vlinkColor	JavaScript 1.0	Indicates the color of links that have been visited, corresponding to the VLINK attribute.

Methods

Method	Introduced	Description
close()	JavaScript 1.0	Closes an output stream and forces data to display.
open()	JavaScript 1.0	Opens a stream to collect the output of write() or writeln() methods.
write()	JavaScript 1.0	Writes a string of HTML to the document.
writeln()	JavaScript 1.0	Writes a line of HTML to the document.

The event Object

The `event` object represents a JavaScript event. Introduced in JavaScript 1.2, JScript 3.0. These objects are created automatically when an event occurs, and cannot be created programmatically. We can retrieve a reference to the event by passing `event` in as a parameter to the event handler:

```
<FORM NAME="myForm" onsubmit=catchEvent(event)>
<INPUT TYPE=SUBMIT VALUE="Click me!">
</FORM>
<SCRIPT LANGUAGE="JavaScript">
function catchEvent(objEvent)
{
alert(objEvent.type);
}
</SCRIPT>
```

Properties

Not all of these properties are relevant to each event type.

Property	Introduced	Description
screenX	JavaScript 1.2	Indicates the horizontal position of the mouse pointer, relative to the user's screen.
screenY	JavaScript 1.2	Indicates the vertical position of the mouse pointer, relative to the user's screen.
type	JavaScript 1.2	Indicates the type of the current event.
x	JavaScript 1.2	In Navigator, this indicates the width of the object when passed with the resize event, or the horizontal position of the mouse pointer, relative to the layer in which the event occurred. In IE, it indicates the horizontal position of the mouse pointer relative to the parent element.
y	JavaScript 1.2	In Navigator, this indicates the height of the object when passed with the resize event, or the vertical position of the mouse pointer, relative to the layer in which the event occurred. In IE, it indicates the vertical position of the mouse pointer relative to the parent element.

The FileUpload Object

Represents a file `<INPUT>` element. Introduced in JavaScript 1.0, JScript 3.0. Created with an HTML `<INPUT>` element with the TYPE attribute set to "FILE":

```
<FORM NAME="myForm" onsubmit=fnSubmit()>
    <INPUT NAME="myFile" TYPE=FILE>
</FORM>
<SCRIPT LANGUAGE="JavaScript">
function fnSubmit()
{
    var objFile = document.forms['myForm'].elements['myFile'];
}
</SCRIPT>
```

The `FileUpload` object supports the following event handlers:

- ❑ onblur
- ❑ onfocus

Properties

Property	Introduced	Description
form	JavaScript 1.0	References the form to which the `FileUpload` object belongs.
name	JavaScript 1.0	Indicates the name of the `FileUpload` object. Corresponds to the `NAME` attribute.
type	JavaScript 1.1	Indicates the type of element, corresponding to the `TYPE` attribute. This will return "file".
value	JavaScript 1.0	Indicates the value of the element, corresponding to the `VALUE` attribute.

Methods

Method	Introduced	Description
blur()	JavaScript 1.0	Causes the element to lose focus.
focus()	JavaScript 1.0	Causes the element to receive focus.
select()	JavaScript 1.0	Selects the input area of the `FileUpload` object.

The Form Object

Represents an HTML form. Introduced in JavaScript 1.0, JScript 1.0. Form objects are created with the HTML <FORM> tag and referenced through the `forms` property of the `document` object:

```
<FORM NAME="myForm" onsubmit=fnSubmit()>
<INPUT TYPE=SUBMIT VALUE="Click me!">
</FORM>

<SCRIPT LANGUAGE="JavaScript">
function fnSubmit()
{
var objForm = document.forms['myForm'];
}
</SCRIPT>
```

The `Form` object supports two event handlers:

- ❑ onreset
- ❑ onsubmit

Properties

Property	Introduced	Description
action	JavaScript 1.0	Contains the URL to which the form will be submitted and corresponds the ACTION attribute.
elements	JavaScript 1.0	Returns an array of the elements in the form.
encoding	JavaScript 1.0	Indicates the encoding type for the form and corresponds to the ENCTYPE attribute.
method	JavaScript 1.0	Indicates the HTTP method to be used to submit the form ("post" or "get") and corresponds to the METHOD attribute.
name	JavaScript 1.0	Indicates the name of the form. Corresponds to the NAME attribute.
target	JavaScript 1.0	Indicates the window at which the contents will be targeted and corresponds to the TARGET attribute.

Methods

Method	Introduced	Description
reset()	JavaScript 1.1	Resets the form to its default state.
submit()	JavaScript 1.0	Submits the form.

The Frame Object

JavaScript actually represents a frame using a window object. Every Frame object is a window object, and has all the methods and properties of a window object. However, a window that is a frame differs slightly from a top-level window. To create and reference a frame, we use the HTML <FRAMESET> and <FRAME> elements and the frames property of the window object.

The Hidden Object

The Hidden object represents a hidden HTML input element, used to send information to the server, which you don't want to appear on the page (but note that this information is appended to the URL when submitted). Introduced in JavaScript 1.0, JScript 1.0. The Hidden object is created with an HTML <INPUT> tag with the TYPE attribute set to "hidden" and referenced through the forms property of the document object:

```
<FORM NAME="myForm">
<INPUT NAME="hidden" TYPE=hidden VALUE="You can't see this!">
</FORM>

<SCRIPT LANGUAGE="JavaScript">
var objHidden=document.forms['myForm'].elements['hidden'];
</SCRIPT>
```

Properties

Property	Introduced	Description
form	JavaScript 1.0	References the form to which the Hidden object belongs.
name	JavaScript 1.0	Indicates the name of the Hidden object. Corresponds to the NAME attribute.
type	JavaScript 1.1	Indicates the type of element, corresponding to the TYPE attribute. This will return "hidden".
value	JavaScript 1.0	Indicates the value of the element, corresponding to the VALUE attribute.

The history Object

The history object is used to contain information about the URLs the user has previously visited. Introduced in JavaScript 1.0, JScript 1.0. The history object cannot be created programmatically but can be referenced through the history property of the window object:

```
var objHistory=window.history;
```

Properties

Property	Introduced	Description
length	JavaScript 1.0	Indicates the number of entries in the history list.

Methods

Method	Introduced	Description
back()	JavaScript 1.0	Loads the previous URL in the history list.
forward()	JavaScript 1.0	Loads the next URL in the history list.
go()	JavaScript 1.0	Loads the specified URL from the history list.

The IMG Object

Represents an image in the HTML page. Introduced in JavaScript 1.1, JScript 3.0. The IMG object can be created with the Image constructor:

```
var objImage=new Image();
```

Alternatively, it can be created with an HTML <IMG> tag and referenced with the images property of the document object:

```
<IMG SRC="myPicture.gif" NAME="myPicture">
<SCRIPT LANGUAGE="JavaScript">
var objImage=document.images['myPicture'];
</SCRIPT>
```

The IMG object supports the following event handlers:

❑ onabort

❑ onerror

❑ onload

Properties

Property	Introduced	Description
border	JavaScript 1.1	Indicates the width of the border around the image and corresponds to the BORDER attribute.
complete	JavaScript 1.1	Indicates whether the browser has completed loading the image.
height	JavaScript 1.1	Indicates the height of the image and corresponds to the HEIGHT attribute.
hspace	JavaScript 1.1	Indicates the size of the horizontal margin and corresponds to the HSPACE attribute.
lowsrc	JavaScript 1.1	Indicates the URL for a lower resolution image to load before the 'real' image is displayed, and corresponds to the LOWSRC attribute.
name	JavaScript 1.1	Indicates the name of the image. Corresponds to the NAME attribute.
src	JavaScript 1.1	Indicates the URL for the image and corresponds to the SRC attribute.
vspace	JavaScript 1.1	Indicates the size of the vertical margin and corresponds to the VSPACE attribute.
width	JavaScript 1.1	Indicates the width of the image and corresponds to the WIDTH attribute.

The Link Object

Represents a link to another page or to another part of the same page. Introduced in JavaScript 1.0, JScript 1.0. Created through the `link()` method of the `String` object or through HTML `<A>` or `<AREA>` tags; in the latter case, it can be referenced through the `links` property of the `document` object:

```
<A HREF="http://www.wrox.com">Wrox Press</A>

<SCRIPT LANGUAGE="JavaScript">
objLink = document.links[0];
</SCRIPT>
```

Note that the `Link` object cannot be referenced through its `NAME` attribute, either in Navigator or in Internet Explorer.

The `Link` object supports the following events:

- ❑   `onclick`
- ❑   `ondblclick`
- ❑   `onkeydown`
- ❑   `onkeypress`
- ❑   `onkeyup`
- ❑   `onmousedown`
- ❑   `onmouseout`
- ❑   `onmouseup`
- ❑   `onmouseover`

Properties

Property	Introduced	Description
hash	JavaScript 1.0	Indicates the anchor part of the URL.
host	JavaScript 1.0	Indicates the hostname and IP address of the URL.
hostname	JavaScript 1.0	Indicates the hostname from the URL.
href	JavaScript 1.0	Indicates the entire URL.
pathname	JavaScript 1.0	Indicates the path and filename of an object.
port	JavaScript 1.0	Indicates the port number in the URL.
protocol	JavaScript 1.0	Indicates the transport protocol to use (such as "http:" or "https:"), including the colon.
search	JavaScript 1.0	Indicates the query string appended to the URL.
target	JavaScript 1.0	Indicates the window at which the contents will be targeted and corresponds to the TARGET attribute.

The location Object

The location object represents the web page currently being displayed in the browser. Introduced in JavaScript 1.0, JScript 1.0. The location object cannot be created programmatically, but can be referenced through the location property of the window object:

```
var objLoc = window.location;
```

Properties

Property	Introduced	Description
hash	JavaScript 1.0	Indicates the anchor part of the URL.
host	JavaScript 1.0	Indicates the hostname and IP address of the URL.
hostname	JavaScript 1.0	Indicates the hostname from the URL.
href	JavaScript 1.0	Indicates the entire URL.
pathname	JavaScript 1.0	Indicates the path and filename of an object.
port	JavaScript 1.0	Indicates the port number in the URL.
protocol	JavaScript 1.0	Indicates the transport protocol to use (such as "http:" or "https:"), including the colon.
search	JavaScript 1.0	Indicates the query string appended to the URL.

Methods

Method	Introduced	Description
reload()	JavaScript 1.1	Reloads the current document.
replace()	JavaScript 1.1	Loads the specified URL over the current history entry.

The navigator Object

This object represents the browser and contains information about the type and version of browser in use. Introduced in JavaScript 1.0, JScript 1.0. This object cannot be created programmatically, but can be referenced through the navigator keyword:

```
var objNav = navigator;
```

Properties

Property	Introduced	Description
appCodeName	JavaScript 1.0	Returns the code name of the browser. This is "Mozilla" for both Navigator and Internet Explorer.
appName	JavaScript 1.0	Returns the name of the browser. This is "Netscape" for Navigator and "Microsoft Internet Explorer" for IE.
appVersion	JavaScript 1.0	Returns information about the browser, including the version number and the platform on which it is running.
mimeTypes	JavaScript 1.1	Returns an array of the MIME types supported by the client. Included for compatibility only in IE, and returns an empty array.
platform	JavaScript 1.2	Returns a string indicating the operating system on which the browser is running (for example, "Win32").
plugins	JavaScript 1.1	Returns an array of the plug-ins installed. Included for compatibility only in IE, and returns an empty array.

Methods

Method	Introduced	Description
javaEnabled()	JavaScript 1.1	Indicates whether Java is enabled.
taintEnabled()	JavaScript 1.1 (removed 1.2)	Specifies whether data tainting is enabled. Data tainting is not supported by IE, so this always returns False.

The Option Object

Represents an option in an HTML <SELECT> element. Introduced in JavaScript 1.0, JScript 1.0. An Option object can be created in two ways; it is created by the <OPTION> tag or it can be created on the fly with the Option constructor. The following code demonstrates both methods, creating a <SELECT> element with options for "Yes" and "No", and adding a third "Don't know" option on the fly:

```
<FORM NAME="myForm">
<SELECT NAME="mySelect">
<OPTION>Yes
<OPTION>No
</SELECT>
</FORM>

<SCRIPT LANGUAGE="JavaScript">
var objSelect=document.forms['myForm'].elements['mySelect'];
var objOption=new Option("Don't know");
objSelect.options[2]=objOption;
</SCRIPT>
```

Properties

Property	Introduced	Description
defaultSelected	JavaScript 1.1	Indicates whether the option is selected by default when the page is loaded.
index	JavaScript 1.0	The zero-based index position of an option in the array of options for the selection list.
selected	JavaScript 1.0	Indicates whether the option is currently selected.
text	JavaScript 1.0	Indicates the text for the option.
value	JavaScript 1.0	Indicates the value of the element, corresponding to the VALUE attribute.

The Password Object

Represents a password input element. Introduced in JavaScript 1.0, JScript 1.0. Created through an HTML <INPUT> element with the TYPE attribute set to "password" and referenced through the elements array of a Form object:

```
<FORM ONSUBMIT=fnSubmit()>
<INPUT NAME=myPWD TYPE=password>
<INPUT TYPE=submit>
</FORM>

<SCRIPT LANGUAGE=JavaScript>
function fnSubmit() {
var objPwd=document.forms[0].elements['myPWD'];
}
</SCRIPT>
```

Beware! Passwords entered in this way are not secure; they are appended to the URL as a query.

The Password object supports two events:

❑ onblur

❑ onfocus

Properties

Property	Introduced	Description
defaultValue	JavaScript 1.1	Indicates the default value for the password.
form	JavaScript 1.0	References the form to which the Password object belongs.

Table continued on following page

Property	Introduced	Description
name	JavaScript 1.0	Indicates the name of the `Password` object. Corresponds to the NAME attribute.
type	JavaScript 1.1	Indicates the type of element, corresponding to the TYPE attribute. This will return "password".
value	JavaScript 1.0	Indicates the value of the element, corresponding to the VALUE attribute.

Methods

Method	Introduced	Description
blur()	JavaScript 1.0	Causes the element to lose focus.
focus()	JavaScript 1.0	Causes the element to receive focus.
select()	JavaScript 1.0	Selects the input area of the `Password` object.

The Radio Object

Represents a radio button in a form. Introduced in JavaScript 1.0, JScript 1.0. A number of radio buttons can be created with an array of HTML `<INPUT>` elements with a TYPE attribute set to "RADIO" and with the same name; assigning different names will cause the radio buttons to belong to different groups, so the user will be able to select any number. The array of radio buttons can be accessed through the `elements` array of a `Form` object; an individual button can then be accessed through an index of this array:

```
<FORM ONSUBMIT=fnSubmit()>
<INPUT TYPE="RADIO" NAME=radBtn>Yes
<INPUT TYPE="RADIO" NAME=radBtn>No
<INPUT TYPE="RADIO" NAME=radBtn>Don't care
<INPUT TYPE=SUBMIT>
</FORM>

<SCRIPT LANGUAGE=JavaScript>
function fnSubmit() {
   var arrRad=document.forms[0].elements['radBtn'];
   var objRad=arrRad[2];
   if (objRad.checked==true) {
      alert("'Don't care was made to care'");
   }
}
</SCRIPT>
```

The `Radio` object supports the events:

❑ onblur

❑ onclick

❑ onfocus

Properties

Property	Introduced	Description
checked	JavaScript 1.0	Indicates whether a specific radio button is currently checked.
defaultChecked	JavaScript 1.0	Indicates whether a specific radio button is checked by default.
form	JavaScript 1.0	References the form to which the Radio object belongs.
name	JavaScript 1.0	Indicates the name of the Radio object. Corresponds to the NAME attribute.
type	JavaScript 1.1	Indicates the type of element, corresponding to the TYPE attribute. This will return "radio".
value	JavaScript 1.0	Indicates the value of the element, corresponding to the VALUE attribute.

Methods

Method	Introduced	Description
blur()	JavaScript 1.0	Causes the element to lose focus.
click()	JavaScript 1.0	Simulates a mouse-click on the element and fires the onclick event.
focus()	JavaScript 1.0	Causes the element to receive focus.

The Reset Object

The Reset object represents a reset button in a form. Introduced in JavaScript 1.0, JScript 1.0. A Reset object is created with an HTML <INPUT> element with the TYPE attribute set to "RESET" and referenced through the elements array of a Form object:

```
<FORM>
<INPUT TYPE="RESET" NAME="myReset">
</FORM>

<SCRIPT LANGUAGE=JavaScript>
var objReset=document.forms[0].elements['myReset'];
</SCRIPT>
```

The Reset object supports the events:

- ❏ onblur
- ❏ onclick
- ❏ onfocus

903

Properties

Property	Introduced	Description
form	JavaScript 1.0	References the form to which the Reset object belongs.
name	JavaScript 1.0	Indicates the name of the reset button. Corresponds to the NAME attribute.
type	JavaScript 1.1	Indicates the type of element, corresponding to the TYPE attribute. This will return "reset".
value	JavaScript 1.0	Indicates the value of the element, corresponding to the VALUE attribute.

Methods

Method	Introduced	Description
blur()	JavaScript 1.0	Causes the element to lose focus.
click()	JavaScript 1.0	Simulates a mouse-click on the element and fires the onclick event.
focus()	JavaScript 1.0	Causes the element to receive focus.

The screen Object

Represents the client's screen and contains information about the display capabilities of the client. Introduced in JavaScript 1.2, JScript 3.0. The screen object is created automatically and can be referenced through the screen keyword:

```
alert("Available area: "+screen.availHeight+" x "+screen.availWidth+
      "\nTotal area: "+screen.height+" x "+screen.width);
```

Properties

Property	Introduced	Description
availHeight	JavaScript 1.2	Indicates the vertical range of the screen potentially available to the browser (in pixels).
availWidth	JavaScript 1.0	Indicates the horizontal range of the screen potentially available to the browser (in pixels).
colorDepth	JavaScript 1.0	Indicates the number of bits used for colors on the client's screen.
height	JavaScript 1.0	Indicates the vertical range of the screen (in pixels).
width	JavaScript 1.0	Indicates the horizontal range of the screen (in pixels).

The Select Object

Represents a selection list in a form. Introduced in JavaScript 1.0, JScript 1.0. Created with an HTML `<SELECT>` element and referenced through the `elements` array of a `Form` object:

```
<FORM ONSUBMIT=fnSubmit()>
Please select your favorite food:
<SELECT NAME="mySelect">
<OPTION>Black pudding
<OPTION>Broccoli
<OPTION>Caviar
</SELECT>
<BR><INPUT TYPE=SUBMIT>
</FORM>

<SCRIPT LANGUAGE=JavaSCript>
function fnSubmit() {
   var objSelect=document.forms[0].elements['mySelect'];
   if (objSelect.selectedIndex==0) {
      alert("Mine too!");
   }
}
</SCRIPT>
```

The `Select` object supports the events:

❑   onblur

❑   onchange

❑   onfocus

Properties

Property	Introduced	Description
form	JavaScript 1.0	References the form to which the `Select` object belongs.
length	JavaScript 1.0	Returns the number of options in the selection list.
name	JavaScript 1.0	Indicates the name of the `Select` object. Corresponds to the NAME attribute.
options	JavaScript 1.0	Returns an array of the `Option` objects in the selection list.
selectedIndex	JavaScript 1.0	Returns the index of the first selected option.
type	JavaScript 1.1	Indicates the type of element, corresponding to the TYPE attribute. This will return "select-multiple" for a multiple selection list or "select-one" if only one item in the list may be selected.

Methods

Method	Introduced	Description
blur()	JavaScript 1.0	Causes the element to lose focus.
focus()	JavaScript 1.0	Causes the element to receive focus.

The Submit Object

The Submit object represents a submit button in a form. Introduced in JavaScript 1.0, JScript 1.0. Created with an HTML <INPUT> element with the TYPE attribute set to "SUBMIT" and referenced through the elements array of the Form object:

```
<FORM ONSUBMIT=fnSubmit()>
<INPUT NAME="sbmtBtn" TYPE=SUBMIT>
</FORM>

<SCRIPT LANGUAGE=JavaScript>
function fnSubmit() {
var objSubmit=document.forms[0].elements['sbmtBtn'];
objSubmit.value="Don't touch me again!";
}
</SCRIPT>
```

The Submit object supports the events:

- ❑ onblur
- ❑ onclick
- ❑ onfocus

Properties

Property	Introduced	Description
form	JavaScript 1.0	References the form to which the Submit object belongs.
name	JavaScript 1.0	Indicates the name of the submit button. Corresponds to the NAME attribute.
type	JavaScript 1.1	Indicates the type of element, corresponding to the TYPE attribute. This will return "submit".
value	JavaScript 1.0	Indicates the value of the element, corresponding to the VALUE attribute.

Methods

Method	Introduced	Description
blur()	JavaScript 1.0	Causes the element to lose focus.
click()	JavaScript 1.0	Simulates a mouse-click on the element and fires the onclick event.
focus()	JavaScript 1.0	Causes the element to receive focus.

The Text Object

Represents a textbox. Introduced in JavaScript 1.0, JScript 1.0. Created with an HTML <INPUT> element with the TYPE attribute set to "text" and referenced through the elements array of the Form object:

```
<FORM ONSUBMIT=fnSubmit()>
<INPUT TYPE="text" NAME="myText">
<INPUT TYPE="SUBMIT">
</FORM>

<SCRIPT LANGUAGE=JavaScript>
function fnSubmit() {
    objText=document.forms[0].elements['myText'];
    if (objText.value=="") {
        alert("You must enter a value.");
    }
}
</SCRIPT>
```

Text objects support the following events:

- ❏ onblur
- ❏ onchange
- ❏ onfocus
- ❏ onselect

Properties

Property	Introduced	Description
defaultValue	JavaScript 1.0	Indicates the default value for the textbox.
form	JavaScript 1.0	References the form to which the Text object belongs.
name	JavaScript 1.0	Indicates the name of the textbox. Corresponds to the NAME attribute.
type	JavaScript 1.1	Indicates the type of element, corresponding to the TYPE attribute. This will return "text".
value	JavaScript 1.0	Indicates the value of the element, corresponding to the VALUE attribute.

Methods

Method	Introduced	Description
blur()	JavaScript 1.0	Causes the element to lose focus.
focus()	JavaScript 1.0	Causes the element to receive focus.
select()	JavaScript 1.0	Selects the input area of the Text object.

The Textarea Object

Represents a textarea in a form. Introduced in JavaScript 1.0, JScript 1.0. Created with an HTML <TEXTAREA> element and referenced with the elements array of the Form object:

```
<FORM ONSUBMIT=fnSubmit()>
<TEXTAREA ROWS=5 COLS=30 NAME="myText">
Enter your text here.
</TEXTAREA>
<INPUT TYPE="SUBMIT">
</FORM>

<SCRIPT LANGUAGE=JavaScript>
function fnSubmit() {
   objText=document.forms[0].elements['myText'];
   if (objText.value=="") {
      alert("You've got to enter something");
   }
}
</SCRIPT>
```

The Textarea object supports seven events:

- ❏ onblur
- ❏ onchange
- ❏ onfocus
- ❏ onkeydown
- ❏ onkeypress
- ❏ onkeyup
- ❏ onselect

Properties

Property	Introduced	Description
defaultValue	JavaScript 1.0	Indicates the default value for the textarea.
form	JavaScript 1.0	References the form to which the Textarea object belongs.
name	JavaScript 1.0	Indicates the name of the textarea. Corresponds to the NAME attribute.
type	JavaScript 1.1	Indicates the type of element, corresponding to the TYPE attribute. This will return "textarea".
value	JavaScript 1.0	Indicates the value of the element, corresponding to the VALUE attribute.

Methods

Method	Introduced	Description
blur()	JavaScript 1.0	Causes the element to lose focus.
focus()	JavaScript 1.0	Causes the element to receive focus.
select()	JavaScript 1.0	Selects the input area of the Textarea object.

The window Object

Represents a window or frame in the browser. Introduced in JavaScript 1.0, JScript 1.0. A window object is automatically created for every browser window open, and can be referenced with the window keyword. However, we can call the methods and properties of the window object without explicitly naming the object, so, to see whether the current window is closed, we can write:

```
alert(closed);
```

instead of:

```
window.alert(window.closed);
```

The window object supports six events:

- ❑ onblur
- ❑ onerror
- ❑ onfocus
- ❑ onload
- ❑ onresize
- ❑ onunload

Properties

Property	Introduced	Description
closed	JavaScript 1.1	Indicates whether a window is closed.
defaultStatus	JavaScript 1.0	Indicates the default text displayed in the window's status bar.
document	JavaScript 1.0	Returns a reference to the document object in the current window.
frames	JavaScript 1.0	Returns an array of the frames in the window.
history	JavaScript 1.1	Returns a reference to the history object for the window.
length	JavaScript 1.0	Returns the number of frames in the window.
location	JavaScript 1.0	Returns the location object for the current window.
name	JavaScript 1.0	Indicates the name of the window. Corresponds to the NAME attribute.
offscreenBuffering	JavaScript 1.2	Specifies whether offscreen buffering is to be used to update objects in the window before they are made visible.
opener	JavaScript 1.1	Returns a reference to the window that called the current window.
parent	JavaScript 1.0	Returns a reference to the window or frame to which the current frame belongs.
self	JavaScript 1.0	Returns a reference to the current window.
status	JavaScript 1.0	Indicates the current message in the status bar.
top	JavaScript 1.0	Returns a reference to the topmost window.

Methods

Method	Introduced	Description
alert()	JavaScript 1.0	Displays a dialog box containing a message and an OK button.
blur()	JavaScript 1.0	Causes the element to lose focus.
clearInterval()	JavaScript 1.2	Cancels an interval set with the setInterval method.
clearTimeout()	JavaScript 1.0	Cancels a timeout set with the setTimeout method.

Method	Introduced	Description
close()	JavaScript 1.0	Closes the window.
confirm()	JavaScript 1.0	Displays a dialog box containing a message and OK and Cancel buttons.
focus()	JavaScript 1.1	Causes the element to receive focus.
moveBy()	JavaScript 1.2	Moves the window by the specified number of pixels on the x- and y-axes.
moveTo()	JavaScript 1.2	Moves the top-left corner of the window to the specified position on the x- and y-axes.
open()	JavaScript 1.0	Opens a new window.
print()	JavaScript 1.2	Prints the contents of the window or frame.
prompt()	JavaScript 1.0	Displays a dialog box with a message, an input area, and OK and Cancel buttons.
resizeBy()	JavaScript 1.2	Resizes the window by the specified x- and y-offsets by adjusting the position of the bottom-right corner.
resizeTo()	JavaScript 1.2	Resizes the window to the specified dimensions by adjusting the position of the bottom-right corner.
scroll()	JavaScript 1.1	Scrolls the window to the specified coordinates.
scrollBy()	JavaScript 1.2	Scrolls the window by the specified x- and y- offsets.
scrollTo()	JavaScript 1.2	Scrolls the window to the specified coordinates, such that the specified point becomes the top-left corner.
setInterval()	JavaScript 1.2	Evaluates the given expression every time the specified number of milliseconds elapses.
setTimeout()	JavaScript 1.0	Evaluates the given expression (once only) after the specified number of milliseconds has elapsed.

Online discussion at http://p2p.wrox.com

Latin-1 Character Set

This appendix contains the Latin-1 character set, and the character codes in both decimal and hexadecimal formats. As explained in Chapter 2, the escape sequence "\xNN", where NN is a hexadecimal character code from the Latin-1 character set, below, can be used to represent there those characters that can't be typed in directly in JavaScript.

Decimal Character Code	Hexadecimal Character Code	Symbol
32	20	Space
33	21	!
34	22	"
35	23	#
36	24	$
37	25	%
38	26	&
39	27	'
40	28	(
41	29	)
42	2A	*
43	2B	+
44	2C	,
45	2D	-
46	2E	.
47	2F	/
48	30	0

Table continued on following page

Decimal Character Code	Hexadecimal Character Code	Symbol
49	31	1
50	32	2
51	33	3
52	34	4
53	35	5
54	36	6
55	37	7
56	38	8
57	39	9
58	3A	:
59	3B	;
60	3C	<
61	3D	=
62	3E	>
63	3F	?
64	40	@
65	41	A
66	42	B
67	43	C
68	44	D
69	45	E
70	46	F
71	47	G
72	48	H
73	49	I
74	4A	J
75	4B	K
76	4C	L
77	4D	M
78	4E	N

Decimal Character Code	Hexadecimal Character Code	Symbol
79	4F	O
80	50	P
81	51	Q
82	52	R
83	53	S
84	54	T
85	55	U
86	56	V
87	57	W
88	58	X
89	59	Y
90	5A	Z
91	5B	[
92	5C	\
93	5D	]
94	5E	^
95	5F	_
96	60	`
97	61	a
98	62	b
99	63	c
100	64	d
101	65	e
102	66	f
103	67	g
104	68	h
105	69	i
106	6A	j
107	6B	k

Table continued on following page

Decimal Character Code	Hexadecimal Character Code	Symbol
108	6C	l
109	6D	m
110	6E	n
111	6F	o
112	70	p
113	71	q
114	72	r
115	73	s
116	74	t
117	75	u
118	76	v
119	77	w
120	78	x
121	79	y
122	7A	z
123	7B	{
124	7C	|
125	7D	}
126	7E	~
160	A0	Non-breaking space
161	A1	¡
162	A2	¢
163	A3	£
164	A4	¤
165	A5	¥
166	A6	¦
167	A7	§
168	A8	¨
169	A9	©

Decimal Character Code	Hexadecimal Character Code	Symbol
170	AA	ª
171	AB	«
172	AC	¬
173	AD	Soft hyphen
174	AE	®
175	AF	¯
176	B0	°
177	B1	±
178	B2	²
179	B3	³
180	B4	´
181	B5	µ
182	B6	¶
183	B7	·
184	B8	¸
185	B9	¹
186	BA	º
187	BB	»
188	BC	¼
189	BD	½
190	BE	¾
191	BF	¿
192	C0	À
193	C1	Á
194	C2	Â
195	C3	Ã
196	C4	Ä
197	C5	Å
198	C6	Æ

Table continued on following page

Decimal Character Code	Hexadecimal Character Code	Symbol
199	C7	Ç
200	C8	È
201	C9	É
202	CA	Ê
203	CB	Ë
204	CC	Ì
205	CD	Í
206	CE	Î
207	CF	Ï
208	D0	Ð
209	D1	Ñ
210	D2	Ò
211	D3	Ó
212	D4	Ô
213	D5	Õ
214	D6	Ö
215	D7	×
216	D8	Ø
217	D9	Ù
218	DA	Ú
219	DB	Û
220	DC	Ü
221	DD	Ý
222	DE	Þ
223	DF	ß
224	E0	à
225	E1	á
226	E2	â
227	E3	ã

Decimal Character Code	Hexadecimal Character Code	Symbol
228	E4	ä
229	E5	å
230	E6	æ
231	E7	ç
232	E8	è
233	E9	é
234	EA	ê
235	EB	ë
236	EC	ì
237	ED	í
238	EE	î
239	EF	ï
240	F0	ð
241	F1	ñ
242	F2	ò
243	F3	ó
244	F4	ô
245	F5	õ
246	F6	ö
247	F7	÷
248	F8	ø
249	F9	ù
250	FA	ú
251	FB	û
252	FC	ü
253	FD	ý
254	FE	þ
255	FF	ÿ

The IE 4 Browser Object Model

The IE 4 Dynamic HTML Object Model contains 12 **objects** and 19 **collections**. Most of these are organized into a strict hierarchy that allows HTML authors to access all the parts of the browser, and the pages that are loaded, from a scripting language like JavaScript or VBScript.

The Object Model in Outline

The diagram overleaf shows the object hierarchy in graphical form. It is followed by a list of the objects and collections, with a brief description. Then, each object is documented in detail, showing the properties, methods, and events it supports.

Note that not all the objects and collections are included in the diagram. Some are not part of the overall object model, but are used to access other items such as dialogs or HTML elements.

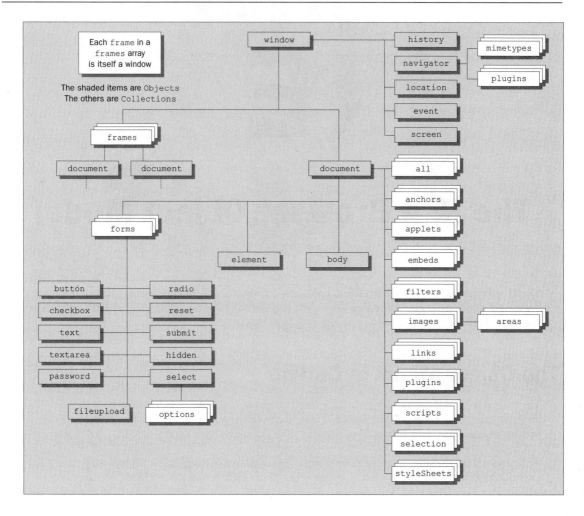

The Browser Objects

Object Name	Description
document	An object that exposes the contents of the HTML document through a number of collections and properties.
event	A global object that exposes properties that represent the parameters of all events as they occur.
history	Exposes information about the URLs that the client has previously visited.
location	Exposes information about the currently displayed document's URL.
MimeType	An object that provides information about a MIME type.

Object Name	Description
navigator	Exposes properties that provide information about the browser, or user agent.
screen	Exposes information about the client's monitor screen and system rendering abilities.
Selection	Represents the currently active selection on the screen in the document.
Style	Represents an individual style element within a style sheet.
StyleSheet	Exposes all the styles within a single style sheet in the styleSheets collection.
TextRange	Represents sections of the text stream making up the HTML document.
window	Exposes properties, methods and events connected to the browser window or a frame.

The Browser Collections

Collection Name	Description
all	Collection of all the tags and elements in the body of the document.
anchors	Collection of all the anchors in the document.
applets	Collection of all the objects in the document, including intrinsic controls, images, applets, embeds, and other objects.
areas	Collection of all the areas that make up the image map.
cells	Collection of all the <TH> and <TD> cells in the row of a table.
elements	Collection of all controls and elements in the form.
embeds	Collection of all the <EMBED> tags in the document.
filters	Collection of all filter objects for an element.
forms	Collection of all the forms in the page.
frames	Collection of all the frames defined within a <FRAMESET> tag.
images	Collection of all the images in the page.
imports	Collection of all the imported style sheets defined for a StyleSheet object.
links	Collection of all the links and <AREA> blocks in the page.
mimeTypes	Collection of all the document and file types supported by the browser.
options	Collection of all the items in a <SELECT> element.
plugins	An alias for collection of all the <EMBED> tags in the page.
rows	Collection of all the rows in the table, including <THEAD>, <TBODY>, and <TFOOT>.
scripts	Collection of all the <SCRIPT> sections in the page.
styleSheets	Collection of all the individual style property objects defined for a document.

The Objects in Detail

This section documents all the properties, methods, and event handlers available for each object in the browser hierarchy.

The document Object

Exposes the entire HTML content, through its own collections and properties. Also provides a range of events and methods to work with documents.

Properties	`activeElement` `alinkColor` `bgColor` `body` `cookie` `domain` `fgColor` `lastModified` `linkColor` `location` `parentWindow` `readyState` `referrer` `selection` `title` `url` `vlinkColor`
Methods	`clear()` `close()` `createElement()` `createStylesheet()` `elementFromPoint()` `execCommand()` `open()` `queryCommandEnabled()` `queryCommandIndeterm()` `queryCommandState()` `queryCommandSupported()` `queryCommandValue()` `write()` `writeln()`
Events	`onafterupdate` `onbeforeupdate` `onclick` `ondblclick` `ondragstart` `onerror` `onhelp` `onkeydown` `onkeypress` `onkeyup` `onload` `onmousedown` `onmousemove` `onmouseout` `nmouseover` `onmouseup` `onreadystatechange`
Collections	`all` `anchors` `applets` `embeds` `forms` `frames` `images` `links` `plugins` `scripts` `styleSheets`

The event Object

The global object provided to allow the scripting language to access an event's parameters. It provides the following properties and collections:

Properties	`altKey` `button` `cancelBubble` `clientX` `clientY` `ctrlKey` `fromElement` `keyCode` `offsetX` `offsetY` `reason` `returnValue` `screenX` `screenY` `shiftKey` `srcElement` `srcFilter` `toElement` `type` `x` `y`
Methods None	**Events** None
Collections `bookmarks` `boundElements`	

The history Object

Contains information about the URLs that the client has visited, as stored in the browser's History list, and allows the script to move through the list.

Properties	`length`
Methods	`back` `forward` `go`
Events None	**Collections** None

The location Object

Contains information on the current URL. It also provides methods that will reload a page.

Properties	`hash` `host` `hostname` `href` `pathname` `port` `protocol` `search`
Methods	`assign()` `reload()` `replace()`
Events	None **Collections** None

The MimeType Object

Provides information about the page's MIME data type.

Properties	`description` `enabledPlugin` `name`
Methods	None **Events** None
Collections	`suffixes`

The navigator Object

This object represents the browser application itself, providing information about its manufacturer, version, and capabilities.

Properties	`appCodeName` `appName` `appVersion` `cookieEnabled` `userAgent`
Methods	`javaEnabled()` `taintEnabled()`
Events	None
Collections	`mimeTypes` `plugins`

The screen Object

The `screen` object provides information to the scripting language about the client's screen resolution and rendering abilities.

Properties	`bufferDepth` `colorDepth` `height` `updateInterval` `width`
Methods	None
Events	None **Collections** None

The Selection Object

Returns the active selection on the screen, allowing access to all the selected elements including the plain text in the page.

Properties	type		
Methods	clear()	createRange()	empty()
Events	None	**Collections** None	

The Style Object

This provides access to the individual style properties for an element. These could have been previously set by a style sheet, or by an inline style tag within the page.

Properties	background backgroundAttachment backgroundColor backgroundImage backgroundPosition backgroundPositionX backgroundPositionY BackgroundRepeat border borderBottom borderBottomColor borderBottomStyle borderBottomWidth borderColor borderLeft borderLeftColor borderLeftStyle borderLeftWidth borderRight BorderRightColor BorderRightStyle BorderRightWidth borderStyle borderTop borderTopColor borderTopStyle borderTopWidth borderWidth clear clip color cssText cursor display filter font fontFamily fontSize fontStyle fontVariant fontWeight height left letterSpacing lineHeight listStyle listStyleImage listStylePosition listStyleType margin marginBottom marginLeft marginRight marginTop overflow paddingBottom paddingLeft paddingRight paddingTop pageBreakAfter pageBreakBefore pixelHeight pixelLeft pixelTop pixelWidth posHeight position posLeft posTop posWidth styleFloat textAlign textDecoration textDecorationBlink textDecorationLineThrough textDecorationNone textDecorationOverline textDecorationUnderline textIndent textTransform top verticalAlign visibility width zIndex
Methods	getAttribute() removeAttribute() setAttribute()
Events	None **Collections** None

The StyleSheet Object

This object exposes all the styles within a single style sheet in the styleSheets collection

Properties	disabled	href	id	owningElement	parentStyleSheet readOnly
	type				
Methods	addImport()	addRule()			
Events	None		**Collections**	imports	

The TextRange Object

This object represents the text stream of the HTML document. It can be used to set and retrieve the text within the page.

Properties	htmlText text
Methods	collapse() compareEndPoints() duplicate() execCommand() expand() findText() getBookmark() inRange() isEqual() move() moveEnd() moveStart() moveToBookmark() moveToElementText() moveToPoint() parentElement() pasteHTML() queryCommandEnabled() queryCommandIndeterm() queryCommandState() queryCommandSupported() queryCommandValue() scrollIntoView() select() setEndPoint()
Events	None **Collections** None

The window Object

The window object refers to the current window. This can be a top-level window, or a window that is within a frame created by a <FRAMESET> in another document.

Properties	clientInformation closed defaultStatus dialogArguments dialogHeight dialogLeft dialogTop dialogWidth document event history location length name navigator offScreenBuffering opener parent returnValue screen self status top
Methods	alert() blur() clearInterval() clearTimeout() close() confirm() execScript() focus() navigate() open() prompt() scroll() setInterval() setTimeout() showHelp() showModalDialog()
Events	onbeforeunload onblur onerror onfocus onhelp onload onresize onscroll onunload
Collections	frames

HTML and Form Elements Cross Reference

Dynamic HTML provides the same integral control types as HTML 3.2. However, there are many more different properties, methods and events available now for all the controls.

The following tables show those that are most relevant to controls.

Control Properties	checked	dataFld	dataFormatAs	dataSrc	defaultChecked	defaultValue	maxLength	ReadOnly	recordNumber	selectedIndex	size	Status	type	value
HTML button	✗	✓	✓	✓	✗	✗	✗	✓	✓	✗	✗	✗	✓	✓
HTML checkbox	✓	✓	✗	✓	✓	✗	✗	✓	✓	✗	✓	✓	✓	✓
HTML file	✗	✗	✗	✗	✗	✓	✗	✓	✓	✗	✗	✗	✓	✓
HTML hidden	✗	✓	✗	✓	✗	✗	✗	✗	✗	✗	✗	✗	✓	✓
HTML image	✗	✗	✗	✗	✗	✗	✗	✗	✓	✗	✗	✗	✓	✗
HTML password	✗	✓	✗	✓	✗	✓	✓	✓	✗	✗	✓	✗	✓	✓
HTML radio	✓	✓	✗	✓	✓	✗	✗	✓	✓	✗	✓	✗	✓	✓
HTML reset	✗	✗	✗	✗	✗	✗	✗	✗	✓	✗	✗	✗	✓	✓
HTML submit	✗	✗	✗	✗	✗	✗	✗	✗	✓	✗	✗	✗	✓	✓
HTML text	✗	✓	✗	✓	✗	✓	✓	✓	✓	✗	✓	✗	✓	✓
BUTTON tag	✗	✓	✓	✓	✗	✗	✗	✗	✗	✗	✗	✓	✓	✓
FIELDSET tag	✗	✗	✗	✗	✗	✗	✗	✗	✓	✗	✗	✗	✗	✗
LABEL tag	✗	✗	✗	✗	✗	✗	✗	✗	✗	✗	✗	✗	✗	✗
LEGEND tag	✗	✗	✗	✗	✗	✗	✗	✗	✓	✗	✗	✗	✗	✗
SELECT tag	✗	✓	✗	✓	✗	✗	✗	✗	✓	✓	✗	✗	✓	✓
TEXTAREA tag	✗	✓	✗	✓	✗	✗	✗	✓	✗	✗	✗	✓	✓	✓

Control Methods	add	blur	click	createTextRange	focus	item	remove	select
HTML button	✗	✓	✓	✗	✓	✗	✗	✓
HTML checkbox	✗	✓	✓	✗	✓	✗	✗	✓
HTML file	✗	✓	✓	✗	✓	✗	✗	✓
HTML hidden	✗	✗	✗	✗	✗	✗	✗	✗
HTML image	✗	✓	✓	✗	✓	✗	✗	✓
HTML password	✗	✓	✓	✗	✓	✗	✗	✓
HTML radio	✗	✓	✓	✗	✓	✗	✗	✓
HTML reset	✗	✓	✓	✗	✓	✗	✗	✓
HTML submit	✗	✓	✓	✗	✓	✗	✗	✓
HTML text	✗	✓	✓	✓	✓	✗	✗	✓
BUTTON tag	✗	✓	✓	✓	✓	✗	✗	✗
FIELDSET tag	✗	✓	✓	✗	✓	✗	✗	✗
LABEL tag	✗	✗	✓	✗	✗	✗	✗	✗
LEGEND tag	✗	✓	✓	✗	✓	✗	✗	✗
SELECT tag	✓	✓	✓	✗	✓	✓	✓	✗
TEXTAREA tag	✗	✓	✓	✓	✓	✗	✗	✓

Control Events	onafterupdate	onbeforeupdate	onblur	onchange	onclick	ondblclick	onfocus	onrowenter	onrowexit	onselect
HTML button	✗	✗	✓	✗	✓	✓	✓	✗	✗	✓
HTML checkbox	✓	✓	✓	✓	✓	✓	✓	✗	✗	✓
HTML file	✗	✗	✓	✓	✓	✓	✓	✗	✗	✓
HTML hidden	✗	✗	✗	✗	✗	✗	✗	✗	✗	✗
HTML image	✗	✗	✓	✓	✗	✓	✓	✗	✗	✓
HTML password	✗	✗	✓	✓	✓	✓	✓	✗	✗	✓
HTML radio	✓	✓	✓	✓	✓	✓	✓	✗	✗	✓
HTML reset	✗	✗	✓	✗	✓	✓	✓	✗	✗	✓
HTML submit	✗	✗	✓	✗	✓	✓	✓	✗	✗	✓
HTML text	✓	✓	✓	✓	✓	✓	✓	✗	✗	✓
BUTTON tag	✓	✓	✓	✗	✓	✓	✓	✓	✓	✗
FIELDSET tag	✓	✓	✓	✗	✓	✓	✓	✓	✓	✗
LABEL tag	✗	✗	✗	✗	✓	✓	✗	✗	✗	✗
LEGEND tag	✓	✓	✓	✗	✓	✓	✓	✓	✓	✗
SELECT tag	✓	✓	✓	✓	✓	✓	✓	✓	✓	✗
TEXTAREA tag	✓	✓	✓	✓	✓	✓	✓	✓	✓	✓

The IE 5 Browser Object Model

The IE 5 Dynamic HTML object model contains 23 **objects** and 29 **collections**. Most of these are organized into a strict hierarchy that allows HTML authors to access all the parts of the browser, and the pages that are loaded, from a scripting language like JavaScript or VBScript.

The Object Model in Outline

The diagram (below) shows the object hierarchy in graphical form. It is followed by a list of the objects and collections, with a brief description. Then, each object is documented in detail, showing the properties, methods, and events it supports.

Note that we haven't included all of the objects and collections in the diagram. Some are not part of the overall object model, but are used to access other items – such as dialogs and HTML elements.

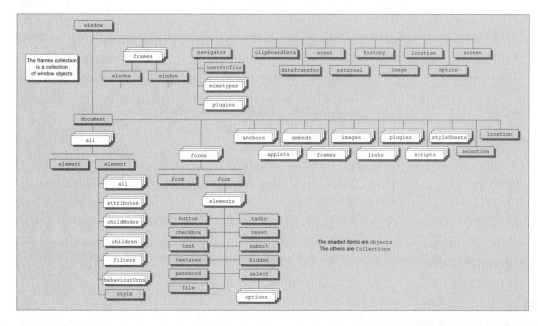

The Browser Objects

Object Name	Description
Attribute	An object-representation of an attribute or property.
ClipboardData	Used with editing operations to provide access to data contained on the clipboard.
CurrentStyle	Represents the cascaded format and style of its parent object.
Custom	A user-defined element.
DataTransfer	Used with drag-and-drop operations to provide access to data contained on the clipboard.
document	An object that exposes the contents of the HTML document through a number of collections and properties.
event	A global object that exposes properties that represent the parameters of all events as they occur.
External	Allows access to the object model of any application hosting Internet Explorer components.
history	Exposes information about the URLs that the client has previously visited.
location	Exposes information about the currently displayed document's URL.
MimeType	An object that provides information about a MIME type.
navigator	Exposes properties that provide information about the browser, or user agent.
Rule	A style (that is, a selector and one or more declarations) within a cascading style sheet (CSS).
RuntimeStyle	Represents the cascaded format and style of its parent object, overriding global stylesheets, inline styles, and HTML attributes. Overwrites the values of the CurrentStyle object but not the Style object.
screen	Exposes information about the client's monitor screen and system rendering abilities.
Selection	Represents the currently active selection on the screen in the document.
Style	Represents an individual style element within a style sheet.
StyleSheet	Exposes all the styles within a single style sheet in the styleSheets collection.
TextNode	A string of text, represented as a node on the document hierarchy.
TextRange	Represents sections of the text stream making up the HTML document.
TextRectangle	A set of the four coordinates that represent the rectangle containing a line of text of a TextRange object.
UserProfile	Allows a script to request read access to, and perform read actions on, a user's profile.
window	Exposes properties, methods, and events connected to the browser window or a frame.

The Browser Collections

Collection Name	Description
all	Collection of all the tags and elements in the body of the document.
anchors	Collection of all the anchors in the document.
applets	Collection of all the objects in the document, including intrinsic controls, images, applets, embeds, and other objects.
areas	Collection of all the areas that make up the image map.
attributes	Collection of all the attributes of the object.
behaviorUrns	Collection of all the behaviors attached to the element (as a set of URN strings).
bookmarks	Collection of all the ADO bookmarks tied to the rows affected by the current event.
boundElements	Collection of all the elements on the page that are bound to a dataset.
cells	Collection of all the <TH> and <TD> cells in a row of a table.
childNodes	Collection of all the object's children.
children	Collection of all the object's direct descendants.
controlRange	Collection of the BODY's elements.
elements	Collection of all controls and elements in the form.
embeds	Collection of all the <EMBED> tags in the document.
filters	Collection of all the filter objects for an element.
forms	Collection of all the forms in the page.
frames	Collection of all the frames defined within a <FRAMESET> tag.
images	Collection of all the images in the page.
imports	Collection of all the imported style sheets defined for a stylesheet object.
links	Collection of all the links and <AREA> blocks in the page.
mimeTypes	Collection of all the document and file types supported by the browser.
options	Collection of all the items in a <SELECT> element.
plugins	An alias for collection of all the embeds in the page.
rows	Collection of all the rows in the table, including <THEAD>, <TBODY>, and <TFOOT>.
rules	Collection of all the rule objects defined in a styleSheet.
scripts	Collection of all the <SCRIPT> sections in the page.
styleSheets	Collection of all the individual style property objects defined for a document.
tBodies	Collection of all TBODY objects in the table.
TextRectangle	Collection of all the TextRectangle objects in the object.

The Objects in Detail

This section lists all the properties, methods and events available for each object in the browser hierarchy. Brief descriptions of these properties, methods and events can be found in Appendix C, and the collections are briefly described above.

It's worth noting that there's a set of attributes that are common to almost all of the DHTML elements. These attributes provide properties, methods, and events for manipulating the specific object. This commonality makes it simpler to use exactly the same scripting style and techniques to deal with nearly every element in the browser object model. Thus, you'll see a certain amount of repetition in these lists.

The Attribute Object

An object-representation of an attribute or property.

Properties	nodeName	nodeType	nodeValue	specified
Methods	None			
Events	None		**Collections**	None

The ClipboardData Object

Used with editing operations to provide access to data contained on the clipboard.

Properties	None	**Methods**	clearData() getData() setData()
Events	None	**Collections**	None

The CurrentStyle Object

Represents the cascaded format and style of its parent object.

Properties	backgroundAttachment backgroundColor backgroundImage backgroundPositionX backgroundPositionY backgroundRepeat borderBottomColor borderBottomStyle borderBottomWidth borderColor borderLeftColor borderLeftStyle borderLeftWidth borderRightColor borderRightStyle borderRightWidth borderStyle borderTopColor borderTopStyle borderTopWidth borderWidth bottom clear clipBottom clipLeft clipRight clipTop color cursor direction display fontFamily fontSize fontStyle fontVariant fontWeight height layoutGrid layoutGridChar layoutGridCharSpacing layoutGridLine layoutGridMode layoutGridType left letterSpacing lineHeight listStyleImage listStylePosition listStyleType margin marginBottom marginLeft marginRight marginTop overflow overflowX overflowY padding paddingBottom paddingLeft paddingRight paddingTop pageBreakAfter pageBreakBefore position right styleFloat tableLayout textAlign textDecoration textIndent textTransform top unicodeBidi verticalAlign visibility width zIndex
Methods	None
Events	None **Collections** None

The Custom Object

A user-defined element.

Properties	accessKey canHaveChildren className clientHeight clientLeft clientTop clientWidth currentStyle dir document id innerHTML innerText isTextEdit lang language offsetHeight offsetLeft offsetParent offsetTop offsetWidth outerHTML outerText parentElement parentTextEdit readyState recordNumber runtimeStyle scopeName scrollHeight scrollLeft scrollTop scrollWidth sourceIndex style tabIndex tagName tagUrn title
Methods	addBehavior() applyElement() attachEvent() blur() clearAttributes() click() componentFromPoint() contains() createControlRange() detachEvent() doScroll() focus() getAdjacentText() getAttribute() getBoundingClientRect() getClientRects() getElementsByTagName() getExpression() insertAdjacentHTML() insertAdjacentText() mergeAttributes() releaseCapture() removeAttribute() removeBehavior() removeExpression() replaceAdjacentText() scrollIntoView() setAttribute() setCapture() setExpression()
Events	onafterupdate onbeforecopy onbeforecut onbeforeeditfocus onbeforepaste onbeforeupdate onblur onclick oncontextmenu oncopy oncut ondblclick ondrag ondragend ondragenter ondragleave ondragover ondragstart ondrop onerrorupdate onfilterchange onfocus onhelp onkeydown onkeypress onkeyup onlosecapture onmousedown onmousemove onmouseout onmouseover onmouseup onpaste onpropertychange onreadystatechange onresize onscroll onselectstart
Collections	all behaviorUrns children filters

The DataTransfer Object

Used with drag-and-drop operations to provide access to data contained on the clipboard.

Properties	dropEffect effectAllowed		
Methods	clearData() getData() setData()		
Events	None	**Collections**	None

The document Object

An object that exposes the contents of the HTML document, through a number of collections and properties.

Properties	`activeElement` `aLinkColor` `bgColor` `cookie` `defaultCharset` `designMode` `documentElement` `domain` `expando` `fgColor` `fileCreatedDate` `fileModifiedDate` `fileSize` `lastModified` `linkColor` `location` `parentWindow` `protocol` `readyState` `referrer` `selection` `uniqueID` `URL` `vlinkColor`
Methods	`attachEvent()` `clear()` `clearAttributes()` `close()` `createElement()` `createStyleSheet()` `createTextNode()` `detachEvent()` `elementFromPoint()` `execCommand()` `getElementById()` `getElementsByName()` `getElementsByTagName()` `mergeAttributes()` `open()` `queryCommandEnabled()` `queryCommandIndeterm()` `queryCommandState()` `queryCommandSupported()` `queryCommandValue()` `recalc()` `releaseCapture()` `write()` `writeln()`
Events	`onbeforecut` `onbeforeeditfocus` `onbeforepaste` `onclick` `oncontextmenu` `oncut` `ondblclick` `ondrag` `ondragend` `ondragenter` `ondragleave` `ondragover` `ondragstart` `ondrop` `onhelp` `onkeydown` `onkeypress` `onkeyup` `onmousedown` `onmousemove` `onmouseout` `onmouseover` `onmouseup` `onpaste` `onpropertychange` `onreadystatechange` `onstop`
Collections	`all` `anchors` `applets` `childNodes` `children` `embeds` `forms` `frames` `images` `links` `scripts` `styleSheets`

The event Object

A global object, that exposes properties that represent the parameters of all events as they occur.

Properties	`altKey` `button` `cancelBubble` `clientX` `clientY` `ctrlKey` `dataFld` `dataTransfer` `fromElement` `keyCode` `offsetX` `offsetY` `propertyName` `qualifier` `reason` `recordset` `repeat` `returnValue` `screenX` `screenY` `shiftKey` `srcElement` `srcFilter` `srcUrn` `toElement` `type` `x` `y`
Methods None	**Events** None
Collections	`bookmarks` `boundElements`

The External Object

Allows access to the object model of any application hosting Internet Explorer components.

Properties	`menuArguments`
Methods	`AddChannel()` `AddDesktopComponent()` `AddFavorite()` `AutoCompleteSaveForm()` `AutoScan()` `ImportExportFavorites()` `IsSubscribed()` `NavigateAndFind()` `ShowBrowserUI()`
Events None	**Collections** None

The history Object

Exposes information about the URLs that the client has previously visited.

Properties	length		
Methods	back() forward() go()		
Events	None	Collections	None

The location Object

Exposes information about the currently displayed document's URL.

Properties	hash host hostname href pathname port protocol search		
Methods	assign() reload() replace()		
Events	None	Collections	None

The MimeType Object

An object that provides information about a MIME type.

Properties	description enabledPlugin name		
Methods	None		
Events	None	Collections	suffixes

The navigator Object

Exposes properties that provide information about the browser, or user agent.

Properties	appCodeName appMinorVersion appName appVersion browserLanguage cookieEnabled cpuClass onLine platform systemLanguage userAgent userLanguage userProfile
Methods	javaEnabled() taintEnabled()
Events	None
Collections	plugins

The Rule Object

A style (specifically, a selector and one or more declarations), within a cascading style sheet (CSS).

Properties	readOnly runtimeStyle selectorText style
Methods	None
Events	None	**Collections**	None

The RuntimeStyle Object

Represents the cascaded format and style of its parent object, overriding global stylesheets, inline styles, and HTML attributes. Overwrites the values of the `CurrentStyle` object but not the `Style` object.

Properties	background backgroundAttachment backgroundColor backgroundImage backgroundPosition backgroundPositionX backgroundPositionY backgroundRepeat border borderBottom borderBottomColor borderBottomStyle borderBottomWidth borderColor borderLeft borderLeftColor borderLeftStyle borderLeftWidth borderRight borderRightColor borderRightStyle borderRightWidth borderStyle borderTop borderTopColor borderTopStyle borderTopWidth borderWidth bottom clear clip color cssText cursor direction display filter font fontFamily fontSize fontStyle fontVariant fontWeight height layoutGrid layoutGridChar layoutGridCharSpacing layoutGridLine layoutGridMode layoutGridType left letterSpacing lineHeight listStyle listStyleImage listStylePosition listStyleType margin marginBottom marginLeft marginRight marginTop overflow overflowX overflowY padding paddingBottom paddingLeft paddingRight paddingTop pageBreakAfter pageBreakBefore pixelBottom pixelHeight pixelLeft pixelRight pixelTop pixelWidth posBottom posHeight position posLeft posRight posTop posWidth right styleFloat tableLayout textAlign textDecoration textDecorationBlink textDecorationLineThrough textDecorationNone textDecorationOverline textDecorationUnderline textIndent textTransform top unicodeBidi verticalAlign visibility width zIndex
Methods	None
Events	None	**Collections**	None

The screen Object

Exposes information about the client's monitor screen and system rendering abilities.

Properties	availHeight availWidth bufferDepth colorDepth fontSmoothingEnabled height updateInterval width
Methods	None
Events	None	**Collections**	None

The Selection Object

Represents the currently active selection on the screen in the document.

Properties	type		
Methods	clear()	createRange()	empty()
Events	None	**Collections**	None

The Style Object

Represents an individual style element within a style sheet.

Properties	background backgroundAttachment backgroundColor backgroundImage backgroundPosition backgroundPositionX backgroundPositionY backgroundRepeat border borderBottom borderBottomColor borderBottomStyle borderBottomWidth borderColor borderLeft borderLeftColor borderLeftStyle borderLeftWidth borderRight borderRightColor borderRightStyle borderRightWidth borderStyle borderTop borderTopColor borderTopStyle borderTopWidth borderWidth bottom clear clip color cssText cursor direction display filter font fontFamily fontSize fontStyle fontVariant fontWeight height layoutGrid layoutGridChar layoutGridCharSpacing layoutGridLine layoutGridMode layoutGridType left letterSpacing lineHeight listStyle listStyleImage listStylePosition listStyleType margin marginBottom marginLeft marginRight marginTop overflow overflowX overflowY padding paddingBottom paddingLeft paddingRight paddingTop pageBreakAfter pageBreakBefore pixelBottom pixelHeight pixelLeft pixelRight pixelTop pixelWidth posBottom posHeight position posLeft posRight posTop posWidth right styleFloat tableLayout textAlign textDecoration textDecorationBlink textDecorationLineThrough textDecorationNone textDecorationOverline textDecorationUnderline textIndent textTransform top unicodeBidi verticalAlign visibility width zIndex		
Methods	getExpression()	removeExpression()	setExpression()
Events	None	**Collections**	None

The StyleSheet Object

Exposes all the styles within a single style sheet in the styleSheets collection.

Properties	disabled id owningElement parentStyleSheet readOnly type
Methods	addImport() addRule() removeRule()
Events	None
Collections	imports rules

The TextNode Object

A string of text, represented as a node on the document hierarchy.

Properties	`data  length  nextSibling  nodeName  nodeType  nodeValue  previousSibling`
Methods	`splitText()`
Events	None **Collections** None

The TextRange Object

Represents sections of the text stream making up the HTML document.

Properties	`boundingHeight  boundingLeft  boundingTop  boundingWidth  htmlText  offsetLeft  offsetTop  text`
Methods	`collapse() compareEndPoints() duplicate() execCommand() expand() findText() getBookmark() getBoundingClientRect() getClientRects() inRange() isEqual() move() moveEnd() moveStart() moveToBookmark() moveToElementText() moveToPoint() parentElement() pasteHTML() queryCommandEnabled() queryCommandIndeterm() queryCommandState() queryCommandSupported() queryCommandValue() scrollIntoView() select() setEndPoint()`
Events	None **Collections** None

The TextRectangle Object

A set of the four coordinates that represent the rectangle containing a line of text of a `TextRange` object.

Properties	`bottom  left  right  top`
Methods	None
Events	None **Collections** None

The UserProfile Object

Allows a script to request read access to, and perform read actions on, a user's profile.

Properties	None
Methods	`addReadRequest()  clearRequest()  doReadRequest()  getAttribute()`
Events	None
Collections	None

The window Object

Exposes properties, methods, and events connected to the browser window or a frame.

Properties	`clientInformation  clipboardData  closed  defaultStatus dialogArguments  dialogHeight  dialogLeft  dialogTop dialogWidth  document  event  external  history  length location  name  navigator  offscreenBuffering  opener  parent returnValue  screen  screenLeft  screenTop  self  status  top`
Methods	`alert() attachEvent() blur() clearInterval() clearTimeout() close() confirm() detachEvent() execScript() focus() moveBy() moveTo() navigate() open() print() prompt() resizeBy() resizeTo() scroll() scrollBy() scrollTo() setInterval() setTimeout() showHelp() showModalDialog() showModelessDialog()`
Events	`onafterprint  onbeforeprint  onbeforeunload  onblur  onerror onfocus  onhelp  onload  onresize  onunload`
Collections	`Frames`

HTML and Form Controls Cross Reference

Dynamic HTML provides the same integral control types as HTML 3.2. However, there are many more different properties, methods, and events available now for all the controls.

The following tables show the properties, methods, and events that are most relevant to HTML form elements.

Control Properties	checked	dataFld	dataFormatAs	dataSrc	defaultChecked	defaultValue	maxLength	ReadOnly	recordNumber	selectedIndex	size	status	type	value
HTML button	✗	✓	✓	✓	✗	✓	✗	✗	✓	✗	✓	✗	✓	✓
HTML checkbox	✓	✓	✗	✓	✓	✓	✗	✗	✓	✗	✓	✓	✓	✓
HTML file	✗	✓	✗	✓	✗	✓	✗	✗	✓	✗	✓	✗	✓	✓
HTML hidden	✗	✓	✗	✓	✗	✓	✗	✗	✓	✗	✗	✗	✓	✓
HTML image	✗	✓	✗	✓	✗	✓	✗	✗	✓	✗	✓	✗	✓	✓
HTML password	✗	✓	✗	✓	✗	✓	✓	✓	✓	✗	✓	✗	✓	✓
HTML radio	✓	✓	✗	✓	✓	✓	✗	✗	✓	✗	✓	✓	✓	✓
HTML reset	✗	✓	✗	✓	✗	✓	✗	✗	✓	✗	✓	✗	✓	✓
HTML submit	✗	✓	✗	✓	✗	✓	✗	✗	✓	✗	✓	✗	✓	✓
HTML text	✗	✓	✗	✓	✗	✓	✓	✓	✓	✗	✓	✗	✓	✓
APPLET tag	✗	✓	✗	✓	✗	✗	✗	✗	✓	✗	✗	✗	✗	✗
BUTTON tag	✗	✓	✓	✓	✗	✗	✗	✗	✓	✗	✗	✗	✓	✓
FIELDSET tag	✗	✗	✗	✗	✗	✗	✗	✗	✓	✗	✗	✗	✗	✗
LABEL tag	✗	✓	✓	✓	✗	✗	✗	✗	✓	✗	✗	✗	✗	✗
LEGEND tag	✗	✗	✗	✗	✗	✗	✗	✗	✗	✗	✗	✗	✗	✗
SELECT tag	✗	✓	✗	✓	✗	✗	✗	✗	✓	✓	✓	✗	✓	✗
TEXTAREA tag	✗	✓	✗	✓	✗	✓	✗	✓	✗	✗	✗	✗	✓	✓
XML tag	✗	✗	✗	✗	✗	✗	✗	✗	✗	✗	✗	✗	✗	✗

Control Methods	add	blur	click	createTextRange	focus	item	remove	select
HTML button	✗	✓	✓	✓	✓	✗	✗	✓
HTML checkbox	✗	✓	✓	✗	✓	✗	✗	✓
HTML file	✗	✓	✓	✗	✓	✗	✗	✓
HTML hidden	✗	✗	✗	✓	✗	✗	✗	✗
HTML image	✗	✓	✓	✗	✓	✗	✗	✓
HTML password	✗	✓	✓	✓	✓	✗	✗	✓
HTML radio	✗	✓	✓	✗	✓	✗	✗	✓
HTML reset	✗	✓	✓	✓	✓	✗	✗	✓
HTML submit	✗	✓	✓	✓	✓	✗	✗	✓
HTML text	✗	✓	✓	✓	✓	✗	✗	✓
APPLET tag	✗	✓	✓	✗	✓	✗	✗	✗
BUTTON tag	✗	✓	✓	✓	✓	✗	✗	✗
FIELDSET tag	✗	✓	✓	✗	✓	✗	✗	✗
LABEL tag	✗	✓	✓	✗	✓	✗	✗	✗
LEGEND tag	✗	✓	✓	✗	✓	✗	✗	✗
SELECT tag	✗	✓	✓	✗	✓	✗	✗	✗
TEXTAREA tag	✗	✓	✓	✓	✓	✗	✗	✓
XML tag	✗	✗	✗	✗	✗	✗	✗	✗

Control Events	onafterupdate	onbeforeupdate	onblur	onchange	onclick	ondblclick	onfocus	onrowenter	onrowexit	onselect
HTML button	✗	✗	✓	✗	✓	✓	✓	✗	✗	✗
HTML checkbox	✓	✓	✓	✗	✓	✓	✓	✗	✗	✗
HTML file	✗	✗	✓	✗	✓	✓	✓	✗	✗	✗
HTML hidden	✗	✗	✗	✗	✗	✗	✓	✗	✗	✗
HTML image	✗	✗	✓	✗	✓	✓	✓	✗	✗	✗
HTML password	✗	✗	✓	✗	✓	✓	✓	✗	✗	✗
HTML radio	✗	✗	✓	✗	✓	✓	✓	✗	✗	✗
HTML reset	✗	✗	✓	✗	✓	✓	✓	✗	✗	✗
HTML submit	✗	✗	✓	✗	✓	✓	✓	✗	✗	✗
HTML text	✗	✗	✓	✓	✓	✓	✓	✗	✗	✓
APPLET tag	✗	✗	✓	✗	✓	✓	✓	✓	✓	✗
BUTTON tag	✗	✗	✓	✗	✓	✓	✓	✗	✗	✗
FIELDSET tag	✗	✗	✓	✗	✓	✓	✓	✗	✗	✗
LABEL tag	✗	✗	✓	✗	✓	✓	✓	✗	✗	✗
LEGEND tag	✗	✗	✓	✗	✓	✓	✓	✗	✗	✗
SELECT tag	✗	✗	✓	✓	✓	✓	✓	✗	✗	✗
TEXTAREA tag	✓	✓	✓	✓	✓	✓	✓	✗	✗	✓
XML tag	✗	✗	✗	✗	✗	✗	✗	✓	✓	✗

The NN 4 Browser Object Model

The Dynamic HTML Object Model for Netscape Navigator contains 29 **objects** and 16 **arrays**. Most of these are organized into a strict hierarchy that allows HTML authors to access all the parts of the browser, and the pages that are loaded, from a scripting language like JavaScript.

The Object Model In Outline

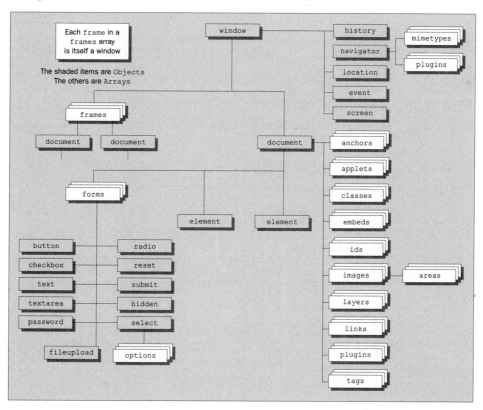

The diagram shows the object hierarchy in graphical form. It is followed by a list of the objects and arrays, with a brief description. Then, each object is documented in detail, showing the properties, methods, and events it supports.

Note that not all the objects and arrays are included in the diagram. Some are not part of the overall object model, but are used to access other items such as dialogs or HTML elements.

The Browser Objects

Object	Description
Anchor	An object that represents an anchor created with <A NAME="..."> in the document.
Area	An area created within a <MAP> element by an <AREA> tag.
Button	An object that represents a control created with an <INPUT> tag where TYPE=button.
Checkbox	An object that represents a control created with an <INPUT> tag where TYPE=checkbox.
document	Exposes the contents of the HTML document through a number of arrays and properties.
Element	An object that represents a control in the array of all the controls on a <FORM>.
event	The global event object exposed for accessing an event's parameters.
FileUpload	An object that represents a control created with an <INPUT> tag where TYPE=file.
Form	An object that represents the section of a page contained within a <FORM> tag.
Frame	An object that represents a <FRAME> within a <FRAMESET>.
Hidden	An object that represents a control created with an <INPUT> tag where TYPE=hidden.
history	Contains information on the URLs that the client has visited.
IMG	An object that represents an element created with an <IMG> tag.
Layer	An object that represents a <LAYER> or <ILAYER> in a document.
Link	An object that represents a link created in the page with an <A HREF="..."> tag.
location	Contains information about the current URL being displayed.
MimeType	Contains information about the MIME types supported by the browser.
navigator	An object representing the browser itself, and its properties.
Option	An individual <OPTION> item in a list created by a <SELECT> tag.

Object	Description
Password	An object that represents a control created with an `<INPUT>` tag where `TYPE=password`.
Plugin	An object that represents the features of an installed plugin component.
Radio	An object that represents a control created with an `<INPUT>` tag where `TYPE=radio`.
Reset	An object that represents a control created with an `<INPUT>` tag where `TYPE=reset`.
screen	Contains information about the client's screen and rendering abilities.
Select	An object that represents a list control created with a `<SELECT>` tag.
Submit	An object that represents a control created with an `<INPUT>` tag where `TYPE=submit`.
Text	An object that represents a control created with an `<INPUT>` tag where `TYPE=text`.
Textarea	An object that represents a text area control created with a `<TEXTAREA>` tag.
window	An object that provides information about the current browser window.

The Browser Object Arrays

Array	Description
anchors	Array of all the anchors in the document.
applets	Array of all the objects in the document, including intrinsic controls, images, applets, embeds, and other objects.
areas	Array of all the areas that make up an image map.
arguments	Array of all the arguments supplied to a function.
classes	Array of all the style classes defined in the document.
elements	Array of all controls and elements in the form.
embeds	Array of all the embed tags in the document.
forms	Array of all the forms in the page.
frames	Array of all the frames defined within a `<FRAMESET>` tag.
ids	Array of all the individual element styles defined in the document.
images	Array of all the images in the page.
layers	Array of all the layers in a document or another layer.

Table continued on following page

Array	Description
links	Array of all the links and <AREA> blocks in the page.
mimeTypes	Array of all the supported MIME types.
options	Array of all the items in a <SELECT> list.
plugins	Array of all the plugins available.

The Browser Objects in Detail

This section documents all the properties, arrays, methods, and events available for each object in the browser hierarchy. The JavaScript objects are covered at the end of this reference section.

The Anchor Object

An object that represents an anchor created with <A NAME="..."> in the document.

Property	name		
Methods	eval() toString() valueOf()		
Events	None	**Arrays**	None

The Area Object

An area created within a <MAP> element by an <AREA> tag.

Properties	hash host hostname href pathname port protocol search target
Methods	eval() handleEvent() toString() valueOf()
Events	onDblClick onMouseOut onMouseOver
Arrays	None

The Button Object

An object that represents a control created with an <INPUT> tag where TYPE=button.

Properties	form name type value
Methods	blur() click() eval() focus() handleEvent() toString() valueOf()
Events	onBlur onClick onFocus onMouseDown onMouseUp
Arrays	None

The CheckBox Object

An object that represents a control created with an <INPUT> tag where TYPE=checkbox.

Properties	checked defaultChecked form name type value
Methods	blur() click() eval() focus() handleEvent() toString() valueOf()
Events	onBlur onClick onFocus
Arrays	None

The document Object

Exposes the entire HTML content through its own arrays and properties, and provides a range of events and methods to work with documents.

Properties	alinkColor bgColor cookie domain fgColor lastModified linkColor referrer title URL vlinkColor
Methods	captureEvents() close() eval() getSelection() handleEvent() open() releaseEvents() routeEvent() toString() valueOf() write() writeln()
Events	onClick onDblClick onKeyDown onKeyPress onKeyUp onMouseDown onMouseMove onMouseUp
Arrays	anchors applets classes embeds forms ids images layers links plugins tags

The Element Object

An object that represents a control in the array of all the controls on a <FORM>.

Properties	checked defaultChecked defaultValue form length name selectedIndex type value
Methods	blur() click() eval() focus() handleEvent() select() toString() valueOf()
Events	onBlur onChange onClick onFocus onKeyDown onKeyPress onKeyUp onMouseDown onMouseUp onSelect
Arrays	None

The event Object

The global object provided to allow the scripting language to access an event's parameters. It provides the following properties, and the three standard methods:

Properties	data layerX layerY modifiers pageX pageY screenX screenY target type which
Methods	eval() toString() valueOf()
Events	None **Arrays** None

The FileUpload Object

An object that represents a control created with an `<INPUT>` tag where `TYPE=file`.

Properties	form name type value
Methods	blur() eval() focus() handleEvent() toString() valueOf()
Events	onBlur onChange onFocus
Arrays	None

The Form Object

An object that represents the section of a page contained within a `<FORM>` tag.

Properties	action encoding length method name target
Methods	eval() handleEvent() reset() submit() toString() valueOf()
Events	onReset onSubmit
Array	elements

The Frame Object

An object that represents a `<FRAME>` within a `<FRAMESET>`.

Properties	length name parent self window
Methods	blur() clearInterval() clearTimeout() eval() focus() handleEvent() print() setInterval() setTimeout() toString() valueOf()
Events	onBlur onFocus onMove onResize
Array	frames

The Hidden Object

An object that represents a control created with an `<INPUT>` tag where `TYPE=hidden`.

Properties	name type value	
Methods	eval() toString() valueOf()	
Events	None	**Array** None

The history Object

Contains information about the URLs that the client has visited, as stored in the browser's History list, and allows the script to move through the list.

Properties	current length next previous	
Methods	back() eval() forward() go() toString() valueOf()	
Events	None	**Array** None

The IMG Object

An object that represents an element created with an `<IMG>` tag.

Properties	border complete height hspace lowsrc name prototype src vspace width
Methods	eval() handleEvent() toString() valueOf()
Events	onAbort onError onKeyDown onKeyPress onKeyUp onLoad
Array	areas

The Layer Object

An object that represents a `<LAYER>` or `<ILAYER>` element in a document.

Properties	above background below bgColor clip.bottom clip.height clip.left clip.right clip.top clip.width document left name pageX pageY parentLayer siblingAbove siblingBelow src top visibility zIndex
Methods	captureEvents() eval() handleEvent() load() moveAbove() moveBelow() moveBy() moveTo() moveToAbsolute() releaseEvents() resizeBy() resizeTo() routeEvent() toString() valueOf()
Events	onBlur onFocus onLoad onMouseOut onMouseOver
Arrays	None

The Link Object

An object that represents a hyperlink created in the page with an <A HREF="..."> tag.

Properties	hash host hostname href pathname port protocol search target
Methods	eval() handleEvent() toString() valueOf()
Events	onClick onDblClick onKeyDown onKeyPress onKeyUp onMouseDown onMouseOut onMouseOver onMouseUp
Arrays	None

The location Object

Contains information on the current URL. It also provides methods that will reload a page.

Properties	hash host hostname href pathname port protocol search
Methods	eval() reload() replace() toString() valueOf()
Events	None **Arrays** None

The MimeType Object

Provides information about the page's MIME data type.

Properties	description enabledPlugin name suffixes
Methods	eval() toString() valueOf()
Events	None **Arrays** None

The navigator Object

This object represents the browser application itself, providing information about its manufacturer, version, and capabilities.

Properties	appCodeName appName appVersion language platform userAgent
Methods	eval() javaEnabled() toString() valueOf()
Events	None
Array	mimeTypes plugins

The Option Object

An individual <OPTION> item in a list created by a <SELECT> tag.

Properties	defaultSelected index length selected selectedIndex text value
Methods	eval() toString() valueOf()
Events	None **Arrays** None

The Password Object

An object that represents a control created with an <INPUT> tag where TYPE=password.

Properties	defaultValue form name type value
Methods	blur() eval() focus() handleEvent() select() toString() valueOf()
Events	onBlur onFocus
Arrays	None

The Plugin Object

An object that represents the features of an installed plugin component.

Properties	description filename length name
Methods	eval() refresh() toString() valueOf()
Events	None **Arrays** None

The Radio Object

An object that represents a control created with an <INPUT> tag where TYPE=radio.

Properties	checked defaultChecked form length name type value
Methods	blur() click() eval() focus() handleEvent() toString() valueOf()
Events	onBlur onClick onFocus
Arrays	None

The Reset Object

An object that represents a control created with an <INPUT> tag where TYPE=reset.

Properties	form name type value
Methods	blur() click() eval() focus() handleEvent() toString() valueOf()
Events	onBlur onClick onFocus
Arrays	None

The screen Object

The screen object provides the scripting language with information about the client's screen resolution and rendering abilities.

Properties	availHeight availWidth colorDepth height pixelDepth width
Methods	eval() toString() valueOf()
Events	None **Arrays** None

The Select Object

An object that represents a list control created with a <SELECT> tag.

Properties	form length name selectedIndex type text
Methods	blur() eval() focus() handleEvent() toString() valueOf()
Events	onBlur onChange onFocus
Arrays	None

The Submit Object

An object that represents a control created with an <INPUT> tag where TYPE=submit.

Properties	form name type value
Methods	blur() click() eval() focus() handleEvent() toString() valueOf()
Events	onBlur onClick onFocus
Arrays	None

The Text Object

An object that represents a control created with an <INPUT> tag where TYPE=text.

Properties	defaultValue form name type value
Methods	blur() click() eval() focus() handleEvent() select() toString() valueOf()
Events	onBlur onChange onFocus onSelect
Arrays	None

The TextArea Object

An object that represents a text area control created with a <TEXTAREA> tag.

Properties	defaultValue form name type value
Methods	blur() eval() focus() handleEvent() select() toString() valueOf()
Events	onBlur onClick onFocus onKeyDown onKeyPress onKeyUp
Arrays	None

The window Object

The window object refers to the current window. This can be a top-level window, or a window that is within a frame created by a <FRAMESET> in another document.

Properties	closed defaultStatus document innerHeight innerWidth length location locationbar menubar name opener outerHeight outerWidth pageXOffset pageYOffset parent personalbar scrollbars self status statusbar toolbar top window
MethodName	alert() back() blur() captureEvents() clearInterval() clearTimeout() close() confirm() disableExternalCapture() enableExternalCapture() eval() find() focus() forward() handleEvent() home() moveBy() moveTo() open() print() prompt() releaseEvents() resizeBy() resizeTo() routeEvent() scrollBy() scrollTo() setInterval() setTimeout() stop() toString() valueOf()
EventName	onBlur onDragDrop onError onFocus onLoad onMouseMove onMove onResize onUnload
Array	frames

HTML Controls Cross Reference

Dynamic HTML provides the same integral control types as HTML 3.2. However, there are more properties, methods, and events available now for all the controls.

The following tables show those that are relevant to controls.

Control Properties	checked	defaultChecked	defaultSelected	defaultValue	form	index	length	name	seleced	selectedIndex	text	type	value
Button	✗	✗	✗	✗	✓	✗	✗	✓	✗	✗	✗	✓	✓
Checkbox	✓	✓	✗	✗	✓	✗	✗	✓	✗	✗	✗	✓	✓
FileUpload	✗	✗	✗	✗	✓	✗	✗	✓	✗	✗	✗	✓	✓
Hidden	✗	✗	✗	✗	✗	✗	✗	✓	✗	✗	✗	✓	✓
Option	✗	✗	✓	✗	✗	✓	✓	✗	✓	✓	✓	✗	✓
Password	✗	✗	✗	✓	✓	✗	✗	✓	✗	✗	✗	✓	✓
Radio	✓	✓	✗	✗	✓	✗	✓	✓	✗	✗	✗	✓	✓
Reset	✗	✗	✗	✗	✓	✗	✗	✓	✗	✗	✗	✓	✓
Select	✗	✗	✗	✗	✓	✗	✓	✓	✗	✓	✓	✓	✗
Submit	✗	✗	✗	✗	✓	✗	✗	✓	✗	✗	✗	✓	✓
Text	✗	✗	✗	✓	✓	✗	✗	✓	✗	✗	✗	✓	✓
Textarea	✗	✗	✗	✓	✓	✗	✗	✓	✗	✗	✗	✓	✓

Control Methods	blur	click	eval	focus	handleEvent	select	toString	valueOf
Button	✓	✓	✓	✓	✓	✗	✓	✓
Checkbox	✓	✓	✓	✓	✓	✗	✓	✓
FileUpload	✓	✗	✓	✓	✓	✗	✓	✓
Hidden	✗	✗	✓	✗	✗	✗	✓	✓
Option	✗	✗	✓	✗	✗	✗	✓	✓
Password	✓	✗	✓	✓	✓	✓	✓	✓
Radio	✓	✓	✓	✓	✓	✗	✓	✓
Reset	✓	✓	✓	✓	✓	✗	✓	✓
Select	✓	✗	✓	✓	✓	✗	✓	✓
Submit	✓	✓	✓	✓	✓	✗	✓	✓
Text	✓	✓	✓	✓	✓	✓	✓	✓
Textarea	✓	✗	✓	✓	✓	✓	✓	✓

Control Events	onBlur	onChange	onClick	onFocus	onKeyDown	onKeyPress	onKeyUp	onMouseDown	onMouseUp	onSelect
Button	✓	✗	✓	✓	✗	✗	✗	✓	✓	✗
Checkbox	✓	✗	✓	✓	✗	✗	✗	✗	✗	✗
FileUpload	✓	✗	✓	✓	✗	✗	✗	✗	✗	✗
Hidden	✗	✗	✗	✗	✗	✗	✗	✗	✗	✗
Option	✗	✗	✗	✗	✗	✗	✗	✗	✗	✗
Password	✓	✗	✗	✓	✗	✗	✗	✗	✗	✗
Radio	✓	✗	✓	✓	✗	✗	✗	✗	✗	✗
Reset	✓	✗	✓	✓	✗	✗	✗	✗	✗	✗
Select	✓	✓	✗	✓	✗	✗	✗	✗	✗	✗
Submit	✓	✗	✓	✓	✗	✗	✗	✗	✗	✗
Text	✓	✓	✗	✓	✗	✗	✗	✗	✗	✓
Textarea	✓	✗	✓	✓	✓	✓	✓	✗	✗	✗

JavaScript Style Properties

These properties provide access to the individual styles of an element. They could have been previously set by a style sheet, or by an inline style tag within the page.

JavaScript Style Properties	align backgroundColor backgroundImage borderColor borderBottomWidth borderLeftWidth borderRightWidth borderStyle borderTopWidth borderWidths() clear color display fontFamily fontSize fontStyle fontWeight height lineHeight listStyleType marginBottom marginLeft marginRight marginTop margins() paddingBottom paddingLeft paddingRight paddingTop paddings() textAlign textDecoration textIndent textTransform verticalAlign whiteSpace width

The ASP 3.0 Object Model

The ASP object model is made up of six objects. The following diagram shows conceptually how these objects relate to the client and the server, the requests made by the client and the responses sent back to them from the server:

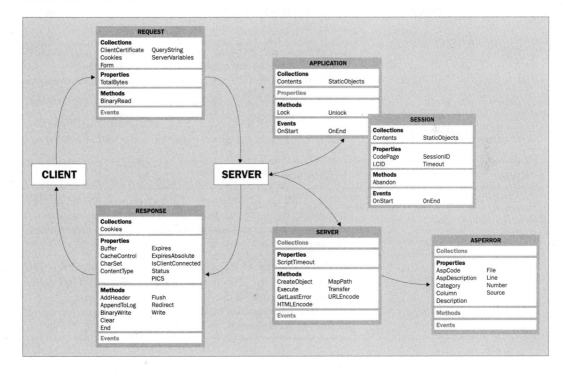

The Application Object

The Application object is created when the ASP DLL is loaded in response to the first request for an ASP page. It provides a repository for storing variables and object references that are available to all the pages that all visitors open.

Collection	Description
Contents	A collection of all of the variables and their values that are stored in the Application object, and are not defined using an <OBJECT> element. This includes Variant arrays and Variant-type object instance references.
StaticObjects	A collection of all of the variables that are stored in the Application object by using an <OBJECT> element.

Method	Description
Contents.Remove ("variable_name")	Removes a named variable from the Application.Contents collection.*
Contents.RemoveAll()	Removes all variables from the Application.Contents collection.*
Lock()	Locks the Application object so that only the current ASP page has access to the contents. Used to ensure that concurrency issues do not corrupt the contents by allowing two users to simultaneously read and update the values.
Unlock()	Releases this ASP page's lock on the Application object.

* You *cannot* remove variables from the Application.StaticObjects collection at run-time.

Event	Description
onStart	Occurs with the first instance of a user requesting one of the web pages in the application, before the page that the user requests is executed. Used to initialize variables, create objects, or run other code.
onEnd	Occurs when the ASP application ends, that is, when the web server shuts down. This is after the last user session has ended, and after any code in the onEnd event for that session has executed. All variables existing in the application are destroyed when it ends.

The ASPError Object

The ASPError object is a new object in ASP 3.0, and is available through the GetLastError method of the Server object. It provides a range of detailed information about the last error that occurred in ASP.

Property	Description
ASPCode	*Integer.* The error number generated by IIS.
ASPDescription	*Integer.* A detailed description of the error if it is ASP-related.
Category	*String.* Indicates the source of the error: such as, ASP itself, the scripting language, or an object.
Column	*Integer.* The character position within the file that generated the error.
Description	*String.* A short description of the error.
File	*String.* The name of the file that was being processed when the error occurred.
Line	*Integer.* The number of the line within the file that generated the error.
Number	*Integer.* A standard COM error code.
Source	*String.* The actual code, where available, of the line that caused the error.

The Request Object

The Request object makes available to the script all the information that the client provides when requesting a page or submitting a form. This includes the HTTP server variables that identify the browser and the user, cookies that are stored on the browser for this domain, and any values appended to the URL as a query string or in HTML controls in a <FORM> section of the page. It also provides access to any certificate that they may be using through **Secure Sockets Layer** (SSL) or other encrypted communication protocol, and properties that help to manage the connection.

Collection	Description
ClientCertificate	A collection of the values of all the fields or entries in the client certificate that the user presented to our server when accessing a page or resource. Each member is read-only.
Cookies	A collection of the values of all the cookies sent from the user's system along with their request. Only cookies valid for the domain containing the resource are sent to the server.
Form	A collection of the values of all the HTML control elements in the <FORM> section that was submitted as the request, where the value of the METHOD attribute is POST. Each member is read-only.

Table continued on following page

Collection	Description
QueryString	A collection of all the name/value pairs appended to the URL in the user's request, or the values of all the HTML control elements in the <FORM> section that was submitted as the request, where the value of the METHOD attribute is GET or the attribute is omitted. Each member is read-only.
ServerVariables	A collection of all the HTTP header values sent from the client with their request, plus the values of several environment variables for the web server. Each member is read-only.

Property	Description
TotalBytes	*Integer*. Read-only value holding the total number of bytes in the body of the request sent by the client.

Method	Description
BinaryRead (*count*)	Retrieves *count* bytes of data from the client's request when the data is sent to the server as part of a POST request. It returns as a Variant array (or SafeArray). This method *cannot* be used successfully if the ASP code has already referenced the Request.Form collection. Likewise, the Request.Form collection *cannot* be successfully accessed if you have used the BinaryRead method.

The Response Object

The Response object is used to access the response that is being created to send back to the client. It makes available the HTTP variables that identify the server and its capabilities, information about the content being sent to the browser, and any new cookies that will be stored on the browser for this domain. It also provides a series of methods that are used to create the returned page.

Collection	Description
Cookies	A collection containing the values of all the cookies that will be sent back to the client in the current response. Each member is write-only.

The Response object provides a range of properties that can be read (in most cases) and modified to tailor the response:

Property	Description
`Buffer =` `True│False`	*Boolean.* Read/write. Specifies if the output created by an ASP page will be held in the IIS buffer until all of the server scripts in the current page have been processed, or until the `Flush` or `End` method is called. It must be set before any output is sent to IIS, including HTTP header information, so it should be the first line of the `.asp` file after the `<%@LANGUAGE=..%>` statement. Buffering is on (`True`) by default in ASP 3.0, whereas it was off (`False`) by default in earlier versions.
`CacheControl =` `"setting"`	*String.* Read/write. Set this property to `"Public"` to allow proxy servers to cache the page, or `"Private"` to prevent proxy caching taking place.
`Charset = "value"`	*String.* Read/write. Appends the name of the character set (for example, `ISO-LATIN-7`) to the HTTP **Content-Type** header created by the server for each response.
`ContentType =` `"MIME-type"`	*String.* Read/write. Specifies the HTTP content type for the response, as a standard MIME-type (such as `"text/xml"` or `"image/gif"`)If omitted the MIME-type `"text/html"` is used. The content type tells the browser what type of content to expect.
`Expires = minutes`	*Number.* Read/write. Specifies the length of time in minutes that a page is valid for. If the user returns to the same page before it expires, the cached version is displayed. After that period it expires, and should not be held in a private (user) or public (proxy) cache.
`ExpiresAbsolute =` `#date[time]#`	*Date/Time.* Read/write. Specifies the absolute date and time when a page will expire and no longer be valid. If the user returns to the same page before it expires, the cached version is displayed. After that time it expires, and should not be held in a private (user) or public (proxy) cache.
`IsClientConnected`	*Boolean.* Read-only. Returns an indication of whether the client is still connected to and loading the page from the server. Can be used to end processing (with the `Response.End` method) if a client moves to another page before the current one has finished executing.
`PICS =` `("PICS-label-string")`	*String.* Write-only. Creates a PICS header and adds it to the HTTP headers in the response. PICS headers define the content of the page in terms of violence, sexual content, bad language, etc. to enable content filtering
`Status = "code` `message"`	*String.* Read/write. Specifies the status value and message that will be sent to the client in the HTTP headers of the response to indicate an error or successful processing of the page. Examples are `"200 OK"` and `"404 Not Found"`.

Method	Description
AddHeader ("name", "content")	Creates a custom HTTP header using the *name* and *content* values and adds it to the response. Will *not* replace an existing header of the same name. Once a header has been added, it cannot be removed. Must be used before any page content (text or HTML) is sent to the client.
AppendToLog ("string")	Adds a string to the end of the web server log entry for this request when W3C Extended Log File Format is in use. Requires at least the URI Stem value to be selected in the Extended Properties page for the site containing the page.
BinaryWrite (*SafeArray*)	Writes the content of a Variant-type *SafeArray* to the current HTTP output stream without any character conversion. Useful for writing non-string information, such as binary data required by a custom application, or the bytes to make up an image file.
Clear()	Erases any existing buffered page content from the IIS response buffer when Response.Buffer is True. Does *not* erase HTTP response headers. Can be used to abort a partly completed page.
End()	Stops ASP from processing the page script and returns the currently created content, then aborts any further processing of this page.
Flush()	Sends all currently buffered page content in the IIS buffer to the client when Response.Buffer is True. Can be used to send parts of a long page to the client individually.
Redirect ("url")	Instructs the browser to load the page in the string *url* parameter by sending a "302 Object Moved" HTTP header in the response.
Write ("string")	Writes the specified *string* to the current HTTP response stream and IIS buffer so that it becomes part of the returned page.

The Server Object

The Server object provides a series of methods and properties that are useful in scripting with ASP. The most obvious is the Server.CreateObject method, which properly instantiates other COM objects within the context of the current page or session. There are also methods to translate strings into the correct format for use in URLs and in HTML, by converting non-legal characters to the correct legal equivalent.

Property	Description
ScriptTimeout	*Integer*. Has the default value 90. Sets or returns the number of seconds that script in the page can execute for before the server aborts page execution and reports an error. This automatically halts and removes from memory pages that contain errors that may lock execution into a loop, or those that stall while waiting for a resource to become available. This prevents the server becoming overloaded with badly behaved pages. You may need to increase this value if your pages take a long time to run.

Method	Description
CreateObject (*"identifier"*)	Creates an instance of the object (a component, application, or scripting object) that is identified by *"identifier"*, and returns a reference to it that can be used in our code. Can be used in the global.asa page of a virtual application to create objects with session-level or application-level scope. The object can be identified by its ClassID ("{CLSID:FDC8-...-37A9}") value, or by a ProgID string such as "ADODB.Connection".
Execute (*"url"*)	Stops execution of the current page and transfers control to the page specified in *"url"*. The user's current environment (session state and any current transaction state) is carried over to the new page. After that page has finished execution, control passes back to the original page and execution resumes at the statement after the Execute method call.
GetLastError()	Returns a reference to an ASPError object that holds details of the last error that occurred within the ASP processing, that is, within asp.dll. The information exposed by the ASPError object includes the file name, line number, error code, etc.
HTMLEncode (*"string"*)	Returns a string that is a copy of the input value *"string"* but with all non-legal HTML characters, such as '<', '>', '&' and double quotes, converted into the equivalent HTML entity –<, >, &, ", etc.
MapPath (*"url"*)	Returns the full physical path and filename of the file or resource specified in *"url"*.
Transfer (*"url"*)	Stops execution of the current page and transfers control to the page specified in *"url"*. The user's current environment (session state and any current transaction state) is carried over to the new page. Unlike the Execute method, execution *does not* resume in the original page, but ends when the new page has completed executing.
URLEncode (*"string"*)	Returns a string that is a copy of the input value *"string"* but with all characters that are not valid in a URL, such as '?', '&' and spaces, converted into the equivalent URL entity – '%3F', '%26', and '+'.

The Session Object

The Session object is created for each visitor when they first request an ASP page from the site, and remains available until the default timeout period (or the timeout period determined by the script) expires. It provides a repository for storing variables and object references that are available just to the pages that this visitor opens during the lifetime of this session.

Collection	Description
Contents	A collection of all the variables and their values that are stored in this particular Session object, and are *not* defined using an <OBJECT> element. This includes Variant arrays and Variant-type object instance references.
StaticObjects	A collection of all of the variables which are stored in this particular Session object by using an <OBJECT> element.

Property	Description
CodePage	*Integer*. Read/write. Defines the code page that will be used to display the page content in the browser. The code page is the numeric value of the character set, and different languages and locales may use different code pages. For example, ANSI code page 1252 is used for American English and most European languages. Code page 932 is used for Japanese Kanji.
LCID	*Integer*. Read/write. Defines the locale identifier (LCID) of the page that is sent to the browser. The LCID is a standard international abbreviation that uniquely identifies the locale; for instance 2057 defines a locale where the currency symbol used is '£'. This LCID can also be used in statements such as FormatCurrency, where there is an optional LCID argument. The LCID for a page can also be set in the opening <%@..%> ASP processing directive, and overrides the setting in the LCID property of the session.
SessionID	*Long*. Read-only. Returns the session identifier for this session, which is generated by the server when the session is created. Unique only for the duration of the parent Application object, and so may be reused when a new application is started.
Timeout	*Integer*. Read/write. Defines the timeout period in minutes for this Session object. If the user does not refresh or request a page within the timeout period, the session ends. Can be changed in individual pages as required. The default is 20 minutes, and shorter timeouts may be preferred on a high-usage site.

Method	Description
Contents.Remove("*variable_name*")	Removes a named variable from the Session.Contents collection.*
Contents.RemoveAll()	Removes all variables from the Session.Contents collection.*
Abandon()	Ends the current user session and destroys the current Session object once execution of this page is complete. You can still access the current session's variables in this page, even after calling the Abandon method. However the next ASP page that is requested by this user will start a new session, and create a new Session object with only the default values defined in global.asa (if any exist).

* You *cannot* remove variables from the Session.StaticObjects collection at run-time.

Event	Description
onStart	Occurs when an ASP user session starts, before the first page that the user requests is executed. Used to initialize variables, create objects, or run other code.
onEnd	Occurs when an ASP user session ends. This is when the predetermined session timeout period has elapsed since that user's last page request from the application. All variables existing in the session are destroyed when it ends. It is also possible to end ASP user sessions explicitly in code, and this event occurs when that happens.

Online discussion at http://p2p.wrox.com

Useful Resources

This appendix contains a compendium of useful resources relating to JavaScript and associated topics.

Wrox Links and Books

We'll start with various links to other Wrox materials.

Wrox Home Page

www.wrox.com

Code Download

http://www.wrox.com/consumer/store/download.asp

Books

Professional JavaScript by Nigel McFarlane et al. (ISBN 1-861002-70-X)
Beginning XML Programming by David Hunter (ISBN 1-861003-4-21)
XML IE5 Programmer's Reference by Alex Homer (ISBN 1-861001-5-76)
JavaScript Objects by Alexander Nakhimovsky and Tom Myers (ISBN 1-861001-89-4)
Beginning Active Server Pages 3.0 by David Buser et al. (ISBN 1-861003-38-2)
Windows Script Host Programmer's Reference by Dino Esposito et al. (ISBN 1-861002-65-3)
ADSI ASP Programmers' Reference by Stephen Hahn et al. (ISBN 1861001-69-X)
Professional ADSI Programming by Simon Robinson et al. (ISBN 1861002-26-2)

Product Download Links

The following are links to product download pages for various pieces of software that we have discussed in this book.

Microsoft Internet Explorer

http://www.microsoft.com/downloads/search.asp?

Netscape Navigator

http://home.netscape.com/computing/download

Mozilla

```
http://www.mozilla.org
```

Macromedia (Shockwave and Flash)

```
http://www.macromedia.com
```

Realnetworks.com (Real Player Basic and Real Producer Basic, which you can use to produce your own Real Audio files)

```
http://www.real.com
```

TextPad (an excellent Windows text editor – you can download a free trial version from this site)

```
http://www.textpad.com
```

Web Standards

In Chapter 13 we mentioned several of the standards that are currently associated with the JavaScript field. The following links will enable you to find out more about these standards.

ECMAScript Standard

```
http://www.ecma.ch/ecma1/stand/ecma-262.htm
```

W3C (World Wide Web Consortium) Web Site

```
http://www.w3.org
```

DOM Level 1 Specification

```
http://www.w3.org/TR/1998/REC-DOM-Level-1-19981001/
```

DOM Level 2 Specification

```
http://www.w3.org/TR/2000/CR-DOM-Level-2-20000510/
```

HTML 4.01 Specification

```
http://www.w3.org/TR/REC-html40/
```

XHTML Specification

```
http://www.w3.org/TR/xhtml1/
```

XML 1.0 Specification

```
http://www.w3.org/TR/2000/REC-xml-20001006
```

JavaScript Reference Web Sites

JavaScript and JScript are primarily developed by Netscape and Microsoft, so more information can be found on their sites.

Netscape JavaScript Reference

```
http://developer.netscape.com/docs/manuals/js/client/jsref/index.htm
```

MSDN JScript Homepage

```
http://msdn.microsoft.com/scripting/default.htm?/scripting/jscript/default.htm
```

Other Sites that may be of Interest

There are many sites on the Internet that may interest you and further your knowledge of the topics discussed in this book. They include the following:

Internet Related Technologies

```
http://www.irt.org
```

Hot Syte

```
http://www.serve.com/hotsyte/
```

WebReference

```
http://www.webreference.com
```

WebMonkey

```
http://hotwired.lycos.com/webmonkey/
```

SQL Course

```
http://www.sqlcourse.com/
```

Online discussion at http://p2p.wrox.com

Support, Errata, and P2P.Wrox.Com

One of the most irritating things about any programming book is when you find that bit of code you've just spent an hour typing simply doesn't work. You check it a hundred times to see if you've set it up correctly and then you notice the spelling mistake in the variable name on the book page. Of course, you can blame the authors for not taking enough care and testing the code, the editors for not doing their job properly, or the proofreaders for not being eagle-eyed enough, but this doesn't get around the fact that mistakes do happen.

We try hard to ensure no mistakes sneak out into the real world, but we can't promise that this book is 100% error free. What we can do is offer the next best thing by providing you with immediate support and feedback from experts who have worked on the book and try to ensure that future editions eliminate these gremlins. We also now commit to supporting you not just while you read the book, but once you start developing applications as well through our online forums where you can put your questions to the authors, reviewers, and fellow industry professionals.

In this appendix we'll look at how to:

- ❏ Enroll in the peer to peer forums at p2p.wrox.com
- ❏ Post and check for errata on our main site, www.wrox.com
- ❏ e-mail technical support a query or feedback on our books in general

Between all three support procedures, you should get an answer to your problem in no time flat.

The Online Forums at P2P.Wrox.Com

Join the JavaScript mailing list for author and peer support. Our system provides **programmer to programmer™ support** on mailing lists, forums, and newsgroups all in addition to our one-to-one e-mail system, which we'll look at in a minute. Be confident that your query is not just being examined by a support professional, but by the many Wrox authors and other industry experts present on our mailing lists.

How To Enroll for Support

Just follow this six-step system:

1. Go to p2p.wrox.com in your favorite browser. Here you'll find any current announcements concerning P2P – new lists created, any removed and so on:

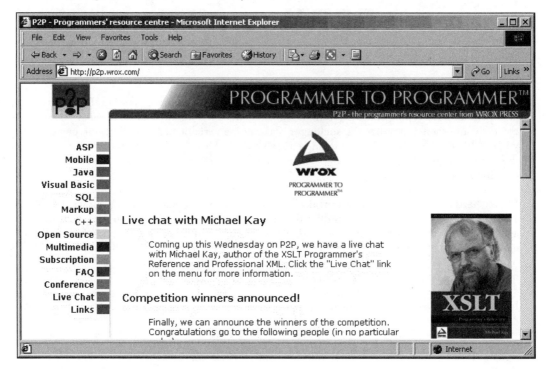

2. Click on the Markup button in the left hand column.

3. Choose to access the javascript list.

4. If you are not a member of the list, you can choose to either view the list without joining it or create an account in the list, by hitting the respective buttons.

5. If you wish to join, you'll be presented with a form in which you'll need to fill in your e mail address, name, and a password (of at least 4 digits). Choose how you would like to receive the messages from the list and then hit **Save**.

6. Congratulations. You're now a member of the JavaScript mailing list.

Why This System Offers the Best Support

You can choose to join the mailing lists or you can receive them as a weekly digest. If you don't have the time or facility to receive the mailing list, then you can search our online archives. You'll find the ability to search on specific subject areas or keywords. As these lists are moderated, you can be confident of finding good, accurate information quickly. Mails can be edited or moved by the moderator into the correct place, making this a most efficient resource. Junk and spam mail are deleted, and your own e mail address is protected by the unique Lyris system from web-bots that can automatically hoover up newsgroup mailing list addresses. Any queries about joining, or leaving lists, or any query about the list should be sent to: `listsupport@p2p.wrox.com`.

Checking The Errata Online at www.wrox.com

The following section will take you step by step through the process of posting and viewing errata on our web site to get help. The sections that follow, therefore, are:

❑   Finding a list of existing errata on the web site

❑   Adding your own errata to the existing list

❑   What happens to your erratum once you've posted it (why doesn't it appear immediately)?

There is also a section covering how to e-mail a question for technical support. This comprises:

❑   What your e-mail should include

❑   What happens to your e-mail once it has been received by us

Finding an Erratum on the Web Site

Before you send in a query, you might be able to save time by finding the answer to your problem on our web site – `http:\\www.wrox.com`.

Each book we publish has its own page and its own errata sheet. You can get to any book's page by clicking on it's category from the selection at the top of the page, in this case, click on JavaScript.

This will bring up a list of all the books in that category. You then need to click on the tile of the book to bring up its details, as shown overleaf:

If there are any errata for the book, then there will be a link for them underneath the book details. Click on this link to brink up a list of the errata, as shown opposite:

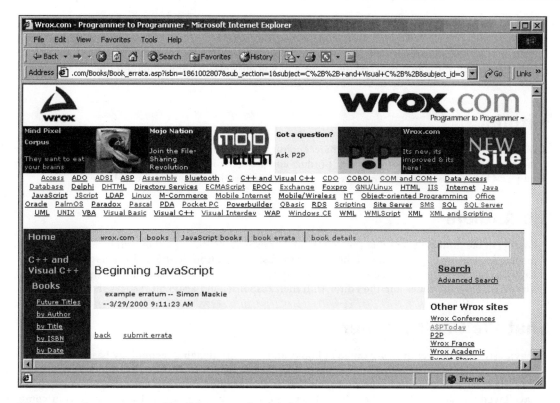

Clicking on the erratum itself will bring up the details.

Add an Erratum: E-mail Support

If you wish to point out an erratum to put up on the web site or directly query a problem in the book with an expert who knows the book in detail, then e-mail support@wrox.com with the title of the book and the last four numbers of the ISBN in the subject field of the e mail. A typical email should include the following things:

❑ The **name**, **last four digits of the ISBN,** and **page number** of the problem in the Subject field.

❑ Your **name**, **contact info,** and the **problem** in the body of the message.

We won't send you junk mail. We need the details to save your time and ours. When you send an e-mail it will go through the following chain of support:

Customer Support

Your message is delivered to one of our customer support staff, who are the first people to read it. They have files on most frequently asked questions and will answer anything general immediately. They answer general questions about the book and the web site.

Editorial

Deeper queries are forwarded to the technical editor responsible for that book. They have experience with the programming language or particular product and are able to answer detailed technical questions on the subject. Once an issue has been resolved, the editor can post the erratum to the web site.

The Authors

Finally, in the unlikely event that the editor can't answer your problem, they will forward the request to the author. We try to protect the author from any distractions from writing. However, we are quite happy to forward specific requests to them. All Wrox authors help with the support on their books. They'll mail the customer and the editor with their response, and again all readers should benefit.

What We Can't Answer

Obviously with an ever-growing range of books and an ever-changing technology base, there is an increasing volume of data requiring support. While we endeavor to answer all questions about the book, we can't answer bugs in your own programs that you've adapted from our code. So, while you might have loved the chapters on file handling, don't expect too much sympathy if you cripple your company with a routine which deletes the contents of your hard drive. But do tell us if you're especially pleased with the routine you developed with our help.

How to Tell Us Exactly What You Think

We understand that errors can destroy the enjoyment of a book and can cause many wasted and frustrated hours, so we seek to minimize the distress that they can cause.

You might just wish to tell us how much you liked or loathed the book in question. Or you might have ideas about how this whole process could be improved. In which case, you should e-mail feedback@wrox.com. You'll always find a sympathetic ear, no matter what the problem is. Above all you should remember that we do care about what you have to say and we will do our utmost to act upon it.

Online discussion at http://p2p.wrox.com

Index

A Guide to the Index

The index is arranged hierarchically, in alphabetical order, with symbols preceding the letter A. Most second-level entries and many third-level entries also occur as first-level entries. This is to ensure that users will find the information they require however they choose to search for it.

C

D

995

U

undefined variables
  common mistakes, 366
unescape() function
  cookie value, retrieving, 428
  JavaScript functions, 423
UPDATE statement, 692
  Access database, 692
  creating, 692
  databases, changing information in, 706
  SQL queries, 692
  WHERE clause, 692
URLs, getting information passed in
  example, 634
  hyperlinks, 636
  onclick event, Button object, 637
  Request object, 633
user sessions
  definition, 658
  Session object, 658
userAgent property
  navigator object, 173, 176, 178
UserProfile object
  Internet Explorer 5 BOM, 942
  methods, 942
users, redirecting
  logon system example, 647
  Response object, 647

V

valid HTML, 528
valid XML, 528
validation
  forms, getting information posted by, 631
  HTML Forms, 197
  isNaN() function, 201
  onsubmit event, 711
  onsubmit event, Form object, 631, 650
  preventing errors, 396
VALUE attribute
  <INPUT> tag, 193, 196, 207
  <OPTION> tag, 224
value property
  Button object, 193
  form element objects, 191
  Option object, 214
  Text object, 196
  TextArea object, 203, 247
value, cookie string, 419
  getCookieValue() function, 426
  retrieving with unescape() function, 428
  setting with escape() function, 423
valueOf() method
  Date object, 227
var keyword
  variables, declaring, 33
variable names, 33
  case sensitivity, 33
  Hungarian notation, 33
  reserved words, 33

variables, 32
  application variables, 660
  assigning values, 34
    alert() function, 35
    initializing, 36
    literal values, 35
    other variable values, 36
  compared to arrays, 55
  declaring, 33
    var keyword, 33
  global variables, 245
  lifetime, 105
  reference objects, 116
  scope, 104
  server variables, 638
  session variables, 659
  undefined variables, 366
  using, 42
  variable names, 32
VBArray object, 883
  methods, 883
VBScript
  compared to JavaScript, 10
  default language for ASP, 616
version information
  ActiveX controls, 600
  CODEBASE attribute, <OBJECT> tag, 600
  Plugin object, 601
  plug-ins, 601
virtual directories
  aliasing, 613
  creating
    Internet Explorer, 614
    PWS console, advanced section, 613
  definition, 613
  PWS console, advanced section, 613
  Trivia Quiz application, 662
  web servers, 613

W

W3C
  see World Wide Web Consortium.
warnings
  compared to error messages, 369
weakly typed languages
  compared to strongly typed languages, 29
  JavaScript, 29
web browsers
  see browsers.
web servers, 9, 605
  clients, 9
  hosting web services, 9
  HTTP, 9
  IIS, 607
  IP addresses, 9
  PWS, 607
  server-side scripting, 606
  virtual directories, 613
web sites
  personalization, 411
    cookies, 411

p2p.wrox.com
The programmer's resource centre

A unique free service from Wrox Press
with the aim of helping programmers to help each other

Wrox Press aims to provide timely and practical information to today's programmer. P2P is a list server offering a host of targeted mailing lists where you can share knowledge with your fellow programmers and find solutions to your problems. Whatever the level of your programming knowledge, and whatever technology you use, P2P can provide you with the information you need.

ASP — Support for beginners and professionals, including a resource page with hundreds of links, and a popular ASP+ mailing list.

DATABASES — For database programmers, offering support on SQL Server, mySQL, and Oracle.

MOBILE — Software development for the mobile market is growing rapidly. We provide lists for the several current standards, including WAP, WindowsCE, and Symbian.

JAVA — A complete set of Java lists, covering beginners, professionals,and server-side programmers (including JSP, servlets and EJBs)

.NET — Microsoft's new OS platform, covering topics such as ASP+, C#, and general .Net discussion.

VISUAL BASIC — Covers all aspects of VB programming, from programming Office macros to creating components for the .Net platform.

WEB DESIGN — As web page requirements become more complex, programmer sare taking a more important role in creating web sites. For these programmers, we offer lists covering technologies such as Flash, Coldfusion, and JavaScript.

XML — Covering all aspects of XML, including XSLT and schemas.

OPEN SOURCE — Many Open Source topics covered including PHP, Apache, Perl, Linux, Python and more.

FOREIGN LANGUAGE — Several lists dedicated to Spanish and German speaking programmers, categories include .Net, Java, XML, PHP and XML.

How To Subscribe

Simply visit the P2P site, at **http://p2p.wrox.com/**

Select the 'FAQ' option on the side menu bar for more information about the subscription process and our service.

wrox

PROGRAMMER TO PROGRAMMER™

Wrox writes books for you. Any suggestions, or ideas about how you want information given in your ideal book will be studied by our team. Your comments are always valued at Wrox.

Free phone in USA 800-USE-WROX
Fax (312) 893 8001

UK Tel. (0121) 687 4100   Fax (0121) 687 4101

Beginning Javascript - Registration Card

Name _____

Address _____

_____

_____

_____

City_____ State/Region _____

Country_____ Postcode/Zip _____

E-mail _____

Occupation _____

How did you hear about this book? _____

☐ Book review (name) _____

☐ Advertisement (name) _____

☐ Recommendation _____

☐ Catalog _____

☐ Other _____

Where did you buy this book? _____

☐ Bookstore (name)_____ City _____

☐ Computer Store (name)_____

☐ Mail Order _____

☐ Other _____

What influenced you in the purchase of this book?

☐ Cover Design

☐ Contents

☐ Other (please specify) _____

How did you rate the overall contents of this book?

☐ Excellent   ☐ Good

☐ Average   ☐ Poor

What did you find most useful about this book? _____

What did you find least useful about this book? _____

Please add any additional comments. _____

What other subjects will you buy a computer book on soon? _____

What is the best computer book you have used this year?

_____

Note: This information will only be used to keep you updated about new Wrox Press titles and will not be used for any other purpose or passed to any other third party.

4060   *Check here if you DO NOT want to receive support for this book* ☐   4060

wrox

PROGRAMMER TO PROGRAMMER™

NB. If you post the bounce back card below in the UK, please send it to:

Wrox Press Ltd., Arden House, 1102 Warwick Road,
Acocks Green, Birmingham B27 6BH. UK.

———— *Computer Book Publishers* ————